PLATE I

THE PIRAEUS LION: NOW IN VENICE
A GREEK CARVING WITH RUNIC INSCRIPTION ON FLANKS
Height about 12 feet. See p. 176.

A HISTORY OF
THE
VIKINGS

T. D. Kendrick

Illustrated

DOVER PUBLICATIONS,INC.
Mineola, New York

Bibliographical Note

This Dover edition, first published in 2004, is an unabridged republication of
the work originally published in 1930 by Charles Scribner's Sons, New York.

Library of Congress Cataloging-in-Publication Data

Kendrick, T. D. (Thomas Downing)
    A history of the Vikings / T. D. Kendrick.
        p. cm.
    Originally published: New York : Charles Scribner's Sons, 1930.
    Includes bibliographical references and index.
      ISBN 0-486-43396-X (pbk.)
    1. Vikings. I. Title.

DL65.K27 2004
909'.0439501—dc22

                                            2003070109

Manufactured in the United States of America
Dover Publications, Inc., 31 East 2nd Street, Mineola, N.Y. 11501

PREFACE

THE vikings are still awaiting their English historian. I do not mean that there is no full account of their doings in Great Britain, for of course there are many excellent books by Englishmen dealing with this special aspect of viking history, and among them are the well-known works of Palgrave, Freeman, Oman, and Hodgkin; I mean that there is no substantial book in English exclusively devoted to the vikings and setting forth the whole of their activities not only in the west and the far north, but in the east and south-east as well; for Paul du Chaillu's [1] long and discursive book *The Viking Age* can hardly rank as serious history, interesting and informative though it is, and I am confident that Professor Allen Mawer would want his admirable little work *The Vikings* to be regarded only as a brief and introductory sketch. I know, needless to say, that there is one important English book concerned with our subject in its larger aspect and that is *The Vikings in Western Christendom*, by Charles Francis Keary, a fine work of real beauty and a masterpiece of expositional style which I take a special pleasure in praising since Keary was once, as I am now, a member of the staff of the British Museum [2]; this classic work was published as long ago as 1891, but by common consent it is still, and will long remain, the most valuable study of viking history in our tongue; nevertheless, as the title explains, its scope embraces western Europe only, and therefore I repeat that the northern peoples have not yet found an English historian to record within the compass of a single book the full story of their achievements in the Viking Period.

For my part, I must explain that I have not set myself the task of writing the English history of the vikings that I should like to read, for it should be a great and gallant book, not over-

---

[1] Du Chaillu, a French Canadian, is best known as the African explorer who rediscovered the gorilla; he was born in 1835 and died in 1903.

[2] Keary, who was novelist, poet, and philosopher, besides historian and numismatist, was on the staff of the Medal Room from 1872 until 1887 and also assisted the Museum for a short time during the War.

burdened with footnotes nor embarrassed by the inclusion of too much perplexing controversial matter. On the contrary I want merely to be the forerunner of some luckier author of the future and I have done my best for him by trying to set down the complete narrative, as it is at present understood, in a severely plain and useful form. The fact is that were I not convinced that there is really a need for a general history of the vikings of this sort I should have abandoned my project on the grounds that the time was badly chosen for writing a general summary of viking history. Even for such quiet folk as students of early history these are stirring days ; veteran certainties of the text-books are dissolving into the miasma of legend while new inter-pretations of the historical material are assuming the semblance of established, and often astonishing, facts. It has been dis-covered for example that the customary condensed version of the first sagas in *Heimskringla* provides not only an insufficient but a misleading account of the formation of the kingdom of Norway, and I recommend to those who know only the traditional tale a most provocative and disconcerting little book by Johan Schreiner called *Olav den hellige og Norges samling* (Oslo, 1929). So, too, in Denmark and Sweden the last few years have witnessed a drastic revaluation of the evidence derived from the earliest written records. And this is not all, for recent archaeological research has afforded with a prodigality that I confess surprises me a wealth of trustworthy data that ultimately cannot fail to enlarge our knowledge of viking history. Naturally I have tried to keep apace with these vigorous advances in learning, but know-ing as I do the energy and thoroughness with which historical and archaeological investigations are now being prosecuted by scholars in the northern countries and in the lands that were colonies of the vikings, I am bound to anticipate the publication of many important and revolutionary contributions to the history of the Northmen in the course of the next few years. This is as it should be and I am glad. But I shall fail in my duty to the reader if I do not warn him that even now large slices of this history are being industriously shovelled into the melting-pot by my learned colleagues and friends.

I want most gratefully to record the help I have obtained from these scholars. They are many and they live far-scattered —in this country, in Scandinavia and Denmark, in Iceland, in Germany, in France, and in America ; to one and all of them I offer my thanks ; but I name here only Mr. Jón Stefánsson and Professor Halldór Hermannson, who have been kind enough to help with the proof-reading and to whom I am indebted for some valuable suggestions. I must also acknowledge gratefully the assistance of another and indispensable proof-reader, my wife, and in conclusion, I desire to thank the Trustees of the British Museum for permission to reproduce illustrations from one of the Museum guides, and Dr. P. Nörlund, Mr. S. Bengtsson, Mr. W. Berthelsen, and Mr. O. Böhm for permission to use photographs taken by them.

T. D. K.

20, BRAMHAM GARDENS
   LONDON
    August, 1930

LIST OF ABBREVIATIONS

Aarb.. . . . . Aarbøger for nordisk Oldkyndighed og Historie (Copenhagen).

A.T.S. . . . . Antikvarisk Tidskrift för Sverige (Stockholm).

An. S.B. . . . . Altnordische Saga-bibliothek (Halle).

C.S.H.B. . . . . Corpus Scriptorum Historiae Byzantinae (Bonn).

J.M.N.P. . . . . Jurnal Ministersta Narodnaga Prosveshcheniya (Journal of the Ministry of Public Instruction, St. Petersburg).

K. Vitt. Ant. Akad. Handl. Kunglige Vitterhets Historie och Antikvitets Akademiens Handlingar (Stockholm).

M.G.H. . . . . Monumenta Germaniae Historia, ed. G. H. Pertz (Hanover) : SS. = Scriptores, folio series.

Mem. Soc. Ant. du Nord. . Mémoires de la Société royale des antiquaries du Nord (Copenhagen).

CONTENTS

LIST OF PLATES

LIST OF ILLUSTRATIONS IN THE TEXT

* Figures 3, 4, 5, 7, and 8 are reproduced from the British Museum *Guide to Anglo-Saxon Antiquities,* by permission of the Trustees.

A HISTORY OF THE VIKINGS

INTRODUCTION

THE barbarians of the distant and little-known north, of Scandinavia, that is, and of Denmark, became notorious in the ninth and tenth centuries as pests who plagued the outer fringes of the civilized world. In chief, this was because the coasts and river-valleys of Frisia and Francia, then a part of the western Roman Empire ruled by the house of Charles the Great, suffered heavily from their onslaughts ; but it was not only the monks and merchants of these two countries whose voices, lifted in shrill lamentation over the smoking ruins of plundered monasteries and towns, added to the disquiet of a Christendom already preoccupied with its own disorderly affairs ; for the loud cry of terror was heard re-echoing from the religious houses of Ireland, and it was told how half Saxon England had fallen into the hands of these ruffian robbers from the north. Even Constantinople herself, the lordly capital of the Eastern Empire, then ruled by the Iconoclast and Macedonian dynasties, was shocked suddenly into recognition of these wild and redoubtable heathens ; only once seriously affrighted, and never persistently assailed, but twice or thrice compelled to come to terms with the Swedes of Russia, and thereafter willing to enlist such splendid warriors in her service.

These adventurous people of Scandinavia and Denmark are known to history as the *vikings*. It is a word that was often heard in the talk of the Northmen themselves, for among them a man could not hope for sweeter praise than to be called by his fellows *víkingr mikill*, a great seafarer, while to go *í víking* was their accustomed expression for the favourite enterprise of trading and plundering across the waters. Yet to employ this word viking as a collective name for the three peoples of the north, whether at home or abroad, to speak of the viking nations, or even of the Viking Period, these are only modern uses of the word. For in antiquity, though the name may have been current not only in Scandinavia and Denmark but also through-

1

out the whole Germanic north, it does not find its way into the chronicles and histories of either of the two Roman empires, nor into Celtic and Saxon annals, as the designation of the northern buccaneers, even during and after the time of their most notable exploits ; in fact it was only after it had long dropped out of ordinary use that scholars, who from the seventeenth century onwards had become familiar with the term in the sagas, perceived its fitness to do duty in historical works as the keyword of the most remarkable period in the whole story of the northern lands.

The Northmen employed the name in the sense of ' one who fared by sea to his adventures of commerce and of war ', and, later on, with the debased meaning of ' robber ' or ' brigand ' ; among the Frisians and the English the word viking seems to have been a synonym for ' marauder from across the ocean ', and in England it was so used at a date considerably earlier than that when the Viking Period, as it is ordinarily defined, begins.[1] But what exactly it meant originally, whether ' men of the camps ' or ' men of the creeks ', is uncertain; [2] it cannot even be said positively that it is of Norse and not of Frisian or English coining. That which is now assured is simply that it was current among Germanic folk in general as a name for filibustering rovers of the sea, and that it is merely a convenience of modern historical machinery to monopolize the name for the three peoples of Norway, Sweden, and Denmark in the amazing centuries of their outpouring upon improvident Christendom.

[1] Examples of the English use of the word *wicing* in the early eighth century will be found in the Saxon poetic version of Exodus (*Bibl. der A. S. Poesie*, ed. Grein, v. 333), in Widsith (II. 47, 59), where it appears as an alternative tribal name for the Heathobards, and also in certain glosses (cf. E. Björkman, *Festskrift K. F. Johansson*, Göteberg, 1910, p. 7). The OFris. form is *witsing* or *wising* ; for its occurrence, see K. v. Richthoven, *Altfriesisches Wörterbuch, s.v. wiking.*

[2] According to the favourite derivation, the element *vik* is to be connected with the word still current in the Scandinavian and Danish tongues for *creek* or *bay*, the vikings therefore taking their name from the haunts whence they sailed and where, in the unhappy lands of their robberies, they best loved to beach their boats. Another supposition, much less likely, is that the word means *warriors*, the first element, on this view, being derived from ON. *vig*, meaning strife or battle. A third and the best etymology (that of E. Björkman) connects *vik* with OE. *wic*, a camp, which in turn is a borrowing of the Latin *vicus*, an inhabited place. As it is easily understandable that the name, bestowed in England and Frisia, should mean the *folk of the camps*, it seems unnecessary to insist that the primary meaning was *townsmen*, with the rider that it was a result of the seafarings and depredations of the merchants from the German towns that the name was subsequently applied to the Northmen in the

As a collective name, then, for the Norwegians, Swedes, and Danes during a certain period of their history, the *vikings*, though not always theirs exclusively, is sanctioned by modern usage and must remain, of course, unchallenged. But viking enterprise is even less a special phenomenon of this period than is the occurrence of the word itself ; for the vikings did not invent their favourite employment of sailing the seas in search of fortune and adventures ; they were not the first shipbuilders of the north nor the first great maritime folk of these waters. Seafarings in search of plunder had long been familiar exploits in the dark Germanic world, and the Baltic had been crossed and crossed again by warrior-bands and the North Sea coasts had been pirate-haunted from the earliest centuries of the Christian era. The Angles, the Jutes, and the Saxons, those persistent raiders of the luckless ' Saxon shore ', had all been vikings in their day ; in the middle of the fifth century the Heruls of Denmark had made a piratical descent not merely on the coast of France but upon Spain, and in the year A.D. 516, nearly three centuries before the Viking Period begins, there had taken place the raid of the Scandinavian Hygelac (or Chlochilaic, as the Franks called him) upon Frisia ; he had attacked the lower Rhine country, laid waste a part of the realm of Theuderic, King of the Franks, and had taken many prisoners and loaded his boats with plunder before he was caught and overthrown by Theuderic's son.

Nevertheless the Viking Period of history-books, as is everywhere understood, does not extend backwards to include such early exploits but begins only at the end of the eighth century when the Scandinavian peoples and the Danes show unwonted activity and more than usual daring and persistency in their robberies across the seas. The actual beginning, so far as history can tell, belongs to the last two decades of that century, and the first appearance of the Northmen that has been recorded took place some time between the years 786 and 793 in the

debased sense of robbers from overseas (cf. E. Wadstein, *Le mot Viking, Mélanges de Philologie offerts à M. J. Vising*, Göteborg and Paris, 1925, p. 381). A fourth etymology, suggested by W. v. Russow, declares the word viking to mean *seal-catcher*, the first element being connected with *wikan*, a seal, in the dialect of Runö in the Gulf of Riga. As the etymology is dubious there are no means of deciding whether the word is to be pronounced rhyming with *licking* or *liking*. Continental historians usually keep the i short ; in England the long i is an accustomed pronunciation. It is, however, better to learn to say vīking rather than vĭking, if only for the convenience of being instantly understood when referring to the early Northmen in the presence of the living scions of their stock.

reign of King Beohtric of Wessex when three Norwegian boats put in to the Dorset coast and the crews murdered the king's reeve. But in 793 there was a much more serious and ominous happening, namely the plundering and destruction of the Lindisfarne monastery on Holy Island off the Northumbrian coast and the massacre of some of the monks. This outrage by the Norsemen surprised and frightened the English; ' it was not thought possible that they could have made the voyage ', wrote Alcuin, the Northumbrian scholar at the court of Charles the Great, and ' never before ', he said, ' in the three hundred and fifty years that we and our forefathers have dwelt in this fair land has such a horror appeared in Britain as this that we have just suffered from the heathen '. It was, however, the grim announcement that a reign of terror had begun ; in 794 the monastery of Jarrow was robbed and that of Monkwear-mouth threatened ; marauding Northmen landed in Scotland, Ireland, and Wales in 795, and in the Isle of Man in 798, and in the Aquitaine province of France in 799. The opening of the next century saw these raids continued ; the almost empty Orkneys and Shetlands were seized by emigrant Norsemen ; the Hebrides were infested with the pirates from over the sea ; Columba's monastery on Iona was burnt in 802 and again in 806 ; in the following year the mainland of Ireland was the scene of a prolonged and vicious foray by the Northmen. And on the Continent, too, the evil hour that witnessed the coming of the viking terror had struck ; as early as the year 800 Charles the Great had been compelled to look to the defences of the Frisian coast, and in 808 the Danish king declared himself the open enemy of the emperor by an attack upon Charles's Slavonic allies, the Obotrites of Mecklenberg and western Holstein ; in 810 with a fleet of 200 ships the Danes descended upon the coast of Frisia, a prelude to the shattering and ferocious onslaught so soon to assail this tempting and unhappy country. And while this was happening, the Swedes had begun to raid the East Baltic coasts, had found their way up into the Gulf of Finland and were winning for themselves a province around the Ladoga lake, where they built a stronghold on its shores close to the modern town of Novaya Ladoga, some 70 miles west of Leningrad.

The end of the Viking Period, according to the usual reckon-ing, comes in the middle of the eleventh century, and between this point of time and the end of the eighth century the three viking peoples did many brilliant and astonishing things. The Norwegians created and owned towns in Ireland and possessed themselves of most of the Scottish islands ; they colonized the

Faroes, Iceland, and Greenland ; they discovered America ; at home they made themselves into a Christian nation united under one king. The Danes extended their authority over Frisia and won all England for their keeping ; like the Norwegians

eland and like them they too became
m. In France a rich and pleasant
Western Empire by Danish and Nor-
east the Swedes took large tracts of
y became lords of the Dnieper basin
state, they dared even to assail Con-
mercial treaties with the emperors of

simplest terms, is unquestionably a
, and though its real worth will
tion, it establishes plainly enough the
not only thieves and destroyers of
earliest times onwards a folk soberly
the necessary task of winning lands
y outset of the Viking Period there
ng movement, namely the westward
Norwegian peasant population to the
, and the settlement of more adven-
brides, while only shortly afterwards
oriously upon another territory ; for
brides was immediately followed by
the attacks upon Ireland that culminated during the '30s of the ninth century in the substantial conquests of the illustrious Turgeis.

The vikings, therefore, were not only buccaneers, they were often invaders intent upon securing a dominion for themselves, and they could also live as colonists in foreign or empty lands, peaceably settled, while others of them, filibustering merchant-adventurers, circulated between the mother-country, the colonies, and the neighbouring states. In certain areas it is possible to distinguish phases in their history during which one or other of their rôles prevailed, as for example in England when random marauding gives way to the great invasion that preceded the first establishment of the Danelaw and this in turn is followed by a short period of earnest colonization in the new-won province ; but on a larger canvas such phases are seen to have only local and episodic value, and viking history as a whole does not lend itself to a schematic presentation on this basis. For from the beginning to the end most of the vikings remained oppor-tunists, and as a result the first glimpse of their history should reveal a disorderly and kaleidoscopic picture, showing a long series of strivings, isolated and concerted, after new conquests, of expeditions and the rumours of expeditions, of plans frustrated by desertion and treachery, of settlements weakened by feud and suspicion, by robbery and by arson. So great indeed is the surface confusion of their story that the real aim and attainments of the three northern folks are momentarily obscured in the clash and clamour of this tumultuous time and they seem at first to be the most restless, ineffectual and irritable creatures that ever sought power and dominion in lands other than their own.

Their history, in its baldest outline, must be set forth by selecting certain main episodes of migration, attack, conquest, and defeat, and stringing these together in catalogue form. But for their easier presentation they may be grouped into five time-periods or phases.

PHASE I.   A.D. 785–820 :
   (a) Minor raids upon the west and the first plundering of the monasteries.
   (b) Settlement of Norsemen in the Scottish Islands.
   (c) The Danes appear as a military power on the continent and threaten Frisia with invasion.
   (d) The Swedes explore the Russian waterways and found the Ladoga settlement.

In this opening phase there was but little sustained fighting ; indeed the far-off grumblings of the gathering storm were not sufficient to warn Christendom of the danger at hand, and only Charles the Great, who feared for the safety of Frisia, cast anxious eyes upon the darkening horizon. But in the second phase, suddenly and terrifically the storm bursts, and in the west the grand attack upon Christendom begins.

PHASE II.   A.D. 835–865 :
   (e) Danish raids upon Frisia (834–850) ; the country over-- run by vikings and Dorstad ceded to Rorik.
   (f) Twenty-four years (841–865) of sustained attack by vikings, chiefly Danes, upon the monasteries and towns along the coasts and river-valleys of Francia.
   (g) Thirty-one years (834–865) of assault upon southern England.
   (h) Conquests of Turgeis in N. Ireland ; foundation of the viking harbour-towns in Ireland and establishment of the kingdom of Dublin by Olaf.

(*i*) 850–860. Swedish conquests in East Baltic lands, southward movement of Swedes who occupy the Slavonic
towns of Russia and become masters of the waterways.
First raid upon Constantinople.

In these thirty years of the second phase, a period of bloodshed, rapine, and terror, the vikings possessed themselves of
new homes in Russia, on the Irish coast, and in Frisia. The
Swedes laid a part of the East Baltic states under them, but took
little profit of their victory, having their eyes upon the Russian
trade-routes and intent upon the rule of the inland river-towns ;
but in southern England and Francia the attacks failed and no
permanent conquests were made, even though a footing was
won by the establishment here and there of fortified strongholds
to serve as winter quarters. Yet this double failure only served
to divert the Danish attack to a new quarter, and the third
phase opens with a most notable success, the outright conquest
of the eastern half of England.

PHASE III. A.D. 866–896 :
(*j*) Great Danish invasion of Northumbria and eastern
England (867) and beginning of the conquest of the
Danelaw ; renewed viking attack upon Wessex (870–
896) which fails after twenty-five years fighting.
(*k*) Ravages of Loire vikings in West Francia (866–869).
Renewed attack upon northern Francia (876–882).
(*l*) Godfred becomes lord of Frisia (882), but at his death
(886) Danish power in this country comes to an end.
(*m*) Beginning of Harald Fairhair's rise to power in Norway
(*c.* 890) ; Norse colonization of Iceland begins (874).

The thirty years of this phase have England as the theatre
of the principal struggle by the vikings to win new dominions.
There is still fighting in Ireland and the Celtic lands, but already
a change is noticeable, for the vikings of the Irish coast are now
living in partly Christian communities that rank as the equals,
and sometimes the allies, of the Irish kingdoms, even though after
the departure of Olaf of Dublin in 870 their prestige and their
numbers most seriously declined. Here the period of the sacking
of the religious houses is almost over, but in Francia the terror
of the vikings is unabated in the towns and monasteries of the
Loire valley and up the Seine. In Russia the Swedish state has
flourished and is becoming more and more orientated towards
the Byzantine Empire. In the north the empty country of
Iceland is discovered and colonized by Norsemen of the Celtic

lands and of Norway, and there is increased emigration to the Norse settlements overseas as a result of the rigorous rule of Harald Fairhair, would-be lord of all Norway.

PHASE IV. A.D. 900–926 :

> (*n*) Harold Fairhair completes subjection of Vestland (*c.* 900) and Norsemen settle in N.W. England ; English reconquer the Danelaw (910–926).
>
> (*o*) Rollo invades Francia and Normandy is ceded to him (911) ; renewed attack on the Loire country (919).
>
> (*p*) Fresh incursions of vikings into Ireland (914–926).
>
> (*q*) Oleg of Kiev attacks Constantinople (907) and a treaty is made between Russians and Greeks (911). The Volga Swedes raid the Caspian lands of the Caliphate (910, 914).

The chief territorial gain of the early tenth century is the winning of Normandy, the buffer-duchy whereby Charles the Simple sought to defend his realm from a repetition of the horrors of the preceding century.   But this success is followed by an almost complete eclipse of Danish power in England, and for some sixty years the vikings made no other notable land-winning in the west and no devastating attacks upon the countries that were not already their own.   Yet in the final phase of the history of their expansion it is England that succumbs to their greatest and most formidable attack.

PHASE V. A.D. 980–1050 :

> (*r*) Danish conquest of England ; Svein and Cnut as kings of England. Decline of Danish power after Cnut's death (1035).
>
> (*s*) Vladimir the Great and Yaroslav of Kiev raise the Swedish-Russian principality to its greatest power.
>
> (*t*) Colonization of Greenland by the Icelanders (*c.* 986).
>
> (*u*) Brian Boru, the high-king of Ireland, defeats a great levy of the western vikings at Clontarf (1014) ; but the Irish vikings retain their hold upon the harbour-towns.

The fifth phase is first of all remarkable for the sudden and dramatic entry of the northern people into the European commonwealth of Christian states.   About A.D. 970 Denmark became for the first time a single kingdom and the Danes were made converts to Christianity by their sovereign, Harald Gormsson ; about 990 Vladimir the Great ordered the conversion of his Kievan principality in Russia and in 995 Olaf Tryggvason began to enforce the new faith on the hundred-year-old realm of Norway, while Olof Skotkonung at this same time likewise sought, though much less successfully, to convert the ancient kingdom of Sweden. But it was only in Denmark and in Russia that this new importance of the northern nations as Christian powers brought a prosperity commensurate with so notable an advance.

For under Svein and Cnut in England, under Vladimir and Yaroslav in Russia, the vikings abroad won the most substantial success and the most honourable status in all their history; indeed in the first half of the eleventh century the Anglo-Danish kingdom and the Kievan Principality were alike powers of European importance, bodies politic of a significance never attained elsewhere in the outside viking world, not even in Normandy, so soon Frenchified, nor in Frisia, and certainly never attained in Ireland nor in the lonely islands of Scotland, nor in far-off Iceland. But this brilliant period was of short duration, in England a bare thirty years and in Russia not much more than eighty, so that after the beginning of the second half of the eleventh century nearly all that remained of viking power abroad was vested in the Norse colonies in the Celtic lands and in the Faroes, Iceland, and Greenland.

Few problems of viking history are more difficult than the determination of the nationality or nationalities of those engaged in any one operation, for the adventurous spirits of the folk of each country sent them forth roaming at random, ready to take their share in whatever fighting was afoot or to beach their boats wherever trade seemed good. In general terms it is true enough that in the west the viking forays and armaments were those of Norwegians, Danes, and Swedes from Scania, who were then counted as Danes, while in Russia the settlers were mostly Swedes; but once the viking movement was begun many of the attacking forces in the west began to lose their national character, for viking enterprise, as will be shown, was never in the early days an expression of a considered national foreign policy, and was seldom engineered, equipped, and controlled by kings in Norway, Sweden and Denmark. Nevertheless while allowing for this sometimes inextricable mingling and for the capricious character of many ventures, there remains a discernible national movement in each instance indicative of the parts played by the three peoples in the viking movement, and this may be summarized here and now.

The Swedes were the folk who achieved the mightiest and most remarkable triumph of viking history, namely the creation of an independent Swedish-Russian state. This they did not by force and fury, but by the orderly development of trade through the eastern Slavonic country along the river-routes familiar to their forefathers and by the undeniable statesmanship of the early Swedish princes of Kiev. They governed and protected the wavering Slavs, and they opened for them, and held open, the golden but dangerous road to Constantinople. It was of Swedish choosing that the influence of the Byzantine Empire shaped Russian modes and manners and thought, and that the Patriarch of Constantinople became the spiritual father of the Russians ; therefore this noble and amazing episode whereby the destiny of Russia was determined assuredly takes rank as the most important adventure of the vikings in constructive politics and was certainly the most fateful and significant part played by them in the great drama of European history.

The Danes, except for the Jomsborg outpost and for certain wars along the Baltic littoral, turned to the west and south-west. Frisia was their first prize and the grants to their leaders of fiefs in this province were the most important of their early gains ; but in the second half of the ninth century, after the long and bloody ravaging of the coasts of France and England, they achieved a more remarkable success, for they won Northumbria and founded the English Danelaw. At this time, too, they made a bid for the control of the Norwegian towns of Ireland, but at the end of the century fortune went everywhere against them and it was not until Rollo's army, which was mostly Danish, suddenly and surprisingly won Normandy in the second decade of the tenth century that success once more attended their arms. Normandy, however, was very rapidly swallowed up in France and lost its identity as a viking province, so that even if its winning can be counted as a Danish achievement it cannot be deemed so remarkable a triumph for the Danes as the second conquest of England in the early eleventh century, a magnificent success that was won under the leadership of Svein, King of Denmark. This was the first occasion on which a viking campaign was a deliberated act of national policy engineered and led by the monarch himself, and Svein's victory was crowned by the formation of a huge and powerful Anglo-Danish kingdom under his son Cnut. Yet it was but a short-lived triumph, for when Cnut died in 1035 once again Danish power declined and with the death of Hardecnut in 1042 their dominion over England ended.

The Norwegians sailed westwards and north-westwards. Beginning with the peopling of the Orkneys and Shetlands they spread rapidly over the Western Sea, taking the Hebrides, over-running Man, and establishing themselves in Scotland and Ireland ; in the early days of the tenth century some of them also settled in north-western England, and just before this there began a migration to the Faroes and to Iceland, this being fol-lowed later by the colonization of Greenland and the wonderful discovery of America. The Norse colonies, however, were all of them remote from the main pulse of European life and there-fore have a history different from and much longer than those of Sweden and Denmark ; thus it comes about that when the Anglo-Danish kingdom was no more and after the principality of Kiev had become wholly Slavonic, the Norse earldom of Orkney and the Norsemen of the Scottish islands and Ireland were still playing a dominant rôle in the history of north Britain. The most brilliant period in the story of the Orkneys was the reign of Earl Thorfinn, who died in 1066, and the Norse kingdom of the Isles and Man was more important at the end of the eleventh century than ever before ; indeed, at the beginning of the twelfth century the might of Norway in the west was proved by the coming of King Magnus Barefoot with the purpose of creating from the Norse colonies a realm that should submerge Scotland and rival the kingdom of England. In the thirteenth century the Irish towns were seized by the English and the fate of the remaining Norse and Danish colonists in Ireland sealed ; but the kingdom of the Western Isles and the earldom of Orkney remained as a menace to Scottish power and so continued until the fateful days when King Haakon Haakonsson came west intending to establish decisively the fact of Norse supremacy in Scotland. But Haakon failed, and after his death in the Orkneys Norse colonial power in the Western Seas came quickly to an end ; henceforth, now that further military aid from the mother-country was no longer to be expected, these poor Norse-men could not hold their own as rivals of the Scots, nor could Norway herself make any serious struggle to retain their alle-giance, and so in 1266 Man and the Western Isles were ceded to the king of Scotland, and a century later there followed the mortgage of the Orkneys and the Shetlands. Only in the far north did the colonies of Iceland, the Faroes, and Greenland, endure miserably to represent the great land-winnings of the early Norsemen. And not all of these survived, for cut-off and forgotten in their cold and remote land the men of Greenland were left to die in horrid starvation and neglect, so that by the middle of the fifteenth century the colony was extinct ; but in Iceland and in the Faroes the scions of the Norsemen still possess

the lands that their viking ancestors took at the end of the
ninth century, and so to this day they remain, proud and uncorrupted communities that witness to the ancient greatness of the
viking world.

As buccaneers, thieves, and murderers, the Northmen horrified
all western Christendom, startled even the Greek Empire, and
more than once shocked the Muslim people of the Caliphate.
In this respect they were no worse than other robbers and pillagers
of history, either before their day or long after it, yet it is an
idle and dishonest task to attempt to defend them against the
charge of plundering and massacre. 'Merry, clean-limbed,
stout-hearted gentlemen of the Northlands' one of their Scottish
historians [1] has called them, and such indeed upon occasions
they may have been, but history also knows them as bloodthirsty and abominable barbarians, enemies of society capable of
infamous, indefensible outrages of arson and slaughter.

The Christian world of the ninth and tenth centuries did not
perhaps deem them to be the most terrible of the enemies of
civilization, for the Saracens and the Hungarians, striking at
the heart of the Christian world, were worse and more dangerous
foes, and it must have seemed a small matter that in 846 the
Frisian town of Dorstad should be sacked by Northmen and the
little Noirmoutier monastery plundered, when in this same year
a Muhammedan force lying before the gates of Rome pillaged
the church of St. Peter and profaned the Apostle's hallowed
tomb. Nevertheless the towns and religious houses of Francia
and Frisia, the monasteries of England and Ireland, and the
tiny outpost of Christianity on Iona, lived for many dark years
in urgent terror of the vikings, and in the churches was heard
that piteous invocation, *A furore Normannorum libera nos,
Domine.* After the pillaging of the monastery of Abingdon in
Berkshire [2] a monk wrote, ' O what misery and what grief !
And who is there of so dull a head, so brazen a breast, and so
hard a heart that he can hear of these things and not dissolve
into tears ! ' In Ireland a Celtic chronicler said, ' In a word,
although there were an hundred hard steeled iron heads on one
neck, and an hundred sharp, ready, cool, never-rusting, brazen
tongues in each head, and an hundred garrulous, loud, unceasing
voices from each tongue, they could not recount or narrate or

---

[1] R. L. Bremner, *The Norsemen in Alban*, Glasgow, 1923, p. 26.
[2] Probably during the Danish invasion of Wessex in 871. There is a
tradition that the charters and treasures had previously been removed
to safety.

enumerate or tell what all the Gaedhil (the Irish) suffered in common, both men and women, laity and clergy, old and young, noble and ignoble, of hardship and of injuring and of oppression, in every house, from those valiant, wrathful, purely-pagan people.' In Frisia and Francia the terror was still worse, for here there were towns for plundering, and so again and again the monks tell the wretched tale of massacre and smoking ruins. Such appalling outrages as the sack of Nantes in 843 that saw the murder of the bishop at the cathedral altar and the butchering of the congregation and the firing of the great church, or the razing of Quentovic two years before to a desert of smoking ruins, or the awful ravages of the grim years between 853 and 858 when Nantes, Poitiers (twice), Angers, Tours (twice), Blois, Orleans (twice), Paris, Bayeux, Chartres, and Évreux were all sacked by vikings, can neither be condoned nor excused ; they were the work of savages angered against a civilization that they were too few to overpower and too ignorant to understand.

The worst atrocities were those committed in the west. For the Russian-Swedes found themselves established in an environment where it was more profitable to develop rather than to extinguish the little towns of their subject Slavs, and, moreover, they were too much occupied in protecting their small world from the Patzinaks and the Khazars to devote themselves to an orgy of plundering and massacre such as delighted the vikings in western Christendom. But they did contemplate greedily the taking of one rich prize, and that was Constantinople. Six times they turned their presumptuous arms against the lovely ' Queen of Cities ' ; yet though this may seem to reflect the age-old barbarian longing to damage a higher and a nobler civilization, there was nevertheless in this instance a worthier motive animating them than that of mere greed, because it was necessary for them to protect either by force or by treaty the Russian-Byzantine trade upon which the prosperity of the Kievan state depended. It is only much farther to the east, on the shores of the Caspian Sea, that the Russians (and no doubt the Volga-Russians more than their Dnieper brethren) appear as sea-rovers intent merely upon plunder and the ruthless slaughter of all those whom they encountered.

But even in the west the reign of terror that was the result of the ravages of the Norsemen and the Danes (most of all the Danes) was not of long duration, and therefore the horrified lamentations of the monks and all the noisy outcry of alarm and hatred that sounds shrilly through the pages of the ninth-century chronicles must be read as a verdict only upon a short and temporary phase in viking history. For sustained pillage and arson ceased with the accomplishment of land-winning, and in the tenth century, after a hundred years of contact with Christendom, the fury of the attack upon towns and churches was spent and the vikings took up arms only either to increase or to defend their holding. There was never, of course, a complete abandonment of the ancient sea-roving habit. Long after the Viking Period was over the Norsemen of the Scottish Isles were still accustomed to fare forth on spring or autumnal cruises to harry and plunder as their forefathers had done of old, and all through the tenth and eleventh centuries there were Norse and Danish chieftains, King Olaf Tryggvason, King Olaf the Saint, and King Svein Forkbeard, for example, who went west-over-sea on viking cruises in their youth. But after the ninth century had run its course these viking princes were merchant-adventurers rather than looters and there are no glaring examples of sustained and villainous piracy until the dark days of the fourteenth century when the German ' Victual Brothers ' of Stockholm terrorized the Baltic world.

Even in the ninth century not all the Danes nor all the Norsemen who sailed the western seas were robbers of the most violent sort ; probably many of the first Norwegian settlers in the Orkneys and Shetlands were peaceful folk, and this in spite of the disadvantage that all the Scottish islands were notorious haunts of Norse pirates who plagued not only the Celtic lands but their own mother-country ; certainly some of the early colonists in Ireland were desirous of maintaining themselves in tranquil and orderly settlements, and they were no doubt men of a peaceable mind who first took land in the Faroes and Iceland. The ninth-century vikings were likewise far from being preoccupied in an unremitting assault upon church and monastery ; thus in England when Halfdan had finally estab-lished his authority by the awful ravaging of Bernicia in 875 those that were left of the religious houses within the Danelaw suffered no harm until 945, in which year an English king came north and sacked Ripon. The truth is that the viking once settled became quickly tolerant of the Christian faith and its institutions, and it was only during forays in wild Ireland or in unconquered Francia that the plundering of monasteries remained a regular practice throughout the greater part of the century. Theft, sacrilege, and massacre, therefore, were not the invariable characteristics of viking operations abroad, and that which was really a typical viking raid in the western seas, a raid such as was repeated again and again throughout the whole of the

Viking Period, was a mild and almost innocuous progress ; a packing-up when the hay was in or the harvest gathered ; the loading and the manning of the boat ; a hazardous journey over the high seas ; then a spell of adventurous trading, a rough-and-ready commerce that often included the exchange of hard knocks, for there was always the chance of a fight with rival boats making for the same market or of landing among strangers who were suspicious and unfriendly.

Much will be heard of viking trade in the narrative that follows, for the Northman was at heart always more of a chapman than a robber, and is deemed to have played no small part in the development of European commerce. As far back as the first century of the Christian era the North Germans had sold furs and amber to the Roman world, and the vikings in their turn were no strangers to continental trade ; but, as of old, their best-organized and most lucrative commerce was that following the great river-routes of East Germany and Russia whereby the Goths of the Black Sea had traded with their fellow-Germans of the north, teaching them the new and flashy eastern modes and selling to them the precious stuffs and wares of the Orient and of Greece. It was, in fact, a desire to retain and to consolidate this ancient German trade across Russia that led to the Swedish settlements on the Volga, the river-way to the Khazar world and the Arabic east, that occasioned the exploitation of the Dnieper basin and the establishment of the Kievan state, and that was the reason for the foundation of Swedish settlements on the Weichsel mouth in the dangerous borderland between the Slavonic Wends and the East Baltic folk.

In the west viking trade was irregular and ill-organized, if indeed it can be said to have been controlled at all. The Danes made but poor use of their capture of the Frisian markets and of their temporary supremacy on the famous route along the North Sea coast to the Baltic ; the Norwegians depended on an intermittent and wasteful commerce. The little boats plied, as they had done of old, across the North Sea, and along the Channel or round Scotland into the Western Sea and to the Irish coast on their seasonal journeys or on bolder trading-ventures lasting for two or three years ; the sea-port settlements in Ireland and South Wales became busy marts ; the viking chapman became familiar to Celt, Englishman, and Frank ; but his was always a petty commerce of private enterprises and of the laborious exchange of wares in little quantities. Nevertheless though it

were casual and difficult trade, though the great protected
convoys of merchant-vikings such as made the Constantinople
journey were unknown in the west, yet the bartering overseas
was precious and necessary to the Northmen and they well
knew the worth to them of such a market as Dublin where vikings
from Norway and from the Scottish Isles and Man and even
from Iceland could pile their goods upon the wharves and obtain
in exchange Irish slaves, grain or cattle, or rarer stuffs come up
from the land of the Franks or from the east.   So it came about
that when the safety of Dublin was threatened by Brian Boru
there hurried from all over the viking world boatloads of warriors
to Dublin Bay to do battle with the Irish at Clontarf and to
defend this main market of the west.

The western trade did not, of course, benefit the vikings only.
For their daring on the seas and the frequency of their visits
gave to trans-ocean traffic an altogether new stability and a
vastly wider scope, so that for the first time in history there
was a regular and stimulating circulation of commodities down
the western fringe of Britain and across the Irish Sea, and in
this improved commerce, which led ultimately to the foundation
by the vikings of the sea-port towns of Ireland and the Welsh
towns along the north coast of the Bristol Channel, the Celt
co-operated with enthusiasm, soon realizing the economic advantages of a viking settlement upon his shores.   Indeed it may
have happened more than once that the continued tenure of
these settlements often depended less on the might of the Norse
arms than on the prospect of the regular arrival of viking boats
to take native wheat or honey or malt or slaves, and to pay in
return for them warm furs and hides, whale oil, walrus tusks,
butter, cheese, dried fish, and coarse woollen cloth.

It has been said that the vikings abroad take their place
in history as conquerors of foreign lands and as colonists, but
it is easy in the modern mood of romantic affection for all
ancient barbarians to err in the direction of overpraising their
achievements in these capacities.   To take first of all the matter
of their land-winning : Frisia, the natural prey of the Danes,
was never adequately defended against them by the Carolingian
emperors, always preoccupied with dangers greater than the
menace of the vikings.   Northern and eastern England, easily
overrun, was nothing but a pitiful turmoil of warring little princes,
and against Wessex, so long as it was stoutly defended, the
vikings failed.   Ireland may have been rich in learning and
monasteries, but the invading Northmen found her a heptarchy

of jealous states incapable at first of organized resistance, and even so they could only hold on with difficulty to their harbour-strongholds on the west and southern coasts. Wales the vikings never conquered. France, sorely harassed in the north and west, was betrayed, like Frisia, by her rulers ; even the cession of Normandy to Rollo was an unexpected weakness on the part of Charles the Simple that a sterner and less embarrassed monarch would have scorned, nothing but a chance consequence of European politics of the hour and in no sense the logical result of a long and brilliant campaign on the part of Rollo. The East Baltic provinces were sparsely populated by a folk no better equipped than the Swedes who subjugated them, and it was only by invitation of the Slavs that the Swedish city-states in Russia were founded. The few inhabitants of the Scottish islands were defenceless, and as for the Faroes, Iceland, and Greenland, these were empty and unwanted wildernesses of the north. For the taking of these the vikings deserve only the credit of the fine seamanship that brought them thither.

It is understood, of course, that mere feebleness of the opposition does not necessarily rob the viking military achievements of all merit, and, setting aside their many audacious and successful raids, there were several occasions in the long story of their operations in enemy countries when beyond all doubt they possessed an effective and dangerous army. Such forces were Halfdan's Danish mounted infantry in England, the armies of Turgeis and Olaf of Dublin in Ireland, Ragnar Lodbrok's army in France in 845, and the huge army of 40,000 men in 700 boats that laid siege to Paris forty years later, the Swedish force that conquered Kurland, the Russian armies of Svyatoslav, Vladimir, and Yaroslav, and the redoubtable hosts of Svein Forkbeard and Cnut the Great. But except when they were under the leadership of such men of military genius as these, it is doubtful whether they would ever have obtained any notable successes against a resolute and united opposition. As it is, whenever a real show of force was mustered against them, whenever they were pitted against a skilfully led army, such as that of Brian's Irishmen, or the English forces of Edward and Æthelstan, or the host of the Emperor John Zimiskes, the vikings crumbled and were scattered. Even the little Spanish kingdom of the Asturias proved that unity of purpose and a brave front could avert the viking menace, and of the west it may be said that whatever the fate of poor Britain might have been, if the Frankish empire had possessed so brave a defender as did the eastern empire in Basil II Bulgaroctonos, who freed Byzantium of the Bulgar peril, then the towns and monasteries of Francia would thereafter have had little to fear from the pirates of an impotent and terrified north.

The chief source of the viking weakness in serious military operations lay in the fact that most of their onslaughts upon foreign countries were not the expression of a national policy, but were merely private enterprises that were also, as often as not, calculated gestures of dissatisfaction with the government of their country. This, of course, is not true of such grand enterprises as the conquest of Svein and Cnut in the fifth phase of viking history and not true of some of the Danish raiders in the time of King Horik, and never true of the Russian wars, but it is true of many of the big viking operations of the ninth and tenth centuries; for in those days the kings of the north were more often embarrassed than gratified by the surprising exploits of their own countrymen abroad, and though they were no doubt willing to take whatever taxes they could succeed in collecting from the newly won possessions of their folk, their own domestic affairs gave them small chance of maintaining discipline abroad, of protecting the would-be settlers, or of reinforcing their armies. Therefore a well-equipped expeditionary force of vikings, once departed from the mother-country, was obliged to feed, pay, and maintain itself with ·little hope of succour from without, a disadvantage that often converted it in a short space of time into an isolated and precariously situated marauding band. Such a lack of support, moreover, was liable to rob the Norsemen of the advantages that were theirs by virtue of their skill as warriors, their clever preliminary espionage and reconnoitring, their strategical sense, their use of camouflage and ruse, their mobility (for they turned themselves into a mounted force wherever horses were available), their unusual battle-tactics and their memorable bravery. It is, of course, a common thing to read in the chronicles how a viking attack was followed by the advent of new fleets of invaders from the north; but these vikings coming afterwards did not always love those who had first arrived and usually weakened rather than strengthened the position of the Northmen abroad. Thus the various Norse and Danish settlements in Ireland were as likely to war with one another as with the Irish; the Danes and the Norse quarrelled in Northumbria; some vikings were prepared to take English pay and enlist against their own countrymen; in Francia one viking fleet could be bribed to fight against another.

It is probably not true that the vikings were any worse fighters by land than they were afloat, but it counted against them in the west that they seldom had the opportunity of fighting foreigners on the sea where they were absolutely and incontestably supreme. The Russian-Swedes certainly failed, as indeed they were bound to fail, against Greek warships and 'Greek fire'; but in north-western Europe none of the kingdoms or empires against whom the vikings fought could oppose them with an efficient fleet; thus when King Alfred built a navy to fight the Danes, his hired sailors bungled in their management of the new boats and the English fleet failed; so, much later, did the expensive and pathetic armament collected by Æthelred at Sandwich, this being miserably scattered by storm and incompetence before a blow was struck. There was, moreover, one consequence of the supremacy at sea that was an additional source of weakness to the viking armies, for since the fleets of the Northmen might fare anywhere unmolested, there was no necessity for them to proceed only in huge armaments; therefore the viking strength was perpetually in danger of being frittered away by the desertion of discontented adventurers who could safely traverse the seas by themselves, either homewards or to fresh foreign lands. In an age of unrest, amid the endless flow and ebb of their folk, it was a hard thing to hold steadfastly to one scrap of conquered land, should their tenure be threatened, or to obey the dictates of wisdom in a world where fortune and folly beckoned to them on every side. Only under the few iron rulers of men, the great vikings, did Northmen rise superior to their chaotic environment and prove themselves redoubtable conquerors and diligent colonists.

The success of their colonial enterprise depended in an even greater measure than that of their wars upon the leaders. Some of these certainly showed a political sense of a high order, such as Rurik of Novgorod or the Kievan princes Oleg, Igor, Vladimir, and Yaroslav, or again Halfdan in England, King Olaf of Dublin, Sigurd and Thorfinn, the Orkney earls, or Rollo in Normandy, or the great Svein and Cnut in Denmark; but these men were exceptions, and of the vikings in general it must be admitted that they failed as colonists. The fault lay in the lack of proper administration and organization, a reluctance to submit to the rule of a single chieftain in a society where most men deemed themselves the equal of one another, and in a lack of zeal for the commonwealth that is common among new settlers who have their own private fortunes to make; thus the grand Danelaw of Halfdan lasted only fifty years before it submitted to an English king; Dublin likewise fell to the Irish after half a century of Norse rule and was for some years under the rule of Cearbhall of Ossory; Frisia was lost by the Danes three years after it had been ceded to Godfred by Charles the Fat; Normandy was Frenchified out of recognition within a century of its granting to Rollo. But these isolated instances of failure within the Viking Period itself are only symptoms of the lack of colonial sense, and the real instability of the achievement of the Northmen as colonists is best shown by the dismal continuation of the story in the twelfth century and afterwards; for the Middle Ages witness the collapse and poverty of the Scandinavian powers, the dwindling and extinction of the Ostmen in Ireland, the loss of the Scottish islands, the complete collapse of Danish rule in England, the unspeakable miseries of deserted Iceland, the shameful end of the Greenland Norsemen, and the vanishing into Slavonic civilization of the few remaining Swedish folk of the Kievan state in Russia. All these events, the immediate sequel to the Viking Period, are a necessary complement to the successes of the ninth and tenth centuries; for the fall of the viking peoples most cruelly illuminates their rise, revealing it not as a stately and stable advance, but as a sickly capricious thing, a triumph not for political sense, but merely for audacity, enthusiasm, and lust.

An incomplete and erroneous impression of the Viking Period must inevitably result from any account that is confined to the fortunes of the buccaneers and colonists abroad. The real story of the time is that of the political development of the three northern countries concerned, and as a background to the plunderers and the emigrants faring over the high seas there remain always the kings of Norway, Sweden and Denmark, ruling as best they could a conservative and long-established folk who clung tenaciously to their ancestral estates. For these hard-working folk, jealous of their traditional freedom and privileges, were the real substance of the viking world, and not only as emigrants but as stay-at-homes, as men of peace as well as men of war, they contribute their share to the history of the time.

In their own countries the Northmen were ruled either by a high-king who was undisputed lord of a nation, or by petty kings or great noblemen who were masters only of the people among whom they dwelt; next in rank to the kings was a rural aristocracy of jarls (earls) and hersir (lesser nobles), and next a vast and respectable middle class of landed farmers known as the bönder (yeomen [1]), while below these were two lower orders of freedmen (cottagers) and thralls (slaves). It was the aristocracy that supplied most of the great viking leaders, and some of these, like Turgeis the Norwegian, Rorik the Dane, and Ingvar Vittfarne the Swede, even came of the royal families, so that it is not hard to understand how domestic political disputes and the rivalry of princes may have been responsible for the departure of these and many other malcontent grandees who left their country in order to win dominions abroad. But the great bulk of the viking emigrants, the colonists and the merchants, were men of the bonde class, a hard-working, orderly agricultural folk of decent birth, dwelling on their ancestral lands, proud of their lineage and their rights, and possessing through the *things* (district courts), of which each was a member, a voice in the economic and political destiny of their folk. The bonde, like the noble, was a free man, owner of the land he lived on, and oppressed by none of the obligations of feudalism, yet though he was a worthy and well-intentioned person, there were two factors that made him not quite such a comfortable and trust-worthy member of the social order as his position warranted ; the first of these was that his favourite odel system of land tenure on a family basis, intended to prevent the alienation of the estate to strangers, either led to its rapid division among the heirs into too many uneconomic units, or left the superfluous younger sons of the family compensated out of the ancestral exchequer, but without an estate at all ; in the second place the bonde was abnormally jealous of his rights and sensitive in a most unusual measure to the real or supposed tyranny of the king.

In these two weaknesses there lie causes of the unrest that provoked these stalwart farmers into the viking enterprises of land-winning and plundering abroad. For a system of land-tenure ill-adapted to the needs of a vigorous and increasing stock in a country where the supply of arable land and pasturage is far from inexhaustible leads inevitably to over-population, and over-population is a potent incentive to migration. A roving life abroad with the promise of quick-won booty, or the adventure of settlement in the colonies, were alike preferable to a difficult and undistinguished existence on the too-crowded family estate, and therefore those men who were not the principal heirs to their fathers' lands took to viking enterprise not merely as an

---

[1] There is no exact equivalent for the Norse *bonde* ; I prefer yeoman to farmer, but any word implying feudal obligations is, of course, misleading.

outlet for their valorous and greedy passions, but of necessity, so that they might win wealth and a home. That over-population was indeed the cause of one migration from the north, an out-pouring of the Gotlanders about the year A.D. 500, is attested by the *Gutasaga* itself, and Dudo, the Norman historian of the eleventh century, likewise attributes the migrations of the Danes and other German folk to the same cause ; but Dudo believed that the over-population was the result of polygamy, and this was certainly a practice of many viking nobles in the early days that must also be reckoned with as contributing to the peopling of the northern lands with spirited and well-born youths who could not hope to inherit the great estates of their fathers.

On the second count, since the freedom of the noble and the bonde led them both to resist stubbornly any attempt to interfere with their ancient privileges, it was inevitable that in an age destined to see the birth of the northern nations as monarchies bowed beneath the rule of one paramount and all-powerful lord, these tender-skinned folk should find themselves assailed by royal commands, by new vexations, new restrictions, and evil consequences of the royal displeasure such as neither they nor their ancestors had known before ; so they took ship, many of them, vowing to make their homes in other countries where a man might manage his affairs as he would and owe allegiance to none other. Thus in Norwegian history there is a tradition, vouched for by Snorri Sturlason, that the severity of Harald Fairhair's rule, after he had made all Norway his, resulted in the migration of the Norse bönder to the Faroes and to Iceland.

But even with this much said it is still impossible to explain in final and satisfactory terms the huge outpouring of the northern peoples that is known as the viking expansion. It may well be that over-population, lack of land, and political grievances were the most urgent motives, yet the relative forces with which they operated cannot be measured, and it must be conceded that neither severally nor together do they seem sufficient to explain migrations so considerable and so long-sustained. Perhaps, after all, sheer and ugly greed must be reckoned as the spur that constantly and unfailingly provoked the Northmen to their viking exploits ; but there may have been other factors likely to result in emigration that were beyond men's control and that are wholly unknown, a long succession of bad harvests, for example, or the temporary failure of the hunting and the fishing.

PLATE II

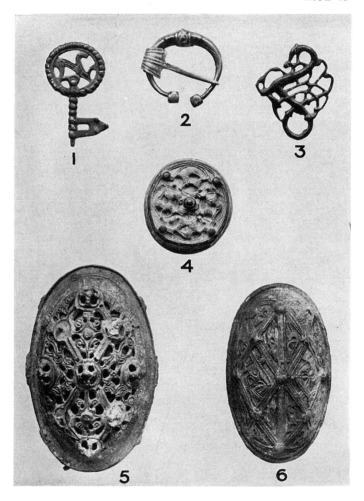

KEY, BROOCHES, AND OPENWORK ORNAMENT: BRONZE AND SILVER ($\times \frac{1}{2}$

For details, see List of Plates

In short, since there is no solution of the problem the historian must perforce accept the phenomenon of the viking movement without further questioning, just as the earlier and unexplained movements of the Migration Period are accepted. For to these the viking expansion is an inevitable sequel, and as in the earlier centuries the East Germans and the West Germans poured out from their homes in an inexplicable onrush, so in the ninth and tenth centuries the North Germans roused themselves in their sea-girt lands, looked forth upon the world, and set sail to ransack Europe in the old barbarian way.

Yet though he was a barbarian the viking was not wholly a savage. It is true that he could not write, even though here and there men could scratch out a few runes on wood or stone, and therefore he had no literature ; but nevertheless he had composed tales and poetry of a kind that even to-day can thrill and astonish. He sang of the gods of his forefathers, endowed by him with personalities akin to those of the viking warrior himself, and in the Edda poems he told of their adventures, their origin, and their struggle with the giants, of their nimble wit and of their loves and quarrels. All men knew the grand Bjarkamal, the Danish heroic lay that St. Olaf caused to be recited to him before the battle of Stiklestad ; the histories of the kings and viking chiefs were learnt by heart for recitation by the *scalds* (professional bards and reciters), and already in the tenth century the Icelanders had begun to weave the stories that are now enshrined in the enchanting literature of the sagas. But the Northman could boast something else besides a taste for heroic and dramatic recitation, for he had wit ; dearly he loved the saucy remarks and lampoons that could be composed during the daily round, and the best of these he was at pains to memorize and circulate, as the sagas show ; likewise he enjoyed the curious and baffling scaldic verse of which the sagas are so full and wherein the poet cloaked his meaning by a prodigal use of synonyms of the most extravagant and far-fetched kind.

In craftsmanship the vikings were expert at the carving of wood and bone and like materials, and there were among them many admirable smiths Iron they could get for themselves and so they were possessed of a wealth of iron tools of sorts and sizes that other nations of western Europe may well have envied, and the viking smith could also do beautiful and delicate work in gold, silver, and bronze. His woman could weave a good cloth ; but her pottery was rough and prehistoric-looking in Sweden and Denmark, and the finest vessels were clumsy copies

of Frankish vessels that have been found in the Sleswig borderland ; most of the household utensils were made either of iron,
or horn, or wood, or stone, and in Norway a special pot-stone
was quarried for this purpose, being employed in making large
basins and long-handled bowls. Similarly in poverty-stricken
Greenland soapstone was the favourite material for cups and
dishes.

The abundance of iron tools and the plentiful supply of wood
made plank-work easy and cheap so that the viking became
proficient to an extraordinary degree in timber-architecture and
shipbuilding, especially the latter. Even before the Viking
Period, as the larger of the two Kvalsund boats [1] shows, the
Northmen could make strong, well-proportioned, clinker-built
craft that were as much as 50 feet in overall length and about
9 feet wide amidships. It was to this type of boat, built of
unpainted oak and clinched with iron nails, broad and shallow,
of easy entrance and run, with a deep rockered keel and a steep
sheer, that the viking shipbuilder always remained faithful ;
but he learnt to build much bigger boats, and of the larger
warships there is a noble example preserved in Oslo to this day,
namely the Gokstad ship, [2] a boat that was in commission during
the reign of Harald Fairhair at the end of the ninth century.
Her overall length is nearly 80 feet and her displacement about
30 tons ; she had a mast capable of being raised and lowered,
and a large square sail, but she did not depend only on the wind
and could be propelled also by 16 pairs of oars worked through
circular oar-ports ; the boat must have had a crew of perhaps
40 men and no doubt could carry 60 or 70 persons in all. She
had a tall, good-looking prow and stern, rising boldly up from
the water and alike fore and aft, and her rudder was fixed
over the starboard quarter. She carried three small dinghies,
had five portable berths forward and a striped tent as shelter
amidships when not at sea ; the great circular shields of the
warriors, painted yellow or black, lined her gunwales on the
outside. In fair weather she could perhaps exceed 10 knots.

The Gokstad boat was of the ' long-ship ' or man-of-war
class, and since speed was required of her she had less freeboard

[1] Her length (54 feet) is estimated only, as the frame is incomplete.
These two boats are dated fifth to eighth century and are now at Bergen.
Pictures of them will be found in Dr. A. W. Brøgger's *Ancient Emigrants*,
Oxford, 1929 ; but for a full description, see H. Shetelig and F. Johannesen,
Kvalsundfundet, Bergens Mus. Skrifter, N.R. II, 2 (1929).

[2] Found at Gokstad, Sandefjord, Norway, in 1880. N. Nicolaysen,
The Viking-Ship discovered at Gokstad, Oslo, 1882 (in English and Danish).

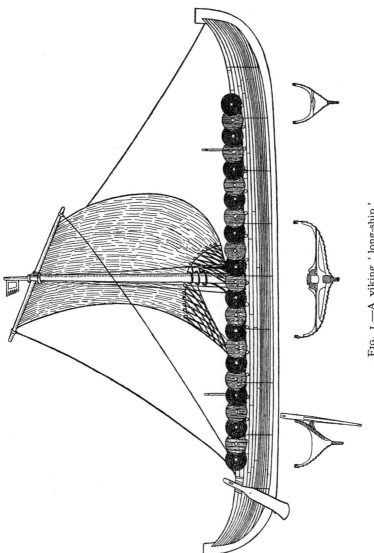

FIG. I.—A viking 'long-ship'

(Type of the Gokstad boat: overall length, 80 feet)

than the ordinary viking craft ; these 'long-ships' were not intended for great voyages upon the open sea, but that a boat like the Gokstad vessel could cross the North Sea or the Baltic comfortably was proved in 1893 when a crew of Norwegians piloted a replica of her over the Atlantic to America, taking four weeks for the crossing and finding no fault with their craft. She was far from being the biggest boat of her kind, for the most famous example of the class, the *Long Serpent* of Olaf Tryggvason, was propelled by 34 pairs of oars and was 160 feet in overall length, a noble ship that perhaps bore to her last tragic sea-fight off Svold (A.D. 1000) as many as 250 men under the great king who was her captain. The carving on the Stenkyrka stone (Pl. IV) from Gotland shows two other 'long-ships' ; the greater of these has the line of round shields on the bulwarks such as lined the gunwales of the Gokstad boat, very curious multiple sheets, and a 'dragon' head adorning the prow. This was a favourite figure-head for the vikings' boats, but unhappily no actual example has survived.

The boats, commonly called 'knörrs', that were used on the big viking expeditions overseas and the long, hazardous trips to Ireland, Greenland, and America, were different craft from the 'long-ships' of the kings and chieftains, being shorter, sturdier, and carrying a higher freeboard and having a great beam and a wide bottom. They depended almost entirely upon sail-power, using their oars only as auxiliaries if the wind deserted them, and they were capable of travelling about 75 miles a day, so that the journey from Norway to Iceland probably took on an average 9 days and the crossing of the North Sea 3 days. They carried about 20 to 30 men as crew, but some of the knörrs were obviously big boats and could take much larger numbers, or could accommodate 40 or so human beings with live-stock besides, and food and fodder sufficient for several weeks. Such boats must have had a displacement of 50 tons or thereabouts.

No viking boat hitherto found has better illustrated the truly admirable skill of the northern shipbuilder than Queen Asa's yacht, the lovely 'Oseberg Ship' that was built about A.D. 800 and in which the queen herself was subsequently buried.[1] The

[1] Like Gokstad, Oseberg is situated on the Vestfold side of the Oslo fjord ; the boat was excavated in 1904 and is described in that mighty work *Osebergfundet*, Oslo, 1917–1928 ; for shorter accounts (in German and English), F. A. van Scheltema, *Der Osebergfund*, Augsberg, 1929 (*Führer zur Urgeschichte*, 7), A. W. Brøgger, *The Oseberg Ship*, Saga-Book of Viking Society, X, i (1919–24), p. 1, and H. Shetelig, *Queen Asa's Sculptures*, *ib.*, p. 12.

PLATE III

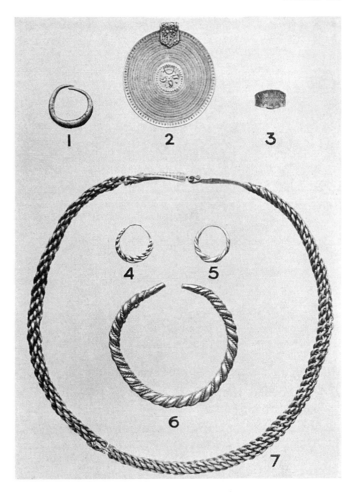

PERSONAL ORNAMENTS OF GOLD AND SILVER
(ALL REDUCED TO SLIGHTLY UNDER HALF SIZE : THUS NO. 7 IS 8 INCHES IN OUTSIDE
DIAMETER)
For details, see List of Plates

craft was designed only for cruising in the quiet waters of the fjords, but she was over 64 feet long and 15 feet broad amidships, and had a mast and sail and accommodation for 15 pairs of oars ; most of all she is remarkable for her graceful lines and her tall curved prow with its richly carved stem and gunwales and its delicate volute-tip. As most travellers to Oslo know, the funeral chamber on this beautiful boat was filled with Queen Asa's treasures, a marvellous array of carved wooden furniture that has made the discovery of the royal grave one of the most astonishing and illuminating archaeological finds of this century ; no visitor to the museum gallery where these beautiful things are set out, no one who has looked at the ship herself in her

FIG. 2.—Detail of brooch from Kaasta, Sweden (¼)

hall on Bygdö, can ever again think of the ninth-century Norsemen as completely vile and soulless barbarians.

Nor dare man assert that the Swedes and the Danes loved fine ships and beautiful ornament less than those Norwegian vikings whose splendid vessels have thus been so luckily preserved for posterity. It is true that the Greeks often affected to despise, as well they might, the open craft of the Russians, referring to them contemptuously as *monoxyla*, mere dug-out canoes ; but the sagas and the rune-stones attest that the Swedish and the Danish vessels were the equals of the Norse, and the lesson of the smaller articles of the Viking Period, brooches, weapons, and the like, is that all three northern peoples shared a taste for the same variety of ornament and could have differed but little from one another in the matter of arts and crafts.

The favourite decoration of the Northmen was an intricate arrangement of animal-forms, knots, and worm-twists. This has survived chiefly in its miniature variety on small metal brooches and so forth, but it was employed also in works of a grander sort such as in the carvings on the Oseberg ship, or upon the woodwork of the mast-churches and the hall-pillars and gables of houses, or upon the great rune-stones that commemorate the noble dead. The history and development of this northern ornament have been studied with exemplary thoroughness by Scandinavian and Danish archaeologists who have pieced together a story of unusual interest.

At the beginning of the Viking Period the craftsmen of the north were using for their pattern-making a formula known as the *Late Vendel*[1] style, a beautiful animal-ornament in the

FIG. 3.—Bronze oval brooch, with detail, from Bergen ($\frac{2}{3}$)

form of a writhing network of a creature's limbs, head, and body, seen in profile, but twisted and contorted almost out of recognition ; it is illustrated here (Fig. 2) by an often-published drawing of the detail of a brooch from Kaasta in Uppland, Sweden, and also (Fig. 3) by a drawing, with detail above, of an .oval brooch from Bergen in Norway that is illustrated again in half-tone (Pl. II, 6). But it was not long before new influences began to alter the work of the viking craftsmen as they became increasingly familiar with the weapons and ornaments of foreign folk and saw something of the handicrafts of the far-away Byzantine-Oriental world. One result of this was the introduction of some severity and restraint in design, so that instead of the overloaded and crowded work of the Migration Period

[1] So-called because it is seen typically in the famous cemetery of boat-graves close to Vendel church in north Uppland, Sweden. *Late Vendel* is the equivalent of *Style* III in B. Salin's renowned analysis of the Germanic animal-ornament.

PLATE IV

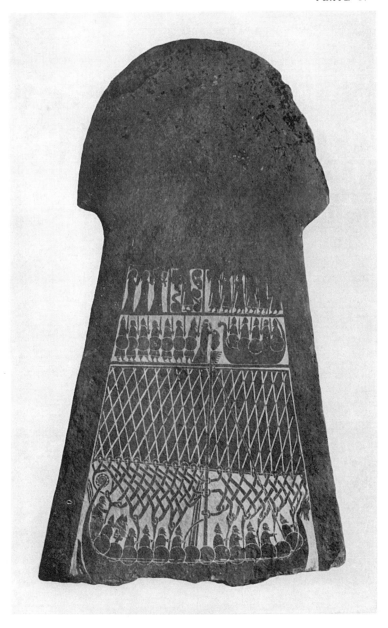

SCULPTURED STONE, STENKYRKA GOTLAND
Height, 8 feet 4 inches

there appear such noble pieces as those carved by the great Oseberg artist whom Dr. Shetelig has called the Academist. But the feeling for classical simplicity and the inclusion of occasional geometrical and foliate forms did not seriously combat the northern love for animal forms, and the outcome was that the viking began to contrive patterns of half naturalistic human or leonine little creatures clutching hold of one another in a semi-plastic style of stumpy, solid forms that was quite unlike the purely linear design of Vendel art. Thus there arose the ninth-century viking style of the *Gripping Beast* that is illustrated here by the top of a box-brooch from the island of Gotland (Pl. II, 4) and that is a style of three phases ; the first, *Viking I* (or *Early Oseberg*), is represented on the brooch, and then there is the succeeding *Viking-Baroque* (or *Late Oseberg*), and thirdly the Borre [1] phase which begins at the end of the ninth century and carries the gripping-beast style over into the tenth century, where it survives in elaborate and altered forms like the decoration on the oval brooch from Santon in Norfolk (Pl. II, 5). This ' gripping-beast ' style, in so far as it reveals a new taste for substance and modelling in surface pattern, was probably a result of the influence of Carolingian and Byzantine wood-carving and sculpture, and the spirit of the new designs with its ' clutching ' forms is quite plainly derived from the illuminated manuscripts, ivories, and metalwork of the English, the Irish, and the Franks.

But the experiment with the poor little gripping-beast forms had not satisfied the Scandinavian artist who was often unsuccessful in controlling and adapting the new *motif*. As the Oseberg and Gokstad ships show, some northern craftsmen still remained faithful to their old love, the linear animal, and were carving heads in profile and even drawing the linear animal itself throughout the period when the gripping beast was the fashion. Gradually the semi-plastic forms gave way before the revived profile animal, but by the end of the ninth century these designers were beginning to know something about Celtic art with its enchanting animal-drawings, and so when the profile creature began once more to be the main theme of the northern patterns, it was in an altered and Irish-looking form ; thus late in the ninth century was born the splendid *Jellinge Style* [2] that was

---

[1] Borre is in Vestfold, Norway, north of Oseberg. This art-convention (it is not really a distinct *style*) was named and defined by H. Shetelig, *Osebergfundet*, III, 295.

[2] Jellinge is near Veile in Jutland, Denmark ; it is the site of the royal barrows and runestones (Pl. VI) described on p. 100. The typical and early ' Jellinge ' animal-ornament is to be seen on a little silver cup from one of the great barrows.

to dominate viking art throughout the tenth century and to live on until the eleventh had wellnigh run its course.

The new Jellinge animal was contorted into the old tangle of limbs and body, but this time the northern artists did not occupy themselves exclusively with twisted writhing animals, for they also set themselves to work out new patterns of intertwining plant-scrolls, snakes, and ribbons, and in order to perfect these they borrowed many details from both eastern and western art. This gave them the opportunity of simplifying and empha- sizing their beloved animal-theme, since the twists and twirls could now be introduced independently, and so by the end of the tenth century they had learnt to prefer a ' Great Beast ', of the kind they had seen on Anglian monuments, that they drew according to their own spirited formula and surrounded by and enmeshed in the sprays and knots which represented, despite the foreign origin of the elements, the feeling for delicate and intricate patterns that was inherited from Vendel art. The Jellinge style in this ' Great Beast ' phase that begins in the '70s or '80s of the tenth century is illustrated here (Pl. VI) by the renowned memorial stone at Jellinge set up by King Harald Gormsson.

Even in the eleventh century the Jellinge style, still with its ' great Beast ', can be recognized in such lovely and fantastic things as the wood-carvings of about A.D. 1080 that adorn the outside and inside of the Urnes mast-church at the end of the Sogn fjord in Norway, and this beautiful ' Urnes ' phase is represented here in miniature by a small ornament in openwork bronze from Norway (Pl. II, 3). This style is, however, matched and excelled in the contemporary Irish metalwork and there is no doubt that it owes as much to direct influence from Ireland as it does to the native Jellinge tradition.

In the first half of the century, however, in the days of King Cnut's Anglo-Danish kingdom and of the busy traffic across Russia with the Byzantine world and the Arabic east, the character of the now beloved foliate and ribbon ornament changes, and in the period A.D. 1000–1050 this is executed in what is known as the *Ringerike Style*.[1] The new convention seems to be most of all influenced by English design, but its graceful leafwork is also to be found in symmetrical palmette- like patterns that are probably of oriental origin and that seem to have been so sufficient and satisfactory in the eyes of the

[1] Ringerike is a district of the Buskerud province of Norway and lies immediately N.W. of Oslo and the Tyri fjord. A group of carved sandstone monuments here has given the style its name.

northern artists that they were now prepared to abandon their ancient animal-theme; yet in the beginning the new style was employed in designs of the Jellinge taste as background to the great beast and it is so displayed upon the well-known viking

FIG. 4.—Bone pin from the Thames (½)

grave-stone from St. Paul's Churchyard that is now in the Guildhall Museum in London. Moreover, Ringerike designs were often enriched by the addition of animal heads as terminals for the scrolls and tendrils, and this can be seen in the half-Jellinge carving of the St. Paul's Churchyard slab or, as a reminder of Jellinge animal-art, in the lovely bronze panel, perhaps part of a viking weathervane, that is now preserved at Winchester. The Ringerike style, however, is really more notable because it represents a break with the old animal-tradition than because of its occasional blending with Jellinge animal-ornament; for it is as something new to northern art that it appears in the simple and solitary decoration of such small objects as the bone pin (Fig. 4) found in the Thames or in the more elaborate designs carved on the London grave-stone now in the British

FIG. 5.—Design on gravestone from Bibury, Gloucs. (⅛)

Museum and on the Ringerike stones themselves; it is a departure from tradition, again, in such a piece of sculpture as the gravestone (Fig. 5) with the mask-terminals from Bibury, Gloucestershire; but the Ringerike style is perhaps best of all exemplified as a new and virile art when it was adopted as the favourite formula of the clever Swedish designers who employed it so effectively upon their rune-stones and who so cunningly worked its patterns in silver on sword-hilts and the sockets of iron spear-heads. At the end of the Viking Period a new and mediaeval-looking animal appears in northern art, and though the old tradition was then vanishing and the conventions of the Middle Ages taking its place, yet this beast was sometimes drawn in a graceful, fiery Ringerike manner, as upon the gilt weather-

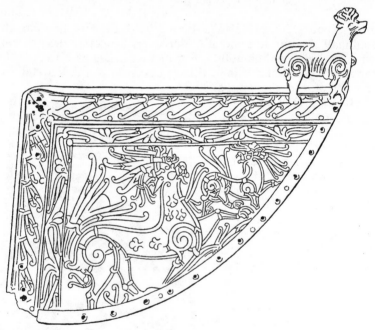

FIG. 6.—Bronze weather-vane from Hedden, Norway ($\frac{1}{3}$)

vane (Fig. 6) from Hedden Church, Norway; this is probably a work of the late eleventh century and it shows how the spirit of viking art lived on to invigorate a continental mediaeval design.

So short a summary as this of the leading northern decorative styles does not by any means cover the whole field of viking art. In a fuller account something would have to be said of the Northman's feeling for colour, of the way whereby he used paints to heighten the effect of his carvings in wood and stone, and of the gay and vigorous painting, now only just recognizable, on the flat panels of the Oseberg chair, on the Jellinge woodwork, and in the interior of the mast-churches. Likewise it would be necessary to speak of the attempts (sometimes rather clumsy) to carve upon the memorial stone figure-scenes of men and animals such as are to be found on some of the viking crosses in the Isle of Man. Worthy of mention too would be the much more successful carvings of the Northman's beloved and beautiful boat. One famous stone depicting a magnificent ship of the ninth century is reproduced here (Pl. IV). It comes from Stenkyrka in the island of Gotland and must be rated among the noblest monuments of the north ; yet it is a piece of sculpture that is emphatically not the work of an artist bound by the conventions of the ' styles ', but of a master-sculptor of a Swedish school that was intent upon the composition of balanced pictorial works according to its own stately tradition.

In spite of some aesthetic sensibility and a real cleverness in the designing of surface-ornaments, the Northman did not achieve any remarkable triumphs in such fields as that of architecture or sculpture in the round. Nevertheless his peculiar skill in the ship-yards had given him some encouragement to experiment in timber-architecture, and the few remaining mastchurches of early Norway such as that at Garmo near Lom and the better-known Urnes church, both of eleventh-century date, are witness to the grandeur of many a vanished hall of the Scandinavian kings and chieftains. But elaborate ornamental structures of that kind can scarcely be called typical homes of the viking folk, and the ordinary northern house was probably of a much simpler sort, timber-built as a rule in Scandinavia, but often made half of turf and stone, especially in the treeless countries of Iceland and Greenland. The furniture, which was usually carved in the homes of wealthy men, was wooden, and the rest of the household equipment simple in the extreme, consisting of pots and pans of iron and vessels of horn and wood ; there were, however, plenty of iron tools, such as knives, sickles, scythes, and pincers, but in addition to these there were stone implements for the roughest work. Poor ' Burnt Njal ' of Iceland, whose homestead at Bergthorshvoll has been excavated and whose pathetic and charred belongings can now be seen in the museum at Reykjavik, seems to have lived a life that cannot have been very much of an improvement upon that of neolithic man. He had iron tools, certainly, but his house contained a large assortment of perforated stone hammers of various sizes [1] and a mass of grooved stone line-sinkers and stone door weights ;

---

[1] Dr. Thordarson tells me that many of these were probably *fisksleggjur*, fish-hammers, and were used for crushing dried cod-heads.

pottery he had none, though he did keep in the house a huge rectangular clay-lined trough to serve him as a bath.

In arms and equipment the viking aped the Frank and the Saxon, and his skill in metallurgy permitted him to copy in profuse quantity the foreign weapons that he so much admired, even if he could not always imitate their quality. He possessed indeed a rich and varied armoury and was in this respect better equipped than the East Baltic and the Slavs, and better off than the Celts whose chronicles admitted the superiority of the viking gear.

Most beloved of all were the sword and the axe, and these, if they were not bought or stolen abroad, were made according to the prevailing continental types that the German smiths had evolved. A single-edged pointed sword was still in use among the northern peoples in the ninth century, but the favourite blade of the Viking Period is two-edged and heavy, with a deep wide fuller. The details of the pommel-shape and quillons vary with the period, but characteristic shapes that occur commonly are illustrated by four viking swords in a little group of weapons (Pl. V) chosen from the Iron Age Gallery of the British Museum. The magnificent axe shown in this same picture is probably the work of an eleventh-century Anglo-Danish smith and is the end of a long and varied series of viking axe-forms which need not be paraded here ; the axe was indeed an almost indispensable companion of the Northmen and it won for the Scandinavians in the Varangian Guard at Constantinople the name of the 'Axe-bearing Barbarians' and singled them out from the other foreign troops in their imperial master's service. The three iron spearheads in the group belong in all probability, like the axe, to the end of the Viking Period, but they illustrate a favourite variety, long narrow blades with sharp shoulders and handsome-looking, such as Svein's soldiers may have borne.

Of the viking shield little is known except that there were two varieties, the one long so that it would cover a man when he knelt behind it, and the other, which was by far the commoner type, round. This last was a light wooden disc about 3 feet in diameter, metal-edged and painted, with a central boss of bronze or iron ; they were shields of this kind, painted alternately yellow and black, that lined the bulwarks of the Gokstad ship (Fig. 1) and that are borne by the warriors carved on the Stenkyrka stone (Pl. IV), and they were such shields, if English examples are wanted, that were carried by the vikings depicted on the Lowther hogback tombstone in Westmoreland and the

PLATE V

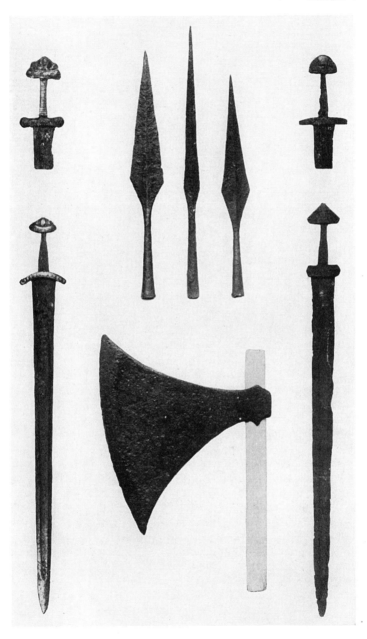

IRON SWORDS ($\times \frac{1}{5}$), SPEAR HEADS ($\times \frac{1}{2}$) AND AXE ($\times \frac{1}{3}$)
For details, see List of Plates

Gosforth hogback in Cumberland. As for armour, chain-mail was not unknown and an attempt to represent this in a little bone carving is shown here (Fig. 7); but probably it was rarely used except by the richest chieftains until the eleventh century, and before that a leather cuirass was the ordinary man's protection for the body; the kings and leaders likewise wore a helmet, a simple pointed casque sometimes provided with a nose-guard and often surmounted by a crest, but never having the funny wings or horns of the picture-book vikings. The profile of these helmets can be seen on the Stenkyrka stone (Pl. IV) and on many other memorials.

The sagas have little to say of bows and arrows, but most of the nobles and *bönder* of the north were practised archers and there is a quiver full of arrows included in the rich furniture

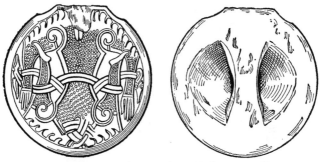

FIG. 7.—Bone carving (front and back) from the Thames ($\frac{2}{3}$)

of a tenth-century viking boat-grave found at Hedeby in Sleswig that is now to be seen in the Kiel Museum. Yet the bow seems to have been comparatively little used except for the rich man's hunting, and it plays but a small part in the saga-stories of battles. But if the ordinary viking was no great archer he was certainly a good horseman, and although an Arab author said of the Volga-vikings that they rode but little, in the west the northern soldiers were accustomed to ride on horseback during their cross-country expeditions, as the chroniclers of both Francia and England testify. The harness and other horse-gear of the vikings have been found on many occasions, and a drawing is shown here of a stirrup of the type they wore (Fig. 8); it is a handsome iron hoop inlaid with gleaming bronze and was found in the Thames; probably this example, which is in the British Museum, was made in England late in the ninth century and its owner may perhaps have been an Englishman, for it is only in shape that it is typical of viking stirrups.

It is no easy matter to pass judgement on the viking abroad or to label him according to the manner of man he was. That he could be a grand and noble adventurer, that he could be valorous in battle, wise in council, and law-abiding, all this the saga-reader cannot doubt ; in like manner his love of poems and stories, his taste for rich and handsome ornaments, his pride in well-built and beautiful boats, his delight in a good sword or a keen axe, these veil him decorously in the mists of romance so that often he figures in history books only as a mettlesome

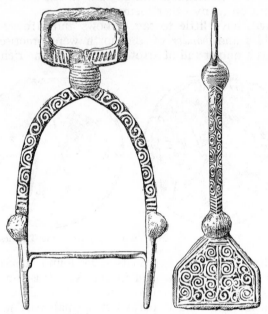

FIG. 8.—Inlaid iron stirrup from the Thames at Battersea ($\frac{1}{3}$)

and admirable person who was lavishly caparisoned, a proud, chivalrous son of the sea, who had come that he might revive with his sturdy northern civilization the effete and characterless folk of the west. But a wealthy viking on his best behaviour can scarcely be taken as typical of all his northern brethren, and neither can his most extreme counterpart, the shameless professional robber, nor the poor squalid settler working on some stolen lands in a foreign country or struggling to develop a bleak, inhospitable territory of the far-off north. It is, of course, true that the viking was often a worthless rascal leading a sordid and miserable existence ; one contemporary Arab writer describes the domestic life of the Volga-vikings in terms that show them to have been objectionable and filthy creatures of a peculiarly repulsive kind, and another Arab agreed that they were veritably the dirtiest of all men. But this glimpse is only of a part of an enormous whole and is insufficient to condemn all the Northmen as entirely despicable barbarians.

For the viking, whatever he may have done abroad, whatever his social behaviour was, despite his heathendom and the polygamy of his chieftains, must be seen against a cultural background that deserves respect. He came of a people who were for the most part sober and industrious agriculturists, a people who were endowed with considerable aesthetic sensibility and who were in some trades, such as shipbuilding and ironwork, craftsmen of more than ordinary skill. Therefore though it is profitless to look for such a thing as a typical viking, since throughout the whole of their history the vikings were exactly what their circumstances made them, robbers, colonists, and traders, yet it is a nearer approach to the truth to believe of them that they were an orderly and sensible civilized folk than that they were bloody and destructive brutes.

It has been said that neither the conquests abroad made by the vikings nor their colonial enterprises command an unreserved respect. It remains, therefore, to ask what was the worth of the viking movement and what permanent good or lasting harm these Northmen did.

So far as eastern Europe is concerned the vikings undoubtedly played an important and beneficial rôle in the foundation of the Russian state and in the subsequent orientation of this upon Constantinople ; herein, beyond all question, was their most significant and remarkable achievement. But in the west there is less to be said for them. Certainly the fact that Iceland and the Faroes are now peopled by a flourishing and happy folk must be regarded as a result of Norse enterprise in the Viking Period ; yet the discovery of Greenland brought few men profit, and the amazing discovery of America was so much adventure and courage wasted. On the other hand, the seaport town-system of Ireland was not only established but developed by the Northmen and this contributed materially to the well-being of the country in the early Middle Ages ; in Ireland, indeed, the usefulness of the vikings ended only with their extinction after the Norman invasion, and this perhaps is also true of the northern shores of the Bristol Channel where the vikings had developed a lively trade and were settled in no small numbers. In England the establishment of the Danes meant the addition of a large foreign element to the population, and though this had no permanent effect upon the southern Danelaw between the Thames and the Welland, it was not without considerable influence upon the social structure of East Anglia, and was of even greater significance in the northern Danelaw of Northumbria where, until the Norman conquest and even later, a peaceable and semi-foreign rural society contrived to hold themselves apart from the rest of the English, aware of their individuality and differing from their neighbours in law and custom. For though the original Danelaw lasted only half a century as an independent Danish colony and though the Anglo-Danish kingdom of Cnut was likewise short-lived, neither the re-conquest of the Danelaw by Edward the Elder nor the collapse of Cnut's realm meant the actual expulsion of the unambitious resident countryfolk of Danish blood. To them the fall of the Danelaw in 920 was but a change of overlord, and the coming of the Normans no worse than the arrival of new masters ; so they survived as only half-English folk, possessors of their ancient *wapentakes*, until at last they disappear in the Norman world of the Middle Ages, leaving behind them a rich legacy of Old Norse personal names and place-names as witness to the foreign blood in them.

As to the effect of the expansion of the Northmen upon the march of civilization, it is easy to exaggerate the harm done by the pillaging and destruction of the monasteries that was the first result of the viking invasion ; for although it is now a commonplace of history that the vikings checked and finally crushed the Carolingian renaissance on the fringes of the western empire and in Britain and Ireland, though it is indubitably true that the destruction of manuscripts and the flight of monks were consequences of their early raids, yet it is questionable whether the increased activity in the world of art and learning that had been encouraged by Charles the Great had had, or was likely to have, any appreciable effect on the remote countryfolk whose lands were now attacked by vikings ; moreover, it is open to doubt whether the destruction of the monasteries, or even of Frankish towns, really interrupted the progress of learning, inasmuch as it was only for a very short time that the monkish studies were checked and the influence of monastic life denied to the layman. One of the most surprising features of this short and horrible period in history is the extraordinary recuperative powers of the ransacked ruined monasteries and the plundered towns ; only a few religious houses were destroyed utterly and only one town Quentovic, on the south shore of the Channel, blotted out of existence. The story of the little monastery of

Noirmoutier in Francia shows how the monks returned again and again to rebuild their homes and how most of their precious belongings had been taken away or hidden before the vikings arrived ; for this was several times plundered in the period 814 to 819, and in 834 the monks, fearing further attack, removed the relics of their patron St. Philibert to safety on the mainland ; in 835 the new onslaught came ; the place was plundered and many monks slain ; in 843 the vikings seized the island and wintered there, but by 846 the monks were back, for in that year the abbey was burnt again. Noirmoutier now became one of the viking strongholds, but still some monks stayed on and did not finally abandon the monastery until 871, when the bones of St. Philibert were translated to St. Pourçain (Allier), where these much-harassed ecclesiastics possessed henceforth a new and safer home. So, too, in Ireland, the monasteries of both Armagh and Clonmacnois were sacked nine or ten times and yet survived, while that of Kildare was not abandoned even after being pillaged on sixteen occasions. And like the monks, the townsmen too crept back to their burnt dwellings, for the chroniclers tell how both civilian and monk trusted loyally and faithfully in the might of the Christian arms to defend them from further peril. Thus Dorstad, the first butt of the Danes, was plundered in 834, again in 835, and again in 836, yet the town survived to pass into the hands of the invaders to be held as fief in 846, and it was rather as a result of viking mismanagement than because of their devastations that the fortunes of this great mart declined.

It is also well to remember that the vikings did not remain for long the ferocious enemies of religion and learning that they certainly were at first ; in England, for example, Wulfhere, the Archbishop of York when the Danish armies took possession of Deira in 867, returned to his archbishopric, though it was still under Danish rule, some ten or twelve years later ; so too the see of Lindisfarne, though the monastery on Holy Island was destroyed in 875, was re-established with its headquarters at Chester-le-Street near Durham in 883, by which time the Danes had learnt not only to tolerate but to accept the Christian faith.

After the middle of the tenth century instead of assessing the harm done to European civilization by the viking movement it is more profitable to ask in what degree the Northmen shared and assisted in the Ottonian renaissance. Perhaps not much ; yet before the eleventh century had begun four determined princes, Harald Gormsson of Denmark, Olaf Tryggvason of

Norway, Olof Skotkonung of Sweden, and Vladimir of Kiev, had deliberately brought their realms within the embrace of Christendom by ordering the conversion of their subjects. There were still lonely and ignorant boors among the vikings, the buccaneering was not magically ended, but of the leaders of the Northmen it may be said that after about A.D. 950 their aim was definitely to rank themselves and their followers as equals of the Christian peoples whom previously they had pillaged. Thereafter they sought and welcomed all the benefits that civilization could bestow. Their ships spread its learning and its comforts more rapidly than these had ever before been propagated to the outlying parts of the empire and to the British Isles, to the Faroes and to Iceland, and to the viking countries themselves. Indeed the Northman who first had terrified the monk with sword and firebrand had now become his courier, his conveyor, and his defender. Therefore whatever debt they may have owed to Europe from the first century of the ravages, they now paid back to the full by providing the missionary and bookish world with a transport service so safe and so swift that the northern waters had never known the like before.

But if the memorial to the vikings in the British Isles and in the western empire is indeed nothing more than a parcel of names and a few fossil customs, there is yet one contribution that they have made to western society of which no man can properly assess the value. For who is to say of what significance either in the past or even in the present is the Scandinavian or Danish blood pulsing in the veins of Saxon, Frank, or Celt? What stamp the vikings have left in countenance and colouring, what added zest for conquest and adventure, what new nobleness was born of them, what valour and what wisdom came of the crossing with their stock, all this is hidden from the historian. A final verdict upon them must reckon therefore with this unknown contribution to western society, and it may be that the judgement of the future will declare the vikings not only harmful and villainous guests in the lands of the Celt and Saxon and Frank and Frisian, but as lion-hearted visitors whose destiny it was to fan the embers of western Christian civilization with the cold winds of the north and kindle from them once more a bright and vigorous flame.

PART I

THE LANDS OF THE VIKINGS

CHAPTER I

EARLY SCANDINAVIA AND DENMARK

AT the dawn of European history the brightening day that illuminates with welcome suddenness the Graeco-Roman world breaks only as a grey and impenetrable twilight over the far-off northern lands where later the viking peoples lived. But to the night-eyes of those trained to see in the full darkness of prehistory these countries of the north were already thronged stages whereon had been enacted dramas of cultural changes and altering populations no less interesting than those that were a prelude to the development of the historical civilizations of early Greece and Rome. Therefore, here in the north as elsewhere it is necessary to have some knowledge of the buried and forgotten past as revealed by archaeological research, in order to have a proper appreciation of the antecedents of the vikings, to know the stock whereof they came and to understand the forces that had moulded them and given them the stamp of a race apart. For of such poor and dubious stuff are the beginnings of their written story made that only with the help of archaeological data is there hope of interpreting correctly the first glimpses of them, or of their forefathers, that are discernible in the half-lights of the earliest records or in the full illumination of the risen sun of history.

The Stone Age in Scandinavia and Denmark, in the formal sense of this term as a definitive era wherein the use of metal was everywhere unknown, was a long period that lasted according to present reckoning from about 7000 B.C. to about 1800 B.C., the date when bronze was first commonly employed in Denmark and Sweden. This immense stretch of time is divided into two periods, and of these the first extends from the beginning of the Stone Age until 4000 B.C., or thereabouts, and is considered by most archaeologists to have witnessed the initial population of the land. This was effected, it is thought, by a series of immigrations from the south and south-east, all these first adventurers to the north being tribes of hunters that were forced into the cold wilderness left bare after the retreat of the ice-cap by new races who were gradually driving them from their homes in Central and Eastern Europe.

Originally such a Central European folk, and the bearers of a late palaeolithic hunting-culture, were the Maglemose or Ancylus people (*c.* 6500 B.C.) who represent one of the first established Stone Age [1] folk in these northern lands.[2] To these succeeded in the sixth or fifth millennium B.C. the well-known Kitchen-Midden, or Ertebölle, people, who were as firmly established in Norway [3] and southern Sweden as in Denmark itself. That the Ertebölle folk were the direct descendants of the Ancylus people has been disputed, and the immigration of a new race invoked to explain the hiatus that is at present thought to separate the two cultures. But it is a fact that the likeness between the simple equipment of stone and bone tools utilized by both peoples is remarkable, and it is always to be remembered that the subsidence of the land that took place during the Ertebölle stage has occasioned the loss of the greater part of the ordinary trusty racial criteria, both archaeological and anthropological. Thus it seems that it is impossible as yet to reach a decision on this point, and that there is at least a likelihood, if not a probability, that the Ertebölle folk were in fact the direct descendants of the Ancylus people.[4] But here it is sufficient merely to record an advance in the arts of life in this Ertebölle culture, as notably in the first introduction of pottery.

(Marginal note: MAGLE-MOSE AND ERTE-BÖLLE CULTURES)

[1] Or ' Bone Age ', as this early period might well be styled owing to the heavy preponderance of bone tools as against those of stone.

[2] An earlier population of Denmark and the extreme south of Sweden, the Lyngby people, is posited by a small band of archaeologists led by Dr. G. Schwantes and Dr. Gunnar Ekholm. For this Lyngby Culture, see Ebert's *Reallexikon der Vorgeschichte*, but cf. H. C. Broholm, *Aarb.*, 1924, p. 138 (French trans. in *Mem. Soc. Ant. du Nord*, N.S., 1926–27, p. 120). For an excellent account and bibliography of the earliest Stone Age cultures of the north, including descriptions of some important and little-known industries, see G. Schwantes, *Mitt. Museum Volkerkunde, Hamburg* (*Festschrift*, 1928), p. 159.

[3] The Nöstvet culture is held to be an independent but counterpart development of the same epipalaeolithic civilization.

[4] See Friis Johansen, *Aarb.*, 1919, p. 235 ff., and H. C. Broholm, *ib.*, 1924, p. 142 (French trans. in *Mem. Soc. Ant. du Nord*, N.S., 1926–27, p. 124) ; also Mr. Miles Burkitt's opinion in *Our Early Ancestors*, Cambridge, 1926, pp. 40, 45.

The end of the Ertebölle culture, about 4000 B.C., closes the first period of the Stone Age that thenceforward includes not only settlements of a folk who lived by hunting and fishing, but peoples who had added the profitable occupation of agriculture to their means of livelihood. Yet this introduction of agriculture does not seem to have involved, nor to have been caused by, a revolutionary and sudden change, and it is best explained as the most important of the new arts acquired in the course of the gradual introduction of the neolithic NEOLITHIC culture ; for by this time the attractive and enviable PERIOD advantages of neolithic civilization were becoming known among all the remaining hunting-peoples of Europe. Thus, some of the kitchen-middens of the Ertebölle culture themselves supply proof of the influence of these neolithic fashions on the Ertebölle folk, and such a midden is the Signalbakken, near Aalborg in Denmark, that yielded axes with pointed butts, and decorated potsherds with a white inlay to show off the pattern.[1] Again, many of the Stone Age dwelling-sites in Denmark show the same fusion between the Ertebölle and the ' full Neolithic ' culture.[2]

It is, in fact, the dwelling-sites that first present the new agricultural civilization of Scandinavia in its developed form with an equipment of polished stone implements and well-made decorated pottery ; indeed, in Sweden (as far north as Norrland) and in Denmark, and more doubtfully in Norway, a ' dwelling-site culture ' is now recognized that is held by some archaeologists to represent the earliest stage of the full neolithic culture in Scandinavia,[3] but it is not by any means established that this ' dwelling-site ' phase can really be differentiated in southern Scandinavia and Denmark as a chronologically distinct prelude to the full neolithic civilization which includes the earliest stage

[1] A. P. Madsen and others, *Affaldsdynger fra Stenalderen i Danmark*, 1900, p. 157 (p).

[2] C. A. Nordman, *Skaldyngernes stenyxor*, *Aarb.*, 1918, p. 137.

[3] In Norrland the counterpart ' dwelling-site culture ' is at first sight different in character and seems to be linked with that of Finland on the one hand and of Norway on the other ; formerly these northern Scandinavian sites, as opposed to those of southern Sweden and Denmark, were attributed to a special ' Arctic Culture ', representing either an indigenous non-Indogermanic people such as the Lapps or a distinct immigration from the east. It is now clear, however, that the apparent specialization of this culture is due merely to geographical remoteness and is a parallel development of the ' stone and bone ' industries of southern Scandinavia rather than the token of a different race. Cf. H. Shetelig, *Primitive tider i Norge*, 1922, p. 272 ff., and *Préhistoire de la Norvège*, 1926, p. 26 ff.

of the ' megalithic ' culture. The remarkable stone-built tombs
MEGA-   known in English archaeological jargon as *megaliths*,
LITHIC   and that give this culture its name, begin in the north
CULTURE   with the simple *dolmen* form, and there is a long and
interesting series of them that from start to finish most certainly
represents an established and prosperous people ; their distribution shows that this megalithic culture was to be found at
its most brilliant in the Danish islands, especially in Zealand,
and is confined to southern Scandinavia, the megalithic area
including, in addition to the whole of Denmark, all the provinces
of Götaland in Sweden, and the islands of Öland and Gotland,
while there is a north-western extension of the cist-graves (the
latest megalithic tomb-type) into Norway in Östfold and in
the neighbourhood of the Oslo Fjord. But the influence of the
megalithic culture extended far beyond those districts wherein
the big stone tombs, that give the culture its name, are to be
found.   Throughout northern Scandinavia fashions plainly
derived from the megalithic zone can be detected in the dwelling-
sites of the agricultural neolithic population. In Norway, for
instance, flint implements of Danish manufacture were imported
in large quantities, not only axes and smaller tools, but also many
of the magnificent flint daggers that are the most remarkable
of the products of the astonishing megalithic flint-industry.
To this may be added the certainty that it is to the inspiration
of the megalithic culture in southern Scandinavia that must be
attributed the real and effective propagation of the knowledge
of agriculture in the northern and more remote districts of the
peninsula. One thing alone the folk in northern Scandinavia
did not copy from their neighbours in the south, and that was
the custom of building communal burial-places ; on the contrary,
they remained true to their old-fashioned single interments
which were frequently found on the sites of the habitation-
places themselves.

The origin of the megalithic civilization in Scandinavia has
been the subject of a considerable controversy, some regarding
this surprising cultural development as the direct result of an
invasion, or at least a strong cultural influence, from the outside
world, while others deem it to be an autocthonous achievement
that was itself the example that inspired the building of similar
tombs elsewhere in Europe. This last view, however, although
it has not lacked redoubtable exponents, is becoming increasingly
difficult to defend. For this Scandinavian megalithic culture is
but a part, albeit the most brilliant part, of a large North European megalithic culture extending from the river Weichsel to

the Zuider Zee, and there is no doubt that the larger culture is, despite the tombs, closely linked with—one might even say founded upon—the contemporary, but non-megalithic civilization of Central Europe.   Moreover, this northern province is culturally quite distinct from the western megalithic provinces where the typical Scandinavian tomb-equipment is lacking.   Only the custom of megalith-building unites the Atlantic and the Northern European megalithic civilizations, and megalith-building, as can be demonstrated in Scandinavia itself, is a curiously localized and capricious fashion.   It is better, therefore, since these two great civilizations of Northern and Western Europe are in other respects dissimilar, to explain their megalithic tombs as being due rather to a common stimulus from the Mediterranean world than to invention and enterprise in the north.[1]   On the whole, then, the rise of the megalithic culture in Scandinavia should probably be read as the result of outside influence—and by *influence* is meant the ordinary results of trade and minor adventurous enterprises—acting upon the descendants of the Ertebölle people, for there does not seem to be any compelling reason to suppose that a large and sudden invasion of a new folk is involved.

An invasion, however, is the most probable explanation of the origin of another people who appear in Scandinavia during the period of the megaliths.   These are the ' Single Grave '
'SINGLE-   folk whose burial-practice, as the name implies, was
GRAVE '   directly opposed to that of the megalithic people who
FOLK   favoured communal burial in a large tomb.   The Single Graves were almost as unpretentious as the megaliths were grand, for they were nothing but tiny mounds covering a body laid on its side or back in a clumsy oval or rectangular enclosure of big pebbles.   Furthermore, the tomb-furniture is entirely different from that of the big communal graves, characteristic finds in the Single Graves being stone battle-axes and beaker pottery with cord-ornament.   In Jutland these graves are found in the central and south-western part of the peninsula, whereas the megaliths are clustered in the northern part and along the eastern coast.   Single Graves of the same type as those in Jutland have been found in the extreme south of Sweden, and many battle-axes of related forms have been discovered elsewhere in that country ;   there are also graves and battle-axes representing a parallel culture in Finland.

The explanation that best fits the facts assumes the Danish

[1] I have written something on this subject in my little book, *The Axe Age*, London, 1925, Ch. IV.

Single Graves to be a later and distinct manifestation of an alien 'Battle-Axe Culture' that is represented in Finland by 'BATTLE- an earlier and separate invasion. This culture is AXE' CUL- thought to have originated in Central Europe—where TURE the copper battle-axes of Hungary perhaps served as models for the stone battle-axes that give the culture its name— under an influence coming from South Russia or Asia. It then spread northwards by various movements, and thus it is that the Danish graves seem to represent newcomers travelling by the Elbe-valley route, while the Finland Battle-Axe Culture is likely to be the result of a direct and different movement to the Baltic by a route leading through the Danzig neighbourhood. In Sweden the new culture seems to be due to a separate branch of this Baltic invasion, launched perhaps from north-east Germany.

This interpretation, however, does not hold the field un-challenged. For it has been argued that the Battle-Axe Culture in Scandinavia is not of Central European origin,[1] but is rather an indigenous Nordic civilization having its roots in the Ertebölle culture. Thus it is asked whether it is not likely, if the communal graves represent a foreign custom, that the single graves might well be the ordinary native burial-places : and, furthermore, it is contended that some of the Danish Single Graves are at least as old as the Dolmen Period,[2] that is to say the earliest stage of the Megalithic Culture, and that a study of the pottery can provide the necessary link between the Ertebölle Culture and that of the Single Graves. Moreover, it is argued that a map showing the distribution of the battle-axes suggests a northern centre of expansion. Such arguments, however, seem to lose importance in face of the decisive fact that the Battle-Axe Cultures of Denmark, Sweden, and Finland are so far different from one another that a common origin in the north itself is in the highest degree unlikely, and that in each area it is not hard to find plain evidence of continental sources that suggest separate invasions from north Germany and the eastern Baltic coast. It is possible, naturally, to admit the existence of an indigenous element in both the Battle-Axe Culture and the Megalithic Culture, particularly in the last-named, since there is good reason

---

[1] The chief exponent of this view is Gunnar Ekholm ; see, for instance, *Uppsala Univ. Årsskrift*, 1916, I (*Studier i Upplands bebyggelsehistoria*), p. 92, and *Fornvännen*, 1926, p. 422. A convenient expression of the orthodox view will be found in that admirable compilation (one of the best general works on prehistoric Europe) *De Förhistoriska Tiderna i Europa*, Stockholm, 1927, Chap. VIII (C. A. Nordman).

[2] *Aarb.*, 1917, p. 131.

to suppose, as has been said, that the Ertebölle folk survived into the Megalithic Period ; but no argument hitherto adduced lessens the probability that the Battle-Axe Culture was imposed on these northern lands by invading hosts. It only remains, therefore, to note here that battle-axes representing both the Danish and the Baltic invasion found their way into Norway, but without the accompanying characteristic pottery, so that it must have been at second hand that the stimulus of this new culture reached that country.[1]

No new invasion, so far as can be determined, brought about the establishment of the full Bronze Age in Scandinavia. But this period, lasting from 1800 B.C. to about 600 B.C., is a time wherein a medley of extraneous influences was profoundly altering the northern culture. The strongest link remains always, it is true, with Central Europe, and Hungary is considered to have been the source of much of the raw metal that was used in the north before the native copper resources were exploited ; but despite this general attachment to Central Europe, and to the Aunjetitz Culture in particular, there are many other influences discernible, their variety being customarily explained on the grounds that the newly established amber-trade introduced the men of the north to fashions current in far-off lands.

BRONZE AGE

One of the earliest of these culture-contacts, one that was in fact established considerably earlier than the beginning of the Bronze Age, is that between the north and the British Isles. Indeed, it might almost be said that during the late Stone Age eastern England shared in the north German and Baltic Culture-Province, while at the very end of the Megalithic Period the ' porthole entrance ' in the Swedish cists has been thought to stand as evidence of a connexion through the medium of north Germany and north France with megalithic Brittany and western England, districts that were at that time included in an Atlantic Culture-Province. In the Bronze Age, however, a less equivocal link with Great Britain is the finding of flat metal axes of an

---

[1] The archaeologist should not fail to note Otto Rydbeck's interpretation of the Stone Age in Scandinavia. This author distinguishes three main cultures : A, the original Dwelling-Place, or Hunting, Folk ; B, the ' Megalith ', or Agricultural, Folk from western Europe who arrived *c.* 2700 B.C. ; C, the ' Battle-Axe ' Folk who arrived from central Europe *c.* 1800 B.C. He maintains that culture A persists in recognizable form in N. Sweden and Norway after the superposition of cultures B and C in S. Sweden and Denmark. See *K. Hum. Vet. Lund Årsberättelse,* 1928, p. 35 ; *Fornvännen,* 1930, p. 25 ; *Acta Archaeologica,* I, 1930, p. 55 (in English).

English-looking type in Denmark, while, for a rather later period, there is the discovery in the same country of two gold lunulae of the Irish kind. But there were other influences of an equal, if not greater, importance. Thus, Italian axes and an Italian fashion in swords, attest cultural relations extending across the Alps into the north Italian plain, while there is also small doubt of a connexion in the early Bronze Age between the north and the cultures of the Aegean world, this being discernible not merely in a few imported articles, but, it is thought, in the ornament that was used to decorate many of the northern bronzes.

New fashions of the Bronze Age in Scandinavia are the oak-tree coffin burials, a northern custom that is found also on the eastern shores of England, and the gradual introduction of cremation and of urn-field burials. Of a high interest, too, is the appearance at the end of the Bronze Age of 'Boat Graves'. These are found most of all in the island of Gotland, where over eighty are known. They consist of large enclosures, some over a hundred feet in length, in the shape of a ship, and are edged by big standing stones

BOAT GRAVES

FIG. 9.—Plan of boat-grave, Levide, Gotland
(Length, 130 feet)

(Fig. 9), or, if the 'boat' is of small dimensions, by round boulders. Inside were one or more burials, sometimes cremation-deposits and sometimes inhumations. Although the special development of this Boat-Grave cult in Gotland is in itself a remarkable proof of the individuality of the island-culture, it is most of all likely that the custom itself is but a manifestation of the widespread primitive belief in the water-barrier separating the world of the dead from the world of the living, and it may well have an origin that must ultimately be traced to the Ancient East. Here in the north, it is best deemed to be a part of a group of religious ideas, much resembling that of Ancient Egypt ; for whereas these graves presumably represent the Boat of the Dead, the contemporary rock-carvings seem to show that the 'Sun Boat' too was already a familiar idea in this early northern mythology.

The northern ship of the Bronze Age, as pictured on the rock-carvings of the Bohuslän province of Sweden (Fig. 10), had a curious bifid prow,[1] but in other respects it so closely resembles the viking boat of later days, that it will inevitably

[1] For some interesting analogies see *Man*, 1928 ; i, 41, 78.

be asked whether the Bronze Age Boat Grave is the direct ancestor of the famous 'Ship Burials' of the vikings. Certain it is that many of the Boat Graves, especially those on the mainland of Sweden, are of unknown date, and may well belong to the Early Iron Age, while one or two seem actually to have been used by vikings, even though it is hard to prove that they were erected in the Viking Period. But 'Ship-Burial' itself, that is to say the well-known viking burial-custom of cremation or interment in the actual boat (as distinct from burial in a boat-shaped enclosure) can be traced back only into the Migration Period, for the earliest instances are not older than the seventh century A.D., so that there is an interval of at least a thousand years in length separating them from the Boat-Burials of accredited date. Moreover, the Boat Graves cannot have been anything but a rare and laborious method of sepulture reserved for the distinguished dead, whereas the viking ship-burials, of which more than a thousand have been found in Scandinavia, represent not a special but an ordinary method of disposing of the corpse; therefore the absence of a full and chronologically established

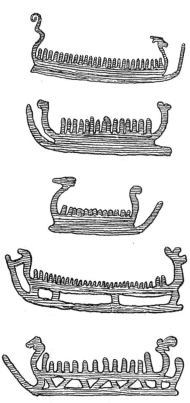

Fig. 10.—Rock-carvings of Bronze Age boats, Bohuslän, Sweden
(Length from 2 to 3 feet)

series of graves showing unmistakably the connexion between the viking burial-fashion and that of the Bronze Age does, perhaps, militate seriously against the chance that Ship-Burial is a part of the heritage of the vikings from their Bronze Age ancestors.[1]

---

[1] On the origin of Ship-Burials, see Knut Stjerna, *Festskrift till Professor Schück på hans 50 års-dag*, Stockholm, 1905 ; Haakon Shetelig, *Saga Book of the Viking Club*, IV, p. 326 ff., and *Osebergfundet*, I (Oslo, 1917), p. 243 ; Albany F. Major, *Folklore*, XXXV (1924), p. 113.

The Bronze Age, however, may justly be described as a period wherein a Scandinavian culture was evolved of so great an import that it may be deemed the basis of the subsequent cultures of the north. It was a development of the Scandinavian peoples, albeit under strong foreign influences, that was sufficiently pronounced to stamp its descendants in the succeeding centuries as sprung from its stock. In a word, the Bronze Age is the time of the segregation of the northern peoples into the characterized cultural and ethnic group from which, over a thousand years later, came forth the viking peoples. It is a period not only distinguished for the ready acceptance of outside fashions, but also for a plain and unmistakable resistance to the domination of these fashions, a brilliant period concluding in the final triumph of a northern spirit that moulded according to its own will and to suit its own purpose the cultural influences of the outside world.

IMPOR-
TANCE
OF THE
BRONZE
AGE

Denmark was the headquarters of this northern Bronze Age, and no one who has visited the National Museum at Copenhagen needs to be reminded of the huge collection of grand gold and bronze objects of this period that attest by their richness and variety the splendour of the Danish Bronze Age. Less remarkable was the Bronze Age in Sweden, though the Kalmar province and Öland, and also Bohuslän and the neighbourhood, have yielded a respectable wealth of finds of the period. It is important, however, to note that at this time begins the cultural prominence of the Mälar region, for not only are the finds from Central Sweden concentrated in Uppland, but it is possible to recognize a special Mälar type of bronze axe. Moreover, the great Uppland barrow, King Björn's Mound at Haaga near Uppsala, is the finest memorial of its kind in the late Bronze Age of Scandinavia, while the rich grave-goods accompanying the king laid to rest beneath it, and the bones of slaves and animals sacrificed at the funeral, speak plainly for the wealth and importance of the Mälar chiefs. Further, the Mälar type of axe has been found in Finland and Russia ; indeed, it has been found in sufficient numbers in the Kasan district to suggest a direct colonization of this particular area from central Sweden.

The Early Iron Age (c. 600 B.C.–A.D. 500) in Scandinavia is commonly divided into two periods, the division taking place in this rough and easy chronological scheme at the year A.D. 1. In the first the north stands isolated from the rest of Europe, while in the second it shares, although at second hand, in the dramatic cultural revolution imposed on the outlying territories

of western and northern Europe by the conquering armies of Rome. It is customary, therefore, to speak of a pre-Roman and a Roman Iron Age, and seldom has archaeological nomen-
PRE-   clature better mirrored the exact and vital significance
ROMAN   of the inevitable sub-divisions of an age. Towards
IRON AGE the end of the Bronze Age a few small trifles made of iron appear among the grave-goods in Scandinavia, and it is certain that the use of the new metal was introduced only gradually into the north. No conquering invasion of an iron-using folk demonstrated its advantages to the peoples of Scandinavia, and they were left undisturbed to exploit the novel metallurgy. The first period of the Iron Age was therefore a direct continuation of the Bronze Age, and it is to be expected that the robust civilization of the period that was ended would now advance to even greater wealth and power. On the contrary, it collapsed suddenly to an enfeebled and backward culture, poverty-stricken and isolated.

Various are the attempts that have been made to explain this downfall. One theory, though it is demonstrably inadequate as an explanation, lays the blame upon the ruin of the Scandinavian amber-trade occasioned by the transference of the monopoly of the market to the East Baltic and Prussian territories ; another is the much-discussed suggestion of Dr. R. Sernander that the climate at the beginning of the Iron Age deteriorated and thus was the cause of considerable emigration [1] and of a much-degraded culture. This notion of climatic variation,[2] warranted as it is by sound geological evidence, may reasonably be counted as one of the causes of the decline of the north, but the decisive factor must assuredly be sought in the political conditions of contemporary Europe. For at this time the people of the north were shut off from their long-standing intercourse with southern Europe by the growth of the great Celtic confederacy that was now established across, and controlled, the accustomed trade-routes. It is perhaps an exaggeration to suppose that the Celtic peoples in Central Europe,

[1] The emigrations that depleted the miserable population of Scandinavia and Denmark during the pre-Roman Iron Age are of considerable importance in the story of the early Germanic world, but beyond a statement of the fact that there was an outpouring of the peoples of the north in this period they require little notice here. The principal emigrants are named in the next chapter (pp. 64–5).

[2] R. Sernander : *Die schwedischen Torfmoore als Zeugen postglazialer Klimaschwankungen* (*Die Veränderungen des Klimas seit dem Maximum der letzten Eiszeit*. Publ. of 11th Int. Geologenkongress, Stockholm, 1910, p. 197 ff.).

south Germany, and Gaul, were actuated by some special hostility towards the men of the north, and as a result of a deliberate policy excluded them from contact with the rich lands of the south,[1] but there is little doubt that the Celts during the period of their maximum power and widest expansion (fifth–third century B.C.) usurped for themselves the greater part of the trade that had hitherto found its way to the north. As a result, the people of Scandinavia were cut off from the direct influence of the great civilizations of Greece and Italy that ruled the Mediterranean and Aegean world from the sixth century B.C. onwards. A fine bronze vessel, possibly of Italian origin and of fourth century date, having the Greek palmette as ornament, that was found in Möen Island off Zealand, is one of the few witnesses in this period to contact with the classical world.

It would be wrong, notwithstanding, to represent Scandinavia as being entirely unaffected by exterior influence in the pre-Roman Iron Age. Many of the Hallstatt fashions in personal ornaments enjoyed a vogue in the north, and the effect of Celtic (La Tène) art on later native craftsmanship can be seen in the ornament on the four-wheeled ceremonial car from Dejbjerg in Denmark, while the Celtic spirit of much of the detail of the famous silver cauldron from Gundestrup in the same country has long been recognized. Moreover, there are two cultural provinces within the Scandinavian area itself ; thus in Denmark and on the western coast of Norway the old Bronze Age burial-fashion of simple cremation prevails, as also in north-west Germany ; but in Ostfold in Norway and west of the Oslo Fjord, on the south Baltic coast of Scandinavia, and in Bornholm, there was a new burial-fashion introduced, namely the pell-mell interment of both the burnt bones and the ashes of the funeral pyre. This new custom seems to have been derived from the eastern side of the Baltic in the neighbourhood of the Oder and the Weichsel. But this is, after all, a small matter of local differentiation affecting only the northern peoples themselves, and it alters in no way the proper estimate of the Early Iron Age in Scandinavia as a period of cultural degradation and isolation. As witness to the poverty of the time, it is only necessary to contrast the many finds of costly gold articles of Bronze Age date with the one or two paltry gold objects that represent in the Scandinavian museums the wealth of the succeeding period.

[1] S. Lindqvist, *Fornvännen*, 1920, p. 113 ff.

The Roman Iron Age, as it is termed, that is to say the first four centuries of this era, was, on the other hand, a busy period of cultural advance towards the high standard of civilization achieved in the Empire itself. This was not, of course, the result of outright conquest by Roman armies, nor ROMAN IRON AGE of formal alliance with the Caesars, but was merely a natural reflex of the continued movements of Roman forces and Roman merchants in the borderlands of the Empire, especially on the Rhine frontiers. It is, indeed, truly remarkable how Roman control led to an apparent, if not real, cultural unity in the barbarian provinces within the Empire, and it would be astonishing if the north, closely involved as it was in the fortunes of the southern and western German tribes, had not taken advantage of many Roman fashions. Even a relentless hostility between two folk is no bar against the inflow of ideas borrowed from the enemy, but here, between the Germans and the Romans, there was not always hostility; thus the powerful Marcomanni, who were established by the end of the first century in Bohemia, boasted themselves the friends of the Romans, while many were the gifts bestowed by Roman generals on German chieftains whose help, or temporary neutrality, they sought. It was in such a way, perhaps, rather than as plunder, that costly objects of Roman workmanship reached even to the north, and there is a rich find in the National Museum at Copenhagen that is a notable example of these Roman presents. This is the lovely pair of Augustan silver goblets that was found with other valuable treasures in a grave at Hoby in the island of Lolland in Denmark, and that was, it is just conceivable, a gift to some northern chief from Silius, the legate in Upper Germany from A.D. 14 to A.D. 21.[1]

Whatever the exact origin of the Hoby treasure may have been, it is at least certain that in the first two centuries of this era Roman material was being imported in considerable quantities into the northern lands, above all into Zealand, a district that must have been at this time the seat of a powerful and progressive folk. Glass beakers and bronze vessels of Roman manufacture seem to have been the favourite novelties that attracted the northern traders as an exchange for their furs and amber; but Roman influence can be detected in many other ways. Roman weapons were imported, and the northern smiths set themselves diligently to the copying of these new

---

[1] For the Hoby find, see *Nordiske Fortidsminder*, II, 3rd hft. The two silver cups are inscribed on the foot with the name Silius; they have also the artist's signature on the side.

forms ; a more serviceable plough of Roman model was introduced ; the distaff, the spindle-whorl, and metal shears were
employed for the first time ; breeches and sandals were copied
from the Roman fashions ; the balance and the steelyard arm,
both of Roman model, came into use, while the weight system
adopted was itself based upon the Roman denarius.[1]

The course of events in Scandinavia in the first two centuries
of the Roman Iron Age is, in fact, the simple story of a steady
cultural renaissance that was directly due to the spread of the
mighty civilization of the Empire. But not all the period of
the Roman Iron Age is thus accounted for. Indeed, in the two
succeeding centuries influence from another quarter can be
discerned as a new and important factor in the development of
Scandinavian culture. This novel culture-influence is to be explained not by the advent, or proximity, of a new folk, but by the
migration of a section of the Scandinavian peoples who, when
the emigrants were finally established at the far-off terminus of
their wanderings, maintained a close connexion with their homeland along the route of their migration, and thus transmitted
to the north many of the characteristics of the peculiar civiliza-
THE GOTHS tion that was the result of their sojourn in strange
lands. These emigrants were the Goths. They had
begun to leave their northern home (Götaland in Sweden, rather
than the island Gotland) towards the close of the last century
before Christ, and after sojourning in the land around the
Weichsel mouth they had moved in the second century up this
great river and finally made their way to the steppes bordering
the Black Sea between the Don and the Danube. At least some
of their number are known to have arrived here by A.D. 214,
for in that year they came into collision with the Romans on the
borders of Dacia.

The attacks of the Goths on the Roman Empire begin in the
middle of the third century, but before the period of the Gothic
invasion no doubt much that was Roman was absorbed into
the Gothic civilization from the provinces of Dacia and Moesia.
It is well known that along the Gothic migration-route in north
Germany and in Russia numerous hoards of Roman denarii of
the late second and early third century have been found, and
it is these coins that afford proof of the relations between the
Scandinavians and the Goths, for big hoards of them have also
been found in the Baltic islands, principally in Gotland that
was at this time the leading trading-station for commerce with

[1] A. W. Brøgger, *Ertog og Øre*, Oslo, 1921, especially chap. I.

eastern Europe ; in much smaller numbers the denarii have also occurred in the Scandinavian mainland and in Denmark.[1]

But it is not the Roman influence upon the Goths that matters here, nor even the fact, and it is of greater importance, that in their new homes these people came into contact with the enfeebled civilization of the Greek colonies on the Black Sea coast. For the event of chief interest is that the Goths lived side by side in south Russia with the Sarmatians, a group of oriental nomads of Iranian stock and akin to the inhabitants of northern Persia. These Sarmatians, who were earlier immigrants into south Russia than the Goths, had wrested their lands from the Scythians who had preceded them in this movement westwards, and who were likewise, it is now believed, Iranians. From them the Sarmatians had acquired a distinctive art, peculiar as regards the representation of animal forms and as regards the style of jewellery affected, both this animal form and this jewellery being derived from the arts of the Persians, the Assyrians, and the Egyptians. The Goths, soon after their arrival on the Black Sea, acquired from the Sarmatians a taste for their gay multi-coloured personal ornaments [2] : in fact, this jewellery, distinguished by flashy mosaics of semi-precious stones set in cells, and the bold use of large gems, is sometimes called ' Gothic ', the reason being that as a result of its adoption by the Goths it was destined to become a widespread and notable fashion throughout barbarian Europe.

There is, then, the possibility of a quasi-oriental influence acting upon Scandinavia by way of the Weichsel trade-route and through the agency of the Goths. Such an influence can, in fact, be detected in the ready adoption of the ' Gothic ' polychrome jewellery, for this seems to have reached the north directly from the Goths by way of the Weichsel route, rather than from Hungary at a later period after the Gothic invasion of the Empire. An effect of such an influence upon small personal ornaments of this kind may seem, indeed, to be unimportant, but actually it is of considerable interest because viking art itself is thought by some to owe not a little to orientalizing tastes.

With the polychrome jewellery another innovation was transmitted from the new Gothic territories back to the north,

[1] For the denarius-hoards in northern Europe and Russia, see T. J. Arne and O. Almgren in *Oldtiden*, VII (1918), pp. 207–212.

[2] On this subject see the magnificent pioneer-study by Professor Rostovtzeff, *Iranians and Greeks in South Russia*, Oxford, 1922, especially chap. VIII.

namely the brooch with the ' returned foot '. This was either invented by the Goths, or an adaptation by them of the provincial Roman or Greek brooches they saw in use, and once introduced into northern Europe it was there copied and developed to an extraordinary extent, being, in fact, the prototype of a long and important series of Teutonic brooches.[1]

More important among the outside contributions to northern civilization in this period is the introduction of the art of writing. The Runic alphabet, or *furtharc* as it is commonly

RUNES   called,[2] was at first used merely for the scratching of an owner's or artist's name on small personal belongings or for memorial inscriptions of the simplest kind, but it is of high antiquity and seems to have been employed in Scandinavia as early as the middle of the third century A.D. The question of its origin has been the subject of elaborate and sustained discussion, but the verdict of Dr. Carl Marstrander, who has studied the problem with a thoroughness that must

F   U TH   A,O   R   K   H   N   I   A   S   T   B   M   L   R

FIG. 11.—The later runic furtharc (800–1100 A.D.)

everywhere command respect, declares that the characters were borrowed from the German Marcomanni, the first people to devise this clumsy but adequate system of letters. An alternative, but orthodox, view attributes the evolution of the furtharc and its transmission into the northern world either to the Goths of south Russia, or to the Heruls,[3] emigrants from south Jutland and Fyen who had followed in the wake of the Goths but yet maintained a close connexion with the large body of their tribe left in their Danish home. The friends of this theory are of the opinion that the Runic characters are nothing but stiffened and modified forms of Greek cursives with the addition of a few Latin letters ; but Dr. Marstrander claims that the furtharc is demonstrably older than the Germanic empires in south

---

[1] For the origin of the brooch with the ' returned foot ', see Bernhard Salin, *Die altgermanische Thierornamentik*, Stockholm, 1904, chap. I.

[2] Because the first letters of the Runic system are not a, b, but f, u, r, th, a, r, c.

[3] The word *erilar* is found in five early Runic inscriptions in the north. It is likely that many of the oldest inscriptions here are the work of travellers rather than of the native population.

Russia and he finds the closest affinities to the Runic characters not in the Greek alphabet, but in Celto-Latin alphabets of the Alpine regions. These last he believes to be based on north Etruscan and Latin systems, and it is the Marcomanni, he contends, situated on the borders of the Romano-Celtic world and already a powerful and important people in the first century, who must have turned them into runes and passed them on to their still unlettered brethren of the north.[1]

No influx of new people in significant numbers altered the character of the population of the north in the Roman Iron Age, and in an archaeological sketch it is sufficient to remark upon the cultural renaissance that took place in this period and that is plainly to be ascribed to an indirect knowledge of Roman civilization. At the same time there is evidence of an unrest disturbing the dwellers in the north, as illustrated by the emigration of the Goths, and at the end of the Roman period, as counterpart to these outward movements, there seems to have been a considerable infiltration of continental Germans, men, that is, of an allied culture and of the same

---

[1] Dr. C. J. S. Marstrander's notable paper, *Om runene og runenavnenes oprindelse* (with French summary) will be found in *Norsk Tidsskrift for Sprogvidenskap*, I (1928), p. 85. It should be compared with the work of Holger Pedersen (*Aarb.*, 1923, pp. 37–82 ; French trans. *Mem. Soc. Ant. du Nord*, Copenhagen, 1920–4, p. 88 ff.), who advocates a Latin origin for Runes through the medium of Gaulish instruction and likewise suggests the Rhine borderlands as the place of invention ; in company with Dr. Marstrander he remarks upon certain analogies between the Runic and Ogam systems and thinks that both the Germans and the British Celts derived their alphabets from a common Gaulish source. The leading exponent of the theory of a Latin origin was Ludwig Wimmer (*Aarb.*, 1874, p. 1 ff. ; German version, *Die Runenschrift*, Berlin, 1887), and the theory until recently widely held of a Greek origin, with the inclusion of a few Latin letters, has been propounded by Otto von Friesen (*Om runskriftens härkomst*, Uppsala, 1904), and cf. the same author's article in Hoops, *Reallexikon der Germ. Alt.*, IV, 1918–19, *s.v. Runenschrift*, and his *Rö-stenen i Bohuslän och runorna i Norden under folkvandringstiden*, *Uppsala Univ. Årsskrift*, 1924, and by S. Bugge (*Norges Indskrifter indtil Reformationen*, *Afd.* I, Oslo, 1905–13). The reader should also note a paper by Sigurd Agrell (*Arkiv f. Nordisk Filologi*, XLIII, 1927, p. 97), who admits the influence of Greek cursives but is of the opinion that the furtharc is really a reflection of Mithraic symbolism and magic, and that it was evolved in the second century by German soldiers serving in the Roman army ; on this subject see also the important studies of Magnus Olsen, e.g. in *Rev. de l'hist. des religions*, XCVI (1927) and *Edda*, 1916, and of Magnus Hammarström, *Studier i nordisk Filologi H. Pipping*, XX (Helsingfors, 1929), I, who emphasizes the Celtic influence on the development of the furtharc. For a short discussion of recent theories and a criticism of Marstrander's views see H. Shetelig, *Bergens Museums Årbok*, 1930, *hist.-ant. r.*, 1.

racial stock. These new arrivals first become important in the subsequent 'Migration Period' (see p. 66) and they seem to have sought western Norway in particular, for more than one rune-stone on the Vestland coast attests their presence and shows them to have been men from the regions of the upper Rhine, Frisia, and Francia. Indeed, their coming was, in all probability a result of the development by the Frisians of a great trade-route between western Christendom and the Scandinavian north and, as such, it was not without importance in the cultural history of these far-off lands ; thus grave-customs, especially in Norway, and pottery types altered under their influence and the northern peoples found themselves linked to the west Germans by a commercial bond that was to survive, firm and unbroken, into the Viking Period.

But the naming of the Germans and the Goths has already involved the narrative in the faint and uncertain beginnings of history, and henceforward the tale must be elaborated by knowledge derived from historical sources. The time has come, therefore, to assemble the simple facts already brought to the notice of the reader and to conclude the archaeological account.

The summary can be easily stated. The Stone Age in the north was pre-eminently a period of immigration, of successive SUMMARY arrivals of folk driven from the central plains of Europe to seek new homes. In a word, it was the period of the population of the north. The Bronze Age, on the other hand, was a static period that witnessed the consolidation of these various folk into a single and admirable northern civilization, distinct from that of southern lands, though always intimately connected with the civilization of north Germany by both a cultural and a racial bond. The pre-Roman Iron Age saw a serious degeneration of this northern civilization, together with a partial emigration of its peoples, but the Roman Iron Age itself was the time of a cultural renaissance that re-established the northern civilization as a powerful and well-equipped group of tribes, albeit a restless people with eyes turned enviously upon the richer lands of the south.

Throughout this length of time the real power and wealth of the north was centred in Denmark, and in Southern and Central Sweden, and the Baltic islands of Gotland and Bornholm, and it is, of course, in these places that the 'ages' of the customary archaeological classification can best be distinguished and defined. But northern archaeology is in reality much more complex than this simple division into periods has suggested, and no work in recent years has done more to show how danger-

ous such glib classification may be than the brilliant and penetrating study by Dr. A. W. Brøgger, *Det Norske folk i oldtiden*.[1]
Dr. Brøgger has shown that in Norway, at any rate, the life
of the people is well-nigh independent of the usual archaeological
machinery of ' ages ' and culture-periods. The introduction of
agriculture during the Stone Age and the much later introduction
of iron are, in his eyes, the chief events of domestic importance ;
in fact, except for changes in habits and pursuits thereby involved, the life of the Norwegians continued little altered from
the Stone Age until the Viking Period ; indeed, in many respects,
as notably in the matter of equipment, it remained little altered
until late historic times.   Occupied in a long-established seasonal
routine of hunting, fishing, and tilling the land, the Norwegians
in their far-off isolated homes had little to gain by a greedy
search for new fashions in the simple tools and weapons they
required.   Thus, throughout the Bronze Age of Denmark, the
Norwegians were content with what was almost entirely a lithic
equipment, and the ' Stone Age ' lasted in a sense right up to
the beginning of the Roman Iron Age.   And there is no need,
observes Dr. Brøgger in parenthesis, to be surprised at con-
servatism in the far past, since late in the last century, and
long after the introduction of the grenade-harpoon, the peasants
in the Skogsvaag near Bergen continued hunting the whale
with bow and arrow.

The truth is that culture-divisions are applicable only where
they can be directly observed, and they must never, without
strict examination, be held as automatically valid for adjacent
communities.   Thus it is probable that in other remote parts
of Scandinavia, just as in many districts of Norway, the period-
narrative given in these pages is a meaningless confusion of a
simple story.   Therefore the culture-changes indicated must be
held to apply only to the rich and vigorous peoples of certain
geographically favoured parts of Denmark and Scandinavia, and
as a background there remains always the steady and little-
changed peasant-life of the Stone Age folk.   Indeed, even in
Denmark it may be that the periods are too severely defined,
for a Bronze Age habitation-site has been found at Voldtofte,
close to Assens on Fyen Island, whereon lay sufficient of stone
implements to suggest forcibly that stone was still in common
use in the late Bronze Age.   As a complement to this find there

---

[1] Oslo, 1925 :   German trans. *Kulturgeschichte des norwegischen
Altertums*, Oslo, 1926.   Mr. Reginald Smith has given a summary of
this work in a review, *Antiquaries Journal*, VII, 542 ; cf. my own review
of the book, *Antiquity*, II (1928), p. 253.

is a bronze founder's hoard from Haag near Randus that contained, in addition to the usual bronze material, a few flint tools.

As an end to this chapter a word must be said on the subject of the peopling of the neighbouring lands across the Baltic and the Gulf of Bothnia. The civilization of north Germany, of course, must be deemed a veritable extension of the northern civilization that has been described, for the folk of north EAST Germany, Denmark, and southern Scandinavia were BALTIC of one and the same racial stock. But the Baltic PEOPLES coast from Prussia to the Gulf of Finland forms, in the Early Iron Age at any rate,[1] a distinct archaeological province. Here there were already settled peoples of Finno-Ugrian race, the ancestors of the Livonians, Esths, and Finns, whose culture, at the beginning of the Iron Age, though poor and ill-represented, is characterized throughout the whole extent of the province by east German fashions. The Roman influence was slight, and was exerted at second hand through German intermediaries, but in the third and fourth centuries of this era there is, as is to be expected, plain evidence of Gothic influence, the result not only of movement along the trade-route to south Russia, but of the actual settlement of the Goths, before and during their migration period, in the neighbourhood of the lower Weichsel. In the sixth century this great group of Finno-Ugrian, yet partly Germanized, folk was broken by the incursion of two new peoples of an Indogermanic race, namely the Lithuanians and the Letts, who seized the country south and west of the Gulf of Riga ; thus the East Baltic littoral had a heterogeneous population, consisting of diverse Finno-Ugrian and Indogermanic folk at the end of the Migration Period. At this time the influences from north Germany weaken and finally disappear, leaving the Baltic province isolated from western Europe, but henceforward influenced to an ever-increasing extent from Scandinavia and Finland.

In Finland, the Stone Age had already witnessed the arrival of a palaearctic Finno-Ugrian population (the comb-pottery people) and also of an Indo-European folk, the bearers of the Boat-Axe Culture. The resultant civilization had, as elsewhere FINLAND in the north, degenerated during the first period of the Iron Age into a poverty-stricken group of peoples, sparsely represented by finds, and the first cultural amelioration was brought about by the immigration into west Finland in the

---

[1] For the Stone Age, see the convenient summary by C. A. Nordman, *Journ. R. Anthr. Inst.* LII (1922), 26 ff.

early centuries of this era of Finnic peoples from the Baltic Province, a folk whose culture was largely influenced by that of the Goths. So strong, in fact, is the Gothic character of this new element in the population of Finland, that the ' Gothic Iron Age ' has been proposed as a better name for the ensuing period than the customary term Roman Iron Age.[1] In the fifth and sixth centuries, on the other hand, Swedish influence becomes manifest, and there may even have been Swedish colonies at this period in east Bothnia. It is certain that Swedish colonies were established in the succeeding century, but the Scandinavian influence weakened again in the eighth century, and in the Viking Period it becomes almost negligible, doubtless by reason of the preoccupation of the Swedes with their newly established colonies in Russia. There was, however, a fresh immigration from Esthonia into Finland about this time, and the newcomers, amalgamating with the original Finno-Gothic people, and the descendants of the Stone Age folk, developed into the Finns of historical times.

In the north of Scandinavia and Finland dwelt the Lapps, a separate palaearctic people of the Samoyed brachycephalic group, isolated at some remote, but unknown period, and, by the time of the Iron Age in south Scandinavia, already long acclimatized as children of the high latitudes. Very THE LAPPS little is known of them in antiquity, though an Iron Age hunting-station of the Lapps has been identified in the Varanger fjord. This shows a culture that is mainly confined to bone implements and weapons, though these primitive objects were accompanied by a few simple tools of iron. It is accordingly supposed, as indeed is likely, that the Stone Age, or Bone Age rather, of the Lapps, passed directly into an Iron Age. The earliest unmistakeable signs of trade between the Lapps and the outside world are some Teutonic ornaments and coins of the Migration Period, but the nomad life of these people has made it excessively difficult to study their past by ordinary archaeological method. It is known merely that the Lapps were already established in the far north before the opening of the present era, and that their remote nomadic life continued uneventful and uninterrupted during the turbulent centuries when Scandinavian seamen ruled the northern waters and the shadows of the viking invasions darkened over Christendom.

[1] C. A. Nordman, *Kultur och folk i Finlands forntid*, Helsingfors, 1928 (in *Svenska Litteratursällskapets Förhandlingar, N.F.* 4).

CHAPTER II

THE NORTH GERMANS

HERODOTUS did not know of the Germans, and the first appearance of these people in history may perhaps have been the mention of a tribe dwelling on the north German coast that was included in a lost book *The Ocean* by a Massiliot Greek, Pytheas, the merchant-explorer whose famous voyage to Ultima Thule and the North Sea [1] took place in the fourth century B.C. But by the time of Poseidonios (135 B.C.–45 B.C.), the Stoic of Apamea, it seems, even though this writer's work is likewise lost, that many of the German peoples were well known in the classical world, and, furthermore, if Athenaeus has repeated a fragment of Poseidonios verbatim,[2] that the word Germani was already in use as a collective term. At any rate, from the days of Julius Caesar onwards, the name, betokening a distinct race of men, was commonly employed, and it is current in the writings of Caesar himself, and of Pliny, Livy, and Tacitus. As a race-name, however, it was at first rather loosely employed in a not always successful attempt to distinguish certain groups of people from the Celts of Gaul [3] ; but by the time of Tacitus, who wrote the *Germania* in A.D. 98, it was clearly understood to refer to the numerous population living between the Rhine and the Elbe, and also believed to inhabit lands even further to the north and east, a huge confederacy of tribes of which many at this late period were well known to the Romans. Tacitus himself described the territories of the Germans in the opening paragraph of his book. He says :

[1] Pliny, *N.H.*, XXXVII, 35. It is sometimes said that the Guiones of Pytheas, the tribe in question, lived in Jutland ; his amber-island Abalos may be Heligoland. See M. Cary and E. Warmington, *The Ancient Explorers*, London, 1929, p. 38.

[2] IV, 153e.

[3] Cf. *B.G.*, II, 4, 1 and 10 ; VI, 32, 1. Note that Strabo (VII, 290) also refers to the Germans and gives a fanciful derivation of their name. For a general summary of the early classical references, see G. Schütte, *Our Forefathers*, I, Cambridge, 1929, p. 17 ff.

' The real Germany [1] is divided from the lands of the Gauls, the Raeti (in east Switzerland and Tyrol), and the Pannonii (in Austria and Hungary), by two rivers, the Rhine and the Danube ; from Sarmatia (south-west Russia and lands east of the Weichsel) and from Dacia (Rumania and north-east Balkans) it is divided by mountains (the Carpathians), and also by the fact that the Germans and the people of these countries live in dread of one another. The rest of Germany has the sea as boundary, and this part of the country includes broad promontories (? Jutland) and great islands (? Scandinavia, that was at first thought to be an island) ; here our military expeditions have lately discovered various peoples and their kings.'

These Germans, who now take up their appointed rôle in history, were the children of the neolithic and Bronze Age civilization of southern Scandinavia, Denmark, and the neighbouring lands between the Elbe and the Oder. Perhaps the first nucleus of the Germans as a race was the amalgamation of the peoples of this area during the Stone Age into the distinctive ' Megalithic Culture ' (p. 44) and the subsequent fusion of this culture with that of the ' Single-Grave ' or ' Battle-Axe ' people, who had arrived in the north at the end of the Stone Age. For, on most counts, it seems likely that the proto-Germans of the last period of the Stone Age, if so they may be called, were Germans by the time the Bronze Age was fully established, and that whatever outside influences may have contributed to the evolution of the typical German, the basis of the stock was the long-established population of the north. On this view, the Indogermanic element that gave the decisive turn to the racial development of the northern peoples was most probably supplied by the Battle-Axe folk.[2]

In early historical times there were three main divisions of the German peoples. In the first place, there were the North Germans of Scandinavia, whose history, since it is they from whom the vikings are sprung, will be the main interest of this chapter ; and there were also the East Germans—an offshoot from the North Germans—and the West Germans.

[1] Germania omnis (cf. *B.G.*, I, 1, 1). Tacitus does not include the transrhenan provinces of Germania superior and Germania inferior ; he refers, if one may express the distinction in modern terms, to ' Germany Proper ' as opposed to ' Greater Germany '.

[2] On the difficult question of the origin of the Germans, see R. Much in Hoops, *Reallexikon, s.v. Germanen* ; among recent books on the subject, T. A. (formerly Fr.) Braun, *Die Urbevölkerung Europas und die Herkunft der Germanen*, Berlin, 1922 ; S. Feist, *Indogermanen und Germanen*, Halle, 1924 ; G. Kossinna, *Ursprung und Verbreitung der Germanen in vor- und frühgeschichtlichen Zeit*, Berlin, 1926. An admirable work in English is *The Aryans* by Prof. V. G. Childe (London, 1926) ; another, and indispensable, book is *Our Forefathers* by G. Schütte (Cambridge, 1929).

The last-named folk were tribes that, at some time shortly after 1000 B.C., had pushed westwards and south-westwards into the territories of the Celtic peoples, and, by about 200 B.C., had advanced the German boundary to the Rhine and the Main.

WEST GERMANS   There was also a steady movement of the West Germans up the Elbe valley, and in the first century A.D. these folk had occupied most of southern Germany.   It was these West Germans, of course, who came into collision with the Romans, and, since they alone were under continued observation from the north-western provinces of the Empire, it is to the West Germans beyond a doubt that the descriptions of the German people by Caesar and Tacitus must, in the main, apply. Their history, after their first clash with Rome, is remarkable for the change from a pastoral manner of life to busy agricultural pursuits, and for the development of great federations of tribes within their own West German society.   The Alamanni, the Saxons, and the Franks are famous names of the composite tribal groups (nations, one might almost say [1]) thus formed.

The East Germans were a branch of the German peoples who migrated, probably at some period about or after 500 B.C., to the lands between and around the Oder and the Weichsel, and who pressed southwards during the following two centuries

EAST GERMANS   along these rivers until they approached the foothills of the Carpathians.   This folk, whose progress was not stayed by the frontiers of the Roman empire, could expand their territory almost at their will, and they were thus able to preserve, in contrast with the West Germans, the accustomed pastoral life of their race.

Most of the East Germans were of Scandinavian origin, and their migration to the Continent during the pre-Roman Iron Age is the counterpart of that noticeable deterioration of the Scandinavian culture during this period to which archaeology can bear witness (p. 51).   Among these emigrants were many folk from the island of Gotland, the Lombards from Scania, the Burgundians from Bornholm, and the Rugians from Rogaland in south-west Norway ; but the best known of them were the Goths whose original home was situated in the northern provinces (Öster- and Västergötland) of Götaland in Sweden.[2]   The

---

[1] See the late Professor J. B. Bury, *The Invasion of Europe by the Barbarians*, London, 1928, pp. 10–15.

[2] Not the island Gotland : see Birger Nerman, *Fornvännen*, 1923, p. 165.   For a most excellent general account of these emigrations, see Nerman, *Die Herkunft und die frühesten Auswanderungen der Germanen*, III F., *K. Vitt. Ant. Akad. Handl.*, I, 5 (Stockholm, 1924).

East Germans also included in their number the Vandals, a name perhaps bestowed in north-east Germany on a large group of emigrants from Denmark,[1] the Gepids, and the Heruls, these last-named folk being distinguished from the other migrants by the fact that while a section of them followed the Goths to south Russia a large body of them remained in their Danish home (probably south Jutland and Fyen) so that they still counted in the ensuing centuries as a people of the north until they were conquered by the invading Danes (p. 73).[2]

The tendency of the East Germans in the third and fourth centuries was to advance slowly into Europe, moving chiefly in a south-easterly direction towards the Black Sea. Here in southern Russia lay the new territory of the Goths, and it was here that these people divided into two great bodies, the Ostrogoths and the Visigoths, a division that was no doubt governed by the order of the arrival of the successive migrating bands.[3] And it was from this region that was launched the great Gothic attack on the Roman empire that began about A.D. 247.

[1] In the Vandal group were the *Silingi* whose name can be perhaps connected with *Zealand*. It has been suggested that the term *Vandal* itself may be derived from the name Vendsyssel in north Jutland, but Kossinna believes that *Vandal* is a sobriquet meaning *merchant*. See the references on p. 241 of his paper *Die Wandalen in Nordjütland, Mannus* 21 (1929).

[2] The Heruls were an interesting people, and are deemed to have played an important part in the development of Scandinavian and Danish civilization. Those who had migrated to the shores of the Black Sea won for themselves considerable notoriety as pirates in the third century. Like the Goths, these South Russian Heruls were driven from their settlements by the Huns, and they subsequently established themselves in Hungary where they remained until the beginning of the sixth century. Then they were driven forth once more, this time by fellow-Germans, the Lombards (p. 74). But throughout all their wanderings they seem to have maintained a close connexion with their countrymen in Denmark, and the introduction of many southern fashions into the north has been explained as the result of the coming and going between the migrants and the stay-at-homes. The Heruls remaining in Denmark were also redoubtable pirates, for Hieronymus has recorded that in the fifth century parties of them raided the coasts of France and Spain, and much of their power must have been derived from the fact that the great trade-route from the mouth of the Rhine to the Baltic crossed directly over their territories. For the Heruls, see O. v. Friesen, *Rö-stenen*, Ch. III, *Uppsala Univ. Årsskrift*, 1924, I, and L. Schmidt, *Geschichte der deutschen Stämme*, I (1910), p. 333 ff.

[3] It has been suggested (Schück, *Svenska folkets historia*, I, p. 96, note) that these names are not to be interpreted as meaning *East* Goths and *West* Goths, even though it is common ground that the Visigoths dwelt to the west of the Ostrogoths; but I confess I find the alternative interpretation difficult to accept.

The migration of certain sections of the Scandinavian peoples across the Baltic Sea in the pre-Roman Iron Age and at the beginning of this era is not a happening that must be regarded only as a curious and isolated episode in the early history of the north. For it was, in fact, a prelude to, if not actually a part of, that larger and much more significant movement of the German peoples that took place in what is commonly called the Migration Period.

This Migration Period (A.D. 400–800) was the time of the chief successes and maximum expansion of the Germans. Visigoths, Ostrogoths, and Lombards were pressing into Italy ; the Vandals, Burgundians, Franks, and others of the Visigoths conquered Gaul, Visigoths and Vandals invaded Spain, the Vandals continuing even into north Africa ; the Alamanni founded a powerful state on the middle Rhine and in the Alplands, and the Angles, Saxons and Jutes invaded Britain. The first half of the period, the two centuries between 400 and 600 A.D., witnessed this tremendous and shattering onslaught on the Roman world, and saw the inception and evolution of a novel and characteristic German culture. This was born of the recently established German confederacies in Central and Western Europe, but it spread rapidly among all the German peoples, and nowhere was it more vigorously developed than in the north itself.

The history of the North Germans, the ancestors of the vikings, in their homeland in Scandinavia and Denmark is fragmentary and difficult to follow in its earlier stages. Pytheas, already mentioned, can hardly be credited with the discovery of these northern lands, and the first assured information about them must have been that won by a NORTH GERMANS Roman fleet that sailed in the reign of Augustus, probably about 25 B.C., to the furthest lands of the Cimbri, where, it is recorded, no Roman had ventured before. As a result of this enterprise the Cimbri, the Charydes, the Semnones, and other northern German tribes that are not actually named, sought the friendship of the Roman people.[1] Fuller details of this exploit of the fleet are given by the elder Pliny (d. A.D. 79). The Romans, he says,[2] rounded the Cimbric peninsula (Jutland) and reached the Codanian Gulf (the Kattegat) wherein there

[1] This is set forth on the Monumentum Ancyranum, the famous narrative of the public career of the Emperor Augustus that is inscribed both in Latin and in Greek on the walls of the temple of Augustus and Roma at Ancyra in Galatia, Asia Minor. *C.I.L.*, III, 769 ; Mommsen, *Res Gestae Divi Augusti*, Berlin, 1883 ; cf. Sandys and Campbell, *Latin Epigraphy*, Cambridge, 1927, p. 258.

[2] *N.H.*, IV, 96.

were many islands of which the most famous was Scatinavia.[1] The real size of this island, he goes on to say, was as yet undetermined, but in the part of it that was known there dwelt the Hilleviones who lived in five hundred villages in a land that they themselves deemed to be a separate (*alterum*) world.

That the Romans mistook the great Scandinavian peninsula for an island is not in itself remarkable, but it is certainly a curious thing that nothing further is heard of the Scandinavian people whom Pliny called the Hilleviones. It has accordingly been suggested [2] that Pliny's phrase *Hillevionum gente* is a misreading of the words *illa Suionum gente*, and, in consequence, that the folk to whom he was referring were none other than the Suiones, that is to say the Swedes. This ingenious emendation involves no extraordinary assumptions, for it is established that the Swedes were already known to the Romans about this time since they are described by Tacitus in the *Germania* [3] (written A.D. 98). The following passage is a translation of his account of the peoples of Scandinavia.

TACITUS

" Beyond these people (the Rugii and the Lemovii) are the states (civitates) of the Suiones, but these are in the ocean itself (i.e. on an island and not, like the Rugii and Lemovii, on the South Baltic coast of the mainland). The Suiones are distinguished not merely for their arms and men, but for their powerful fleets, though the style of their ships is unusual in that there is a prow at each end so that the boat can advance head-on in either direction. Moreover, they do not use sails, and the oars are not fixed in rows along the sides, but are detachable, and are removed on certain rivers ; they can also be reversed, if occasion demands.[4] These people respect wealth, and one man among them is supreme, there being no limits to his power and no question as to the full obedience due to him. Promiscuous carrying of arms is not allowed here, as it is among the other Germans, but weapons are kept shut up in the charge of a

[1] Scadinavia is a variant ; other later readings are Sandinavia and Scandinavia. Scania (Scåne), the present name of the southernmost district of Sweden, is the same word in another form, although it must be observed that this equation has been opposed with some force by H. Lindroth, *Namn och Bygd*, 1915, p. 10. Note that Mela in his *De Situ Orbis* (III, 6, 54), written some thirty or forty years earlier than Pliny's *Natural History*, did not give the word Scadinavia although it appears in some editions of his work. The name in the oldest text of Mela is Codannovia.

[2] V. Grienberger, *Zeitschr. f. deutsches Altertum*, 46 (1902), p. 152.

[3] *Germania*, 44, 45.

[4] The fragmentary Als boat (? pre-Roman Iron Age) of Denmark and the Nydam boat of the third–fourth century A.D., also recovered from the peat in Denmark, are the surviving specimens of a northern ship nearest in date to those described by Tacitus, and to them the account in the *Germania* might well apply.

slave who acts as guard.[1]   This is because the sea prevents sudden inroads from enemies, and because bands of armed men who have nothing to do often become unruly.   It is not found expedient for the king (regia utilitas) to place a nobleman or a freeborn man, or even a freedman, in charge over these arms. . . .   Next to the Suiones are the tribes of the Sitones who resemble the Suiones in all respects except that the Sitones have a woman as ruler.[2]

The identification of the Suiones with the Swedes (Svear) is a matter of certainty, but there has been considerable doubt as to the identity of the Sitones.   Some writers have believed them to be the Finns and not a people of Scandinavia, yet it is just as likely that they were a Germanic folk of Swedish culture inhabiting Vesterbotten and the northern shores of the Gulf of Bothnia.[3]   That they are said to ' continue ' the Swedish people and were like to them in most respects seems to confirm this ;   moreover an archaeological discovery at Storkaage near Skellefteaa has provided proof of a flourishing trade between this Vesterbotten district and Estland in the latter part of the Roman Iron Age,[4] so that there is good reason why the Sitones, if they dwelt on the Norrland coasts, should be mentioned in conjunction with the Swedes.   For Tacitus in all probability derived his information concerning the people of Scandinavia from Roman amber-merchants and others who traded with the north, and he presumably names these two peoples of Scandinavia and no others because his informants obtained their own

[1] This is doubtless a garbled version of a custom at *things* or fairs such as might easily attract the notice of foreign traders and yet have little real significance.

[2] *quod femina dominatur*.   This could mean that their then ruler was a woman or that their sovereigns were always women (my interpretation and the usual one) or that the Sitones were an Amazon tribe where ' the woman rules '.   Professor Maurice Hutton (Tacitus, *Dialogus*, etc., Loeb Library, p. 353) argues that the epigram immediately following these words, i.e. *in tantum non modo a libertate sed etiam a servitute degenerant*, enforces this last interpretation.

[3] The district that in medieval times was called Kvänland.   Adam of Bremen (eleventh century) is thought to refer to this selfsame territory when he speaks of the ' land of women ', *terra feminarum* (IV, 17, 224 ; IV, 19, 228 ; cf. III, 15, 134).   It is then arguable that the Latin expression may be a punning translation, or even a misunderstanding, of the tribal name Kvän which was confused with ON. *kván*, woman.   The words *terra feminarum*, if not due to an accident of this kind, confirm the statement of Tacitus about the Sitones *quod femina dominatur*, and strengthen, as Professor Hutton sees, the interpretation of this phrase as ' where the woman rules ', thus implying that the Sitones were an Amazonian society.

[4] See Erland Hjärne, *Fornvännen*, 1917, pp. 147, 203 (for Kvänland, p. 216 ; and for the Sitones, p. 223).

FIG. 12.—Southern Scandinavia

knowledge of these folk from the mainland tribes of the East
Baltic, who were well acquainted with the Swedes and Sitones,
their nearest neighbours in the peninsula, but who had little or
nothing to do with the inhabitants of southern and western
Sweden.[1]

The history of the north opens, then, with the *civitas* of
the Swedes already formed, a state that must accordingly take
honourable rank as the second earliest monarchy in the Germanic
world [2] and one that, since it can be counted as a forerunner of
the modern realm, gives Sweden to-day title to claim herself
the oldest state in Europe. This ancient kingdom of Svitjod,
as it was later styled, must have embraced all the folk of
Uppland and the Mälar and Hjelmar country, and perhaps
many of the people of Norrland south of the territory of the
Sitones.

The next witness after Tacitus is Ptolemy the Geographer
(*c.* A.D. 150). East of the Cimbric peninsula, he says,[3] are four
islands called Skandiai. Three of these (perhaps the west
Danish islands) are small, but the fourth, which is
PTOLEMY the easternmost and lies opposite to the mouth of
the Weichsel, is a big island ; this is the one that is properly
called Scandia. In the western part of it dwell the Chaideinoi,
in the east the Fauonai and Firaisoi, in the north the Finnoi,[4]
in the south the Goutai and the Daukiones, and in the centre
the Leuonoi.

These queer-sounding and unexpected tribal names have been
the subject of much speculation. The only reasonably certain
identification is that of the Finnoi with the Lapps, for in this
instance there is a wealth of corroborative evidence from other
sources ; but as to the rest of the tribes mentioned, it has been
found exceedingly difficult to connect them with any peoples
named elsewhere in history, or even, as a last resort, with place-
names. It is, however, common ground that the Goutai must
be either the Goths of Götaland or the inhabitants of the island
of Gotland, and the mention of the Chaideinoi in this passage
has been allowed to attract considerable sentimental interest as
being, it is thought, the first appearance of a Norwegian people
in history, namely the Heiner, or folk of the Hedemark in central

[1] Cf. J. V. Svensson, *Namn och Bygd*, 1917, p. 154.

[2] A Frisian *civitas* comes first, see G. Schütte, *Our Forefathers*, Cambridge, 1929, p. 51. Note that Curt Weibull, *Hist. Tidskrift f. Skåneland*,
VII (1920), pp. 304–5, denies the existence of this early Swedish kingdom.

[3] *Geog.* II, ii.

[4] Actually this name is recorded in only one MS. See the editions
of the *Geography* by Müller (Paris, 1883) and Otto Cuntz (Berlin, 1923).

Norway.[1] The most surprising thing about Ptolemy's account is that there is no mention of the Swedes (Suiones), so that it is reasonable to suppose that one of the names he gives must be the distorted title of these already famous people, and it now seems that the central Leuonoi are the most likely folk to be the inhabitants of Svitjod.[2]

There is a long interval of four centuries between Ptolemy's *Geography* and a further mention of the people of Scandinavia by a writer of the outside world. For Jordanes is the next JORDANES author to speak of the Scandinavians, and his *Getica*, or *History of the Goths*, was written in the middle of the sixth century. The new evidence is not really that of Jordanes, who was a native of the Eastern Balkans, but that of the distinguished Roman statesman Cassiodorus who, some thirty years earlier, had written a work, now lost, called *The Origin and Exploits of the Goths* ; this was a big book in twelve

[1] But if this identification be correct, it is astonishing that Ptolemy should know of these dwellers in the remote inland, and yet have nothing to say about the busier coastal folk. It is true that the Hedemark, as Dr. A. W. Brøgger has observed (*Kulturgeschichte des Norwegischen Altertums*, Oslo, 1926, p. 198), affords some archaeological evidence of a high prosperity before and just about the time of Ptolemy, but there is also evidence of a larger population living around the mouth of the Oslo Fjord, and the absence of their name from Ptolemy's list cannot fail to arouse some misgivings about this common belief that the Chaideinoi were a people of interior Norway.

[2] For apart from their stated geographical position, from τα δὲ μεσ A/CYIONOI by misreading AC as AE and IO as Ω ΛΕΥΩΝΟΙ is produced at once, and this without exaggerating the ordinary chances of such textual error if the archetype manuscript were written, as is almost certain, in uncials. This is the ingenious suggestion of J. V. Svensson, *Namn och Bygd*, 1919, p. 12, in a paper that must be read without fail by all interested in the Ptolemaic Scandinavian tribe-names. The author urges that Ptolemy's sources must surely have been the same as those used by Tacitus, namely the Roman amber-merchants who traded with the Prussian coast and the south Baltic districts, and the information given to him would accordingly concern the *eastern* Scandinavian folk ; if the Leuonoi be taken for the Swedes, it is possible to identify the Fauonai and Firaisoi as the inhabitants of the south-west and west coasts of Finland, a district that would easily be confused at this early time with Scandinavia itself. The Chaideinoi, to the west of the Swedes, may then legitimately be placed not in Norway, but in the Dalarne and Gestrikland districts of Sweden, where indeed there are plenty of place-names containing the *hed* (heath) element to justify the shift from Hedemark in Norway. Further, the Daukiones are not necessarily the Danes (Dankiones—Daneiones), but, by abandoning Δ as a foreshortened enclitic, the Aviones (meaning *islanders*, cf. Germanic *awi*), well-known in the *Germania*, and perhaps a name borne by the inhabitants of Öland at this time. As a complement to this it is simple to accept the Goutai as the people of the island Gotland.

volumes, and the *Getica* of Jordanes is simply an abridgement of it. Cassiodorus himself derived much of his information from a still earlier work by an unknown writer Ablabius, but in the passage describing Scandinavia he doubtless repeats much that was told him by the various northerners who had travelled to Italy and whom he had met. One of these must have been the Scandinavian king Rodvulf, who, not liking his own kingdom, transferred himself with a band of his followers to the court of Theodoric the Great, the very court where Cassiodorus was a much-honoured man.

The description of Scandinavia, the large island Scandza,[1] begins with the remark that it contains ' many and diverse nations ', the term *nationes* referring, of course, to small independent peoples with a king or chieftain at their head. In the northernmost part were the Adogit, perhaps the folk of Halogaland (lat. 68°, Nordland, Norway), who enjoy forty twenty-four-hour days of unbroken daylight in the summer and a like period of unbroken darkness in the winter. The account then names another northern people, the Screrefennae (Lapps), who were content to live without corn, eating only animal flesh and birds' eggs. The next folk to be mentioned are the Suehans (Swedes) ; they were famous for their fine horses, and it was they who supplied the black fox skins that came eventually to the Roman markets. They were a poor people, but nevertheless they wore fine clothes. Then comes a group of peoples who dwelt in a great and fertile plain where they suffered much from the constant attacks of their enemies. They are the Theustes (perhaps from the Tjust district near Kalmar),[2] the Vagoth, the Bergio, the Hallin (dwelling in Halland), and the Liothida (perhaps from Lödde near Lund, or Luggude, Hälsingborg). The next group of people mentioned are the Ahelmil, the Finnaithae (from Finnveden in Småland), the Fervir (from Fjäre, North Halland), and the Gautigoth (inhabitants of

---

[1] Jordanes, *Getica*, ed. Mommsen, *Mon. Germaniae historica*, V, Berlin, 1882, p. 58.

[2] On the difficult subject of the tribe-names of Jordanes, see Von Grienberger, *Die nordischen Völker bei Jordanes, Zeit. f. deutsches Altertum*, 45 (1901), 128 ; J. V. Svensson, *De nordiska folknamen hos Jordanes, Namn och Bygd*, 1917, pp. 109–157 ; B. Nerman, *Det svenska rikets uppkomst*, Stockholm, 1925, pp. 33–52, and Lauritz Weibull, *Arkiv f. nordisk Filologi*, 41 (1925), p. 213, a most interesting and important paper. I have given here, in brackets, some of the suggestions of these writers in the instances where there is a general agreement, but I ought to say that Weibull's views diverge considerably from those of the other authors. He believes, for instance, that the whole of the Theustes-Liothida group is to be located in a small area in north-west Scania.

Västergötland), all brave and warlike folk ; with them are named the Evagreotingi.[1] The folk of this group dwelt (like animals, says Jordanes) in rock-hewn fortresses.[2] Beyond them were the Ostrogoths (inhabitants of Östergötland) and the Suetidi, who are the Suehans, or Swedes, again, though now they are given another form of the name. They are said, at this second reference to them, to excel all other folks in stature, yet, the account goes on to say, the Danes, who are sprung of the same stock as the Swedes and now occupied the lands of the Heruls whom they had driven from their home, also boasted that they were the tallest of the Scandinavians. In this group with the Ostrogoths and the Swedes Jordanes names the Raumariciae (from Romerike in south-east Norway), the Ragnaricii [3] (from the ancient Ranrike, now the Bohuslän), the peace-loving Finni,[4] and the Vinoviloth. Finally, there comes a group of Norwegian peoples, the Granni (of Grenland), the Augandzi (of Agder), the Eunixi, the Taetel, the Rugi (of Rogaland), the Arachi, and the Ranii. It was over these folk that the Rodvulf, who subsequently lived at the court of Theodoric the Great, was king.

The double mention of the Swedes is not, of course, a proof either of the importance or large dominions of these people, being merely a consequence of the mishandling by the author of information derived from more than one source. Yet it is clear that the Swedes were still a powerful folk ruling big territories. The existence of the skin-trade suggests that their dominion extended over a large part of Norrland, and it may also be inferred from the manner of their mention that their lands considerably exceeded the modern Uppland, probably extending both westwards to Vermland and in the south-east into Östergötland. The reference to the Danes who were of the same race as the Swedes, and yet were compelled to emigrate, suggests the vigour of the parent stock. Again, although by the Roman standard the Swedes were judged a poor folk, yet they were noticeable for their rich dress, and this in itself

---

[1] The text (Mommsen) reads *dehinc mixi evagre otingis* ; this is emended *dehinc mixti evagreotingis.*

[2] *Excisis rupibus quasi castellis* ; this must refer to the hill-forts of fourth to sixth century dates that are common in Central Sweden, especially in Bohuslän and Östergötland. See B. Schnittger, *Die vorgeschichtliche Burgwälle in Schweden, Opuscula arch. O. Montelio sept. dicata,* Stockholm, 1913, p. 335.

[3] The text (Mommsen) reads *raumarici, aeragnaricii.*

[4] Probably a folk of the boundary lands between Sweden and Norway, and neither the Finns of history nor the Lapps. ' Finn ' may be a descriptive term meaning *seeker, collector, gatherer.*

is a striking testimony that they possessed much wealth according to the humbler standards of the north.

But they must by this time have had serious rivals in their struggle for supremacy in central Sweden. The warlike Gautigoth of Västergötland are now in the picture, and it is worth noting that the Swedes and the Vinoviloth are expressly said [1] to be on an equal footing with the Ostrogothae and the other peoples of the same group. Furthermore, there can be little doubt of the notable increase in political importance of the tribes of south-east Norway. It is not surprising, therefore, that another, and contemporary author, should make no mention of the Swedes at all.

This was Procopius of Caesarea, who lived in the reign of Justinian (A.D. 527–565). He was the legal adviser and secretary of the general Belisarius and was an experienced man of PROCOPIUS affairs who had travelled in Africa and Italy and in the East. He accompanied Belisarius in the wars against the Vandals and the Ostrogoths, so that he knew something of the German peoples, and, in fact, it is in connexion with a German folk, the Heruls (see p. 65), that he finds occasion to mention the dwellers in the north. [2] The Heruls, about A.D. 505, had been defeated in battle by the Lombards, and in their retreat from their territory in Hungary they had divided into two parties, the one settling across the Danube in Illyricum and the other journeying northwards through the lands of the Slavs into the country of the Danes. There they reached the sea, and then, sailing over to Thule, they established themselves on that 'island'. Thule, said Procopius, is very large, being more than ten times the size of Britain, and was situated a long way to the north of the last-mentioned island. Most of the land of Thule was barren, but in the inhabited districts there lived thirteen nations (ἔθνη), each comprising a very large population and having a king at its head. After describing the midnight sun, Procopius goes on to say that among the inhabitants of Thule were the Scrithiphinoi, a people whose primitive manner of life was akin to that of beasts. They lived by hunting, and knew nothing of agriculture nor of wine ; they did not wear shoes, and their dress was simply the skins of the animals they had slain ; moreover their infants were not breast-fed as among other nations, but were nourished from birth onwards by marrow from animal bones. Nevertheless the other inhabitants of

---

[1] Though this, a matter of punctuation, could be challenged. See, however, Von Grienberger, *Zeitschr. f. deutches Altertum*, 46, pp. 137, 138.

[2] *History of the Wars*, VI, xv.

Thule, Procopius says, did not differ very much from the rest of men. One of the most numerous nations was the Gauti, and it was close to this people that the incoming Heruls settled. There is little doubt that Thule in this context was Scandinavia and that the Scrithiphinoi (the Screrefennae of Jordanes) were the Lapps. The Gauti must have been either the Gautigoth of Jordanes, who dwelt in Västergötland, or a generic term for the inhabitants of Götaland, and the naming of them by Procopius as one of the most numerous peoples of Scandinavia and the fact that it is they alone, apart from the Lapps, who are thought worthy of mention, confirms the impression already given by Jordanes, namely that at this period the centre of power in Sweden lay no longer in Svitjod, but had shifted, or was shifting, to Västergötland and the southern and western provinces of Götaland.

This short summary of the evidence of the historians of the outside world represents the whole of the direct information concerning early Scandinavia, and the gist of these fragmentary and incomplete accounts can be stated in a few words. SUMMARY During the first and second Christian centuries it seems that the leading people of the north were the Swedes of the Mälar lands and that they owed much of their prosperity to a flourishing trans-Baltic trade in skins which were destined for the Roman market. So great was their increase in numbers that eventually a section of them, afterwards called the Danes,[1] were forced to migrate to south Jutland, a place that from this time onwards became their home, though they subsequently increased their territories by the conquest of all Denmark and also of certain southern territories in the mainland of Scandinavia. On this subject, it may be inferred from the archaeological evidence that the migration of the Danes was no remarkable displacement of peoples, but merely the movement to Jutland of adventurers strong enough to fight their way into the position of the ruling caste and to bestow their own tribal name upon the natives of their adopted country. Not all the power and the wealth, however, lay with Sweden. Southern Scandinavia was

---

[1] The Swedish origin of the Danes depends on the plain statement of Jordanes and I see no good reason to doubt his information on this point. It has, however, been challenged, see Lauritz Weibull, *Arkiv f. nordisk Filologi*, 41 (1925), p. 244 n., and Axel Olrik, *Heroic Legends of Denmark*, New York, 1919, p. 34. The reader should be informed that this very great authority, the late Axel Olrik, not only claimed that the Danes were an indigenous folk in Denmark but also denied that the Heruls were its original inhabitants. This is the direct opposite of the views expressed in this book.

rapidly establishing a connexion, independent of Swedish activity, with the mainland of Germany, and early in the second century many other North German peoples dwelling in southern and western Sweden and in southern Norway were known to exist as separate nations, living much like the rest of men. Again, further to the north of these lived the curious and primitive Lapps of whom strange tales were told by travellers returning to the Roman world. Excepting the Lapps, all the Scandinavian peoples are spoken of as nations or states ruled by a king or chieftain (in one instance a queen), and, as to the political relations between them, at least it can be inferred that by the time of the sixth century the kingdoms of Götaland, particularly that of the Västergötar, had risen to such strength and power that they seriously challenged, if indeed they had not over-thrown, the supremacy of the Swedes.

It is possible to add something to this short and simple story by a study of early Germanic literature and the traditional history of the north such as is embodied in the sagas. In the forefront of the material of this kind stands the English poem Beowulf. The oldest version of it is a manuscript of tenth-century date, but the poem was composed, it is confidently BEOWULF believed, in England, probably by an Anglian poet, in the early eighth century. Its interest here, of course, is that it has a Scandinavian theme, and that it is plainly a version of a Scandinavian epic or of a group of Scandinavian lays. The background of the poem is a series of actual happenings in Scandinavian history, as is shown by the fact that the four-times-mentioned raid of Hygelac, king of the Geats, upon the Frisian Chattuari (about A.D. 520) is an event that is independently chronicled by Gregory of Tours in the *History of the Franks*.[1] The nations that are concerned with the principal episodes of the story are the Geats (also called the Weders, or Weder-Geats), the Swedes, and the Danes. The question of the identity of the Geats has occasioned a long dispute as to whether they were the Goths (Gautar, Götar) or the Jutes, but the arguments on each side are too elaborate for the case to be tried here.[2] There is little doubt, however, that after a review of the evidence an impartial jury would decide that the Geats of the poem were not the Jutes but the Goths. It may be that the term refers in particular to the Västergötar whose territories

[1] III, 3.
[2] For a summary, see R. W. Chambers, *Beowulf, An Introduction*, Cambridge, 1921, pp. 8–10, 333–345 ; cf. B. Nerman, *Det svenska rikets uppkomst*, Stockholm, 1925, p. 108 ff.

at this time perhaps extended from the borders of Svitjod in the north to the Bohuslän in the south-west and to the Danish territories in the south. But it is more likely that it is a generic name including all the peoples of Götaland excepting the Danes of Halland and Scania in the extreme south of Sweden.

The poem relates the adventures of its hero Beowulf, who was the nephew of Hygelac, king of the Geats. In the first part of the tale he crosses the sea to the Danish land (Zealand) and there slays the murderous Grendel, a monster that was terrorizing the court of Hrothgar, the king of the Danes. Hrothgar was of the Scylding dynasty, being the great-grandson of Scyld, its founder. In his first speech Hrothgar refers to his own people as the West Danes, but one of his honorific titles was Chief of the East Danes, and this means that though his kingdom was in Zealand he was overlord of the Danes who still dwelt in the south of Sweden.[1] In the second part of the poem Hygelac, and also his son, are dead, and Beowulf is king of the Geats. The story now concerns his contest with a dragon that was devastating his own realm, but it contains many allusions to fierce struggles between the Geats and their neighbours the Swedes, who were ruled by a Scylfing (ON. Ynglinga) dynasty of kings. The poem closes with the death of Beowulf and a prophecy of further wars with the Swedes and also with the Franks and Frisians.

The poem provides, therefore, a corroboration of the suspected rivalry between powerful states in Götaland and Svitjod in the early sixth century, and demonstrates the almost equal importance in Scandinavian affairs at this time of a Danish kingdom established in Zealand and Scania. It introduces, however, the names of the kings who ruled these states and gives considerable information concerning the royal dynasties to which they belonged. As a consequence upon this introduction of personalities, the history of the early Scandinavian peoples necessarily assumes an altered aspect. Henceforward the ancestors of the vikings stand ready for individual summoning as actors in the drama, and where there were formerly but the dim and uncertain shadows of the tribes, now at last the stage has brightened and the people move at the spoken direction of their several chiefs.

---

[1] But E. Wessén rightly attaches little significance to the use of such terms as East Danes and West Danes. See his fine essay, *De nordiska folkstammarna i Beowulf, K. Vitt. Ant. Akad. Handl.*, 36 : 2 (Stockholm, 1927), p. 51.

CHAPTER III

THE BIRTH OF THE VIKING NATIONS

I T may be that not all the royalties and nobles of *Beowulf* were historical personages, but it is certain that some of them at any rate really lived and played the parts assigned to them in the poem. That this is so is proved not only by the record in Frankish history of Hygelac's raid, but by the mention of some of the Beowulf names, coupled with accounts of their doings resembling those chronicled in the poem, in the traditional Scandinavian history that is preserved in other works. Chief of these is the *Ynglingatal*, a Norse genealogical poem said to have been composed in the middle of the ninth century, but probably an altered version of an earlier Swedish poem.[1] Another, but less important, document is Snorri Sturlason's *Ynglingasaga*, incorporated in the *Heimskringla*, that was written in Iceland in the thirteenth century, and there is also the *Historia Norwegiae* that was written about the same time and was based on the older and lost *Íslendingabók* [2] of Ari Thorgilsson that had been compiled at the beginning of the twelfth century.

Of the early Yngling kings of Svitjod there is little need to speak, for fancy alone can say whether they were real people or not.[3] But the *Ynglingatal* and *Ynglingasaga*, after giving EARLY the names of fifteen rulers of the Swedes, make KINGS OF unquestionable allusions to some of the personalities SVITJOD and some of the events that are mentioned in *Beowulf*. The Yngling king Ottar is Ohthere of *Beowulf*, and king Adils (Eadgils of the poem) is his son who made war upon king Ali

---

[1] The poem was incorporated by Snorri Sturlason in the *Ynglingasaga*. In the prologue to the *Heimskringla* Snorri says that the *Ynglingatal* was composed by Thjodolf of Kvinesdal, the scald (court-poet) of Harald Fairhair. The genealogy is not, however, traced to Harald, but terminates with an early Vestfold (Norwegian) king Ragnvald Heidumhar, a cousin of Harald's according to Snorri. There is a good edition of the poem, with a critical commentary, by Adolf Noreen, *K. Vitt. Ant. Akad. Handl.*, 28 : 2 (1925).

[2] A recension of this by Ari, the *Libellus Islandorum*, is also known as *Íslendingabók* and has survived ; but it deals only with Icelandic history.

[3] But see Birger Nerman's brave struggle with this problem, *Det svenska rikets uppkomst*, Stockholm, 1925, p. 29 ff., 137 ff.

(Onela), his uncle, and slew him at the Battle on the Ice. It is true that king Ali of Uppland is presented in the *Ynglingasaga*, and also in the *Skjöldungasaga* of the Danish kings,[1] as coming from Norway, but this is easily explained as the result of a confusion on the part of the Icelandic authors who, writing many centuries later, did not realize that the struggle between Adils and Ali was a civil war, and consequently assumed that Uppland was not the Swedish Uppland but Opland in Norway.

Adils, according to the dead reckoning that alone can be used to find the approximate chronology of the kings of the Ynglinga line, died in the first half of the sixth century, and that is a date corresponding with the time of Eadgils's death according to the Beowulf chronology.[2] He was a mighty king and much is heard of him in the northern sagas and chronicles. They tell that he fought with Helgi, a Danish king (p. 82), some saying that he attacked Denmark and took scatt from the Danes,[3] while others aver that it was Helgi who was the invader.[4]

The most famous of the Yngling kings was Ingjald Illradi who was the great-grandson of Adils and who reigned in the seventh century. It is said[5] of him that he increased his dominions by the simple expedient of inviting the petty kings whose power and possessions he coveted to a feast where he deliberately burnt them alive. But one invited king, Granmar of Södermanland, did not attend the feast and so escaped the fate of the others. Ingjald accordingly went to war with him, but he found that Hogne, king of Östergötland, had allied himself with Granmar, and Ingjald got the worst of the battle that took place between the rival forces. However, he succeeded at length in overcoming Granmar by treachery and thereupon annexed his lands ; but the king of Östergötland he was never

[1] It is known only in a Latin epitome. Ed. A. Olrik, *Aarb. f. nordisk Oldkyndighed*, 2 S. IX (1894), p. 116.

[2] The counting here is so inexact that the agreement of the two chronologies really carries little weight. B. Nerman, it should be noted, puts the death of Adils at about A.D. 575, *Det svenska rikets uppkomst*, p. 138. It is possible that Adils may have been one of the kings who were buried in the three royal barrows of Uppsala, see Nerman, *Vilka konungar ligga i Uppsala högar ?* Uppsala, 1913 ; his father Ottar is thought to have been buried in the Ottar-barrow at Vendel, Uppland, despite Snorri's account of his horrible obsequies in Jutland. For the excavation of this barrow and a discussion of the problem, see S. Lindqvist, *Forn-vännen*, 1917, p. 127 ; the barrow contained a coin of A.D. 476 or 477.

[3] *Leire Chronicle*, ed. M. Cl. Gertz (*Script. min. hist. Danicae*, Copenhagen, 1917), Cap. V, p. 48.

[4] *Ynglingasaga*, ed. F. Jónsson, Copenhagen, 1912, p. 36 ; *Skjöldung-asaga*, ed. A. Olrik, *Aarb. f. n. Oldkyndighed*, 1894, p. 114

[5] *Ynglingasaga*, ed. F. Jónsson, 1912, K. 34–40.

able to subdue. Finally he burnt himself in order to avoid falling into the hands of Ivar Vidfadmi, the king of Scania.

Among the kings summoned to the feast where they were to be destroyed by fire was Algaut of Västergötland, and it is said afterwards that there were men from Västergötland in Ingjald's service. This suggests that Västergötland ceased to be an independent kingdom during Ingjald's reign at Uppsala and came under the Swedish sovereignty. On this supposition Ingjald has acquired much fame as a ruler who welded the lands of modern Sweden into a political whole, and it has been found possible to adduce other statements from the sagas that seem to reveal him as the founder of the present Swedish kingdom. But, although there is a certain sentimental interest in the enquiry, little profit is to be gained from a discussion of Ingjald's claim to this honourable title, for it is obvious that his achievements have been overstated. It is very unlikely, for instance, that the important island of Gotland had passed at this early period under Swedish rule,[1] and it is quite clear from the sagas themselves that Östergötland at any rate resisted his supposed pan-Swedish policy. Indeed, except for the instance of Västergötland, there is no reasonable evidence that any large tracks of Götaland, such as Småland and Blekinge, accepted his rule. And certain it is that the territories won by him were soon in danger of being lost to Sweden, for at his death another and a greater king was threatening his realm.

This was the conquering Ivar Vidfadmi. It is said of him

[1] An attempt has been made to prove by means of archaeological evidence that Sweden conquered Gotland in the sixth century. Knut Stjerna was the first to suggest that the cultural equipment of Gotland assumed an altered complexion in the middle of the sixth century and that thenceforward brooches, pins, and pottery favour the Swedish fashion as opposed to those previously current in Götaland, *Essays . . . on Beowulf, Viking Club Extra Series, III* (1912), esp. p. 72. This contention is warmly supported by Birger Nerman, *Det svenska rikets uppkomst*, 197, but I must confess that at present I do not attach much weight to these archaeological arguments. Dr. Nerman, however, tells me that the greater part of the Gotland material has yet to be published, and I respect the judgement of this great authority on Gotland antiquities sufficiently to know that a verdict must accordingly be postponed. All that history tells us here is that Gotland indubitably belonged to the Swedes about A.D. 850 (Wulfstan's narrative in Alfred's *Orosius*, ed. Sweet, 1883, p. 20). Tradition, however, does suggest that the island was under Swedish rule at a rather earlier date than this, for it is recorded in the *Gutasaga* that the men of Gotland first paid scatt to the Swedes in the days of a legendary king Awair Strabain ; but this, of course, proves very little (*Gutasaga*, ed. H. Pipping, 1905–7, p. 64 ; also in Prof. E. V. Gordon's *Introduction to Old Norse*, Oxford, 1927, p. 158).

that he overthrew Ingjald, who is described as the last of the Ynglings, and usurped the Swedish throne. This is perhaps an overstatement, but it is impossible to doubt that Ivar won for himself considerable power in Scandinavia. It is not by any means clear that he did overthrow the Yngling dynasty, for it is said in the *Historia Norwegiae* [1] that Ingjald's son, Olof Tretelgja, died in *Swethia* after a long and peaceful reign, while the great Icelandic historian, Ari Thorgilsson, whose works were one of the sources of the *Historia*, calls him *Suía-konungr*, king of Svitjod. [2] But Snorri says of Olof that he was an exile in Vermland after the death of Ingjald, becoming king of that country and dying there. [3] It is just possible to explain this discrepancy on the grounds that Ari and the author of the *Historia* wrote loosely, deeming Vermland a part of *Swethia* in Olof's time as it most certainly was in their own day ; so that on the whole it is tempting to read something of fact into Snorri's evidence which thus points to a break in the line of Swedish kings at the very period of Ivar's sudden rise to power. [4]

Before following the history of Svitjod and its dependencies under Ivar Vidfadmi, it is necessary to say something of the early kings in Denmark, though the accounts of them are exceedingly difficult to follow and have only a small historical THE value. As an aid to the understanding of their affairs DANES it will be profitable to recall the manner whereby the country of Denmark had become the land of the Danes, namely the migration of a section of the Swedes, styling themselves Danes, from the Mälar region of Svitjod direct to South Jutland, and the subsequent conquest by these emigrants of the Heruls who were the native peoples of south Jutland and Fyen. [5] This movement was rapidly followed by an extension of the Danish conquests until the invaders possessed not only all the Danish islands but also Scania in South Sweden, and perhaps Halland as well.

---

[1] Ed. G. Storm, *Monumenta Historica Norwegiae*, Oslo, 1880, p. 102.

[2] *Íslendingabók*, ed. W. Golther, Halle, 1892, p. 2.

[3] *Ynglingasaga*, ed. F. Jónsson, K. 42, p. 48.

[4] Snorri's version of the story is adopted as historical fact by Birger Nerman, but is vigorously contested by other authorities. Cf. A. Noreen, *Ynglingatal, K. Vitt. Ant. Akad. Handl.*, 28 : 2 (1925), 245. Professor Sune Lindqvist, *Fornvännen*, 1921, 178, in discussing this question rightly observes that it is ridiculous to suppose that Ivar introduced the boat-grave custom into Svitjod, for the earliest Vendel graves are much earlier than Ivar's time.

[5] E. Wessén, *K. Vitt. Ant. Akad. Handl.*, 36 : 2 (1927), 7 ; also Otto v. Friesen, *Uppsala Universitets Årsskrift*, 1924, p. 47.

The date at which this Danish incursion took place is uncertain. It may have been as early as the third century, this corresponding with the first appearance of the Heruls on the Continent, but the manner of the reference to the event by Jordanes (p. 73) suggests, on the other hand, a period not very long before that in which he himself wrote. It seems, therefore, that a date about A.D. 450–500, and after the migration of the Jutes from Jutland and the Angles from Sleswig, is a more probable one. It is, of course, certain that the Danes were firmly established in their new home in the middle of the sixth century, and it is to be expected that their rulers, as portrayed in *Beowulf*, should be presented as stalwart and powerful kings of an ancient house. It is thus, indeed, that they are described, yet Hrothgar did not boast the long series of mythological ancestors that decorated the family tree of the contemporary Yngling, and it is reasonable to suppose that in the early sixth century the Danes and their kings were not far from being newcomers to Denmark.

Of the Danish kings mentioned in *Beowulf* the first, and the founder of the Scylding dynasty, is Scyld Scefing, an entirely mythical personage. But his grandson, according to the poem, EARLY was Halfdan (Healfdene), and with Halfdan begins KINGS IN the real history of the Scylding line of kings. Half-DENMARK dan, following now the Danish versions of their story, had two sons Hroar or Ro (Hrothgar) and Helgi [1] who, after the death of their father, ruled simultaneously, each taking a separate portion of the kingdom. Helgi is said to have warred with Adils in Sweden ; the chronicles also relate of him that he unwittingly contracted an incestuous union with his own daughter Yrsa, the son of this terrible marriage being that famous person Hrolf Kraki (*c.* A.D. 650–700), the great hero-king of the Scyldings.

Hrolf's court was at Leire, now a small village near Roskilde [2]

---

[1] Saxo (ed. Müller, 1839 ; II, 80) says of Helgi that he killed a Saxon prince by name Hunding and this has naturally suggested that he was really the renowned hero Helgi Hundingsbane of the elder *Edda*. If this was so Helgi the Scylding must be credited with considerable foreign conquest ; but it is much more likely that Hundingsbane was not the Danish chief but a king of Östergötland. Cf. S. Bugge, *Home of the Eddic Poems* (Grimm Library 11), London, 1899, p. 126 ff. ; T. Hederström, *Fornsagor och Eddakväden*, II, Stockholm, 1919, pp. 1–124 ; E. Wessén, *Fornvännen*, 1927, p. 64 ff.

[2] For a long time it was erroneously supposed that Roskilde was founded by Ro (Hróar) ; see E. V. Gordon, *Introduction to Old Norse*, Oxford, 1927, p. 230, n. 14.

in Zealand, a place that was also the site of Hrothgar's hall Heorot, the scene of Beowulf's contest with Grendel. Of Hrolf Kraki, Snorri wrote, ' Among the kings of old his was the most gentle disposition, his the most fearless nature, and none was more dearly loved than he ' [1] ; and Saxo Grammaticus said, ' All the ages after him have honoured his great name and the lustre of his deeds.' [2]

There is a story connected with him, that concerns the Swedes and their Yngling king Adils. This is the tale of Hrolf's visit to Uppsala. The cause, so Snorri's *Edda* declares, was that Adils had refused to pay the reward due to Hrolf's berserks for their help in his struggle against king Ali (Onela) and had declined to send fitting presents to Hrolf in acknowledgement of the loan of these fighters.[3] Hrolf took his twelve berserks with him and set off for Uppsala. On his arrival he and his party were led to lodgings and entertained. But king Adils's men heaped so much wood on to the fire that the clothes were burnt off Hrolf and his companions. And they taunted the Danes, crying, ' Is it true that Hrolf Kraki and his berserks are not afraid of iron and

FIG. 13.—Denmark

fire ? ' Thereupon Hrolf and his men sprang to their feet and flung their shields on to the fire so that it blazed still higher, and one after another they leapt over the fire and, seizing Adils's men, they forced them into the flames. Then Yrsa, Hrolf's mother and here said to be the wife of Adils,

[1] *Edda, Skáldskaparmál,* 48.

[2] II, 82 (ed. Müller).

[3] *Edda, Skáldskaparmál,* 43. There are other explanations in the *Hrólfssaga* and Saxo's *Gesta Danorum.* The most likely theory is that it was because Ali had married Hrolf's aunt and because H. therefore desired to avenge the death of his relative by marriage that he undertook the expedition ; see A. Olrik, *Danmarks heltedigtning,* Copenhagen, 1903, p. 38.

gave to Hrolf a horn full of gold and a famous ring called
Sviagris, and bade him ride away.   But Adils with a party of
Swedes pursued Hrolf and his men who were now in full flight
across the Fyris plain.   Hrolf therefore flung the gold down on
to the road, whereat the Swedes checked their pursuit in order
to recover it.   But Adils bade them ride on, and himself began
to draw near to the fleeing Hrolf.   So Hrolf took the ring and
threw it towards Adils, telling him he might receive it as a gift.
Adils rode at the ring and recovered it at the point of his spear.
Then Hrolf Kraki looked back and, seeing how Adils bent down,
cried out, ' Now I have made him who is mightiest of the Swedes
bent as a swine is bent ! '

Such is the story in the prose *Edda,* and it is retold in an
expanded and different form in the *Hrólfssaga* and also by
Saxo Grammaticus.   Yet each version ends with the flight of
Hrolf Kraki and his men from Uppsala, so that it may well be
that the narratives enshrine the memories of a serious war
between the Swedes and the Danes at the end of the seventh
century, a war in which the Danes, though ultimately driven off,
were the attacking party.   It is possible, moreover, that the
Danes themselves had suffered from Swedish oppression shortly
before Hrolf's rise to power, for a curious legend has survived
to the effect that before Hrolf came to the throne the Swedish
king Adils, taking advantage of Denmark's weakness after the
death of the brothers Hroar and Helgi, imposed a dog-king
upon the Danes [1] and acted in every way as the master of Danish
politics.   This preposterous tale can perhaps be connected with
the attacks said to have been made by Adils on the Danish
coast near Sleswig that are described by Saxo Grammaticus, [2]
and the fighting between Helgi, the Danish king, and this same
Adils that is recorded in the sagas.

In addition to the tales of the kings at Leire, Danish tradition
has likewise something to say of kings in Jutland.   It was at
the court of one of these kings, Feng by name, that Ambloth
lived, Ambloth who is known to all the world as Hamlet, Prince
of Denmark.   It is hard to say if there really was a long dynasty
of Jutish kings still ruling in Jutland after the migration of
the principal body of the Jutes, and possessing their country
as a kingdom entirely distinct from that of the eastern Danes
in Scania, Zealand, and the islands ; for it may well have been

---

[1] *Leire Chronicle,* ed. M. Cl. Gertz (*Script. Min. Hist. Danicae,* Copenhagen, 1917), Cap. V, p. 48, and cf. *Gesta Danorum,* ed. M. Lorenzen,
Samfund t. udgivelse af gammel nordisk litt., XVIII, p. II.
[2] IV, 162 (ed. Müller).

that the kings in Jutland were chieftains of Jutish blood who had won only some transitory independence, either by revolt against the Leire king or as a gift from him. Thus, indeed, of Hamlet's father and uncle it is said that it was Rorik Slenganboge, a king in Leire after Hrolf Kraki, who had made them chiefs in Jutland.[1] The chronicles also name two other kings as ruling Jutland, Vermund and Offa. Vermund is said to have been a contemporary of the Swedish king Adils and there are records of two raids by the Swedes on the Danish coast near Sleswig during his reign. But both he and Offa, his son, were in all probability Angles, as indeed their names suggest, who ruled in Sleswig before the migration of the Anglian folk.[2] The Danes tell the grand story of how Saxon aggression was frustrated by Offa's personal valour in defeating single-handed two chosen champions of the enemy ; but they doubtless believed Offa to be a Dane because this famous exploit is described as having taken place on the Eider banks in what was later Danish territory, whereas the earlier *Widsith* poem establishes him as an Anglian prince.

The relations between the Jutland kings and the Scyldings at Leire are perplexing enough, but there is yet another complication in the affairs of early Denmark. For it is clear from the poems *Widsith* and *Beowulf* that the Scyldings and their folk were principally occupied by a long-sustained and bitter feud between themselves and a dynasty of Heathobard kings. Who these Heathobards were is uncertain, and all that is known about them is that they were a Baltic people, perhaps living in Jutland itself. At first sight it may seem convenient to make a single problem of the double difficulty of Jutish and Heathobard kings by supposing that the Heathobards were in fact the Jutland division of the Danes, a people whose kings soon begin to figure in Danish history of a little later date, and who eventually encompassed the downfall of the Scyldings ; but such a view implies the outbreak of a prolonged civil war between two sections of the Danes not long after their arrival in Denmark as invaders struggling for a foothold in a hostile land. This objection naturally leads to the

HEATHO-
BARDS

---

[1] *Gesta Danorum*, ed. Lorenzen (op. cit.), p. 17.

[2] Professor H. M. Chadwick has removed some considerable chronological difficulties here by supposing that the Adils who attacked Vermund's kingdom was not the sixth century king of Sweden but Eadgils, prince of the Myrgings, who is mentioned in the *Widsith* poem, this giving Vermund a date in the middle of the fourth century. *Origin of the English Nation*, Cambridge, 1907, p. 135 ; cf. R. W. Chambers. *Widsith*, Cambridge, 1912, p. 93.

consideration of a rival theory which supposes that the Heathobard attack on the Leire kings represents the revolt of the
indigenous population against the Danish invaders, this indigenous folk being the Heruls, or rather the remnant of them
now left in the Cimbric peninsula.[1] Against this last view it
may be fairly urged that the equation of the Heathobards with
the Heruls makes the events of the two poems an exact reverse
of the historical fact that the Danes attacked and drove out
the Heruls. For it is the Heathobards who are the attacking
party and it is the Scyldings who are defending their father-
land [2]; moreover, Procopius has attested that a section of the
Heruls, returning from the Continent, marched peacefully
through the land of the Danes at the beginning of the sixth
century, and this is very unlikely to have happened if the Danes
were at war in this very period with their stay-at-home brethren.
The failure of these views, and also of the hypothesis that the
Heathobards were the Lombards, has suggested to Dr. Elias
Wessén the arresting and revolutionary idea that it was the
Heathobards who were the Danes and that the Heruls with
whom they strove and whom they eventually conquered were
none other than the people ruled by the Scylding princes at
Leire.[3] This interpretation, though it is one to be treated with
considerable caution, has the merit of explaining several of
the puzzling features in the Scylding legends. Thus if the
Scyldings were really Heruls it is not hard to understand why
their immediate ancestor, being of the pre-Danish population
and yet within the Danish realm, bore the name Halfdan (half-
a-Dane),[4] and why the story ends with disaster hanging over
the Scylding house which seems to end with Hrolf Kraki. Again
the ancestor of the Heathobard kings, Frode and Ingjald, was
Dan who came, says the *Leire* Chronicle,[5] from Uppsala in
Svitjod just as did the Danes themselves; moreover, the
Heathobard dynasty twice contains the rare name Frode, which
can perhaps be connected with the Swedish god Frö, the
mythological founder of the Ynglings, the royal dynasty of
Svitjod. It is therefore an undeniably important theory that
Dr. Wessén has suggested, but it is very easy to see that there
are two weak points in it. The first of these is that in societies

[1] K. Müllenhoff, *Beowulf*, Berlin, 1889, p. 31, and cf. R. W. Chambers, *Beowulf*, Cambridge, 1921, p. 24.

[2] *Beowulf*, 913.

[3] E. Wessén, *K. Vitt. Ant. Akad. Handl.*, 36 : 2 (1927), 25.

[4] Cf. an essay by Kemp Malone, *Danes and Half-Danes, Arkiv f. nordisk Filologi*, 42 (1926), p. 234.

[5] Ed. M. Cl. Gertz, Cap. I, p. 43.

where feuds were common it is very unwise to overpress coin-
cidences of results into evidence as to the race of the participants ;
the second is that no ingenuity can explain away the fact that
the people who on this view were really the Danes were in fact
called Heathobards, whereas the people who were called the
Danes were not Danes at all, but Heruls.[1]

There will be little profit gained by a further discussion here
of these difficult matters, for it is plain that no satisfactory account
can as yet be given of sixth-century Denmark, despite the many
legends of its heroes and the attempts of the early mediaeval
chroniclers to weld together separate dynasties into a single
and imposing line of Danish kings. Certain is it, nevertheless,
that the whole of Denmark was not a united state ruled by one
all-powerful dynasty, but rather was the country an arena for
the struggles between warring and contentious tribes. That
the power passed eventually into the hands of the Danes in
Jutland may be inferred, but these folk can have acquired no
permanent dominion over the whole peninsula and the Danish
islands. Indeed, in the seventh century, the eastern Danish
kingdom (Scania, and perhaps the Danish islands) must surely
have been included in the confederacy of states established by
that conquering prince, Ivar Vidfadmi, who has already been
named in connexion with the affairs of the Ynglings of Svitjod.

Ivar came of the Danish line of the Scyldings, for his father
Halfdan Snjalli, brother of the king of Scania, is said by two
medieval genealogies to have been the great-grandson of king
Hrothgar of the Beowulf poem. According to the *Hervarar-
saga*,[2] he also belonged to the royal family of a main-
IVAR   land division of the Goths who dwelt in Reidgötaland,
VIDFADMI
KING OF   a district that has been identified almost with certainty
DENMARK   as part of north-east Germany, probably East Prussia
AND   and Poland.[3] His conquests were considerable, if
SWEDEN
               the sagas are to be believed. He is said not only to
have subdued Sweden and the Danish kingdom, but also to have
held very extensive dominions on the mainland, this being doubt-
less a result of his descent from the Reidgothic kings, and to
have conquered the East Baltic states of Kurland and Estland.
He is also credited with conquests in England, the *Hervararsaga*
explaining that he ruled over the part of the island that is called
Northumberland.

---

[1] For the argument on these points see E. Wessén, loc. cit., p. 32.
[2] Ed. S. Bugge, *Norske Oldskriftselskab Samlinger*, VI (Oslo, 1864),
p. 290.
[3] Otto v. Friesen, *Rökstenen*, Stockholm, 1920, p. 108 ff.

Ivar's realm, however, was probably a loosely knit confederacy of vassal states. Indeed, if it is correct to identify
the Hogne and Granmar of the Helgi Lays in the elder *Edda*
with the kings of the same name in the *Ynglingasaga* (p. 78),
it might be argued that Ivar was rather the ally than the conqueror of the states of Östergötland and Södermanland. At
his death, however, the confederacy, if such it was, collapsed,
and confusion reigned until Ivar's grandson once more united
the several states under a single direction. This new chieftain
of eastern Scandinavia was Harald Hilditönn.

All the saga-sources agree that Harald won back by slow
degrees his grandfather's vast kingdom, but though he lived
to an old age he met his death in battle and as a result his
possessions were seized by an upstart ruler. This was one of
HARALD   the great battles of early Scandinavian history, a
HILDI-   contest that was long remembered by the scalds and
TÖNN   chroniclers. It was fought at Bravalla, probably
close to Norrköping in Östergötland, about the middle of the
eighth century, and the issue of the battle affected very considerably the distribution of the balance of power in Scandinavia. The difficulty, however, is that while modern scholars
do not deny the historicity of the battle,[1] the personality and
nationality of the protagonists is by no means easy to decide.
There has, indeed, been a wide divergence from the saga-
BATTLE   traditions in the attempts to square the accounts of
OF   the battle with the supposed political condition of
BRAVALLA the time. It is, however, little short of perverse to
claim that Harald Hilditönn was anything other than king of
' Greater Denmark ', a ruler of Denmark and Scania whose sway
extended by right of conquest over a very large area of Sweden,
even perhaps over Svitjod itself. Many of these districts within
his kingdom were ruled by sub-kings who had sworn allegiance
to Harald, and his adversary at Bravalla, Sigurd Hring, must
assuredly have been one of these sub-kings risen in rebellion
against him. But who was this Sigurd Hring ? The *Hervararsaga*, which is of thirteenth-century date, declares that he was
a nephew of Harald and a sub-king in Denmark itself.[2] The
Sögubrot, written about 1300, agrees that Hring was a nephew

[1] See, for instance, A. Olrik, *Namn och Bygd*, 1914, p. 297 ; A. Nordén,
Saga och sägen i Bråbygden, 1922, pp. 28–52 ; and *Östergötlands Järnålder*,
1929, I, 196 ; E. Hjärne, *Namn och Bygd*, 1917, p. 56 ; T. Hederström,
Fornsagor och Eddakväden, I, 1917, pp. 20–60 ; B. Nerman, *Det sve nska
rikets uppkomst*, p. 253.
[2] Ed. S. Bugge, 1864, p. 292.

of Harald, but says that Harald had made him king of Svitjod and Västergötland.[1] Saxo Grammaticus, writing about 1200, also makes Hring to be Harald's nephew (but by his sister, not his brother) and describes him as king of Sweden.[2] The slightly earlier *Leire* Chronicle (late twelfth century) is another source in which Hring is described as king of Sweden,[3] but there is one saga, that of Herrand and Bose which was written in the fourteenth century, that depicts Hring, who is not said in this account to be a close relative of Harald, as the ruler of Östergötland.

Without entering into a full argument as to the exact situation of Sigurd Hring's country, it seems to be a safe inference from the united testimony of these sources that the great Bravalla battle represented the secession from the Danish confederacy of one or more of the northern states that had submitted to Ivar Vidfadmi and to Harald Hilditönn. The long accounts of the battle, and the description of the vast hosts and mighty heroes alleged to have taken part in it, are sufficient to show that it was fought to decide great issues and that its result must have been a turning-point in Scandinavian history. Harald met his death, the Danish supremacy came to an abrupt end, and once more the states of central Sweden, Västergötland, Östergötland, and Svitjod, now perhaps coalesced under the rule of Sigurd Hring, were free to shape their own destiny, to increase and to prosper until at length they stood before the world as the united

SVITJOD
BECOMES
KINGDOM
OF
SWEDEN

kingdom of Sweden. It would be doubtless a serious overstatement to declare that the immediate sequel to Bravalla was the foundation of the modern Swedish state, for the gain to Svitjod from this victory cannot accurately be assessed. But at least it is certain that in the next century the Danes held only the extreme south of Sweden in addition to their own territories, and that the old distinction between Swedes and Goths as peoples of separate kingdoms had disappeared, the names Swedes and Sweden henceforward embracing the Goths and Götaland.[4]

[1] Ed. C. Petersen and E. Olson, *Samfund t. udgivelse af gammel nordisk litt.*, XLVI, p. 15.

[2] VII, 367 (ed. Müller).

[3] Cap. IX, p. 53 (ed. Gertz, SS. Min. Hist. Dan., 1917).

[4] The fact that the missionary Anskar, who preached in Sweden, refers only to the Swedes and the Swedish kingdom, seems to be proof of this, for Anskar had a detailed knowledge of Scandinavian affairs. It is true that the travellers and missionaries who supply our meagre information about Scandinavia in the ninth and tenth centuries all seemed to have approached Sweden by its eastern Baltic coast, so that

It is an unfortunate thing for the purpose of the present narrative that the formation of the state of Sweden in the dark centuries following upon the battle of Bravalla should be an event that is lost to history ; but there is no escape from this conclusion inasmuch as the paucity of records after the battle makes any conjecture as to the full story a rash and unprofitable enterprise. It must be sufficient to say that from the end of the eighth century onwards there may have been a single kingdom of Sweden possessing, except for some territories in the extreme south and west, almost the whole of the lands of modern Sweden.

The time has come, then, to turn once more to the story of early Denmark, though, first, a preliminary word must be said concerning affairs on the Continent.

The long and bitter struggle between the Saxons and the Franks that had endured throughout the eighth century ended with the triumph of the now Christian and cultured Franks over their dour heathen adversaries. In 772 Charles the Great DENMARK himself invaded the lands of the Saxons and destroyed AND THE that focus of their pagan worship, the Irmensul in FRANKS its sacred grove, at the same time forcing the reluctant heathen to admit his missionaries. For twenty more years they resisted him still, but when Charles at length resorted to mass deportations the Saxon power was broken. Henceforward their revolts became less frequent and feebler until in the middle of the ninth century they had ceased.

The Danish lands, therefore, after Bravalla, were subject to a new influence, namely the advent near the Danish frontier of the Franks themselves. It was a circumstance of no little importance. This was no contact with mere brother Germans, rough heathens of the same calibre as the Danes themselves or their familiar neighbours the Saxons and Frisians. The Franks, on the contrary, were a civilized and instructed people, inheritors of a rich legacy of Roman culture and determined evangelists of the Christian faith. Their relations with the people of Denmark could not fail, therefore, to bring upon the uncouth Danes all the disturbing consequences, both social and political, that

it is possible that they had little experience of Götaland proper ; but all the same it is very unlikely that there would have been no reference to a Götaland kingdom in their accounts if such a state had existed independently of Svitjod. Again, it is true that there are various references to the Goths and Götaland, and even to chiefs who ruled in Götaland, in the Icelandic sagas ; but this surely does not prove the existence of an independent Gothic state. One might as well deny the union of England and Scotland on the grounds that the Scots and Scotland retained their names after 1603.

so often follow the throwing together of a rich and powerful people, intent upon spreading the gospel of their own religion, with a humbler folk. Of this clash between the Danes and the Franks something may be learnt from the Frankish chronicles.[1]

The history of the Danes as derived from these sources opens with the flight of the Saxon chief Widukind in 777 to Denmark; there he took refuge with a Danish king called Sigfred who subsequently entered into diplomatic relations with Charles the Great. At the beginning of the ninth century Sigfred had been succeeded by Godfred, a very powerful king.[2] He collected an NINTH- army to oppose Charles, being fearful perhaps of the CENTURY loss of his revenues as a result of the appearance of DANISH the Franks upon the Frisia-Baltic trade-route, and KINGS in 808 he overthrew the emperor's allies, the Obotrits, a Slavonic people living in the modern Mecklenberg region, and built a defensive dyke extending half-way across the country from the Baltic coast near Sleswig to the Hollingstedt swamps, this being the renowned Danevirke[3] (Fig. 14). Two years

[1] Chief of these for ninth-century Denmark are the *Annales Einhardi* (Pertz, *M.G.H.*, SS. I, pp. 157, 191 ff.), *Annales Fuldenses* (ib. p. 354 ff.), and *Annales Bertiani* (ib. p. 424 ff.).

[2] This was the Godfred identified by N. M. Petersen, P. A. Munch, and G. Storm with the Vestfold (Norwegian) king Gudröd (see p. 106) who is mentioned in the *Ynglingatal*; see Storm's *Kritiske Bidrag til Vikingetidens Historie*, Oslo, 1878, p. 34 ff. The case for a partial conquest of Denmark at this period cannot, however, be seriously maintained; indeed, the identification was abandoned by Storm himself, *Arkiv f. nordisk Filologi*, XV (1898), 133–5. This matter of Godfred's supposed Yngling ancestry must not nevertheless be allowed to prejudice the question of the subsequent existence of a Dano-Norwegian kingdom.

[3] There is a large literature dealing with the Danevirke. The principal authoritative account is that by S. Müller and C. Neergaard, *Fortidsminder*, I (1903), but it is important to consult Vilh. La Cour's *Danevirke*, Copenhagen, 1917, and *Geschichte des schleswigschen Volkes*, I, Flensburg, 1923, and other recent descriptions such as that by Hans Kjaer, *Vor Oldtids Mindesmaerker*, Copenhagen, 1925, p. 177 ff.; cf. furthermore, the references to papers by S. Lindqvist and E. Wadstein (p. 97). Godfred's Danevirke consists of the Vestervold and the Ostervold, though this last has now almost completely disappeared. The earthwork was 8½ miles long, and in its best preserved portion is now over 60 feet broad and 9 feet in height; it has no ditch. The port of Hedeby was situated on the coast of Hedeby Nor 2 miles to the east of the Danevirke; it was enclosed by a semicircular dyke shutting off an area of 54 acres and connected with the main Danevirke by a dyke without a ditch. South of Hedeby and running westwards to the southern bulge of the Danevirke is another fortification, the Kurvirke or Kograv, a dyke 3¾ miles long with a ditch on its south side; this is obviously a forward extension of the frontier protecting Hedeby. It is supposed that the connecting dyke between Hedeby and the Danevirke

later he is said to have operated with his fleet against the Frisian coasts. His relative (nepos) Hemming succeeded him, and for the time being a peace was established between the Franks and the Danes. In 812, following upon the death of Hemming, there was a long struggle for the throne between Godfred's descendants and those of an earlier king called Harald. After fortune had favoured both sides with temporary success the crown passed eventually to one of Godfred's five sons, but Harald, a namesake and descendant of the earlier Harald, appealed to the emperor, now Charles's son Louis (814–840), for help. He was eventually reinstated as co-regent with one of Godfred's sons (or possibly allotted a portion of the Danish

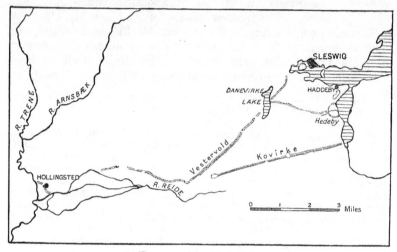

FIG. 14.—The Danevirke

realm), but, later on, he was once more expelled. This time he made certain of the lasting favour of Louis the Pious by adopting the Christian faith (826) ; but even this did not prevent his second expulsion from Denmark, and he then settled in some lands at the mouth of the Weser that he held in fief from the Frankish emperor (p. 196).

proper was built by Harald Gormsson (late ninth century), but the date of the Kurvirke is uncertain. It is probably a late structure, although E. Wadstein regards it as the original Godfred's dyke. The Vestervold itself is complicated by the addition of a massive stone revetment, popularly attributed to Thyra, king Gorm's queen (mid ninth century), and, later, by an additional frontal wall constructed by Valdemar the Great (twelfth century).

In the 30's and 40's of the ninth century, Horik, another of Godfred's sons, is named as Danish king, a personage who is also mentioned in the life of Anskar, the missionary, and plays a not inconsiderable part in Frankish politics of this period (p. 195). It is said of Horik that, although at one period he was sole king of Denmark, in 850 he was forced to concede two portions of his kingdom to relatives who had attacked him, and that four years later all three kings fell in a war with Horik's nephew Guthorm. The crown then passed to relatives of Harald, but in 857 a second Horik is named as king. At the same time, however, a part of the realm was possessed by another king called Rorik who plays a famous part in viking history and who was Harald's brother. Much later, in 873, there is further mention of two Danish kings, Sigfred and Halfdan,[1] ruling simultaneously, each of them making peace with the Frankish emperor Louis the German.

It seems plain that throughout this period there can have been no such thing as a single and undivided kingdom of Denmark, except perhaps for short lengths of time when some powerful chieftain won for himself a temporary supremacy. But, for the most part, the country's history is one of a turmoil of warring princes who struggled continuously for the possession of increased dominions at their neighbour's expense, sometimes courting the favour of the Franks or sometimes standing forth in armed revolt against them.[2]

This reading of the state of affairs in ninth-century Denmark can in a small measure be confirmed by appeal to another source of information, namely two travellers' accounts of Scandinavia. Shortly before the year 900 the English king Alfred the Great made a translation of a history of the world written five hundred years earlier by Orosius, and to this he added some general information about Europe and also the narratives OTTAR of journeys made in northern Europe by two men, AND Ottar (Ohthere) and Wulfstan. In his own remarks WULFSTAN upon the northern countries Alfred distinguishes between the South Danes living in a land having the North Sea on the west and the Baltic on the east (i.e. Jutland, and presumably central Jutland in view of his further remarks) and

[1] They were perhaps sons of Ragnar Lodbrok (pp. 203, 231) and probably of the house of Harald.

[2] On this difficult subject of the ninth-century Danish kings, see W. Vogel, *Die Normannen*, Heidelberg, 1906, p. 57 ff., p. 403 ff., and Jan de Vries, *De Wikingen in de lage landen bij de Zee*, Haarlem, 1923, esp. Ch. V and appendix I, p. 351.

the North Danes who lived to the east and north of them, both on the Continent (this must mean north Jutland and not Scania) and on islands (Zealand and the Danish archipelago).[1]

Ottar, the first of the two travellers, was a northern trader from Halogaland in Norway. He said that to the south of his country at a distance of a month's sail, always with a fair wind and riding at anchor each night, was a port Sciringes-heal (Skiringssal), now known to have been situated near Tjölling at the mouth of the Oslo fjord. From that port a sail of five days took one to Haethan (Hedeby), near the modern Sleswig, and this town, he said, belonged to the Danes. For the first three days of the journey there was open sea to starboard and ' Denmark ' on the port side, but for the last two days Jutland and Sillande (south Jutland) and many islands lay to starboard. To port now were islands (Zealand and others) that belonged to Denmark.[2]

Hedeby was the point of departure for Wulfstan, the second traveller. He went to Truso at the mouth of the Weichsel, taking seven days and nights on the journey. Wendland in north-east Germany was on his starboard side, and to port were Langeland, Laaland, Falster, and Scania, all of which belonged to Denmark. Then he came to Bornholm, an island having a king of its own, and after that he left on the port side Blekinge, Möre, Öland, and Gotland, tracts of the Scandinavian mainland and two large islands that all belonged to Sweden.

These accounts, in conjunction with Alfred's own observations, are sufficient to show that there was as yet no single kingdom of Denmark and that the Danes were divided into two states, the one occupying the greater part of Jutland, and the other comprising Zealand and the islands, the Scania district of southern Sweden, and, perhaps, some territory in north Jutland. At the end of the ninth century, then, Denmark had not achieved the political solidarity already won by the Swedish state, and another century must run more than half its course before the Danes can be counted as a nation united under one rule.

[1] Alfred's *Orosius*, ed. H. Sweet, Early English Text Soc., 1883, p. 16.
[2] As proof that the coastal tracts of Sweden and the country up to and including Vestfold in Norway were under Danish control in the ninth century, the *Einhardi Annales* (Pertz, *Mon. Germ. Hist.* SS. I, 200) are often quoted, e.g. *Camb. Med. Hist.*, III, 313. But I am not sure that in the passage concerned *Westarfolda*, the extreme district of the realm of the joint Danish kings Harald and Ragnfröd, is really Vestfold in Norway. The context suggests that a district in Jutland is more likely.

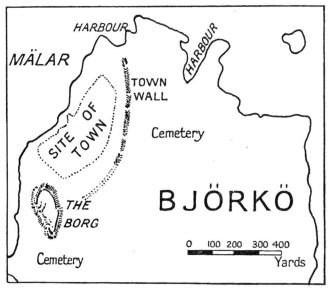

Fig. 15.—Site of the ancient town Birka, near Stockholm

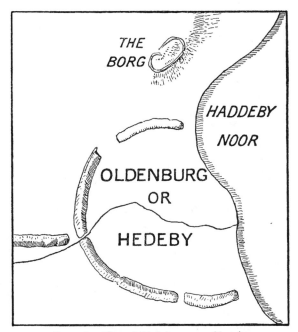

Fig. 16.—Site of Hedeby, near Sleswig

The late ninth and early tenth centuries, however, witnessed one very important event in the economic history of the North, and that was the rise to fame of notable and busy ports at BIRKA   Birka in Sweden and Hedeby in Denmark. Birka AND   (Latin form of Björkö) was situated on the little HEDEBY   Björkö island on the Mälar lake west of Stockholm, and was, at the time when it was visited by the missionary Anskar, a seat of the Swedish king. The town lay within a fortified area of some nineteen acres and seems to have been occupied from the ninth century until about 1050. Hedeby stood, as has been said, on the coast of Haddeby Nor in Sleswig, outside Godfred's Danevirke and in territory that had been left sparsely populated by the migration of the Angles ; it was

FIG. 17.—Silver coins and coin-pendants from Birka
(Late ninth or early tenth century A.D.)

defended by a semicircular dyke enclosing an area of 54 acres. The excavation of the place yielded a rich harvest of finds, now in the Kiel Museum, that suggest an occupation lasting from the late ninth century to the middle of the eleventh century.

The most probable of the theories concerning the origin and interconnexion of the two towns is that both of them were first and foremost market-places established as a result of the enterprise of the Frisian merchants who traded so busily with the north in the ninth century and who bartered the weapons, glass, and fabrics of western Europe for the native furs ; yet it is likely that they were built by the viking folk and that from the beginning they were peopled largely by them, for the fortunes of Frisia declined rapidly soon after their establishment and the northern people were left to dispute among themselves for the control of the profitable trade-route leading across Sleswig to the Baltic and to the Vik.[1] The supreme economic importance of this route was demonstrated more than once in northern history, as when a later king of Denmark, Harald Gormsson, and the then ruler of Norway, Jarl Haakon, united in 974 to defend this Danevirke district against the attacks of the German emperor, Otto II, but its immediate interest is that even in this early period at the beginning of the tenth century there was a struggle between the Swedes and the Danes for the

[1] It was Knut Stjerna, *Hist. Tidskrift f. Skåneland*, III (1909), p. 176 ff., who first suggested the Frisian origin of Birka, and there is something to be said in favour of his view ; thus there were some distinctive pottery jugs found there that have exact parallels in Frisia, and the resemblance of the well-known Birka coins (Fig. 17) to Frisian prototypes has been demonstrated by P. Hauberg. It is not, however, by any means certain that the relatively common placename Björkö, which occurs not only in Sweden but in Norway, is of Frisian origin and betrays, as is sometimes said, the northern marts of this merchant-folk, for only at the Mälar Björkö is there any sign of an important settlement in the ninth and tenth centuries, and it is possible, as E. Wessén has suggested, that the word is simply an Old Swedish form for *Birch Island*. Note that H. Schück, *Birka*, 1910, and, more recently, S. Lindqvist, *Fornvännen*, 1926, p. 4 ff., have denied the Frisian origin of Birka. For this town, see Lindqvist's excellent little guide, *Björkö, Svenska fornminnesplatser* 2, Stockholm, 1930, and A. Schück, *Det svenska stadväsendets uppkomst*, Stockholm, 1926, p. 51 ff. and p. 348 ff., a most important book. Hedeby also can show pottery that has Frisian analogies (I refer to the curious ' bar-lip ' fragments) ; for this town, see O. Scheel and P. Paulsen, *Schleswig-Haithabu*, Kiel, 1930 (containing all the historical references to Hedeby and a full bibliography of recent literature). Here the problem of its age and origin is made all the more difficult in that it is bound up with the theories concerning the archaeology and history of the Danevirke. The argument that because the site lies south of Godfred's dyke Hedeby must be a non-Danish foundation is of no importance, as the existence of a frontier does not preclude further territorial expansion ; moreover, E. Wadstein, *Fornvännen*, 1927, p. 253, has tried (I do not think successfully) to prove that it is the Kurvirke, lying south of Hedeby, and not the Vestervold to the north, that was Godfred's original fortification. Professor Lindqvist will have it, *Fornvännen*, 1926, p. 1, that Hedeby is not older than about A.D. 900 and that it was founded by invading Swedes, being planned on the model of Birka ; but I have seen an oval brooch among the Hedeby finds that ought to be older than 900, and I should like to stress the very important evidence of the Norwegian Ottar (see above) who knew Haethan, which must surely be Hedeby, as a Danish town before the end of the ninth century. Lindqvist would no doubt retort that this Danish town was on the north of the Slien, probably on the site of the modern Sleswig, and not the Hedeby in the ' semicircle ' ; Wadstein, however, opposes this and declares that Hedeby in the semicircle was the early Sleswig (Sliesthorp or Sliaswich), *Fornvännen*, 1927, p. 255.

possession of Hedeby. The first hint of this rivalry is to be discovered in an account of certain Danish kings given in an historical treatise that it is now proper to cite.

The Frankish chronicles have nothing to say of the kings of Denmark in the period immediately after 873, and it is not until the beginning of the tenth century that Danish royalties are mentioned again. The new source is the *Hamburg Church History* of Adam of Bremen, and his testimony, although brief, is of more than ordinary interest in that he derived his facts, as he himself remarks, from the mouth of Svein II Estridsen, king of Denmark, about the year 1075. According to this authority a king named Helgi ruled in Denmark about A.D. 900, and this Helgi was succeeded by an Olof who came from Sweden and seized the kingdom by force. Olof's sons, Knubbe and Gurd, reigned after him, and in due course the throne passed into the possession of Knubbe's son who was called Sigtryg; but when he had reigned a short time Hardegon Svennson, coming from ' Nordmannia ', wrested the kingdom from him. But, adds Adam, it is uncertain whether all these kings reigned in succession one after the other or whether some of them ruled at the same time.

The significance of the statement that Olof came from Sweden is not immediately obvious, but the fact that there is such a large number of objects of patently Scandinavian origin and of about his date among the Hedeby finds suggests at once HEDEBY A that it was in fact at Hedeby that he established his SWEDISH Swedish invaders, having possessed himself of this COLONY district, and the town dominating the old Frisian trade-route, by right of conquest. On this point there is something more than the witness of Adam of Bremen. For Widukind's chronicle relates how the Emperor Henry I fought against Knubbe (here called Chuba), Olof's son, to punish him for piratical raids on the Frisian coast,[1] and this Knubbe's name, together with that of his son, Sigtryg, is inscribed on two memorial stones near Hedeby, one of which was set up on the coast of Haddeby Nor and betrays Swedish dialectical peculiarities.[2]

The fate of the Swedish colony at Hedeby when Sigtryg was defeated and slain by the invading Hardegon in the early

[1] *M.G.H.* (Pertz), SS. III, p. 435.
[2] L. Wimmer, *Danske Runemindesmaerker*, 70. It is also related in the greater Olaf Tryggvason saga that Knubbe was slain by the Danish king Gorm (*Fornmannasögur*, I, 115) ; this is a late and dubious tradition, though it is likely enough that Gorm did war against the Hedeby Swedes.

'30s is not known, for who exactly this newcomer was Adam of
Bremen does not say.   But he was evidently not a Dane since
he arrived ' from Nordmannia ', and the natural conclusion is
that he was a Norwegian, or, just conceivably, another Swede.[1]
Thus it is probable that Hedeby under Hardegon and his house
was still a foreign settlement outside of the Danish dominion,
and so, indeed, it continued to be even after the next change
in the ruling dynasty, which took place in the '80s of the tenth

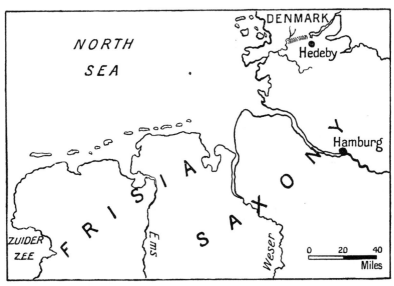

FIG. 18.—Hedeby and the neighbouring lands

century when King Eric Segersäll of Sweden took possession of
the town ; but by this time the adjacent realm of Denmark

[1] There has been considerable argument as to his identity and nationality.   Formerly his name was assumed to be Hardecnut and he was
believed to be either the father of the Danish king Gorm (who is known
to have been so called) or Gorm himself.   Everything depends, of course,
upon the interpretation of the name of his country Nordmannia, for this
might be translated Normandy, and therefore it is not impossible that
Hardegon was a Dane returned from the colony overseas ; but the fact
remains that according to chronicle-usage Norway is much more likely
to be the correct translation.   It is worth noting, however, that Adam
of Bremen uses the name Nordmannia in one instance as though it
applied also to eastern Scandinavia, that is Sweden.   For Hardegon's
identity see L. Jacobsen, *Svenskevaeldets Fald*, Copenhagen, 1929, and
the reviews of this notable book, e.g., S. Lindqvist, *Namn och Bygd*,
1929, p. 1, and V. La Cour, *Hist. Tidsskrift*, Copenhagen, 9 R. VI, 3,
p. 459.

had become a powerful state and the foreigners' hold on the border-town was not destined to endure much longer. The end came about A.D. 995, when the Swedes were driven out by the Danish king, Svein Forkbeard, and the once busy mart was utterly destroyed.

The story of Denmark's development into the formidable kingdom ruled by Svein begins in the days of his grandfather Gorm, a monarch whose achievements history has unhappily failed to chronicle although his reputation as a mighty man has survived into saga-tradition. He was the last of the heathen kings of Denmark and reigned about the years A.D. 930–940, having his court at Jellinge in Jutland. Here it was that Gorm was laid to rest beneath a great barrow that can still be seen, and here too stands the grave-mound, or cenotaph,[1] of Thyra, his queen, a royal lady who has been honoured in later days as a noble defender of the Danevirke.[2]

KING GORM

The great royal mounds of Gorm and Thyra stand about 200 feet apart and between the two is a stone carved at the order of Gorm's son Harald. It is richly ornamented, bearing on one face a figure of Christ and on another face an animal, each framed in an elaborate twisted loop of rope-pattern and enmeshed in heavy interlacing ribbons and twisting tendrils; on the third face, and continuing along the bottom of the other two

HARALD GORMS-SON, FIRST KING OF A UNITED DENMARK

[1] On the subject of the Jellinge barrows, see S. Lindqvist, *Fornvännen*, 1928, p. 257.

[2] A stone stands at Jellinge bearing a Runic inscription that until recently was interpreted *Gorm, the king, made this memorial for Thyra, his wife, Denmark's protector*, and it was believed to prove that Thyra had directed and inspired her countrymen on some occasion when the safety of their land was threatened. The expression *DanmarkaR bót* has been the subject of much argument, but it is now held that this epithet does not justify Thyra's latter-day fame since it may well apply not to Thyra but to Gorm, the inscription then reading *Gorm the king, Denmark's benefactor, made this memorial to Thyra, his wife*. See Hans Brix, *Acta phil. Scand.*, II (1927), p. 110; and cf. H. Brix, Lis Jacobsen and N. Möller, *Gorm Konge og Thyra, Runernes Magt*, Copenhagen, 1927; but note that Finnur Jónsson has opposed this new reading. The stone in question is now in the churchyard at Jellinge and there is considerable doubt as to its original position. Possibly it was not connected with Thyra's grave-mound but was erected during her lifetime by her husband, for Saxo (I, 486) and the sagas (e.g. *Fornmanna sögur*, I, 119) say plainly that Thyra outlived Gorm. On the other hand, it is known that there was once a stone on the top of Thyra's mound; for the Jellinge stones, see L. Wimmer, *Danske Runemindesmaerker*, I, 2, pp. 8, 17, and cf. an important essay by Lauritz Weibull, *Nordens hist. o. år* 1000, Lund, 1911, p. 1 ff.

PLATE VI

MEMORIAL STONES ERECTED BY KING GORM AND KING HARALD GORMSSON (TWO VIEWS) AT JELLINGE, DENMARK

Heights, 8 feet 3 inches and 4½ feet

faces, is a Runic inscription that reads, ' Harald the king set up this memorial to Gorm, his father, and Thyra, his mother ; that Harald who won for himself all Denmark and Norway and who made the Danes Christian.'

These are the words of a great king and, indeed, it is to Harald Gormsson, or Bluetooth (*blátönn*) as he is often called, that must be ascribed the honour of founding the Danish kingdom as a united and enduring whole. Tradition, from the saga-period onwards, has given Gorm the credit of this achievement, but the inscription on the Jellinge stone proves that Harald deemed himself in some special sense the founder of the Danish kingdom, perhaps by the consolidation of his father's territorial gains and the firm administration of newly acquired lands in Norway. His kingdom consisted of the Danish islands and Jutland as far south as the Danevirke, of Scania, and perhaps of a part of the Halland coast of Sweden, and of the Ranrike province and the Vik district of Norway. His boast that he counted this country also as a part of his realm was not merely a fiction of Danish imagination, even though it is certain that he never conquered nor controlled the whole of Norway ; but he most assuredly became a dominating personality in Norwegian affairs. His influence here dates back to the time when the widow of Eric Bloodaxe, Gunnhild, and her sons were fighting against Haakon Æthelstan's-fosterson for the possession of Harald Fairhair's throne, for Harald Gormsson was Gunnhild's brother, and in return for the aid he lent her he became lord of the Ranrike on the east side of the Vik. Subsequently there was hostility between Gunnhild's sons and their too powerful uncle, so that Harald took the side of the usurper Jarl Haakon, who eventually overthrew them, and thereby increased his authority in Norway. Haakon was, in fact, his liegeman and was summoned to assist Harald when Otto II attacked the southern boundaries of Denmark ; henceforth all the Vik lands were under the direct control of the Danish king and they were no doubt included in the missionary activities that were a sequel to Harald's conversion to the Christian faith. Haakon's loyalty weakened as the years passed and there seems to have been war between him and Harald, a clash between newly Christian Denmark and still heathen Norway, but the Danish yoke was never completely thrown off and Harald Gormsson died master of the Vik.

The political success of the Danish king in his own realm is inseparably connected with his conversion to Christianity, an event that is described by the tenth-century monk Widukind

of Corvey in his chronicle.[1] During a feast at which the king
was present there arose, Widukind relates, a dispute about the
worship of the gods. The Danes conceded that Christ was
veritably a god, but they avowed that the old gods were stronger
than Christ because they revealed themselves to mortals with
more powerful tokens and wonders. Thereupon Bishop Poppo
testified that the Father, the Son, and the Holy Ghost were
one God, and that there was no other god, the so-called gods
of the heathen being only demons. Harald asked if Poppo
would prove his faith by ordeal and without hesitation Poppo
replied that he would willingly do so. On the next day the king
commanded a heavy piece of iron to be made red-hot and bade
Poppo hold this as an evidence of his faith. This Poppo did
for as long as the king desired, and when he was allowed to
loose his hold of it he displayed for all to see hands that were
unscathed by the hot metal. Thereupon the king said that he
would honour Christ alone as the true God, and he commanded
that the people over whom he ruled should abandon the heathen
gods and worship the Christ.

The historicity of this picturesque story is negligible, but
as to the main fact of Harald's conversion there can be no
dispute. Equally certain is it that he did attempt to impose
Christianity upon his dominions, even though it might be
questioned if he was as successful in this attempt as the boast
on the Jellinge stone pretends. It is possible that a wise foreign
policy [2] led him to take this step, for there can have been no
surer method of winning the lasting favour and support of the
German emperor than by professing the Christian faith. Thus
it may well be that Harald's major claims to greatness, the
winning of a united Denmark and the conversion of the Danes
to Christianity, ought to be considered as two noble achievements
inspired by a single dominating purpose, namely the desire to
rule a kingdom that could rank among the civilized states of
Europe. Nevertheless, in this aim, if such an ambition really

[1] III, 65 (Pertz, *M.G.H.*, SS. III, p. 462).
[2] There is a truly remarkable letter (Pertz, *Mon. Germ. Hist.*, Dip.
regum I, 294) purporting to have been written by Otto the Great in 965,
the supposed year of Harald's baptism, in which the emperor promised
that any lands in the mark or kingdom of the Danes at that time owned,
or subsequently acquired, by the bishoprics of Sleswig, Ribe, and Aarhus,
should be held free of all taxes and duties payable to Otto ; furthermore
he enjoined that the dependents and tenants on these lands should be
responsible to no master other than the bishop. But this letter is probably an invention of the sixteenth century, see Hauck, *Kirchengeschichte
Deutschlands*, III, p. 102 ; and J. Steenstrup, *Danmarks Sydgraense*, p. 54.

inspired him, he must be judged to have failed, for the time and the conditions within his realm were against him.

Although his relations with Otto the Great seem to have been for the most part amicable, it is said that immediately before the emperor's death Harald was under suspicion of plotting some mischief against the Germans,[1] and in 974, when the old emperor was dead and while Otto II was concerning himself with Bavarian politics, the Danes began to ravage the country beyond the Elbe. It is not unlikely that their raids were instigated by Harald, for it is possible that the Danish king believed that a favourable opportunity had arrived to increase his kingdom and to rid it of a now oppressive German yoke.[2] Otto's anger was aroused and he collected an army. Driving back the invading Danes, he marched upon Denmark to exact reprisals, although Harald at once attempted to stop him with bribes and entreaties for peace. At length Otto reached the Danevirke, where he found that Harald had barred his further progress by an army of Norwegians under Haakon. An indecisive action was fought, but the Norwegians, who had got the better of the fight and had no wish to take part in a protracted winter campaign, boasted themselves the victors and soon afterwards returned to their own land. Meanwhile Otto directed a new attack on the Danevirke at a point in the fortifications where there was a gap called Wieglesdor, and he succeeded in breaking through. Harald thereupon sued for peace, which was granted upon the condition of his paying a heavy tribute. Before his return Otto built a fortress on the frontier, a place that has been doubtfully identified as a camp in the line of the Danevirke close to the Danevirke lake. The whole campaign lasted about three months and took place in the early winter.[3]

Harald died about A.D. 986, the single lord of all Denmark, and with his reign the goal of the present chapter, so far as his country is concerned, has been reached. The formation of the Swedish state in the dark years following upon the battle of Bravalla in the eighth century has already been recounted and the time has come, therefore, to tell the genesis of the kingdom

---

[1] Pertz, *Mon. Germ. Hist.*, SS. XX, 787.

[2] The chronicler calls him *incentor malorum* and describes him as having himself taken part in the raids (Pertz, *Mon. Germ. Hist.*, SS. XX, 788).

[3] The accounts are conflicting and the details hard to follow. There is an excellent study of the campaign by Henrik Ussing, *Festkrift til Finnur Jónsson*, Copenhagen, 1928, p. 140 ; this should be compared with K. Uhlirz, *Otto II and Otto III*, *Jahrb. des deutschen Geschichte*, Leipsig, 1902, pp. 55, 56.

of Norway, and to describe a struggle to achieve unity of rule that had begun in that country nearly a full hundred years before Harald Gormsson's death. It is a fortunate thing that this welding of Norway into a single state was an event that had a special personal interest for the Icelandic historians, and it is in a sudden and unexpected flood of light from early northern literature that the winning of the sovereignty of all Norway can be watched.

The story is concerned principally with the adventures of the redoubtable Harald Fairhair (*hárfagri*), who reigned in the last half of the ninth century and in the first half of the tenth. But the reason why the Icelanders had memorized with such care the events of this period was not only because the glamour attaching to the king's deeds required the constant repetition of his saga ; rather was it because they believed that Harald's conquests and confiscations in Norway had caused the emigration of some of the proud Norwegians who would not bear his yoke, and that a number of these, sailing away with their families and possessions, had founded the republic of Iceland.

Before the time of Harald's great achievement, Norway was divided into districts, or states, variously governed and independent of one another. The Tröndelag was one of the most important of these. The lands around the modern Trondhjem (Nidaros) are geographically favoured as a centre of EARLY population, and here dwelt eight ' folks ', each with FOLKS IN its own chieftain and its own *thing*, but united in NORWAY the observance of a common code of laws ; a corporate religious life also bound the people together, for in this district there were two principal places of public worship, one for each group of four folks. To the north of the Tröndelag lay Halogaland and Namdal, famous for their rich fisheries and prosperous skin-trade, where a notably adventurous population was likewise divided into folks governed by chiefs or petty kings. South of the Tröndelag were the poorer districts of Nordmör, Romsdal, and Söndmör, where there were also small independent kingdoms, but further down the coast lived the three great peoples of Vestland, the folks of Nordfjord and Sogn, and the renowned vikings of Hordaland, all three folks observing a common law that was administered at the Gulathing. South again lay Rogaland, the seat of another powerful folk, and in eastern Norway was an important confederacy of petty kingdoms established in the Hedemark, Romerike, Hadeland, and Ringerike.

It was not, however, any of these folks who were destined to assume dominion over the whole of Norway. Vestfold was

the seat of Harald Fairhair's conquering dynasty.   Here on the
west of the Oslo fjord was a kingdom that had shared in the
KINGDOM   long-established prosperity of the Vik, being closely
OF VEST-   connected with Denmark and knowing something of
FOLD   the advantages of a continental trade.   Even at an
early time, as far back as the period from the fourth to the sixth

FIG. 19.—The Vik district of Norway

century, there is archaeological warrant for the existence of a
rich and independent Vestfold state occupying the province
between Brevik and Tönsberg, and it seems a natural thing
that in this territory should dwell the royal line that aspired to
control the destinies of all Norway.

But this was not achieved by the scions of the most ancient dynasties of the Vestfold kings, for the history of the country opens with the passing of their realm into the hands of a royal family who were foreigners to the land.

It was the purpose of that much-discussed poem the *Ynglingatal* (p. 78) to declare the descent of these new Vestfold kings from the ancient Yngling dynasty of Svitjod. According to the poem, the first of the foreign Vestfold line was Halfdan Hvitbein, the son of Olof Tretelgja who was the son of the Svitjod king Ingjald Illradi (p. 79). Olof had been an exile in Vermland after the death of his father and had married a woman of Solör, a district north of Vermland and on the eastern boundary of Norway ; the son of this marriage was Halfdan Hvitbein[1] who eventually became lord of the Vestfold kingdom ; it is related of him that he fell at Toten in the Hedamark and was buried at Skiringssal, so it may well be that he was the conqueror not only of Vestfold but of Ringerike and Hadeland, and was engaged in an attempt to extend his conquests further to the east when he died.

Eystein Halfdansson succeeded his father and, after his death, was likewise buried in Skiringssal.[2] He was followed on the throne by Halfdan Eysteinsson. This third king had his capital at Holtar, the present Holtan in Borre, and he was buried at Borre.

The fourth king in Vestfold was Gudröd.[3] He began his reign just about A.D. 800 and was murdered by a retainer of his second wife Asa (the queen who was buried in the Oseberg ship) somewhere about A.D. 840.

The next king, Olof Geirstada-alf, is said to have been the son of Gudröd by his first marriage. He is praised in the *Ynglingatal* for having ruled firmly over the wide land of Vestmar,

[1] But the ancestry of Halfdan, in spite of this account, is necessarily dubious, for his name constitutes a break in the alliterative series of names in the Yngling royal stem—Egil, Ottar, Adils, Eystein, Yngvar, Anund, Ingjald, Olav : Halfdan. See A. W. Brøgger, *Vestfoldminne*, I (1925–6), p. 15.

[2] A much-disputed point, for Snorri in the *Ynglingasaga* says he was buried at Borre ; but see the essay on this subject by O. A. Johnsen, *Festkrift til F. Jónsson*, Copenhagen, 1928, p. 121. A. W. Brøgger, however, upholds Snorri's version, op. cit.

[3] His name breaks the alliterative line of his three predecessors and has decidedly a Danish sound, so that it is open to question whether this Vestfold Gudröd was really in the direct Yngling line and not an usurper. This Gudröd has been fancifully, and probably incorrectly, identified with the Danish king Godfred (p. 91) who was the opponent of Charles the Great.

and the verses about him begin so proudly that he seems to be emphasized as the brightest ornament of the Yngling line in Norway [1]; but Vestmar is only the southern portion of Vestfold, and Snorri in the *Ynglingasaga*, though he calls Olof a bold and mighty man, reveals him as a king who lost a great part of his father's possessions, and who was forced in the end to divide what remained of his kingdom with his half-brother Halfdan. Olof died in the middle of the ninth century and was buried at Geirstad.[2] He was succeeded by his son, Ragnvald Heidum-har, the king in whose honour the *Ynglingatal* is said to have been written. Of all the kings of Vestfold, however, he is the least known to history. This curious circumstance is not easy to explain, but it may be that the king was a busy viking who gained his honours on the high seas and in far-off lands,[3] thus playing but little part in the affairs of Vestfold. This would to some extent explain why it is that the manner of the king's death and the place of his burial are now unknown.

Halfdan the Black, said to have been a son of Gudröd and his second wife Asa, meanwhile ruled in his allotted portion of the Vestfold kingdom. His first exploit was a reconquest of part of the Vingulmark, and he followed up this success with a series of wars whereby he won back the lost possessions in Romerike, Hadaland, Toten, and the Hademark. Nor did his conquests end here, for he is said to have extended his kingdom into the west of Norway, this being largely the result of his marriage with the daughter of the king of Sogn, since at this king's death Sogn fell easily into his hands.

At what period and by what means he took all Vestfold for himself history does not record, but it is clear that the partition of the kingdom ended in his reign. At his death, therefore, which took place about the year 880, he was undeniably a great and powerful king ruling over a very large dominion in southern Norway. His hold over Sogn seems to have been a temporary

---

[1] H. Schück, *Studier i Ynglingatal*, Uppsala, 1905–10, pp. 38, 52, suggested that these verses in reality applied not to Olof Geirstada-alf but to Olof Tretelgja. Cf., however, A. Noreen, *Ynglingatal, K. V. Ant. Akad. Handl.*, 28 : 2 (1925), 251.

[2] This has been identified, naturally enough, with the existing Gjerstad near Tjölling and close to Skiringssal. But there is a possibility that it was really Gjekstad, close to Gokstad on the Sande fjord, and there is accordingly a further possibility that the renowned Gokstad ship-burial was the grave of Olof Geirstada-alf. The highly ingenious argument for this identification, first discussed by N. Nicolaysen (*Viking-ship discovered at Gokstad*, Oslo, 1882, p. 70), has been restated by A. W. Brøgger, *Vestfoldminne*, I, 1925–6, p. 175, and *Borrefundet*, 1916, p. 55.

[3] See A. W. Brøgger, op. cit., p. 186.

affair, for the Sogn people were an independent folk again in the early years of his son's rule, but even without Sogn Halfdan's realm was of vast extent and there can be no doubt that he was a great king. Thus in the *Heimskringla* he is the first monarch to have a whole saga to himself, and in the *Fagrskinna*, another thirteenth-century history of Norway, his reign is the starting-point of the country's story.[1] Moreover, he is remembered as a just man and a wise law-maker, honoured especially for his system of assessing weregilds (blood-money).

Halfdan's achievement in winning his vast dominion in the south-east was, as the medieval historians knew, the direct prelude to the formation of the united kingdom of Norway. Whether by a wise administration he had imposed a more stable constitution upon his realm than any conqueror before him, whether the sanction of his might enforced a greater solidarity than as yet had been obtained, there are no means of telling. But not all the credit for the winning of a united Norway belongs to his splendid and adventurous son, for Harald Fairhair built his larger kingdom upon the foundations laid by Black Halfdan.

The date at which Harald came to the throne is usually said to be about A.D. 860. According to one group of northern histories his reign lasted from 852 to 923, but, following the better chronology of Ari Frode, Harald was king

HARALD
FAIRHAIR

from 862 to 932. A new dating, however, has been proposed by Professor Halfdan Koht,[2] who, after computing the probable length of the generations between Harald and the later kings whose date is certain, arrives at the conclusion that Harald's birth must be set as late as A.D. 865–70, and his reign must therefore be defined as lasting from 875–80 to 940–45. This chronology depends principally upon the date given in the Anglo-Saxon chronicle for the arrival of Harald's successor, Eric Bloodaxe, in England (p. 254), and although it is in the highest degree doubtful whether the dead-reckoning employed in this method of calculating by generations is a sufficiently delicate instrument to prove an error in the chronological reckoning of so careful an historian as Ari,[3] yet it is certainly true that

[1] *Ágrip*, another early history of Norway, also begins in the reign of Halfdan the Black, but the opening passages of the book are missing.

[2] *Innhogg og utsyn i norsk historie*, Oslo, 1921, p. 34 ; *Norske Historisk Tidskrift*, 5 R. VI (1924), p. 146, also XXVIII (1929), p. 425. Cf. an earlier attempt to discredit the traditional chronology by G. Vigfússon, *Corpus Poeticum Boreale*, Oxford, 1883, II, p. 487.

[3] See Johan Schreiner's criticism of Koht's chronology, *Norske Historisk Tidskrift*, 5 R. VII (1928), p. 161 ff., and F. Jónsson, ib., 5 R. VI (1924), p. 1.

this new dating is better in accord with the facts of outside history than was Ari's; therefore it seems that in respect of Harald's reign the new chronological system, though perhaps open to certain misgivings, may for the present hold the field.

Harald Fairhair was the son of Halfdan and Ragnhild, daughter of a petty king of Ringerike and said to be related to the Danish royal family; he was a mere boy, probably only ten years old when he came to the throne. Immediately upon the great king's death, the jealousy and envy of the small princes outside and within his father's realm threatened the safety of his throne. The first to attack was Gandalf of Ranrike, but the chieftains of Vestfold not only repulsed Gandalf, but later drove the war into this king's country, slew him, and took possession of all his realm. Thus at the outset of his reign Harald acquired the great stretch of country on the east side of the Skagerak that extended southward almost to the modern town of Göteborg in Sweden, a valuable length of coast long coveted by the Swedish kings. In the meantime, a group of Opland chiefs had rebelled, but Harald's generals invaded Opland, took the rebels by surprise, and burnt them to death in the house where they were lodging. The Toten district, the Hedemark, and Romerike lay thenceforth under the young king's power.

It is at this stage in the saga of Harald that Snorri relates that often-repeated story of how the king was first fired with the determination to conquer all Norway. He had fallen in love with a girl, Gyda, daughter of a king in Hordaland, but when he sued for her hand the girl replied contemptuously to Harald's envoys that she would not waste her maidenhood on a king who ruled over but a few peoples. 'Marvellous it seems to me', she said, 'that there is no king who will make Norway his own, and be sole ruler thereof, as King Gorm has done in Denmark, and Eric in Uppsala.' When this answer was told to Harald, he said that the girl had spoken well. It seemed to him strange, indeed, that he had not already thought upon the conquest of all Norway, and he vowed there and then that he would neither cut nor comb his hair until this end was achieved. Thus his splendid golden hair was allowed to grow to great length and earned for him the nickname 'Fairhair'.

The story of Gyda and her taunt is assuredly fictitious, but the time had come when the great ambition was formed in Harald's mind. Whether the whispers of his councillors inspired him, whether the enthusiasm of his own people or the friendly overtures of the chieftains of northern Norway supplied the incentive to his enterprise, history does not record; but it is plain that Harald, who found himself in early manhood a king whose prestige stood high and whose dominions were already large, realized the enormous economic importance of uniting under a single leader the several trading-communities of the country, and himself determined, as paramount lord, to direct and safeguard the rich but dangerous commerce of Norway. These were the years when the Frisian traders trafficked constantly between the markets of western Europe and the fishermen and hunters of the north, and when Swedish merchant-princes were established along the waterways leading to the Arabic East and to Constantinople; but Norway, because of internal jealousies and the bitter piratical warfare waged by neighbour upon neighbour, took less than was her due by way of profit from this busy trade, so that the wisest heads, with gallant young Harald to urge them, had begun to understand that the development of Norway's commerce was a task that could be accomplished only by a supreme and resolute warrior-lord. It was to this grand and enviable position that Harald now dared to raise himself.

His first move was a direct and uncompromising attack upon the troublesome pirate-folk of the Sogn district of Vestland,[1] and the sequel to it was an alliance with the grateful Jarl Haakon Grjotgardsson, who was lord of a vast stretch of the western littoral that included all Halogaland, Namdal, the outer Tröndelag and most of north Möre; likewise with the chieftain of the adjacent coastal territory, the jarl of Möre, Harald concluded a peace. But the demonstration against Sogn had not achieved its purpose, for the Vestland people further to the south still held themselves aloof contemptuously from the new combination and remained a serious danger to the shipping that coasted along this country of the great fjords, so that now Harald, for the fulfilment of his purpose, found himself faced with a war against the redoubtable vikings of Hordaland and Rogaland. Of the length and character of the struggle nothing is known, but of its result there is no doubt, for the victory was to Harald. Utstein in Boknfjord became a residence of the conqueror, and Avaldsnes, a little to the north in Karmsund, another of his strongholds.[2] Yet even so, the war in the west was not over, for Jaeder

---

[1] And probably not, as *Heimskringla* relates, an onslaught upon the Tröndelag by way of Dovre. Harald's aim was to secure the friendship of the Tröndelag by ridding her merchants of the menace of the Vestland pirates.

[2] *Heimskringla*, after recounting a conquest of Möre that includes the two battles of Solskel, interrupts the story of the war against Vestland

still held out against him and was supported by restive chieftains of Agder and rebels from the conquered fjordlands, so that the opposition to Harald's further advance stiffened. Finally ships and an army were collected, and the full strength of south-west Norway summoned to resist him ; the names of many of the leaders who rallied against Harald are recorded in the sagas, some of them being no doubt the usual inventions that in the course of the centuries were added to most of the battle-rôles of early history. But the one man who was certainly the mainspring of these warlike preparations was Kjötve, a king either in Jaeder or Agder, and with him was a warrior Haklang, sometimes called Kjötve's son and thought by Gustav Storm and others to have been the viking Olaf of Dublin.[1]

Harald's preparation had been no less thorough than those of his adversaries, and about the year A.D. 900 [2] the memorable battle took place that was to decide the fate of the vikings still outside his dominion. His armament sailed suddenly south from the Tröndelag while his foes were concentrating in Jaeren, and when their assembly was almost complete and they proceeded to their appointed station in Hafrsfjord, they found that Harald had outsailed them and was there waiting for them, his fleet marshalled and prepared.

Long and hard was the battle that followed. There is no proper description of the fight, but the sagas tell of the great slaughter on both sides, the deaths of many chieftains of Vestland, and the flight of Kjötve. Harald had won and Vestland was fallen. Hafrsfjord was a decisive battle, and the fame of Harald's victory was henceforward numbered among the dearest themes of the scald and chronicler. Thus sang the poet Hornklofi:

BATTLE OF HAFRS-FJORD

Hast thou heard how yonder in Hafrsfjord the high-born king (Harald) fought with Kjötve the wealthy ?
Ships came from the west, ready for war, with grinning heads and carven beaks. They were laden with warriors, with white shields,

by taking Harald off to fight Eric Segersäll, king of Sweden, who had invaded Ranrike and Vermland. Six years elapsed before Harald returned to western Norway.

[1] See n. 2, p. 280. The new dating for Hafrsfjord, of course, completely wrecks this identification.

[2] Or, according to the old dating, c. A.D. 870. I myself believe that a date about 890 is nearer the mark, since on the evidence of Grettir's saga Hafrsfjord was fought within three years of a date when Cearbhall of Ossary (p. 282) was living, and this great Irishman died in 888. The evidence in the introduction to Eyrbyggja saga according to which Ketil Flatneb (p. 304) was dead by 884 must be disregarded.

with western spears and Welsh swords. They tried their strength against the eager king, the lord of the Eastmen that dwells at Outstone, and he taught them to flee. The king launched his ship when he looked for the battle. The berserks roared in the midst of the battle, the wolfcoats howled and shook the iron (spears).[1]

Harald was now master of every state in Norway. But there were still many dangers ahead of him ; the mutterings of the conquered people in Vestland, the emigration of the wealthy landowners who would not endure his rule, and the frequent return of these emigrants on piratical raids, were plain proof that he did not as yet command a united and contented nation. Two or more years elapsed before his title as overlord was every-where recognized and his authority no longer disputed. Then, at last, Harald, deeming his great task achieved, allowed his shock of hair to be cut and combed.

The king spent much of these two years in the district that gave him the most trouble, Vestland. Here, especially in Sogn and Nordfjord, he was for a long time occupied in a series of minor and undignified struggles, and of these the sagas have many tales to tell, tales that usually end with the death or flight of some rebellious landowner. Such a one was Thorolf Kveldulfsson, an erstwhile hench-man of the king's who had fought by Harald's side at Hafrsfjord. He had subsequently become an exceedingly wealthy man with a home at Sandness in Halogaland, but as he was rash enough to entertain Harald surrounded by a retinue exceeding in numbers that of the king, he very soon aroused the jealousy and anger of his sovereign. Harald's enmity made of Thorolf a rebel and a viking, and it was not long before he provoked the king's utmost fury by an audacious act of plunder-ing in the Vik. Harald despatched two warships and two hundred men in pursuit of Thorolf to Halogaland, and himself followed with four ships and a large body of men. Thorolf was slain in the gallant defence of his burning home before the people of Halogaland and Namdal could rally to his cause. And there is little doubt that with this tragic fight at Sandness a possibly serious insurrection in the north was crushed. Not

HARALD LORD OF ALL NOR-WAY

---

[1] G. Vigfusson and F. York Powell, *Corpus Poeticum Boreale*, Oxford, 1883, I, p. 256. Welsh (*valskr*) means *foreign*, especially *Gaulish*. Lord of the Eastmen refers to Harald as king of the Norwegians east of Vest-land, but Harald's manor of Outstone (Utstein) was on an island in Boknfjord. *Berserks* and *wolfcoats* were warriors in Harald's army ; the names seem to have been interchangeable, but *berserks* are usually described as battling in a ferocious frenzy.

for the first time had swift action been the secret of Harald's success.

The king's consolidation policy was not confined to domestic struggles. The Norwegians in the Scottish islands, who by this time included in their number many exiles and malcontents, were beginning to raid the western coast of Norway with increasing severity, and it became necessary to take steps to prevent these turbulent folk from becoming a serious menace to the security of Harald's new realm. The tale of how the king succeeded in destroying these nests of pirates is one that is complicated by many confusions and inaccuracies,[1] but it seems that about 910 he appointed Ketil Flatneb (p. 304) as governor of the Hebrides, while in the '20s, still profoundly dissatisfied with the behaviour of the western vikings, he himself undertook a serious punitive campaign. He set sail with a large fleet and accompanied by some of his bravest warriors ; first he made for the west coast of Scotland, everywhere seeking out the viking settlements and putting the inmates to the sword ; then he continued his progress and drove out the viking chiefs from the Hebrides ; it is said that he even descended upon the Isle of Man. Next he went north to the Orkneys and Shetlands, which he laid under him, and Sigurd, brother of Ragnvald the jarl of Möre, was given the earldom of these two archipelagos, remaining behind when Harald and his host returned to Norway.

Harald has often been credited with the introduction of a revolutionary system of government in Norway, some novel and efficient system of central government that bound the various folks firmly together in a single political unit. This notion is in the main founded upon Snorri's enthusiastic chapter in the *Heimskringla* [2] wherein he describes the administrative system in the reign of Harald in such a way as to suggest it was the invention of the king. Actually, Harald made little contribution to the methods of government in Norway, and the old partition of the land into folks, the old legal alliances between these folks, the old judiciary functions of the *things*, all these were left unchanged. He did, however, treat his conquered provinces with something of the severity exercised by the vikings in the administration of the territories they won abroad, and it may well be that the effect of such treatment on the hitherto

[1] For the difficulties, and an excellent attempt to resolve them, see D. W. H. Marshall, *Sudreys in Early Viking Times*, Glasgow, 1929, p. 32 ff.
[2] *H. hárfagri*, 6.

independent folks was an acute sense of their altered government.[1]

The state of Norway at the time of its beginnings under
Harald was in most respects very like any other early Germanic
kingdom, such as that of Charles the Great or that of Alfred in
England. Like them, it was to suffer from all the weaknesses
inherent in a constitution founded upon the personal authority
of the king, and though Harald certainly did create a kingdom
that was to endure, its subsequent history is the long inevitable
tale of dissensions and interior strife, interrupted not only by
more than one collapse into separate states but also by both
wholesale and partial foreign dominion. Even in Harald's
old age the trouble was beginning, and it was not long after his
death that the unity of his realm was seriously threatened.

It has not been the intention of this chapter, however, to
follow the history of the formation of the nations of Sweden,
Norway, and Denmark, beyond the point at which their peoples
first possessed real sense of national unity. Its purpose, rather,
was to show at what period it is first permissible to use the nation-
names and to handle their history in its national aspect. That
purpose is now achieved. First in the dark period after the
battle of Bravalla, between the end of the eighth century and
the end of the ninth, Sweden emerges as a single kingdom ;
then Harald Fairhair at the turn of the ninth and tenth centuries
makes of Norway one state ; finally, Harald Gormsson, late in
the tenth century, won all Denmark for himself. The three
great viking countries are born ; another chapter must see the
continuation of their story.

Yet one matter remains for short mention here, and that
is a statement of the connexion between these three separate
births of the viking kingdoms and the appearance in history of
the three northern peoples as vikings harassing, conquering, and
possessing lands abroad. The outstanding difficulty is, of course,
one that has already been discussed, namely the impossibility

---

[1] The sagas make much of the heavy taxation imposed by Harald
and of his confiscation of odel property ; but it is doubtful if he really
did collect taxes on a large scale or everywhere turn the freeholders into
his tenants by taking absolute possession of the land. On this subject
see the study by Eggert Briem, *Um harald hárfagra*, Reykjavik, 1915,
who summarizes the saga-evidence and most of the discussions thereon.
There is also an important paper by E. Bull, *Historisk Tidskrift (Norsk)*,
5 R. IV (1917–20), p. 481, and this should be compared with J. Schreiner's
paper, ib. 5 R VII (1928), p. 208. In English there are some admirable
pages on this subject in Mr. G. Gathorne Hardy's book *Norway* (London,
1925, p. 37 ff.).

of determining an absolute beginning for the period of piracy and colonial enterprise abroad ; but although throughout all the stormy centuries of national development the folk of the three nations had found delight in buccaneering expeditions, the immediate task must be to review the story of the kingdoms in relation with the historically accepted and plainly observable outburst of viking activity that suddenly opens in the decades just before and after the year A.D. 800.

With this limit set to the enquiry it is at once obvious that the first expansion of the viking Swedes, their conquest of certain East Baltic states and the early establishment of Swedish outposts in Russia, must be divorced by at least half a century in point of time from the political upheavals that led to the formation of the Swedish state, and in what degree the struggles of Svitjod for complete ascendancy in eastern Scandinavia was the indirect result of this outpouring of Swedish adventurers is a subject upon which history is silent. Yet it will be shown that the early conquests abroad coincide with a period of dual rule (p. 191) under a king in Birka and another in Uppsala, so that it is not improbable that the conflict of the princes of these two houses was in part responsible for considerable unrest and the resultant foundation of settlements in other lands.

In the instance of Norway there is likewise no room for doubt that a considerable tide of emigration and viking enterprise had taken place before the days of Harald Fairhair. At the beginning of the ninth century the peasants of the Möre and Agder districts had begun to people the Orkneys and Shetlands (p. 303), and it is hard to believe that this can have been occasioned by such factors as the wars of their princes or the beginnings of the struggle for supremacy between the young Vestfold state and its rivals. Yet it is also a fact that in the first half of this century (800–850), during the long period of political disturbances in Vestfold before and during the reign of Olof Geirstada-alf, a more audacious and aristocratic people than these poor farmers had seized the Hebrides and had possessed themselves of harbour-strongholds in Ireland, where they had won much wealth ; indeed, as both of the two most illustrious chieftains of the early vikings in Ireland, Turgeis (Thorgest) and Olaf of Dublin, were sprung of the Vestfold royal house, it seems that among these more spirited adventurers of the west there were many whom dissensions at home, and not only the mere lust of conquest, had urged abroad.

Similarly, historians have attested that a second wave of emigrants departed west-over-sea, or went further on to the

Faroes and to Iceland, at the time of Harald Fairhair's achievement of the high-kingship of Norway. It is possible, notwithstanding, to exaggerate the effects of his sudden and severe
rule, and it is certainly an overstatement to declare that such
notable events as the colonization of Iceland and the Faroes
were the result of no other cause than Harald's harsh and hated
supremacy in his new-won realm (p. 340). But that a Norwegian
aristocracy, discontented and resentful, materially swelled during
Harald's reign the flood of adventurers and exiles who sought
homes in foreign lands and formed the bulk of the emigrants
from Norway in the late ninth century is an axiom of every
history book.

In Denmark, on the other hand, the beginnings of the viking
attacks upon Frisia and Francia long antedate the foundation
of the Danish kingdom by Harald Gormsson and belong to the
period of strife in the early ninth century when the contest for
supremacy among the Danish princes was first becoming acute.
Over a century and a half was to pass before the line of Gorm
and Harald was rid of all rivals and ruled alone, yet it was during
the first throes of Denmark's birth that the outcast royalties in
their rage and anger fell upon the Western Empire to win for
themselves, if they could, the territories and power that were
denied to them in their own country.

It is abundantly clear, then, that not only the potent factors
of over-population and an innate spirit of adventure, but the
domestic political situation must be taken into account in
estimating the cause of the viking movement.   For though history
fails, except in the instance of Norway, to show that the contest
for a single and undisputed throne sent the spirited malcontents
abroad as vikings, yet both in Sweden and Denmark too, it is
likely enough that political disturbances consequent upon, or
a prelude to, the creation of a single kingdom also played their
part in urging the wrathful and ambitious sons of the north to
their conquests overseas.

CHAPTER IV

SCANDINAVIA AND DENMARK IN VIKING TIMES

THE rest of the story of these three northern kingdoms, their fortunes during the Viking Period and in the centuries following upon this, can very easily be summarized in the course of a recital of their rulers ; for among the viking peoples, perhaps to a larger degree than in any other society of their time, the history of the three nations tends to be a mere record of the policies and achievements of their great men.

Setting aside, then, as of no immediate concern here a study of the social life and altering conditions of the various classes, it will be sufficient to recount the chief activities of the famous rulers who helped their country to prosperity and whose names are likely to be found in viking history abroad, or, alternatively, to record those periods of decline and depression when no such strong man was there to govern and direct. The territorial expansion of the vikings and the establishment of their colonies abroad will be described in subsequent chapters, so that here there is no need to do more than indicate the course of home affairs in the three countries ; yet it will be as well, for the sake of completeness, to continue the outline of their history down to the time of the union of the three nations at the end of the fourteenth century, because thus far at least it will be necessary in later chapters to follow the history of such viking colonies as Iceland and Greenland.

DENMARK

Harald Gormsson, or Bluetooth, who died in the viking stronghold of Jomsborg by the Oder mouth, was succeeded by his rebel son, Svein I (986–1014), commonly known as Svein
SVEIN I   Tjuguskegg, that is Forkbeard ; the new king of Denmark was a redoubtable warrior, far-famed as the organizer and leader of viking expeditions ; but above all he is known as the stern and implacable foe of England, and it was at the head of his armies in England, in the very year of his

complete triumph over that unhappy country, that he died. He was followed on the throne of Denmark by Harald II, his eldest son, and when Harald died in 1018 the next king was Svein's second son, a prince who in respect of his achievement, in respect of wisdom, statesmanship, and military genius, must take rank as the greatest of all the vikings.

This was Cnut I (1018–1035) ; for a year before his accession to the throne of his fathers he had been king of England, and he died ruler not only of the mighty Anglo-Danish realm, but also as overlord of Norway. He was a monarch held in high repute throughout all Europe ; England was his home and he was most of all occupied with English affairs, but in the kingdom of Denmark his power was absolute and even in Scandinavia the authority of this great lord was respected. He fought the united armies of Norway, under Olaf the Saint, and Sweden, under Anund Jacob, and withstood their challenge to his supremacy ; in his turn he carried the war into their countries, conquering much of southern Sweden,[1] while in 1028 he deposed King Olaf of Norway, setting up in 1030, after Olaf's return and defeat at Stiklestad, young Svein, Cnut's son by an Englishwoman, as regent of the country. True that Cnut's overlordship of Norway and this regency were insecure and dangerous, but in England and Denmark he ruled until the day of his death supreme and unassailable, a dignified and beloved monarch whose reign is an honourable page in the history of the two realms he governed.

CNUT I

With the passing of Cnut the glory of the Danish royal house, previously distinguished by Gorm, Harald Gormsson, and Svein, suffered eclipse, for Hardecnut, his son, was an unworthy successor. The English kingdom, ruled for a while by another son, Harald Harefoot, and afterwards by Hardecnut, regained its independence on this prince's death, so that the mighty realm of Cnut was sheared in half, and in the same year that Hardecnut died (1042) and England was returned to her own kings, Magnus of Norway, son of Olaf the Saint, was chosen to fill the empty throne of Denmark, so that Norsemen and Danes might unite to resist the threat of the Slavonic Wends against their lands and commerce.

Young Magnus, already a powerful king in his own country, had previously warred against Denmark and was, moreover, son

[1] This is uncertain ; Cnut certainly called himself lord of the land of the Swedes, but it may be that after the fight off Holy River, in which the united fleets of Norway and Sweden seem to have got the better of him, he gave up his claims to Swedish territory.

of the king whom Cnut had expelled. He had no reason, then, to love the Danes whose fallen kingdom he now added to his own, yet during the five years of his rule (1042–1047) he dealt justly by them. It is true that in 1043 he utterly destroyed the rebellious Danish stronghold at Jomsborg, but in the same year he delivered his new dominion from an appalling peril by routing a huge host of the Wends who had invaded Denmark and threatened to crush this almost defenceless state out of existence. Furthermore, he chose as his regent of this country, Cnut's nephew, Svein Estridsson, though this friendly gesture proved to be a mistaken policy for, so soon as the danger of the Wendish attack was removed, Svein conspired against him and raised armies to overthrow the power of Norway. The regent obtained the help of Swedish troops and was aided by Harald Sigurdsson Hardradi of Norway, so that when Magnus died no man questioned his right to become king of Denmark, and as Svein II (1047–1076) he maintained against Magnus's successor, Harald Hardradi, the struggle with Norway ; but the fortunes of war continued against him until a peace was made in 1064, whereupon Svein, abandoning warfare, settled down to rule over Denmark in comparative security. He died a much-honoured monarch, having lived for twelve years at peace with his neighbours, a period wherein he worked ceaselessly to strengthen the crown's authority by remodelling the ecclesiastical organization of his kingdom and ruling it according to the enlightened precepts of his friend Adalbert, the Archbishop of Bremen.

Svein II Estridsson died in 1076 and for four years afterwards the country continued at peace under the rule of his son Harald III. But when a second son, Cnut II, came to the throne conditions changed, for the brother was at heart a soldier and had long dreamt of the reconquest of the fair country that had been a possession of the Danish crown in the days of the illustrious great-uncle whose name he bore. The contemplated attack on England came to nothing, as indeed other Danish attempts in Svein II's day to rob William the Conqueror of his new realm had failed, and the taxes and tribulations that were the result of Cnut's military ideals, his arrogant and ridiculous conception of his kingly rights, so dissatisfied his own people that the peasants revolted against him and the end of his reign came in 1086 when he was assassinated in the church of Odense. Yet in 1095 his bones were disinterred and reburied in honour under the high-altar of the church, and in 1101 he was canonized as a saint.

With the ignominious dismissal of the force whereby St. Cnut was hoping to attack England, the viking days of Denmark, in the ordinary historical sense of a Viking Period, come to an inglorious end. But this outline story must be carried a stage or so further, though the shortest possible summary will suffice.

St. Cnut was succeeded on the throne by his brother Oluf, whose grim nickname Hunger tells of the famine that wasted Denmark in his day; but in 1095, when Eric I, fourth son of Svein II, came to the throne, the country returned to its ancient prosperity; so, too, during the greater part of the long reign of Eric's successor Niels (1104–1134), a fifth son of Svein, Denmark enjoyed peace and plenty, although in these days there was fighting against the Wends. It was at the end of Niels's reign that serious troubles once more befell the state, for Magnus Nielsson murdered Cnut Lavard, a son of Eric I, and a civil war broke out that ended in 1134 at the Battle of Fodevig where Magnus was slain. Niels himself died shortly afterwards and the crown passed in the year of the battle to Cnut Lavard's brother, Eric II. Three years later the new king was murdered at the *thing* in Roskilde, and his nephew, Eric III, reigned in his stead; but the unhappy country was still torn by domestic quarrels and when Eric died in 1146 an utterly disastrous period known as the *Wars of the Princes* opens. The three leaders who now struggled for the mastery were Cnut III, grandson of Niels, Svein III, son of Eric II, and Valdemar, the son of Cnut Lavard, who triumphed in the end over his two adversaries; in 1157 Valdemar the Great at last found himself the sole and undisputed ruler of Denmark. His reign was long and glorious and when he died in 1182 he had become the hero of his people, a brilliant figure still famous to this day as the deliverer of his country from the fury of the Wends.

After Valdemar the Great the only Danish king who need be mentioned is Valdemar Atterdag (1340–1375), who was the great-grandson of Christopher I (1252–1259), the grandson of Valdemar the Great. And the reason that Valdemar Atterdag comes into this story is that his daughter, Margaret, married in 1363 King Haakon VI of Norway, for the result of this marriage was that some thirty years later this very remarkable Danish woman found herself in the position to effect by her astonishing genius for statesmanship the union of Norway, Sweden, and Denmark under a single king, her great-nephew, chosen by herself.

NORWAY

Harald Fairhair had had many wives and many children; but late in life, when he found himself a powerful king ruling over a united Norway, he made one profitable and important alliance such as befitted his high station, a marriage with the Danish princess, Ragnhild, daughter of Eric of Jutland, and he put away from him the numerous undistinguished Norwegian ladies who hitherto had been his consorts. The son of this marriage with Ragnhild was Eric Bloodaxe whom Harald regarded as the only legitimate heir to Norway and whom he married to Gunnhild, King Harald Gormsson's sister, thus strengthening the already existing bond between the royal houses of Norway and Denmark. But Eric knew that his sole hope of becoming supreme king in his father's place lay in his ability to destroy by fair means or foul those of his half-ERIC brothers who were likely to contest the inheritance, BLOODAXE and therefore both before and after his father's death he and his mettlesome wife set themselves to kill off their rivals. When in due course Eric came to the throne, he soon found that he was regarded on all sides with hatred and suspicion, and as he was far too hot-headed a man to cope intelligently with the reaction against a centralized monarchy that now swept over the land, after a short and troubled reign he was forced to abandon the throne and fly from Norway. He was succeeded by one of his half-brothers, young Haakon, the son of a serf-woman and a child of Harald's old age, who had been fostered in England at the court of Æthelstan. This was in the '40s of the tenth century.

Haakon the Good was a wise and generous prince, and though he estranged the folk of the Tröndelag by an ill-advised attempt to introduce Christianity, yet his position was from the outset so secure that the other surviving sons of Harald made no challenge against his supremacy. But it was other-HAAKON wise with the sons of the exiled Eric Bloodaxe, for THE GOOD after their father's death in England (954) they deemed themselves the rightful heirs to the Norwegian throne and would not leave the country at peace under the usurper Haakon. Urged on by their determined Danish mother, they enlisted the support of Harald Gormsson in Denmark and with the forces he gave them they invaded Norway; there was much fighting and at first Haakon triumphed, but in the end the sons of Gunnhild and Eric slew him. This took place about 960.

Harald Ericsson Greycloak, eldest surviving son of Eric,

became king in Haakon's stead, but once again Norway was plunged into a turmoil of civil war. Harald himself was a HARALD fine man, a brave and adventurous viking whose most GREY- notable exploit as king was a brilliant attack upon CLOAK the territories of the Düna mouth and the Archangel country in the White Sea ; but in his own realm he had naturally to admit Harald Gormsson of Denmark as his overlord and to delegate much of his authority to his mother and brothers, while many of Haakon's staunchest friends, such as the powerful Jarl Sigurd of Lade in the Tröndelag, lived in open rebellion against the new regime. There was, in consequence, much fighting and discontent in Norway during this supremacy of the sons of Gunnhild and Eric, and the end of nine years of unrest was that Jarl Haakon Sigurdsson of Lade, whose father had been burnt alive by Harald Greycloak, excited the Norwegians to the pitch of rebellion. Jarl Haakon went to Denmark and won over Harald Gormsson to his side ; then he engineered the murder of Harald Greycloak and had himself appointed regent of Norway with the king of Denmark as his master and with Svein, Harald Gormsson's heir and the future conqueror of England, as temporary lord of the Vik provinces.

Jarl Haakon, not even of the blood royal, was unquestionably a usurper, but his personal influence and authority were sufficient to restore order in the land, and, like Haakon the Good before him, he ruled wisely and well ; he was not afraid to delegate JARL the duties of government to other jarls and even to HAAKON petty kings such as Harald Grenske of Vestfold and Agder, a powerful man since Svein's return to Denmark, and in consequence of this there was but little opposition to the benevolent supremacy of so brave and distinguished a nobleman. In 971 he crushed the last revolt of the sons of Gunnhild and so gave peace to the land ; but after the Battle of the Danevirke in 974, where he and a Norwegian army fought on the side of Harald Gormsson against the Emperor Otto II, he quarrelled with the king of Denmark, who subsequently invaded Norway and took outright possession of the Vik lands. It was because of this quarrel that the Jomsvikings (p. 182) swore to King Svein, Harald's son, that they would kill Jarl Haakon and fared forth in the winter of 986 to the stirring battle of Jörundfjord, where Haakon routed these famous fighters. The long reign of the Jarl of Lade nevertheless ended disastrously, for as he grew old he began to offend his people by his increasing tyranny and loose-living, so that there was a revolt against him and Norway hailed gladly as her king, after Haakon's ignominious death in 995, a young Christian prince who was lately returned from a viking expedition in England and the western seas. This was Olaf Tryggvason.

The new king was of the line of Harald Fairhair, his father, Harald's grandson, being King Tryggve of the Vik whom the sons of Gunnhild had put to death, and his short reign of five years is memorable for one of the most remarkable missionary OLAF enterprises in the history of northern Europe. For TRYGG- this young giant, a man of immense physical strength VASON and endowed with a most masterful personality, by sheer force and persistence made his realm a Christian state, and not only converted the unwilling heathen masses of Norway, but saw to it that the even more stubborn Norse colonists of the Faroes, of Iceland, and of Greenland, likewise accepted the new faith. In reality, Olaf's robust methods of conversion and his complete failure to organize a proper teaching of the Christian doctrines left Norway as much heathen at heart after these wholesale compulsory baptisms as before them, so that his achievement is admirable less because of its effect than because of its grandiose scale and the uncompromising thoroughness whereby it was carried out ; for with Olaf his own zest and energy were sufficient to win the respect of his subjects, to ensure obedience to his strange whim of ordering the baptism of all and sundry, and to make of him a brilliant and successful king ; but of the art of government, of the way to consolidate and preserve his great-grandfather's mighty kingdom as a lasting and law-abiding state, he knew and cared nothing.

Thus when he fell in the year A.D. 1000 at the tragic sea-fight of Svold (p. 184), betrayed by the Jarl of Jomsborg into the hands of his enemies, the jealous kings of Sweden and Denmark and the rebel Jarl Eric Haakonsson of Norway, his realm, ill-organized and defenceless, was divided, unresisting, among the victors. Svein I of Denmark took the southern provinces and Opland, Olof Skotkonung of Sweden the south-east lands of Bohuslän from the Göta River to Svinesund together with the west-coast provinces of Möre and central and southern Tröndelag, while Jarl Eric and his brother Svein, the sons of Jarl Haakon, ruled over the rest of the country. But in 1015, when Eric left the country in order to fight for Cnut the Great in England, a new claimant to the throne of Norway appeared, another prince of Harald Fairhair's line. This was OLAF THE Olaf Haraldsson the Stout, son of Harald Grenske of SAINT Vestfold. He, like Olaf Tryggvason before him, came to Norway from the west where he had been on a viking expedition, having fought in England first against the forces of Æthelred the Unready and afterwards on the English side against the Danes. There was opposition to his seizing the throne of Olaf Tryggvason, but the armies of Denmark were too fully occupied in England to take the field against him in the north, and after he had defeated Jarl Svein in battle in the same year of that victory, 1016, he was acclaimed as king throughout all Norway.

Olaf showed himself to be an earnest and not unenlightened statesman. Early in his reign he recovered Opland and the other territories ceded to the kings of Sweden and Denmark, and this important task done, he soon revealed his intention of turning his still reluctant country into a properly Christian state, supplying priests and churches throughout all the land and insisting upon the universal observance of a Christian code of behaviour. He did much to strengthen his own power by installing priests who looked directly to him, and to him alone, as their master ; but he tried further to consolidate his own kingly authority by suppressing the remaining sub-kings and generally undermining the powers of the aristocracy, taking away from them their titles to govern locally and bestowing the offices they held by an almost hereditary right upon officials of common birth who were chosen by himself. Even the dignitaries of his own simple court were deliberately selected from among the Icelanders and from the lower ranks of Norwegian society rather than from among the leading nobles of the land.

It was not long, then, when once this policy was established, before Olaf found himself with many enemies among the aristocratic families, and it was this general discontent among the chief land-holders that emboldened Cnut the Great, after he had become king of England, to assert that he was entitled, as ruler of Denmark, also to be the overlord of Norway. Olaf refused even to consider Cnut's claim, and, having successfully made an ally of the Swedish king, he rashly threatened to attack the all-powerful Danish realm. Cnut prevented their contemplated invasion of Denmark by fighting the allied fleets near Holy River off the coast of Scania, and in the year 1028 he sailed at the head of 1,400 warships for Norway where he was enthusiastically welcomed by the Norwegians, for they had lately been outraged by the murder of one of the best-loved members of the old nobility, Erling Skjalgsson, and they respected Cnut as lord of the great trade-routes to the west ; at *thing* after *thing* he was hailed as king of Norway, and Olaf, seeing that the whole country was turned against him, fled to Russia. He remained for a year at the court of Yaroslav, the Swedish Grand Prince of Kiev, but when he heard that Cnut's regent in Norway, another Jarl of Lade by the name of Haakon, had been summoned to England, Olaf thereupon returned through Sweden to the Tröndelag, where his remaining friends, some Icelanders and many Norwegians of the poorer classes, joined themselves to the little band of Swedish auxiliaries, mostly adventurers and outlaws, that the exiled monarch had collected. It was with this ill-armed and undisciplined force that the king confronted in Verdal the large peasant-army of the rich Norwegian landed proprietors that had been gathered to oppose his further progress. The renowned Battle of Stiklestad took place on the 29th July, 1030, and there Olaf the Stout fell after an heroic struggle against better and more numerous troops.

Olaf died, having lost the kingdom that he had governed too strictly, despised and rejected by the majority of his countrymen ; but his labours had not been in vain and already a national consciousness was stirring. Yet it was above all of his piety and his constant championing of the Christian faith that men first of all thought, and when a year after the battle they disinterred his wonder-working body and found it lying in uncorrupted beauty, then they knew that he was indeed a man of God whose spirit would forever comfort and encourage his people. They gave him a new and honourable burial at Nidaros and henceforward this failure of a king has lived on immortal in the memory of his countrymen, Olaf the Holy, the patron saint of Norway.

King Cnut put young Svein, his son, to rule Norway after Olaf's death, but it was really Aelfgifu of Northampton, the prince's mother, who held the power. Very quickly these two made themselves unpopular, for now Danish taxes were introduced, Danish laws enforced, and preference was everywhere given to Danish interests. This was the chief reason for the awakening of the national sentiment that made the fallen Olaf into a saint and the explanation of the recall from Russia, as soon as Cnut was dead, of Olaf's son, the boy Magnus.

MAGNUS OLAFSSON Upon the return of Magnus Olafsson in 1035 and the rising of the people against them, Svein and Aelfgifu fled, so that Magnus was elected king of Norway unopposed. And now prosperity returned to the country, for the supremacy of Denmark was ended and in 1042, according to an amicable arrangement between the two countries, Magnus the Good was appointed to fill the Danish throne left vacant by the death of Hardecnut. In 1043, after the destruction of the independent Danish fortress of Jomsborg and the routing of the Wends, for the first time in the history of Scandinavia the king of Norway was beyond all dispute the mightiest monarch of the north.

But Denmark did not long submit to Norwegian rule, for the regent whom Magnus in all good faith, but most unwisely, had entrusted with the government of his new kingdom was Svein Estridsson of the Danish royal family, and this prince, who made only a temporary show of loyalty, was soon striving to throw off the Norwegian yoke. And in Norway, too, the tenure of the king was no longer secure, for in 1046 Olaf's half-brother had returned, that most glorious prince of adventurers, the great viking Harald Hardradi (p. 172). In the end Magnus shared his kingdom with Harald, but himself died in the following year (1047), and until 1066 Harald ruled alone, a great king who, by virtue of his complete victory over the always rebellious Opland and Tröndelag folks, was more truly the master of a united Norway than any other sovereign before him. These were turbulent years of war and excitement ; a desperate and nearly successful attempt to wrest Denmark back from Svein Estridsson, a daring voyage of discovery made by the king into the polar waters, the expedition to aid Tostig of Northumbria against the English Harald, and that last adventure, the winning of a grave's length of England for Hardradi at Stamford Bridge, where this most amazing viking fell.

A long period of peace followed under Olaf Kyrre, Harald Hardradi's son, who reigned over Norway until 1093. By this time, as also in Denmark, the restlessness of the viking age seemed to be over, and in these thirty years the OLAF KYRRE Norwegians, under a generous and enlightened government, found time to copy many fashions and customs of England and the Continent, to build churches, to establish at the king's prompting the merchant-port of Bergen as a centre for the now important cod-fisheries of the west coast of Norway, and to develop the towns of Nidaros and Oslo. But Magnus Barefoot (1093–1103), Olaf's son and successor, had the old MAGNUS BAREFOOT viking temperament and planned conquests abroad on a noble scale, hoping to win both Scotland and Ireland for Norway. He commanded three naval expeditions in the western seas and re-affirmed the sovereignty of the Norwegian crown over the unstable Norse colonies in the Scottish islands and Man, added a part of Anglesey to his dominion, and died fighting in Ireland.

After Magnus's death Norway was divided among his three

youthful sons, Eystein, Sigurd, and Olaf.   The last-named died
in 1115, still a boy, and the government of the country was left
in the hands of the peace-loving Eystein, who stayed dutifully
in Norway, and the much more adventurous Sigurd the Crusader
who was away on his renowned journeys in the Mediterranean,
in Palestine, in the Byzantine Empire, and in central Europe,
from 1108 until 1111 ; once more Norway enjoyed tranquillity
such as she had known under Olaf Kyrre.   But Eystein died
in 1122 and Sigurd in 1130.

The country was then plunged into civil war.   Just before
Sigurd died an Irishman who called himself Harald Gille and
who claimed to be a son of Magnus Barefoot had arrived at
HARALD   Sigurd's court ; he had proved his story by the test
GILLE   of ordeal and had been accepted by Sigurd as a brother,
                though he was made to swear that he would not
claim kingly rank either during Sigurd's life or during the reign
of the heir to the throne, Magnus Sigurdsson.   But a party of
the Norwegian nobles prevailed upon him to break his word
when Sigurd died, and from that time onwards for the space of
110 years the throne of Norway was in dispute.   Harald, a
swarthy and kilted foreigner who could speak little or no Norse,
captured Magnus and blinded him ; then another pretender to
the throne, Sigurd Slembe, who also said he was a son of Magnus
Barefoot, arrived in Norway and murdered Harald.   Sigurd
took the blind Magnus out of prison to make him king, but the
sons of Harald Gille continued the war and killed Magnus in
battle (1139).   Twenty years of chaos followed while the sons
and grandsons of Harald fought among themselves and as a
result the prestige and the power alike of the kings became
negligible ; but at the end of this time the nobles and the clergy
had become strong enough to invest one of their number, Erling
Skakke, who was married to Sigurd the Crusader's daughter,
with almost supreme authority, and in the early '60s the Archbishop of Nidaros crowned Magnus Erlingsson as king, the
great Erling for a while ruling Norway as regent and for a while
giving the country peace.

There was, of course, some opposition.   A grandson of
Harald Gille raised a last and feeble rebellion in 1177 which
was without difficulty suppressed, and it was precisely at this
moment when the power of the Skakkes seemed to be most
securely established that they were suddenly and unexpectedly
overthrown by one of the most remarkable men who ever sat
on the throne of Norway.   For the miserable rebel party, the
Birchlegs, so called because they had been reduced to using

birch-bark in place of shoe-leather, after their defeat invited Sverre Sigurdsson to be their leader. Sverre, who bore a vulgar Faroese name, claimed to be a bastard son of King Sigurd Mouth, a son of Harald Gille; but his mother, a Norwegian lady, had married a Faroese comb-maker and he himself had been trained for the priesthood in the Faroe Islands. He made an efficient army out of a nucleus of 70 Birchlegs and after suffering many hardships and rebuffs he routed the host of the Skakkes, slaying Erling in 1179 and Magnus in 1184. All parties in the state, nobles, churchmen, and peasants, were against him ; pretenders to the throne he had usurped threatened rebellion ; yet Sverre triumphed over all opposition and remained king of Norway until his death in 1202. In an atmosphere of universal suspicion and often of open hostility, excommunicated by the Church, he established himself as an autocratic ruler of unexampled power in Norway and died having created a centralized monarchy that had wellnigh completely undermined the old local authority of the nobles and landed proprietors who, taking advantage of the weakness of the throne during the previous century, had once more attained to a formidable power in the land. In so doing he was but reverting to the policy of St. Olaf, but Sverre's creation of a new nobility of court and government officials and his wholesale confiscation of land were acts not merely directed against the ancient aristocracy but against the *bönder*, or yeomen, themselves whose tenure of their estates henceforth depended upon the king's pleasure and whose share in the control of the country, as exercised at their *things*, was speedily reduced to empty formalities, so that thereby the dawning sense of nationality among them was summarily extinguished.

Sverre, a harsh and dauntless dictator, handed on to his son Haakon a crushed and listless Norway, and two years later, in 1204, on Haakon's death the crown passed to Inge Bardsson, Sverre's nephew. These princes, though patching up the quarrel between the king's party and the Church, relinquished little of the authority held by the founder of the dynasty, nor did the political conditions of the people improve under Inge's successor, the great King Haakon Haakonsson (1217–1263). Haakon was Sverre's grandson and was only a boy when he came to the throne ; but when he had attained manhood he was forced to concede a third of his realm to Skule, a brother of King Inge. Skule was killed in 1240, a year later, and with his death there ended that long period of civil war and bitter internal strife that with only rare interruption had distressed Norway since the death of Sigurd the Crusader.

Norway, still in the unrelaxing grip of her over-centralized government, was now at peace, and Haakon's reign is memorable not for domestic affairs so much as for the king's vigorous foreign and colonial policy ; in his day the viking people of Iceland and Greenland for the first time agreed to live under the direct rule of the Norwegian crown, Norwegian rights in Finland were established by treaty, and it seemed that the Norwegians as a nation, whether living in Norway or abroad, were to be welded into a single political unit under this true autocrat of Sverre's line ; for Haakon's last enterprise, made with the intention of asserting his overlordship of the viking settlements in the Scottish Isles and Man, was a bold and formidable expedition against Scotland. Luck turned against him at the so-called ' battle ' of Largs, and Haakon, having given unmistakable proof of Norway's power, went off to winter in the Orkneys where he suddenly fell sick and died.

But Haakon's son, Magnus Lagaböter (1263–1280), the great jurist of Norway, realized the hopelessness of effectively controlling from Norway the Western Isles. One of his early acts MAGNUS (1266) as king was to cede the Hebrides and Man to LAGABÖ- Alexander of Scotland in return for a yearly payment TER of money, and it is with this surrender that the disruption of the far-flung viking commonwealth of Norwegian peoples begins. He was followed on the throne by his son Eric (1280–1299) and afterwards by his second son Haakon V (1299–1319) ; Haakon married his only legitimate heir, a daughter, to the son of King Magnus Ladulås of Sweden, and the son of this union in due course inherited the thrones both of Sweden and Norway. This was Magnus Ericsson (1319–1355), whose reign marks the first serious stage of the national decline, a period of poverty and mercantile failure MAGNUS that was speedily reflected in the fortunes of the ERICSSON unhappy colonies of Greenland and Iceland that were now dependent upon Norway for the imports without which life in these remote places was almost impossible. The union itself was of little advantage and only of short duration, for in 1355 Magnus ceded the throne of Norway to his young son Haakon VI (1355–1380), himself remaining king of Sweden ; yet a greater and more disastrous coalition was at hand, for Haakon married Margaret, the daughter of King Valdemar Atterdag of Denmark, and this marriage led to a union of Norway and Denmark that lasted until 1814. For Valdemar died without sons in 1375, whereupon Haakon and Margaret had their five-year-old son chosen as king of Denmark ; then Haakon died in 1380, so that the young Olaf, with his mother MARGARET for regent, became king of Norway as well as king OF DEN- of Denmark. In the meantime his grandfather had MARK AND been deposed from the throne of Sweden and this THE UNION Magnus's nephew and successor, Albert of Mecklenberg, had become so unpopular that the Swedes made it plain that they would prefer Margaret's rule. It seemed certain that rather than continue under the hated Mecklenbergs they would take little Olaf for king, when this young prince suddenly died. The occasion was one when the fate of all Scandinavia hung in the balance, but Margaret faced the crisis with magnificent wisdom. She had herself elected formally as regent of Norway and Denmark until such time as these two countries could agree upon a successor to Olaf, and then without hesitation she invaded Sweden. Albert and his Germans were beaten near Falköping in 1389 and the country was soon in her hands ; then she chose her youthful great-nephew, Eric of Pomerania, as the king who was to rule the three realms, and in 1397 at the Swedish city of Kalmar Eric was solemnly invested with the crown of a united kingdom of Norway, Sweden, and Denmark. And thus it came about that after the reign of Haakon V the neglected Norsemen of Greenland and Iceland could expect aid only from kings who were foreigners to them, unsympathetic and pre-occupied monarchs who gave little heed to the failing fortunes of the wretched children of the vikings in the far-off colonies of the north.

SWEDEN

The history of the kings of Sweden, after the foundation of the single kingdom, begins again in the early ninth century with King Björn who in 829 sought alliance with the Emperor Louis by inviting Christian missionaries to his realm, for Björn had expelled his brother and co-regent Anund, and Anund was plotting revenge with King Horik in Denmark. Then in the '50s of this century a King Olof of Birka is named who is re-nowned as the conqueror of Kurland, but it seems that a King Eric, likewise a conqueror of East Baltic territories, ruled simul-taneously in Uppsala ; thereafter the story is a blank until seventy years have passed and a King Ring is mentioned, though before his day another king called Olof (p. 98) appears and obtains mention in the Frankish chronicles as the conqueror of Hedeby in Sleswig, which was held as a Swedish colony for several decades early in the tenth century ; later, about A.D. 970, another king is named, Emund Ericsson, who was a contemporary of Harald Gormsson and Svein Forkbeard in Denmark and Jarl Haakon in Norway. This is perhaps the Emund Slemme who made a celebrated bond with Svein of Denmark whereby the boundaries of their realms were formally declared.

The first half of this century witnessed a weakening of Swedish power in the north, for Blekinge, North Halland, and Bornholm were lost to the Danes in the time of Emund and his predecessors, but it seems that somewhere about A.D. 980, there was a revival in the fortunes of the country when, according to tradition, Harald Gormsson invaded Sweden and was defeated on the Fyris Plain near Uppsala. Indeed, on Svein Forkbeard's accession to the throne of Denmark, King Eric Segersäll, who was the successor, and probably the son, of King Emund, attacked Denmark and won a dominion there that was held until Svein drove the Swedes out of Hedeby in 995.

Eric, who died in this same year, was succeeded by his son Olof Skotkonung (the Tax-King) and at the end of the century there was a sudden reversal of Swedish foreign policy, for Olof joined forces with Svein of Denmark and Jarl Eric of Lade OLOF against the great king of Norway, Olaf Tryggvason. SKOT- The Swedish Olof took part in the Battle of Svold KONUNG in the year A.D. 1000, where the Norwegian king was drowned, and after this victory he received a part of Norway as his spoils, the provinces immediately north and south of Nidaros and the Bohuslän coast from the Göta River to Swinesund. But Sweden was not long destined to hold these new territories ; her possession of Möre and the central and southern Tröndelag amounted to little more than the receipt of taxes paid by the Norwegian governor, Jarl Svein Haakonsson, and in 1015 Olaf Haraldsson the Stout became king of Norway and drove out Svein, so that the payment of these taxes ceased. The Bohuslän was more precious and necessary to Sweden, but the new king of Norway soon revealed his intention of re-conquering this province and after four weary years of fighting a treaty was made whereby Norway recovered at least certain rights over these eastern Vik lands. During this time Olof Skotkonung had become increasingly unpopular, and eventually he was forced to retire to Västergötland, setting his son Anund Jacob in Uppsala as his co-regent.

Anund became sole king after his father's death in 1021. In the following year the mighty Cnut, now king of both Den-

mark and England, came sailing into the Baltic and there conquered Samland (the Königsberg peninsula on the east side
of the Gulf of Danzig), whereat the sudden menace of
his almost overwhelming power became so serious both
to Norway and Sweden that Anund and Olaf the
Stout hastily combined together and in 1025 or 1026 made
preparations for an attack upon Denmark. Cnut knew of their
plans and forestalled them; there was an indecisive engagement off the coast of Scania opposite Holy River and then speedily
retribution followed their overboldness. For afterwards Cnut
went on to the conquest of a great part of southern Sweden
and obtained the submission of Anund, even styling himself
on his coins as ' King of the Swedes '[1]; Olaf he drove from
Norway and himself became lord regent of that country.

ANUND
JACOB

With the fall of Denmark after the death of Hardecnut,
Anund recovered some of his former power and, except for the
Bohuslän and Scania, he regained most of the Swedish territory
that Cnut had won; yet the new period of prosperity was
short-lived and a prelude to two disastrous centuries of civil
war. Anund was followed on the throne by a half-brother,
Emund, who died after only a brief reign, and at his death,
which took place about A.D. 1060, the ancient Yngling line of
Uppsala kings was ended, for Emund was succeeded by Stenkil,
a man of Västergötland, who had married a daughter of the
last of the Ynglings. It was when Stenkil died in 1066 that the
long and devastating struggle for the throne began.

The story of the early Middle Ages in Sweden, of the long-
continued strife between the house of Stenkil and princes of
the old royal family, there is no need to relate. For the only
king in the first hundred years of the civil wars whose reign,
though it lasted but a few years, is worthy of record in this
context is Eric Jedvardsson, better known as Eric the
Saint, who was the husband of a great-granddaughter
of Stenkil. As a warrior and as an evangelist he was beloved
of his people, ever famous as the man who led a crusade against
the heathen Finns whom he converted to Christianity at the
point of the sword; but in 1160 he was murdered in Uppsala
on his way from mass and subsequently he was admitted into
the calendar of saints, there to join the company of those two
other royal vikings, St. Olaf of Norway and St. Cnut of Denmark.
Eventually he became the patron saint of Sweden, the legendary
and knightly symbol of a golden age.

ST. ERIC

The last king of the direct line of St. Eric died in the middle

[1] But see n. 1, p. 118 above.

of the thirteenth century and his successor was Valdemar Birgersson, whose mother, a princess of Eric's family, had married Jarl Birger Magnusson, the great nobleman and soldier who was regent of the country on his son's behalf until 1266 and whose firm rule at length gave peace to the long-troubled and weary land. In his day Sweden prospered ; a trade-agreement with the Hansa made possible a new development of Swedish commerce ; relations with Norway and Denmark became more friendly ; a new and successful Swedish settlement in Finland was established ; and this prosperity lasted through the reign of Birger's second son, Magnus Ladulås (1275–1290), and afterwards throughout the regency of that noble Swede Thorgils Cnutsson. But troubles began again with the accession of the three-year-old Magnus Ericsson Smek in 1319. This young prince, a month after he came to the throne of Sweden, also became king of Norway on the death of his grandfather, Haakon V, and in 1333, by redeeming Scania which had been mortgaged to the Count of Holstein, Magnus found himself ruler of the whole Scandinavian peninsula ; the result of these enormous acquisitions of new territory was the complete financial breakdown of the Swedish government and Magnus was soon forced to realize the impossibility of maintaining order throughout his huge realm. In 1343 he surrendered Norway to his son Haakon and henceforth devoted himself to the difficult task of ruling Sweden and Scania ; he governed courageously, giving the land a common law and doing much to strengthen the crown's authority at the expense of that of the nobles and clergy, but his reign ended in civil war and the loss of Scania to Denmark. The Folkung dynasty was overthrown and the crown of Sweden conferred by the selfish and discontented nobles upon Albert of Mecklenberg, the son of Magnus's sister, in 1363 ; thereupon Haakon VI of Norway, Magnus's son, at once took up arms against the German usurper and the struggle between them was the immediate prelude to the sudden and astonishing union of the three kingdoms of Norway, Sweden, and Denmark, by Queen Margaret.

MAGNUS ERICSSON

THE UNION

Such in their simplest outlines are the stories of the ruling dynasties of the three viking countries, but to a summary of the chieftains' deeds and politics there must be added a brief statement concerning two other matters of northern history that will be seen to have some bearing upon the course of viking affairs. The first of these new topics is the conversion of the peoples of the north to the Christian faith and the second is the

decline of their shipping and commerce in the face of the competition of the redoubtable Hanseatic League of German
merchants.

THE INTRODUCTION OF CHRISTIANITY

Eight hundred years after the birth of Christ these northern
folk, except perhaps for a few adventurous travellers, were still
heathens. Their religion was polytheistic, yet not wholly rid
of an older and baser animism that found expression in various
forms of nature-worship ; also the cult of ancestors and of the
spirits of the noble dead had its ardent devotees. But most of
all they loved the gods. Of these Thor, the Thunderer and
Hammer-Wielder, was dearest to them, for he was the friend
and protector of mankind, a patron of farmers, a peacemaker
at the *things*, and a mighty comforter in battle and the guardian
of bold warriors. Then there was Odin, too, in later days a deity
especially beloved in Sweden and Denmark, whose cult had
found its way to the north in the time of the folk-wanderings ;
he was the fount of valour and wisdom, the supreme and almighty
father of gods, the lord of the warrior-dead in Valhalla. Also
there was Frey, god of fruitfulness and prosperity, and Njord,
an ancient god of plenty, but now the patron of fishermen and
merchants ; there were, in addition, many minor and local gods
included in this changeable and uncertain pantheon. To these
deities, above all to the three first named, temples were built
and to them sacrifices were made, these being conducted at the
major festivals by the kings themselves in their capacity as the
religious heads or chief priests of the people. Not animals only,
but human beings too, were the victims of these rites.

Like other barbarous religions of its kind, it was in certain
respects a comfortable one, for it enjoined no stringent moral
code upon its adherents. Every bloodthirsty and abominable
act of slaughter and pillage, except those that involved the
death of relatives, could be committed at the sole risk of human
vengeance, and sweet to Thor and Odin were the clash and
clamour of any fight, the smoke of all burning dwellings, and
the vainglory of each victor. An eye for an eye, these gods
demanded, a tooth for a tooth. But it was precisely this freedom to battle and to ravage without incurring the wrath of
heaven that Christian teaching sought to end ; therefore, though
a viking might without serious misgivings allow himself to be
persuaded to acknowledge Christ as his heavenly master instead
of the dear gods of his fathers, it was a vastly more difficult
thing to complete his conversion by making him pay a proper

respect to Christian teaching. To fight for Christ he was often willing enough, but to hold back from fighting, to forbid himself the bloodshed that had pleased Thor, to offer the other cheek to him that smiteth, this was asking of him an almost insupportable restraint.

The conversion of the northern lands, then, falls into two periods, the first of mere acknowledgment of Christ, of lip-service to Him, and the second of real spiritual reconciliation to the Christian doctrine. It is in this second phase that the results of the conversion are most of all likely to lead to observable alterations in the habits and behaviour of the viking peoples.

When the Viking Period opens, that is to say at the turn of the eighth and ninth centuries, the northerners, or at any rate their chiefs and nobles, were already aware that the Christian faith was not the special religion of one particular foreign nation but was rather some tremendous and all-pervading belief that bound together the diverse peoples of two huge empires. Everywhere that travellers from the north went, whether they journeyed south or west, when they entered the civilized world they found themselves among Christians. Their brother Germans, they knew, were already forsaking the old gods ; the Franks and the Frisians had long been Christians ; the Saxons were now Christians ; the English were Christians ; only in the darkest and furthermost shadows of the barbarian domains did heathendom still linger. Christianity was a passport into a world of wealth and splendour, a permit to tread safely upon the golden roads that led to the markets of Byzantium and the court of the western Emperor.

The kings of the north were not slow to perceive the advantages of adopting the new faith, and in Louis the Pious (814–840) they discovered an emperor who prized a convert dearly. Harald of Denmark (p. 92), whose kingdom had already been visited by the missionary Archbishop Ebbo of Rheims, was the first to become a Christian and he was baptized at the imperial palace of Ingelheim, close to Mainz, in 826 with several hundreds of his followers amid scenes of pomp and enthusiasm over which Louis himself presided. Then in 829 came a Swedish delegation to the emperor asking for missionaries to be sent to Sweden, for King Björn, like King Harald none too sure of his throne, needed the friendship of the Frankish empire ; so the missionary Anskar, who for two years had been preaching the gospel in Hedeby, was bidden to move on to Birka, and there he built a church. But neither these kings, nor the missionaries whom they introduced, made any substantial progress in overthrowing the heathendom of the north. Certain kings changed their faith, and no doubt their courts did likewise ; the missionaries, established and protected by these kings, preached ; yet the people remained pagan and indifferent. Moreover, succeeding kings themselves turned from Christianity, preferring their fathers' ancient faith. Indeed, heathendom must have seemed established in unassailable strength when, at the end of twenty years of Christian endeavour, a huge Danish fleet under Horik seized Hamburg (p. 203) and drove Anskar, now an archbishop, from this his archiepiscopal seat.

During the viking raids, the trading enterprises, and the colonial expeditions of the ninth century, the adventurers who stayed to bargain or take land abroad found themselves dwelling in close contact with Christians, and this not only on the shores of the Western Empire or on the borderlands of the Byzantine world, but also in the fervently Christian provinces of Ireland and Scotland, and in north England, where the Northumbrian Danes had their own Christian king at York, one Guthred, as early as 883. Some of these Northmen in foreign countries took Christian women to wife ; by the '50s many prominent viking aristocrats had themselves become converts, and one result of this was that when Iceland was colonized in the last quarter of the century there were Christian families among the new settlers. Also a number of Swedish and Danish merchants who were accustomed to trade with such Christian ports as Dorstad in Frisia received baptism and on their return became members of the tiny Christian colonies in Birka and Hedeby, the chief trade-towns of the north ; indeed, on the island of Gotland, as the *Gutasaga* attests, it was the missionary work of the returning merchants of Gotland that first introduced Christianity into the island. Yet these small Christian communities had little real influence ; for the early Christianity of Iceland was engulfed and lost in the heathendom of the majority, and in Scandinavia the worship of that new and potent deity Christ made no significant progress, lessening in no wise the common respect for friendly Thor and Odin. Nearly two hundred years were to pass since the day when Ebbo had first preached in Denmark before the heathen Northmen were suddenly bidden by their rulers to abandon, one and all, their old faith and to receive baptism in the new.

It was, in fact, wellnigh at the end of the Viking Period that the peoples of the north awoke to find themselves assailed not merely by the entreaties of a few venturesome missionaries as of old but by the thunder and majesty of the king's own command ; for within the space of the ever-memorable half-century that began about A.D. 970 three great princes stood forth determined there and then to enrol their countries among the Christian nations of the world. It was King Harald Gormsson (died 986) ' who made the Danes Christian ', as he declares of himself on the Jellinge stone (p. 100) ; it was King Olaf Tryggvason who in the five amazing years before the tenth century closed bullied his Norwegian subjects into accepting the new faith, and saw to it, moreover, that the Norse colonists of the Faroes, Iceland, and Greenland, likewise accepted Christianity ; it was King Olof Skotkonung (995–1022) who no less energetically, though much less successfully, sought to convert the Swedes.

It may well be that each prince was impelled to the surprising task of turning his people into Christians as much by the hope of immediate political gain as by a pure and disinterested evangelical zeal. Harald Gormsson, though his own conversion preceded Otto II's Danish war in A.D. 974, must have realized after his defeat by the emperor that the success of his efforts to create a united state of Denmark largely depended on Otto's friendship and that only as the head of a Christian state could he hope to remain in the emperor's favour.[1] Olaf Tryggvason was a returned exile with at first only a precarious hold upon his throne ; but he was a much-travelled man, converted during a viking expedition in the west ; he had been a companion of the Christian prince Svein of Denmark ; he knew that the lordly Vladimir of Kiev, with whom he had spent his boyhood, was now a Christian and was compelling all his Russian subjects to follow his example ; therefore because Olaf knew that as a Christian country his new-won realm of Norway would have powerful friends abroad and that the tenure of his throne depended upon her prosperity, he forthwith turned with all his magnificent energy to the task of converting his subjects. Olof Skotkonung, baptized about A.D. 1008 at Husaby in Västergötland by English missionaries who had come to the north in the followings of Svein and Cnut, was watching jealously the growing strength of Denmark and Norway ; he dare not run the risk of isolation at the head of a still heathen folk and therefore he too bade his people change their faith.

Against this formidable campaign of three anxious and

---

[1] Adam of Bremen certainly implies that Harald, in making Denmark a Christian state, was acting according to the terms of a promise made to Otto the Great ; but cf. L. Weibull, *Nordens hist. o. år* 1000, Lund, 1911, p. 37 ff.

determined kings only the Uppland Swedes offered a serious resistance, for they, when Olof Skotkonung burnt the great heathen temple at Uppsala, so bitterly resented the desecration of this ancient and beloved fane that the king, knowing that they would otherwise renounce their allegiance to him, abandoned them to their heathen ways and took up his residence in Västergötland where the English missionaries had better prepared the ground for his so unpopular task. Yet even in Uppland it was not long, as the rune-stones prove, before the aristocracy surrendered to the inexorable advance of the new religion.

Up to this point the conversion of the Northmen had been for the most part an affair of social expediency and a result of a salutary respect for the king's personal authority; for the king's much-vaunted God had been matched against the old gods and by the king's strong arm it had been effectively demonstrated to all who doubted that Jesus Christ was indeed a more powerful deity than Thor or Odin. But of Christian doctrine the Northmen, as yet unprovided with sufficient priests and without any proper ecclesiastical organization, knew next to nothing. It was the work of a new generation of leaders, in particular of Saint Olaf of Norway (p. 123) and Bishop Odinkar of Denmark, to found national churches that were able in a small measure to control popular opinion according to the precepts of Christ, and this second phase in the conversion of the north, the years wherein a respect for Christian conduct gradually replaced the lawless spiritual freedom of pagan life, began about A.D. 1020 and lasted far into the Middle Ages. But in the very first century that Christian precept began to influence public thought the Viking Period came to an end.

It is not true, of course, that Christian teaching was in itself sufficient to put a stop to bloodthirsty and unnecessary adventures overseas. Yet unquestionably some allowance must be made for the effect of the preaching of the newly imported clergy inasmuch as the preachers were for the most part drawn from countries, England and Germany in particular, that had had sore experience of viking attacks; therefore when the character of northern warfare changes, when expeditions abroad are only undertaken as affairs of grave national import, the possible influence of the holy fathers of the Church must count for something. But it can only have been very slowly that their influence made itself felt, and as a factor directly contributing to the surrender of viking habits the Church acted imperceptibly rather than noticeably; for it is not until the twelfth century, when the Viking Period was past and the Middle Ages begun, that there are momentous signs of Christian piety governing the warlike inclinations of a viking chief. Then it was that King Sigurd of Norway sailed forth not to harry his neighbours but to seek adventures as a crusader in the Holy Land, and that the mettlesome patron saint of Sweden, Eric, sought his beloved fighting not in the territories of his fellow-Christians, but instead found outlet for his martial zeal in war against the heathen Finns, leading his armies to battle under the banner of Christ Militant.

THE HANSA

The usurpation of viking trade by the Hanseatic League of German merchants demands a short notice here inasmuch as it has a bearing upon the fate of the viking colonies in the north and west. For it will be related in subsequent chapters how, after the Viking Period was ended, Iceland fared miserably, how the Norsemen of Greenland starved and died in shameful neglect, how the Ostmen of the Norse towns in Ireland received no succour against the English, and how Norway surrendered to Scotland her faithful subjects in the Orkneys, the Hebrides, and Man. Various causes contributed to this downfall of the colonial system ; the increasing strength of Scottish and English arms, the Black Death that most cruelly ravaged Norway in 1349, the unsympathetic government of Norway by foreign kings after the Kalmar union in 1397, all these play their part in the story of distress and poverty in the mother-country that ended either in the cession or ruin of her colonies in the fourteenth and fifteenth centuries. Yet most of all was the Hansa responsible, for these foreign merchants wrecked utterly the busy viking trade that had for so long nourished and sustained the distant settlements of the viking peoples.

In the days of the great king Sverre of Norway (1184–1202) the Germans who, together with Danes, Swedes, and English, frequented Bergen, were the least popular of the foreign traders who thronged the wharves of this prosperous centre of Norwegian commerce ; but with the growing importance and riches of the towns whence they came, the numbers of these Germans steadily increased and within a hundred years of Sverre's death they had unmistakably become a power in the land, both the merchants of Lübeck and of Bremen having received charters from Magnus Lagabøter and assurances of the special friendship of the king. With the whole wealth and the formidable organization of the Hanseatic League to support them they soon aimed at securing as the maximum benefit of the royal patronage a complete control of Norwegian sea-trade and it was not long before they were able to give a startling demonstration of their power ; for in the reign of King Eric Magnusson (1280–1299) it was suddenly revealed that the newly established Hansa held Norway in its grasp. It happened that a Norwegian noble of these days, turned pirate, had begun most persistently to assail the German shipping and the principal north German towns of the League thereupon united in equipping a fleet that in retaliation undertook a stringent commercial blockade of Eric's realm ; Norway, whose discouraged and indigent merchants with their few obsolete boats found themselves shut helpless in their harbours, was speedily faced with a calamitous and complete economic ruin so that the king had no other course than to submit himself to the will of the League. He was made to pay a huge indemnity for the piratical outrages and to grant the Germans increased trading-privileges ; shortly afterwards he was even compelled to suppress the little native guilds that had unwisely attempted to compete with the Hanseatic merchants. His successor, Haakon V (1299–1319), still further strengthened the power of the Hansa in his country by his foolhardy policy of discouraging trade with England ; it was not long, therefore, before the all-powerful Germans found themselves without competitors and thereat the busy Norwegian merchant-town of Bergen was delivered into their hands.

Among the most profitable commercial enterprises in the north, and equal in importance to the cod-fisheries of the Norwegian coast, was the herring-trade of the Baltic, for it was in this sea that the herring used to spawn ; therefore the chief anxiety of the German merchants was to control the fisheries in these waters in order that it might be they, and they alone, who supplied northern Europe with the huge quantities of herrings for which the fasts prescribed by the Church had now created a voracious market. In the middle of the thirteenth century the Swedes under Jarl Birger and the German traders managed to come to terms, and it was Denmark who was most affected when the merchants of Lübeck began to divert the wealth of Scania, chiefly acquired by this fishing, from the coffers of the Danish king to the German counting-houses ; but under the bold government of two great kings, and inspired by hatred of Sweden no less than by jealousy of the Germans, Denmark was for a while successful in thwarting the ambitious merchants of north Germany who so much coveted the monopoly of trade in the Baltic. The struggle began as early as the reign of Valdemar the Great (1157–1182), who openly opposed the activities of the Germans and who, in the year 1203, captured Lübeck, a town which the Danes then held for twelve years.   Subsequently the fortunes of Denmark declined ; Scania of her own accord sur-rendered herself to Sweden (1333), who remained an enemy and tolerated the Hansa ; but success and prosperity returned temporarily in the fourteenth century when Valdemar Atterdag (1340–1375), after recovering Scania from the Swedes, went on his conquering way to Gotland and there, in 1361, captured the Hanseatic town of Visby.   Yet in the end the strength of the League, supported in this contest both by Norway and by Sweden, prevailed over that of Denmark, and before the '60s closed the united fleets of the German towns gained a decisive victory of which the Treaty of Stralsund was the outcome.   This gave vastly increased privileges to those members of the League who traded along the coasts of Denmark and Scania, recognized the temporary possession by the Hansa of fortified towns like Helsingborg and Malmö that controlled the Sound between Zealand and Scania, and accorded to the Council of the League a deciding vote in the appointment of Valdemar's successor. There followed four years of peace wherein the Hansa developed its Baltic and Norwegian trade in comfortable security, and although in the tumultuous days after Valdemar's death and before the union of the three kingdoms (1397) the League was compelled to defend its merchants against more than one attempt by Norwegians and Danes to break loose from the economic stranglehold of the Germans, the astute diplomatists of the Hansa saw to it that the League remained established in its northern harbours with augmented prestige and undiminished security throughout the twenty years of swift and astonishing political changes that ended in the election of a woman as the regent over all three countries.

Queen Margaret had been at first an enemy of the Hansa, though she had courted the friendship of Lübeck, and there was no doubt of her intention to recover the portions of Scania held as security by the League after the war with Valdemar.   But upon the fall of Albert of Mecklenberg, Stockholm, garrisoned by his German adherents, held aloof from her dominion and became a terror to all the traders of the north, Germans, Danes and Scandinavians alike.   This was the doing of the so-called ' Victual Brothers ', pirate-gangs of these Stockholm Germans, who in the space of six years almost succeeded in bringing Baltic commerce to a standstill ; they took possession of Gotland, established themselves in the coastal towns of Mecklenberg, attacked Denmark, and on two occasions, once in 1393 and again in 1395, even sailed up the Norwegian coast and sacked Bergen. The safety not only of Hanseatic trade but of the northern government itself was threatened, and in consequence Margaret and the Hansa, in the face of this unexpected and paralysing assault upon law and order, at last took council together and agreed to act in concert. Through the mediation of the German Hanseatic towns a treaty (1395) was arranged between Margaret and her sworn foe, Albert of Mecklenberg, whereby it was agreed that Stockholm should be surrendered to the Hansa for a term of three years and that after this period it was to be handed over to the Queen. And when this bond had been made the Hanseatic and Scandinavian fleets together set about the task of hunting down the Victual Brothers and driving them off the seas ; Gotland was reconquered in 1398 and in that same year Stockholm was restored to Margaret's triple realm.

Thus the Victual Brothers by their lawless raiding provided the Hansa with an opportunity of interfering in the politics of the north, of re-affirming the rights of the League, and of earning the gratitude of the Queen. But it was in Norway that the pirates had served the Hansa best ; for during the reign of Haakon VI Magnusson (1355–1380) the hold of the League upon the Norwegian ports had become much less secure than in the days of his predecessors, and the two sacks of Bergen by the Victual Brothers, crowned by a third outrage against this unhappy town in 1428 that was the doing of the League's own agents, wrecked totally the forlorn revival of native Norwegian commerce that Haakon had encouraged and that would have meant so much to the starving viking colonies. Henceforth, for the space of wellnigh a hundred years, the Hanseatic towns possessed an almost exclusive control over Norwegian shipping, and so it came about that in this dark century Iceland came dangerously near to ruin and the miserable colony of Greenland was left to perish utterly.

PART II

THE VIKINGS ABROAD

CHAPTER V

RUSSIA AND THE EAST

THERE are few features in European geography more remarkable than the network of riverways that traverse the huge extent of Russia and allow light craft to find their way, with only an occasional portage of the boats overland, across the whole length of the country from the Baltic coast far away south to the Black Sea and the Caspian. It was a river-system of more than ordinary commercial importance, as the North Germans had known ever since the Goths had taken up their abode in south Russia, but when the Viking Period begins most of the Goths had long departed from their Black Sea home, and the movement of the Slavs into Russia had further contributed to the breakdown of the old trade with the north ; therefore the vikings found profit and adventure in re-establishing this ancient commerce and in so doing they embarked upon what was destined to be the most remarkable and historically important of all the exploits of the Northmen abroad. This was the winning of the Dnieper basin and the foundation of the Russian state.

It was not the work of a single mighty conquest, nor was it even the result of a deliberate and carefully planned campaign of many years' duration ; yet it was achieved with almost dramatic suddenness before the ninth century had run its course. Of the first event in this memorable Swedish adventure there is

SWEDES FOUND ALDEIGJU-BORG ON LADOGA, *c.* 800–50

no historical record, but archaeology has made it evident that the tale opens with the establishment of a small Swedish colony in the first decades of the century on the south shore of Lake Ladoga. The stronghold here, Aldeigjuborg, was reached by sailing to the end of the Gulf of Finland, where Leningrad is now, and then down the Neva for some thirty miles into the lake and

143

along its coast into the mouth of the Volkhov, where the settlement was established eight miles south of the lake. It was placed, therefore, at the head of a fine water-road to distant lands, for the Volkhov led to Novgorod, and Novgorod was a gateway leading by the route of the Lovat to the mighty Dnieper and so, past Kiev, to the Black Sea and the Greek colonies and to Constantinople herself; or from Novgorod boats might fare by way of

FIG. 20.—The waterways of Russia

the Syas and the Mologa to the Volga and thence to the Caspian Sea and the markets of the Saracen East. But of the life of the early Swedish settlers at Aldeigjuborg,[1] established like the Jomsvikings in a fortress and, like them, surrounded by a foreign folk, nothing is known; nor are the adventures recorded of the vikings who stayed first in Novgorod or further south in Smolensk.

[1] For the archaeology of this and other viking settlements in Russia see a convenient summary by T. J. Arne, *Det stora Svitjod*, Stockholm, 1917, p. 37 ff. Cf. also the same author's *Suède et l'Orient*, Uppsala, 1914.

The story of the Scandinavians in north Russia, as history relates it, does not begin until A.D. 859. In this year, as a passage in the Russian Nestor Chronicle [1] relates, the Varangians [2] (northerners) came ' from the other side of the (Baltic) sea ' and laid under them not only the Baltic lands of the Tchuds but also the territories of various neighbouring Slavonic folk. The story goes that the Varangians were expelled from their new dominions in 862 and that after the Swedish suzerainty was thus ended, anarchy reigned among the native people; clan battled against clan, and so disastrous was this internal strife that the Slavs voluntarily invited the Swedes to return and rule them. Three brothers [3] from among the Varangians were chosen to undertake this task and in the same year, 862, they came back at the head of the ' Russians ', [4] for so the chronicle calls the

LEGEND OF THE FOUNDATION OF THE SWEDISH STATE IN RUSSIA, A.D. 859

[1] Commonly known as the *Ancient Chronicle*. The authorship thereof used to be attributed to a monk of Kiev, Nestor, who lived at the end of the eleventh century and at the beginning of the twelfth ; actually it contains Nestor's original chronicle only in an abridged form and is a compilation edited by Abbot Silvester of Kiev about A.D. 1116. The passage mentioned here will be found in Chaps. XIV, XV (ed. Leger, Paris, 1884).

[2] This word *varjagi* was a synonym in Russia and Greece (βάραγγοι) for northerners, Scandinavians ; it is supposed to be the equivalent of ON. *váeringi* and AS. *wáergenga*, and probably meant originally ' sworn men ' or ' men of a brotherhood '. For a review of the various etymologies suggested and a discussion of the problems connected with this word, see R. Ekblom, *Archives d'Études Orientales*, XI (1915), p. 30.

[3] A ' three brothers ' legend (*Chronicle*, Ch. VI) is also part of the story of the Slavonic foundation of Kiev.

[4] The chronicler says that the Varangians (northerners) concerned in this episode were called Russians, but he does not use this name as the equivalent of Swedes, for he adds that other Varangians were called Swedes, Normans, Angles, and Goths. This supports the view that these Varangians of the ' Nestor ' chronicle were not Swedes who came direct from Sweden, but Swedes who came from the Ladoga settlement, a view, however, that is in conflict with the express statement that the ambassadors of the Slavs journeyed ' over the sea ' to invite the return of their former rulers. On the other hand, the chronicler's use of the word Varangians here might be taken as support for the theory that the founder of the Russian state was not a Rurik of Sweden but Rorik of Denmark (see note 1, p. 206). The derivation of the word Russia is uncertain. The territory of *Rus*, as known to the Greeks, was the Kiev district, and by ' men of Rus.' the Greeks quite certainly were referring to ' Scandinavians ' ; Liudprand, *Ant.*, V, 15, is explicit on this point and says the name Russ meant ' fair ' or ' ruddy ' men ; ' we ', he says, ' from the position of their country call them Nordmanni '. Subsequently the Greeks used the name to denote the upper classes, whether Scandinavian, Slavonic, or both, of the Russian cities. Possibly the folkname *Russians* is a Slavonic form of a Finnish *ruotsi*, itself derived from

Northmen, to rule the Slavs ; the eldest, Rurik, took up his abode in Novgorod and after the death of his brothers became possessed of their provinces,[1] so that he ended his days as lord of all north-west Russia from Rostov to Pskov.

Concerning this legend it may be said at once that it is beyond a doubt a muddled and chronologically dubious description of an actual event, and that it may indeed be correct in so far that a Scandinavian noble of the name of Rurik did become lord of Novgorod in the middle of the ninth century ; but it is unlikely that the tale represents more than a solitary episode in the early story of Scandinavian Russia and it cannot therefore be accepted as a complete and truthful version of the beginnings of viking dominion in this great country. It is not, however, lacking in importance, for its unequivocal testimony, all the more noteworthy since it comes from a Slavonic source, is almost in itself sufficient to demonstrate that a ruling caste of Scandinavian vikings obtained control of the Russian merchant-towns.[2] How and when this first happened is not told. But there is reason to believe that the infiltration of the vikings began many years before Rurik came to Novgorod ; indeed it is probable that there were resident Scandinavians settled on the upper reaches of the Volga and the Dnieper, and in such important river-towns as Kiev, as early as the beginning of the ninth century.[3] Possibly a Kievan state, controlled by the vikings, was

ON. *roðsmenn*, river-folk or rowing-folk, which was the special name of the Swedes of Roslagen, the *rowing-law* district. For a discussion of the various etymologies see R. Ekblom, *Arch. d'Études Orientales*, XI (1915), p. 6 ; cf. also H. Jacobsohn, *Nachrichten K. Gesell. d. Wissenschft., Göttingen, Phil. Hist. Klasse*, 1918, p. 310 ; and E. König, *Zeitschrft. d. deutsch. morgenländischen Gesell.* 70 (1916), p. 22, who considers that the name Rus was applied by eastern peoples to a folk in the south-east of Russia *before* the arrival of the Varangians. This seems to be the solution of the difficulty arising from the various mentions by Greek and Arab authors of ' Russians ' prior to the appearance of the Scandinavians in the ninth century, for distinct from the *Rus* of the north there was probably a Caucasian folk known by a name etymologically different but almost identical in pronunciation.

[1] Their capitals are said to have been at Byelozero and Izborsk.

[2] This, of course, has been contested by philo-slav authors who have tried to show that the Varangians of this passage were not the vikings or a Germanic folk at all, but Slavs. Other writers have argued that they were Khazars or the descendants of the Goths and Heruls still living in S. Russia. For a summary of the controversy and references see L. Niederle, *Manuel de l'antiquité slave*, I, Paris, 1923, p. 200, n. 2.

[3] Probably the Persian Ibn Hordâdbêh (wrote *c.* 845) refers to the vikings and not the southern Rus when he describes the Russians as established traders in the Greek and Caspian worlds, *Book of Routes, Journ. Asiatique*, 6S. V (1865), 154. Of course, Nizami (twelfth century)

in existence by about 840, and if this was so the legend of the invitation to Rurik may represent an appeal for succour made to the Swedes by the peoples of the Novgorod neighbourhood who were at war with the new principality of Kiev ; on this view Rurik and his Varangians ' from across the sea ' came at first to defend the northern peoples and then remained to rule them, and it was Rurik's royal house that by triumphing in the end over the Kievan Russians provided in 880 a lord-paramount of all Russia in the person of Oleg (p. 151).

The explanation of the settlement of the Swedes on the Ladoga shore and their gradual expansion across Russia, first south to Novgorod and then eastwards to the Volga and southwards along the Lovat to the Dnieper, is that the vikings and not the Slavs were the rightful heirs to the long-sustained and flourishing commerce that of old had united the Baltic with the Black Sea, namely the four or five hundred years of trade between the German peoples of the north and the German emigrants who in the third century A.D. had gone to dwell in the Dnieper basin and on the northern coasts of Pontus. On the other hand the Slavonic peoples of South Russia were newcomers, for it was not until the fifth and sixth centuries that they had taken the place of the Goths and other German folk in the Dnieper valley, and though now in the ninth century these Slavs dwelt in river-towns that the Germans had occupied before them, though they had usurped, as had done the Germans in their turn, the markets and the trade-routes of the ancient Scythians and Sarmatians, though they stood sentinel at the gateway between Byzantine civilization and the outer darkness, yet the shattering effect upon them of their wars with the Asiatic Avars and Khazars, added to the serious disadvantages of their own cultural backwardness, presented the daring Scandinavians who sailed their rivers with all the opportunity that such eager and pugnacious Germans required in order to re-assert the ancient supremacy of their forefathers over the golden waterways of Russia.

There was a need, then, for the strength of viking arms in order that the great trade-route of the Dnieper might be made safe ; for the Khazars and Patzinaks of Asia terrorized the Slavs to the south of Kiev and blocked the way across the Steppes to the Black Sea. And it was not only the Slavs, but the vikings too, who found the lower Dnieper dangerous. Thus in 839 when certain Swedish ambassadors reached the court of the Emperor

who brings the Scandinavians to Azerbaijan temp. Alexander the Great has simply attributed the defeat of the Berdaa vikings of 943 to his hero (*Sikandar Nama*, ed. Clarke, London, 1881).

Theophilus at Constantinople, they reported that in coming thither they had had to pass through countries inhabited by peoples so cruel and so dangerous that to prevent a repetition of this hazardous journey Theophilus sent them home by way of the Frankish court at Ingelheim with a recommendation to Louis the Pious that he should give them safe conduct through his realm.[1]

In soliciting the friendship of Theophilus the Swedes showed themselves aware that the development of the Dnieper trade-route depended largely upon the co-operation and goodwill of the Byzantine Greeks, but the viking spirit of their Scandinavian leaders in these early days of sudden power was too urgent and unruly to permit the practice of a wholly conciliatory policy. At the beginning of the ninth century an army from ' Rus ' under a prince named Bravlin had begun the struggle for the command of the lower Dnieper by a long campaign that ended after many years' fighting with the capture from the Khazars of lands in the Cherson district,[2] and just before the year 842 another fighting force from Rus had raided the southern coasts of the Black Sea and plundered Amastris in Paphlagonia.[3] Such

[1] *Ann. Bert. M.G.H.* (Pertz), SS. I, p. 434. Theophilus called them ' men of Rhos ' and said that they had come to him with a message of friendship from their khagan (chacanus), a word that is the Khazar equivalent of king. Louis ascertained that his visitors were Swedes and as he already knew something of vikings he regarded them with the utmost suspicion, throwing them into prison until he was satisfied that they were not spies.

[2] But this may not have been a Scandinavian venture. Theophanes, for example, records the presence of hostile Russian vessels in the Black Sea about A.D. 765 (*Chron. C.S.H.B.*, XXVI, p. 691) and this most certainly must refer to the southern and non-Scandinavian ' Russians ' who are first heard of in the Caucasus neighbourhood as early as the sixth century.

[3] The authorities for these two raids are the legendary biographies of St. George of Amastris (early ninth century) and St. Stephen of Sugdaea (eighth century), published in V. G. Vasilievsky's *Russko-Vizantiyskiya Izsledovaniya*, St. Petersburg, 1893. The ' Russian ' passage in the life of St. George (Greek text with German commentary) is given by E. Kunik, *Bull. Hist.-Phil. Acad. Imp. des Sciences*, St. P., III (1847), 3, col. 33 ff., who identifies the raid there described with that of Bravlin in the life of St. Stephen and dates it 866. A Latin version of the passage in St. George's life will be found in *Acta Sanctorum (Boll)*, Feb., III, p. 282. For the Russian passage in St. Stephen's biography see A. Vostokov, *Opisanie Russ. y Sloven. Rukopysey Rumyantsovskago Muz.*, St. P., 1842, p. 689 (cf. nos. CLXVIII, CLXIX), and for further discussion see D. Pogodin, *Zapysky Odesskago Obshchestva*, I (1844), p. 191. On the general question of the date of these biographies, see W. von Gutzeit, *Bull. Acad. des Sciences*, St. P., XXVII (1881), p. 333, and E. Kunik, ib., p. 388, V. Jagitch (reviewing Vasilievsky), *Arch. f. slav. Phil.*, XVI (1894), p. 216 ;

reckless warfare could only lead, of course, to friction with the Greeks, and in 860 a quarrel between Greek merchants and the now presumptuous traders of Rus was followed by an impudent and astonishing attack upon Constantinople herself. The Queen of Cities, surpassing all others in luxury and magnificence, lay at a distance of about ten days' sail from the Dnieper mouth along the western coast of the Black Sea ; her thronged wharves were the centre of the world's commerce, and travellers' tales of this fabled metropolis of the Eastern Empire had long enthralled and amazed her barbarian neighbours ; no richer prize ever tempted the vikings to their wars. But when in 860 the Varangian princes of Kiev, said to be two brothers named Askiold and Dir, led forth a flotilla of 200 of the little Russian boats to threaten the city, it may be that they dared hope for no other reward than a renewal of those trading-privileges that were essential to the prosperity of the Dnieper town. The time, however, was well chosen, for the viking leaders had learnt that the weakling emperor Michael III and his resolute uncle Bardas had left the capital to fight the Saracens, and it was a dark hour for the Greeks when the Russian fleet sailed suddenly into the Bosphorus and lay at anchor before the lovely city of Constantine. What exactly happened is unknown ;[1] the town walls were strong, and the remaining garrison was sufficient in numbers to preclude all danger of the capture of the city by the viking force. But the Greeks were certainly taken by surprise and seriously alarmed. It seems that the emperor returned hastily and had some difficulty in passing through the cordons of Russian boats ; but when the Byzantine and the Russian armaments were face to face the Greeks soon gave proof of their overwhelming superiority in ships and in equipment, so that the ' rude ($ὠμός$) and barbarous ' invaders, as the Patriarch Photius called them, met with a crushing and complete defeat. Yet Photius himself admits that the Russians gained great renown as a result of this raid upon Constantinople, and their own chronicle avers that the Greeks and their city only escaped because of a storm that rose suddenly and wrecked the viking fleet, this storm being the

(In the margin:)
FIRST RAID ON CONSTANTINOPLE
A.D. 860

also F. Golubinsky, *J.M.N.P.*, 187 (1876), p. 78 and the same author's *Istoriya Russkoy Tserkvy* (Moscow, 1901), I, pp. 54, 57. For a valuable discussion of Bravlin and his raid in English, see N. T. Belaiew, *Saga-Book of Viking Soc.* X, Pt. 2, p. 272.

[1] The accounts of this raid are summarized by C. de Boor, *Byzantinische Zeitschrift*, III (1894), p. 445. The date of the raid, as de Boor points out, is fixed by a passage in *Anecdota Bruxellensia*, I, *Chron. Byz. MS.* 11376, Ghent, 1894, p. 33.

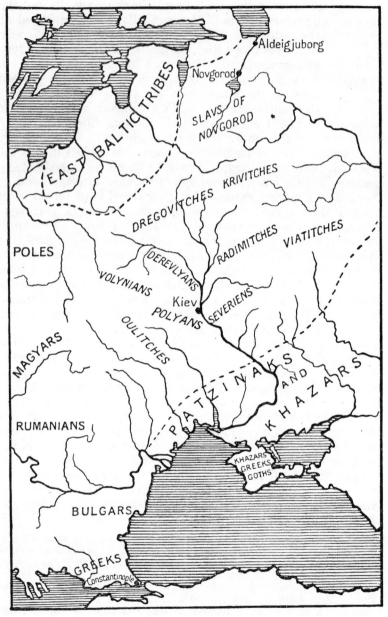

FIG. 21.—The Slavs of the Dnieper basin and their neighbours

generous gift of the Virgin in answer to the urgent prayers of the terrified inhabitants.[1]

Askiold and Dir, the reputed leaders of this expedition, are said to have been the founders of the Varangian state of Kiev; but the Russian chronicle is at fault in the matter of the date assigned to the beginning of the Swedish supremacy over this town, for its first masters are described as companions of Rurik when he established himself in Novgorod, and this did not happen until two years after the raid from Kiev took place. The fact emerges, however, that the Polyane city under its earliest foreign lords remained independent of the Swedish rulers of Novgorod until the year (c. 880) when Rurik's successor, Oleg, himself went south with an army and, after taking Smolensk and Lyubetch, captured this new prize, slaying Askiold and Dir. Thereafter Kiev, the master-city of the Dnieper and the route to the Black Sea, became the capital of the ' Russian ' state.

The half-legendary Oleg, though unknown to foreign writers, was, if the Russian stories of him are true, one of the greatest, bravest vikings who ever ruled a Slavonic state. His power OLEG OF and his dominion were alike enormous, for soon after KIEV, Kiev fell to him and the ' mother of Russian cities ' c. 880–912 became his capital, he found himself the sovereign of a mighty political confederacy of town-provinces; all the eastern Slavonic tribes now looked to him as their protector and to Kiev as their rallying-point, wherefore Oleg began the building of fortifications to prevent the inroads of the Khazars and the Patzinaks, and set himself to achieve, knowing it to be a matter of paramount urgency, the safeguarding of the Russian merchants on their annual and most perilous journey to Constantinople.

It was the custom of the royal convoy of merchantmen, loaded with furs, honey, wax, and slaves, to depart from Kiev in June [2] and sail a short distance downstream to Vitichev, where a halt was made until such time as all the traders from far-off towns like Novgorod, Smolensk, Lyubetch, Tchernigov, and Vishgorod had joined the flotilla. From Vitichev the great convoy descended the Dnieper, each day in increasing peril of attack from the lawless peoples on their left flank, until the eastern

---

[1] For the two homilies of Photius dealing with the Russian raid of 860 see *Frag. Hist. Graec.* (ed. Müller), V, i, p. 162. For other references, see F. Dvornik, *Les Slavs, Byzance, et Rome au 9e. siècle*, Paris, 1926, p. 58, n. 2, and cf. A. A. Vasiliev, *Hist. Byz. Emp., Univ. Wisconsin Studies* 13, Madison, 1928, p. 337.

[2] This account is based on the well-known description by the Emperor Constantine VII Porphyrogenitus (912–959), *De Administrando Imperio,* IX.

bend of the river was reached, where for forty miles progress was stayed by the necessity of passing seven cataracts in quick succession.[1] It was only with the utmost difficulty that these obstacles were overcome ; at some points armed detachments had to be sent out to the flanks to ward off the Patzinaks while the slaves were marched overland past the rapids, and to circumvent the worst of the falls not only the cargoes, but also the boats themselves, had to be dragged along the banks. Then, when the cataracts were safely passed and the grateful traders had duly sacrificed to the gods, a journey of four days took the convoy to the island of Berezan [2] at the mouth of the Dnieper estuary, where two or three days were spent in fitting out the ships for a voyage that was henceforth by sea. But the convoy was compelled to hug the shore and until it reached Sulina, at the middle rivermouth of the Danube delta, the Patzinaks patrolled the coast ready to take advantage of storm-driven or disabled Russian ships that were forced to put in to land ; but once past the Danube mouth nothing more was to be feared from the Patzinaks ; only tempest and piracy on the high seas henceforth threatened the convoy with disaster as it made its slow way past Constanza, Varna, and Misivria to the New Rome.

No doubt it was some quarrel between Greeks and Russians, some infringement of a trade-agreement made in or after 860, that gave Oleg pretext for the master-stroke of his career. Yet it was no mere retaliatory raid that he led against SECOND Constantinople in 907, but a solid and carefully planned RAID ON demonstration of Russian might. The force he had CONSTAN- collected for this great expedition was indeed a large TINOPLE one, and is said to have consisted of 80,000 men in no A.D. 907 less than 2,000 boats, together with a cavalry detachment proceeding overland, a naval and military array that represented more than the full fighting strength of the Kievan state and included contingents of Tchuds and other peoples of the north.

[1] This is the number given by Constantine ; actually there are 9 or 10 ' great ' rapids and another half-dozen that are less formidable ; for an account of them see T. J. Arne, *Det Stora Svitjod*, Stockholm, 1917, p. 38. Some of the rapids were known to the Greeks not only by Slavonic, but also by ON. names ; thus the second cataract, says the Emperor, was called ' island-cataract ', *ostrobruniprach* (ostrovŭnyj pragŭ) in the Slavonic tongue ; in ' Russian ' it was *ulborsi* (holm-fors). For the philology of the cataract-names see the literature cited by L. Niederle, *Manuel de l'antiquité slave*, I, Paris, 1923, p. 206, n. 3. It is worth remarking that apart from these there are no Norse place-names in the Dnieper basin of South Russia.

[2] For the relics of the vikings here, which include a Runic inscription on a memorial stone, see N. Cleve, *Esa*, IV (1929), p. 250.

On this occasion the Greeks were prepared for trouble from the Russian quarter and Oleg found the Bosphorus barred against him by a chain. But a fleet of light ships that had successfully navigated the Dnieper rapids was not to be hindered thus, and the story goes that Oleg had his ships drawn overland past the barrier and so arrived with his huge fleet before Constantinople. There was reigning at this time the Emperor Leo VI, and this wise man, acting in accordance with the customary Byzantine policy of conciliation and toleration, showed himself disposed to welcome rather than resist the threatening armament before his walls. The Russians had already plundered churches and palaces in the neighbourhood of the city, but there was no fighting before Constantinople ; mediators from the emperor arrived ; they suggested that the maintenance of friendly relations with the empire and the stimulus of Byzantine trade were alike indispensable to the well-being of the state of Russia ; on their part they admitted that they had need of the commodities that the Russian traders brought to their doors ; they showed themselves prepared to listen sympathetically to Oleg's grievance and made proposals for a generous commercial treaty.[1]

Oleg professed himself satisfied and was entertained hospitably ; presents were lavished upon him and the chieftains in his train ; gifts were made to his ships' crews, both Scandinavian and Slavonic ; moreover, subsidies were paid by the Greeks to each of the several Russian towns where dwelt princes who were under Oleg's authority. And so he returned to Kiev, having struck no blow against the Greek forces, but having laid enduring foundations of commercial prosperity for Russia and having thrown open the

TREATY
BETWEEN
GREEKS
AND
RUSSIANS

[1] Oleg's attack upon Constantinople is not mentioned in any Byzantine source nor is Oleg himself named, and for this reason some authors believe that the account of his expedition in the Russian chronicle is apocryphal ; but there can be no doubt that the story of the treaty is based on historical fact. Thus, much later, the Emperor John Zimisces avowed to Svyatoslav that Igor of Kiev, Oleg's successor, had disregarded the *sworn agreements* by attacking Constantinople in 941, and this can only refer to the treaty made between Leo VI and Oleg (see A. A. Vasiliev, op. cit. p. 389). I find it hard to believe that this treaty was not the sequel to some sort of demonstration by the Russians and I have therefore incorporated the story of the raid in my narrative ; but I admit that the strength of Oleg's force may be much exaggerated. A supposed reference to Oleg and a mention of a reluctant Russian raid upon Constantinople occurs in a twelfth-century Hebrew document concerning Khazar history (*Jewish Quarterly Review*, N.S. III, 1912–13, p. 196 ff., pp. 217, 218, and cf. P. K. Kokovzev, *J.M.N.P.*, 1913, p. 150) ; but the chronological difficulties in connexion with identification of Oleg are most formidable and it is much more likely that the events referred to belong to the time of Igor.

gates to the flood of vivifying Byzantine inspiration that was destined for so long to be the mainspring of art, thought, and fashion in the Russian state. The commercial treaty was not concluded until four years afterwards (911), when Oleg entrusted the final negotiations to fifteen envoys, all of whom bore Scandinavian names. According to the preliminary agreement following the expedition itself, the Russian traders were to have quarters outside the walls in the St. Mamas (now Béchik-Tach) suburb [1] of Constantinople during their annual visit, were to receive a maintenance allowance, and were to be absolved from the payment of taxes on their merchandise ; but they were only allowed to enter the city itself by one specified gate and in detachments of not more than fifty men, all unarmed. To these fundamental principles that gave the Russian visitors to the Greek capital a recognized, though restricted, status, the treaty itself added various clauses defining their legal position during their sojourn among the Greeks and governing Greco-Russian international relations in general.[2]

To Oleg, as Grand Prince of Kiev, there succeeded in the second decade of the century Igor, the son of Rurik. He too went warring against the Greeks, this happening at the end of a long reign that had seen Russia at peace, except for the endless struggle with the Patzinaks. The cause of Igor's quarrel with Byzantium is unknown, but that he suddenly resolved to attack Constantinople is certain, and in the early summer of 941, when the Greek navy was away fighting against the Saracens, the Russian prince led a flotilla of 1,000 boats [3] over the Black Sea to raid the city. Once again the Greeks were at a disadvantage, but the Emperor Romanus Lecapenus caused fifteen old barques to be patched up and fitted out with apparatus for discharging Greek Fire ; these he put under the command of the Protovestiarius Theo-

IGOR AND THE THIRD RAID ON CONSTANTINOPLE A.D. 941

---

[1] On this, see J. Pargoire, *Échos d'Orient*, XI (1908), p. 203.

[2] The text of the treaty is recorded in the Russian chronicle, ch. XXII ; the 944 treaty of Igor is given in ch. XXVII. This later treaty adds the conditions that the Russians were to bear passports and were not to spend the winter at St. Mamas, on Berezan, or at the Dnieper mouth, but were to return to their own country. An excellent summary of the treaties is given by J. C. S. Runciman, *Romanus Lecapenus*, Cambridge, 1929, p. 110, but for a detailed study, see D. Mejcik, *J.M.N.P.*, 1915, Parts 57, 59, 60 ; 1916, Pts. 62, 66 ; 1917, Pt. 69.

[3] I am following here the Italian Liudprand (*Antapodosis*, in *Op.* ed. Pertz, Hannover, 1839, p. 139) instead of the Greek authors who give the number as 10,000 or even 15,000 ; the Russian chronicle also says Igor had 10,000 ships. For references to the Greek texts and an English account of the expedition, see J. C. S. Runciman, loc. cit., p. 111 ff.

phanes and sent them forth to guard the Bosphorus. They came
upon the Russians near the east coast of the strait at Hierum,
and there the overbold venture of Igor, so far as the safety of the
capital was concerned, came to a sudden and humiliating end ;
for the Russians would not face the all-destroying fire that was
belched against them from the grim old hulks of Theophanes
and in terror they took to flight, scrambling out of the Bosphorus
as best they could and rallying later on the north coast of Asia
Minor.[1] When they had recovered from their fear they abandoned themselves to a reckless and bloodthirsty harrying of the
provinces of Paphlagonia and Bithynia in the accustomed viking
manner of their Swedish leaders. But while they thus robbed and
murdered, the Greeks collected an army and at length they surprised and cut to pieces a landing-party of the Russians ; this
prevented all further forays and was the prelude to a decisive
success, for when in the autumn the invaders sought to return
to their own country they found their escape barred by Theophanes, this time commanding not fifteen creaking old boats, but
a huge and majestic armament of Byzantine warships. Igor's
little craft were a helpless prey ; as though it were the visible
wrath of Heaven the terrible fire poured down upon them from
the Greek boats, and amid foul scenes of panic, drowning, and mad
flight the Russians were broken and destroyed. A few, including
Igor, escaped, and a large number were taken as prisoners to
Constantinople where they were executed ; but the rest were
either burnt to death in the sea-battle or drowned.

Igor returned to Kiev shocked and humiliated, but planning
revenge. Soon he began to recruit a new army, this time sending
to Sweden for reinforcements and enlisting under his banner
levies of the easternmost Slavonic tribes and hired hordes of the
Patzinaks. In 944 the new and formidable Russian fleet, accom-
IGOR   panied by a cavalry detachment on land, set out upon
AGAIN   the great expedition ; but once again Igor failed to
THREA-   reach Constantinople. For the Emperor Romanus,
TENS CON-
STANTI-   who had received a timely warning from the Bulgars
NOPLE   of the movements of the huge host, sent off ambassa-
A.D. 944   dors to Igor bearing messages of conciliation and
friendship, and these Greek envoys intercepted the invading force
at the Danube delta. Igor was won over by costly gifts and

---

[1] The Russian chronicle, followed in this respect by most historians,
makes the arrival of the Russians in Asia Minor precede the attack on
Constantinople. But this is an extremely improbable sequence of events
and one that is contrary to the express statements of Cedrenus, Zonaras,
Theophanes, and Liudprand.

promises ; he left his Patzinak troops, no doubt with the ready consent of the Greeks, to plunder at their will in Bulgaria, and himself led the Russians home ;[1] diplomatic discussions followed his return to Kiev and in 945 another treaty was concluded between Russia and Byzantium on the same lines as that of 911, SECOND though this time the foreign policy of the principality TREATY of Kiev was controlled, for Igor swore that in return BETWEEN for occasional military aid from the Greeks he would GREEKS AND RUS- neither permit the Bulgars to invade the Chersonese, SIANS now dominated by the Russians, nor allow his own A.D. 945 countrymen to molest the Khazars who went fishing in the Dnieper mouth. Fifty Russian commissioners and merchant-delegates attended the negotiations that preceded this treaty and their names are recorded ; the majority of them are in unrecognizable forms, but sixteen are unmistakably Scandinavian and only three are certainly Slavonic ; it is also said that some of these envoys were Christians, for among the Varangians, so the chronicle relates, there were now many converts and in Kiev itself there was already a cathedral.[2]

When Igor died his son was but a boy, and it was his widow, Olga, who governed Russia after his death. This princess, the OLGA OF ἀρχόντισσα of Russia as the Greeks called her, was one KIEV of the Christians among the Varangians and during her regency proved herself an enlightened and industrious ruler ; but her chief title to fame was won by the celebrated diplomatic visit paid by her in the year 957 to the court of Constantine Porphyrogenitus at Constantinople where she was received with a pomp and magnificence that have been described by the emperor himself.[3] After her the next ruler of the Russians

[1] It is commonly stated that he consoled them by taking them across the Caucasus to ravage Azerbaijan and that his was the army that took Berdaa (p. 162) ; but the date of the Berdaa expedition is given by Ibn Miskawaih in the *Tadjarib-el-Oman* as 943 and it therefore antedates Igor's second war against the Greeks.

[2] The conversion of the Russians is said to have begun at least as early as the '60s of the ninth century, and the Patriarch Photius, who considered the introduction of Christianity into the Russian state to have been one of the most notable achievements of the Byzantine Church in his day, even gave them a bishop (*Epist.* I, xiii, ed. Migne, P. Graec. 102, cols. 736–7). But whether there was really any appreciable inclination on the part of the Russians to desert heathendom so early as this is a little doubtful. On this subject, and for full references, see F. Dvornik, op. cit., p. 145 ; for an English summary based upon E. Golubinsky's monumental *History of the Russian Church* see M. Spinka, *Journal of Religion*, VI (Chicago, 1926), p. 40.

[3] *De Cerem. Aulae Byz.*, II, sect. 344 (ed. Migne).

was Svyatoslav, her son and Igor's; he was the first prince of Kiev to bear a Slavonic name, but he was made of the stuff of his viking forefathers and spent the greater part of his reign in fighting, in the beginning with the praiseworthy intention of establishing new trading-depots in the east for the Russians,[1] and subsequently in the grand and dangerous hope of extending his Russian dominion over the Balkans. He defeated the Khazars and captured Sarkel near the delta of the Don at the head of the Sea of Azov and thereupon inaugurated a Russian protectorate of the Crimean Goths that endured until his death; afterwards he carried his victorious arms into the Kuban; in the north-west of his principality he attacked the Vyatiches of the Oka banks and forced them to pay tribute to Kiev; in the south-west he crossed the Danube and declared war upon the Bulgarians. This last campaign began in 967 and was the sequel to his failure in founding new trade-routes up the Don and Volga, for the Grand Prince eventually realized that his hardest task was to be the defence of the old Constantinople trade-route in the face of the rivalry and hostility of the Bulgars.

SVYATOSLAV OF KIEV 957–972

RUSSIAN INVASION OF BULGARIA

The war was actually inspired, so the tale goes, by the Emperor Nicephorus Phocas, for the Byzantine government needed allies against whom the anger of its relentless foes in Bulgaria might be diverted while he himself led the Greek armies forth upon the mighty struggle that was to end half a century later in the brilliant triumph of Byzantium over all her enemies.[2] But Svyatoslav, who knew the commercial importance of the Danube mouths, needed little urging and the Russians descended in a mighty host upon their new prey. The invasion was at first successful; all northern Bulgaria fell to them and at Pereislavets, near the modern Preslav at the mouth of the Danube, the Grand Prince endeavoured to establish a new capital, for he perceived the trading-possibilities of this town lying closer to central Europe and closer to Greece than did his own city on the Dnieper. But during his absence the Patzinaks attacked Kiev, so that Svyatoslav was forced to return. In the summer of 969

[1] For Svyatoslav and his eastern foreign policy, see N. Znojko, *J.M.N.P.*, N.S. XVIII (1908), p. 258.

[2] The tale goes that the emperor's envoy was a Chersonese Greek named Calocyr and that this man tried to persuade Svyatoslav to withdraw his support from the reigning emperor, suggesting that the Grand Prince should be allowed to hold Bulgaria for himself while the hatcher of this plot, with the Russians as his helpers, should usurp the imperial crown. The story has little historical importance, but for a full account and discussion, see N. Znojko, *J.M.N.P.*, N.S. VIII (1907), p. 229.

he invaded Bulgaria again, this time leaving the Russian state divided into three portions, each under the nominal rule of one of his young sons, and as he had now collected an enormous army that included even Patzinak and Magyar auxiliaries, this time he swept victoriously through Bulgaria and descended upon Philippopolis on the Maritza, which town he took, massacring the inhabitants.   But this brilliant raid was his undoing, for there-

SVYATO-SLAV THREAT-ENS CON-STANTI-NOPLE
after in his pride he saw himself not only the conqueror of the Bulgars but master of the Greeks themselves, and so he dared even to advance against Constantinople. It was an act of wild barbarian folly ; Nicephorus at once levied the Greek armies, equipped squadrons of armoured cavalry, saw to the defences of the capital, and barred by a huge chain its sea-approach.   It was not, however, Nicephorus, but his murderer and successor, that great general the Emperor John Zimisces, who drove the Russians back, who finally compelled Svyatoslav to sue for peace after the Byzantine army had trapped the retreating barbarians in Silistria and had defeated again and again the bloody and desperate sallies of the imprisoned Northmen and Russians.[1]   The Grand Prince of Kiev was made to renew the terms of the existing treaties and in addition to declare that henceforth he would neither invade Bulgaria nor the Greek Chersonese ; thus ended his dreams of a mighty Russia made by his strong arm mistress of Balkan and eastern commerce, and thus was the valour of his followers squandered and the fruits of his conquests wasted.   And in the gloom of this reverse the adventurous reign of the ambitious warrior-prince closed, for on his way back to Russia in the year (972) after the capitulation at Silistria Svyatoslav was slain near the Dnieper cataracts during a sudden onslaught of a marauding troop of Patzinaks.

The principality of Kiev and the Dnieper trade-route, though the early history of Russia is almost exclusively occupied with them, were not the only scenes of Scandinavian commerce in this THE VOLGA vast country.   For there was another great waterway TRADE-ROUTE   well known to the men of the north even in the dark days at the beginning of the ninth century before the voyage down the Dnieper had become an attractive adventure to the Swedes, and this was the Volga.   Here the vikings sailed south to traffic with the White Bulgars and the Khazars, or dared to venture through the lands of these folk far south into

---

[1] For an account of the Russian war up to the time of the death of Nicephorus, see G. Schlumberger, *Un empereur byzantin au* 10e *siècle,* 1923, pp. 461–474, 610 ff.

PLATE VII

ILLUSTRATIONS OF THE RUSSO-BULGARIAN WAR, *c.* 970

Above : RUSSIANS PUT THE BULGARIANS TO FLIGHT

Below : BULGARIANS ROUT THE RUSSIANS

From a fourteenth-century Bulgarian MS. (see List of Plates), but perhaps copies of earlier miniatures

' Sarkland ', the country round the Caspian Sea,[1] and thus visit the markets of the East ; by this route the majority of the huge quantity of Arabic silver coins found in Russia and in Sweden travelled from the provinces of the Caliphate into the viking world, and along this mighty stream Bulgars, Khazars, and, may be, Arabs too, themselves sailed up to visit the cold north. The Volga was the first trans-Russian waterway of the vikings, and throughout the ninth and tenth centuries it continued to be the most important trade-route for the merchants of Sweden and Gotland, this because the rival Dnieper was soon in the hands of an independent and jealous group of Swedish settlers who would not allow their countrymen a free and unhindered passage to the south.

There is no doubt of the existence of small Swedish settlements in the upper Volga basin north of the White Bulgars and the Steppes in the ninth century, but the history of their inhabitants is almost unknown. These Volga-Russians, however, ARABIC AUTHORS are mentioned by Arabic authors, so that at least it ON THE can be discovered how they appeared to the cultured VOLGA-RUSSIANS travellers of the East. One writer who names them was Ibn Dustah (sometimes called Ibn Roste) who inserts no very flattering picture of them in a work [2] composed by him in the first decade of the tenth century ; they were, he says, bold and handsome barbarians, but dressed in dirty clothes, though the men wore heavy gold armlets ; their sole occupations were fighting and bargaining, their only merchandise consisted of skins and slaves ; they were always armed, and were quick-tempered and pugnacious ; they were excellent sailors, but rode little on horseback. Another Arabic author, Ibn Fadlan,[3] described the Volga-Russians from personal knowledge of them, having accompanied in 921 an embassy of the Caliph al-Maktadir to the king of the White Bulgars, whose capital was situated on the Volga between Kazan and Simbirsk.

---

[1] The word Sarkland probably means ' land of Saracens ' and denotes the Muslim countries south-west and south of the Caspian (Azerbaijan and N. Persia). It has been suggested, however, that the Norse name referred originally not to the Saracens but to the Khazar town of Sarkel which was built in the '30s of the ninth century as a defence against the Russian attacks.

[2] An encyclopedia ; Vol. VII, containing the description of the Russians, has been translated into Russian (Kiev, 1870).

[3] Quoted by Yâqût, the thirteenth-century geographer, in his lexicon ; the passage concerning the Russians is printed with translation and copious notes by C. M. Frähn, *Ibn-Foszlan's . . . Berichte über die Russen älterer Zeit*, St. P., 1823.

Ibn Fadlan said that he had seen the Russian traders arriving by river and thought that never before had he beheld such big and ruddy men. They wore cloaks and each man bore an axe, a knife, and a sword, this last being of European work and often ornamented ; the women wore brooches and neck-chains ; they were one and all especially fond of glass beads and willing to pay a big price for them. Ibn Fadlan declared that they were the dirtiest people that God ever made and so lax in certain specified matters of personal cleanliness that he could only liken them to wild asses. He goes on to say that these Russians, when they had arrived, built themselves wooden booths, each holding from ten to twenty people, and that they spent much time in wor-shipping and making presents to a large wooden idol that stood in a sacred place surrounded by other idols and posts. Thereat follows the amazing and often-quoted description [1] of a Russian chief's funeral, the ritual burning of him in his boat surrounded by rare and costly merchandise, with rich foods and strong drink, with a dog, horses, oxen, and poultry, and with the dead body of a slave-girl, whose sacrifice, that her soul might journey forth with her master's, is the culmination of the ceremonies and the horrible prelude to the firing of the ship. Ibn Fadlan said that the boat had been drawn up on land for the burning and that the last act of all was the piling up over the charred remains of an earthen mound upon which was set a wooden memorial bearing the name of the dead man and the name of his king.

A third Arabic author who writes of the Russians was Mas'ûdî, a celebrated traveller and story-teller who died in 956 or 957. He said [2] that the nation was made up of several dis-tinct peoples, that their trade took the Russian merchants to Spain, Rome, and Constantinople, and the Khazar world (the lower Volga and north-west coast of the Caspian), and that their sailors were the masters of the Black Sea ; then he tells of a great raid carried out by the Kievan Russians. Some time after the year 912, probably in 914, a fleet of 500 of their ships, each manned by a hundred men, sailed through the Sea of Azov into the Don ; when they had secured, either by force or bribery, a promise from the Khagan of the Khazars that he would not interfere with them, they went up the Don and then made their way across country, dragging their boats overland, until after a week or so of this labour they

RUSSIANS AND THE CASPIAN A.D. 914

---

[1] An English translation arranged by A. F. Major will be found in *Folklore*, XXXV (1924), p. 135 (and see n. 40).

[2] *Meadows of Gold and Mines of Gems*, Eng. trans. by Aloys Sprenyer, London, 1841, I, p. 416 ff.

had reached the Volga ; then they sailed downstream and out past the town of Itil (near Astrakan) into the Caspian Sea. They attacked first the Persian coast in the south and afterwards the western Azerbaijan country ; they found that the inhabitants were defenceless and for months the Russians remained in the Baku district, plundering, massacring, and stealing children for the slave-trade. The Muslims, however, raised an army and, after suffering one defeat, this levy of Islam was enlarged by

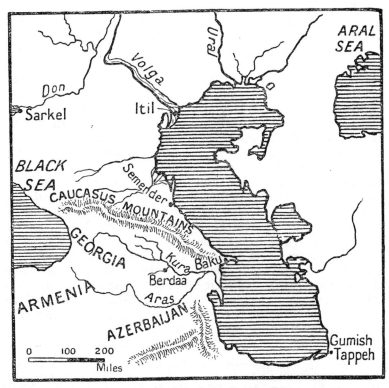

Fig. 22.—Region of the Caspian Sea

reinforcements from Itil of Christian and Mohammedan Khazars who were likewise desirous of ridding the Caspian of these barbarian interrupters of the accustomed peaceful trading between Itil and the Caliphate. A great battle, lasting for three days, was fought near the Volga mouth and in the end the Russians were overthrown and almost annihilated. Only a small remnant of their host escaped and this too perished in the course of the hazardous journey back to the Black Sea.

This was not the only expedition made by the Russians against the northern and western coasts of the Caspian. As early as A.D. 880, or thereabouts, a band of Russian pirates had seized a town near the modern Gumish Tappeh, far away in the south-east corner, and had been slain one and all by the Muslim levies ;[1] again in 910 a fleet of 16 Russian ships plundered the Persian coasts, but after committing a long series of violent robberies the crews were caught divided between ship and land and met with disastrous defeats from which not one of them escaped alive. But the most serious raid took place in 943,[2] some thirty years after that described by Mas'ûdî. On this occasion the Russians arrived at the mouth of the river Kura in Azerbaijan and sailed some 200 miles up-stream to Berdaa on the Terter, a southern tributary. This town, the ancient capital of the Arran province, they took, after defeating a levy of 5,000 Mohammedans, and subsequently they put most of the wretched inhabitants to the sword ; after this the Muslim governor, El-Marzoban, collected an army of 30,000 men from out of his province and threatened the Russians. His attacks were beaten off, but by this time the Russian ranks were being thinned to an alarming degree by an epidemic of dysentery, and as it soon became certain that they could not withstand another attack, they made off without waiting for the encounter. As soon as they had gone, the Mohammedans dug up the male corpses of their enemies to secure the fine weapons that these northern warriors had borne with them into the grave, for even during the ravaging of the disease the Russians had buried their dead, according to custom, armed and accompanied by a wife or a slave. The remainder of the Russian army returned to their homes seriously depleted in numbers, but bringing with them a noble spoil.

RUSSIANS CAPTURE BERDAA, A.D. 943

Another occasion when the Russian fleets crossed the Caspian

[1] The sources for this and other Caspian raids are set forth and discussed in a long paper by B. Dorn, *Caspia ; über die Einfälle der alten Russen in Tarbaristan*, Mem. Acad. Imp. des Sciences, St. P., 8 S. XXIII (1877), 1.

[2] For this, see Ibn Miskawaih (French trans. by C. Huart in *C. R. Acad. des Inscriptions*, 1921, pp. 182–191). In the opinion of B. Dorn and others this expedition took place in 944, which was the year of Igor's second attack upon the Greeks, and it is suggested that the Caspian raid provided an outlet for the fighting lust of his enthusiastic mercenaries (cf. Dorn, loc. cit., p. 302). This is unlikely in view of Miskawaih's evidence that the Caspian expedition occurred in 943 and not 944. But it is possible that the events referred to in the Khazar document mentioned above (p. 153, n. 1) may be connected with Igor's movements in 944.

was in 969 at the time of Svyatoslav's wars with the Bulgars on the Danube. For in the east the Volga-Russians, descending the river in armed hordes, captured the capital of the White Bulgars RUSSIANS and the Khazar town of Itil at the river-mouth; CAPTURE there they embarked and sailed over the Caspian to ITIL, sack another Khazar town, Semender, near the modern A.D. 969 Petrovsk. Yet another incursion of the vikings into the Caspian region was the far-famed expedition of the royal Swedish viking Ingvar Vittfarne, whose illustrious name appears on more than twenty rune-stones in his country. This prince, with a following of Swedes, made a daring voyage down the INGVAR whole length of the Volga, fighting on the way, so VITT- his saga tells, dragons and serpents and monsters of FARNE all kinds, until at last he came to Sarkland where he died in the year 1041 at the young age of twenty-five. A memorial-stone in Södermanland is thus inscribed, ' Tola set up this stone for her son Harald (or Havald), Ingvar's brother; in far-off lands they sought wealth boldly; in the east their battles spread food before the eagle; south in Sarkland they died.' [1]

Svyatoslav, for ever busy with his wars, had left the principality of Kiev divided into three parts, each committed to one of his sons, but after his death in 972 there was dispute among them and eventually the eldest, Yaropolk of Kiev, slew the second brother, Oleg, Prince of the Derevylans. At this the third son, Vladimir of Novgorod, fled to Sweden. He returned, however, in 980 with a Swedish army to the town that was his heritage and after rallying the northern Russians to his banner he marched south and overthrew Yaropolk, thus securing the whole dominion of his father for himself.

Vladimir the Great of Russia is an outstanding figure in the early history of his country. First and foremost he was a warrior; he was everywhere successful in re-imposing Kievan authority VLADIMIR upon those Slavonic tribes whose allegiance had THE wavered during the turbulent years of Svyatoslav's GREAT wars and in the subsequent period of unrest; Estland 980–1015 and the East Baltic lands were made to acknowledge his suzerainty; he proved his might by carrying the Russian arms into enemy countries; he fought the Bulgars in two victorious campaigns; he fought King Boleslav of Poland, and is even said to have invaded Eastern Galicia; also he built and garrisoned a new chain of forts to prevent the inroads of the Patzinaks. Yet it is above all as a statesman that he is renowned, for it was

[1] E. Brate, *Runverser* 84, p. 194 (A.T.S., x, 1887–91); for Ingvar, see F. Braun, *Fornvännen*, 1910, p. 99.

Vladimir who decided the destiny of Russia when he became a
convert to Orthodox Christianity and delivered the young soul
of the country into the keeping of the Patriarch of Constantinople.

He was, of course, at the outset of his reign a heathen, and
moreover a zealous one, since he owed the winning of Svyatoslav's throne to his heathen army from Sweden and he had therefore good reason to be distrustful of and antagonistic to the
CONVER-   small Christian element in the population of Kiev
SION OF   who had been the subjects of Yaropolk. But with
RUSSIA   the increase of his power and authority he began to
understand that heathendom was hindering himself and his
barbarian people from enjoying the advantages of what he now
believed to be the proper due of the Russian state, namely the
respect and confidence of the civilized world. He knew that in
Denmark at this very time King Harald Gormsson had secured
the valuable friendship of the Emperor Otto by making Christians
of the Danes, and Vladimir, no less prudent, likewise realized that
the Christian faith, whether Roman or Greek, and the faith of
Islam and also the Jewish religion, which last was now gaining
ground among the Khazars, all possessed one common property
of inestimable value in that their followers could gain admittance
on terms of equality into civilized communities where a heathen
would be abhorred. The story goes that Vladimir anxiously
debated the merits of these many religions, even sending commissioners into foreign countries in order to report how the
worshippers in each conducted their services, and that in the end
the stately and lavish splendour of the divine ceremonies in the
churches of Constantinople turned the scale in favour of Greek
orthodoxy. But it is probable that the Prince of Kiev was less
influenced by questions of dogma and ritual than by the cogent
demands of a sudden political opportunity.[1] For it happened
that the Byzantine emperor, Basil II Bulgaroctonos, sought in
988 the assistance of the Russians against the Greek rebel Bardas
Phocas, whereupon Vladimir, swollen with pride, promised the
help required of him on the condition that he received in marriage
the hand of the emperor's sister Anna. A Russian army of 6,000
men was duly despatched to serve under the emperor, and Vladimir announced his conversion to the faith of the Orthodox Church ;
nevertheless Basil, when Phocas had been killed, kept most of the

[1] The date and manner of Vladimir's conversion are both uncertain.
The chief authority is E. Golubinsky, *Istoriya Russkoy Tserkvy*, Moscow,
1901-4, I, and a summary of his views is given by M. Spinka, *Journal of
Religion*, Chicago, VI (1926), p. 40. According to Golubinsky, Vladimir
was baptized in 987, that is to say two years before the attack on Cherson.

Varangians in his employ and showed considerable hesitation in the matter of bestowing Anna upon the new convert who had been so recently not only a heathen but a polygamist of a most unsavoury sort.[1] The delay incensed Vladimir and he straightway led a force down the Dnieper and captured the Greek town of Cherson in the Crimea (989) ; the occasion was well chosen, for the Greek emperor had become involved in a war with the Bulgars and so could not come to the rescue of the colony ; therefore he found it wisest to placate the ambitious and powerful lord of Kiev by sending the princess to him and conceding Cherson as her dower.

Thereafter Vladimir showed himself no less zealous for the cause of his new faith than had been Harald Gormsson in Denmark. He was determined that his realm, willing or unwilling, should be incorporated in Christendom, that he at its head, the brother-in-law of an emperor and the most important viking prince alive, should enjoy the respect and friendship of all Christian rulers, and that in consequence he should be in a position to extract the uttermost advantage from the trade that now flourished upon the Russian rivers. Accordingly he commanded the immediate conversion of all his people, and though perhaps he did not meet with the same astonishing success that Olaf Tryggvason was to have a few years later in Norway, he nevertheless succeeded in making clear to the world that Christianity was henceforth the official religion of the Russians. It was a conversion of much the same order as that famous change of faith enacted upon Thingvellir in Iceland in 1030 when nearly all men promised to declare themselves followers of Christ, but were yet allowed to practise privily their ancient and beloved rites. For heathendom still lingered in Russia, especially among the wild and remote Vyatiches and Kriviches, even though in name at any rate most men consented to become Christians. And in thus bringing Russia within the fold of the Greek Church Vladimir completed the memorable work of Oleg. Henceforth, heart and soul, his country was to become the foster-child of Byzantium. He turned roughly aside the wooing of Rome and held the young Russian Church in steadfast allegiance to the Patriarch. So there came to his principality the Greek hierarchy, Greek prayerbooks and sacred literature, Greek education, and Greek ecclesiastical architecture and art.

Sviatopolk the Accursed succeeded to the throne of his father

---

[1] Vladimir's regiment of wives and concubines was of such notorious dimensions that a German chronicler calls him *fornicator immensus et crudelis* (*M.G.H.*, Pertz, SS. III, p. 859).

Vladimir, and he, wedded to the daughter of Boleslav of Poland and sure of Polish support, cared but little for the love of his own people. He murdered shamelessly and brutally two brothers and was afterwards so hated by the Russians that the prince and his city fell an easy prey to the armies of another son of Vladimir, Yaroslav of Novgorod. The new prince reigned, at first with a brother Mstislav as colleague, from 1019 until 1054, and in this period the state of Kiev advanced to a prosperity and brilliance such as it had not yet attained. Like his great contemporary, Cnut of England and Denmark, Yaroslav made his realm into a power of European importance. He overthrew the Patzinaks in a decisive battle and rid himself for ever of the danger from their raids ; he increased his territories westwards, taking Belz in Galicia and subduing the peoples of the Polish frontier ; he reconquered the Tchuds and founded Dorpat. Also he made important alliances with the royal houses of foreign countries ; the daughter of Olof Skotkonung of Sweden was his wife ; he married his sister to the king of Poland ; he married a daughter to King Henry I of France, another to King Andrew I of Hungary, another to Harald Hardradi of Norway ; three of his sons wedded German royalties, while a fourth married a princess of the Byzantine court. But it was not because of his conquests nor because of the brilliant alliances made by his family that Yaroslav is remembered with gratitude and that Kiev became a noble city ; it is because he beautified his capital with fine churches and monasteries, including the lovely cathedral of St. Sophia ; because he filled the town with scholars and artists ; because he built ecclesiastical schools ; because he ordered the translation of books into the Slavonic tongue ; because he sought earnestly to revise, to codify, and to enforce the legal system of the Church and State.

Yet there was one venture of Yaroslav's, a foolhardy war with the Greeks, that ended in most disastrous failure. The origin of the quarrel was the murder of a Russian nobleman following upon a riot in Constantinople, and Yaroslav, believing that this was an occasion for him to make a final and supreme demonstration of his power, for the Byzantine empire was in the hands of the weaklings Michael IV and Michael V, prepared an enormous armament wherewith to attack the Byzantine capital ; this force he entrusted to his own son Vladimir and despatched him on the luckless enterprise in 1043. The numbers of the Russians and their Scandinavian reinforcements were large, but their little boats were no match for the Greek triremes, even for the out-of-date

(marginal notes:)
YAROSLAV
1019–1054

RAID ON
CONSTAN-
TINOPLE
A.D. 1043

and discarded ships that had to be recommissioned to oppose them, and they were to discover, moreover, that they were about to attack no irresolute foe ; for when they arrived before Constantinople, it was to find that Michael V had been replaced by Constantine Monomarch. At first this great emperor, when Vladimir arrived near the capital, sought to avoid battle by negotiations, but the Russians refused to parley with him, and thereupon the Byzantine fleet was marshalled against them ; once more the emperor invited his enemy to accept compensation for the murder of their countrymen, and again the Russians answered contemptuously, demanding impossible concessions. Then Constantine ordered three of his triremes to advance to the attack and immediately they destroyed seven Russian boats with Greek Fire ; the rest of the Russian fleet took to flight, but a Greek detachment pursued them and finally Vladimir's army was overwhelmingly defeated on land. The prince himself escaped and made his way back to Russia, but most of his men who were not slaughtered on the field were captured and taken by the Greeks to the prisons of Constantinople. Seldom in all the long story of viking overboldness has an assault upon the strongholds of civilization met with defeat so crushing ; seldom have the folly and presumption of a barbarian people been rewarded with a chastisement so salutary and so severe.[1]

During Yaroslav's reign the bond uniting the state of Kiev with Scandinavia not only remained unbroken but was strengthened by an increased intercourse between Scandinavians and Russians. The prince of Kiev had taken to wife the daughter of the king of Sweden ; the fortress of Aldeigjuborg was granted RELATIONS to Ragnvald, jarl of Västergötland ; the brother-in-BETWEEN law of Yaroslav's Swedish wife, King Olaf the Saint KIEV AND of Norway, after his expulsion by Cnut, fled to the SCANDIN- Russian court, and it was with a force given to him by AVIA Yaroslav as the nucleus of his army that he set forth upon the ill-fated endeavour to recover his lost kingdom that ended in the battle of Stiklestad. The young Magnus Olafsson, before his recall as king of Norway, spent many years with Yaroslav ; Saint Olaf's half-brother, the splendid Harald Sigurdsson Hardradi, who had become a fugitive after Stiklestad, went

[1] Michael Psellos, *Chron.*, ed. Renauld, Paris, 1928, II, p. 8 ff. Michael Attaliota, p. 20 (*Corp. SS. Hist. Byz.* 34), Cedrenus, II, 551 (ib. 24). Note that the Russian chronicle (LVI) prefers to attribute the defeat of Vladimir's armament to a storm instead of the Greek Fire ; it admits, however, that the remnant of the Russians was chased by fourteen of the emperor's ships.

to Russia and was made a captain in Yaroslav's army ; later he set off upon his famous adventures in Constantinople and the Mediterranean, but it was to Yaroslav that he sent his booty and prizes and it was to the Kievan court that he returned, there to wed the Grand Prince's daughter Elisabeth, before he journeyed back to his own country and won a crown in Norway. Small wonder, then, that although the Russian state was becoming more and more Slavonic as the years passed Thietmar of Merseburg could refer in 1018 to the inhabitants of Kiev as ' Danes '.[1]

Yet by the end of Yaroslav's reign the debt of Russia to her early Scandinavian princes was determined. They had given her political form, had organized and developed her river-trade, had chosen her creed, and had bidden her fashion herself upon the illustrious model of Byzantium. After his day the Slavonic element began to overshadow the Swedish in Russian society ; intermarriage with the Slavs had left the aristocracy no longer of purely Scandinavian blood ; Slavonic speech had become the official tongue of the Church ; the Scandinavian visitors in the Russian towns passed through and did not settle therein, so that only the Slavonic and not the Swedish population increased. *Svitjod hin mikla*, Great Sweden, as Russia, the land of Kaenugard (Kiev) and Holmgard (Novgorod) was called, knew no more the armies of northern vikings who had laid the foundations of her fortunes, and now the multitudes of Slavs assumed the government and control of the country that as a result of Swedish daring and Swedish perspicacity had already won an honourable place among the Christian lands of Europe.

The memorable achievement of Yaroslav was to a large extent undermined by a complicated law of succession of his own making and by the muddling and quarrelling of his sons and grandsons. Unity vanished and a confederacy of small provinces, ruled by members of the ancient Scandinavian dynasty, but almost wholly Slavonic in speech and spirit, was left to battle with the disastrous and terrible invasion of the Polovtzi Turks that now began to break down the established trade-routes and was soon to cut off Russia from the Byzantine mainspring of her inspiration. Only Vladimir Monomarch (1113–1125) and his son Mstislav I (1125–1132) of Yaroslav's house regained at Kiev the power and glory that had been won by their viking ancestors, and with the death of Mstislav the great days of the principality ended.

The breaking of the Swedish connexion with north Russia did

[1] *M.G.H.* (Pertz), SS. III, 871.   The word *Danes* is here an equivalent of Scandinavians.

not occur until long after the closing of the trade-routes due
to the Polovtzi invasion. In Novgorod Scandinavian settlers
remained and there at Gutagard the merchants of Gotland had
an emporium and a guild-house in the twelfth century. But this
trade across the Baltic lasted only until the fourteenth century
when the Hansa League made it impossible for an independent
Scandinavian settlement to survive in a foreign town. Then
was the place named Novgorod and an end came to the long
centuries wherein trader-Swedes had made their home in Russia.[1]

One reason for the decline in power of the Swedish aristocrats
who ruled Russia was the everlasting sapping of their strength
by Constantinople. For the Queen of Cities, rich beyond com-
parison and luxurious beyond description, was always the goal
of the viking's dearest and most adventurous ambitions and one
that tantalized him into the supreme enterprise of seeking his
fortune not in the dim trading-booths of the Russian rivers or
in the barbarian wildernesses of northern Europe but within the
golden gates of the fairest city in Christendom. To Mikligard
or Tsarigrad, as the Northmen and the Russians called the
Byzantine capital, the Swedish merchants had found their way
long before the control of the Russian waterways passed into
their keeping, and the safety of the Russian travellers
thither, and their status when arrived, was the chief
concern of the first viking princes of Kiev, the object
of their demonstrations against the Greeks, and the main
content of the diplomatic conversations between the two
peoples. But it was not so much the advantages of trade within
the walls of Constantinople that enticed the Swedish lords of
Russia to take leave of their city-states, it was the opportunity of
embarking upon a career wherein honour and wealth might be
won nobly by sword and axe in a gallant company whose headquarters was the royal palace itself. This corps was the emperor's
Varangian Guard.

Even in the early days of the Swedish supremacy in Russia
there had been Scandinavian mercenaries in the Greek forces in
addition to the many other foreigners who were bought into the
armies of Byzantium.[2] In 911 as many as 700 Russians had been

CONSTAN-
TINOPLE
AND THE
VARANGIAN
GUARD

---

[1] For the survival of Swedish sagas in Russian folk-tales (bylins), see S.
Roznieski, *Varaegiske Minder i den russiske Heltedigtning*, Copenhagen, 1914.

[2] Miss Katherine M. Buck has reminded me that there is some evidence
for the appearance of northerners in Constantinople long before the Viking
Period and it is therefore possible that the Varangian Guard has a history
that goes much further back than is commonly supposed (see her *Wayland-
Dietrich Saga*, nos. 91–96, p. 156, n. 3 and Index vol. to Pt. 1, p. 173,
n. iv).

enlisted in a Greek expedition under the admiral Himerius against Crete,[1] and in the '30s, during the reign of Romanus Lecapenus, over 400 of them in seven ships took part in a Greek invasion of southern Italy ;[2] indeed, the proper treatment of such Russian auxiliaries and the supply of them had been regulated in the treaties with Byzantium made by the princes Oleg and Igor of Kiev. In 949 another Greek force collected for an attack upon Crete was strengthened by nine boats containing over 600 Russians, while seven more Russian boats patrolled the coasts of Dalmatia,[3] and in 956 there were Christian Russians at the emperor's court on the occasion of the reception of the Caliph's ambassadors. There had been Russians in the Byzantine armies during the Mesopotamian wars against the Caliphate in the late '40s and '50s, and in 986 the Italian Liudprand noticed two Russian ships included in the imperial fleet.[4] The Greeks, therefore, had had throughout the tenth century a full opportunity of recognizing the worth and prowess of these hardy giants from the north and their Slavonic followers, and no one better appreciated their value than the emperor himself.

The establishment of a large and permanent Russian company in the regiments of the imperial guard was probably the work of the Emperor Basil II Bulgaroctonos, who had enlisted the services of 6,000 men sent to him by Vladimir of Kiev in 988 (p. 164). For a considerable time before this the guard had included a corps of foreigners made up of detachments of Russians, Khazars, and others, but this Varangian *druzhina*, or brigade, of Vladimir's, consisting no doubt mainly of Swedish volunteers, was assuredly the nucleus of that special company of Scandinavians that became the Varangian Guard of history.[5]

The worth of these northerners for the emperor lay not so much in their unquestionable valour and fighting-skill as in their

[1] Constantine Porphyrogenitus, *De Cerem.*, II, 44 (*C.S.H.B.*, p. 651, and cf. pp. 654–5).

[2] Ib. p. 660.

[3] Ib. (II, 45), p. 664. There were 584 Russians and with them 42 others, boys and servants.

[4] *Legatio*, ed. Pertz, 1839, p. 198.

[5] The most detailed study on this subject, including a full account of the Norse material and Harald Hardradi's adventures, is a long essay (in Russian) by V. G. Vasilievsky entitled ' The Varangian-Russian and the Varangian-English corps at Constantinople in the eleventh and twelfth centuries ' (*J.M.N.P.*, 1874, Pt. 176, p. 105 ; 1875, Pt. 177, p. 394, and Pt. 178, p. 76) ; this is reprinted in the *Works*, St. P., 1908, I, p. 176, where it is accompanied by another paper on the same subject, p. 378. Cf. also a paper (in Danish) by G. Storm ' Harald Hardradi and the Varangians ', *Hist. Tidskrift*, 2 R. IV (1884), p. 354.

disinterested zeal for the fulfilment of their duty. Moreover, because they were not sprung of races living close upon the borders of the eastern empire their presence in the palace and their attachment to the person of the emperor occasioned none of the heart-burnings and jealousies that resulted from favours shown to Armenians, Bulgars, Arabs, Turks, and Georgians, and because the land of their birth lay thus far away the chances of disloyalty among them, should they be called upon to fight against their own countrymen, were minimized.[1] In addition to this, they had yet one other recommendation to the imperial favour, for the Varangians knew little or no Greek and were therefore not likely to be corrupted by court intrigues or to become disaffected during those dangerous periods when sedition was rife among the Greek-speaking regiments of the line. It was for these reasons that the Scandinavian detachment was preferred to the other companies of foreign mercenaries and entrusted with the honour of being the sovereign's personal guard.

The Icelandic saga-writers of the early Middle Ages believed that two of their countrymen had served in this guard as early as the middle of the tenth century,[2] and they also tell how a third Icelander had won fame in this body at about the same time of its first appearance in Byzantine history.[3] But the value of their evidence is in this instance but slight, and there is no good reason for thinking that a special Scandinavian company of the palace-guard was in existence before the beginning of the eleventh century. In fact, in Greek history they are not heard of until Cedrenus describes the events connected with the accession of Michael IV the Paphlagonian in 1034,[4] but it is clear from the nature of his allusion to them that they must have been a recognized body in the brigade of guards during the reign of Michael's predecessor Romanus II (1020–1034). The Varangians are mentioned on the occasion of the dismissal of some of them, probably those who were serving in the army of George

---

[1] But that they should be required to do so was not out of the question, for there were Scandinavians in other armies than the Greek, particularly in the Norman hosts. Thus Bohemund of Antioch, son of Robert Guiscard, had ' men of the island of Thule ' in his train in 1107 when he invaded Albania and was besieged by Alexius Comnenus. Note that Anna Comnena says of these men that they were accustomed to fight for the Greeks (Alexiad, C.H.S.B., 25, ii, p. 172), for some take this to mean that these men of Thule were deserters from the Varangian Guard ; but this is very unlikely.

[2] Hrafnkelssaga, ed. Hannaas, 1907, pp. 10, 28.

[3] Laxdaelasaga, ed. Kaalund (AN. S.B. 4), LXIII. But this reference to Bolli Bollason is almost entirely apocryphal.

[4] Cedrenus, Syn. Hist., C.S.H.B., 24, ii, p. 508.

Maniaces in Asia Minor, into winter-quarters, this suggesting that they were then only ordinary mercenaries ; but the historian afterwards uses the expression ' Greek and Varangian palace-guards ', adding that the Varangians were of ' Celtic ' stock.[1]

One of the most famous personages who served in this guard, and one who is sometimes said to have been its founder, was the royal Norwegian Harald Sigurdsson Hardradi (p. 126). The prince was born in 1015 and while still a boy had fought for his half-brother St. Olaf at Stiklestad (1030), where he was HARALD HARDRADI wounded ; after Olaf's fall he fled first to Sweden and then to Russia, where he entered the service of Yaroslav, as has been related, and became in a very short time a trusted and redoubtable captain in the Russian army. But when he was only twenty years old he embarked upon the supreme adventure of a visit to Constantinople and there he arrived with 500 men in his train in 1034, the very year when the Varangian corps is first mentioned in Byzantine history. The Greeks hailed him as the ' King of Varangia ',[2] but the emperor Michael IV the Paphlagonian (1035–1041) and the Empress Zoe, after welcoming him, at once gave him the opportunity of proving his prowess in the field by inviting him to take part in the Arab wars in Asia Minor. Harald and his men proceeded to the theatre of war where the brilliant young general George Maniaces commanded, and here the ardent Norwegian prince soon covered himself with glory. The campaign took him in 1035 east to the Euphrates and it is said [3] of him that he captured 80 strongholds of the Arabs and then turned south to threaten Jerusalem, harrying on both sides of Jordan as he approached the town. But after the capture of Edessa by Maniaces in 1031 the emperor had begun negotiations with the Caliph, and in 1036 a treaty was made with the Muslims whereby the Christians secured access to its holy places without waiting for Harald's attack upon Jerusalem.

The Norwegian prince returned to Constantinople, but his sojourn there was a short one, for his next adventure was a

[1] Cedrenus, ib., p. 613.

[2] See an anonymous *Book of Advice* edited with the *Strategicon of Cecaumenos* by V. G. Vasilievsky and V. Jernstedt, St. P., 1896, p. 99. Harald is referred to as Ἀράλτης βασιλέως βαραγγίας.

[3] *Heimskringla, H. harðráði*, III–XV, contains the Norse version of Harald's adventures in the Greek service. As the account was derived from his comrade and countryman Halldor Snorrason it might be expected to have considerable historical value, but the saga-writer's ignorance of eastern geography and of Byzantine affairs has reduced Halldor's story to a muddled rigmarole of dubious worth. It is chiefly interesting for the account of the rivalry between Harald and Maniaces that culminated in Harald acting independently of his commander-in-chief in Sicily.

share in the Greek attempt in 1038 to win back Sicily from the Arabs, and again George Maniaces was his commander-in-chief. The new campaign, in which a number of Norman soldiers also took part, opened with a series of fine victories and it was not long before Messina and Syracuse, with all the eastern part of Sicily between them, fell into the hands of the Greeks. But Maniaces in this hour of triumph was rewarded only by the jealousy and suspicion of his imperial master and was recalled to the Byzantine court, there to languish in disgrace ; then the Norman auxiliaries departed after a quarrel about their pay and Harald's Scandinavians likewise became discontented. Subsequently all the newly conquered territory, except for the town of Messina, was recovered by the Saracens and in 1041 the Greek general who had supplanted the too-successful Maniaces removed the Greek army to southern Italy to fight against the Normans. Harald took part in this short Italian campaign and then went back in the middle of this same year to Constantinople. The sick and troubled emperor loaded him with honours, making him *manglavite,* a high official of the imperial entourage, and with Michael Harald and the Varangians shortly afterwards set off to take a part in the Bulgar war that was fought in the late autumn. On the return he was promoted to the rank of *spatharocandidate,* the third highest grade of officials in attendance upon the emperor, and his position at the palace seemed to be one of enviable pre-eminence and security ; but at the end of this fateful year Michael died. He was succeeded by Michael V Calaphates, a stranger to the Macedonian dynasty, and at once the court was in a turmoil of intrigue and revolt. Four months later, after the upstart's senseless persecution of Harald's aged friend the Empress Zoe, there was a revolution. The infuriated mob flung themselves upon the palace walls and after two days and two nights of fierce and bloody battling the people burst their way into the imperial apartments. The emperor and his hated uncle had fled, but the mob discovered their whereabouts and surged angrily after them, eventually to batter their way into the Stadion Church where they had taken refuge. It was Harald Hardradi, captain of the guard, who, when the fugitives were dragged to the Sigma, upon the prefect's bidding gouged out their eyes.

After these terrible days of carnage in April of 1042 Harald did not remain long in Constantinople, and in the days of Constantine IX Monomarchus he decided to return to his own country where his nephew Magnus was now king. It is said that he was refused permission to leave the Greek capital and that he was cast in prison, perhaps under the suspicion of having connived at the luckless Russian raid upon Constantinople in 1043 ; but he was able to escape and to make his way back to Yaroslav in Kiev, to whom he had already despatched a great part of the booty won by the prowess of his arms.

But the Varangian Guard was not dissolved either by the shattering disaster of the revolution or by Harald's departure, for fresh adventurers continued to arrive from the north to swell their numbers, and the corps remained a permanent and privileged part of the army.

These Varangians were known to the Greeks as the ' axe-bearing barbarians ', and more than once Anna Comnena refers to them by this name in the *Alexiad*, the ponderous biography that she wrote of her father the Emperor Alexius (1081–1118). She paid a high tribute to their loyalty, saying they deemed themselves bound to the emperor's service by inviolate ties that were already an ancestral tradition among some of them, being handed down from father to son, and she declared that they would not hearken to a single treacherous word ; [1] she tells also of their foolhardy gallantry at the battle of Durazzo (1082), when the Varangian corps under a captain named Narbites was cut to pieces. [2] Another historian, Zonaras, describes the loyalty of the Varangian guard to their master Alexius at the time of his death, [3] yet it seems that there was some reason to suspect that the fidelity of this illustrious corps was not always unshakeable ; for it is certain that the Varangians mutinied in the reign of Alexius's predecessor, Nicephorus III Botaniates (1078–1081), [4] and Alexius himself on the occasion (1103) when he entertained the Danish king Eric I is said to have been seriously afraid that the Varangians would transfer their allegiance to the northern king who could address them in their own tongue. [5] He took considerable precautions to prevent this, but Eric, when at last he was allowed to address some of the guard, congratulated them on having attained the highest honour to which a northerner could aspire ; they were, he said, far more fortunate than their stay-at-home brethren and therefore he charged them to fit themselves for their high office by the constant practice of virtue and sobriety. To his own countrymen he promised rewards upon their return commensurate with their services to the Byzantine emperor,

[1] *Alexiad*, C.S.H.B., 25, i, p. 120 (II, 9 : 62).
[2] Ib., p. 211 (IV, 6 : 116).
[3] *C.S.H.B.* 29, iii, p. 763 (Epit. XVIII, 29, 1–10).
[4] Ib. p. 722 (Epit. XVIII, 7–8).
[5] *Saxo*, ed. Müller, XII, p. 610. Cf. *Knytlingasaga*, ed. Petersens and Olson, 81, p. 192, where the incident is not mentioned.

while if they fell in battle he pledged himself to take care of their families.

At first these Northmen of the guard were well paid, for quarters and food were free and each man received as much as 10 to 15 gold solidi for a month's service, together with various special grants and prize-monies, so that soon the Scandinavians and other northerners who came to Constantinople with the intention of joining this favoured band of foreigners had to pay heavily for their commission in the guard. Of its normal strength and of its officers little is known, but in the field the corps was commanded by a chieftain (ἡγεμών) of Varangian blood, while in the palace the chief authority was vested in an official,

FIG. 23.—Seal of Michael, Pansebastos of the Varangians (½)

probably a Greek, known as the *pansebastos* and *megalodier-meneutes*, who, as the title of his office explains, was the supreme officer-in-command and principal interpreter of the corps, and one whose duty must have been the administration of the regiment on behalf of the Byzantine government. An impression in lead of the seal (Fig. 23) of one of these civil administrators, a man named Michael, still exists [1] ; upon the obverse is the figure of his patron the archangel and on the reverse are his titles ' pansebastos, sebastos and megalodiermeneutes of the Varangians ' with a representation below this of the famous axe that gave the Varangian Guard their sobriquet of πελεκυφόροι, the ' axe-bearers ' ; but this seal is probably no earlier than the thirteenth century, and though the blade of the axe is not unlike those of the late Viking Period that have been found in the north (cf. Pl. V), the weapon here is probably meant to be a version of some special variety of medieval pole-arm that resembled the Scottish lochaber in appearance ; or, perhaps, as the drawing on the seal

[1] A. Mordtmann, *Archives de l'orient Latin*, I (1881), p. 698 ; G. Schlumberger, *Sigillographie de l'empire byzantin*, Paris, 1884, p. 350.

suggests, it was a short-handled battle-axe of eastern European variety.[1]

The fighting skill of the splendid northern warriors and their own adventurous spirit was sufficient to ensure that these vikings in the service of the Greek emperor were not merely household troops and guards of parade. They fought abroad when their THE master willed it and many were their adventures. The PIRAEUS disastrous and complete annihilation of the Varangian LION section of the Greek army at the battle of Durazzo, the result of their improvident ardour in the fight, is described in the *Alexiad*, but the most remarkable witness to the exploits of the Scandinavians in the Greek world is not to be found among the writings of an historian ; it is the great white marble lion that now stands sentinel, with three companions, outside the gates of the Arsenal in Venice (Frontispiece). The two largest of these four lions are known as the Piraeus lions because they were brought back to Italy in triumph from the Piraeus harbour [2] of Athens by the Doge Francesco Morosini at the end of the seventeenth century ; the bigger of the two, a huge beast squatting on his haunches and measuring about 12 feet in height, is a Greek carving probably of the second or third century A.D., and near to it when it stood in its original position in Greece some Scandinavian soldiers upon at least one occasion were encamped ; for its two flanks are defaced by ribbons of their ugly runes. The carving of this inscription on the lion was done, as its style shows, in the second half of the eleventh century and there is little doubt that it is the work of Swedes.[3]

Except in the illustrious instance of the Norwegian Harald Hardradi, little or nothing is known of the names or deeds of the Scandinavians who served in the Varangian Guard and who took part in the emperor's wars ; for it is likely that most of them,

[1] Miss Katherine Buck has shown me a picture of a Frankish pole-arm that should be compared with the axe on the seal. It is figured in H. Testard's ed. of Thierry, *Recits des temps mérovingiens*, London, 1888, frontispiece, and has a curved blade like a hockey-stick with an axe projecting from the side (all cast in one piece).

[2] For the original position of the large lion, see C. C. Rafn, *Antiquités de l'Orient*, Copenhagen, 1865, p. 62 ff.

[3] Eric Brate read the inscription as a memorial to the Swede Horsa (Haase), already commemorated on an Uppland rune-stone as an adventurer who went to Greece to win fame and fortune ; for this and for earlier readings see *A.T.S.*, XX (1919), 3, and for an English rendering of Brate's version see E. V. Gordon, *Intr. Old Norse*, Oxford, 1927, p. 172. Brate claimed that he read the runes under exceptionally favourable conditions, but there is little doubt that the inscription, except for a few isolated phrases, is really illegible. Haakon Shetelig (*Fornvännen*, 1923,

since the route to Constantinople lay along the waterways of Russia, were Swedes whose Swedish sagas had no interest for the Icelandic historian of later days. But on rune-stones in Sweden there are inscriptions telling of a few of these men, and the best known is one at Ed near Stockholm that commemorates the mother of a man named Ragnvald who had been a military chief in Greece.[1] From the style of the runes it is clear that Ragnvald must have served in Constantinople during the days of the earlier Comneni, either in the reign of Isaac or Alexius, and perhaps was in the city in that fateful year of 1058 when the Varangian Guard, acting under the orders of the Emperor Isaac, arrested the Patriarch Michael Cerularius.

As an episode in viking history the story of the Varangian Guard is but of slight interest after the middle of the eleventh century ; for when Maniaces returned to Constantinople from his short governorship of south Italy in 1042 he brought with him many Norman adventurers who were recruited for the Greek army and subsequently drafted into the guard. Indeed, after 1066 the ranks of the guard were filled not so much by Scandinavians as by the numerous Englishmen and Danes who fled from England after the Conquest and by discontented Norman soldiers who deserted from France or Italy to Greece ; so it came about that it was as an English and Norman-French body rather than as a Scandinavian corps that the guard ended its short but eventful history at the time of the fall of Constantinople to the Latins in 1204.[2]

In addition to the Scandinavian visitors in the Greek capital who came either to soldier or to trade, there were many other NORTHMEN Northmen who found their way thither when the AND THE call to the crusades provided the spirited folk of Scan- CRUSADES dinavia and Denmark with a new field for adventure. It was a party of these ' Jerusalem-farers ', men of Norway,

p. 201) was brave enough to declare that this is so, and though Brate, just before his death, defended his reading (ib., p. 222), and though archaeologists have been warned not to meddle in the domain of the runologist, I must also state that after a careful examination of the lion under varying lighting conditions I came to the opinion that only by supernatural inspiration can sufficient characters be recognized among these worn and feeble letters to make an intelligible legend.

[1] á Griklandi liðsforungi (A.T.S. 10, p. 84) ; the usual translation ' chief of the bodyguard ' is a trifle bold.

[2] For references to the English in the Varangian Guard see Vasilievsky, op. cit. (p. 170), and also G. Buckler, Anna Comnena, Oxford, p. 366, n. 1. Mr. Robert Byron makes an interesting reference to the often-mentioned tombstones of the Varangians on p. 147 of his Byzantine Achievement (London, 1929).

Orkney, and Shetland, who, halting in the Orkneys in the first
winter of their expedition (c. 1152), broke into the huge prehistoric
cairn of Maeshow and scratched many lines of feeble runes and
a little drawing of a wounded dragon upon the walls of the magnificent, but empty, burial-chamber that they found.   Many
crusaders were illustrious folk whose names are familiar in
northern history,[1] and the most famous of them were King Eric
of Denmark and King Sigurd Magnusson (Jerusalem-farer) of
Norway, who both arrived in Constantinople during the reign of
Alexius Comnenus, Eric, as was told above, about the year 1103
and Sigurd some eight years later.   This Norwegian king left his
country in 1108, spent the winter in England, and then journeyed
with his host to France and Spain, passing his second winter in
Galicia ; in 1110 he sailed for the Mediterranean and arrived in
the Balearic Islands, where he inflicted a heavy defeat upon the
Saracen population ; thence he went to southern Italy, where the
Normans showed themselves willing to take him for their chief,
but Sigurd remained faithful to his purpose and in the same year
he reached Palestine.   In 1111, after fighting in the Holy Land,
he came to Constantinople and there he was received at the Golden
Gates by the emperor himself, who welcomed him with all the
prodigal and glittering magnificence of Byzantine state ceremonial.   It was a visit never to be forgotten by the Norsemen
in Sigurd's train ; they were housed in splendour, overwhelmed
with costly gifts, and entertained with banquets and with games
in the great hippodrome where these simple souls took the statues
for gods.   Sigurd left for the north again as a devoted adherent
of the emperor and at their parting gave to him the dragon-head
from the prow of his own ship, a work of northern craftsmanship
that was once erroneously believed to have found its way back
from the warm south and to be none other than the dragon that
to this day scowls down from its cold belfry-summit in Ghent
over the roofs and gables of a Flemish city.

[1] The evidence is set forth in the notable work by Paul Riant,
Expéditions et pèlinerages des Scandinaves en Terres Saintes, Paris, 1865.

CHAPTER VI

THE SOUTH AND EAST BALTIC COASTS

IN the middle of the tenth century Denmark, under that restless and ambitious king, Harald Gormsson, was chief of the northern powers. Both Norway and Sweden knew her might, but there was a third land that had learnt to fear her and that was the country of the Wends, a group of recently arrived Slavonic people who had established themselves during the seventh century in the country between the Elbe and the Weichsel. Here, in the district where that thronged trade-route between north and south, the river Oder, reached the sea, these Wends had a town by name of Jumne (or Vineta) and thither flocked merchants and adventurers from Scandinavia and Russia, from Germany and from Central Europe, from the East even, for the purposes of barter and exchange. Great was the wealth that passed through this people's hands.

To Wendland, somewhere about the year A.D. 960, came Harald with fire and sword, soon to make himself master of the Oder mouth, and that this new and profitable dominion might not easily slip from under his suzerainty, that the many pirates who haunted the Oder and Peenemunde flats might no longer vex his own kingdom, he built close to Jumne a stronghold, or fortified harbour, that was known as Jomsborg.[1] It was, according to later accounts, a mighty place ; 360 warships could ride at anchor shut within the port, this having a harbour-entrance of stone that could be closed by iron doors and that was bridged over by an arch with a tower above bearing giant catapults for its defence. Probably, as at Hedeby and elsewhere in the north, a huge semi-circular vallum guarded the land-area of the fortress.

[1] That Harald founded Jomsborg (*Knytlingasaga* and *Fagrskinna*) is more likely than the tale in *Jómsvíkingasaga* to the effect that it was built by Palnatoki, the Danish viking from Wales, who had won the friendship of Boleslav, king of the Wends. The best study of the historical material relating to Jomsborg is that by L. Weibull, *Nordens hist. o. år* 1000, Lund, 1911, p. 178, who comes to the unwelcome conclusion that Jomsborg and the Jomsvikings never existed at all. The student should not fail to make himself acquainted with this author's cogent arguments, for there can be no doubt that the whole story of the Danish fortress and its vikings must rest under suspicion.

Exactly where this great stronghold was no man knows.   At one time it was confidently believed to have been on the Silberberg just to the north of Wollin, for this town has the name of Julin in Latin, which is enough like Jumne to suggest at any rate that the site of the market-town of the Wends was Wollin itself ; but subsequent criticism has overthrown this identification, while as

FIG. 24.—The Jomsborg district

for the view that Jomsborg and Silberberg are the same, archaeological research has satisfactorily established the certainty that there was no viking settlement here close to Wollin. Another hypothesis is that the fortress of Jomsborg stood on land, since submerged, off the north-west point of Usedom, either the Peenemunde shoals or the isolated Veritas Grund, on the south coast of Greifswalder Bodden between Ruden Island

and Greifswalder Oie,[1] and though under present conditions archaeology can neither prove nor disprove the existence of Jomsborg upon this lost land,[2] at least there is no doubt that once there were vikings in this locality, for five gold armlets such as they wore were found in 1905 at the extreme end of the Peenemunde peninsula. They are now in the Stettin Museum.

It seems that the Wends very quickly accustomed themselves to the overlordship of the Danish king, finding that this great fortress of the vikings protected them from the attacks of pirates and gave to the trading-town of Jumne a sense of security that it had hitherto lacked. Their rulers, therefore, were at some pains to keep on friendly terms with the governors of Jomsborg and the Danish royalties, and it was doubtless in order to cement this alliance between the Danes and the Wends that Duke Mesko of Poland, the father of that noble prince Boleslav Chrobri, married one of his daughters to Jarl Sigvaldi of Jomsborg and another to Harald Gormsson's successor, King Svein. Thus the fortunes of Wendland were closely bound up with the affairs of viking Denmark so that soon the interests of Jomsborg and Jumne were identical, and it is perhaps this circumstance that accounts for the story that Jomsborg was built by Palnatoki who received the land whereon it stood as a gift from the king of Wendland ; it is certainly for this reason that the stronghold and the town were later believed to be the same place, the Norse sagas never mentioning Jumne, but Jomsborg only, while the German histories refer always to Jumne and not to Jomsborg. And that there should be confusion here is all the more likely because the viking stronghold had but a short life of some eighty years only.

In spite of the friendship between the Wends and the Danes, Jomsborg itself was inhabited by a purely viking garrison, and legend tells that this society within the fortress was governed by strict rules. There were no women at all allowed inside and each one of the men was a warrior of tested valour, not older than fifty years of age nor younger than eighteen. Courage, and courage alone, won admission to their company, and in that company a self-sacrificing loyalty to each and all of one's fellows was demanded of the Jomsvikings, slander of any kind was

---

[1] On this subject see Sofus Larsen, *Aarb. f. nordisk Oldkyndighed og Historie*, III R., 17 (1927), p. 1 ; this paper is continued, ib., 18 (1928), p. 1. See also C. Schuchhardt, *Sitzungsberichte der preussichen Akad. der Wissenschaften*, 1924, p. 176.

[2] On the supposed ' ruins ' of Usedom—which until the middle of the nineteenth century were identified as the lost city of Vineta, see R. H. Major, *Archaeologia*, XXXVI (1855), p. 85.

prohibited, and the private retention of booty forbidden. Military efficiency was the sole object of their organization and regulations, and though no single man might be away from the fortress for more than three days without special licence, each summer the Jomsvikings were abroad together fighting, and so widespread did their fame become that soon they were counted as the greatest warriors of the North.

These redoubtable vikings of Jomsborg made more than one appearance in history before they and their fortress were destroyed in 1043. The first occasion, and the most memorable, was in the year 985 or 986 when Jarl Sigvaldi was governor. It was the time of the civil war in Denmark between Harald Gormsson and his son Svein, he who was later conqueror of England, and the story begins with the death of Harald at Jomsborg and the restoration of peace between the Jomsvikings and the Danes under King Svein. This was confirmed by a visit of the Jomsvikings to Denmark where they were present at a funeral feast given by Svein in memory of Harald. Ale flowed freely, talking and boasting grew wild, and after Svein had gloriously declared that he would conquer England, Sigvaldi, not to be outdone, swore on his part that before three years were passed he would either kill Jarl Haakon of Norway or drive him from the land ; thereupon many of the other Jomsvikings at once pledged themselves to accompany their leader on this mad enterprise and to perform various deeds of daring on their own account in Norway. Next morning they all agreed that the preposterous boasting of their drunkenness had involved them in an undertaking that was of almost suicidal idiocy, but to the Jomsvikings their oaths were sacred ; they were pledged to attack Haakon in Norway and it seemed to them that their only hope was to invade the country at once before the great Jarl got news of their intention and while his forces, since it was in the depth of winter, were disbanded. Late in December, accordingly, with a fleet of sixty magnificent long-ships they sailed to Norway in the hopes of surprising Haakon, and after making their way plundering up the west coast they came at length to Hareidland in Söndmör, where they were told by a Norwegian farmer the gratifying news that Haakon, accompanied by only one or two ships, lay in the neighbouring Jörundfjord. Into the fjord, then, sailed the fleet of the Jomsvikings, joyfully assured that the Jarl was now their easy prey ; but the sight they saw must have chilled even their brave hearts, for they came upon Haakon and his son Eric, long warned of the impending attack, waiting for them with a huge fleet of 180 ships.

Yet after the first shock of seeing this enormous levy of Norwegian strength in grim readiness for them, they had no reason to fear disaster; for they knew themselves the hardest fighters among all vikings, while their sixty great warships were worth more than all Haakon's miserable and hastily collected little craft. So they ranged themselves for battle and advanced boldly to the conflict. Fierce, indeed, was the mighty battle of Jörundfjord, and at first it was the Jomsvikings who seemed likely to gain the day; but Haakon sacrificed (his son, so it is said) to the gods, Eric rallied the scattering Norwegian boats, and in the end the Danes, fighting with glorious valour but hopelessly outnumbered, knew themselves faced with defeat; so thirty-five of their ships, with Sigvaldi at the head, broke from the battle in flight. Twenty-five of the Jomsborg ships were captured or sunk by Haakon, and many Danish prisoners, some of them famous chiefs, fell into the hands of the Jarl. One of these was Vagn Aakeson of Fyn, and the story of the brave contempt for death shown by eighteen of his followers when one by one they were beheaded by Thorkel Leira, the executioner appointed by Harald, how Vagn himself slew Thorkel and won, as he had sworn he would, Thorkel's daughter, this is the splendid finale of the *Jómsvíkingasaga* and is a tale that is also told by Snorri in the *Heimskringla*, where it is to be counted among the most exciting and dramatic passages in that noble history.

That the Jomsvikings turned their arms against Sweden too is likely enough, but the fantastic legend of their adventures in that country under the leadership of their governor Styrbjorn, in company with Harald Gormsson's troops, when they fought against King Eric Segersäll (died c. A.D. 995) and were defeated on the Fyris Plain near Old Uppsala, cannot be history. More credible is the story how under the double-faced Sigvaldi the Jomsvikings played a part in the downfall of King Olaf Tryggvason of Norway in A.D. 1000.

The last adventure of the Norwegian king's crowded life opens with his sudden appearance in Wendland at the head of a fleet of warships, this move presumably being the prelude to a mighty crusade against heathen Denmark or heathen Sweden, for both these countries, jealous of his ever-increasing power, had become his enemies. He made an alliance with Boleslav I (992–1025) of Poland and then paid a visit to Sigvaldi at Jomsborg. Now Sigvaldi, who was a Dane and an ally, if not a vassal, of the Danish king, received Olaf well, but he lost no time in informing Svein of the Norwegian strength and purposely delayed Olaf in Jomsborg with excuse after excuse until the Danes, the Swedes under Olof Skotkonung, and a company of Norwegians under the rebellious Jarl Eric, had had time to unite their forces.

But at last Olaf heard rumours of the movements of his enemies and became suspicious of his long entertainment in Jomsborg, so he set sail with a fleet of seventy-one long-ships. The main body headed for the open Baltic under separate orders, but Olaf with eleven of his largest warships steered on another course, hugging the land on the advice of Sigvaldi, who had lent him some ships manned by Jomsvikings and claimed that he knew the shoals and currents of the north German coast better than any other pilot. So Sigvaldi skilfully led the king towards the mouth of the Svold inlet on the mainland coast somewhere in the neighbourhood of Rügen where he knew that the fleets of Olaf's enemies were concentrated ; he had sailed a little way ahead with his own Jomsborg contingent and when he approached the fleets of the allies he lowered sail and rowed behind an island into the sound where they lay at anchor. Olaf, following with his few ships, likewise turned into the sound and there he discovered himself face to face with the full battle-array of his foes. Then followed the famous sea-fight that ended in the death by drowning of King Olaf Tryggvason.

The Jomsvikings were also known in the west, though their name is not actually recorded in the German and English chronicles. Yet it is certain enough that a large band of them not only plundered and harried in Holland and England, but even entered the service of the king of England and fought for him against their fellow-Danes. For Olaf the Saint, in the course of a viking expedition made in the days of his youth before he was king of Norway, arrived in Jomsborg, where he discovered a great fleet being fitted out by Thorkel the Tall, Sigvaldi's brother, and to this force the future saint joined his own ship.[1] The Jomsborg expedition was preparing to go a-viking in the west, probably at the bidding of King Svein who was now bent upon the conquest of England and is said to have provided men and boats to increase the strength of Thorkel's armament ; when it was ready for sea in the year A.D. 1009, this flotilla steered for the coast of Frisia, sacked the town of Tiel and threatened Utrecht,[2]

[1] It is quite likely that Olaf did not really join Thorkel's fleet until this was already operating in England, for the chronology and accounts of his movements are by no means clear. The suggestion that the Jomsvikings attacked Jutland on their way to Frisia and England is scarcely to be credited and it is more probable that this was a private enterprise of Olaf's.

[2] For the tangled story of the Dutch raids, see Jan de Vries, *De Wikingen in de lage landen bij de Zee*, Haarlem, 1923, p. 304 ff.

and then descended upon the luckless kingdom of Æthelred the
Unready (p. 264). The Jomsvikings plundered pitilessly in the
south of England, wintered on the Thames, and made more than
one attack upon London ; then in 1010 they went into East
Anglia, defeated the local levies, plundered inland to Northampton
and burnt that town ; in 1011 they moved south again and
sacked Canterbury. They murdered the archbishop, after holding
him to ransom, and when at length Æthelred had bribed them with
sufficiently enormous sums of money Thorkel, with forty-five of
his ships, and Olaf too, abandoned their maraudings and suddenly
professed themselves willing to take up arms on behalf of the
English king. In the wars with Svein in 1013 these Jomsvikings
and Norwegians helped Æthelred to defend London against the
invading Danes, but when in 1014 the English cause seemed to
be hopeless Thorkel, though he received yet another payment
from Æthelred, sailed off to Denmark and placed himself and his
vikings at the disposal of King Cnut.

It was in the year 1043 that young Magnus Olafsson the Good,
king both of Norway and Denmark, put a sudden end to the great
stronghold of Jomsborg and its famous vikings. They were, he
must have believed, endangering the existence of his flimsy
double-kingdom, for the Jomsvikings did not consider that they
owed Magnus allegiance nor that the homage paid to him by
Svein Estridsson of Denmark affected their own imagined independence ; moreover, it was clear to Magnus that they might
at any time throw in their lot with the numerous and powerful
Wends who were now threatening hostilities against the Scandinavian power. Therefore he sailed at the head of a mighty fleet
and took Jomsborg, then under the command of Harald Thorkels-
son, by storm ; he destroyed it utterly, burning the buildings to
the ground and putting the captured vikings to the sword.

So ended in fire and massacre the stronghold that Harald
Gormsson had built, the fortress whose fierce and terrible warriors
had been renowned above all other vikings. But though Magnus
had shown the strength of his arm in Wendland, the peaceful
town of Jumne, for over eighty years defended by the vanquished
Jomsborg, remained. And the Wends rose in this same year ;
with a huge army they invaded Denmark and there on Lürschau
Heath, west of Hedeby, they pitted themselves against the
conqueror of the Danish fortress that had for so long protected
their coast-lands. The victory went to Magnus, and so it came
about that the fall of Jomsborg was the immediate prelude to the
decisive battle that for ever put an end to the further expansion
of the Slavs northwards and westwards.

All the east German coast from Jomsborg to the Kurisches Haff lay exposed to the attacks of Danish and Swedish buccaneers, but except for the commercial importance of the river-mouths neither merchants nor marauders found much induce-

NORTH-EAST GERMANY ment to exploit these flatlands where west of the Weichsel dwelt the Wends and where in East Prussia a partly Baltic and partly Germanic folk, who had resisted the Slavonic invasion, maintained a precarious existence.

In Wendland, apart from the Jomsborg, there are no signs of occupation by the vikings. Mecklenburg has next to no archaeological material as witness to their presence,[1] and in Pomerania only a few viking graves have been found ; in this last-named province, however, some discoveries unconnected with burials have been recorded, mostly gold ornaments and combs of viking types, and from the bed of the Oder viking swords have been dredged up, while on the coast near Leba the hull of a viking ship was found.

But further to the east the Weichsel, the great river that had borne so many of the Scandinavian emigrants on their way to the south, was a trade-route known to the men of the north from ancient days, and here on the lower reaches that were the boundary between the Slavs and the German and Baltic people there are still three or four Scandinavian place-names [2] to attest the existence of viking settlements at the head of this important thoroughfare. There is, indeed, no doubt that the vikings took their share of the trade along this river, for up-stream far inland near Mewe there was discovered the grave of a viking merchant who lived in the latter part of the eleventh century that contained not only his sword and spear but his weights and scales as well.

In the Gulf of Danzig and along the coast of East Prussia the Swedes were jealous rivals of the Danes,[3] but in the second half of the ninth century when the Englishman Wulfstan made his celebrated voyage to Truso (Meislatein) near Elbing, this famous mart was in the undisputed possession of the native folk.

---

[1] A summary of the viking antiquities found in north-east Germany is given by G. Kossinna, *Mannus*, XXI (1929), p. 97 ff. For East Prussia, see also W. Gaerte, *Urgeschichte Ostpreussens*, Königsberg, 1929, p. 320 ff.

[2] W. La Baume, *Volk u. Rasse*, I (1926), p. 93. Note that the suggested etymology for Danzig is the merest surmise and cf. A. Brückner, *Arch. f. slav. Philol.*, XXXVIII (1923), p. 44. For other problematical viking place-names containing the element *vaering* (Varangian) near Gnesen, Cracow, and Lemberg, see R. Ekblom, ib., XXXIX (1925), p. 185 and cf. G. Kossinna, *Mannus*, XXI (1929), p. 105 ff.

[3] But the Swedish *sýsla* of the *Ynglingatal* I assume to have been not here but in Kurland, West Latvia (see *infra*, p. 190).

It was not until a century later that the vikings arrived in formidable array, and then, so Saxo Grammaticus relates,[1] Haakon,
a son of King Harald Gormsson of Denmark, invaded the East
Prussian lands and laid under him Samland, the ' amber coast '
peninsula north of Königsberg. But of this Danish conquest
there is, as it happens, no certain archaeological proof and the
single important witness to viking settlement here in the Königsberg peninsula suggests the dominion of the Uppland Swedes
rather than of the Danes. This is the large graveyard at Wiskiauten near Cranz that contains sufficient viking burials among its
more than two hundred graves to establish the fact that there
was a colony of Swedes in the neighbourhood during the ninth
and tenth centuries.[2] Moreover whatever may be the significance
that is to be attached to the first Danish conquest of Samland,
there can be no doubt that the province was speedily lost to the
Danes, for it is known that Cnut the Great added Samland to
his huge realm [3] somewhere about the year 1020. In all probability the Danes thenceforth possessed the province until Cnut's
death when the ancestors of the Prussians recovered their country
and began to prepare for the coming struggle with the Poles.

In the East Baltic states of Lithuania, Latvia, and Esthonia
the viking adventurers, whether merchants or marauders, were
almost all of them either Swedes or Gotlanders. Yet though
EAST   the voyage thither was not a long one and though
BALTIC   there was a busy coming and going across the Baltic
STATES   of Swedes journeying to the Russian cities or to the
lands of the Saracens and Greeks, here on the east Baltic shores
there was no properly established Swedish colony in the first two
centuries of the viking expansion, for the antiquities of Scandinavian type dating from this period that have been found in
the lands between the Kurisches Haff and the Gulf of Finland [4]
are so scarce and come from sites so far apart that they are
insufficient to establish the existence of even a few noteworthy
settlements ; indeed it is not until the first half of the eleventh

---

[1] P. 485 (ed. Müller). Cf. note on p. 288 of Part II of this ed. and
for some general remarks concerning the early Danish wars in Samland
see J. Langobek, *Scriptores Rerum Danicarum*, II, p. 157, note q.
[2] See W. Gaerte, op. cit., pp. 347–9 and G. Kossinna, op. cit., p. 102.
Dr. Birger Nerman tells me he agrees as to the general Swedish character
of the Wiskiauten finds and suggests that the colony may possibly have
been derived from Birka.
[3] Saxo, ed. Müller, p. 508 ; see especially note 3.
[4] These have been studied in detail by Dr. Birger Nerman, *Die
Verbindungen zwischen Skandinavien und dem Ost-Baltikum in der
jüngeren Eisenzeit, K. Vitt. Ant. Akad. Handl.*, 40 : 1 (1929).

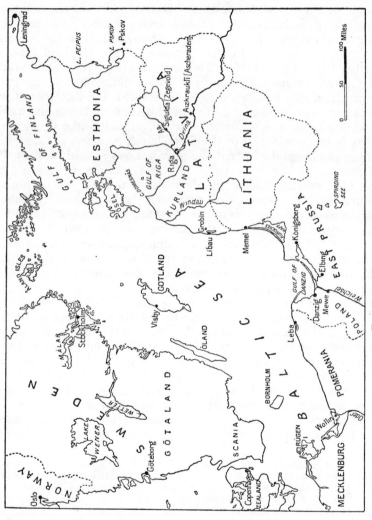

FIG. 25.—The Baltic coasts

century that the Swedes and Gotlanders began to establish trading-posts along the east Baltic littoral.

Weapons and ornaments that date from this later time and that were made according to the fashions of Sweden and, more often, Gotland have been discovered in relatively large numbers in these countries. They come most of all from Ösel Island (Saaremaa) and Moon Island (Muhu), from the south-west coast of Esthonia, and from the banks of the rivers Aa, Düna, and Windau (Venta) in Latvia, and they prove plainly enough that SWEDISH at the end of the Viking Period resident traders from SETTLE- across the Baltic, particularly Gotlanders, were dwelling MENTS, among the native population, while the large cemeteries *c.* A.D. 1000 of mixed East Baltic and viking character, such as that at Ascheraden on the Düna or that at Zegevold on the Aa, demonstrate the very considerable influence that viking fashions in personal ornaments exercised upon the native craftsmen just before and after the year A.D. 1000. The cause of this sudden activity of Scandinavian merchants here and of this viking stimulus to the life and arts of the East Baltic folk is not easy to determine ; but hitherto these poor coastal lands had been but thoroughfares, crossed hurriedly by northern traders eager to reach the flourishing towns of the new Russian state or to travel further south either to visit the markets of the East or to visit the great city of Constantinople, and it happened that about the time these settlements on the east Baltic coast were first established there had been a breakdown in what was for Sweden and Gotland the most important trade-route, namely the Volga-route across Russia to the Saracen East, this being due to the political failure of the Caliphate and the consequent stoppage of the mints that had for so long filled the coffers of the Swedes with the much-prized silver coins of the Arabic world. The result of this must have been that Swedish traffic with the Kievan cities of Russia increased, but these, though partly Swedish and controlled by a Swedish aristocracy, were governed by their own autocratic and independent Grand Prince ; in his realm itinerant merchants from Scandinavia could not move as they would, but must pay taxes to this lord and obey his rule. Therefore, with the Volga trade failing and too keen a competition in Kiev, the town that controlled the Dnieper route, the Swedes found it more profitable not to seek these distant markets themselves but to be content with the rôle of middle-men, accordingly developing trading-stations of their own along the northern littoral and exploiting the none too wealthy sources of the east Baltic lands.

But setting apart Scandinavian merchant-enterprise, early

and late, there are not lacking records of Swedish military opera-
tions, sudden raids and conquests, in these provinces towards
SWEDISH   the close of the Migration Period and during the
CONQUEST   Viking Period. As far back as the seventh century
OF KUR-   Sweden had possessed a tax-paying dependency in
LAND AND
ESTHONIA. Kurland (West Latvia),[1] a *sÿsla* as it is called in
7th AND   *Ynglingatal*,[2] where the praises are sung of King
9th CEN-   Yngvar of Svitjod who died fighting against the
TURIES   ' Esths ', and of King Anund, his son, who also warred
in their country. The great Ivar Vidfadmi, king of the united
realms of Svitjod and Denmark, must certainly have ruled a
part, if not all, of the east Baltic lands in the second half of this
century, and so, perhaps, did his successor Harald Hilditönn,
though these provinces seem to have regained their freedom in
the eighth century after the fall of Harald at Bravalla. Nevertheless the next century was to witness a new period of Swedish
aggression in the east Baltic countries, for Archbishop Rimbert
in his biography of the missionary Anscar tells [3] how the Danes,
at the time of Anscar's second visit to Sweden, that is to say about
A.D. 854, had raided Kurland and suffered defeat ; but the Swedes,
he says, came following upon their heels and, led by King Olof,
took this land which had been in the past, as Rimbert knew,
a sysla of Sweden.

There are other witnesses to the crossing of the Baltic about
this time by expeditionary forces from Sweden. One is a passage
in the Russian Chronicle that relates how in A.D. 859 the Varangians came ' from the other side of the (Baltic) sea ' and
demanded that the Tchuds and various Slavonic peoples of north
Russia should pay them indemnities. In 862, the chronicle
continues, these vikings were driven out of the conquered territories and forced to return to their homes ; thereupon follows
the celebrated legend of the recall by invitation from the leader-
less Slavs of three viking brothers who recrossed the Baltic to
govern the chaotic native tribes. The Tchuds (foreigners) were
Finns who lived in Esthonia west of Lake Peipus, and it was in

[1] Kurland is defined by Birger Nerman as the district west and south-
west of the Gulf of Riga except for the northern fringe of land projecting
to Cape Domesnes where there dwelt a distinct group of Livs.

[2] *v.* 18. There has been dispute as to the locality of the sysla and
some believe it to have been in East Prussia. Cf. H. Schück, *Uppsala
Univ. Årskrift*, 1910, p. 145 ff., for the whereabouts of the ' Esths ' named
in this passage.

[3] *M.G.H.* (Pertz), SS. II, 714. The ' Seeburg ' mentioned here has
been identified at Grobin near Libau ; it contains cemeteries of Uppland
Swedes and Gotlanders, and is now being excavated.

their territory, or close to it, at Izborsk, south-west of Pskov, that one of the three Swedish brothers took up his abode with his following ; thus to the evidence of Rimbert must be added that of the Russian chronicle as showing that at a period shortly after A.D. 850 Sweden was boldly intent upon conquest abroad, taking to herself the east Baltic provinces of Kurland and Esthonia. And this is not all, for Olof, who was king at Birka, had a contemporary Eric, an Uppsala king, who likewise led Swedish armies eastwards across the Baltic ; it is the Icelandic historian Snorri Sturlason who testifies to this ; for in the Saint Olaf saga of the *Heimskringla* he puts into the mouth of Thorgny Lagman a remarkable speech in which the indignant old councillor, upbraiding Olof Skotkonung for his arrogance, declares (this was about 1016) that his (Thorgny's) grandfather could remember Eric, the renowned conqueror of Finland, Karelia, and Estland ; the prowess and glory of Eric, he says scornfully, was greater than that of Olof Skotkonung, yet Eric was less haughty and, unlike Olof, would hearken to the advice of others.   Doubtless it was Rimbert's Olof of Birka, and not Eric, who was the conqueror of Kurland ; but it is abundantly plain that Eric's forces, perhaps the Varangians of the Russian Chronicle, also gained notable successes in the east Baltic area and that a part of the lands of Finland and the modern Esthonia were won, temporarily at least, for the dominion of the Uppsala king.

Yet, as has been said, archaeology offers no proof of serious colonization by the Swedes of the provinces, Finland and Karelia included, that the royal raiders had subdued in the ninth century.   The kings came with their armies, conquered, and took an indemnity, afterwards returning with most of their warriors to Sweden, and though perhaps a jarl was left to act as governor, it can only have been in a loose and irregular manner that the overlordship of the Swedish monarchs was exercised during the next hundred years.   In the days of Eric Segersäll (*c.* 980–995) Estland and Kurland, on the indirect evidence of Thorgny Lagman's speech, may possibly have acknowledged the suzerainty of the Swedish king, but in the reign of Olof Skotkonung (995–1022), a monarch more interested in western politics and his quarrel with Norway than with eastern affairs, these provinces had most certainly recovered their independence, even though it was at this time that they tolerated, or were forced to tolerate, the establishment of Swedes and Gotlanders in settlements along their shores or along their rivers.

When the ninth century was over they lay an easy prey to the prospering Swedish state in Russia and to the plundering of vikings other than the Swedes. At the beginning of the tenth century two Norwegian princes, sons of Harald Fairhair, raided Estland, and to Kurland about this time came the celebrated Icelander Egil Skallagrimsson with his brother Thorolf. But the increasing power of the Russians is not discernible until the '70s of this century, the time when Olaf Tryggvason, afterwards king of Norway, spent some years of his boyhood in Estland, and it was only a short time after this that the indifference of the Swedish Olof Skotkonung was all too plainly demonstrated by his allowing Jarl Eric Haakonsson of Norway, who was on good terms with him, to ravage Ösel Island and Kurland about the year A.D. 1000 and to burn the Aldeigjuborg, the stronghold of the Russian Swedes to the south of Lake Ladoga. Nevertheless in the eleventh century, in the reigns of Anund and Emund and when the all-important trade with the east had broken down, then once more Sweden found occasion to seek wealth in the lands across the Baltic ; this was the time when Swedish traders made their settlements here and the time when Swedish buccaneering again distressed these coasts. Seven Runic inscriptions upon Swedish memorial-stones of this period (1020–1060) tell of Swedes who fell in these countries, and it was in these decades that the royal viking Ingvar Vittfarne descended upon and captured the western and southern coastlands of the Gulf of Riga. By 1070 Kurland, and probably Esthonia, were again under Swedish dominion,[1] but it was not for long that Sweden held these provinces inviolate ; for Cnut II of Denmark ravaged Kurland and Estland about ten years later, and after a short period of Danish supremacy they passed again into the keeping of their own Baltic folk.

[1] Adam of Bremen, *Hamburg Church Hist.*, IV, 16.

CHAPTER VII

THE WESTERN EMPIRE

IT was in the second decade of the ninth century, soon after the death of Charles the Great, that the first shock of viking aggression warned Louis the Pious of the danger from the north now menacing the calm and prosperous lands of the huge Frankish Empire. Just south of the mouth of the Loire on the big tidal island of Noirmoutier was the monastery of St. Philibert, not perhaps a provokingly wealthy institution, but one of some prosperity inasmuch as the island was a port of call for the barques employed in the salt-trade that was then, as now, the chief industry of the Breton marsh-lands. As such, Noirmoutier was doubtless well known to the northern adventurer-merchants, and it was this place that became the first goal of northern pirates in the Atlantic waters.

It may have been Norwegian vikings from Ireland, rather than Danes coming by the Channel route, who first of all plundered the abbey, but it was not long afterwards that the Danes found their way round Ouessant and sailed into the Bay of Biscay. Whether from Ireland or from Denmark, several times between NOIRMOUT- the years 814 and 819 viking fleets appeared suddenly IER 814-819 off the island and sacked the monastery, so that the abbot was compelled eventually to build temporary quarters for his monks inland on the Grand-lieu lake near Nantes, and here they were able to shelter during the months they soon learnt to recognize as the raid season. Later, Noirmoutier itself was fortified against the vikings, but the dangers of its island-position made defence against a viking fleet a peril worse than precipitate flight. Eventually the wretched and often ruined buildings of the monastery were abandoned, and the island became a viking-headquarters where the pirates could pass the winter; but this happened some twenty years after the early raids, and, as the opening of the viking attacks, it is sufficient to record the first plunderings of the abbey and also the sack about the same time of another monastery much further to the south on Ré island off Rochelle.

Louis may have paid little heed to these sudden and unexpected raids on the remote Atlantic islands, but it was not long before the Franks were to hear something of the itinerary of these viking expeditions and could thus gauge the seamanship and audacity of the pirates.   In 820 a small fleet of thirteen ships appeared off the Flanders coast where, after effecting a landing, they burnt some houses and stole a few cattle ; thence the little armament made for the mouth of the Seine, but the crews failed in an attempt to land in that neighbourhood, losing five men in the enterprise.   Undaunted, the fleet straightway sailed round the Brittany peninsula and fell upon and destroyed the town of Buin on the shores of the Bay of Biscay.   Thence, laden with a rich booty, the pirates made off to their home, perhaps paying a visit to Ireland on the way back.[1]

There followed a period wherein the Danes were occupied by internal struggles in their own country and their viking enterprise checked, maybe, by the deliberate policy of their leaders who were anxious to win the emperor's favour (p. 135) ; so it happened that for thirteen years Louis had no trouble from pirates, even though throughout all this time the Norwegians were terrorizing Ireland.   In 834, however, the rich merchant-province of Frisia, that had already been a victim of the Danish pirates in the time of Charles the Great, was attacked by Danes who ravaged a part of the land and finally plundered, and partially destroyed by fire, the wealthy town of Dorstad, an important Frankish-Frisian mart on the site of the modern Wijk-bij-Duurstede in the fork of the Lek and the Kromme Rhine, where they slew many of the inhabitants and carried off others as prisoners.   Here they were not merely reckless adventurers, for political conditions had given their erstwhile king Harald (p. 92) and his brother Rorik a footing in Frisia, and it was possibly a result of their intrigues with the emperor's son, Lothar, who was at strife with his father, that there took place this plundering of the country outside their grip by Danish pirates.   But whatever the cause, the menace to the Empire from the viking movement was now becoming serious.   In the following year Noirmoutier was attacked again and Frisia revisited by the Danes, and in the year afterwards, 836, Noirmoutier had to be abandoned by the monks, who were forced to dig up and remove to a place of safety the bones of their founder St. Philibert ; at the same time Frisia suffered from a third and more severe onslaught, Antwerp and

FRISIA
834–839

---

[1] It happens that Howth near Dublin and the islands in Wexford Haven were plundered in this year and a number of Irish women carried off ; but the identity of the raiders is, of course, unknown.

Witla at the mouth of the Meuse being burnt, Dorstad plundered, and a tribute demanded from the now terrified inhabitants of the country.

There was another attack on Frisia in 837 and Louis was at last forced to take action. He had been purposing an expedition to Italy, but he gave up his plans and marched instead to Nimeguen with the intention of driving the vikings out of Frisia. But they escaped before he arrived and he could do

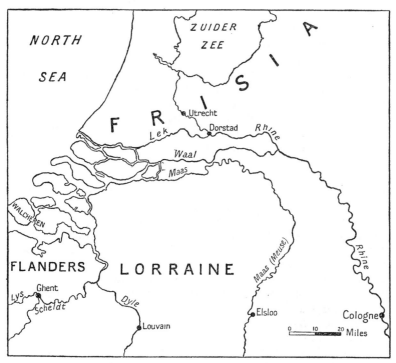

FIG. 26.—Map of the Dorstad region

nothing except make some pretence of setting in order the defences of the country, now a matter of considerable difficulty inasmuch as some of the Frisians, in despair of obtaining effective aid from the emperor, seemed disposed to seek safety by siding with the vikings. The Danish king Horik I (p. 93) had denied all knowledge of the earlier raids, telling the emperor that he had seized and executed some of the pirates responsible for them, and he even went so far as to demand in return blood-money for those of his countrymen who had been slain during these plunderings. Exactly how he justified this preposterous demand is not known, but it is easy to believe that at this period he was not the instigator of the raids, and Louis, recognizing the impotence of even a strong Danish king to curb this viking enterprise, itself probably a result of Horik's tyranny in his own state, had to content himself with a diplomatic indication that he would hold Horik responsible for any further acts of piracy committed by his countrymen.

A storm, happily for the Frisians, destroyed a Danish fleet that set off to ravage their country in 838, and Louis, seeing that further attack was to be expected, now ordered the building of some boats to patrol the coast so that at least there might be some warning of the raids. Nothing happened for the rest of that year, but there was a renewal of the viking plunderings in 839. Their ravages, however, were overshadowed by a horrible disaster of another kind, for on Boxing Day of this year the sea broke over the dykes and poured into the land, destroying, it is said, over two thousand four hundred homesteads and drowning a large number of men and animals. But the emperor was now in no mood to concern himself with the unhappy state of this country, for he was already heavily involved in the desperate political jealousies of his sons, and during the stormy domestic quarrels of 839 he gave no heed to the further viking raids on Frisia and up the Rhine. It may be that he bought some peace for the Frisians by the grant of Walcheren to the Danish insurgent Harald and of Dorstad to his brother Rorik, wasting no more time on wordy exchanges with Horik ; but the troubles within the empire were now increasing, and the menace from Danish pirates was the least of the urgent anxieties that beset the Franks on that summer morning of A.D. 840 when Louis the Pious, the second Carolingian emperor, died.

The empire was at once in a turmoil, and for a year the threats and hostile demonstrations of the three warring sons of the dead emperor left the Frankish territory at the mercy of an invader. Events marched rapidly to the dreadful and bloody climax at Fontenoy (25th June 841) when Charles the Bald and Louis the German amid scenes of revolting carnage defeated Lothar, and thereby sealed the fate of the empire as a majestic and indivisible whole. For two more years Lothar struggled, but all his efforts to become sole emperor were in vain, and in 843 by the treaty of Verdun the three brothers made the partition of the empire an accomplished fact. Lothar, who retained the imperial title, took the middle kingdom, that is Italy and the long stretch of land reaching from the Alps to the North Sea between the Rhine and the Scheldt ; Louis the German had the lands east of this, except Frisia which was allotted to Lothar, and so possessed a sea-coast from the Weser to the Eider ; Charles had France from the Meuse to the Loire, together with rebellious Aquitaine and the Toulouse country.

The Danes had been quick to take their opportunity, and Frisia now lay helpless in their power. They had even meddled to a small extent in the great civil war, the turbulent Harald, in return for a renewed grant of Walcheren, serving in Lothar's

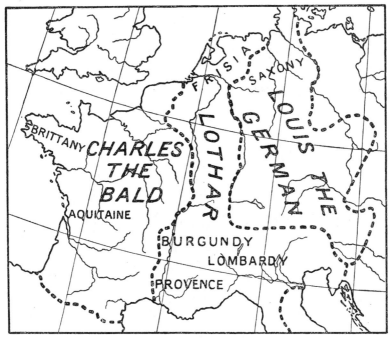

FIG. 27.—The Western Empire in 843

army on the Moselle in 842, and bringing, either through fear or treachery, disaster upon his ally. But this was an isolated political enterprise, and an earlier and serious act of piracy had shown that the vikings saw in the death-throes of the empire the chance of plunderings and conquests further afield. In May of 841 a large fleet under a chieftain called Asgeir[1] suddenly appeared on the Seine and hurried up-river to Rouen

---

[1] Commonly called Oscar. The name is given in the chronicles as Oscheri or Hoseri.

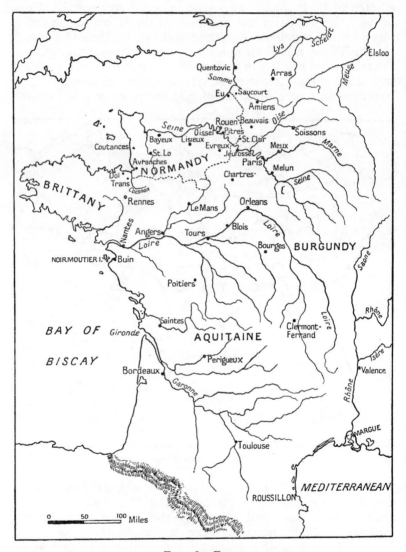

FIG. 28.—France

which was stormed, plundered, and fired. The abbey of St. Ouen close at hand shared a similar fate, and down-stream, a few days later, the monastery of Jumièges was forced to buy its safety at a heavy price. Then the vikings slipped down to the open sea and disappeared, refusing to risk an engagement with a Frankish force that attempted to waylay them. In the following year a viking fleet, it may have been the same one, after an attack on London, crossed the Channel and swooped down on Quentovic, a busy and important mart at the mouth of the Canche near Étaples ; the pirates sacked the defenceless town with the utmost ferocity, leaving only amid the smoking ruins some few houses that had bought their safety by bribes. From Quentovic this remarkable fleet sailed back to England and plundered Rochester.

THE SEINE AND QUEN-TOVIC 841–842

The disasters that had befallen Rouen and Quentovic, terrifying though they were, were eclipsed in 843 by the appalling fate of Nantes. The capture of this strong and guarded city was made possible by interior dissension in Brittany,[1] and a fleet of sixty-seven ships, not from Denmark but from Vestfold in Norway,[2] was able to sail up to the town walls unsuspected and unobserved, the wretched Nantais thinking only of the dangers threatening them from the land-side where Count Lambert was busy stirring up the country against Charles the Bald. It was St. John's Day, and the town was full to overflowing on the occasion of the festival. Without any warning the vikings poured in, putting to the sword all whom they encountered and firing the houses on every side. They burst into the cathedral and hacked down the bishop at the altar itself ; they butchered the huge and terror-struck congregation and then burnt the building. Only at nightfall did the awful slaughter and the pillaging cease, the vikings escaping unharmed with a rich booty and many prisoners. They made their way back to the sea, plundering recklessly as they went, and finally landed at Noirmoutier, which they had chosen as their base, and where, in fact, they passed the winter. It was the beginning of a new and dreadful phase of the viking attacks. No longer could the creatures be counted upon to go scurrying home when their terrible work was over ; now they dared to lurk close at hand watching over their miserable prey.

SACK OF NANTES 843

In 844 the vikings appeared on another great river of France,

[1] The story that the vikings were conducted to the attack by a pilot in the employ of the rebel Count Lambert is no doubt an invention.

[2] The pirates were called Westfaldingi, *Ann. Engolism.* 843 (Pertz, *M.G.H.*, SS. XVI, 486), *Chron. Aquit.* 843, 3 (SS. II, 253).

the Garonne. Here, as on the Loire, they found a land dis-
tracted by civil war, for the young Pepin had not given up
THE GAR- his pretensions to the throne of an independent
ONNE AND Aquitaine. The viking attack was well-timed, and
SPAIN 844 the pirates were able to sail up-river, plundering
without hindrance until they were within a short distance of
Toulouse. The town had lately been besieged unsuccessfully by
Charles the Bald, and the vikings must have learnt that the
garrison was too strong for them ; so they made no attack,
and, instead, sailed off suddenly. Whether they had deliberately
chosen Spain as their new goal, or whether it was a storm that
drove them out of their course, is now hard to say, but Spain
it was where the viking fleet, 150 ships strong, next appeared.
They made first for the northern coast, landing near Gijon,
and plundering there and in the neighbourhood of Corunna.
But the little kingdom of the Asturias showed a high courage
in the face of this danger, and proved to the world in what
large measure interior political dissension and irresolute leadership had contributed to the humiliations inflicted on the Franks
by these northern buccaneers. An army was rapidly collected,
the viking land-force heavily defeated, the survivors pursued
to their boats, and a number of these (it is said as many as seventy)
burnt. The pirates fled in confusion and, rounding Cape Finis-
terre, sailed down the western coast of the peninsula, pillaging
as they went. Their surprise attacks were successful, but they
were soon to find themselves opposed by a new and redoubtable
foe, the Arab conquerors of Spain. At Lisbon the vikings
(called *majus* by the Arabs) had a fleet of about a hundred sail,
and they were able to hold on for thirteen days in the vicinity,
plundering and occasionally fighting with Moorish detachments.
In the first exchanges they seem to have got the better of their
adversaries, who rapidly became seriously alarmed by the in-
cursions of the northern pirates. Then the vikings set off southwards ; a part of the fleet visited Arzilla on the North African
coast, but the main body sailed to Cadiz, and thence made their
way inland to Medina Sidonia where they encountered and
defeated a Moorish force. After this they returned to the sea,
and then, with reckless courage, made their way up the Guadalquivir towards Seville. This audacious stroke was successful,
and, when two engagements had been fought, the town, except
for the garrison in the citadel, fell to them. Thereupon the
vikings, holding Seville as their base, even dared to go ravaging
far inland in the direction of Constantina, Cordoba, and Moron.
But the Arabs, after the first weeks of panic and flight, were

rallied by their chiefs at Carmona, and when Seville had been in the hands of the vikings for six weeks, a large raiding party of the pirates was ambushed and massacred, and almost immediately afterwards the city was retaken by the Moors. The surviving vikings realized the overwhelming danger of their position and forthwith took to their boats, but there was a delay in gathering in the scattered bands of marauders and some haggling over the exchange of prisoners, while the Moors were daily growing in strength. The result was that before they could escape to the sea the vikings were caught by the full

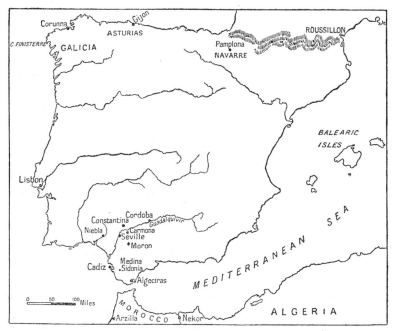

FIG. 29.—Spain

Moorish force at Talayata near Seville, where they met with a crushing defeat, losing many men and thirty of their ships. The survivors made off at once and, reaching the open sea, headed for the mouth of the Tinto ; they then sailed up that river to Niebla, but they were speedily driven off by the Moors. This time they escaped without serious loss, and sailed away to attempt a second raid on Sidonia. The resolute and energetic opposition of the Moors was, however, too much for them, and when, a day or two after their arrival, they heard that the fleet of the Emir 'Abd-ar-Rahmān had arrived in Seville, they were forced to make off to their boats in precipitate flight. Some of them were driven across to the African coast by a storm, but others made their way at once up the western side of the peninsula, plundering as they went. At the end of the year the remnants of the expedition were reunited in the mouth of the Gironde.

A curious result of this expedition was the temporary establishment in the middle of the ninth century of some kind of diplomatic relations between the Arab Emir of Spain and the king of the *Majus*. The Emir is known to have sent an ambassador to the court of the viking chief, and, although the nature of the mission of this man, Ghazâl, is not recorded, his adventures during a two months' sojourn at the viking royal palace and the gallant court paid by him to the viking queen Noud [1] have been described in some detail. [2] The land whither Ghazâl went was a great island in the ocean where there were flowing waters and gardens ; it lay at a distance of three days' journey from the mainland (the point of departure is, unhappily, not specified) and contained a large population of *majus* ; in the neighbourhood were many other isles of various sizes, all inhabited by *majus*, and the adjacent territories of the mainland belonged also to them.

But where was this island and who was the king ? In all probability it was, as is to be expected, Horik in Zealand whom Ghazâl visited, but the account of the itinerary does not by any means establish this as certain, and there remains the chance that the Emir's ambassador did not go to Denmark at all, but to Ireland. In that event his mission would have been to the court of the great viking chieftain Turgeis (p. 276), who had won for himself enormous power in Ireland and who was drowned in 845, the year after the Spanish expedition. This view is to a small extent supported by the circumstance that the name Noud would just pass as a version of Aud (Auðr), the name of the wife of Turgeis, whereas the name of Horik's wife is not known from the northern sources. But this is flimsy evidence, and it seems on the whole most likely, on the grounds of the geographical description of the lands of the *majus*, with their territory on the adjacent mainland (Scania), that Ghazâl was sent to the Danish court.

[1] In the Arabic script the d was not aspirated. Tuda and Nuda are variants of the name.

[2] R. Dozy, *Recherches sur l'histoire et la littérature de l'Espagne*, 3rd ed., Paris, 1881, II, p. 267 ; and cf. A. Fabricius, *Actes du 8e. congrès int. des orientalistes*, 1889 (Stockholm and Oslo), I, p. 121.

This year of the Spanish raid, 844, saw another attack on Quentovic, and the fate of that unhappy Channel town was thereby sealed ; Étaples sheltered its escaped merchants, and henceforth took over its trade.   In 845 all three kingdoms of the former Carolingian empire were assailed by vikings.   Horik, the Danish king, now abandoning a pretence of friendship CAPTURE   towards Louis the German,[1] despatched a fleet of no OF HAM-   less than 600 ships to the Elbe and seized Hamburg. BURG 845 For two days the Danes remained plundering and burning in the town, and though, ultimately, they were repulsed with considerable loss by a Saxon levy, they had struck Christendom a cruel blow, not only materially by their wanton destruction and slaughter, but morally by driving the great missionary Anskar, now Archbishop of Hamburg, into exile.   Frisia also suffered from Danish piracy in the same year.

Cruel, too, was the humiliation that befell Charles the Bald, for now there descended upon his realm one of the most renowned vikings of all time, Ragnar Lodbrok, a scion of the Danish RAGNAR   royal family.   In the beginning of March this robber-LODBROK   hero reached the Seine at the head of a Danish fleet, ON THE   120 ships strong, and sailed straight up-stream to SEINE 845 Rouen, where he tarried only two days, and then on to Carolivenna (now Chaussy) near St. Germain-en-Laye and about nine miles from St. Denis.   Charles heard of his coming and marched at once with a moderate-sized army against him ; but, on approaching the enemy, he made the mistake of dividing his force, sending the two detachments down the river on opposite banks.   The vikings fell upon one of these parties and drove it back in confusion, taking many prisoners ; these, said to have been 111 in number, they hanged on an island in the Seine in full view of the second detachment that was advancing against them, and then fell in fury on the now unnerved Frankish troops.   The result was a big victory for Ragnar, and Charles, with the remnant of his army, was compelled to take refuge in the abbey of St. Denis and there to watch events.   Ragnar, after terrorizing and devastating the neighbourhood, eventually sailed boldly past the little cooped-up Frankish force, and, at the end of the month, arrived before the walls of Paris.

Paris, though in those days not much more than an island-city in the Seine, was already beginning to count among the chief towns of the kingdom, and the prize now offered to the Danes was a rich one.   On the approach of Ragnar, the monks

[1] There is, however, nothing in the history of Mohammedan Spain to suggest that this was a result of Ghazâl's mission.

and most of the population took to flight, and the town must have been almost empty when the vikings, on Easter Sunday, FIRST   fell upon it.   Nevertheless, there was a great plunder-
SACK OF   ing, and most of all the monastery of St. Germain-
PARIS   des-Prés suffered.   Then Ragnar gave the order to retire.[1] His position must have been precarious, for Charles, who was behind him and in a position to bar his escape, had lost no time in collecting reinforcements and was now at the head of a considerable host.   It seemed that he had only to take up a proper strategic position, making a full show of his strength, and Ragnar must be lost.   But the necessary courage failed the Christian king, and now came the first of those pitiful and short-sighted weaknesses, those follies of a cowardly states-manship that seem to have passed muster as safe and sane expedients of government in this unhappy century.   Charles bribed the pirates to depart.   Ragnar, therefore, sailed home unmolested, taking with him the plunder of Paris and a danegeld of 7,000 pounds of silver, the price of his promise to leave Charles's kingdom henceforward in peace.

Ragnar's expedition, however, had an inglorious end, for on the journey back a pestilence visited his fleet, and when he returned to the Danish court, Horik, in a fright lest this plague might spread in Denmark, set free some of Ragnar's prisoners and restored to the Franks a part of the viking's plunder.   There is no knowing whether this gesture was intended to placate an outraged Heaven, or whether the dismissal of the prisoners was an ordinary sanitary precaution ; but it is certain that the Danish king showed himself through his embassies to the Paderborn assembly, that was held in the autumn of this year, as being now of a chastened mind, and a peace was made with him that left the Eider districts, at any rate, undisturbed until the '80s.   For six years the Seine, also, was not visited by pirates.

The sack of Paris was not the only disaster that befell West Francia in 845, for there was a sustained pillaging of the Loire regions and Aquitaine from the viking base at Noirmoutier.   In CAPTURE   addition, the returned Spanish fleet, now presumably
OF   augmented, was operating in the Gironde country, and
SAINTES   in this year its crews captured and burnt the inland town
845   of Saintes.   Before the fall of the town the vikings had repelled an attack by a local levy of the Franks, but after the town was theirs they were able to settle unmolested in the

---

[1] A picturesque legend describes a fog falling suddenly upon the impious villains and causing their retreat in confusion and alarm.

Saintonge. Charles, ever careful of the major political anxieties of his difficult realm, was the last person to think of attempting to dislodge pirates from a remote district of rebellious Aquitaine.

Frisia was ravaged again in the following year, Dorstad being once more sacked and burnt, and many abbeys in the Scheldt district plundered. At this point the three kings of the empire, meeting in conference at Meersen near Maestricht, sent a warning to Horik that his subjects must either keep the peace in Frisia or expect an attack from the joint armies of the three kingdoms. Horik knew this for an empty threat, a plain statement of the weakness and misery in the kingdoms of the Franks, for the chances of these three jealous and mutually suspicious rulers acting in concert were obviously negligible. Accordingly, he took no notice and allowed Frisia to be attacked again in both of the two succeeding years. The province of Betuwe fell under viking dominion as a result of these operations.

Brittany was ravaged in 847 by pirates, and an army of the Bretons under Duke Nominoë was defeated by them. But the principal centre of viking activity was now the Gironde where Asgeir, who had taken Rouen in 840, added to the lustre of his former great achievement by investing (847) and capturing CAPTURE (848) Bordeaux. The long siege of this town, and OF BOR- its fall owing to the treachery of the Jews, reflects DEAUX 848 the curious impotence of the Franks to override domestic politics and quarrels for the sake of repelling the invader. Pepin, the pretender to Aquitaine, made no attempt to relieve the city, so Charles the Bald, scenting a big political advantage to himself from the increase of his prestige in this neighbourhood, made a demonstration of doing so. He did actually attack and sink nine viking ships on the Gironde, but he carefully avoided a general engagement, and Bordeaux fell to the invaders without any effective intervention on his part. But his plan succeeded. Pepin was to some extent discredited by the fall of the town, and in the same year (848) Charles had himself solemnly crowned as king of Aquitaine. After Bordeaux was captured the vikings elected to remain in the district, and in 849 they pressed inland as far as Perigueux, which they sacked with their customary viking thoroughness.

In the first decades of the second half of the ninth century, the calamitous and monstrous outrages of the Danes were repeated with increasing and ever more reckless ferocity, so that the miseries suffered by the Franks of the coastal districts and river valleys were terrible indeed. In 850 there was plundering by a great Danish fleet on the Rhine and the Lek and the

Maal, and once more peace had to be bought, this time by a new grant of Dorstad to Rorik, Harald's brother, for this turbulent chief had lately been expelled from the town and had taken refuge in Saxony whence he set forth as a viking to rob his former fief. By reaccepting Dorstad from Lothar Rorik laid himself under the obligation of protecting to some degree his portion of Frisia from further viking attacks, but his promises, perhaps because he lacked the power to fulfil them, were speedily proved worthless and Frisia was repeatedly ravaged by pirates throughout the two following years. Afterwards, however, the unhappy country, by this time almost completely under Danish rule, secured some peace from the raids of mere plunderers.[1]

GRANT OF DORSTAD TO RORIK 850

The autumn of 851 saw a new attack on the Seine country, the vikings concerned being commanded by Asgeir, who had now left Bordeaux. The chief event of this raid was a land expedition from Rouen to Beauvais, which was plundered and burnt, but on the return the vikings were surprised by a Frankish army and lost many of their men. The defeat, however, did not drive them from the Seine, and at the beginning of the next year the Fontanelle monastery near the river-mouth was burnt to the ground by the same vikings. In the summer of 852 they returned to Bordeaux, but in October of that year a Danish fleet led by two vikings called Sigtryg and Godfred appeared on the Seine to continue the plunderings of the vikings who had left. The new arrivals used as their headquarters an old camp known by the name of Givold's Fosse, probably at Jeufosse on a bend of the river between Vernon and Bonnières.

RAIDS UP THE SEINE 851–852

Charles and the Emperor Lothar had by this time no illusions as to the real danger of the viking menace, and it seemed that a chance had come when by concerted action they might reasonably hope to teach the Danes a salutary lesson. Accordingly, they each assembled an army and together laid siege to Givold's Fosse. There ought to have been no doubt as to the result, yet, probably because of the inevitable Frankish jealousies, the

[1] Rorik died in 876. In 857, three years after the accession of Horik II, he had also won for himself land near Hedeby, and seems to have been the lord of a large and important realm that included most of Sleswig and North Frisia ; but he seems to have lost his Danish possessions by 862, and, though his Frisian fiefs were restored by Charles the Bald in 873, he never succeeded in establishing a stable colony. For the identification of Rorik with the Rurik who founded the Russian state, see N. T. Belaiew, *Saga-Book of Viking Society*, X, Pt. 2 (1925–7), p. 267, a most valuable and well-documented paper.

siege was not pushed to a victorious conclusion, and in the following year the hostilities ended, hard though it is to believe, in some sort of treaty, the vikings being allowed to make their way back to sea unpunished and at their leisure, and, what is worse, Godfred himself receiving a grant of land in Flanders. ' The heathens ', a chronicler had written four years earlier,[1] ' more and more put the Christians to shame ', and it is easy to imagine how this last contemptible weakness of the Frankish kings must have deepened the terror reigning in the land to a dark and settled despair.

' It is wretched to have to write these things,' said the same chronicler, and, in truth, the long tale of viking raids that followed is a miserable record. Fortunately, however, there is no need to name them here one by one or to report in detail each year's disasters, and it will be sufficient to note any outstanding act of pillage, keeping a watch at the same time for any symptoms of change in the manner and policy of the viking attacks.

Nantes was sacked again by the Loire vikings in 853, Poitiers and Angers were plundered by cavalry raids from a new viking depot well up the Loire, and in November of this year took place that memorable act of sacrilege, the plundering of Tours and its two famous monasteries. One of these was without the walls at Marmoutier (here 126 monks were killed), and the other in REIGN OF the town itself, that beloved and venerated house of TERROR St. Martin, the home of Gregory, the historian of the 853–858 Merovingian Franks. In 854 Blois was burnt, and an unsuccessful attack made on Orleans. Two years later the vikings, issuing from their new depot at Besse, an island near Nantes, returned to Orleans and sacked it. In 857 Paris fell to Björn Ironside, one of the sons of Ragnar Lodbrok, and there was a systematic and terrible burning of its churches, only four escaping destruction. In the same year a party of vikings, in shameful alliance with Pepin of Aquitaine, once more plundered Poitiers, and Tours and Blois were attacked a second time. In Frisia Utrecht was rased to the ground, and in 858 there was viking plundering in an hitherto unmolested region on the Bremer and the Weser. The Seine vikings pillaged Bayeux and slew its bishop ; Chartres and Évreux were sacked ; two prominent ecclesiastics were captured, the abbots of St. Denis and St. Maux, and Charles was compelled to redeem them by the payment of an enormously heavy ransom.

The sufferings of the Franks in the western kingdom were

[1] *Ann. Xant.*, 849 (Pertz, *M.G.H.*, SS. II, p. 229).

now almost beyond endurance, and their king, though he had many more pressing cares, had no other choice than to attempt once again to oust the pirates. Accordingly, in the summer of 858, he attacked the Seine vikings in their stronghold of Oissel, an island opposite Jeufosse. He had prepared for this purpose not only an army, but, more important, a fleet ; and he had enlisted the support of Lothar II, the new lord of that portion of the middle kingdom lying between Frisia and the Alps, and of his own son Charles the Young. Even Pepin of Aquitaine promised his aid. The position of the vikings, when they were blockaded in their island-fastness, was indeed serious, and for a while it seemed that the Christian armies must crush the heathen force. But Charles fell ill, and, once again, the siege wavered. Then, twelve weeks after the siege had begun, there happened a sudden and unexpected event that immediately brought freedom to the vikings ; for Louis the German cruelly chose this moment to invade his brother's kingdom, and Charles had no other course open to him than to withdraw at once from Oissel and to move with all possible speed to Lorraine to oppose his brother.

SIEGE OF OISSEL BY THE FRANKS 858

In the next year a Danish fleet under a viking called Weland appeared on the Somme. The monks fled from the monasteries of the terror-struck countryside and the pirates were left free to plunder where they would ; in the end the great town of Amiens was taken by them and burnt to the ground. This year, 859, also saw the beginning of a celebrated long-distance viking raid. The pirates concerned in it started out from the Seine and are next heard of when they attempted a landing on the coasts of Galicia in northern Spain, where, like the vikings of the earlier Spanish raid, they were promptly driven off with severe loss. Thence, 62 ships strong, they sailed down the west coast of the peninsula and, after being worsted by the Moors at the Guadalquivir mouth, they made their way through the Straits of Gibraltar into the Mediterranean. In passing the Straits they had burnt the mosque at Algeciras, and from here they crossed over to Nekor (Mezemma) on the coast of Morocco, where they defeated a Moorish force that attempted to interfere with their plunderings.[1] After a sojourn of eight days in Morocco, the vikings went back to Spain and continued up the east coast.

SPAIN AND MEDITERRANEAN FRANCE 859–862

---

[1] It seems that a part of the fleet, on leaving Morocco, went off to Ireland, taking with them some Moorish prisoners. These Moors are mentioned in early Irish texts as *fir gorm* (blue men), though the ON. *blámenn* can be exactly translated *dark men*.

They raided the Balearic Islands and then went on to plunder in Rousillon in the south of France ; finally they reached the island of Camargue in the mouth of the Rhône. Here they took up winter-quarters, and subsequently they began pillaging the Rhône valley, even raiding as far up-stream as Valence. In the new year, however, they suffered a defeat at the hands of the Franks and, shortly afterwards, they sailed away. Their subsequent adventures are uncertain. The popular version of the tale takes them to Italy, and describes the sack of Pisa and Luna, which they are said to have mistaken for Rome and where they gained entrance by the picturesque stratagem of carrying in their leader, very much alive in his coffin, for Christian burial ; but this Italian exploit may quite well have been another and different raid carried out not by Northmen but by Saracenic pirates, for Saracens and northern vikings, both heathens, can be easily confused in the Christian chronicles. What is certain is that the vikings landed north of Gibraltar on their homeward journey and subsequently had a sea-battle with the Moors ; then they sailed off to Navarre, where they captured Pamplona, and in 862 they returned to Brittany.

In 860 there had been another act of folly, a shameful betrayal of their weakness, on the part of the Franks, for Charles the Bald attempted to bribe the Somme vikings under Weland to drive their countrymen, the Seine vikings, away. Three thousand pounds of silver he offered ; but he had great diffi-culty in collecting this vast sum, and in the end the Somme vikings departed, unpaid, to ravage England and, afterwards, the Flanders coast. In the next year (861) the Seine vikings attacked Paris and St. Germain des Prés. Then Weland's fleet, over 200 ships strong, returned down the coast and also entered the Seine. Charles, in despair, renewed his offer, and this time the original Seine vikings were besieged by their fellow-Danes in the Oissel stronghold. They bought their freedom for 6,000 pounds of gold and silver, a ransom that is in itself an eloquent tribute to the success of their robberies. But, after a temporary withdrawal, the vikings of both parties were soon marauding again, and in the year 862 Charles was forced to take arms to prevent the further plunderings of Weland. He was too late to stop the capture and burning of Meaux, but he cut off Weland's retreat and, for the first time, inflicted a serious defeat on the pirates. Now, indeed, he acted with the courage and vigour that the poor terrified monks had loyally ascribed to him throughout all their tribulations. His terms were harsh ; all the vikings

CHARLES
THE BALD
DEFEATS
THE SEINE
VIKINGS
862

were summarily expelled from the Seine valley and forced to
release their prisoners instantly.   Then he began serious defensive
measures, building fortified bridges and other works to bar the
river against future raids, and of these the most important and
the strongest was to be a great bridge at Pitres (Pont de l'Arche).
He also appointed two commanders who were responsible for the
protection of the threatened areas, Count Adalhard superintending
the Seine defences, and Robert the Strong, Marquess of Neustria
and founder of the Capetian line of kings, those of the Loire.

For a while there was peace on the Seine, but Robert,
embarrassed by Breton insurrection, was soon attacked by
vikings, and despite the resolute opposition that he offered,
Poitiers and Angoulême fell to the pirates during the two following years.   In 864 Toulouse was threatened.   In 865 Orleans
was sacked and Poitiers ravaged again, while the vikings and
the insurgent Bretons together plundered Le Mans ; but the
year closed with big victories for the Franks, and for one district
at any rate, Aquitaine, the viking menace was ended.   On the
Seine, however, this year 865 was disastrous.   A small
viking fleet forced its way up the river to the Pitres
bridge ;   Paris suffered from a land raid ;   there was
an unsuccessful attack on Chartres.   And then the
little fleet actually broke through the Pitres barrier, probably
as yet incomplete, and for the whole of twenty days the vikings
plundered in and around St. Denis.   Charles superseded Adalhard
and put Robert in his place ; but at the beginning of 866 the
pirates had got past Paris as far as Melun, eluding the Frankish
troops who were pursuing them.   Thereat Charles weakened
and gave in.   Four thousand pounds of silver, together with
large quantities of wine, was the price he paid the vikings to
get rid of them.

FURTHER
RAIDS UP
THE SEINE
865–866

For once the bribe seemed to have achieved its purpose.
The vikings withdrew, the bridge at Pitres was rebuilt, and for
ten years the Seine valley was left unmolested.   But it was not
the bribe so much as the misfortunes of another country (these
were the years of the Danish conquest of eastern England)
that gave respite to the Franks of Neustria.   And there was no
peace for the Franks of the Loire.   Hastein, that
great viking, appears in Brittany in 866, and Robert
the Strong, now recalled to the Loire, was killed in
the battle of Brissarthe, near Châteauneuf-sur-Sarthe, that
followed Hastein's first raid.   The loss of this bold and resolute
man was a serious one, and as a result the vikings remained
unchallenged on the lower Loire.   In 867 Hastein destroyed

HASTEIN
IN BRIT-
TANY 866

Bourges and in 868 he attacked Orleans ; but the relations between the vikings and the Bretons, now familiar with one another by reason of their occasional alliances and by the ordinary trading that inevitably took place in the peaceful intervals between the plundering expeditions, had changed. The vikings had shown that they could be harmless neighbours when it so pleased them, and they had shown that they could even be useful if their strength could be turned against the Frankish king when he threatened Brittany. So, as a result of Breton PEACE and Frankish jealousy, in 869 a rash and experimental BETWEEN peace was made by Duke Salomon of Brittany with VIKINGS Hastein and his pirates. For the first time a viking AND host dwelt in France officially recognized, at any rate BRETONS by its immediate neighbours, as settlers in the land.
869

As was to be expected, this peace did not really remove the distrust and dread of the vikings who had so hardly used the Loire countryside, and in the end, after the arrangement had lasted for three years, Salomon's suspicions were fully justified. The breaking of the peace was one of those daring and impudent exploits that occasionally enliven the records of the Northmen's rapine and arson. In the spring of 872 they suddenly took ship (they were then dwelling on their island-base in the lower Loire), sailed up-river, and then turned up the Maine to Angers. The inhabitants of this luckless town VIKINGS fled precipitately and the vikings entered the empty CAPTURE streets unopposed. It was, of course, expected that AND HOLD they would plunder and burn, and then, following ANGERS their usual custom, depart hastily with their booty. 872-873 But this time the vikings did nothing of the sort. Finding themselves in complete possession of a Frankish town, admirably situated astride the river and easy to defend, they elected to send for their wives and children, and, having done so, they settled down in comfortable occupation of the place. Angers was to be their new home.

Such was plainly their intention. But though vikings in a remote island-fastness of a rebellious province might be tolerated, vikings in complete occupation of a Frankish city, within raiding distance of Tours itself, was more than the often-humiliated ruler of the western kingdom dare permit. For a year, or nearly a year, they were indeed allowed to remain in Angers, but in the summer of 873 Charles marched against them with a great army and he had no difficulty in persuading Salomon and the Bretons to join his expedition. The vikings had set the fortifications in order so it was necessary to lay siege to the town, and Charles immediately set to work by building an elaborate circumvallation. But he could not effect a proper blockade of the Maine, and this left the river-route in and out of Angers open to the vikings, who were thus able to watch the operations of the investing force without undue perturbation. Many were the attacks made on the town walls, and new engines of war were specially invented to help push them home ; but it was all in vain, and the vikings, so long as their escape could be easily made, remained unshaken. Then an epidemic began to rage among the besiegers and the attacks weakened in strength ; the Christian leaders began to despair, and at last, in October, it was realized that if there was to be success at all the viking ships must be destroyed without delay. The plan they adopted was a bold and ingenious measure, nothing less than the diverting of the Maine by cutting a great canal. It succeeded instantly ; the ships were left high and dry, and fell an easy prey to the Franks and the Bretons, whereupon the vikings, now absolutely cut off from retreat or from possible reinforcement, surrendered without more ado.

The terms Charles imposed seem suspiciously lenient, and there is some talk of his having accepted a bribe ; but he did at least extract from the vikings a promise that they would leave his kingdom, and they certainly were sent back at once to their island-home on the lower Loire. But they were granted a few months' respite here, and the upshot was that they did not leave at all, though for a long while they did not dare to trouble the country again, except in the immediate neighbourhood of their base. In plain fact, it was not until ten years later that they finally withdrew, and then it was only to go plundering elsewhere in France.

In 876 took place the seventh viking expedition to the Seine, and, like many viking ventures, it was well timed, for it found Charles away warring in the Aix and Cologne country. The Pitres bridge once more failed to stop the pirates and they DEATH OF made their way up-stream to threaten St. Denis ; CHARLES eventually Charles returned and bought them off for THE BALD 5,000 pounds of silver. This was his last traffic 877 with the Danes, for in the following year he died.

Much had his western kingdom suffered from the great evil of the viking invasion, but it is well to remember that another and greater evil, the ceaseless fraternal jealousies and civil wars of the Carolingians, had occupied him almost to the exclusion of his other cares throughout most of the years of his long reign. Charles, in fact, believed that his paramount duty was to preserve, and, if possible, to increase, the kingdom that was left to him out of his famous grandfather's greater empire. His brothers, not the Danes, were his chief foes, and so long as he could keep the rival kings quiet at his frontiers, it was a small thing if a monastery here and a monastery there, a village or even a town, were sacked by the irresponsible pirates from Denmark. The vikings, he rightly judged, were not as yet a peril that threatened the very safety of his kingdom ; he had not thought of them as would-be colonists, had not dreamed that they might one day win a part of his broad lands for themselves. And so, though he was a brave man, he would not, he could not rather, resist the vikings with the show of force that was necessary to drive them helter-skelter for ever from his land. Untrustworthy vassals, unsuitable military organization, and a lack of suitable equipment, these things combined with the ever-present dread of treachery on the part of his brothers and of insurrection in Brittany and Aquitaine, all made a resolute opposition to the pirates and a systematic and remorseless severity impossible. Charles the Bald was the victim of his times and his conditions, and, though his disastrous bribes to the vikings constitute a shocking record of weakness, it is fairer to blame the bewildering and ever-recurring conspiracies in Frankish politics rather than to impugn the wisdom, or the personal character and valour, of the king.

It was in 877 that he died, and his death was followed by that of his son and successor, Louis the Stammerer, a year and a half later. This last king left two youthful heirs, Louis and Carloman, and a third son, Charles, who was posthumously born. Immediately factions arose in the western kingdom ; Louis of Saxony, a son of Louis the German, interfered ; an independent kingdom of Provence was set up under Boso ; in 880 there was a treaty that allotted Francia and Neustria to Louis III, and Aquitaine and Burgundy to Carloman. Louis III died in 882, and Carloman then became the sole sovereign of the old western kingdom of Charles the Bald, except for Provence. But two years later, in 884, Carloman also died, and, since the third son of Louis the Stammerer was unfit to reign by reason of his youth, the Frankish nobles appealed to the Emperor Charles the Fat, son of Louis the German, and now lord of most of the old middle and eastern kingdoms, to assume the vacant throne. By so doing they completed the union under a single crowned head of the three great kingdoms of the empire of Charles the Great.

In spite of the discord in the western kingdom, it was the

coastal district of the middle and eastern kingdoms, now ruled
by Louis of Saxony, that suffered most from the raids of the
vikings in the period between the death of Louis the
Stammerer and the death of Carloman. In 879 a large
Danish fleet, that had been wintering on the Thames
at Fulham but had found no prospect of successful
plundering in England (p. 240), appeared off the coast of France
and sacked Thérouanne. Then the pirates made for the Scheldt
and established themselves in a fortified camp at Courtrai.
Louis of Saxony heavily defeated a party of them at Thion on
the Sambre in 880, but this did not prevent the burning of Arras
and of Nimeguen, and a viking expedition into Saxony itself.
The Danes also suffered another defeat at Saucourt,
between Abbeville and Eu, this time at the hands of
the young Louis III, a famous battle that is celebrated
in a German *cantilène* that has survived till this day.[1] But,
despite these reverses, the vikings reached the valley of the
Meuse and built themselves a camp at Elsloo. In the following
winter (881–882) they sacked Maestricht and Liège, and plundered
such notable towns as Cologne, Bonn, and Aix, and for three
days they held Trier in their grip. In the meantime Louis of
Saxony had died and Charles the Fat was now master of the
whole eastern kingdom. In the summer of 882 he determined
to rid himself of these troublesome Danes, and, gathering a big
army, marched against their camp at Elsloo ; but
though his strength was considerable, for some reason
his attack did not materialize, and in the end he
resorted to negotiations. It was a shameful weakness ; one of
the viking leaders, Godfred, on the condition of his receiving
baptism, was granted a large part of Frisia, probably Rorik's
ancient holding, as a fief, and the others, Sigfred and Orm,
were bribed to take their men away.

Although Harald and Rorik in the turbulent beginnings of
Danish piracy had failed, as is easily understood, to consolidate
their holding in Frisia, this installation of Godfred, at a later
day, ought to have been a landmark in viking history, the
foundation of a state such as had been won in England and such
as was shortly to be established in Normandy. But
Godfred was not a man of sufficient political perception to build up a stable colony. At heart he was
a viking, and he was soon away on a viking raid in
Saxony, and afterwards he was foolish enough to make impudent

RAIDS
ON THE
NORTH
COAST 879

BATTLE OF
SAUCOURT
880

SIEGE OF
ELSLOO 882

COLLAPSE
OF DANISH
POWER IN
FRISIA 885

---

[1] K. Müllenhoff and W. Scherer, *Denkmäler deutsches Poesie u. Prosa*,
Berlin, 1892, I, 24.

demands of Charles the Fat for a grant of the wine-districts of Coblenz and Andernach. As a result of his intrigues, he was assassinated by Charles's agents and his army was subsequently destroyed. Thus was Frisia lost, a land that had been for so long, from 834 till 876, partially, sometimes almost entirely, under viking dominion, and that was, in a sense, the natural colony of the Danes. Henceforward, the marauding hosts and would-be settlers left this poor troubled country alone.

That part of the viking armies that followed Sigfred and Orm, after some plundering in Flanders and Picardy, now turned to attack the western kingdom, and were bribed by Carloman to leave his realm in peace. But after Carloman's death they deemed themselves absolved from their bond, and, failing to obtain a similar bribe from Charles the Fat, who had succeeded Carloman as ruler of the West Franks, they forthwith attacked the Seine country. This was in the spring of 885.

It was a great force that had been collected, 700 ships and probably as many as 40,000 men, a viking invasion far more terrible than anything France had as yet seen. In July they took Rouen, and, after breaking through a Frankish force sent to oppose them, they concentrated in their full strength before Paris on the 24th of November. And now began one of the most memorable events of all the viking wars, the siege of Paris.

SIEGE OF PARIS 885

Paris was, except for some outlying suburbs, still an island-town, and in 885 there were only two bridges connecting the island with the river-banks. The northern bridge, leading to the north bank of the Seine, was a stone structure, narrow, but well made and strongly fortified with protecting towers at either end. The bridge connecting with the south bank was only made of wood, but it was also defended by towers. Clearly all depended on these bridges, for if they were destroyed the viking fleet could pass unhindered up the Seine, and while they held the Danes could not possibly attain their objective, which was the confluence of the Marne and Seine above Paris and the plundering of the inland Marne country beyond Paris. Yet it must have seemed a forlorn hope to stay their progress, for there were only two hundred men-at-arms in the town.

At first Sigfred tried to negotiate for a passage up-stream, offering to leave Paris in peace, but he was summarily refused by the gallant leaders of the defence, Joscelin, Abbot of St. Germain, and Odo (Eudes), Marquess of Neustria and son of Robert the Strong. They had been bidden by Charles, they said, to bar the Seine against the vikings, and bar the Seine they would ; so the Danes had no other choice than to attempt the capture of the town.   On the morning of the 26th came the first attack, and it was directed against the tower on the right bank of the Seine defending the northern bridge.   All day the furious battle raged ; sling-stones and arrows beat upon its walls ; burning pitch and boiling oil was poured upon the assailants.   But the defence prevailed and at nightfall the vikings withdrew, having lost many men and with nothing achieved. During the night the Parisians, building desperately, added a storey to the tower's defences.   The second day's fight was no less furious than the first ; the vikings brought a battering-ram and a heavy catapult into play, and attempted to undermine the tower's foundations and to fire its wooden walls ; but, once more, they were beaten off with heavy loss.

By the end of the second day the Danes had learnt their lesson and for a while abandoned these disastrous shock-tactics. Their next move was to entrench themselves within a camp that they constructed around the abbey of St. Germain l'Aux-errois, and here they remained for some weeks, harrying the country far and wide in collecting provisions for the winter, while they also occupied themselves in preparing new and more formidable engines of war.   On the 31st of January they advanced again to the attack, menacing the tower with one division of their forces and directing two others against the bridge itself. For three days the battle raged.   The vikings tried every possible stratagem ; they attempted to fill up the fosse round the tower with straw, branches, slaughtered animals, and even with the dead bodies of their prisoners ; on the last day of the fight they filled three of their ships with inflammable material, and, setting fire to them, let them drift against the bridge ; but the vessels burnt themselves out harmlessly against the bastions.   For the third time the Danes were forced to withdraw leaving the defence unshaken.

On the 6th of February came suddenly the winter floods, and the swollen Seine itself swept away the southern wooden bridge, cutting off the tower on the left Seine bank from the island-city.   The disaster must have been foreseen, for only twelve defenders were posted in the tower when it thus fell an easy prey to the vikings.   But with the destruction of the bridge, the river-route was at last open to the Danes, and, so long as a small force remained to invest Paris, the greater part of the viking host was at liberty to pass up-stream, keeping in to the south bank of the Seine, and to plunder the inland country right up to the Loire.   The principal attacks, however, were directed eastwards ; both Chartres and Le Mans were threatened by the Danes at this time, and Évreux fell to them.

Joscelin now sent messengers to Charles, who was in Italy, and to Henry of Saxony, with urgent requests for help. Henry did indeed come to the aid of the Parisians towards the end of February, but his Germans suffered severely during their hard winter-march, and after one abortive attack on the Danish camp they withdrew without bringing any appreciable relief to the inhabitants of the beleaguered town.

As a safeguard against further attacks from the Eastern Franks, the Danes moved their camp to St. Germain-des-Prés on the left bank of the Seine, and now it seemed that all hope of saving the town was extinguished. But already Sigfred himself was tiring of the investment of Paris and consented to be bought off by the paltry bribe of 60 pounds of silver. He could not, however, persuade the majority of his countrymen to accompany him, though he incited them to another fruitless attack on the stone bridge to prove to them the difficulty of taking Paris by direct assault ; in the end he sailed off down the river with his own personal following in the second week of April. But soon after his departure the Parisians were dismayed by what seemed to be the worst and cruellest misfortune that had as yet befallen them, for Joscelin, their beloved bishop and the mainspring of a glorious defence, fell sick and died. Now, in truth, was their position desperate ; their leader was gone, disease was taking a heavy toll of their numbers, and there was scarcely sufficient room on their little island for the burying of all their dead. But there still remained that man of courage, Odo, and he, seeing their terrible plight, secretly left the town at the beginning of June to plead with the Frankish grandees for immediate help, to plead, if necessary, with Charles the Fat himself, for the emperor was by this time back from Italy. His mission was successful ; he returned with an escort that fought a way for him back into the town, and he was able to promise the speedy arrival of the emperor's troops. By the middle of August Charles with a mighty host was moving against the Danes.

At Quierzy the emperor was joined by Duke Henry, but Henry shortly afterwards lost his life in a rash reconnoitring movement, and Charles, much discomfited by this event, delayed his own advance. The Danes, however, were alive to the gravity of the position and determined upon one last and formidable attack on Paris ; with their full strength they flung themselves upon the defences and a last and terrible battle was

fought. But the Parisians fought with the knowledge that help
was at hand, and once again the indomitable courage of the
garrison prevailed. The vikings were beaten off. And then
Charles advanced ; he flung the Danes back on to the south
bank of the river, sent reinforcements into the town, and moved
a part of his army across the Seine to invest the Danish camp.
Finally, in October, he established his main body in an entrenched
position at the foot of Montmartre.

And now, after all this bravery on the part of the Parisians,
this proper show of force on the part of the emperor, once more
was enacted the dismal folly of the Elsloo debacle. Charles
failed to strike a decisive and crushing blow ; instead he opened
negotiations with the vikings, and in the end granted the Danes
a free passage up the Seine and the right to take up winter-
quarters in rebellious Burgundy. Afterwards, in the spring, he
was to pay them 700 pounds of silver on the condition that they
would then finally leave his country. In the beginning of
November a treaty to this effect was concluded, and he thereby
accorded to the Danes all that the wretched Parisians had
fought so hard to withhold from them.

But Odo and the brave people of the town would not be
cheated in this shameful fashion without some vigorous protest.
They indignantly disregarded the treaty, and of their own
accord refused the vikings permission to sail past Paris. They
could not, of course, succeed in holding them back for long,
but they forced the Danes to drag all their ships for some
distance over dry land in order to reach the Seine above the
town.

And as for Charles, when he departed, he heard that Sigfred
was back plundering on the lower Seine, and that Soissons in
the east and Bayeux in the west had fallen to his vikings.

In the beginning of 888 Charles the Fat was deposed, an
event that spelt the final dismemberment of the empire of Charles
the Great. The West Franks thereupon elected as their king
the hero of the siege, Odo, Marquess of Neustria. He was,
indeed, the one man likely to make a brave attempt to rid his
country of the pirates who were now ravaging at their will on the
Marne and Aisne in Burgundy, and at first it seemed that he
would justify the high hopes that were entertained of him. In
ODO AND June of this year he surprised a force of the Danes at
THE SEINE Montfaucon in the Argonne between Verdun and the
VIKINGS Aisne, and, though he was outnumbered and he himself
888–889   wounded in the battle, the impetuous charge of his
men put the vikings to flight. The Danes, however, returned

to Meaux, which had previously fallen to their countrymen, and, subsequently, threatened Paris; but Odo with his army covered the town and there was no attack. Nevertheless in May of 889 they approached Paris to claim the bribe promised them by the deposed emperor, and when they attempted, in defiance of their oath, to go back up-stream for further plundering, their progress was at once barred by Odo and the Parisians. There was skirmishing, and a battle in which the vikings came off worse, but the end was that Odo, like Charles before him, found himself compelled to purchase their withdrawal downstream. This was the last time that a viking fleet visited the island-city, and it was a fleet that must indeed have learnt to stand in awe of the dauntless population of the little town that was destined to become the capital of France.

After the retreat from Paris one section of the great viking force sailed to the mouth of the Vire in the Cotentin and, in 889 or 890, captured St. Lô.[1] But on attempting to move further south, this party of the Danes was heavily defeated and it subsequently made off to Conflans at the junc-

THE COTENTIN AND THE SCHELDT 890–892

tion of the Oise and the Seine. These Northmen afterwards plundered on the Oise, where they were vigorously opposed by Odo, and also on the Scheldt; for a while they ravaged on this last-named river unchecked, but in 891 they met with defeat at the hands of Arnulf, Carloman's son and king of the East Franks, at Dyle near Louvain; and in 892, in the time of a severe famine, the whole force, now only 250 ships strong, sailed off to England, landing at the mouth of the Lymne in east Kent.

Until 882 the vikings of the famous Angers exploit had remained in the Loire country, but in that year Hastein and his fleet left Brittany and sailed off to the Somme, where they

FRANCIA RID OF VIKINGS 892

remained for many years. After the siege of Paris, however, when the Franks were pressing the vikings hard, Hastein found his tenure in Picardy insecure, and about the same time as the battle near Louvain his vikings were defeated by a Frankish army collected by King

[1] History has nothing to say as to the period when the Channel Islands first fell into the hands of the vikings; it may have happened during this Cotentin campaign, but the position of the islands makes it probable enough that they had long been known to the vikings on their journeys to the Loire mouth. The evidence of Danish occupation, as derived from place-names, is overwhelmingly strong and in Guernsey (Warns-ey) a megalithic monument still bears in the modern name Déhus the Danish name for a barrow, *dysse*. See my *Archaeology of the Channel Islands*, I (London, 1928), pp. 15, 16, 132.

Odo. In 892, therefore, Hastein followed the example of the great army and crossed the Channel to England, heading for the Thames mouth. Thus was the land of the Franks free from the viking terror for the first time in forty years.

And the respite seems to have been a long one. After the victory won over the Danes by Alfred the Great in 896, some of the vikings from England may have begun to return to the Seine, and there was a minor expedition up this river about this time under a viking whose name appears in the chronicles as Huncdeus ; but many years elapsed before a force of considerable strength was once more collected on the lower waters of the Seine. The new period of viking aggression begins in 910 when there was a raid in the Sénonais district of Burgundy ; the marauders were defeated by the Bishop of Auxerre, but nevertheless they went farther on, to plunder Bourges, and even contemplated an attack far to the south on Clermont-Ferrand.

INVASION In 911 the same or another band of vikings, commanded
OF ROLLO by Rollo, advanced against Chartres and laid siege to
911   the town. Its defences, however, had been repaired, and its bishop lost no time in appealing to the Frankish grandees for help ; but whether outside aid came or not, when the vikings launched their biggest attack they were driven off with heavy loss and compelled to raise the siege. They retreated hastily to their headquarters on the Seine, and though afterwards some of them were able to make a daring, though abortive, venture in the Nivernais on the upper Loire, they were by this time much more disposed to seek peaceful settlement in the land than riches by means of the old plunderings and robberies that were daily becoming more and more perilous and unprofitable.

Rollo, the chieftain of these Northmen on the Seine, is one of the most celebrated personages of viking history, perhaps, indeed, the only man among all the pirate-princes of the west whose memory has been consistently treasured until this day with honour and affection in the land that he made his home. On the authority of the *Heimskringla*, he is supposed to have been a Norwegian, namely that Ganger-Rolf who was the exiled son of Ragnvald, earl of Möre (p. 306), the trusty liegeman and comrade of King Harald Fairhair, and it is chronologically quite possible [1] that Ganger-Rolf should have played a part in these operations in the country of the West Franks. The difficulty about this identification is that the Norman chroniclers themselves do not seem to have known the name Ganger-Rolf, or even Rolf alone, and the name that they do cite, Rollo, is better

---

[1] Though not according to the reckoning of Finnur Jonsson.

derived from ON. Hrollaugr or Hrolleif rather than from Rolf.[1] But this in itself would not disprove the Norwegian nationality of Rollo, and as guarantee of his Danish origin there is nothing better than the always-to-be-suspected word of that very indifferent historian Dudo of St. Quentin. On the other hand, in St. Olaf's time, according to the *Heimskringla*, a Duke of Rouen, a descendant of Rollo, declared that he well remembered his kinship with the chiefs of Norway ; while Saxo, the persistent panegyrist of the Danes and a writer to whom Dudo's book was known, makes no boast that Rollo was of Danish ancestry. It must be held, therefore, as most likely, though not proven with certainty, that Rollo was Norwegian [2] ; but whether he were Norwegian or Danish, there can be no doubt that the bulk of the army he commanded was composed of Danish vikings and that he had with him at the most only a few Norwegians from Ireland or from Norway itself. In a word, the signal achievement of this army that is now to be described must be counted as a Danish enterprise.

At this time Charles the Simple, the posthumous son of Louis the Stammerer, was king of the West Franks, having succeeded Odo in 898. He was not, despite his surname, a man of no understanding or determination, and after the retreat of Rollo's army from Chartres he acted with statesmanship and precision. He saw that while the Franks were strong enough to keep the vikings in check and could prevent serious and far-flung raids by them, yet it was useless to attempt an organized defence of the kingdom as a whole, or to oust the Danes from their settlement on the lower basin of the Seine. To shield his own most precious dominions, the very heart of his realm, from further peril of viking attacks by way of the Seine and the Oise, he realized that it was necessary under these circumstances not only to tolerate the presence of the Northmen on the lower Seine, but to establish them there in the status of peaceful citizens whose interest it would be to prevent the attacks that he himself feared. And so, at the end of 911, Charles and Rollo made a treaty at St. Clair-sur-Epte on the highroad from Rouen to Paris.

By this treaty Charles offered to Rollo as a fief, on the

---

[1] Which would probably appear in the chronicles as Rodulfus.

[2] For an attempt to prove that Rollo was a Swede, see *Eng. Hist. Review*, III (1892), 214. A summary of the whole debate over Rollo's nationality is given by H. Prentout, *Essai sur les origines et la fondation du Duché de Normandie*, Paris, 1911, p. 153 ff. Cf. L. Weibull, *Hist. Tidskrift f. Skåneland*, IV (1910–13), p. 205, *Rollo o. Gånge-Rolf*.

customary terms of vassalage in the Frankish kingdoms (*terram determinatam in allodo et in fundo*), all the territory that was NOR- later known as Haute Normandie, that is the country MANDY between the Bresle and the Epte and the sea, together CEDED TO with the Rouen, Lisieux and Évreux districts of the ROLLO 911 Seine basin. This offer, which was accompanied by the disgraceful intimation that the Danes might continue to plunder in Brittany, was conditional upon Rollo paying homage to Charles and adopting the Christian faith, conditions that bound Rollo to keep the peace with the Christian king and, more than that, to defend from attack that portion of the Christian kingdom that was offered to him. Rollo agreed, did homage to Charles (with a very bad grace, so the story goes), and became a Christian. Now at last the vikings had won for themselves a permanent and recognized home in France.

Rollo took his new position as the Christian lord of Haute Normandie seriously. He is said to have rebuilt and re-endowed the abbeys that had been pillaged and ruined by the Danes, to have divided the land among his followers, according them the full odel (i.e. freehold and hereditary) rights to their properties, and to have set in order the defences of the towns ; in addition to these measures he formulated some sort of rough-and-ready legal code on the Scandinavian model that was sufficient to guarantee the personal safety of his subjects and the security of their possessions.

In what degree he considered himself master of his new territory it is difficult to say. The chronicles call him *princeps* or *dux*, and, later, *patricius*, and he was doubtless considered by the folk of Scandinavia and Denmark to be the absolute ruler of an independent and self-governed colony. But in Frankish eyes he was certainly nothing more than a new Count of Rouen, the lord of a restricted fief, owing proper allegiance to the king of the West Franks. As such, after the revolt that led to the crowning of Robert of Neustria as king of France, Rollo loyally took up arms in 923 on behalf of Charles the Simple against Robert's son-in-law and successor Raoul, Duke of Burgundy ; but for this recognition of his vassalage, if such it was, he paid dearly, since later on Raoul made a punitive expedition into Normandy, burning and slaughtering in the land of the vikings just as these had been wont to burn and slaughter in the country of the Franks. After this the vikings in their turn began to ravage the provinces across the Oise and in the end a peace was patched up between them and the new royal house on terms that were favourable to Rollo inasmuch as he now received the Bessin and Hiémois districts for the aggrandizement of his existing fief.

There were, however, continual arrivals into the colony of fresh adventurers from the north and it was a long while before occasional outbursts of the old viking temper had ceased to be a danger to the safe tenure of Rollo's Frankish duchy. Thus in 925 there was an invasion of the Beauvaisis by armed bands of the Normandy settlers, a serious attack that culminated in the burning of Arras and Amiens, and as reprisal for this King Raoul marched into Normandy and captured Eu with heavy loss to the Danes. Later in this same year there was a battle at Fauquembergue in Artois between the new colonists and the Franks, and though Raoul himself was wounded over a thousand of the Danes were killed and the remainder put to flight ; after this defeat Rollo's little state was in real danger of dissolution, but fortunately for him Raoul was prevented from consolidating his substantial victories in Normandy by the necessity of withdrawing his troops to repel an invasion of the Hungarians, and the Frankish king was therefore compelled to terminate the Danish war summarily by the old expedient of a bribe.

The granting of Normandy to Rollo, however, had achieved its object in that a desultory border-warfare was the worst evil that was now likely to disturb West Francia from the Channel side, and henceforward the oppressing dread of the formidable viking raids up the Seine was at an end. But there were, nevertheless, other vikings besides those of Normandy FURTHER remaining in Francia. In 897 Odo had come to terms RAIDS ON with some of the Seine vikings, leaving them free to THE LOIRE go off to the Loire, and this they had accordingly 919–939 done. Not being so dangerously situated, in the opinion of the West Frankish king, as were their countrymen on the Seine, they had been ignored by Charles the Simple at the time of the treaty of St. Clair-sur-Epte ; but the Loire valley suffered seriously from their depredations. In 919 Brittany was ravaged with the utmost severity [1] ; Nantes fell again, Angers and Tours were burnt, and Orleans was besieged. Robert of Neustria, the brother of King Odo, drove them out of his duchy in 921, but after a five months' siege of their stronghold he was content to accept hostages from them and to withdraw, leaving them in undisputed possession of the Nantes district. In 923,

---

[1] Nordmanni omnem Britanniam in cornu Galliae in ora scilicet maritima sitam depopulantur, proterunt atque delent, abductis, venditis, ceterisque cunctis ejectis Britonibus (*Ann. Clod.*, Pertz, *M.G.H.*, SS. III, p. 368).

at the time of the outbreak of civil war between the Carolingians and the Capetians, these Loire vikings raided far south into the Aquitaine and Auvergne, and in 924, made bold by their unrestricted progress, they demanded for themselves a fief such as had been granted to Rollo. This was refused them by King Raoul, and thereupon they went off plundering into Neustria, now the territory of Hugh the Great ; in the winter of the same year they even invaded Burgundy, but there they met with a defeat and afterwards retired in confusion to Melun on the Seine, subsequently escaping back to Nantes when both Hugh and Raoul took the field against them. In 927 Hugh the Great set out to attack them in Brittany, but his campaign, which lasted only for five weeks, ended, as Robert's had done six years before, in an agreement whereby the vikings gave hostages and promised to make no further raids on the condition that they were left undisturbed in Nantes. They kept their word for a time and no more is heard of them until 930 when they penetrated into the Limousin country, and there they suffered a crushing defeat at the hands of King Raoul that abruptly ended the long and bloody record of viking onslaught upon the land of France.

For the raiders, when they returned discomfited to Nantes, now found that their position on the Loire was itself no longer secure, since the Bretons, encouraged by Raoul's great victory, were risen against them. In 931, upon the feast of St. Michael, they were caught off their guard and large numbers of them massacred including their leader Felecan, and though a Loire viking named Incon afterwards ravaged Brittany as a reprisal for this slaughter of his fellows, the fighting spirit of the Bretons was not extinguished. In 936 their chief, Alan Barbetorte, returned from England where he had been a refugee, and putting himself at the head of local levies he quickly fired the enthusiasm of his compatriots by crushing victories over the foreigners [1] at Dol and St. Brieuc. He then marched towards the Loire and in 937 his campaign was crowned by a decisive and brilliant coup, the recapture of Nantes. The vikings that escaped with their lives fled from the country, and thereafter Brittany had only to fear her neighbours the Normans. In 939 there was a Norman attack upon Rennes, but the invaders were subsequently

---

[1] The chronicles do not distinguish between Normans, that is to say Danes from Normandy, and the Loire vikings. It is probable that these initial victories of Alan were won in a campaign against the invading Normans who long continued to be dangerous and pugnacious enemies of the Bretons.

annihilated in their fortress of Trans (Trant) near Coësnon, and the victorious Bretons were left, for a time at any rate, as undisputed masters of their own land. Thus after a full century of terror and bloodshed, of humiliation and dismay, of vicious outrage and foul sacrilege, the attack of the Danes upon Francia was ended.

Rollo died about the year 927 and his son, William Longsword, succeeded him. The new duke recognized Raoul as king and did homage to him, once on his succession and again in 933 on receiving the Avranchin and the Cotentin which were in RISE OF that year added to his duchy, perhaps as purchase-THE NOR- price of his continued fidelity. He was a man of MANS Frankish tastes, a devout, though rather irresolute, Christian, having few of the qualities of his viking forefathers, and it is not surprising, therefore, that there should have been a reaction in Normandy when he died in 942, both paganism, with a revival of the cult of Thor, and viking savagery showing themselves plainly under the thin veneer of Frankish culture. Immigrants from Scandinavia and Denmark were no doubt responsible for much of this unrest,[1] but an unsuccessful attack shortly after William's death by the Carolingian Louis d'Outremer, king of France from 936 to 954, helped to restore order in the duchy for the reason that Louis was plainly desirous of wresting Normandy from her young duke. This was Richard (942–996), who at first had been a supporter of the heathen party ; but the Christian Normans rapidly asserted themselves as the political leaders of the duchy, so that the duke, realizing that the ultimate triumph of Frankish civilization was certain, finally concluded a formal alliance, not with the Carolingian, but with Hugh the Great and, later, with Hugh Capet. From this time onwards the distinctively northern character of the people of the duchy, their Scandinavian or Danish manner of life and their old viking roughness, weakens, and only the build and body of the Normans endured as proof of their viking ancestry. For these alliances with the Capetian princes drew Normandy more and more into the political maelstrom of tenth-century Francia, more and more made Christianity necessary as the adopted religion of the duchy, more and more made the law of Normandy Frankish, and more and more the speech of Normandy French.

In what degree the viking blood that was in them contributed to the remarkable vigour of the eleventh and twelfth century

[1] One band of these new arrivals was commanded by ' Haigrold ' and it is not impossible that this chieftain was either King Harald Gormsson of Denmark or King Harald Greycloak of Norway.

Norman stock is a matter upon which no decision can be reached. The duchy certainly, as its history shows, remained a land of adventurers and brave seamen, and the two great events in the subsequent story of the Normans, the conquest of southern Italy and Sicily and the conquest of England, were exploits that superficially may seem to be only a natural sequel to the viking beginnings of the Norman aristocracy ; but, in truth, explanations of these mighty enterprises, simpler and more satisfactory than the mere spur of a lively ancestral tradition, are readily to be found in the contemporary political conditions and in the potent factor of the over-population of the pleasant province of Normandy.

Therefore with the adventures of the Normans in Italy, the first despatch of soldiers in 1016, the granting of Aversa to Rainulf about 1029, the papal confirmation of Robert Guiscard as Duke of Apulia in 1059, the Norman conquest of Sicily, the audacious war with the Greek empire and the fighting on the Illyrian coast in the early '80s, and with the coronation of Roger II as King of Sicily in 1130, with the whole brave story of Norman achievement in the Mediterranean world, this book is not concerned. Nor is there need to recount the familiar tale of how in 1066 the great Norman duke, William the Conqueror, overthrew the English Harald and made of the remote kingdom across the Channel a realm henceforth brought into the daylight of European politics, no longer an outlying, backward country but a land awakened and refreshed by the strong-flowing tide of continental culture and continental thought.

CHAPTER VIII

ENGLAND

BY the end of the ninth century two great Mercian kings, Æthelbald and Offa, had established a political ascendency that made the rulers of Mercia the dominating personalities in English affairs, even though the realm of Wessex and the once mighty state of Northumbria still held themselves aloof. It was during this period of Mercian supremacy that the first recorded viking raids, the sporadic plunderings of Norwegian pirates (p. 4), took place; but after the appearance of vikings near Dorchester and the attacks upon Lindisfarne and Jarrow, England knew no more of the pirates for a period of forty years, and when they began once again to plague this country the power and territories of the English kingdoms had altered. Northumbria remained a rich but sorry state, enfeebled by a turmoil of civil wars; the great kingdom of Mercia had dwindled to only half RISE OF its former size; Wessex had expanded to a large and THE KING- prosperous realm that now embraced all of England DOM OF south of the Thames. The men of Essex had also WESSEX submitted to the West Saxons; but the East Anglians, who had broken away from Mercia, were ruled by their own king as an independent realm.

The man who had accomplished this aggrandizement of Wessex, who had conquered West Wales (Cornwall and Devon), routed the Mercians, and put his own son to rule over the sub-kingdom of Kent, was the ætheling Ecgbert, son of one of the petty kings of Kent. He had been driven out of England by Offa and Beorhtric of Wessex, but on the death of Beorhtric in 802 he returned to be elected king of Wessex in his place. It was in 825 that Mercia collapsed and the growing power of the southern kingdom was transformed into an assured supremacy.

The viking attacks begin again in 834. It was the year of a great Danish attack upon Frisia (p. 194), and many of the Danes who set out then, and later, to harry that country and the French coast also determined to try their fortunes in England. They first appeared at the Thames mouth, where they ravaged the island of Sheppey, but two years later there was another raid,

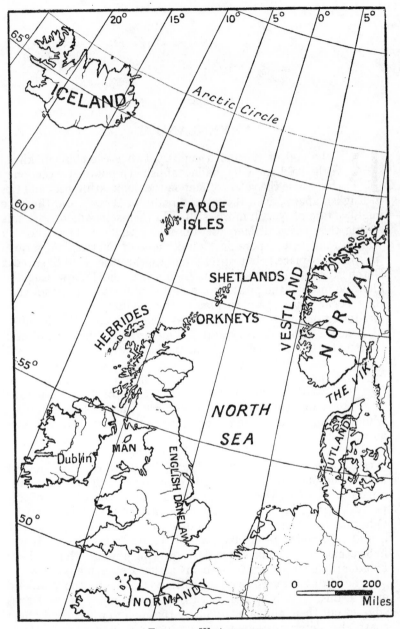

FIG. 30.—West-over-sea

carried out by a detachment of thirty-five ships from a Danish
DANISH   fleet that had been operating against Frisia, and this
RAIDS ON   time the landing was made on the Dorset coast.
SOUTHERN   Ecgbert himself opposed them and fought the pirates
ENGLAND
AND   at Charmouth,[1] but the English were worsted in the
CORNWALL   encounter, though luckily the vikings soon afterwards
834–838   made off without doing any notable plundering.
In 838 there was a third raid, and now the landing was made
in Cornwall. Once more Ecgbert marched to meet the invaders,
and though the discontented Cornish had risen in arms to join
them, he overthrew the united forces of the vikings and the
rebels at Hinxton Down near Callington.

Ecgbert died in 839 and Æthelwulf, his son, succeeded him
as lord of Wessex. In the year after the accession of this much
weaker, though devout and well-intentioned king, the Emperor of
the Franks, Louis the Pious, died and the disruption of his great
            empire began. This was the signal for a renewed out-
RAIDS ON   burst of viking activity, and just as the Franks were
SOUTHERN
AND   now to know the full terrors of the Danish invasions,
EASTERN   so too in England from this time onwards the raids
ENGLAND   became more frequent and the menace of the Danish
840–842   attack grew more and more serious. In 840 a fleet
of thirty-three viking ships was defeated at Southampton with a
great slaughter of the pirates, but in another raid, directed against
Dorset, the Danes won a big victory at Portland. In 841 others
of the Danes won a fight in Romney Marsh on the south coast of
Kent, and in that same year they ravaged not only on the south
coast, but in Lincolnshire and East Anglia. In the following
year the Danes of the celebrated Quentovic fleet (p. 199) pillaged
London, and, after the sudden dash across the Channel to the
unhappy town of Quentovic, these same Danes returned to
plunder Rochester.

During the next decade the Danish pirates were so fully
occupied with their increasingly audacious raids into the heart
of the western Frankish kingdom and so greedy for the easily
obtained plunder from the rich monasteries of the Continent
that they left England in peace. But towards the end of 850
a Danish fleet of 350 ships, returning from a continental plundering, arrived off Thanet and wintered there, and in the beginning
of the next year the crews began to ravage the country. The
great horde of pirates first took Canterbury, and then captured
London, putting Beortwulf, the king of Mercia, to flight. After

[1] Or at Carhampton, in which case the vikings landed in Somerset
or N. Devon.

this they crossed the Thames and invaded Surrey ; but this was
DANES   the end of their adventures, for at Oakley[1] they were
DEFEATED met by Æthelwulf and the West Saxon army and there
AT OAKLEY they suffered an overwhelming defeat.   In the same
851   year the men of Devon defeated a viking band, and
another Danish force was put to flight at Sandwich in Kent,
losing nine of its ships.

Yet these victories over the Danes did not check the viking
invasion.   In 853 the united levies of Kent and Surrey were
called out to fight the pirates in Thanet ; in 855 one party of
vikings made a daring raid into Mercia and went plundering in
the upper Severn valley ; in the same year the Danes wintered
in Sheppey.   In 861 a great fleet that had been operating on the
Somme landed a pirate force on the Hampshire coast, and,
marching inland, this army took Winchester by storm ; but the
men of Hampshire and Berkshire rose up against them and the
Danes were soon driven out of the country.   Four years later
another band of vikings took up their quarters in Thanet and
began to negotiate for a peace with the men of Kent who were
now prepared to bribe the Danes not to attack them ; but before
a bargain was struck the vikings lost patience and forthwith
ravaged East Kent far and wide.

This, for the time being, was the end of the sporadic raids
on Wessex, but England was now confronted by a much graver
peril than these occasional viking attacks, however serious the
pillaging and destruction that resulted from them.   The new
danger was nothing less than a great and purposeful invasion
that had as its objective the conquest and settlement of the land,
and it was a danger that was all the more urgent in that the blow
fell not upon the strong kingdom of Wessex, that might have
successfully resisted the attack, but on the weaker realms of
East Anglia and Northumbria.   The few years' respite from
Danish attacks that gave Wessex breathing-space after the final
expulsion of the Thanet pirates in 865 were years wherein a storm
was gathering on the borders of the kingdom, a storm so fearful
that when it broke over Wessex, as inevitably it had to, it was only
the courage and tenacity of a hero-king, Alfred the Great, that
saved England from passing completely under Danish dominion.

The large army of Danes that in 866 established itself in
East Anglia was, according to Scandinavian tradition, a force

[1] I am adopting here the usual identification of Oakley with Ockley,
south of Dorking, but I believe the site of the battle is as likely to have
been Oakley on the Thames near Gravesend.   For the claims of Ockley
Wood near Merstham, Surrey, see *Surrey Arch. Collns.*, XXV, 136.

made up of the followings of the three sons of Ragnar Lodbrok
(p. 203), namely Halfdan, Ivar, who had arrived from Ireland,
(p. 279), and Ubbe ; and a further tradition, though it is scarcely
THE INVA- to be believed, tells that they had come to avenge
SION OF   the death of their father, who is said to have been
866   killed in an earlier raid on Northumbria. That these
three chiefs were indeed the sons of Ragnar is probable enough,
but as to the motive that inspired this great invasion it is more
likely that they came with the plain intention of winning land
for themselves and their men. For this is certainly what they
set themselves to do. The first action of the Danes after they
had made themselves secure in East Anglia was to obtain horses,
and when they were properly equipped as cavalry for a cross-
country expedition, they made a circuit round the fens and then
moved northwards across Lindsey into the province of Deira.
As usual in this period of her political and military decline,
Northumbria was in a state of civil war, and in 867 the Danes
DANES   captured York without meeting any serious opposition.
CAPTURE   The two rival kings, Ælle and Osbeorht, were now
YORK 867   uncomfortably aware that there would be no English
kingdom of Northumbria for them to fight for if they did not
at once make common cause against the invaders ; so they
patched up a peace and marched off together to recapture York.
But it was too late ; the attempt failed and both the English
kings were killed in the fighting.

The Danes made York (*Jórvík* it was now called in place of
the English name *Eoforwic*) their stronghold, and soon all Deira
lay under their dominion. Nor was it long before they were
in a position to extend their conquests. Bernicia, to the north,
did not attract them, and so was allowed to remain for a time
under the rule of its English princes ; but to the south-west lay
the richer lands of Mercia, and thither a large force of the Danes
advanced. Their route took them down the valley of the Trent
to Nottingham, and seizing that town, they remained there
for the winter. In the meantime the king of Mercia, Burhred,
appealed to Æthelred, the fourth son of Æthelwulf and now king
of the West Saxons, for help, and the Wessex king, with his
brother Alfred, marched with an army to join Burhred in an
attempt to win back Nottingham. The English laid siege to the
town, but there was no pitched battle and in the end the Mercians
bought a peace, the viking host thereupon retiring to York.
For a year the whole Danish force remained in Deira, but late in
869 a Danish army rode south, burning the fenland monasteries
and plundering recklessly on all sides, until it arrived at Thetford

FIG. 31.—England and Wales

in East Anglia, where it made preparations to pass the winter.
There Edmund, King of East Anglia, met them in battle, but
the English force was decisively beaten, Edmund himself being
CONQUEST captured by Ivar the Boneless and Ubbe and, it is
OF EAST said, cruelly put to death at Hoxne because he would
ANGLIA not become the vassal of a pagan. The exact cir-
869 cumstances of Edmund's death are unknown and the
familiar story of his martyrdom cannot rank as more than legend,
but there is no reason to doubt that some cruel and cold-blooded
act of Danish barbarism attended the death of this unfortunate
petty king ; for, insignificant though he was, few events in the
whole of the history of the viking wars so profoundly impressed
a horror-struck Christendom. The memory of Edmund, henceforward Saint and Martyr, was soon venerated not only by the
vanquished Anglians, but throughout all England ; the stream
of pilgrims to his shrine, the jealous protection of his relics, and
the very naming of him, perpetuated the shame of his murder
and made of Edmund's martyrdom a constant reproach to the
Danes, even to Cnut, the great Danish king who ruled in England
in the eleventh century.

After the fall of Edmund, East Anglia had perforce to submit
to the heathen invaders, and now the greater part of the eastern
plain of England was held fast in the grip of the Danes. The
time had come when central and southern England was to tremble
lest it shared a similar fate. Halfdan and a chief by the name
of Bagsecg were the commanders when the Danes next advanced,
DANES this time to attack Wessex. Their object was to
ATTACK surprise Æthelred by a winter attack, and it was late
WESSEX in December of 870 when they marched into the Thames
870-871 valley and descended upon Reading, where they made
for themselves a fortified camp at the confluence of the Kennet
and the Thames. In January of 871 there was a skirmish with
a small English force at Englefield, six miles west of Reading,
in which the Danes were worsted, but four days later when King
Æthelred and his brother Alfred together assailed the Danish
stronghold at Reading the English were beaten off. Another
four days passed, and then a second battle took place between
Æthelred and Alfred and the whole force of the Danes who were
drawn up on the slopes of Ashdown,[1] some 25 miles to the west
of Reading. The result of the battle was a big victory for the
English, and Bagsecg and many of the viking chieftains were
slain ; but Æthelred did not follow up his success, and only a

[1] The exact site of the battle is uncertain. See H. J. E. Peake, *The
County Archaeologies : Berkshire*, Ch. XI.

fortnight later the English were beaten in a third encounter that took place at Basing in Hampshire. In March there was yet another pitched battle between the two Wessex princes and the Danes, this time in Wiltshire at the village of Marton on the outskirts of Savernake Forest ; for the greater part of the day the English held the upper hand, but they could not put the enemy to flight, and, after heavy slaughter on both sides, they were forced to withdraw leaving the Danes in possession of the field.

In the spring of this year, and with the Danes pressing hard upon his realm, Æthelred died. As the two children that he left were only infants, the crown did not pass in the direct line to his eldest son ; instead, he was succeeded on the throne by one of the greatest men England has ever produced, his brother Alfred. It was a situation of the utmost gravity that faced the new king.

ALFRED THE GREAT 871–899 Deira, Alfred knew, was lost to the Danes ; East Anglia was theirs ; Mercia had only escaped for the time by the humiliating purchase of a peace ; and now the Danes had already been four months in Wessex. At such a time and in such a crisis even a powerful and experienced ruler might have wavered ; but Alfred the Great was only a youth of 23 years when he came to the throne and a prince possessing neither rude strength nor robust health. He had, however, already proved his courage. He had fought the Danes ; he knew the manner of their warfare ; and his own people trusted him. So the young king never faltered, but led his army straightway against the pagan host. The first battle took place at Wilton ; it was hard fought, but as before at Marton, the English at first drove back the Danes, only to be themselves repulsed at the end of the day. Despite this failure, Alfred did not once relax his close watch upon the movements of the enemy nor the determined opposition whereby he countered them ; in this year, 871, he fought no less than nine pitched battles against the Danes, and at last the invaders, who were losing many of their men in this constant fighting, realized that the conquest of Wessex was not likely to be effected in the present campaign. The result was that Alfred was able to make a peace with Halfdan and the viking army withdrew across the Thames. For the time, at any rate, Wessex was saved.

But this freedom for Wessex was bought at the expense of Mercia, and in the next year the Danes determined upon the conquest of Burhred's kingdom. This prince, since he had been occupied in a struggle with the Welsh, had not come to the assistance of Wessex in the hour of its peril, and Alfred in his turn, either because of his bond with the Danes or because the better organization of his own kingdom demanded his full attention, left Mercia to its fate. Halfdan's first move was to march with his vikings to London, where they spent the winter 871-2, and while they remained there Alfred posted a small observation force on his side of the Thames. But it was Burhred who was compelled to take some action, for he could not permit the Danes to hold this important Thames mart unchallenged, and as he dare not attack Halfdan, he too made a peace with the enemy, ransoming the town by the payment of a heavy tribute. The Danes thereupon temporarily withdrew from south-eastern Mercia; but after a return to Deira they came south again into Lindsey and spent the winter 872-3 at Torksey on the Trent near Lincoln. Then began a terrible ravaging of Mercia, and by the following winter the Danes had established themselves in the heart of the kingdom at Repton, where they destroyed the mausoleum of the Mercian kings. At the end of 874 the overthrow of the wretched kingdom was finally completed. Leicester, Nottingham, Lichfield, and Tamworth had fallen,[1] and Burhred had abandoned his country to its fate. He fled to Rome, where he died soon afterwards, and Halfdan set up in his stead on the Mercian throne a man called Ceolwulf, an English thane who was instructed to govern the country on behalf of the Danes as long as it so pleased them to entrust it to him. Halfdan's army then retired from Repton, and in doing so divided, one portion under Halfdan himself returning to Deira to winter on the Tyne, while the other, commanded by Guthrum, Oscytel, and Anwind, went to Cambridge.

DANISH INVASION OF MERCIA 873-874

Halfdan thereafter (875) set about the conquest of Bernicia, whose inhabitants had rebelled against their prince, Ecgberht, a vassal of the Danes, and Ricsig, another ruler appointed by the foreigners ; he ravaged the country north of the Tyne and west to Carlisle, burnt and looted monastery after monastery, was the cause of the bishop of Lindisfarne abandoning his see, and even penetrated into the lands of the Picts and the Strathclyde Welsh. He did not succeed in crushing all resistance from the independent Northumbrian princes at Bamborough, but when at length he was satisfied that little or no danger was to be anticipated from the north, he returned to Deira, and in 876 began the initial organization of what was clearly intended to be a stable and law-abiding colony. His first action was to portion out the province of Deira among his followers, and he made these new Danish

[1] There is, however, no reference in the Chronicle to the fate of these towns. They can hardly have offered any conspicuous resistance to the Danish advance.

masters of the land responsible for the continued cultivation of their holdings. In the next year he added to the territory thus under direct Danish ownership a large tract of Mercia, namely that part of the kingdom east of a boundary extending from the Peak district in Derbyshire to Tamworth in Warwickshire and then south-east along the Watling Street as far as the northern boundary of Northamptonshire. Here, as in Deira, Danish ownership of the land, and Danish law and social organization, were imposed on the English, but there was also an important political reorganization of the district, for this Mercian territory was divided into five portions, each under a jarl who was instructed to maintain an army for the defence of his area, and each having as its centre a specially fortified town that was known as a *borough* (OE. *burh* = fortified place). These viking headquarters were the towns of Lincoln, Stamford, Nottingham, Derby, and Leicester, and together they form a famous historical group giving the name of the ' Five Boroughs ' to these lands in Danish Mercia and Lindsey.

THE DANE-LAW AND THE 'FIVE BOROUGHS' 876

Thus were the foundations of the Danish colony in England, the Danelaw,[1] laid. But while Halfdan and the vikings of Deira and the Five Boroughs were intent on the proper colonization of the important territories that were now their own, Guthrum and the Danes who had settled at Cambridge coveted a larger dominion than their present holding in East Anglia. And so once more they set out upon the conquest of Wessex.

Except that in 875 a tiny fleet of six viking ships had been defeated in a sea-battle, the kingdom of Alfred the Great had been left in peace for a space of five years. But now the troubles of Wessex were to begin again, and in 876 a force described as the 'western army', and probably composed of vikings from Ireland, landed near Poole Harbour in Dorset. This was a move in a preconceived attack of a very

SECOND INVASION OF WESSEX

---

[1] It is convenient to employ this term loosely as a designation for the whole strip of eastern England possessed by the Danes in the ninth century; the northern Danelaw comprises the kingdom of York and the country between the Yorkshire borders and the Welland, while the southern Danelaw, or East Anglian kingdom, extends westwards to include Northamptonshire and (prior to the treaty of 885) Buckinghamshire and Middlesex. *Dena-lagu* is, of course, really the name of a district wherein *Danes' Law* was administered, that is to say it is a legal province, and its geographical extent naturally altered with changing political conditions ; for its significance in Saxon and early mediaeval documents, see F. Liebermann, *Gesetze der Angelsachsen*, II, p. 347 ; H. M. Chadwick, *Studies on Anglo-Saxon Institutions*, Cambridge, 1905, p. 199 ; F. M. Stenton, *Oxford Studies in Social and Legal History*, II, Oxford, 1910, p. 3.

serious kind, for the Irish host was promptly joined by Guthrum's army that had marched overland from Cambridge and that had successfully evaded the Wessex force collected to oppose its progress. Together the two bands of Northmen plundered the neighbourhood, and finally they seized the town of Wareham, which they made their headquarters. Alfred, although his army was mobilized, was not prepared to undertake the proper siege of the place, and he deemed it wisest to make a peace, the vikings giving hostages and swearing that they would leave Wessex at once in return for a money-payment. But Guthrum, in spite of the solemn nature of his oath, broke his word ; the Danish cavalry slipped out of Wareham by night and made its way hastily not out of Alfred's kingdom, but to Exeter. At the same time the viking fleet sailed down the coast with the intention of turning up the mouth of the Exe to join the rest of the force.

It was plainly the intention of the vikings to ravage Devon, but fortune was now (877) on Alfred's side. While the Wessex king, who had marched at once in pursuit to Exeter, succeeded in keeping the land-force shut up in the town, the fleet that was to bring this Danish army reinforcements met with a terrible disaster off Swanage where in a great tempest over 120 of its ships foundered. Guthrum in Exeter had now no other course than to surrender, and Alfred, having accepted hostages, allowed him and his army to escape into Mercia. Possibly the Danes had promised to return to East Anglia ; but if so, they broke their word once more. For they settled down in Gloucester close to the Wessex frontier.

With a viking host so near, it was idle to pretend that Wessex was saved a second time, and, in truth, the hour of its direst peril was at hand. In mid-winter of 877–8 Guthrum suddenly struck with his full force against Chippenham where Alfred had a royal residence and where perhaps he was living for the Christmas season, and early in the following year Halfdan's brother Ubbe arrived from Wales on the north coast of Devon with a fleet of 23 ships and an army of 840 men. The effect of this double COLLAPSE stroke, made at a season when invasion was little feared, OF was overwhelming. Alfred, indeed, escaped from WESSEX Guthrum, but all organized resistance broke down and 878 a terrible devastation of Wessex began. So serious was the plight of the land that many of the West Saxons fled across the Channel, and at last it seemed a certainty that Wessex must fall within the Danelaw. All England, so men thought, must now pass irrevocably into the hands of the invaders.

But the king remained in Wessex, and the king did not yet

despair. Escaping from Chippenham with a small personal following, he collected a little army during his retreat into the Somerset marshes, and finally, at Eastertide of 878 he established himself in a stockaded fort on the island of Athelney.[1]

ALFRED IN ATHELNEY Throughout the months of his hiding in the marshes he had not ceased to consider how he might best make a counter-attack upon the Danes, and during the seven weeks that he was encamped at Athelney he worried the enemy with an incessant guerilla-war and at the same time completed the difficult preliminary arrangements for the plan he had in mind. Then came the good news that the men of Devon, under their alderman Odda, had defeated Ubbe's vikings who were laying siege to ' Cynwit ', a fort either in north Devon or in Somerset,[2] and had not only almost annihilated the Danes but had slain their leader Ubbe himself.[3]   This success was exactly the encour-

[1] It is difficult to see any connexion between the name Athelney and Alfred's sojourn on the island ; the old form is *Æthelinga-ig*, usually translated ' isle of the princes ', though the first element may conceivably be the corrupted form of a proper name. The site of Alfred's fort is supposed to be the Borough Mump, a lofty knoll with a sham ruined church on its summit, about halfway between Othery and Ling, and just north of the confluence of the Tone and the Parrett ; it is connected by a causeway with the high ground between Othery and Middlezoy and is well placed as a centre for the military control of the marshes, being readily convertible by means of a palisade into an almost impregnable fortress. But as the knoll bears no certain traces of artificial fortifications, and as the only archaeological material from the site is some Roman pottery that was found at the foot of the Mump in Borough Bridge, there must remain some doubt as to its identification with Alfred's fort. The ' Isle of Athelney ', a low and elongated platform of land, lies about a mile to the south-west and is assumed to be the site of the monastery subsequently founded by Alfred as a thank-offering for his victories.

[2] The site has not been satisfactorily identified, but ' Kenwith Castle ', an earthwork in the parish of Abbotsham near Bideford, Devon, and the scarped knoll about one mile north-west of Cannington near Bridgwater, Somerset, have both been suggested ; in fact, Cannington Knoll is now honoured on the current 1 inch O.S. map with the name of Cynwit and the date of the battle. Both identifications are valueless (in spite of the bones found in the Warren field at Cannington), and a third suggestion that Cynwit is Countesbury, near Lynton, can also be neglected (see W. H. Stevenson, *Asser's Life of Alfred*, Oxford, 1904, p. 262).

[3] This was the battle of the ' Raven Banner ', a celebrated standard that was said to have been woven by the daughters of Ragnar Lodbrok between dawn and dusk in a single day ; it had a raven blazoned upon it that seemed to flutter if the army was advancing to victory, but drooped and was still if defeat was in store for the vikings: *Saxon Chronicle, Laud MS. E.*, s. a. 876, *Annals of St. Neots, ed. with Asser's Alfred*, W. H. Stevenson, Oxford, 1904, p. 138. For a description of a Norse magical banner of the same kind, see *Flateyjarbók, Olaf Trygg.*, 186.

agement that was needed, and so in the middle of May, at the date appointed in the messages that he had sent secretly throughout this south-western portion of his kingdom, Alfred moved suddenly from Athelney to a rendezvous somewhere just to the east of Selwood Forest,[1] and was there joined by the levies of Wessex men that had been hastily raised in Somerset, Wiltshire, and Hampshire. Great was the joy of these loyal West Saxons at being thus reunited under their beloved king, and it was amid demonstrations of enthusiasm and affection that Alfred now set out to recover Wessex from the Danes.

Swift action counted for much, and two days after the concentration of the army, Alfred, pushing rapidly forward with the troops thus collected, fell upon Guthrum's army that had by this time moved out from Chippenham to oppose him. The rival forces met at Ethandun (the modern Edington in Wiltshire, ALFRED'S 12 miles south of Chippenham)[2] and the result of the VICTORY battle was a complete rout of the Danes, who were AT ETHAN- driven back, after suffering heavy losses, to their DUN 878 camp. Without hesitation Alfred followed them there and laid siege to the place. It was the bold action of a great leader and it was successful, for two weeks later the remnant of the Danish army in Wessex, though a short time before a complacent and victorious host, surrendered unconditionally to the man who was deemed to be a fugitive and helpless king.

The peace treaty that followed was of the kind that the Christian monarchs of Europe considered a full reward for their occasional victories over the pagan invaders. The vikings gave hostages, swore solemnly that they would leave the kingdom, and Guthrum himself promised to become a Christian. And TREATY having by this time a wholesome dread of Alfred, they OF CHIP- carried out their promises. Guthrum was baptized in PENHAM June at Aller near Athelney, and this ceremony was followed by a chrism-loosing (the laying aside of the white band of the catechumen) at Wedmore near Glastonbury ; here the Danish chief abode for twelve days with the Wessex king, who now received him as his son by adoption and loaded him with

[1] At *Ecgbrihtes stan*, but the site has not been identified. *Brixton* Deverill is etymologically unsatisfactory.

[2] This identification has been warmly contested and the Somerset Edington, near Athelney, has been preferred by certain authorities, among whom the Rev. C. W. Whistler and Mr. Albany Major were the foremost ; but in this instance ancient variants of the name show that an equation with Ethandun is difficult to defend ; for the arguments in favour of this identification see *Arch. Journ.* 75 (1918), p. 178 and *Antiquaries Journal* I, p. 104.

gifts. After this Guthrum and his vikings were permitted to winter in Wessex, but in the next year, faithful to their bond, they withdrew from the kingdom. Their first move was to Cirencester, just inside Mercia.

The *Treaty of Chippenham*, or *Peace of Wedmore* as it is often called, had at least put an end to any serious danger of a viking conquest of Wessex, but, just as had happened on the last occasion when Alfred rid his country of the Danes, their retreat from Wessex boded disaster for the neighbouring kingdom of Mercia. The move to Cirencester was plainly an indication that Guthrum had as yet no intention of leaving the midlands, and that Gloucestershire and Worcestershire were now in peril of being added to the Danelaw. But the two chief men of this Hwicce province, Æthelred, Duke of Gloucester, and the Bishop of Worcester, knowing that it was useless to turn to Halfdan's creature Ceolwulf, their so-called king, for aid, offered their allegiance to Alfred the Great, and this dramatic step (it put an end to the existence of the old independent kingdom of Mercia) had the anticipated effect on the Danes, for Guthrum made off without fighting a battle and marched back into East Anglia. In the summer of the previous year a fleet of viking ships had arrived in the Thames, apparently with the intention of plundering in southern England, perhaps even of joining forces with Guthrum ; but the now considerable prestige of Alfred made any sort of expedition, even into Mercia, dangerous, and the newcomers accordingly remained for the winter at Fulham. In 880 when Hwicce passed under Alfred's protection and Guthrum had abandoned his hopes of conquest in the midlands, this fleet likewise changed its plans and sailed off to plunder on the Continent (p. 214).

Guthrum, finding himself back in the east of England, had perforce to be contented with the territories of Hendrica and East and Middle Anglia. Following Halfdan's example, he apportioned out the land among his followers ; he established boroughs under independent jarls, each with his own army, at Northampton, Huntingdon, Cambridge, and Bedford, while he himself controlled a large province that embraced the towns of London, Colchester, Ipswich, Thetford, and Norwich, a province including not only Hendrica but a half (corresponding roughly with the modern Buckinghamshire) of the district of Chilternsaete.

The most significant result of the *Treaty of Chippenham* was that this Danelaw, now a vast belt of country stretching across England from the Tees in the north to the Thames in the south, had been recognized and, in part, defined by Alfred as the proper and permitted realm of the Danish leaders. As such it prospered and an Archbishop returned to York to resume the interrupted ecclesiastical government of northern England. Of the great Wessex kingdom of Ecgbert, his grandfather, Alfred had abandoned to the vikings only London and Essex, a big concession, but one that the occasion demanded, for the Danes, thus established, were now inclined to live peaceably within their own territory, while Alfred had a corresponding term of leisure wherein to set his realm in order. He was thus enabled to effect various pressing military reforms, notably a reorganization of the fyrd, or national levy, the enlistment of Frisian sailors for the strengthening and better management of his fleet, and the building of fortified strongholds on the model of the Danish boroughs, each the headquarters and rallying-point of districts that were subdivisions of the older shires.

The *Treaty of Chippenham* was made in 878 and it was not until 882 that Alfred was forced to take arms against the vikings once more, and on this occasion it was only to drive off four pirate ships. But there was a more serious disturbance in 885 when a viking host landed in Kent and attacked Rochester, for this was followed at once by a breach of the peace on the part of Guthrum who evidently believed that another opportunity had come for an attack upon Wessex. But Alfred drove off the Rochester vikings, who were forced to abandon their prisoners and the horses that they had brought with them from Francia, and he despatched his fleet across the estuary of the Thames to the mouth of the Stour, where it captured a fleet of sixteen viking ships. Guthrum, however, sent out a larger fleet that succeeded in catching Alfred's boats on their return and putting them to flight, so that the English naval expedition ended disastrously. But Alfred was in no wise daunted and acted at once with characteristic vigour, for he straightway marched up the south bank of the Thames and captured London. It was a bold and famous stroke. Guthrum was forced to make a new peace [1] with the Wessex king, and as a result the boundaries of the southern Danelaw were altered in Alfred's favour, the Danes ceding the North London area together with Hendrica and their portion of Chilternsaete. But even more important than mere territorial gain was the increased prestige that Alfred won by this

SECOND TREATY BETWEEN ALFRED AND GUTHRUM 885

---

[1] A part of the text of this peace between Alfred and Guthrum (not to be confused with the Treaty of Chippenham) has been preserved, F. Liebermann, *Die Gesetze der Angelsachsen*, I, p. 126, and F. L. Attenborough, *Laws of the Earliest English Kings*, Cambridge, 1922, p. 98.

liberation of London ; for when he had restored the town and fortified it, and committed it to the care of his own son-in-law Æthelred, Duke of Mercia, ' all the English, save those in captivity of the Danes ', turned to him eagerly as their leader, and now, in central and southern England, from the Mersey to the south coast, every man looked to him as the redoubtable head of the nation and the deliverer of the people of England.

But in 892 there was a new and most dangerous crisis to be faced, for this was the time when the great army of the siege of Paris left Francia and invaded England (p. 219). The formid-

DANISH able host, embarked in 250 ships, sailed from Boulogne INVASION and landed at the mouth of the Lymne in Kent, whence OF 892 they marched inland and captured a fort at Appledore. At the same time another viking fleet, 80 ships strong, under Hastein, the lusty and terrifying old warrior of the Loire and the Somme, appeared in the Thames and seized the town of Milton-near-Sittingbourne.

Alfred, fearing that there might be a general rising of the Danes throughout all the Danelaw, pledged both the Northumbrian Danes and those of East Anglia (from the latter he also took the precaution of extracting hostages) to abstain from joining in this attack upon his kingdom ; but in spite of their vows they most certainly did send expeditions, as he had foreseen, to swell the numbers of the new invaders in Kent, and, furthermore, they chose this opportunity to land a viking force in Devonshire. The situation was therefore extremely serious when in 893 Alfred took up a position with his army within striking distance of both the enemy camps in Kent and so began an anxious and bitter three years war. At first there was no general engagement, and, after some skirmishes, Alfred tried to treat with Hastein ; but while the negotiations were in progress the Appledore Danes sent their boats to Benfleet in Essex and themselves set out upon

THREE a long circuitous raid through Surrey, Hampshire, and YEARS Berkshire, across the upper Thames, and then east-WAR 893–6 wards to Benfleet. They were, however, intercepted by Alfred's eldest son, Edward, at Farnham and utterly routed in the battle that followed, being driven in confusion across the Thames. They then retreated for 6 miles up the Hertfordshire Colne and took refuge in an island by the hamlet of Thorney in the parish of Iver [1] on the Buckinghamshire side of the river ; here they were besieged by Edward, but the young prince was

---

[1] This identification of Æthelwerd's Thorney was first made by Professor F. M. Stenton, *English Historical Review*, XXVII (1912), p. 512.

soon forced to withdraw as his army's term of service had expired and rations were running short.

Alfred was on his way to relieve his son's army when he heard that the treacherous Danelaw had sent a fleet of over 100 ships to besiege Exeter and another of 40 ships to harry North Devon ; he was compelled therefore to march off to the west country and drive off the vikings encamped before Exeter. Meanwhile Edward, having obtained reinforcements and accompanied by Æthelred with his Londoners, returned to Thorney and, finding the Danes still there, forced them to surrender. He took hostages from them and then allowed them to retreat to Benfleet where Hastein had lately established himself, though the old pirate was on this occasion away on a plundering expedition ; but soon afterwards he and Æthelred followed them there, attacked the Danish camp, and gained an overwhelming victory. The English took many prisoners, including the women and children of the settlement,[1] and they captured the whole viking fleet ; they sent off as many of the enemy boats as they could man to London and Rochester, but the remainder they either broke up or burnt. It was, in short, one of the most complete victories hitherto gained over a viking force on English soil.

The Danes who escaped from this disaster were joined by Hastein at Shoebury and there they made themselves a new camp. It was not long, however, before their numbers were increased by large reinforcements from within the Danelaw, and their next move was to make a dash across England to the Severn valley, presumably to demand the succour of the vikings by this time established in South Wales. They succeeded in reaching the Welsh borders at Buttington before a great levy raised by Æthelred and the aldermen of Somerset and Wiltshire, a levy that even included some of the North Welsh, marched against them. For many weeks the two armies watched one another, but at length the Danes began to run short of provisions and in desperation crossed the Severn to attack the English main body. There followed a big battle and both sides lost heavily, but the result was a defeat for the Danes. Back to Shoebury fled the beaten remnant of the expedition.

But now all the Danelaw was in a ferment, and once again the old hopes of the conquest of western Mercia, perhaps even of Wessex itself, were revived. Fresh bands of warriors collected

---

[1] Among these were the wife and sons of Hastein, but they were subsequently restored to him by Alfred. This was probably because Hastein had become, or had promised to become, a Christian when he was negotiating with Alfred at Milton.

at Shoebury and a second cross-country raid was attempted, on this occasion a forced march along the Watling Street until the army reached a deserted and ruined Roman town, Chester. Æthelred's levy was taken by surprise and could not prevent the Danes from sheltering in safety behind the strong walls of the abandoned city ; but winter was at hand, and it seemed sufficient for the English to destroy everything in the neighbourhood that could possibly provide sustenance for the Danes or their horses. This done, the English force withdrew to watch events.

The result of the stratagem was successful, for in the next year, 894, the lack of provisions compelled the Danes to vacate Chester and to go plundering in Wales. Then they made off with their booty and returned to Mersea in Essex, but in crossing England they were careful to make a wide detour through Northumbria and East Anglia so as to keep out of reach of the English army which is said even to have dared to threaten York in an attempt to catch the retreating vikings. At the same time the viking band that Alfred had defeated in Devonshire was also on its way back to East Anglia ; while they were sailing up the south coast they had tried to plunder in Sussex, but the men of Chichester had risen up against them and routed them, even capturing some of their boats. The remnant, however, found their way to the new camp on the island of Mersea, where they joined the vikings of the Chester raid.

At the end of the year the Danes returned to the attack. A large fleet sailed from Mersea up the Thames and then up the Lea to a point 20 miles north of London where a fortified camp was made and where the fleet remained for six months unchallenged. In the summer of 895 they were attacked by an English force collected in and around London, but the attempt to storm the fortress failed and the levy retired, having suffered serious losses. The vikings were now plundering boldly, and so, in the harvest time, Alfred himself marched to London with his army to protect the neighbourhood while the corn was being cut. He did not attack the Danish camp, but he found a place where the river could be blocked by the construction of two works, one on either bank, and no sooner had he begun to construct them than the Danes realized that their ships were going to be shut in. They did not wait to be caught in the trap, for they abandoned their boats at once and, sending their women safely away into East Anglia, they set off overland on one last desperate raid into Mercia. Their goal was Bridgenorth on the Severn, and there, when they had eluded the pursuing English army, they built a fort and settled down for the winter. In the meantime the men of London had taken the abandoned ships, towing some down to London and destroying the remainder.

The end was now at hand. The Englishmen had shown themselves sufficiently strong to make it certain that there could be no prospect of conquests in Mercia as a result of these irregular and ill-supported raids, while in the Danelaw the settlers were becoming less and less disposed to risk the security of their holding by further offending this most resolute king who opposed them. The veteran Hastein and the viking party, the marauders, were now a discredited minority, and so it came about that the summer of 896 saw the pirate host break up, the Bridgenorth Danes returning some to East Anglia and some to Northumbria ; then those of the vikings who did not succeed in obtaining a grant of land in the Danelaw and those who still chose to lead a pirate life sailed off to renew their ravages on the Seine.

TRIUMPH OF THE ENGLISH 896

The Danelaw, however, even with this unruly element gone, was not a land of peaceful colonists only, for in this very year there were minor raids on the south coast of Wessex, raids from Northumbria and East Anglia that were carried out in the old ships that had brought the Danes to England. To put an end to this buccaneering Alfred ordered the construction of a new fleet of 'long ships' that were nearly double the size of the Danish boats, some having sixty oars and some even more. They were built neither on the Frisian nor the Danish model, but were designed by the king himself and were thought to be swifter and steadier than the foreign craft. This was a courageous experiment, but it seems that the crews, both English and Frisian sailors, found their fine new boats exceedingly difficult to manage, for when nine of these ships of Alfred's engaged six pirate boats the English made a sad muddle of the fight by running aground ('very awkwardly' as the chronicler candidly says). The chronicler also records that twenty ships, crews and all, were lost on the south coast during this same summer, and he was probably referring to English ships. But though these new boats were evidently not an unqualified success, the king was under no delusions as to the proper way to treat these buccaneers when he caught them. In the fight in which the English ships ran aground, three of the Danish boats escaped, and two of these were subsequently driven ashore on the coast of Sussex. The crews were led to Winchester to the king and Alfred hanged every man of them.

He died in October 899, this great king, and for the last three years of his reign Wessex had had peace. Alfred had saved his

kingdom from the Danes, and by saving Wessex he had saved
England. But he had done more than achieve a mere
deliverance of his realm ; for he had toiled ceaselessly
at the interior organization and military equipment of
Wessex, and he left his kingdom a powerful and enlightened state,
no longer the defenceless prey of the Danes but now an avenger
that was to dare to advance to the conquest of the Danelaw.
Over this reborn Wessex his son, Edward the Elder, was now
elected to rule.

At the outset of his reign Edward had a quarrel with his cousin
Æthelwald to whom Alfred had left estates in Surrey and Sussex,
and this prince fled to Northumbria where he took refuge with
the Danes. A few years later he made an alliance with the East
Anglian Danes, whose king was now Eric, Guthrum
having died in 890, and he succeeded in inciting them
to attack Wessex. In 904 a Danish force, with Æthelwald among the leaders, marched out across Chilternsaete, crossed
the upper Thames at Cricklade, plundered in the Braden Forest
district, and returned home unchallenged. But Edward replied
with a vigorous counter-attack, and sending an army of Kentish
men and Londoners into the Danelaw he ordered the devastation
of Middle Anglia. This expedition came to grief as the army
was slow to heed Edward's command to withdraw and was consequently caught by the Danish army under Eric and Æthelwald.
A fierce battle took place at Holme near Biggleswade [1] in Bedford-
shire in which the English came off worse although the Danes
lost both their king and Æthelwald. Another Guthrum succeeded
Eric, and immediately afterwards Guthrum and Edward concluded a peace at Yttingaford, near Linslade in Buckinghamshire,
whereby the older treaty of 886 between Guthrum and Alfred was
re-affirmed, and it was further stipulated that the Danes in the
dioceses of London and Dorchester should become Christians and
pay the proper tithes and church dues to the bishops.

The Danes remained quiet for some years after this show of
force by Edward and they are not heard of again until 910 when
they once more attacked Mercia. Edward was in Kent with his
fleet, but he sent his army immediately to the assistance of
Æthelred so that the Duke of Mercia was able to confront the
invaders with a big force when they began their homeward march.
A battle took place at Tettenhall in Staffordshire and the result
was a complete overthrow of the Danes, who suffered very heavy
losses.

[1] For this identification of the battle-site, see W. J. Corbett, *Cambridge Med. Hist.*, III, p. 361.

This great English victory marks the opening of a new phase in the history of the Danelaw, for it was no longer Mercia and Wessex that lived in fear of attack. It was the Danes now that were in peril. The two directing minds that planned and embarked upon the brilliant but arduous reconquest of the ' Five Boroughs ' were Edward and his sister, the ' Lady of the Mercians ', Æthelfleda, widow of Æthelred who had died soon after the battle of Tettenhall in 911. They moved cautiously, Edward acting against the Danes from the south and Æthelfleda from the west, and as they slowly pushed back the Danish frontier they consolidated their gains by the erection of fortified boroughs. In 913 Edward built such a borough at Hertford and another at Witham, while Æthelfleda made Mercian boroughs of Tamworth and Stafford. In the next year two Danish raids were repulsed by Edward, and Eddisbury and Warwick were fortified in Mercia. In 915 there was a diversion caused by the arrival of a fleet of pirates from Brittany in the mouth of the Severn ; but the men of Hereford, Gloucester, and Wales rose against them and with the assistance of Edward's army drove them out of the country by harvest-time. Edward then continued his campaign against the Danelaw and captured and fortified Buckingham before the year was out. The following year Thurkytel, the jarl of Bedford, capitulated, and the whole of Chilternsaete thus fell into Edward's hands. In the meantime, Æthelfleda, who in her turn had been diverted from her main purpose by a war with the Welsh, established boroughs at Chirbury in Staffordshire (against the Welsh) and at Warburton and Runcorn in Cheshire on the Danish frontier. In 917 she advanced up the Trent valley into Danish Mercia and won back Derby, thus rendering the position of the Danes at Northampton and Leicester, who were already threatened by Edward from the south, more and more precarious. In 918, together with the Danes of Huntingdon, these Mercian Danes attempted a double counter-attack on Edward's boroughs in Chilternsaete and Hendrica, but even the reinforcements brought up by Guthrum failed to push the attacks home. Edward replied by laying siege to Tempsford near Bedford, and soon afterwards he took the town by storm, slaying Guthrum himself and two of the Danish jarls. At this disaster the Danish resistance broke down ; Colchester fell to the Wessex arms, an attack on Maldon was repulsed, and after this Thurferth, the jarl of Northampton, submitted to Edward. His example was followed by all the Danish leaders of Middle Anglia and then by the chiefs of East Anglia ; they hailed Edward as

EDWARD AND ÆTHELFLEDA BEGIN THE RECONQUEST OF THE DANELAW

their protector and lord, promising not to take up arms against him in the future, and the English king in his turn granted them the right to retain their estates and continue to live according to their Danish laws and customs. All the Danelaw south of the Welland was now under English control, and it was at this time that the jarl of Leicester submitted to Æthelfleda without offering further resistance, and it is said that even at York there was serious alarm and promises made of submission to her rule. But in this year the 'Lady of the Mercians' died.

Edward, in the meantime, had advanced to Stamford and had there received the submission of the Danes of Kesteven and Holland, but on hearing of his sister's death he hurried to Tamworth and proclaimed himself as her successor. There was, of course, no heir to the Mercian throne who was likely to resist him and it was in his favour that he had already a proper claim to the overlordship of Hwicce ; furthermore, his was the high prestige of a great warrior-king who had co-operated closely and loyally with Æthelfleda. It is not surprising, then, that the nobles of Mercia readily accepted him as king. But this union of the two realms under Edward was immediately followed by other tributes to his authority, for to him also came embassies from the princes of Gwynedd (North Wales) and Deheubarth (South-West Wales) offering their alliance. A strange and sudden stroke of fortune had transformed Edward, a year ago only the Wessex king, into the lord of all England south of the Humber.

He did not, however, turn aside from his great campaign. In 919 he pushed northwards, building forts at Manchester and at Thelwall in Cheshire ; in 920 he moved into the Peak country and erected a borough at Bakewell. There was now no room for doubt as to the result of this bold and vigorous policy, and the Danes of Northumbria began to fear that a further resistance on their part might even jeopardize their right to remain in possession of the fertile lands that their fathers had won for them half a century earlier. Accordingly, their leader Ragnvald (p. 283), DANES SUBMIT TO EDWARD 920 a viking chief of the Irish branch of the house of Ragnar Lodbrok and only lately established as king of York, now declared himself ready to make a peace with Edward. And it came about that the English king, at this proud end of his long campaign, received the homage not only of Ragnvald, but also of the Anglian princes of Bamborough who were the nominal rulers of Bernicia. Nor was this all, for he even received congratulatory embassies from Constantine III, the king of the Scots, and from Domnhall, the chief of the Strathclyde Welsh, both of whom were now eager to put themselves on friendly terms with the great warrior and redoubtable strategist, the man who had broken the power of the Danes.[1]

Edward had not been in the full sense of the word the conqueror of the Danelaw. He had not interfered with the land-tenure of the colonists nor with the Danish laws and customs obtaining in the colony ; all he had done was to establish himself as the undisputed overlord of the Danelaw and so cripple the military power of the colonists that his own English subjects need no longer live in fear of attack from them. But the winning of this overlordship was in itself a very remarkable achievement, being nothing less than the humiliation and subjection of a young and vigorous colony only fifty years established.

One of the reasons for this downfall of the Danelaw was clearly that the Danes themselves, however anxious they might be for colonial expansion, were utterly lacking in the political experience that is necessary for the founding of a stable colony in a hostile land. Except when such a man as Halfdan led and governed them, the rank and file were at heart nothing but small and unambitious farmers with a taste for an occasional plundering expedition. There was, in plain fact, but little corporate feeling in the Danelaw, and submission to an English overlord was regarded with indifference provided that the ownership of the land was not disputed. Even the jarls, with their boroughs and their armies, shared this apathy and had no proper perception of the co-operation that was required of them when a resolute and sustained attack was directed against the Danelaw. And in addition to this lack of cohesion, the jarls further contributed to the inherent weakness of the colony because their independence was a part of that still greater failing of these chieftains, a viking restlessness. For when fortune turned against them, they were tempted to slip away with their personal following and, as buccaneers once more, to seek a home and riches elsewhere. It happened at this very time when Edward and Æthelfleda began their campaign against the Danelaw that Charles the Simple gave the land of Normandy to Rollo and thus provided a safe and attractive home across the Channel where vikings were allowed to live in peace. It is likely, then, that the numbers of the Danes in the English Danelaw were seriously depleted by the

[1] The very famous entry in the Chronicle (s. a. 923) describing this submission reads: ' And the king of the Scots, and all the people of the Scots, chose him (Edward) as father and lord ; and so did Ragnvald, and the sons of Eadulf (the English earls of Bamborough), and all those who dwell in Northumbria, whether English, or Danish, or Northmen (Norwegians), or others, and also the king of the Strathclyde Welsh, and all the Strathclyde Welsh.'

departure of many of the more adventurous vikings to the new Danelaw on the Continent. Thus the Chronicle records that Thurkytel, the jarl of Bedford, after his submission to Edward in 917, sailed off two years later to Francia together with such men as would follow him.

In the Northumbrian Danelaw there was, however, a special source of weakness, for within the short period of Edward's reign the autonomy of the colonists had been threatened by the rapid

ARRIVAL OF THE NORWEG-IAN AND IRISH VIK-INGS IN NORTH-UMBRIA development of a rival colony of foreigners around and among them. These newcomers were their fellow-vikings, Norwegians and others, partly Norse and partly Danish, from the Irish viking colonies, and Norse-descended folk from the western Scottish isles and Man. Some had come directly from Norway to the Yorkshire coast in the Whitby district, but the majority had arrived from the west and had begun in the early tenth century to settle on both sides of the Solway Firth, in the no man's land of the Cumberland coast, and in the western part of Deira around Morecambe Bay and along the north Lancashire littoral. They came gradually, not in one angry invasion, and as land-takers they were peaceable folk ; but the absence of resistance to their settlement encouraged them to push steadily inland and it was not long before they were securely established in the dales of the Lake District and in part of western Yorkshire, particularly in the Craven region, and also in the western dales of the North Riding and even in the Cleveland Hills.[1] Even so, they probably had no serious intention of ousting the original settlers from their heritage ; but upon their sudden rise to political importance it was inevitable that there should be a disastrous clash of interests within the Danelaw and consequent disturbances that effectively prevented the colony from offering a stout and single-fronted opposition to Edward and his English.

The cause of the trouble was the quarrel between the related royal houses of Dublin and York whose sons, all of the stock of

[1] On the Norsemen of north-west England see W. G. Collingwood, *Lake District History* (Ch. III), Kendal, 1925, and *Publ. Tolson Museum, Huddersfield, Handbook* 2 (ed. 1929) ; E. Ekwall, *Scandinavians and Celts in North-West England*, Lund ; A. H. Smith, *Placenames of the North Riding of Yorkshire*, Cambridge, 1928. These vikings, though of much importance both for history and archaeology, obtain little notice in the written records and their chief claim upon the reader's attention is that they are the subject of Mr. W. G. Collingwood's lovely and memorable romance *Thorstein of the Mere*. This story, which opens with the submission of the vikings to Edward at Bakewell, provides a fascinating and illuminating introduction to the study of viking Northumbria which no one interested should miss.

Ragnar Lodbrok, believed that Dublin and Northumbria should properly be ruled by a single prince of their line. In these jealousies and wars of their kings the settlers, new and old alike, took little interest at first, but the danger of the royal rivalries for the common welfare lay in the fact that the sympathies of the heathen Norsemen and Irish Danes now dwelling in England were clearly with the Dublin claimants, so that in the event of the triumph of one of the Dublin princes over his cousin at York the whole complexion of the Danelaw would be altered and would henceforth have a westward orientation gravely to the disadvantage of the original settlers. This is what had actually happened in 918 when a roving viking of the Dublin house, Ragnvald (pp. 248, 283), came over from Ireland and seized the throne of York. The result was that exactly at the time when the Northumbrian Danelaw should have been rallying its full strength in readiness for the coming struggle with Edward the unhappy province was thrown into chaos by the attempt to impose heathen Irish-Norwegian government upon the Christian Danes of Deira ; small wonder, then, that at the approach of the English, Ragnvald, who had not been able to consolidate his victories, and the Danes who dreaded the losing of their lands and the tyranny of the Norsemen, alike agreed to end the anarchy in Northumbria by accepting the king of England as their overlord.

It was in 920 that the Norwegians and Danes submitted to Edward and for five years afterwards the country was at peace ; then in 925 this great king died, having reigned twenty-six years. ÆTHEL- He was succeeded by his son, the magnificent young STAN prince Æthelstan whose destiny it was to crown the 925-939 achievement of his father and his grandfather by new and stirring successes of the English arms. His first act, however, was to confirm the existing peace between England and the Danelaw, and this he did by meeting the king of York, now Ragnvald's relative Sigtryg Gale who had been king of Dublin before he went to York, at Tamworth and arranging a marriage between this prince, now become a Christian, and his own sister. But Sigtryg died in the following year (926) and Æthelstan immediately marched into Northumbria, expelled the Dublin king Godfred who had come over from Ireland to take the vacant throne, forbade the succession of Sigtryg's son Olaf Cuaran, and himself seized the realm. This actual annexation of the Yorkshire Danelaw seems to have had far-reaching results, for in a peace made at Emmet in Holderness the Welsh kings, the Bamborough prince, and Constantine III, king of the Scots, renewed their pledges of friendship as the subject-allies of the king of England.

But seven years later, in 933, this peace had been broken and Æthelstan was marching northward to fight the kings of Scotland and Strathclyde. The cause of the outbreak of hostilities was, it seems, that the aged Constantine, who no doubt preferred that there should be an independent Scandinavian kingdom of Northumbria between his own realm and that of this most formidable English king, had rashly espoused the cause of Olaf Cuaran, son of Sigtryg Gale and now regarded by vikings and Scots alike as rightful heir to the throne of York. Æthelstan's campaign was successful in that he spread the terror of the English arms far and wide in Strathclyde Wales and Alban ; but he was not able to crush his opponents, and in 937 he learnt that the northern nations were uniting in their preparations for a decisive conflict with the Saxons and counted upon the aid of a large army of Northumbrian and Irish vikings.

RISING OF THE SCOTS AND STRATH- CLYDE WELSH 933

The cause of the war that now broke out was still the affair of the succession at York, and the hostilities opened with an oversea raid by Olaf Cuaran and a party of Scots and vikings upon Northumbria by way of the Humber mouth. The campaign opened brilliantly for the rebels as the Anglophile earls set over the province by Æthelstan were defeated, and this was at once followed by a sympathetic rising of the Welsh, both of North Wales and of Strathclyde. It was, in truth, a formidable combination that now confronted the English king, an alliance showing plainly that North Britain, Celtic, Danish, and Norwegian, pagan and Christian, was determined to stay Æthelstan's growing power and to break free from his overlordship.

But the king, Edward's son and Alfred's grandson, was not the man to allow his authority to be challenged with impunity. Accompanied by his half-brother Edmund, then a boy, and having in his train 300 vikings under the Icelander Egil Skallagrimsson and his brother Thorolf, he marched northward and invited the great allied force commanded by Constantine and Olaf to meet him in battle at Brunanburh, a place that is now generally thought to be Birrenswark, a flat-topped hill in Annandale, nine miles north of the Solway Firth in Dumfriesshire.[1]

BATTLE OF BRUNAN- BURH 937

The Celtic and viking armies arrived at the scene of the combat

[1] For the site of Brunanburh, see Neilson, *Scottish Historical Review*, VII (1909), p. 37, and R. L. Bremner, *The Norsemen in Alban*, Glasgow, 1923, p. 127. The reader should note that there are some serious chronological difficulties in the way of identifying the battle of Vinheid in Egilssaga with Brunanburh.

first and established themselves in an old Roman camp north of the hill upon which the battle was to take place, and the English, coming later, collected their army in a second camp on the south side of the hill. There were many delays and many useless diplomatic exchanges before the armies were fully mustered, and the contest opened unexpectedly with a fight between the impatient Celts and, on the English side, the Northumbrians and Icelanders, wherein the Icelandic leaders, or so at least *Egilssaga* tells, gained a splendid victory, even though the Northumbrian commander shamefully fled from the field. But the battle proper came on the following day and then the complete forces of both sides were paraded. It was fought long and hard, and ended in an amazing and overwhelming victory for the English ; Olaf and the beaten remnant of the Irish vikings escaped to their ships and sailed off to Dublin, while Constantine, the hoary-headed traitor, ' fled to his North again '.[1] Æthelstan's enemies were completely cowed, and the English king henceforth could justly style himself, as he did on his coins and in his charters, *Rex totius Britanniæ*.

He had become, indeed, one of the great kings of north-western Europe, and he was held in high honour by the princes abroad. The Carolingian king, Charles the Simple, by marrying Æthelstan's sister Edgiva, became his brother-in-law, and Louis d'Outremer, the son of this marriage and a future king of France, was reared at the court of the English king ; the Capetian Hugh the Great married Eadhilda, another sister, and Otto the Saxon, the future Roman emperor, wedded Edgitha, a third sister. But such powerful connexions on the Continent do not represent the entire scope of Æthelstan's relations with foreign powers, and it may be that his fostering of Haakon,[2] one of the sons of Harald Fairhair, and Harald's acceptance of a sword from Æthelstan, are, in spite of the embroideries of the *Heimskringla* version of the story, merely tokens of an English foreign policy that aimed at a friendship with the rising state of Norway. There was, indeed, a most unexpected result to this exchange of civilities, for when Eric Bloodaxe, Harald's heir and successor, was on a viking cruise in the west, Æthelstan, remembering his friendship with Eric's illustrious father, sent for him, and offered

[1] From Tennyson's translation of the ballad of Brunanburh, the famous poem that is inserted in the Saxon Chronicle, s. a. 937.

[2] It is not, of course, certain that the Æthelstan who fostered Haakon in England was the great king and indeed there are chronological difficulties in the way of this identification. The Dane Guthrum, baptized after the Treaty of Chippenham, received the name of Æthelstan and it may have been to him that the young Norwegian prince was sent.

to make him, if he would become a Christian, the vassal-earl of Northumbria. Eric accepted this offer, was baptized, and, furthermore, promised to defend his new territories against the attacks of Danes and other vikings. Thus, at the will of the English king, a Norwegian prince ruled at York and held his honourable position until Æthelstan died.[1]

The death of the king took place in 939, two years after the battle of Brunanburh, and he was succeeded by his half-brother Edmund, who was only eighteen years old. The accession of this youth was the signal for a revolt on the part of Olaf Godfredsson, the king of Dublin, who at once hurried over from Ireland to Northumbria where he was received with open arms by the Norwegian settlers and ultimately elected as king in place of Eric Bloodaxe who was summarily expelled. The Yorkshire Danes, whose spirit had long since been crushed, were doubtless anxious for a continuation of the peace they had enjoyed under Æthelstan, but Olaf and his Norwegians were athirst for conquest. Crossing the Humber they easily reduced the Danes of the Five Boroughs to a state of subjection and then forced them to join in a revolt against their English masters. Thereupon Olaf, in 940, dared to cross the Welland and attack Northampton, so that for the time it seemed that the whole Danelaw might be wrested from the English king.

EDMUND
940–946

REVOLT OF OLAF GOD-FREDSSON

But Olaf was beaten off from Northampton, and after a raid on Tamworth he was driven back to Leicester and there besieged by Edmund. He managed, however, to cut his way through the

---

[1] There are serious objections to this account that I have given of Eric's instalment at York by Æthelstan and I must explain that, according to Norse tradition, Eric did not become earl until after Harald's death and his own expulsion from his kingdom of Norway. That means (if we accept the new dating for his accession to the Norwegian throne) that he did not arrive in England until after Æthelstan was dead. I am assuming here, therefore, that Eric became earl of York *during his father's lifetime*, a not impossible adventure to befall this fiery viking prince. That he was appointed to this earldom by Æthelstan is vouched for by the *Heimskringla, Egilssaga,* and *Fagrskinna*; but this can be contested on the grounds that the Saxon Chronicle and other English sources (notably Simeon of Durham) say nothing of Æthelstan's friendly action towards Eric. On the contrary, the Saxon Chronicle does not mention Eric until 948. If Harald Fairhair's death can be put as late as 943–5 (cf. p. 108), and if Eric reigned in Norway for two or three years before his exile, the Chronicle's date would do very well as that of his first appearance in this country. Note that if Harald's death took place about 933 (the old dating), and Eric's exile (say) 935, he may perfectly well have been the vassal-lord of York for the last two or three years of Æthelstan's life and at the same time the exiled king of Norway.

investing army and make good his escape, so that in the end the young English king was compelled to come to terms with him. It was a surprising and disastrous peace that Edmund made, disastrous both for English prestige and for the unfortunate Danes of the Five Boroughs, for Edmund was forced to concede these boroughs, Danish Mercia in fact, to Olaf and his Norwegians, and it was agreed that the boundary between the Danelaw and the English realm in this area should be the Watling Street.

LOSS AND RECOVERY OF THE FIVE BOROUGHS 940–942

Nevertheless this humiliating position was not of long duration. In 941, after a raid upon the territory of his northern neighbour in Bernicia, Olaf died, and Edmund at once attacked his cousin and successor Olaf Cuaran, or Sigtrygsson, who had come over from Ireland to York in the preceding year. In 942 Edmund won back the Five Boroughs. It was an impressive feat, and was hailed with joy throughout England, though few were more thankful for this deliverance then the Mercian Danes themselves, who had no love for the Norwegian vikings. But the power of these Northmen was now weakening, and in 943 Olaf Cuaran submitted to Edmund and consented to be baptized a Christian, though this act the Norwegians regarded as a shameful betrayal and accordingly they drove Olaf out of York, electing his cousin Ragnvald Godfredsson as king in his place. Edmund, thereupon, marched across the Humber and captured York, and with the fall of York all Northumbria passed into his hands. His next move was to march into Cumberland where by a campaign of harrying and burning he hoped to crush the unruly Norwegian settlements round Carlisle, the favourite base of those malcontent Irish vikings who had come to win a kingdom for themselves in England. He did not, however, complete the subjection of this Norse colony, finding it more prudent to depose Domnhall, the last Welsh king of Cumbria, and to consign the district to Malcolm, king of the Scots, who in return promised to keep these Norwegians and Irish Danes in order and to become the ally of the English king. But Northumbria Edward himself controlled as overlord, and this was the position when he died in 946.

EDMUND WINS NORTH-UMBRIA

The next king of England was his brother Eadred, youngest son of Edward the Elder. At the very outset of his reign he made a military demonstration in Northumbria in order to establish his position as overlord, and he took care to renew the alliance with the Scots. But he found himself faced, nevertheless, by a serious insurrection

EADRED 946–955

in the Yorkshire Danelaw in 947. Wulfstan, the then archbishop of York and a man probably of Danish family, seems to have been one of the chief instigators of this revolt that culminated in the setting-up of a rebel king at York, this being none other than its former earl, Eric Bloodaxe, the Norwegian prince (p. 121). Eadred's wrath at this flouting of his authority was terrible, and he straightway began to ravage in Northumbria, even burning the famous minster of Ripon. But the punitive expedition ended in humiliation, for the rearguard of the English force was caught by the rebels and almost annihilated ; whereat Eadred, still more wrathful, immediately turned his army about, and so plainly was it now his intention to devastate the whole of the unhappy province with fire and sword that the Danes promptly drove out Eric and submitted to Eadred.

But Northumbria remained a fickle and uncertain province. In the very next year (949) Olaf Cuaran returned from Ireland, and, aided by the machinations of Wulfstan, he succeeded in making himself king at York. Then, in 952, Eadred imprisoned the treacherous archbishop, and the Norwegians and Danes, once COLLAPSE more taking fright, expelled Olaf. But it was only OF NORTH- to replace him by Eric Bloodaxe,[1] and this was more UMBRIAN than Eadred could tolerate. In 954, after Eric had REBEL- LION AND sat on this insecure and dangerous throne for two years, LAST OF the English king marched north, seized the Yorkshire THE FOREIGN Danelaw, and expelled Eric. There were no half- KINGS OF measures, no bargainings and treaties, this time. All YORK 954 resistance in Northumbria was broken down, and Eadred handed over the whole province to Oswulf of Bamborough as an earldom. The unfortunate adventurer Eric, who met his death this same year, was the last of the kings of York, and once again England became a single realm extending from the Forth to the Channel.

This year, 954, marked the end of the first great episode in the viking history of England. A hundred and twenty years had passed since the vikings had first assailed Ecgbert in Wessex, and, though amid the catastrophic disasters of the first forty-three years of this period it had seemed that the very fabric of English society was threatened with extinction, yet in the brave struggles of the final seventy-seven years that remarkable family of warrior-kings, Alfred, Edward, Æthelstan, and Eadred, had driven back the invaders, humiliated them, and put an end to

[1] It has been suggested that the Eric who was made king of York in 952 was not Eric Bloodaxe, but a Dane, the son of Harald Gormsson. But this identification is very dubious.

PLATE VIII

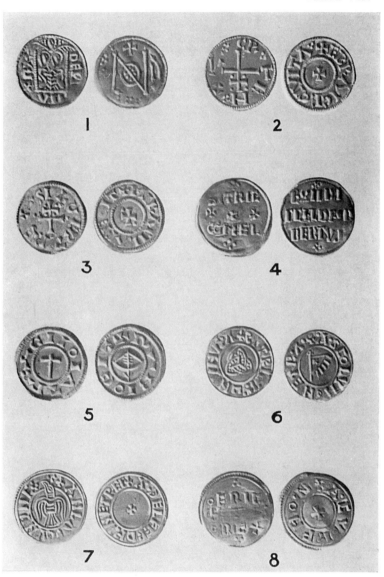

1 2

3 4

5 6

7 8

COINS OF THE VIKING RULERS OF ENGLAND

For details, see List of Plates

them as a political power in the land. The great eastern plain of England, parcelled out among its Danish proprietors, had been an established colony of the foreigners : but it had been won back for England, and, though Danish blood and Danish customs remained in undiminished force to distinguish the Danelaw from the rest of the country, yet, by 954, this province had been victoriously transformed into a quiescent appanage of the English crown.

It is a story of which England may be proud, this splendid show of force under the five great kings. But their achievement in its political aspect, as distinct from their solid military success, must not be rated too highly. For even with the subjugation of the Danelaw and the territorial expansion of the last thirty years, these kings cannot be said to have created an English nation inasmuch as differences in law, manners, and feelings, still preserved the identity of the several provinces that now formed the consolidated kingdom. Thus the Danelaw was governed by its Danish jarls, and governed by them according to the Danish law without any interference on the part of the English king ; clearly the loyalty of these Danes to their English overlord was dependent only on the protection he could offer them and might count for nothing if a stronger master threatened the land.

And now that peace had come, there was no king of England powerful enough to crown the work of Alfred and his descendants by imposing a common law throughout all the realm and so instilling the proper sense of nationality that was needed to make the kingdom a stable and enduring whole. Church reforms under the firm leadership of that great ecclesiastic Dunstan, and the franchises in favour of the monasteries granted by Edgar (959–975), were the main preoccupation of England's rulers in the long period of quiet that followed the death of Eadwig (955–959) ; and when Æthelred, then aged ten, came to the throne in 978 in a land troubled only by the rivalries between clerks and clergy, it was to take his place at the head of a state softened rather than strengthened by twenty-five tranquil years. And this was the England, and this the time, when the second viking episode opens. Once more the pirate craft swoop down on the English coast, harbingers of a second viking invasion not less formidable than that which had threatened to destroy England in the ninth century.

The raids began again in 980. In that year a fleet ' from the North ', coming probably from Ireland or Man, took Chester and its crews ravaged the country around, while another fleet,

no doubt from Scandinavia or Denmark, seized Southampton
NEW AT- and massacred the townsfolk. Thanet was also
TACKS BY plundered by pirates in this year, and in 981 Cornwall
VIKINGS and Devon suffered from similar visitations. In 982
FROM
OVERSEAS London was seized and burnt, and in Dorset Portland
980- 987 was plundered by the crews of three viking ships.
Then followed an interval of five years ; but in 987 Watchet in
Somerset was sacked by buccaneers, and in the year after there
was fighting in Devon.

All these raids were carried out by small parties of vikings
who could be repulsed without difficulty, in spite of the frequent
initial success of their surprise attacks, and they seemed to have
occasioned no great uneasiness in the mind of the king or among
his councillors. But in 991 there was a raid of a much
INVASION more serious kind, one that was to shock England
OF 991 not only into consciousness of her new peril but into a
dismal realization of the weakness of her present rulers. The
fleet that appeared suddenly on the Thames in that year was not a
force of overwhelming strength, but it was ninety-three ships in all
and its commanders were the exiled Norwegian prince and future
king of Norway, Olaf Tryggvason (p. 123), Justin (ON. Jósteinn),
perhaps an uncle of Olaf's,[1] and Guthmund Stegitansson (ON.
Sigitansson or Sixtansson), who was probably a Swede ; its crews
must have been mostly Swedish vikings from Russia where Olaf
had been brought up, and whence he had sailed on this viking
cruise to the western waters.

The attack began by a plundering in the neighbourhood of
Staines. Then the fleet moved to Sandwich, and from there
crossed over to sack Ipswich ; from Ipswich it sailed into the
mouth of the Blackwater. But by this time Brihtnoth, the Duke
of the East Saxons, had collected an army, and without delay
he marched to Maldon, the town that was now threatened.

The Battle of Maldon is described in an epic poem that is
one of the chief ornaments of pre-Chaucerian literature in England,
and as it is thus one of the few battles with the vikings of which
BATTLE OF there is a coherent account it has a special interest.
MALDON But it is not only because it reveals something of the
991 nature of this pirate-warfare that the account in the
poem deserves more than passing mention ; on the contrary it is
important for the greater reason that the battle itself was a
decisive one, marking, as it does, the first overthrow of the English
after a long sequence of victories that had been followed by a

---

[1] Or, possibly, Toste (Tusti), a famous viking whose name appears
on many Swedish rune-stones.

comfortable interlude of peace. It marks, indeed, the opening
of a new epoch in viking history, an awakening for the English
of a rude and bloody kind.

The fight took place close to the island of Northey [1] in the
estuary of the Blackwater about $1\frac{3}{4}$ miles below Maldon. Olaf
and his vikings were encamped on the island which was connected
to the south bank of the river by a causeway that was submerged
at high tide. Brihtnoth led his men at once to this causeway
and drew up his force in battle-array on the river-bank opposite
the vikings who were ranged on the island-side of the narrow
stream. The proceedings opened with an offer on the part of
the vikings that was shouted across the river:

'Send quickly rings for your safety: it is better for you to buy off
with tribute this storm of spears, than that we should share the
bitter war: . . . we will with gold set up a truce. . . . We will go
abroad with the tribute, and sail the sea, and be at peace with
you.' [2]

It was the old cry of the robber-vikings, 'Buy us off'; but
this time the offer of peace was unceremoniously rejected.

'Brihtnoth spoke and grasped his shield, brandished the slender
spear, and, wrathful and unwavering, gave him answer: "Hearest
thou, rover, what this people saith? They will give you in tribute
spears, and deadly darts, and old swords; they will give you the
war-harness that avails you naught in the battle. Seafolk's envoy,
take back this word, tell thy people a crueller story: that here
stands an earl not mean, with his company, who will defend this
land, Æthelred's home, my prince's folk and field: the heathen shall
fall in the war. Too shameful it seems to me that ye should go
abroad with our tribute, unfought with, now that ye have come thus
far into our land: not so lightly shall ye come by the treasure:
point and edge shall first make atonement, grim warplay, before we
pay tribute."'

But it seems that while these high-spirited preliminaries were
in progress the tide had been creeping-up, and presently the causeway was submerged by the inflowing waters. The combatants
were therefore left facing one another over a stream that they
could not cross, and, except for a few arrow-shots, it was plain
that there could be no fighting until the ebb. When at long last
the tide did fall, the impatient vikings tried to cross the causeway,
but Brihtnoth posted three stout-hearted English heroes at its

[1] The real site of the Battle of Maldon was first established by F. D.
Laborde, *Eng. Hist. Review*, XL (1925), p. 161.
[2] From the translation by the late Professor W. P. Ker.

head, and these, like Horatius and his two comrades, held the bridge. The Norwegians saw very quickly that they could not cross the river by fighting their way over the causeway, and accordingly they begged the English leader to retire with his army while they led their companies over and could post themselves ready for battle on his side of the water. The English earl, of his over-boldness, agreed to this plan, and so it came about that the vikings were allowed to cross the stream in safety while Brihtnoth drew up his men anew on some rising ground to the rear. Then, at last, the armies faced each other without any intervening barrier and now a fierce battle began. The fighting from the first went against the English ; Brihtnoth was slain, some of the English fled, and then the remnant, after a last glorious stand, was annihilated. It was over a hundred years since England had suffered so crushing and so significant a reverse.

Æthelred, whose miserable sobriquet was to be ' the Redeless ', the king who was *lacking in counsel*, did not hasten to avenge the death of these loyal men of Essex. Instead it was resolved, THE VIK- on the advice of Sigeric, Archbishop of Canterbury, to INGS make peace with the viking leaders, and by a bribe of BRIBED 991 10,000 pounds of silver to obtain from them a promise that they would not molest the southern English again and that they would help to ward off any other viking attacks that occurred while they and their fleet remained in Essex. But this was not the whole of the shameful bargain,[1] for in addition to the very heavy tribute (danegeld) thus offered, Æthelred further promised to supply rations for the pirate force while the vikings stayed in England. Thus was danger temporarily averted by a cowardly and ill-omened pact. It was not, of course, the first occasion whereupon English money had been paid to the Northmen, but it was the first bribe of the sort that openly revealed the English king as a weakling and his English subjects as no longer a hardy and implacable foe.

Olaf Tryggvason and the viking chiefs who had made this treaty no doubt took themselves off in due course with their own personal followings and their share of this huge tribute, but a part of the viking host nevertheless stayed on in East Anglia, and Æthelred very soon realized that something other than a

---

[1] I take the treaty between Æthelred, on the one hand, and Olaf, Justin, and Guthmund, on the other hand (for the text see A. J. Robertson, *Laws of Kings of England from Edmund to Henry I*, Cambridge, 1925, p. 56) as applying to this 991 peace. The difficulty, of course, is that the treaty text speaks of a bribe of 22,000 pounds of gold and silver.

bribe was needed to rid himself of them ; accordingly, in 992 he collected all his serviceable ships in London and ordered an attack on the viking fleet. But a treacherous alderman gave the enemy warning of the impending attack, and when the vikings and the English did at length engage in a naval battle Æthelred's fleet was beaten. Yet the threat against the security of the enemy base was successful, for the vikings sailed away northwards after this fight, and in the next year, 993, they left southern England in peace. Instead they stormed Bamborough, taking a great booty in that town, and afterwards they ravaged at their will throughout Northumbria and Lindsey. A big army was collected to drive them out, but the courage of the northern English was now failing like that of the southerners, for on approaching the enemy the leaders of this levy took to flight and the army dissolved without offering any resistance to the marauders.

In 994 the Norwegian Olaf, who had been plundering in Anglesey, was joined by Svein (p. 117), King of Denmark, and with a fleet of ninety-four ships they sailed together to attack London. There was a fierce battle outside the town, which the vikings tried to fire, but the Londoners defended themselves with THE VIK- valour and drove the Northmen off with heavy loss. INGS After this reverse, they gave up the attempt to take BRIBED the town, and went off to plunder along the coasts of AGAIN 994 Essex, Kent, Sussex, and Hampshire. Emboldened by the feebleness of the opposition they encountered, they then obtained horses for themselves and began to make inland raids. Æthelred and the Wessex army proved themselves incapable of defending the country, and at last the king and his witan were reduced by these terrible weeks of panic and chaos to offer tribute and rations to the vikings if they would cease from their plundering. The price paid on this occasion was 16,000 pounds. When this bargain was struck, Olaf was then brought in honour to Andover and there baptized with Æthelred himself as sponsor. Once more he promised not to attack England again, and this time he kept his word, for in the following summer he sailed away to make himself king of Norway.

Svein also left England, though he continued his viking cruise and plundered in Wales and in Man before he returned to his own kingdom. But when he was back in Denmark he did not forget the now feeble realm that he had robbed so successfully, and after he had secured his own power he proceeded to organize a series of raids against England that proved to be a prelude to the outright conquest of the country. In 997 Wales and Cornwall were harried, the minster at Tavistock was burnt, and the towns of Lydford and Watchet plundered ; in 998 it was the turn of Dorset, and now the vikings established a base in the Isle of Wight which they provisioned by raids upon Hampshire and Sussex. In 999 it was Kent that suffered, and this is the pitiful description in the Saxon Chronicle of the events of that year.

' The Danes came round into the Thames, and up along the Medway to Rochester. And the Kentish force came against them, and they fought sharply. But, alas, that they all too quickly gave way and fled, because they had not the support that they should have had. And the Danes held the field ; and then took horses and rode whithersoever they would, and ruined almost all West Kent. Then the king with his witan decreed that they should be met both by a navy and a land-force. But when the ships were ready there was delay from day to day, and the wretched crews in the ships were harassed ; and ever, as things ought to have been more forward, they were from one hour to another more behindhand. And ever they let the host of their foes increase ; and ever the English withdrew from the sea, and the Danes followed them up. And then, in the end, neither the navy nor the land-force came to anything, save toil of the people, and waste of money, and encouragement of the enemy.' [1]

In the year 1000 Svein's vikings attacked not England, but Normandy, and during their absence Æthelred, at last determined to take some measures for the protection of his miserable country, made an expedition to the north in order to subdue the vikings settled in Cumberland and in Anglesey. But in 1001 Svein returned with his Danes and once more southern England was in peril. There was a big battle at Alton in which the Hampshire men were beaten after both sides had suffered heavy losses, and from Alton the Danes went to Devon where they were joined by a small army under Pallig,[2] Svein's brother-in-law, who had previously sold his services to Æthelred and now most treacherously broke faith with his English master. In Devon the Danes burned Teignton and many other towns, and at Pinhoe they routed the levies of Devon and Somerset. Pinhoe and Clyst they burnt, and then they returned to Hampshire, where they sacked Bishop's Waltham, and to the Isle of Wight.

This triumphant march of the enemy across south-western England and the unchallenged security of the base in Wight were

[1] Trans. from R. W. Chambers, *England before the Norman Conquest*, London, 1926.

[2] Who has been identified by Steenstrup with Palnatoki, the Jomsborg viking who settled in Wales.

sufficient to reveal the formidable strength of the Danish army
and to drive the English king to the desperate panic measures
THE VIK-   that had already half ruined his country.   He made a
INGS   third offer of a big money payment in return for peace,
BRIBED   and for the price of 24,000 pounds a truce with the
FOR THE
THIRD   Danes was bought.   Then he committed the further
TIME   folly of himself breaking this truce, for hearing, so it
1002   is said, of a Danish plot against his life he utterly lost
his head and gave orders for the massacre of all the Danes in the
south of England, that is those who had been bribed into entering
his service and those, if any, who had become peaceable settlers
in the land.   On St. Brice's Day of 1002 this abominable deed
was duly carried out, and among the victims was Gunnhild, who
was Pallig's wife and Svein's sister.

It was useless now to hope for the peace so expensively bought
earlier in this same year, useless, in fact, to expect anything but
the immediate return of the furious Danish king.   And back
he came, merciless and implacable, and in England he remained
SVEIN'S   for the years 1003 and 1004.   Exeter fell to him in
CON-   Devon, and in Wiltshire he took Salisbury ; Norwich
QUESTS
AND THE   and Thetford were sacked and burnt in East Anglia,
FOURTH   though in this last district the Anglo-Dane Ulfkytel
BRIBE 1007 made a braver show of defending the southern Danelaw
than the King of England had done in Wessex.   In 1005 there
was a famine and while it lasted Svein and his army returned to
Denmark, but in 1006 he sailed back and ravaged Kent with the
utmost ferocity.   Next he moved to his quarters in Wight and
at mid-winter made a great demonstration march across Wessex,
lighting war-beacons as he went.   He sacked Reading and
Wallingford, and because it had been said that if he reached
Cuckamsley Hill he would never return to the sea, to Cuckamsley
Hill he marched ' and there abode as a daring boast '.   On the
way home there was a battle with a local force somewhere in the
Kennet valley that Svein won, and by the end of the year the
English were so completely demoralized that they were willing to
purchase peace no matter what sacrifices the levying of the
immense tribute required might cost them.   Thirty-six thousand
pounds were paid over to Svein in 1007.

Æthelred had once again a short respite, so he emerged from
his hiding in Shropshire and commanded that there should be a
great national shipbuilding campaign.   In 1009 the large fleet
that thus came into being was concentrated at Sandwich, and it
seemed that at last England had a defence that might prevail
against her enemies.   ' But ', says the Chronicle, ' we had not

the good fortune nor the worthiness that the ship-force could be of any use to this land.' For there was quarrelling among its leaders, some of the boats were sunk in the fighting that followed, others were lost in a storm, and the rest of the fleet was shamelessly abandoned by the naval commanders. 'And then afterwards', the Chronicle continues, 'the people who were in the ships brought them to London, and they let the whole nation's toil thus lightly pass away.'

Svein was now occupied by the government of his own country, but he did not relax his grip on the luckless realm of England, and shortly after this suicidal break-up of the fleet his lieutenant, Thorkel the Tall, a viking jarl from Jomsborg (p. 184), landed with a great army at Sandwich, the very port where the fleet had been collected. With Thorkel and his Jomsborg Danes there also landed a young Norwegian prince, a future king of Norway, who was known in his lifetime as Olaf the Stout but who is now famous to history as the great St. Olaf, and he and his Norwegian adventurers were for many years embroiled in the fighting in England.[1] Immediately after the arrival of Thorkel's army, the men of east Kent bought their freedom for 3,000 pounds, but when the vikings had established themselves in the Isle of Wight, Sussex, Hampshire, and Berkshire were ravaged mercilessly from the island-base. Æthelred made some show of opposition, but treachery and mutiny dissipated the force he collected, and the Danes found themselves free to plunder as far afield as Kent. Finally they took up winter quarters on the Thames, pillaging Essex and the home counties in their search for provisions; but when they attacked London, as they did again and again, they there met with a stubborn resistance and each time were beaten off with heavy losses. Yet they did at length succeed in breaking past the bridge that barred the river against them at London,[2] and

[1] Olaf had been plundering in Frisia and came to England after the battle of ' Kinnlimaside ' on the coast of Holland; it is possible that he did not join Thorkel until the time of the attacks on London (*infra*).

[2] The well-known account of the attack on London in the *Heimskringla* (*St. Olaf's Saga*, XI, XII) refers to these battles, but Norse tradition is obviously at variance with the English historical record. It is clear, however, that the key to the town was a castle (evidently on or near the site of the Tower of London) and a fort (probably originally built by Alfred) called the *Sudrvirki* (Southwark), and that a bridge, connecting these two defensive positions, was itself fortified so that it effectively blocked the progress of enemy boats up-river. Olaf's famous feat was the breaking-down of the bridge, and this he accomplished by roofing-over his ships, so that the rowers were protected from the missiles hurled down upon them, and thus sailing right up under the bridge

giving up all hopes of taking the town itself, they made instead an attack through Chilternsaete on Oxford which they burnt. They wintered in the Thames valley, then moved back to Kent to refit their ships and in the year 1010 sailed for Ipswich. East Anglia collapsed before them, and for a space of three months this land that had been a colony of their forefathers, where the folk were half Danish and where Danish law still obtained, was pitilessly ravaged. After burning Thetford and Cambridge, the army struck westwards into Oxfordshire, and then back to burn the town of Bedford, after which the vikings returned to their ships. The wretched English army was grossly mismanaged, and the king and his witan were helpless to stay this insolent plundering ; indeed, late in the year when the Danes made another raid and burnt Northampton, the terrified king gave up all hope of defending the land by battle and in 1011 he sent messengers to the Danes to ask for peace, offering this time a tribute of no less than 48,000 pounds, as well as food-supplies, if they would cease from their plunderings. To collect

FIFTH BRIBE TO THE VIKINGS 1012 such a sum was, of course, a very difficult task and during the inevitable delay there were further disasters. Canterbury was captured, through the treachery of the Abbot of St. Augustine's, and the Archbishop Ælfeah (Alphege) was taken prisoner with many other notable ecclesiastics. The Danes stayed in Canterbury as long as it pleased them to do so and for a while they held the Archbishop to ransom, but finally he was murdered by them at Greenwich. Says the Chronicle : ' All these calamities fell upon us through evil counsel, because tribute was not offered to them at the right time, nor yet were they resisted : but, when they had done the most evil, then was peace made with them. And notwith-

---

he then passed hawsers round the supporting piles and, having done this, rowed hard downstream, the current and the muscles of his oarsmen being sufficient, so says the account, to loosen the piles and bring the bridge toppling down. The *Heimskringla* narrative then goes on to say that Southwark was afterwards taken by storm and that the fortress on the north bank surrendered. The *Heimskringla* version, however, is wholly untrustworthy in that it presents Olaf as fighting for Æthelred against the Danes who, according to this story, were in possession of London, and it puts the date of the battle as being after the death of Svein in 1014. Although it is true that Olaf was in Æthelred's service when the English king was called back from his exile in 1014, there is no record in the English sources of an attack on London such as is described in the Norse saga. It may, indeed, be taken as certain that the Chronicle, so pathetically verbose in these years, would not fail to signalize with proper rejoicings a recapture of London from the Danes by Æthelred.

standing all this peace and tribute, they went everywhere in companies, harried our wretched people, robbed and slew them.'

At last the great tribute was paid and oaths of peace sworn. The Danish force accordingly broke up, but not all of the vikings returned to Denmark, for Thorkel himself with forty-five ships, and the Norwegian Olaf too, remained behind to take service with Æthelred, as the Dane Pallig had done before them. And it came to Svein's ears that Thorkel, rich and powerful, now ruled, so the tale went, over the land subdued with the force that Svein had entrusted to him. It was just such a report as was most likely to enrage the haughty and quick-tempered King of Denmark, and if poor Æthelred believed that Thorkel and Olaf, now bribed to fight for him, would save England from further attack by the Danes, he was to be speedily undeceived. For soon came the great Svein himself, wrathful and jealous, to prove his might by a greater achievement than that of his treacherous lieutenant. In July 1013 he set sail from Denmark with the avowed purpose of seizing the English throne.

His first move was to enlist the support of his countrymen in the Danelaw, and so, instead of attacking Wessex from the Thames or the south coast, he sailed to the Humber. Accompanied by his young son Cnut, who was destined to succeed SVEIN'S him as king of England, he landed at Gainsborough, INVASION and there, as he had expected, Uhtred, the English 1013 jarl of the Yorkshire Danes, offered him allegiance, whereupon Lindsey and the Five Boroughs also submitted to him without any struggle. Svein, therefore, at once found himself accepted as overlord of Northumbria and Danish Mercia, and having thus established himself in the country he crossed Watling Street to attack the territories still loyal to the English king. The result of this march to the south, a savage and terrible punitive expedition, was that first Oxford and then Winchester submitted to him, and after this double triumph he turned eastwards to London with the intention of crowning his achievement by the complete overthrow of Æthelred, Thorkel, and Olaf, who were encamped with their armies in the town. But in fording the Thames he lost many of his men, and when he attacked London itself he was beaten off. Thereupon he altered his plans, being too clever a strategist to waste his strength on further assaults, and, secure in the knowledge that the greater part of the effective English force was concentrated in London, he immediately marched away across Wessex to Bath and there

obtained control of the western country, the aldermen of Devon and all the western thanes at once submitting to him without a struggle. Then he went across England to his ships on the
SVEIN BECOMES KING OF ENGLAND
Humber and was everywhere acknowledged as ' full king ', so that in the end there was no other course left for London but to submit and give hostages to this great Danish warrior. Svein contented himself with exacting a tribute from the Londoners : Thorkel retreated to Greenwich, and Æthelred, after lurking with his fleet off the Thames mouth, fled to the Isle of Wight and ultimately escaped overseas to take refuge with his brother-in-law, Richard II, Duke of Normandy. And so it came about that a Danish king ruled England, while the English king hid as a refugee in the anglophile court of the province that had been, one hundred years before, the French Danelaw.

But Svein, the conqueror of England, did not long enjoy this complete triumph, for he died suddenly at the beginning of 1014 and his death was at once followed by a struggle for
DEATH OF SVEIN 1014
the throne he had won. His own army and fleet at Gainsborough chose his young son Cnut, then only 18 years old, as king, but this choice was not accepted in Denmark where Cnut's elder brother Harald succeeded his father. Nor were the English slow to realize that an opportunity had come to throw off the Danish yoke and they instantly invited Æthelred to return, declaring that no lord was dearer to them than their natural lord, if he would but rule them better than he had done before. It was, in truth, a touching demonstration of the loyalty and affection of the English people that greeted Æthelred when he came back in Lent of this year to take up arms against the Danes, for he was everywhere acclaimed with the joy and thankfulness that was born of their revived hopes.

Æthelred began his operations with an unwonted show of force, and at the sudden approach of the English army to Lindsey Cnut at once went off to Denmark to seek reinforcements. The English king then paid Thorkel and Olaf at Greenwich 21,000 pounds, presumably to ensure the continued fidelity of these uncertain allies, but this payment unluckily turned out to be so much wasted money for Thorkel shortly afterwards sailed away to Denmark to place himself under Cnut's leadership. Nor was the English king able to count for long upon the aid of Olaf and his Norwegians, for although this future saint, after Æthelred's flight, had gone off on a viking raid to France and had now returned in the retinue of the king, he did not fancy the fortunes of the English and soon took himself off on another viking expedition to the Continent.[1]

In the meantime the young Danish prince Cnut had collected a large and carefully chosen army, including a force of Norwegians under Eric, a son of Jarl Haakon (p. 122), and in September of 1015, at the head of a fleet of 200 ships, he came back to England.

Æthelred was ill, and his country was distracted by a bitter feud between the sick king and his son Edmund who was now holding the Five Boroughs as a declared rebel. Cnut, after putting in at Sandwich, sailed down the coast to Wareham and CNUT'S   landed there unopposed. When from this base he INVASION began to ravage in Dorset, Wiltshire, and Somerset, 1015   at length Edmund and the man he most of all hated, Eadric the Grasper, Duke of West Mercia, an evil and treacherous councillor of his father, both gathered forces to resist the Danes, and the two English leaders, though bitter enemies, marched south together to fight Cnut. But when the Danes and English came face to face, Eadric, preferring to harm Edmund rather than save his country, proved such an uncertain ally that the English were in the end compelled to retreat from the presence of the enemy without fighting a battle ; to complete their discomfort the traitor thereupon took forty ships of Æthelred's fleet and went over to Cnut. This was the end of all opposition in Wessex which thus passed without a struggle into Cnut's hands.

In 1016 Cnut, now with Eadric in his train, marched into Mercia and ravaged Warwickshire with the utmost ferocity. Edmund bravely came forth to do his duty ; but the absence of Æthelred, who was now in London, and the known quarrel between king and his son, made it impossible for him to get together a loyal force of sufficient size and finally he was compelled to abandon Mercia and appeal for help to Uhtred of Northumbria. Uhtred and Edmund then came south together to attack the territory of the much-detested Eadric in Staffordshire and Shropshire, but while they were so engaged Cnut, in his turn, pushed northwards and reached York. There was nothing left for Uhtred but to go back and offer his submission to the Dane ; this was accepted, but on Eadric's counsel, Cnut connived at the murder of the English earl and put Eric Haakonsson to be jarl of Yorkshire in his place.

[1] But Olaf's moves are somewhat uncertain. He seems to have returned to England again in 1015 and to have fought in Lincolnshire and Yorkshire before he finally departed for Norway.

After the fall of Northumbria Edmund fled to his father in London, and Cnut, who was now almost master of England, followed him there ; but before the Danish fleet had reached the Thames Æthelred died. The Londoners chose Edmund as king, and at once he hurried off to the west country to collect a new army. In the meantime the Danes had advanced upon London, and by digging a great ditch so as to form a loop behind the south bank they were able to drag their ships past the bridge that barred the river ; after this they trenched round the whole town and shut the Londoners in. But though they attacked often, yet each time the townsmen beat them off.

By this time Edward had collected a sufficiently numerous host to justify an advance eastwards, first to Pen near Gillingham and then to Sherston near Malmesbury where he fought two indecisive engagements with Eadric and a Danish force sent by Cnut to intercept him. But the Danes retreated on London and Edmund was left free to collect a larger army. When this was done he boldly assumed the offensive, relieved London, and two nights later crossed the Thames at Brentford and defeated the Danish army. After this splendid and courageous stroke Edmund then returned to Wessex, and the Danes, when they had made yet one more abortive attack on London, sailed off to the Orwell in Suffolk. From that base they raided both Mercia and Kent, but by this time Edmund had come eastward again and one of the enemy raiding parties in the Medway valley was beaten off after getting the worst of a battle at Otford.

The hopes of saving England were now reviving and even the treacherous Eadric began to feel that after all he had thrown in his lot with the losing side. At this juncture, therefore, he made his submission to Edmund at Aylesford, and the king accepted it. ' Never ', says the Chronicle with bitterness, ' was greater folly than that.' For when King Edmund, reinforced by Eadric and his men from the Welsh border, advanced to battle with the Danes at Ashingdon[1] in Essex, Eadric lost the day for England by his cowardly flight from the field. ' He betrayed his king and lord and the whole English nation,' the Chronicle continues, ' and Cnut won the victory, and with it all England.' The English losses were, indeed, terrible, and among the fallen chivalry of the land was the gallant Ulfkytel of East Anglia. The king of England fled into Gloucestershire ; thereat the last

---

[1] On the site of the battle of *Assandun* see Miller Christy in *Journ. Brit. Arch. Assoc.* NS. XXXI (1925), p. 168.

flickerings of the hope that had burned so bravely but a few weeks earlier flickered down into the ashes and were dead.

Cnut followed Edmund. And there seemed nothing left for the English king to do but to come to terms before the prestige of his earlier victories had been lessened by further defeat. So the young prince and the young Danish king met at Olney near Deerhurst and there they agreed that the realm should be divided, Edmund holding Wessex, and Cnut all Mercia and the Danelaw. As for London, the brave townsmen were granted peace by Cnut in return for a money payment and the Danish fleet took up its winter-quarters in the battle-shaken and splendid town.

It was a situation ominous of another, and even more ferocious struggle yet to come, this division of England into two kingdoms, for what Dane did not know that Cnut, when he had recruited his expeditionary force by drafts from Denmark, would seek to win Wessex? And what Englishman, now that a breathing-space had been bought, would not rally to the banner of his king, Edmund *Ironside* as men had learnt to call him, should he summon them to a last resistance or should he, gallant and lion-hearted, seek in his turn to recover England for the English? For desperate though the situation was, yet that had been a worse peril from which Alfred and Edward the Elder had rescued their country.

But Fate willed that there was to be no struggle. On St. Andrew's Day (30th November) of this same year, 1016, the English king died suddenly at the early age of 22, and when the sorrowing folk of Wessex laid Ironside to his rest, it was with the full knowledge that the passing of their young champion had made the further independence of his kingdom an impossibility. Therefore, early in 1017, the nobles of Wessex turned to the one strong man who could give them peace and security, Cnut the Dane, and, by choosing him as their king, made him lord and sovereign of all England.

CNUT BECOMES KING OF ENGLAND 1017

It was the hour of the greatest triumph in the whole history of the vikings. A Danish king ruled the country, and the Danish army and the Danish fleet were masters of the English lands and the English seas. There could be no rallying, no hero of this last and desperate danger to rescue England, no Athelney to shelter him. For the end had come and the victory was to the Danes.

In the twenty years that followed the crowning of Cnut, England, though sunk to the status of a mere province in an Anglo-Scandinavian kingdom, enjoyed a peace and a prosperity

PLATE IX

KING CNUT AND HIS WIFE AELFGIFU-EMMA
From the New Minster Register 1016-1020

such as she had not known since the days of mighty Æthelstan and Edward the Elder. For the Dane, suddenly altered from a young barbarian pirate into a dignified and benevolent monarch, loved much the country that he had won, and, taking up his abode at royal Winchester, by his piety and statesmanship, by his careful and well-intentioned government, made of Danish tyranny a blessing in all respects preferable to a sickly independence under weakling Saxons such as Æthelred.

In the first year of his reign he wedded Emma of Normandy, the widow of Æthelred, thus gaining the friendship of the neighbouring and powerful Duchy and at the same time earning the approbation of his new subjects by so connecting himself with the English court that had lately ruled at Winchester. Then, fine gesture of the year 1018, he paid off and dismissed the great Danish army that had made the conquest of England possible, and, this done, in addition to the ordinary duties of legislature and executive government, he set himself to the building of churches, honouring especially the poor English martyr St. Edmund, slain by his countrymen in 869, and also St. Alphege, the archbishop murdered by the Danes in 1011 and whose relics Cnut now (1023) translated with all possible pomp and honour from St. Paul's to Canterbury. Yet another notable act of his was a memorable pilgrimage to Rome made in 1026, for the Danish king of England was present with all the great princes of Europe at the coronation of the Emperor Conrad II on Easter Day in 1027 and was well-received by the Pope ; from Rome he addressed to his people that noble letter wherein he declared the concessions he had obtained for his subjects who desired to visit Italy and then assured them how upon his return he would diligently seek to administer an equal justice to all, without favour or oppression, enjoining only of them that they should pay regularly and promptly the dues required of them by the Church. On this journey he did much to restore the lost prestige of England on the continent, and a token of this was the betrothal of his daughter to the emperor's eldest son, a union that subsequently brought to Cnut a full sovereignty over Sleswig and so pushed forward the southern boundary of Denmark to the Eider.

He was already king of Denmark when he conquered England, but he claimed in addition the throne of Norway. And though King Olaf the Saint denied his rights and in 1025, allied with the king of Sweden, opposed Cnut in the famous sea-fight of the Holy River in Scania, yet in 1028 Cnut returned to the north and being joyfully received in Norway, where there was

CNUT AS KING

much discontent at Olaf's rule, he made the country his own without a battle and at a *thing* in Nidaros was acknowledged by all as overlord of the land. Now were Denmark, Norway, and England, confederate states with this mighty king as their single head, and so great was his power then that it is small wonder that Scotland also acknowledged his authority, not actually submitting to him, but nevertheless offering homage.

He died at Shaftesbury in November of 1035, a man of early middle age, and was buried at Winchester. And with him perished this great Anglo-Scandinavian kingdom.

For he left three sons, Svein and Harald Harefoot by Aelfgifu of Northampton, and Hardecnut by Emma. Svein took Norway, Hardecnut Denmark, and Harald England. But the sons of the great king were ruffians, ignorant and boorish vikings, unworthy to succeed their noble father. Harald Harefoot died in 1040, leaving England discontented and rebellious, and Hardecnut, who was then invited to follow him upon the throne of England, died at the age of 25 in 1042. Thus fell the Danish dynasty in England within only seven years of Cnut's death, for now the English chose as their king a prince of the old West Saxon royal line, a son of Æthelred and Emma who had been living in exile in Normandy, Edward the Confessor. And so closed the Danish episode in English history.

Yet one last attempt there was to bring back England under viking dominion, this was the invasion of Harald Hardradi who was half-brother of King Olaf the Saint and had ascended the throne of Norway in 1047. It was in 1066 after King Harald, son of Earl Godwin and himself of half-Danish blood, had succeeded Edward the Confessor, that Hardradi was tempted to essay the conquest of England. He sailed first to the Orkneys where he obtained many recruits from the Scottish Isles and from Man, including the Orkney earls Pall and Erlend, sons of the great Thorfinn; thence he made his way south, joined his forces with those of Tostig, the English king's banished brother who sought to win back his lost earldom of Northumbria, and landed with him in Cleveland. There the invading army plundered for a space, and burnt Scarborough; but finally Hardradi and Tostig sailed for the mouth of the Humber and moved inland to attack York, overthrowing in battle two English earls who opposed them at Fulford, two miles from the city, on the 20th September. They entered York in triumph and a few days later marched eastwards some seven or eight miles to Stamford Bridge on the Derwent where the hostages they had

HARALD HARDRADI, THE LAST VIKING IN- VASION OF ENGLAND

demanded from Deira were to be handed over to them. But at Stamford, only five days after the Battle of Fulford, the English force, collected with amazing suddenness by Harald of England who only a short while previously had disbanded his army, confronted and astonished the invaders. Then followed the famous battle wherein Hardradi's magnificent and adventurous career ended with the winning of his grave-space, that seven foot's room of England or the little more that he, being taller than other men, might require, and in which Tostig also was slain. The triumph of English Harald was complete ; but no matter that the danger of Scandinavian princes attempting to regain the realm of Cnut was thereby ended. For another army gathered for the overthrow of Harald's kingdom stood marshalled and prepared even while Harald and his foes battled at Stamford Bridge. Cnut's kingdom of England was to pass into the keeping of a prince who was neither Scandinavian nor English, though the ancient blood of Scandinavia was in his veins and his people who still bore the name of Normans, *northmen*, had been the children of the vikings. For, most of all, he was a Frenchman, this William the Conqueror, who three days after Stamford Bridge landed at Pevensey.

CHAPTER IX

IRELAND

IT was in Ireland's ' Golden Age ' that the vikings fell upon
Erin. Not only in wealth, but in learning and in intellectual
vigour, was the country rich, and as steadily as Christianity
with its softening of old barbarisms had won its way into the
hearts of the people, firing them with its doctrines of concord
and charity, so there had arisen a sense of Irish solidarity, and a
respect for law and the security that law can give, that, though
it may have had but little flavour of real nationalism, had nevertheless raised the Irish state to a high position in the van of the
civilized countries of north-western Europe.

The island was a heptarchy. Connaught, Munster, and
Leinster (though not with exactly the present boundaries of these
provinces), were three of the kingdoms, the fourth was Meath
(the northern part of modern Leinster), and the other three were
in Ulster, namely Ailech in the west, Ulaidh in the east, with
Oriel (Airgialla) between them. But this heptarchy was not a
chaos of seven quarrelsome and suspicious states, though, in
truth, there were still wars enough in Ireland ; for the control
of the whole country belonged to but two kings, those of Tara
(Meath) and Cashel (Munster), the other sub-kings existing for
the most part upon the favour of these two great chieftains.
There was, therefore, a primary division of Ireland, not into
seven kingdoms, but into two confederacies of kingdoms, that
of the South, looking to the Cashel king as its overlord, and that
of the North, which was ruled from Tara. Nor was this all, for
the Tara king was more than the head of the northern states,
being nothing less than the titular ' King of Ireland ', high-king
of the commonwealth of both the northern and southern confederacies. No doubt his authority depended rather upon common consent than the sanction of his might, for he possessed no
constitutional powers in the kingdoms that were not his own ;
but for all that he was acknowledged as first in rank in the country,
being, potentially at any rate, the chosen head of a united
people.

Yet Ireland, for all these advantages of learning, law, and a high-king, did not present an unbroken front to the invaders from overseas. There was still a jealousy between North and South, and much fighting, viking raids of rapine, between the chiefs of the several states. Plainly enough, in this time of prosperity and comparative quiet, the Irishman's worst foe was his own neighbour, and at the end of the eighth century and at the beginning of the ninth the attacks of the Northmen in their first isolated and little raids were much less to be feared than the sudden and ferocious battles of the rival clans. Had the viking invasion burst upon the country as one huge and shattering blow, then possibly might Ireland have faced the evil single-hearted and resolute ; but the piecemeal raiding of the Northmen discovered the weakness of the land, allowing them to trade upon local jealousies, to take advantage of the personal quarrels of the kings, and so to succeed in winning for themselves settlements in Erin before the Irishmen learnt that the Foreigners had veritably come to conquer and to govern.

The first recorded attack took place in the year 795 when the Northmen, sailing south from Skye, plundered and burnt the EARLY church on Lambey, an island off the Leinster coast just RAIDS north of Dublin. And the opening phase, a period of 795–830 thirty or forty years, of the long struggle between the Gaedhil [1] and the Gaill, [2] of which this raid is the prelude, was for Ireland the same series of intermittent alarms and maraudings as that whereby the Danes were plaguing the kingdoms of England and the great empire of Louis the Pious. It seems that they were Dubhgaill (black strangers), Danes, [3] who made this the first-mentioned attack upon Ireland, but in these early years it was really the Norwegians who most of all ravaged Erin.

Of course, in the beginning neither the audacity of their forays nor the behaviour of the vikings themselves distinguished the Norwegian pirates in Ireland from the Danish buccaneers on the Continent. Hurrying west-over-sea to their summer robberies from the little independent kingdoms that at this time made up their country, these Norsemen were soon attacking Ireland from all sides, sailing up the Shannon in the west, raiding Cork in the south, pillaging the rich monasteries of Ulster in the north, pene-

[1] *Gaedheal*, Irishman.

[2] *Gall*, foreigner (originally, a Gaul, and by application, a viking).

[3] Irish chroniclers, who use a variety of names for the vikings, often distinguish between *dubh* (black) and *finn* (white) foreigners, and this is usually assumed to be a distinction between dark Danes and fair Norwegians. But it is really a distinction of only dubious ethnological value, and though it has been utilized here, according to the custom of Irish historians, I do this not without serious misgivings.

trating inland into Roscommon in Connaught, and daring even to plunder into the heart of Leinster. But the character of the raiding changed quickly and it must have been about 830 that the hitherto sporadic plundering was first followed by the settle-

CONQUEST OF THE NORTH BY TURGEIS 834

ment of some of the vikings in the land, while not many years later, about 834, an event occurred that at once gave the Norse invasion of Erin a different aspect from that of the contemporary viking invasion of England and Francia. This event that led to the opening of a period of serious colonization, not, as yet, attempted by Danes anywhere but in Frisia, was the arrival in Ireland of a chieftain, Turgeis (or Thorgest, as the Norse would have called him), a Norwegian royalty,[1] who sailed to North Ireland with a great ' royal ' fleet and made himself king over the Norwegian settlers in Ulster.

Now it so happened that the coming of Turgeis fell at a time when Feidlimid, the priest-king of Munster, was throwing all Ireland into a turmoil by his monstrous plundering of the monasteries, a long series of outrages that were inspired by his attempt to secure for himself absolute spiritual authority over Ireland and the high-kingship itself. His calamitous behaviour, in every respect as terrifying and as cruel as that of the heathen Norsemen, together with all the conspiracies and jealousies that his quest for power occasioned, left Ireland an easy prey to a determined and able general, and such a man, beyond all doubt, was Turgeis. The capture of Armagh, for it was the chief town of the north and the ecclesiastical centre of Ireland, made this remarkable man, soon after his arrival, one of the powers of the land, and when he drove out the abbot and himself assumed the abbacy, thereby controlling the rich revenues of the monastery, he had achieved a power and dominion such as few vikings of these early years could hope to win. He was not, however, content with a supremacy in Ulster, and spying into the chaos that Feidlimid had made of central Ireland he soon saw opportunity of extending his power. With a fleet that he had sent up the Shannon to Loch Ree he terrorized Connaught in the west and Meath in the east ; he sacked the great monasteries of Clonmac-

---

[1] The identification of Turgeis with Thorgils, a son of Harald Fairhair, is chronologically impossible, although the story of Thorgils as preserved in Norse tradition (*Heimskringla, H. hárfagri*, XXXV) corresponds fairly closely with the Irish account of Turgeis. That this prince was a member of the Yngling family of Vestfold (p. 106) is probable enough. I retain the Irish form of the name here as Thorgils, not Thorgest, may conceivably have been the Norse equivalent.

nois [1] and Clonfert, and all Ireland learnt to dread his name. He did not, of course, conquer the Ui Neill or Fiedlimid's Munster, but he certainly succeeded in establishing the Gaill as a political power in Erin and in threatening the safety of the whole fabric of Irish society. Yet, like many another viking chieftain in the hour of his success, he did not know when to stay his hand and remain content with the dominions already under his sway ; for his relentless and savage campaign against organized Christianity, which culminated in a final outrage when Aud, his wife, gave her heathen audience at the high altar of Clonmacnois, made the prospect of his overlordship so intolerable that at last the faithful men of Meath rose in their dismay and their king, Mael Seachlinn, by trickery rather than fighting, captured him and drowned him in Loch Owel. This was in the year A.D. 845.

Thereafter the Irish were encouraged to defend their country with increasing boldness, but the fall of this great viking did not, nevertheless, free the lands he had won from the Norse yoke that now lay heavy upon them. The fame of Turgeis's conquests had already fired his countrymen, and before FOUNDA- his death fleets of adventurers, ' great sea-cast floods TION OF THE HAR- of foreigners ', were assailing the coasts of Ireland. BOUR- It was this period of the late '30s and early '40s that SETTLE- witnessed the first establishment of the vikings in the MENTS harbour-strongholds of the east and south that became their permanent bases and were later developed into the towns of Dublin, Anagassan (on the coast of Louth), Waterford, Wexford, and Limerick. From these new strongholds, soon to become much more dangerous than the now feeble settlements of the north, the vikings cruelly devastated the country and the death of Turgeis was followed by a decade of hard fighting between the Gaill and the Irish. No strong chieftain took the place of the fallen viking lord, so that many and brilliant were the victories won by the native levies, and this in spite of the continual advent of fresh companies of vikings from Norway. But these successes of the Irish in the end brought further troubles upon the country, for the rumour of disasters to the Norwegians reached the ears of their enemies the Danes, and about the year 849 a fleet, 140 ships strong, of the Dubhgaill (black foreigners, Danes) invaded

---

[1] Dr. A. Mahr very reasonably connects a fine ninth-century sword discovered in 1928 in Ballinderry Bog, Co. Westmeath, with Turgeis's raid upon Clonmacnois (*Mannus, Ergänzungsband* VI (1928), p. 240). This remarkable weapon is of Frankish, not Scandinavian, manufacture and bears the name of a Teutonic smith Hiltipreht ; it was no doubt obtained by the vikings, always greedy for Frankish arms, either by trade or robbery on the Continent.

FIG. 32.—Ireland

Ireland, careless of possible Irish resistance, but determined to crush the power of the Finngaill (white foreigners, Norwegians) and to take the land for themselves. Long and bitter was the fighting between these Danes and the Norsemen. In 851 the Norwegians of Dublin were almost annihilated and their women and treasures seized by the Dubhgaill ; in 852 there was a great battle of three days' duration on Carlingford Loch in which the Danes were finally victorious ; but in 853 the Norwegians regained the upper hand.

This came about through the arrival of another great Norwegian viking, much experienced in raids upon the west, who, like Turgeis, understood something of the art of command and

OLAF OF government. He was Olaf, commonly called Olaf the
DUBLIN White,[1] and was a prince of the royal house of Vestfold,
853–871 being descended from Halfdan Hvitbein (p. 106). With a great fleet he came, and such was his strength that the Danes and Norsemen alike submitted to him, and even some of the Irish were forced to pay him tribute. But most of the Danes, having no stomach for such complete Norse ascendency, went off to plunder Britain, while a few took service with the Irish kings, and this left the Dublin colony that was now ruled by Olaf as the undisputed centre of viking power in Ireland.

The Norse king left Ireland soon after his initial conquests, but upon his return in 856 he was joined in Dublin by two viking

IVAR THE princes, one a Dane, Ivar the Boneless, who was a son
BONELESS of Ragnar Lodbrok,[2] and the other his (Olaf's) brother Audgisl, and these three chieftains having come to terms, they soon set about the plundering of the middle territory

[1] The identity of the Olaf of the Irish chronicles with Olaf the White of Norse tradition is generally accepted, though not by any means certain. It depends on the explicit statement of *Landnámabók* that Olaf the White ' took Dublin in Ireland and Dublinshire and was made king over it '; but there are serious objections to the identification. See A. O. Anderson, *Scottish Annals from English Chronicles*, I, p. 308, n. 1 and D. W. H. Marshall, *Sudreys in Early Viking Times*, Glasgow, 1929, p. 21.

[2] See A. Mawer, *Saga-Book of Viking Club*, VI, pt. 1 (1909), p. 80 ff. Like Olaf, Ivar left Dublin soon after his arrival, going off to take part in the Danish invasion of England where it is alleged that he murdered St. Edmund. But immediately after this he joined Olaf in an invasion of Scotland. It is a curious thing that neither he nor Olaf seem at first to have regarded the Irish port as anything better than a base for further conquests, Olaf in Scotland and Ivar in England. It is because of Ivar's kinship with Halfdan of York that there arose the later quarrel between the reigning houses of Dublin and York, Halfdan thinking himself justified in interfering in the Dublin succession after Ivar's death, and the descendants of Ivar subsequently fighting to possess themselves of York in addition to Dublin.

of Ireland, even ransacking the pre-historic tumuli and the souter-
rains (stone-lined underground passages) in their frenzied search
for treasure. But it so happened that a great Irishman, Aed
Finnlaith, was now high-king, and he so resolutely opposed the
Norse raids, so fearlessly and so successfully carried the war back
to the very gates of the Norse strongholds, that the prudent Olaf
and his fellow-adventurers deemed it best to remain content with
the safeguarding of their own small colony rather than to risk
defeat and expulsion by Aed. They made no attempt, therefore,
to co-operate with the other Norse settlements in attacks upon the
Irish, always supposing that the jealous and independent colonies
could co-operate effectively, and instead made a peace with Aed,
Olaf himself wedding the high-king's daughter, a plain proof of
the secure establishment of Dublin as a Norse realm. From this
time onwards (it was in the late '60s) Olaf's principal viking expeditions were directed overseas against Strathclyde Wales and
Pictland, though his Dublin colonists still went plundering in
Leinster and Munster when the Irish were busy with their own
quarrels, and he himself on one occasion (868) went north to burn
Armagh. In the meantime Ivar the Boneless had sailed for
England to help in the conquest of the Danelaw by his brothers
Halfdan and Ubbe.

Though Olaf did not achieve any notable territorial aggrandize-
ment in Ireland of his Dublin kingdom, he added materially to
its importance by securing a wholesome regard for his personal
authority in Man, in the Hebrides, and on the mainland of Scot-
RISE   land. One of the three women he had taken in
OF THE   marriage [1] was Aud the Deepminded, a daughter of
DUBLIN   Ketil Flatneb, already a famous viking of the Sudreys
KINGDOM   (Hebrides), and another was daughter of Kenneth
MacAlpin, the great king who had brought about in 844 the union
of the Scottish and Pictish monarchies in Alban. Such alliances
must undoubtedly have given him a real, or fancied, right to
intervene in the politics of Scotland and the Isles, and though
he can hardly have won any recognized overlordship, except
perhaps over Man, he extended, nevertheless, most successfully
the sphere of Dublin influence, making of his Irish kingdom the
acknowledged headquarters of viking activity not only in Erin,
but in all the western waters.

But in 871, at the height of his power, Olaf left Ireland for
ever, sailing off to fight in his own country where he fell in battle. [2]

---

[1] Always supposing that Olaf of Dublin was really Olaf the White.

[2] On the other hand, *Landnámabók* says explicitly that Olaf was slain
in Ireland and Scottish tradition affirms that he was killed while fighting

He left Ivar the Boneless, who had been away fighting in England, as king of the Norse colonies in Ireland ' and Britain ', and two years later, at Ivar's death, Olaf's son Eystein became king in his stead. Early in his reign there was an attack by the Danes on Dublin, a small party of the Northumbrian vikings under Halfdan (p. 231), and perhaps Ubbe, his brother, attempting to take Eystein's kingdom from him by guile, this because it had been under the rule of their brother Ivar and they could therefore pretend some claim to add this splendid colony to their rich English possessions. It was the beginning of a long and curious struggle between Dublin and York that was partly based on the natural rivalries of Danes and Norwegians and partly a result of the circumstance that the later rulers at Dublin were of the same family as the Danish kings of York ; in a word, the struggle was not so much a declared war between the two viking states as a series of attempts to unite by force these two states into a single family heritage.

INVASION OF HALF-DAN OF NORTH-UMBRIA

On this first occasion Aed Finnlaith intervened on behalf of the now peaceful Norwegians, so that Halfdan and his contingent took fright and sailed off northwards up the Irish coast where the great Northumbrian chief was killed [1] in a battle with the Norsemen on Strangford Loch. The Danes of his army fled to Scotland, and thence to Wales and Devonshire, and for the time being the Norwegians in Ireland had nothing more to fear from their fellow-vikings.

But at this period, about 877, their power was already on the wane. No longer came great fleets from Norway to reinforce the colonies, for now the Vestfold royal line was aiming at the mastery of all the country and the full strength of the great viking provinces of Vestland was needed at home in order to resist their would-be lords. The Irish settlements, therefore, grew weaker in numbers, and less and less a menace to the native kings and their peoples. It even came to pass that Dublin, the main-

Constantine in Scotland ; for a summary of G. Storm's arguments concerning Olaf's identity with the Thore Haklang who fell at Hafrsfjord, see L. J. Vogt, *Dublin som norsk By*, Oslo (1896), p. 60 ff. Cf. also Sir H. Howorth, *Saga-Book of Viking Society*, IX, pt. 1 (1920), p. 172. The evidence of the *Three Fragments*, s.a. 871 seems to be conclusive in the matter of the country of Olaf's death, but the battle therein mentioned cannot have been Hafrsfjord (new dating *c.* 900) ; it is possible that Olaf made a bid for the Vestfold throne when Halfdan the Black died leaving only young Harald Fairhair to succeed him.

[1] The King Halfdan who died in East Anglia (*Saxon Chronicle*, s.a. 911) was another chief of the same name.

spring of Norse power in Ireland, fell, after the short reigns
DECLINE of the sons of Audgisl and Ivar, under the control
OF THE of Cearbhall of Ossory, who had been an ally of
NORSE IN Ivar. Although Cearbhall's granddaughter married a
IRELAND son of Olaf of Dublin, and his daughter married the
viking Eyvind Eastman, and though he himself was later
counted as the head of the family tree of several distinguished
Icelandic families, this Irish control of Dublin must have been
a sorry business for whatever remained of the old viking pride,
and it is natural enough that about this time the settlement
should have been further depleted by the wholesale migration
of many of the Norse colonists across the Irish Sea to Cumberland
and Northumberland. Small wonder that when Cearbhall, king
of Leinster, attacked Dublin in 902, he captured the place without
difficulty, made a terrible slaughter of the inhabitants, and forced
the beaten remnant of the defending army to seek refuge across
the sea, some going off to plunder Chester and others sailing for
the Loire.

Although, during these forty years after the death of Halfdan,
the viking hold upon Ireland had been steadily weakening, yet
most of their harbour-strongholds on the coast must still have
remained as centres of a semi-Norse population. Even as early
as the middle of the ninth century there existed the Gaill-Gaedhil,
or foreign Irish, and though at first these were merely Irishmen
who had thrown in their lot with the pirates, it is likely enough
that from these recreants had sprung a race of mixed parentage,
THE half Irish and half Norse, in the settlement areas. But
GAILL- the Gaill-Gaedhil, low-born adventurers whose swords
GAEDHIL were for hire,[1] were not the only result of intercourse
between Norse and Irish. On the contrary, there are many
records of the free and peaceable mingling of the two peoples,
the intermarriage of the high-born Norse and the Irish nobility,
and also of temporary alliances between them for battle and
adventure, the Norse sometimes entering with zest into the wars
of the rival Irish kings, while these kings, upon occasion, were
not above taking a part in the viking expeditions in search of

[1] They seem to have been ready to fight for the best paying master ;
thus a party of them under a viking leader, Ketil Find, were defeated
by the Dublin Norse under Olaf in 857. Another group of such semi-
Norse folk dwelt in western Scotland (Kintyre, upper Argyll, Galloway—
the name is derived from *Gall-Gael*—and the Hebrides) ; these were of
mixed Scottish-Scandinavian blood and in Norse source the inhabitants of
Galloway are referred to as *vikingar-skotar*. For the Gaill-Gaedhil, see
D. W. H. Marshall, *Sudreys in Early Viking Times*, Glasgow, 1929, p. 9.

plunder. There remained, therefore, on the Irish coasts a not inconsiderable legacy from the viking conquests of Turgeis and Olaf, even if viking rule had to some extent collapsed, and it needed only the advent of fresh armies of Norsemen to re-establish the colonies where the Norse tongue and Norse manners were still cherished by the enfeebled descendants of the early raiders.

Not that, even in this dark period, the fighting force of the Gaill in Ireland was reduced to complete inactivity. In 879 and 880 they were certainly marauding outside their territory, and in 881 they took part in an attack by Flann Sinna, the high-king, upon Armagh. In 893 (this was after the death of Cearbhall) there was civil war in Dublin among the foreigners, and in 895 Sigtryg, son of Ivar, and now king of Dublin, led the Gaill north to plunder Armagh, the same Sigtryg who in 892 had taken an army across the sea to invade the Scots. Again, in 904, the Dublin vikings under Ivar, who was a grandson of Ivar the Boneless, invaded Alban.

It was not until 914, however, that the new period of viking activity in Ireland begins, this being a time when both Francia and England were virtually closed against viking enterprise, NEW the one because of the concession of Normandy to VIKING Rollo, and the other because of the prestige and power ATTACKS of Edward the Elder. The first notice of the new peril 914–916 threatening Ireland was the arrival of a viking fleet at Waterford, and this was quickly followed by a second fleet under Ragnvald, grandson of Ivar the Boneless, though the leader himself, who had previously been fighting in Scotland and Man, was soon off again to try his fortune as king of York. In 916 came Sigtryg Gale, another grandson of Ivar, who, after making a fortified camp at Cenn Fuait close to Waterford, set out to recapture Dublin, sailing into the Liffey mouth with an immense fleet manned by crews made up of both Danes and Norwegians.[1]

But the Irish had not allowed the sudden challenge of this new viking invasion to shock them from the offering of a brave and well-supported resistance. Their gallant, though luckless,

---

[1] It is unlikely that these early tenth-century invasions were either purely Norse or purely Danish enterprises. The Irish annals certainly suggest that the armies included vikings of both nationalities, and this, indeed, is to be expected if we imagine the attacks on Ireland to be adventures of Danish malcontents from Normandy and Danish and Norwegian emigrants from England and Scotland. Limerick is supposed to have been captured in 920 by Danes, but there were probably Norsemen too in the invading force. Cf. A. Walsh, *Scandinavian Relations with Ireland*, Dublin, 1922, p. 24.

high-king, Niall Glundubh, for he it was who inspired and led the attacks upon the Norsemen, had at once set aside the wars and quarrellings of domestic politics in order to protect Erin from the Gaill. In 917 he fought them, unsuccessfully, at Clonmel, and afterwards, undismayed, he marched off, this time in alliance with the king of Leinster, to attack the foreigners in Waterford. He encamped in a fortified position over against the enemy, and so remained for three weeks, but finally the vikings managed to attack the Leinster men separately and to defeat them, thus forcing Niall to retire without giving battle and leaving the enemy in assured possession of the stronghold at Waterford. In 918, Niall, still resolute in the defence of Ireland, determined upon attacking Sigtryg Gale in Dublin. It was by this time clear to all the Irish that this new establishment of a great host of the Gaill in the old viking capital must mean the beginning of another long struggle with the foreigners, for the position of this important harbour made its occupants a perpetual menace to the safety of Leinster, Meath, and Ulster. Niall, therefore, was able to collect a formidable hosting, a great company of the Irish sub-kings and their followings, and in 919 at the head of this force he gave battle to Sigtryg near Islandbridge on the north bank of the Liffey. But brave fighter though he was, Niall was not destined to be the saviour of Erin. Victory went to the Gaill ; Niall fell, and with him there died twelve of the Irish kings. It was a decisive battle, leaving the foreigners in undisputed possession of Dublin and with Ireland, now that the chief parade of her strength was overthrown, at their mercy. Yet, upon consideration of the uncertain and feeble resistance that opposed elsewhere the great tenth-century invasions of the vikings, it seems no small honour in the annals of Erin that these Norwegians and Danes should win their footing in the land only at the price of a hard-fought battle against a hosting of the chieftains of the land with the high-king at their head.

IRISH RE-SISTANCE UNDER NIALL GLUNDUBH

NIALL FALLS AT ISLAND-BRIDGE 919

The Gaill were not slow to take advantage of the victory, and by 920 they had already begun to ravage the north, pillaging Kells and many of the monasteries of Meath and Ulster, and even occupying Armagh. In the same year Limerick was captured by 'an immensely great fleet, more wonderful than all the other fleets ' that was manned chiefly by Danes and commanded by Thorir Helgason who fortified the place and held it as a settlement entirely independent of, even hostile to, the colony at Dublin. In 921 Sigtryg Gale,

THE DANES IN LIMER-ICK 920

king of Dublin, left Ireland to succeed Ragnvald as king of York,
and his Irish throne was filled by a relative, Godfred, who is said
to have been another grandson of Ivar ; the new king also
assumed command of the Waterford vikings, putting his son
Olaf as king there, and shortly afterwards was busy with the
further devastation of Ulster. But brave Niall's son, Muich-
ertach, king of Ailech, defeated the vikings near Armagh in this
year, and it seemed plain that the Norsemen could make no
permanent settlement in the north of Ireland, though with their
fleets on the rivers and lochs of Ulster they remained for a
while a most serious menace to the whole province.

Yet viking affairs were not prospering everywhere. Ragnvald,
king of York, had submitted to Edward the Elder in 920, and
Sigtryg Gale, when he succeeded him in Northumbria, could not
do other than continue as vassal of the English king, this meaning
that the intended Irish-Northumbrian kingdom, now almost
entirely in the hands of the Danish family sprung from Ivar the
Boneless, never rose to the importance that must have been
intended when Ragnvald usurped the throne of York. And the
annexation of the Kingdom of York in 926 by the English, intro-
ducing a period of almost complete subjugation of the vikings in
Northumbria, robbed the rulers in Dublin of all effective power in
England, and this despite the rebellion of 937 that
DUBLIN culminated in the shattering defeat at Brunanburh,
AND YORK
and the short and unhappy spell of Northumbrian
independence from 939 to 944. The Dublin kings, therefore,
Godfred himself, Olaf Godfredsson from Waterford (who fought
at Brunanburh), and that great adventurer Olaf Sigtrygsson
Cuaran, spent much of their strength in vain endeavours to regain
the viking supremacy in northern England, and it may have been
for this reason, if it was not because of a wholesome fear of the
Irish, that they made no attempt at a serious conquest of large
territories in Ireland. Indeed, the Gaill had begun thus early in
the tenth century to accommodate themselves to the changing and
confused conditions of Irish affairs, the adoption of Christianity
by so many of the Norsemen and the growth of a busy trade
between defenders and invaders resulting in many intermarriages
and alliances so that the viking colonies began to acquire the
status of recognized sub-kingdoms, quarrelsome and dangerous
may be, of the body politic of Ireland.

Nevertheless occasional spells of surface calm in reality did
little towards lessening the deep-seated distrust with which the
Irish regarded the foreigners, and the annals tell that in the years
following Niall's death there was still fighting enough between

Irishman and Gall. His son, Muirchertach, was the worst foe of the Dublin colony when the vikings ventured abroad to plunder, and in 926 this king defeated them at Carlingford. In 927 he gained another victory over them at Anagassan, but the chief adventures of his struggle with the Gaill took place in 939 when he made a successful expedition against the Norsemen of the Hebrides, and yet was himself captured and held to ransom by the Dublin vikings. However, Muirchertach had established an ascendency over the Gaill that was not lightly to be overthrown, and on the occasion of that famous hosting of 941, the great march of his ' Leather Cloaks ' around all Ireland when he, as high-king designate, demanded hostages from every kingdom, he encamped near Dublin, and in the course of this royal and amazing progress took a hostage from the Gaill themselves.

MUIRCHERTACH OF THE LEATHER CLOAKS

Muirchertach of the Leather Cloaks died in 943 and still the struggle continued, sometimes the vikings making daring plundering expeditions, sometimes living at peace, while sometimes they in turn were attacked by the Irish armies. In 944 Congalach became high-king and made a successful raid upon Dublin ; in 946 the foreigners pillaged Clonmacnois ; in 947 Congalach resumed the offensive and won a great victory over the Gaill at Slane in County Meath when he defeated the then king of Dublin, Olaf Cuaran, and exacted a tribute from the Dublin colony. This Olaf was the last of the viking princes in Ireland who sought to win a kingdom in Northumbria, for in his early days he had set himself to gain both the realms that had been ruled by his father, the Sigtryg who had been in turn king of Dublin and king of York. But at the time of his defeat by Congalach he had been expelled from York, where he had for a time set himself up as king, and had been for some years in Ireland ; yet after the complete rout of his army at Slane and the downfall of Dublin, he straightway abandoned his Irish realm and returned to York. He succeeded in getting himself made king there for a second time, but once again the English authority was too strong for him and he was compelled to leave Northumbria. In 951 he went back to Ireland and resumed his position as king of Dublin. He gave up all hope of recovering the throne of York, and, content at last with the single Irish realm, he reigned for some thirty years, the most illustrious and perhaps the best-known of the foreign kings of Dublin. But he never succeeded in restoring the colony to the power that it had enjoyed in the days of his father and of Godfred ; on more than one occasion the Irish attacked and

OLAF CUARAN OF YORK AND DUBLIN

defeated him, and when, in 980, Mael Seachlinn Mor, the high-king, having overthrown Olaf's sons in battle at Tara, forced Dublin to surrender to him, then was the great viking a broken man and he fled from the country, making his way as a Christian pilgrim to Iona where he died.

Olaf Cuaran had married a daughter of Muirchertach, and it was the son of this marriage, a man of mixed blood with the Irish name of Gluniarainn (Iron Knee), who succeeded to the throne of Dublin, assuredly as the sworn vassal of Mael Seachlinn, for the Irish king not only was half-brother to Gluniarainn by reason of this marriage of Olaf's, but was also his conqueror in the field. Yet although in 983 Mael Seachlinn took the Dublin king and the army of the Gaill to fight side by side with him against the king of Leinster and the viking Ivar who was now king of Waterford, nevertheless the relations between the two half-brothers were not always friendly, and in 989 Mael Seachlinn again laid siege to Dublin, forcing it to surrender after an invest-ment of twenty days' duration, the townsmen giving in because of a want of water ; again he demanded a tribute, and, further-more, a tax of an ounce of gold from every building in the place. Gluniarainn died soon afterwards and it seems that his now weakened realm was seized by Ivar, of the old family of Ivar the Boneless, the powerful king of the now independent and rival colony at Waterford ; but in 994 Mael Seachlinn drove him out, taking on this occasion as part of his booty Thor's ring, the holiest treasure of ancient viking heathendom and the focus of pagan rituals of oath and sacrifice, and ' Charles's Sword,' a weapon that was the symbol of Dublin's power and that was believed, no doubt, to have belonged to the great Emperor himself. After the expulsion of Ivar, Sigtryg of the Silken Beard, another son of Olaf Cuaran, became king of Dublin.

But this was the time when the fortunes of the Dublin colony began to be affected by the rapid march to power and fame of Brian Boru, the noblest and the greatest Irishman of his day and the well-beloved hero of the songs and stories of posterity. BRIAN BORU Except perhaps for Alfred the Great, no man of all the princes of the western world has been more honoured as the champion of his people against the vikings, and though it may be that his struggle with the Gaill is of less account than his magnificent achievement of the sovereignty of all Erin, yet the fall of the foreign colonies as powers likely to become supreme in Ireland was in no small measure decided by his adven-tures and strategies, so that the tale of Brian's life is a significant and fateful chapter of the viking history of the country.

He was born in 941 and was the son of Cennetig, king of
Dal gCais, a small province occupying the eastern half of the
modern county of Clare and in the tenth century a border-state
of Munster.   Ever since their early days he and his brother Mahoun had watched with indignation the plunderings and ravages of
the Danes at Limerick, and for many years they had engaged in
a pitiful, though lion-hearted, guerilla warfare with these Gaill,
hiding their tiny forces in woods and caves, and content merely
with embarrassing the progress of the marauding enemy bands.
So heavy, nevertheless, were the losses of the brothers that
Mahoun made a truce with the Danes ; but Brian, bitterly
reproaching him for this weakness, continued the miserable
struggle, careless of the rapid dwindling of his own small following
and fighting on until it is said he had only fifteen men left with
him.   At this point the assembly of the little kingdom was con-
voked in order to decide whether the war should be continued,
and, though their tribulations had been long-lasting and terrible,
the courageous Dalcassians determined upon one final attempt
to rid themselves of the foreigners ; at the same time they
purposed to assert Mahoun's claim to the throne of Cashel, the
chief kingdom of Munster, for the death of the Munster king in
963 presented what seemed to be a favourable opportunity of
making this bid for greater power.   And so, summoning to their
aid allies from Connaught and western Munster, Mahoun and
Brian seized Cashel and, having established themselves there,
prepared for a serious struggle against the Danes.

Five years later, at Sulcoit near Tipperary, came the inevitable
conflict between the two Dalcassian princes and Ivar, the proud
and aggressive king of Limerick, and after a battle lasting from
sunrise until noon the foreigners were overthrown and
driven back in confusion to Limerick.   There the
Danish fort was sacked by the pursuing Irishmen and
the town itself burnt.   Ivar fled overseas, and of the
great band of prisoners taken by Mahoun and Brian,
those who were of military age were put to death and the rest
carried off as slaves.   Seldom had a victory over the Gaill been
more complete, and seldom had its aftermath been so pitiless
and so thorough an extermination of the enemy.

ROUT
OF THE
LIMERICK
VIKINGS
967

But Munster was not for ever freed of the Danes.   The
year after the battle, in 969, Ivar returned from his short exile in
Britain and once more at the head of a very great fleet.   He built
himself a new camp at Limerick and also fortified the islands of
the Shannon, and then, with his own holding thus secured, he
proceeded to make alliances with those Munster chiefs who were

watching with jealous eyes the new political ascendency of the Dal gCais. Mahoun, however, did not wait for the breaking of the storm that was gathering against him and speedily renounced his pretensions to the overlordship of Munster ; yet this submission did not save him from his enemies, and it was with Cashel thus surrounded by foes that in 976 he was mysteriously killed. Brian, heir to the murdered king, immediately and magnificently became the avenger of his brother and the saviour of his people. ' And he was not a stone in the place of an egg ; and he was not a wisp in the place of a club ; but he was a hero in the place of a hero ; and he was valour after valour.' He attacked the islands of the Shannon in 977, killed the terrible Ivar and two of his sons, BRIAN and took a great booty of gold and silver. In the BECOMES next year he raided the territory of Donnabhan of the KING OF Ui Fidgenti in County Limerick, where another of CASHEL Ivar's sons had taken refuge, and there he slew both the viking and Donnabhan himself. In the same year he fought Maelmuadh, king of Desmond and overlord of Munster, at Belach Lechta near Ardpatrick, and in that great fight Maelmuadh fell and with him 1,200 of his men, both Irish and Danes. After this Brian took hostages of Munster ' even unto the sea ', and so became the undisputed king of Cashel and the mightiest chieftain in Munster.

His first concern in the period following the battle of Belach Lechta was to obtain the submission of the Leinster kings, for this neighbouring province, itself at the mercy of the Gaill of Waterford and Dublin, was an ever-present source of danger, unless governed by his own strong hand. When, by 984, he had achieved this overlordship he was master of southern Ireland, and henceforth during the long spell of peace that lasted until the very end of the century he devoted himself above all things to the re-organization and administration of his now great realm and eagerly fostered the once-flourishing arts and scholarship that the coming of the foreigners had ruined. But just as a strong man had stood forth as champion and defender of the south, so too a mighty king, Mael Seachlinn Mor, controlled the north, and the history of the last fifteen years of the peace reveals a growing rivalry between these two powerful rulers. But it was not until 999 that there was any threat of open hostilities on a large scale. In that year a Leinster king made an alliance with the Dublin Gaill and revolted from Brian's overlordship. Brian marched to lay siege to Dublin, and on his way intercepted the united forces of the Leinster men and the Gaill in the pass of Glen Mama in the western foot-hills of the Wicklow mountains ;

there a horrible and bloody battle took place, a slaughter in which the Dublin army was almost annihilated and the men of Leinster routed. The Dalcassians and the Munster force likewise suffered heavily, but when the beaten remnant of the enemy had scattered in flight Dublin lay an easy prey to Brian and at Christmas he took up his headquarters in the town. Sigtryg of the Silken Beard was king, and he, after seeking in vain for succour from the princes of north Ireland, returned to Dublin and submitted to Brian who thereupon agreed to maintain the Gaill in their appointed territory on the condition that they should pledge themselves to fight for him. Moreover, Brian gave his daughter in marriage to Sigtryg, and it was probably at this time that he himself wedded the woman Gormflaith, sister of the king of Leinster, who had been the wife of Olaf Cuaran though she was now the divorced wife of Mael Seachlinn himself.

The vanquished Gaill, therefore, despite the overthrow of their army, were not allowed to remain as unforgiving enemies of the king of Munster ; instead they were offered Brian's friendship and protection, and instructed to recruit their strength so that they might henceforward be counted upon as welcome and trustworthy allies. This clever and conciliatory move on the part of Brian, the conversion of his military supremacy into the overlordship of a friendly state, was, of necessity, prelude to the inevitable struggle between Munster and the North, for the strategical importance of Dublin was enormous and the foreign colony had long been subject to Mael Seachlinn. Brian must have known that a clash was now inevitable and, accordingly, at the end of this same year (999) he himself took the initiative, invading the kingdom of Tara at the head of a great army of southern Irish and reinforced by the Dublin Gaill. But the momentous conflict, a matter rather of military demonstrations and diplomatic exchanges than of battle and surrender, was short ; in 1001 Brian, encamped at royal Tara itself, was demanding the submission of Mael Seachlinn, and by 1002 he had become high-king of Ireland in his stead. Not all the princes of the north acknowledged his overlordship so readily as did the far-seeing and noble Mael Seachlinn and the king of Connaught, but in the end the kingdoms of Ailech and east Ulster also made their peace with him. In truth, it was no vain and empty title that his clerk gave to Brian Boru in 1004 at Armagh when he styled him *Imperator Scottorum*, Emperor of the Irish.

Brian as high-king gave further proof of the wise statesmanship and careful government that had already distinguished his rule in Munster. But of his administration and peace-making, of his love of learning and tradition, and of his modest court (not at Tara or Cashel, but among his own Dalcassians at Killaloe on Loch Derg), there is no occasion to speak here. It is sufficient to note, as evidence of his power, a levying of tribute by him from Saxons, Scots, and Britons, across the sea, and to honour his ceaseless effort to unite the several peoples of Ireland in a confederacy of tranquil states under his own supreme authority.

Not that he could ever prevent, even in the years of greatest calm, those petty struggles and fights that the little kingdoms loved. But he did achieve for Ireland a certain solidarity and sense of security such as she had not known before, and this was rapidly paving the way for a substantial increase in the prosperity of the country when the general peace was rudely shattered by the rebellion of the Leinster king in 1012.

Of the beginnings of the quarrel, the journey of this king, Maelmordha, to Kincora, the evil counsel of his sister, the adventuress-queen Gormflaith, the subsequent bickering with Murchad, Brian's son, there is a close and detailed account. But no matter ; it is sufficient to read how the angry Maelmordha rode home to

REBEL- call an assembly of all the Leinster nobles so that they
LION OF might hear of the dishonour that he conceived himself
LEINSTER to have suffered, an insult, he said, not only to himself
1012 but to his province. For this assembly decided upon

revolt ; an alliance was made with the Gaill at Dublin, and, as though this were not enough to endanger Ireland, the Leinstermen urged the king of Ailech to civil war in the north. Thereupon the whole country was soon in a turmoil of fighting and intrigue. Yet, at first, old Brian himself remained aloof, trusting that patience and mediation might restore order ; but in the summer of 1013, when hopes of conciliating the rebels were vanishing,

BRIAN Murchad, his son, was sent to devastate Leinster.
LAYS Maelmordha fled to Dublin, and there in the autumn
SIEGE TO came Brian to join Murchad and lay siege to the town.
DUBLIN,
BUT WITH- Until Christmas was Dublin invested, but the Gaill and
DRAWS Leinster men held out and Brian eventually withdrew
1013 his army, it is said because of the difficulty of provid-

ing food for his men in these winter months.

But the rebels were growing in strength. Gormflaith had left Brian, and now safe at the court of her son, Sigtryg of the Silken Beard, she was busy plotting the destruction of the high-king. Sigtryg was sent overseas to seek help, for that there was to be serious war could no longer be doubted, and the chief ally he secured was Sigurd, the strong jarl of the Orkneys, whose mother was Irish. The aid of this great man was won by the THE VIK- promise of Gormflaith's hand and the throne of Dublin, INGS and this same promise, dishonourably made anew, PREPARE lured Brodir, another viking chief, and his fleet of FOR THE GREAT twenty ships, from Man to Dublin. And the word of STRUGGLE the impending battle was spread far afield, and from the Hebrides, from Cornwall and Wales, from Normandy and Francia, and from Scandinavia, there came vikings to save Dublin in this hour of danger and so to preserve for the viking world a necessary and profitable trading-mart.

Not all the adventurers invited to come to the assistance of the Dublin Gaill gave their help. Olaf Ospak, Brodir's brother, who was likewise in the Isle of Man, refused to fight against so good a king as Brian and straightway went off with ten ships to give the high-king information of this gathering of the forces against him and to join his little force to Brian's. But, nevertheless, the assembly of the vikings at Dublin meant a formidable increase to the rebel strength and was a safe index of the gravity of the coming struggle.

Yet the challenge that this gathering represented was inspired by the hatred of Gormflaith and the jealousy of Maelmordha, and was directed against the personal authority of Brian. The viking detachments of the great rebel army cannot at any time have hoped for, or threatened, an outright conquest of the whole Irish state. Not that Irishmen had any illusions as to the possible consequences of a determined and well-directed viking invasion in this the very year of Svein's great triumph over England, for they knew that the kingdom of Saxon Æthelred was at last overthrown by the Danish armies ; but it must have been plain that here in Ireland, despite the thrill and stirring of the viking world, and the grand rally of the adventurers in Dublin, the personal relations of the three leaders of the Gaill, Sigtryg, Sigurd, and Brodir (each of the last two promised the kingdom of Dublin), and the Irishman Maelmordha, were not of the kind that fitted them for a serious attempt to secure for any one of them the over-lordship of Ireland. The re-winning of Dublin, freed of the Munster king's control, as a safe and permanent trading-station for the vikings of the northern waters, and a full licence for Maelmordha to rule Leinster as he would, these alone were the objectives of the allied rebels, and if the great battle that now took place was decisive, for a fight between so great a mustering of the vikings and the almost national army of the Irish under Brian must inevitably have been so, it was decisive not in the sense that victory to the rebels would leave Ireland in the hands of a Norse king, but because the aftermath of victory would be the horrors and confusions consequent upon the overthrowing of the stable government of Brian.

This much the high-king must have realized. The security of the Irish kingdom, the laws he had made, the peace he had won, all these were threatened if Leinster seceded from the confederacy he governed, if Dublin became once more a powerful and independent colony of the foreigners. And since he had now information of the numbers gathered against him, he prepared to do battle for his country at once and with all his strength.

It was not only the full force of Munster that the aged Brian led to battle. In these spring weeks of peril in 1014 he roused Ireland to arms, and so there came the chivalrous Mael Seachlinn to join him with the army of the middle kingdom, the chieftains of Connaught and of Oriel with their men, and drafts even of the BRIAN Scottish Irish. It was, indeed, except for rebellious MARCHES Leinster and the neutrality of the Ui Neill of the north, TO BATTLE a national army that Brian commanded when, under 1014 seventy banners and probably some 20,000 strong, his great host was at last concentrated near Grangegorman and Glasnevin, close to Dublin but on the north bank of the Liffey. This was in the week before Palm Sunday, and the viking fleets were already assembled.

Brian, on his arrival, had plundered and burnt in the Dublin territory, but for a while the battle itself was delayed. At last, however, on the morning of April the 23rd, the vikings under BATTLE OF Sigurd and Brodir advanced to battle-position and the CLONTARF, Leinstermen under Maelmordha, with the Dublin 23 APRIL, vikings under Sigtryg's brother Dubhgall, issued from 1014 the fortress, crossed the Liffey, and arrayed themselves in front of the Irish army. Brian's army was established in the narrow tongue of land between the Liffey and the Tolka, and since it faced the sea it was threatening not so much the town and fort of Dublin (for this lay on the south bank of the river) but the vikings newly arrived from overseas, and especially that precious and vulnerable part of their fighting force, the fleet, now riding at anchor close to the Tolka mouth and Clontarf. Sigurd, if he would not lose his boats, his sole hope of escape should he be worsted in battle, must fight with them behind him ; but by so covering the Clontarf Weir, as he was thus compelled to do, he committed his side to operations on a battle-front of nearly two miles in length, for this is the distance between the Weir and the bridge over the Liffey to Dublin, the other vulnerable spot in this far-flung and dangerous line. It is true that the crest

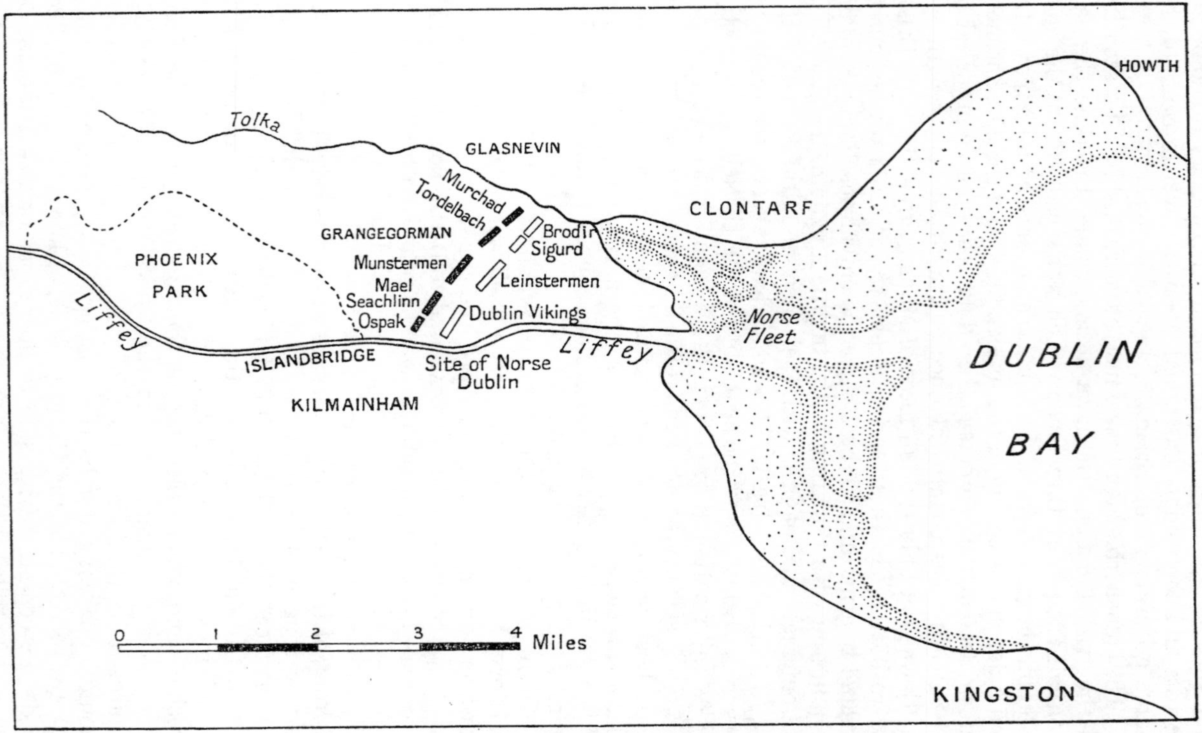

FIG. 33.—Battle of Clontarf

of high ground where to-day are Mountjoy Square and Rutland
Square in modern north Dublin makes the centre of this line a
position of some importance, and this was the posting of Maelmordha and his Leinstermen ; but it was upon the wings, miserably and perilously stationed on the lower ground at some distance
from Maelmordha, that the fate of the battle hung.   Here, on
the right, Sigurd and Brodir covered their fleets from a position
on the extreme Tolka side of the line, while the left wing, composed
of the Dublin Gaill, guarded the Liffey bridge-head.[1] Sigtryg
himself did not come out to fight, but remained in Dublin.

The strange thing is that Brian, likewise, would take no part
in the battle ; but it was Good Friday that the vikings chose for
the combat and on that holy day the great king would not take
up arms.   Instead he gave the command of his armies to his son
Murchad, himself retiring with a few warriors to ' Tomar's Wood ',
perhaps somewhere in the north of Phibsborough, and there he
spread a skin whereon to kneel and pray, leaving the anxious
watching of the battle to his companions.

The disposition of the Irish forces was naturally over a front
of no less extent than that of their adversaries, but some detachments had the advantage of prepared positions and the whole
army could afford to await the enemy attack.   Murchad himself,
in command of the Dalcassians, opposed Sigurd and Brodir on
the extreme left, and he had Tordelbach, Brian's young grandson,
on his right.   In the centre were other battalions of Munstermen,
with Mael Seachlinn and the southern Ui Neill close at hand in
an entrenched position.   On the right of the line, opposite the
Dublin vikings, were the men of Connaught and the Isle of Man
viking, Olaf Ospak, with his contingent.

The Battle of Clontarf, for that is the name of this famous
fight, began in the early morning with a personal combat between
two champions, one from Brodir's division and the other from
Murchad's.   But this was quickly followed by an advance on
the part of Maelmordha and the centre, and the battle-clash of
Murchad and Brodir.   At first the rebels seemed irresistible.

---

[1] For the topography of the Battle of Clontarf, and an excellent account
of the great fight, see J. H. Lloyd, *New Ireland Review*, XXVIII, 1907–8,
pp. 35, 87.   I have followed Mr. Lloyd's account here, but it should be
observed that the disposition of the rival armies in the field is largely
conjectural.   I find it hard to believe that the battle-rules of the early
eleventh century did not demand the massing of the rebel army, even
though this meant leaving the main viking fleet and the Liffey bridge
exposed, instead of the reckless distribution of the force across the two-
mile strip.   Yet I agree that the various descriptions of the battle certainly suggest that the rebels were split into three detachments posted
at a distance from one another.

Maelmordha swept downhill upon the Irish centre, the first charge of the Leinstermen carrying all before it. Brodir drove Murchad back. But in the meantime the Connaught men advanced against the Dublin vikings and, after much fighting, routed them, while on the other flank Sigurd was being pressed back by the Irish under the impetuous young Tordelbach.

With the wings already wavering, all hopes of success for the rebels were soon seen to depend upon the centre. But here too the tide of battle was turning against them, for the conquering Leinstermen, flushed with the brilliance of their fine first charge, had pressed recklessly on, and now Mael Seachlinn, issuing from his trenches on their left, caught them exhausted and scattered by their onrush. In a very short while, therefore, they in their turn were being driven back and flung in confusion upon their right wing. And here too the Irish were triumphing, for Murchad had rallied his men and now attacked the vikings so furiously that Brodir fled into a neighbouring wood, leaving his force to be well-nigh cut to pieces.

It was upon this occasion, with the rebels and vikings in retreat on all sides, that Sigurd showed himself the redoubtable warrior that he was. By his personal example and valour he stayed the rout of his own men ; he collected the refugees from the centre around him ; he despatched a messenger to the Dublin vikings bidding them come to his aid. And then he began to fight his way forward. Whether by design or whether by accident his advance led him towards the Tomar wood, and breaking right through the Irish line, he found himself among the rear-guard and close to the place where the aged high-king of Ireland still knelt in prayer. And the prowling Brodir, who DEATH OF must have joined Sigurd in this rush forward, came BRIAN upon Brian and his tiny company. He took him for a priest at first, but when it was told him that it was indeed the king, he broke easily through the shield-burg made by the few defending warriors and slew him, crying ' Now let man tell that Brodir felled Brian ! '

But Murchad had heard how Sigurd and his vikings had broken through the Irish ranks, and was now returned with Tordelbach. For a while there was hard fighting, but Sigurd had committed his men to a position whence further advance was but to invite total destruction and orderly retreat an impossibility. The brave prince Murchad fell in this last struggle, but when both Sigurd and Brodir also lost their lives the unequal contest came to an end. A few vikings, Thorstein the Icelander was one of them, were given quarter upon their surrender, but the greater part of the beaten force fled desperately towards their ships, and once more the Irish flung themselves in pursuit ROUT OF after the panic-stricken Gaill and the routed Leinster-THE VIK- men. To the Weir of Clontarf was the chase pressed, INGS AND and there, in this frenzied hunting of the fugitives, LEINSTER- the young Tordelbach was drowned, so that upon this MEN luckless day Munster lost not only her king, but his son and his grandson. To the Liffey bridge in the south the chase was also directed, and it is said that only twenty of the Dublin vikings crossed over the river to the safety of their fort. By sunset 7,000 of the rebels, Leinstermen and vikings, lay dead upon the field, and of the victorious Irish 4,000 were fallen. So ended the Battle of Clontarf, Brian's Battle, the overwhelming, though costly, Irish victory that must be ranked as incomparably the most splendid uprising of a wrathful nation to resist the menace of the vikings in all the history of these northern invaders.

Yet the death of Brian, aged though he was, robbed the Irish of the peace and security that this victory should have won for them. His amazing funeral, the honour paid to him in their grief by the whole people of Ireland, whether of the North or of the South, whether Goidel or Gaill, the tributes to him in both Irish and Norse literature, so testify to the power and authority of this noble prince that it is easy to understand how his slaying and the sudden loss of his guiding hand left the Irish as much broken by this desperate battle as were the defeated and fugitive THE IRISH rebels. Almost at once, upon the break-up of the VICTORY Irish host immediately after the battle, there was civil AND ITS war in Munster over the succession to Brian's throne, AFTER- and soon all Ireland was sinking into the old fretful-MATH ness of quarrels and discord, the struggles of smaller-minded men than the great king who was dead. ' Brian fell, but saved his kingdom ', said the Norse poet of him, and this much is true that Clontarf had ended for ever the danger that the Gaill might win Ireland for their own ; but, alas, Brian's fall sent Ireland rocking and tottering back to the soul-destroying chaos of a too-loosely knit heptarchy of little states.

And to the foreigners in Ireland, beyond the smart of the defeat and the shame of Sigurd's downfall, Clontarf meant nothing. There was no expulsion of the Gaill, no restriction even of their civic or personal liberties, and Dublin, the storm-centre of the rebellion, was left to itself after the battle. True that it fell only a year later to Mael Seachlinn, once again high-king, when he marched south to prove to the Leinstermen and Dublin vikings by a show of savage force that further rebellion on their part was useless. But Dublin survived its capture and the line of foreign kings were not immediately deposed ; the colony prospered, there came fresh contingents of Gaill from over-seas to swell its population, and here, as at Waterford, Wexford, Limerick, and Cork, the settlers of Norse and Danish blood remained to contribute, as the years passed, by their trade and wealth, by the very stability of the ' towns ' that they thus developed, not a little to the well-being of the Irish commonwealth. And so it came about that these towns are discovered, hustling centres of merchant activity, when, just over a hundred and fifty years later, there fell upon Ireland that new disaster, an angrier and sorrier blow than ever the Northmen had struck at Erin, the coming of the English.

Of the history of the Gaill in this period after Clontarf the barest outline must suffice. Yet it is true that the entries con-cerning them in the Irish annals are much the same in the century and a half after the battle as in the two centuries that preceded it, the familiar tale of little wars and plunderings, of success and set-back, of conquests and submission. Certainly in the '20s, and close, that is, to the time of Clontarf, the Dublin foreigners did suffer more than one heavy reverse at the hands of the Irish ; but by the '30s their prestige and prosperity were restored, the colony flourishing from this period until its army met with a disastrous defeat in 1052 that led to the flight of the king of the Scandinavian line and the transfer of the crown to an Irishman, Diarmait of Leinster, whose royal house long retained the over-lordship of Dublin.

But under King Torquil, who was of the Scandinavian dynasty, the colony regained in the early twelfth century something of its old political ascendency, and in 1140 the Dublin Norse were engaged in a struggle with the Gaill of Waterford wherein the Irish took no part. Nevertheless, in the following year Dublin fell once more into the hands of an Irishman, Conchobar, king DUBLIN of East Munster, and sixteen years later, in 1157, IN THE Limerick surrendered to Muirchertach MacLochlainn, TWELFTH king of Ireland, who also attempted, though without CENTURY success, to conquer Dublin in 1162. Yet Dublin, also, fell in 1164, Diarmait MacMurchad making himself master of the colony. This prince was the king of Leinster, who is notorious as being the first to bring over the English to Ireland, for he was driven overseas in 1166 and sought the help of the Normans in Wales for the recovering of his kingdom ; in three years' time he had achieved his end, so that he was able in the following year to turn savagely upon Dublin and Waterford, cruelly putting

many of the Gaill to death and filling both towns with the hired
soldiery from abroad. Asgall Torquilsson, who had been king
of Dublin, tried, in company with the old Orkney pirate, Svein
Asleifarson, to retake the town, but he failed, and when Strong-
bow, earl of Pembroke, came to Ireland in that year, both
Dublin and Waterford were a part of the Leinster kingdom he
usurped on the death of Diarmait in 1171.

Thus it happened that it was, in the end, the English who
broke the power of the Gaill in Ireland, for by the year 1200
all the five cities (Dublin, Waterford, Limerick, Wexford, and
Cork) of the Ostmen (for this, meaning *men from the
east*, was the new name of the Norse population) were
in the hands of the newcomers. Some of the unfortunate inhabitants must have sailed off to the Isles where the
descendants of the vikings still lived in colonies that knew only
the king of Norway as their overlord, but many peace-loving
traders remained and these the English expelled from the towns
that their fathers had built, herding them into settlements
without the walls. Yet the trade they commanded and the
important consideration that they were largely non-Celtic in
race did give the Ostmen at first some political significance as
potentially valuable allies both in commerce and war, so that they
received nominally, at any rate, a certain measure of protection
from the English crown. For a while, then, though continually
robbed and cheated by the unruly invaders, they held their own
as independent corporate societies of not unwealthy merchants
in full legal possession of the land whereon they lived. But
towards the end of the thirteenth century these little communities
of Ostmen were dwindling in numbers and the Englishmen began
to buy or seize their lands in the Ostmantowns, so it is small
wonder that these poor and persecuted children of the vikings
should appeal to Haakon Haakonsson, King of Norway, when in
1263 he sailed at the head of his great armada into the western
waters of Scotland, begging him to free them from their English
oppressors. But, alas, Haakon, the deliverer and the master of
the Isles, never came to Ireland, and when he died, when the
Isles fell to the king of Scotland, the last faint hopes of the survival
of independent Scandinavian societies in Erin were abruptly
extinguished. In the fourteenth century the name of an Ostman is
hardly to be found in charter or annal, and thus into obscurity pass
the last unimportant remnants of the old Norse colonies, hounded
from their homes and cheated of their trade by the bullying new
foreigners. For, as were their own viking ancestors in the beginning,
so too these English were *Gaill*, Teuton strangers in a Celtic land.

CHAPTER X

SCOTLAND AND MAN

THERE was no great realm of Scotland in the eighth century, and North Britain, when the vikings first laid hold upon it, was a patchwork of kingdoms inhabited by peoples of different races. There were, first and foremost, the Picts, these occupying the largest part of the land, all the country north of the Firths of Forth and Clyde (except modern Argyllshire) and overflowing into the islands of the west and north, a confederacy of greater and lesser tribes, each with their own sub-king or chief, but having, when their history begins, a high-king at the head of all. Second, and like the Picts long-established, were the Strathclyde Welsh, Brythonic Celts as were their brothers in Wales itself, the whole body being the westward-crowded remnant of the Britons of pre-Roman days. But these Welsh of the north, or of the Cumbrian kingdom as it is sometimes called, were isolated from the Welsh of Wales and separately ruled, their territories being the lands from the Clyde to the Derwent in Cumberland, with Carlisle a chief town of theirs and Dumbarton (Alcluit) on the Clyde their capital ; yet it may be that Galloway was not Welsh entirely, having a more Pictish than British population. Then, third, there were the Scots, newcomers, who were Goidelic Celts and colonists from Ireland : they had first established themselves about the year A.D. 500 in their new home, the district that came to be known as Dalriada and that comprised the whole of Argyllshire including the Kintyre peninsula and the islands of Islay, Jura, Arran, and Bute. Then, fourth, there were those other newcomers, Teutons, the Angles of Bernicia, whose kingdom, with Bamborough as its capital, extended first from the Forth to the Tees and later, when Deira was added, from the Forth to the Humber.

This Anglian kingdom was at first a powerful and dangerous neighbour, but the principal interest of eighth-century history in North Britain is the solid advance of Dalriada, the kingdom of the Scots, as a political force, and the decline of the Picts and the Welsh. Indeed, in the ninth century the four kingdoms were reduced to three by the union in 844 of the Picts and Scots under Kenneth MacAlpin, king of Dalriada. And in the tenth century this united kingdom came into possession of Cumbria, while, in the beginning of the eleventh century, Lothian, the northern part of Bernicia between the Forth and the Tweed, was also annexed. And thus was the great kingdom of Alban, Scotland that is, formed.

Now threefold was the viking menace against her. From the south where the Danes were colonizing Northumbria, from the Irish colonies in the west, and in the north from Scandinavia ; but although Lothian suffered an invasion of the Northumbrian Danes in 875 and the Scots were later embroiled in the wars of the succession to the throne of York, it was most of all as coming from the north and west that Alban knew the vikings, and it was from Scandinavia and Ireland that they came. The settlements were first of all established in the islands. The Orkneys and Shetlands, or Nordreys as the vikings called them, were occupied at the beginning of the ninth century, and so too were the Sudreys, or Hebrides ; but these island-settlements were followed in the late ninth and in the tenth century by minor extensions of the little colonies on to the adjacent mainland coast, especially into Caithness in the north. And it will be seen that the history of the vikings in Scotland, apart from occasional raids and battles, is not much more than the history of the northern and the western island-groups, namely that of the earldom of Orkney (this including the Shetlands) and that of the kingdom of the Sudreys and Man. But there were nevertheless other notable settlements, for from Ireland the vikings established themselves around the Solway Firth, both on the north shore far into Galloway and in the south down the Cumbrian coast, while at an early date Norsemen colonized the coastal fringe of Argyll in the Dalriadic kingdom and the Kintyre peninsula ; in fact the mixed Skotar-viking inhabitants of these districts later came to be known as the *Gall-gael* (Foreign Scots), the name Galloway itself (in the Norse tongue *Gaddgeddlar*) being derived from this.

As to the first settlement of the vikings history is silent, but Dr. A. W. Brøgger, whose happy lot it is to illumine with welcome and unexpected light even the darkest passages in his country's story, has sought to make up for the lack of written record by a study of place-name and linguistic evidence, together with that of the less trustworthy and admittedly scanty archaeological material.[1] Therefrom he argues that in the earliest flood of Norse

[1] *Ancient Emigrants*, Oxford, 1929.

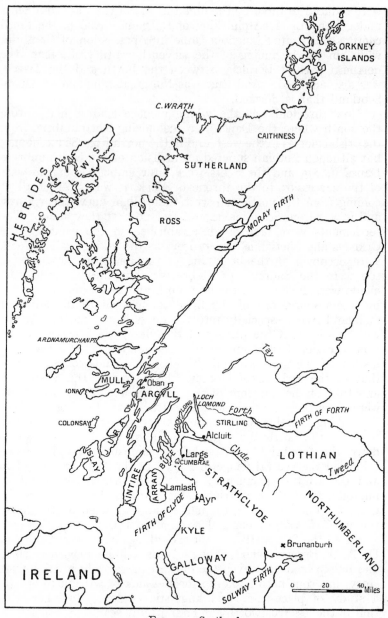

FIG. 34.—Scotland

emigrants to Scotland (here dated 780–850) there were two tides, the first being the outpouring of a harmless peasant folk from the Möre—Tröndelag and Jaeder—West Agder districts into the almost empty islands of the Orkneys and Shetlands,[1] and the second being the separate movement of a band of prouder spirits, nobles in search of wealth and adventure, who took up their abode in the Hebrides in the first decades of the ninth century, viking chieftains of the story-book type, contemporaries and fellows of the great Turgeis who conquered northern Ireland in the '30s. The new world of Norse aristocrats thus formed in this western archipelago was therefore a congenial home for the spirited malcontents whom the harsh rule of Harald Fairhair drove from Norway ; but others also, as Snorri tells in the *Heimskringla*, descended upon the quiet Norse inhabitants of the Orkneys and Shetlands, and from their winter-quarters in these islands they harried their own country until the fearful time when Harald, in his wrath, came west-over-sea to butcher these pests and burn their pirate-homes.

Iona, most beloved and hallowed isle of Columcille, was plundered in 795, and this was the first warning to the Christian world that the vikings had fallen upon Scotland and the Isles. EARLY RECORDED VIKING RAIDS It may have been the Danes who committed this outrage, inasmuch as it is said to have been ' Black Pagans ' who in the same year attacked Lambey and Skye, and, indeed, they may even have reached the Hebrides a year before ; yet, beyond a doubt, it was most of all the Norsemen that perhaps before this time and thereafter harried the Scottish islands and, in the north and west, the mainland of Scotland itself.

There is but little early history of the vikings here, for in these sparsely populated and remote districts, the Norse might rob, and even settle, if so they would, without attracting the notice of the Christian chroniclers. Thus, except for the raid on Skye and four cruel attacks upon Iona, there is nothing heard in the Celtic records of vikings in Scottish waters until the late '30s of the ninth century when a fleet of the pirates, sailing from Dublin, attacked Dalriadic Scotland, and subsequently Pictland. This was just after the great land-winning of Turgeis in Ireland and five years before the triumph of Dalriada over Pictland when Kenneth MacAlpin, the founder of the

---

[1] I say nothing of the theory that the Orkneys and Shetlands were occupied by the Norse at a much earlier date (about 700) as this has not passed the recent test of Dr. Brøgger's examination (*op. cit.*). It depends on linguistic rather than archaeological evidence, see A. Bugge, *Vesterlandenes Indflydelse . . . i Vikingetiden*, Oslo, 1905.

Scottish kingdom, added the realm of the Picts to his dominion. Perhaps Turgeis, as Norse king in Ireland, aimed at a recognition of his authority from the vikings of Scotland, if not from the Scottish and Pictish chieftains themselves, as most assuredly did the Norse Olaf when, fourteen years later, he had made himself king of Dublin.[1]

For Olaf had three wives. One was Aud the Deepminded, daughter of a viking called Ketil Flatneb (to be spoken of below) ; another was daughter of Aed Finnliath, high-king of Ireland ; and the third, whom he married four years before the Irish princess, was a daughter of Kenneth MacAlpin himself, the king of Scotland, this alliance in itself proving that the Norse king of Dublin in his viking days had played some part in the affairs of Alban, perhaps even to the extent of assisting Kenneth against other vikings or against the common enemy, the Picts. At any rate the Scottish marriage must have given him some fancied heritage in Alban, for in 866, some years after Kenneth was dead, Olaf, with Audgisl his brother, invaded Fortrenn, that is the valley of the upper Forth in Pictland, while in 870 Olaf and Ivar the Boneless, son of Ragnar Lodbrok and also from Dublin, attacked the great natural fortress of Dumbarton (Alcluit) on the Clyde, the last stronghold and capital of the Strathclyde Welsh. This, after a four months' siege, they took, and they subsequently returned to Dublin with a huge booty and a large number of prisoners, Welsh, Scottish, and Saxon. Clearly Olaf believed, rightly or wrongly, that most of western Scotland should properly submit to the authority of the Dublin king.

WARS OF OLAF OF DUBLIN IN SCOTLAND 866, 870

Ketil Flatneb, Olaf's father-in-law by his first marriage, was a famous viking of the western waters. He came from Romsdal in Norway, and in his early days, that is in the '40s and '50s of the ninth century, he went off regularly on summer viking expeditions, plundering most of all west-over-sea in the Hebrides. His rise to a position of considerable power came late in life,[2] ten years or more before the great expedition (about 894) of Harald Fairhair to crush the turbulent vikings of the Scottish islands, for it was old Ketil who had been chosen by Harald to rule the Hebrides

KETIL FLATNEB

---

[1] I repeat (see p. 279, n. 1) that the identification of Olaf the White with Olaf the Dublin king is not a matter of certainty.

[2] For the involved and difficult story of Ketil in the Hebrides, see D. W. H. Marshall, *Sudreys in Viking Times*, Glasgow, 1929, p. 32, but note that the chronology employed in this work is based on the old date for Hafrsfjord.

on his behalf. This duty he performed with the zeal and thoroughness that was expected of him, subduing all the still restless vikings of the Sudreys and making himself their acknowledged ruler ; but he very soon incurred the king's displeasure by neglecting to pay the tribute that Harald demanded of him. At once his lands in Norway were seized, and Ketil, then at home, was forced to fly from the country and remain for the short rest of his life an outlaw chieftain in the islands that he knew so well. After his death, the members of his family who were sharing his exile made their way sooner or later to Iceland, and so were the Western Isles left for the time with no lord but far-away Harald.

Another notable viking of the Hebrides in these early days was Önund Tree-foot (for he had a wooden leg). On one occasion, before he lost his leg fighting against Harald at Hafrsfjord, he arrived off Barra with a little fleet of five ships and found there the Irish king, Cearbhall of Ossory ÖNUND (he who was also king of Dublin), also with five boats. TREE-FOOT There was a battle in which the vikings defeated the Irish, so that Cearbhall was forced to escape in his one surviving ship. Önund remained for three years in the Hebrides after this, pillaging shamelessly both in Ireland and Scotland. He went back to Norway for the great Hafrsfjord battle, and then returned to the Sudreys and settled there with his company in contented exile, harrying overseas regularly each summer and becoming just one of those lawless and unprofitable scoundrels whom Harald so much detested. He had a ferocious battle with two other Sudrey vikings of his own kidney who, after a long absence plundering in Ireland, came back unexpectedly with thirteen ships to their old home, and by winning this he must have made himself for a time master of the Hebrides. Yet his authority was recognized neither in Norway nor in Ireland, and eventually he migrated to Iceland, no doubt before Harald's punitive expedition to the Scottish waters.

The appearance of Cearbhall in the Sudreys is to be explained on the grounds that this energetic and far-seeing king had laid plans whereby he might become overlord of the Western Isles and other viking dominions. To this end he had given his daughter in marriage to yet another notable viking of the period, EYVIND Eyvind the Eastman (for his father came from Sweden), THE EAST- and created Eyvind, henceforth his friend and ally, MAN warden of the Irish coasts, a position that seemingly carried with it a considerable authority over the Hebrides, for when Eyvind met Önund Tree-foot he reproached him bitterly

for having broken the peace of king Cearbhall and would have
set upon him, had not Eyvind's brother, who was Önund's
friend, intervened.

A daughter of Eyvind and the Irish princess was married
to Thorstein the Red, a son of Olaf the White and Aud the Deepminded, and grandson, therefore, of old Ketil Flatneb.   Thorstein
seems to have respected Cearbhall's peace in Ireland and the
Isles, but in Scotland he harried far and wide ' and
was ever victorious '.   He settled, after Ketil's death,
with his mother and their company in Caithness,
where he entered into an alliance with Jarl Sigurd
of the Orkneys, and together these two made considerable conquests in the mainland of Scotland, so that
in the end the Scots were forced to cede to the viking chieftains
the north-east corner of Alban.   Thorstein the Red was killed
there (murdered treacherously by the Scots, so it is said) about
the year 900.

THORSTEIN
THE RED
AND JARL
SIGURD
WIN
CAITHNESS

Sigurd was the brother of Ragnvald Möre-jarl of Norway.
Probably many of the Orkney vikings were of their kin and
Ragnvald, who did not choose to live in the islands himself, was
content to let Sigurd be the resident chieftain.   The
story goes that the jarldom was conferred on this distinguished Möre family by Harald Fairhair, first upon
Ragnvald and afterwards, when he declined the honour,
upon his brother, and according to Ari's chronology
this traditional account is satisfactory ;   but it is really more
likely that Harald was still a young boy when Sigurd was first
installed in the Orkneys, perhaps as early as the '70s or '80s,
and therefore the appointment made by Harald must have been
a subsequent confirmation of the existing governorship on the
occasion of his punitive expedition to the western seas in the
'90s.   For by that time Ragnvald and Harald were sworn friends
and the continuance of Sigurd's jarldom would commend itself
to the king once he had satisfied himself of his loyalty and his
power.

CREATION
OF THE
ORKNEY
JARLDOM
c. 875

The first earl (if the reader will allow here and henceforth
in this chapter the use of the more familiar spelling) of Orkney
was a redoubtable warrior, for, aided by Thorstein the Red, he
became master of Caithness and Sutherland, continued his conquests right up to the banks of the Oykell, and, adventuring
farther, is said not only to have subjugated a part of Ross but
also to have built himself a fortress on the south of the Moray
Firth.   When he died, poisoned by a scratch from the tooth
of a decapitated Scottish chief whose head was hung at his

saddle, he was in the mainland portion of his dominion and
was buried near the Oykell; but his death put an end
EARL
SIGURD to the supremacy of the Orkney earl over north-east
Alban, and worse was to come, for a little while afterwards even the authority of the earl in the islands themselves was
challenged. This came about for the reason that Sigurd's son,
Guthorm, died childless after reigning only a year, and Hallad,
a son of Ragnvald the earl of Möre, who was thereupon sent over
from Norway to become earl, proved himself a weak and miserable governor, allowing the islands to be overrun with marauding
vikings; he could give the Norse bönder no protection from
these attacks and himself suffered so many indignities at the
hands of the pirates, who usurped his power and his rights, that
at last he most shamefully abandoned his charge and returned
to Norway.

The youngest son of Ragnvald, Turf-Einar (so called because
he taught the islanders to cut peat for fuel), subsequently replaced Hallad and is the best-known of the early governors.
EARL
TURF-
EINAR His first act was to defeat in battle two Danish vikings
who had recently settled in the Orkneys, and, this
done, he quickly recovered the lost authority of the
earl in all the islands of the archipelago and established himself
as a great and powerful chief. He never sought, however, to
regain the extended dominion that Sigurd, his uncle, had possessed
before him, and on one occasion he even lost the island-earldom,
this happening when one of Harald Fairhair's truculent and
rebel sons, Halfdan Halegg, after assisting in the murder of the
great earl of Möre, fled to the Orkneys and there set himself
up as king. Einar escaped to the mainland of Scotland, but in
the same year he returned, gave battle to Halfdan, and was
victorious, the Norwegian prince himself being captured the
following day and cruelly put to death. This act of vengeance
earned for him the bitter enmity of Halfdan's brothers in Norway, and there were threats of an expedition to the islands;
but Einar cared little until at last King Harald himself sailed
to the Orkneys. Then he fled at once to Caithness. The end,
however, was that a reconciliation was brought about between
Harald and Einar, and the king, who loved the good earl of
Möre and his family, contented himself with demanding a fine
of 60 marks of gold from the islands. Einar offered to pay the
whole of this fine himself if the bönder would surrender their
odel (freehold) rights to him, and this offer these peasant-pro-
prietors of the land accepted. Einar thus became more than
the king's appointed governor of Orkney; he became in addition

the landlord, the owner, of the islands. This must have been somewhere about 940, shortly before Harald's death.

The chief events of viking history in Alban in the very early tenth century were raids from Ireland upon the kingdom of the Scots, now ruled by Constantine III. Thus in 904 Ivar of Dublin, grandson of Ivar the Boneless, ravaged as far north as Dunkeld on the Tay, and in the next year lost his leg in a battle with the Scots near by in the Earn valley. Again, in 912, Ragnvald, likewise a grandson of the first Ivar and he who descended upon Waterford in 917, also attacked Fortrenn, pillaging Dunblane and the country around. In 918 this same viking, after his short visit to Ireland, crossed over to Britain and seized the lands of Ealdred, Earl of Bamborough, whereupon the Englishmen fled into Scotland to beg the help of Constantine. The Scots came south and fought Ragnvald at Corbridge on the English Tyne ; the result of the battle was indecisive, but the Danish viking relinquished his hold upon Bernicia and, moving south in the following year, possessed himself of the kingdom of York.

WARS OF THE IRISH VIKINGS IN SCOTLAND 904-918

Yet the enmity of the Scots and the Irish vikings, and the alliance of the Scots and English of Bernicia, were not of long endurance. This was nearly the time of the great English supremacy under Edward the Elder, and soon, when the king of York was the helpless vassal of the king of England, when the Scots and the Welsh alike were forced to acknowledge his power, then the relationship between the Scots and the Dublin vikings changed from hostility into friendship. For it was plainly to the interest of the Scots, in the face of this English aggression, that Northumbria should be maintained as an independent Scandinavian principality, and when on the death of Sigtryg Gale in York, Æthelstan expelled his would-be successor, Godfred, king of Dublin, and also refused to tolerate the succession of Sigtryg's son, Olaf Cuaran, it was clear enough that the king of England now aimed at the full control of Northumbria. Olaf, therefore, when he fled to Scotland, was welcomed and given in marriage the daughter of Constantine, an alliance that Æthelstan could not help regarding as a direct challenge to the authority of England. And so in 934 came about the invasion of Scotland by the English, and in 937 that great battle, Brunanburh, when the king of England overthrew the united forces of Constantine, the viking leaders, and the Welsh.

ALLIANCE OF SCOTTISH AND IRISH VIKINGS

In the second half of the tenth century the earldom of Orkney once again assumed the importance that it had enjoyed under the first earl Sigurd. Caithness had been added for the second time to the island-dominion by the marriage of one of Turf-Einar's sons with a native princess of the mainland, and the next earl in the succession had further increased the sphere of his influence by marrying the daughter of an Irish king. A period of still greater prosperity began with the accession of the

EARL SIGURD THE STOUT d. 1014

son of this marriage, Sigurd the Stout, he who in part restored the odel rights of the Orkney landholders that had been bought from them by Turf-Einar This second Sigurd confirmed by victories in the field his title to Caithness, and harried far and wide in Scotland and Ireland, even winning a temporary possession of the kingdom of the Sudreys and Man, placing at Colonsay a tributary earl of his own choosing to rule them on his behalf. As his second wife he married a daughter of Malcolm, king of Scotland, and his power in the north at the beginning of the eleventh century was such that when the rebel kingdom of Dublin stood in deadly fear of the attack of Brian Boru, high-king of Ireland, it was the great Sigurd whose help the Irish vikings first sought. And to Dublin with his fleet he sailed, the price of his coming being nothing less than a promise of the Dublin throne, and there at the Battle of Clontarf in 1014 he fell.

The son of Sigurd's second marriage was Thorfinn the Mighty, the grandest figure among all the viking chiefs of Scotland. He was a boy, living at the Scottish court, when his father died,

EARL THORFINN THE MIGHTY d. 1064

but it was not long before King Malcolm made him earl of Caithness and Sutherland. Then there followed a long series of struggles with his three half-brothers who had shared out the Nordreys among themselves, but by the late '20s of the eleventh century only one of these, Brusi, was left to dispute the island-realm with Thorfinn, and these two divided Orkney between themselves, this at the bidding of King Olaf the Saint who very naturally took the opportunity of re-affirming the position of the Norwegian king as overlord of the earldom.

When Malcolm, his grandfather, died, Thorfinn lost a most ·important ally, and he was at once engaged in a war with the new king of the Scots, Malcolm MacKenneth, who sought to recover Caithness, but it needed only a single successful campaign for Thorfinn to re-establish his ascendency in north-east Alban. Then Brusi died and Thorfinn took all the Orkneys: but Brusi's son, Ragnvald, returned to the Nordreys in 1036 with a claim, endorsed by the new king of Norway, Magnus Olafsson, for two-thirds of the island-territory of the earldom. Thorfinn ceded this to Ragnvald without demur, and for eight years the two kinsmen lived at peace, fighting side by side on many viking enterprises in the Sudreys, the firths of western Scotland, Galloway, Ireland, and, in 1041, England. But in the end they quarrelled and a bitter and horrible war between them began. Ragnvald was defeated in a sea-fight and fled to Norway, but he came back and caught Thorfinn unawares, setting fire to the house wherein the earl slept. Thorfinn, unknown to all, escaped from the blazing homestead with his wife in his arms and fled to Caithness, but it was not long before he had his revenge. He crossed over to Orkney at Christmastide, surprised Ragnvald by night, burnt his house over his head, and slew him when he tried to escape. This left Thorfinn as sole earl of Orkney and from this time onward he advanced from power to power until he became lord of a mighty realm extending from the Orkneys over northern and western Scotland to Ireland and was a formidable rival of the Scottish king. He became possessed of nine earldoms in Scotland, these including Ross, a part of Moray, Galloway (where he frequently resided), and the Sudreys, and in addition he laid the Isle of Man under him and also owned estates in Ireland. This vast dominion he ruled with sympathy and patience, for after making peace with his own royal overlord in Norway and visiting Denmark, Saxony, and Rome, he settled down to the quiet government of his northern lands. It must have been in these closing years of his adventurous life that he built Christchurch minster, a building which, if it was not on the site of the present Birsay parish church in Mainland, Orkney, may perhaps be the ruined Brough chapel on an islet off the Birsay coast. This was the first bishop's seat in the Nordreys and it was within the walls of Christchurch, in the year 1064, that this great earl was laid to rest.

Until the advent of Sigurd the Stout, the lordship of Man and the Isles had been a precarious holding, at first ruled by a Norwegian governor on behalf of the king of Norway, then passing into the hands of the Dublin kings, and later, that is in the tenth century, under the control of the Limerick Danes. HEBRIDES Magnus Haraldsson is the first chieftain from the AND MAN, Limerick colony known to have been appointed king TENTH of the Isles, and it was his brother Godfred, his suc- AND cessor, who lost this unruly and difficult realm to ELEVENTH CEN- Sigurd the Stout. The Orkney supremacy weakened, TURIES if it did not entirely cease, some years before Sigurd died, and Ragnvald, son of Godfred, is named as king of the

Isles while Sigurd still lived, though it well may be that he acknowledged the Orkney earl as overlord. The last king of the Limerick dynasty was Svein Kennethsson, and he, after the death of Sigurd in 1014, no doubt broke from the Orkney suzerainty, but at the time of Svein's death in 1034 Thorfinn and Ragnvald Brusason had once more established the supremacy of the Nordreys in these western waters.

Thorfinn died as recognized overlord of all northern and western Scotland, holding these lands in fief for the king of Norway, but towards the end of his life, Malcolm Canmore, who succeeded Malcolm MacKenneth on the throne of Scotia, must have recovered from Thorfinn some of the Scottish earldoms of the south. It was at this time that the Isle of Man fell once again under the rule of the Dublin vikings, a Godfred Sigtrygsson, who took part with Harald Hardradi and Earl Tostig in the battle of Stamford Bridge (1066), being named, two years after Thorfinn died, as king of the island. But the Sudreys, it seems, still paid scatt to the king of Norway, even though the Orkney earls who followed Thorfinn henceforth interfered but little in their government.

When Godfred Sigtrygsson and the little remnant of his fleet returned to Man after the battle of Stamford Bridge there was in his company a fugitive from the defeated army, one Godred Crovan, the son of an Icelander. Now this adventurer, having learnt the attractions of the island and having spied out its weaknesses, after a sojourn in Norway came back to Man some twelve years later at the head of a considerable fleet and overthrew the reigning king, Fingal Godfredsson, thus obtaining outright possession of the island where he forthwith installed himself as king. This, moreover, was not a solitary success, for his conquests outside the island made him monarch of no small realm, and it is said that Dublin and a great part of Leinster fell into his power, while in Scotland he was universally feared and his son Lagman was set up by him as lord regent of the Sudreys. Godred reigned for sixteen years over this great kingdom that he had so splendidly won, dying in the '90s of the eleventh century, and it must have been he, surely, who was the famous King Orry (or Gorry) of Manx legend.

GODRED CROVAN, KING OF MAN 1079–1095

But now a Norwegian statesman and warrior intent upon winning a huge Scottish-Irish state for the possession of Norway, appeared in these western seas and shattered, temporarily at any rate, the newly created realm of Godred Crovan. This was none other than the king of Norway himself, Magnus

Barefoot, who in 1093, 1098, and 1103, crossed the North
MAGNUS Sea with a great fleet and by pillaging and mas-
BAREFOOT sacre of the most outrageous kind successfully
d. 1104   brought Orkney and the Hebrides, the western islands
of Scotland, Kintyre on the mainland (won, it is said, from the
Scottish king by a celebrated and astute piece of cheating),
and Man, under the direct and unqualified overlordship of the
Norwegian throne. Magnus even invaded Anglesey (1098) and
reconquered as much of this island as had been formerly under
Norse sway, and later he attacked Ireland (1103), wintered in
Connaught, and was killed fighting in Ulster in 1104.

After his fall most of the Norse population of Scotland still
remained faithful to the Norwegian king as overlord. True
that in Man and the Sudreys, and perhaps in Galloway too,
the line of Godred Crovan was re-established upon the throne
and that Godred's son Olaf (1113–1153) reigned over them for
forty years. But he was a man of peace and rather than run
the risk of another attack from Norway, he duly acknowledged
her king as his overlord, paying him the proper tribute due on
his succession. And in addition to this prudent act, he so
cleverly courted the favour of the kings of Scotland and Ireland
that none molested the Isles during his reign. Yet there were
domestic troubles at the end of his long life and as a result of these
he was assassinated by a rebel nephew, though after all it was
his own son Godred who eventually succeeded him. This warlike prince for a short period ruled over Dublin in addition to
the Isles, but he soon became so overbearing and tyrannical
that it was not long before there was a movement afoot in
Man to depose him.

King Olaf had married one of his daughters to a powerful
chieftain of Argyll who was of Scottish descent on his father's
side but nevertheless bore the unmistakably Norse name of
Somerled and who had beyond a doubt the blood of the Norse
nobility in his veins, being probably of the family of
SOMERLED Sigurd the Stout, the Orkney earl. To this Somerled
d. 1164   the malcontents of the Isles appealed, begging him
to give them Dugald, his son and Godred's nephew, as their
king. Somerled, grand adventurer that he was, at once agreed,
and immediately there was a struggle between himself and
Godred. A great sea-fight took place on the night of Epiphany
of 1156 ; but though both sides lost heavily, neither could
achieve a complete victory, and in the morning a peace was
patched up, the rival claimants, Godred and Dugald, agreeing
to share the kingdom of the Isles, Dugald taking Kintyre and

Bute, and the islands south of Ardnamurchan Point, while Godred, whose realm was thus split into two separate provinces, retained Man, Arran, and the Hebrides. ' So ', says the Manx Chronicle, ' was the kingdom of the Isles ruined from the time that the sons of Somerled took possession of it ', and it was plain enough that for a while the peace enjoyed under King Olaf was at an end. Two years later Somerled attacked Man and obtained possession of the island, Godred escaping to Norway. But in 1164 Somerled died and Godred came into his own again, taking to himself all his ancient domain with the exception of certain islands on the west of Scotland (Skye and Bute were two of these) that remained in the hands of Somerled's descendants.

After Thorfinn died in 1064 there was for a time no great Orkney earl of equal power and estate, a frequent division of the earldom between brothers or cousins lessening considerably the importance of the Nordreys as a factor in the politics of ORKNEY Scotland, and a result of this was that north-east IN THE Alban fell away from the earldom and passed under TWELFTH the overlordship of the Scottish king. Such joint earls CENTURY were Pall I and Erlend, sons of Thorfinn, and during their reign there was an interruption of the now long-established dynasty of earls founded by Ragnvald of Möre, for when King Magnus Barefoot of Norway invaded the Orkneys he deposed the two earls, setting up his own son Sigurd as earl in their stead. But Sigurd became king of Norway in 1103 and thereafter Haakon Pallsson, grandson of Thorfinn, and Magnus Erlendsson shared the earldom as dependents of the ST. MAG- king of Norway. Magnus Erlendsson the Saint NUS d. 1115 (d. 1115) was indeed after his death a revered and much-honoured personage, but in life he was an obscure personage, ruling only a half of the islands, and it was not until the earl of the other half, Haakon (d. *circa* 1123), had caused him to be put to death and had taken all the earldom for himself that the fortunes of the Orkneys seemed to improve ; for Haakon, after making a pilgrimage of penitence to Rome, governed well, made new laws, and kept his realm at peace. But there was quarrelling after his death between his sons Pall and Harald Smoothtongue (who held Caithness in fief from the king of Scotland), and the earldom was again divided, though Pall (d. 1136) eventually recovered the whole island-dominion of his father. He was a peace-loving and unadventurous man, yet towards the end of his life when Ragnvald Kali (descended from Earl Erlend on the distaff side and named after Ragnvald Brusason) claimed the half of the Orkneys that Saint Magnus Erlendsson had possessed, Pall II refused to share the realm and drove Ragnvald off when he tried to seize his fancied heritage. But there was a second invasion of Pall's earldom, Pall disappeared, and Ragnvald laid the whole of the Nordreys under him. He was a great and a famous figure in Orkney history, illustrious for good government, land reforms, the furthering of the cult of the new saint (canonized in 1135) and the building of the first cathedral.

EARL RAGNVALD

There dwelt at this time in the Orkneys a rich chieftain of noble birth, having estates both in Orkney and Caithness, by name Svein Asleifarson, whose career,[1] though this is in the twelfth century, was a long series of the same sturdy and astonishing adventures that filled the lives of the vikings of three hundred years earlier. As the result of a murder he was outlawed by Earl Pall, and when Ragnvald came for a second time to the Orkneys, Svein suddenly crossed over from Thurso, took Pall captive, and hurried him off to the court of Maddadh, earl of Atholl, who had married Pall's sister. Pall's fate is unknown ; there is a story that he was blinded and put to death by Svein and Margaret, the sister, but it is as likely that he was taken to Atholl to serve Svein's political ambitions, for it is certain that he would have been re-instated with honour in his own domain should Pall recover the earldom. But Pall, it happened, never did go back to Orkney and Svein returned alone to make his peace with the now all-powerful Ragnvald. His next adventure was a daring raid on foot across the Highlands of Scotland from Atholl to Sutherland where he destroyed the home of the man who had slain his father ; after which he plundered the neighbourhood and, regaining his ships, harried round Scotland. On another occasion he went to the Sudreys, on the invitation of Holdbodi, a noble of the Isles, whose lands were being plagued by a Welsh chieftain. Svein and Holdbodi together harried the coast of Wales, but the Welshman who was the cause of this punitive expedition retreated to a stronghold on Lundy Island in the Bristol Channel, and though Svein and Holdbodi pursued him there, they could not capture the place and so returned

ADVEN-
TURES OF
SVEIN
d. 1171

---

[1] The reader should note that the portions of the Orkneyinga saga dealing with Svein must be accepted with misgivings as being for the most part later interpolations and having far less historical value than the rest of this work. Particularly in the matter of Svein's death during the siege of Dublin is the saga to be doubted and the briefer account in the Irish annals preferred.

to Man. Eventually, Holdbodi played traitor to Svein, and when the Orkney viking, after a raid upon Ireland, came back to Man, he found Holdbodi in alliance with the Welshman. There was an attack upon him that he beat off and then he took up his abode for a while in Lewes.   Later he returned to Orkney and prepared an expedition whereby he might wreak vengeance upon Holdbodi ; but though he plundered savagely in the Sudreys in the end he had to return to Caithness without having captured his enemy.   And then misfortune befell him, for he quarrelled with one Thorbjorn, who had accompanied him on the raid, and this led to a quarrel with Earl Ragnvald himself. Svein took refuge in a castle in Caithness and therefrom did much plundering, so that it was not long before Ragnvald crossed over from Orkney and laid long siege to Svein's stronghold. Finally Svein escaped by lowering himself at night over the walls down to the sea and so swimming away.   He then made his way south in a little boat that picked him up and visited the court of the Scottish king, David, in Edinburgh, and the king, after inviting him without success to enter his service, made peace between him and Ragnvald so that Svein could return to the Orkneys.   This was in the '40s.

In 1151 Ragnvald, who left Harald Maddadhsson, his kinsman but a man with much Scottish blood in him, as earl-regent, set off with a small company of laymen and clerics for the Holy Land and was away for two years.   During his absence there were troubles in Orkney : Erlend, son of Harald Smooth-tongue, who had obtained from the new boy-king of Scotland, Malcolm IV, the title of earl and half Caithness, soon came into conflict with Harald, and allied with the turbulent and always dangerous Svein, was struggling to make Harald give up his claim to the isles ; moreover, King Eystein of Norway came to Orkney in 1153, and fearful of the growing ascendency of the Scottish party, he showed greater favour to Erlend than to Harald whom he compelled to become his vassal and whose privileges he restricted.   But when Ragnvald at last came back to Orkney he joined forces with Harald Maddadhsson and declared war upon Erlend and Svein.   In 1154 there was a battle at Knarstoun in Mainland in which Ragnvald and Harald suffered disastrous losses, but Erlend was slain in another engagement at the end of the year and an attempt was made by Ragnvald, who seems to have had a considerable regard for Svein, to reconcile this fiery old ruffian with Harald.   But he had to be fined and threatened with the confiscation of half his lands and his best ship, and Harald, in executing the seizure of Svein's property, so incensed the hot-tempered viking that Svein at once attacked him, and it was only after a year of fighting, hiding, and bargaining, that peace was at last restored. Svein's next adventure was a viking expedition to the Sudreys, and south as far as the Scilly Isles, where he took much plunder from Port St. Mary. In those days it was Svein's custom to winter at his home in Gairsay, where he kept about eighty men at his call, and he worked his company exceedingly hard in the early spring at the tilling and sowing of the land. When this was done he took his men off on a spring-viking expedition, generally to the Sudreys and Ireland, returning home after midsummer. Then he stayed in Orkney until the harvest was gathered, and after it was safely stored he set off again on what he called his autumn-viking.

It was in 1171, after Ragnvald was dead and when Harald was sole earl, that Svein made his last and most memorable expedition. With Harald's son in his company and a fleet of seven long-ships the old pirate sailed off on his autumn cruise, steered first for the Sudreys and then for Ireland, where he joined his forces to those of Asgall Torquilsson, sometime king of Dublin, who had been driven from his realm by Diarmait MacMurchad, king of Leinster. This prince held the town of Dublin with the aid of an army largely composed of Norman soldiers from Wales, where he had sought help during a period of banishment from Ireland, and it was to help Asgall recover his lost kingdom and so re-open the great Irish trading-station to the viking merchants that old Svein had come to Ireland. SVEIN IS Together Orkney adventurers and Asgall's army KILLED IN attacked the town, but though at first they were DUBLIN successful, even to the extent of being able to demand 1171 a ransom and the formal submission of the defenders, yet there followed speedily an uprising within the town so that Svein was ambushed in the streets and killed.[1]

During the reign of Earl Harald the Nordreys came into collision with the kingdom of the Sudreys and Man. In 1198 King William of Scotland, hearing that Harald had taken to himself Caithness without the Scottish king's authority, quar-EARL relled with the Orkney earl and enlisted the support HARALD of Ragnvald, king of the Isles, son of Godred II AND and at this time a most powerful chieftain. Ragnvald RAGNVALD OF THE set out at once with a large force to subdue Caithness, ISLES for this province the Scottish king now promised to him should he be successful in ousting Harald; but though

[1] In the Irish annals he is named as *Eoin* (*Sean*) *mear* (mad John) of Orkney; it is only told that he was killed in the siege of Dublin.

he did for a while obtain the mastery of the north-eastern corner of Scotland, Harald crossed over from the Orkneys as soon as Ragnvald had retired and proceeded to wreak his vengeance upon those who had submitted to the king of the Isles. Then King William himself invaded Caithness, and Harald, even though he had a force of 6,000 men, dared not risk a battle with the mighty host of Scotland so that the struggle concluded with the Caithness men being compelled to pay William a heavy fine and to acknowledge him as their overlord. Yet Harald was still permitted to retain the title of their earl.

Nor was this humiliation on the mainland the only reverse that Harald sustained, for towards the end of his long life, after the vain *Öyskeggene* rebellion (1193) against King Sverre when many Orkneymen and Shetlanders fought in the army of the insurgents, he lost the Shetlands, hitherto included in the Orkney earldom, to the king of Norway. This was effected by the Treaty of Bergen in 1195 which not only transferred the control of the Shetlands and made them share a *lagman* with the Faroes, but also materially increased the powers and privileges of the Norwegian Crown in the Orkneys. He died in 1206, aged 73, having reigned, after Ragnvald Kali's death, for forty-eight years as sole earl.

The great Ragnvald of the Isles was assassinated in 1229, and Olaf the Black, his brother, who succeeded him, dutifully went to Norway to pay the customary tribute and to acknowledge King Haakon Haakonsson as his overlord. But Haakon had become dissatisfied at the loss of revenue from the islands formerly in the western kingdom but now possessed by the descendants of Somerled, and so had despatched one Haakon Ospak to govern the Sudreys and recover, if he could, the islands held by the rebels. This newcomer and Olaf, on his return from Norway, very sensibly joined forces ; but Ospak was killed in an attack upon Rothesay in Bute and the rival Somerledian kingdom remained for the time unshaken and independent. King Harald (1237–1248), his son, succeeded Olaf, and he, like his father, acknowledged the Norwegian overlordship, though this was not before some pressure was exerted upon him. For the new king of the Isles was a person of considerable importance and much-honoured outside his realm ; Henry III, king of England, knighted him in 1247, and in 1248 he was given in marriage the daughter of the king of Norway. But this was the year of his death, for on the return from the wedding Harald and his Norwegian bride were both drowned in a storm off the Shetlands.

Harald's relations with the king of Scotland had been friendly, but already Alexander II had begun to think it was time to put an end to the Norse supremacy on the western and northern fringe of his kingdom ; for the Norse power seemed to be on the SCOTLAND increase inasmuch as Haakon had now won the partial AND NOR- allegiance of the grandsons of Somerled, Eogan and WAY : THE Dugald, himself conferring upon them the title of STRUGGLE FOR THE king and thus bringing almost the whole of the WESTERN ancient kingdom of the Isles under his personal ISLES authority. Alexander's first move was an attempt to acquire the islands of the west from Norway by purchase, but when Haakon most proudly and indignantly refused to sell the heritage of his fathers and when Eogan, in the face of Alexander's entreaties and threats, persisted in his loyalty to the Norwegian king, Alexander thereupon took up arms. He planned an attack upon Eogan's kingdom of Mull and led his army into Argyll ; but he fell sick and died (1249) on Kerrera, the island opposite Oban, and for a while the Scottish attempt to rewin the Sudreys was abandoned. Negotiations with the king of Norway were renewed in 1261 by the young Alexander III, but again Haakon declined to cede the islands to Scotland. In the following year Dugald reported to Norway that his island of Skye had been attacked by the Scots, so that it was soon plain to all that Alexander purposed to achieve his father's ambition of annexing the western islands ; Haakon thereupon decided to make a great demonstration of Norwegian strength by himself sailing to the kingdom of the Isles to assert his supremacy and to overthrow the king of Scotland in a decisive engagement.

Haakon with his great fleet sailed first to Shetland and thence to the Orkneys, and there in July of 1263 he received the submission of the men of Caithness whom he forced to pay him a KING fine. Then in August he rounded Cape Wrath and HAAKON made Lewes, and thence south-east into the sound of HAAKONS- Skye where the new king of the Isles, Magnus, third SON'S EX- PEDITION son of Black Olaf, joined him. Further south, off TO THE Mull, the flotilla was also augmented by the fleet of WEST 1263 King Dugald, but the other Somerledian king, Eogan, would not throw in his lot with the Norsemen, preferring to stand aloof from the struggle on the grounds that he owed allegiance to both the rival suzerains of the Isles and that the bond between himself and the Scottish court was no less strong than that whereby he was pledged to Haakon. Yet from Ireland there came an offer of help, for the Ostmen of the once Norse towns had realized the importance of the impending struggle and begged that the mighty king of Norway in return for a detachment of their fighting men would afterwards come to their aid and free them from the oppression of the English that was now threatening to crush them out of existence. So Haakon sent ambassadors to Ireland to report upon this proffered aid and the condition of the Norse colonies.

By the time the fleet arrived at Kerrera it was at full strength, numbering in all some 160 sail and carrying not many less than 20,000 men, this without Irish reinforcements. It was to be expected that the approach of this huge force would cause serious alarm in Scotland, but money had been raised for the increase of garrisons in the castles situated in the heart of the country and for repairing the fortifications of the towns they guarded; the chief concentration of the Scottish armies was upon the Firth of Clyde in the neighbourhood of Ayr, for this was the coastline that was most of all likely to be attacked.

And, indeed, Haakon's first move showed plainly that this was veritably the danger-point, for he proceeded to lay under him all Kintyre and Bute, and that accomplished, he sailed with the whole fleet round the Mull of Kintyre to Arran where he anchored on the 8th of September in Lamlash harbour opposite the mainland coast. At this stage there began parleys and proposals for peace between Haakon and Alexander, but as the Scottish king, even though he was now prepared to make large concessions, entirely refused to admit Haakon as overlord of Arran and Bute, the long drawn out negotiations came to nothing, and after Haakon and his fleet had moved further into the Clyde mouth to the Cumbrae Islands opposite Largs there was an end of all truces.

It was already autumn and the need for immediate action/ was pressing. So Haakon divided his fleet and sent sixty ships under Magnus up Loch Long and overland to Loch Lomond whence they most successfully ravaged parts of Stirlingshire; but the king of Norway himself lay at his headquarters off the Cumbraes and prepared his force for the coming contest with the Scottish army that was now assembling at Largs and Ayr. After a week or two had passed there came disaster upon the Norse, this being a violent storm that raged on the night of the 1st of October and wrecked ten boats of the Loch Long fleet, while in Haakon's own squadrons many boats broke from their moorings. When daylight came it was found that three of these had been driven ashore on the mainland coast by Largs.

Some Scottish outposts began to shoot when the discomfited

crews scrambled on to land, and Haakon, though the heavy
seas almost prevented him from coming to their aid, managed
to put ashore a small force that succeeded in driving off the
SKIRMISH   Scots. But getting back to the ships was still difficult,
AT LARGS, so the Norwegians passed the night on shore and
OCTOBER were still there on the next day (3rd October) when
1263   a much larger contingent of the Scottish army
approached, this including 500 cavalry with mail-clad horse
and a body of infantry. There were probably about 800 or
900 Norsemen in all on land and of these some 200 were posted
on a hillock, but the rest were miserably stationed on the beach
itself. The Scottish attack at once swept the Norsemen from
the hillock and soon they were retreating in pell-mell confusion
down to the sea. Thereat panic seized the little army on the
beach and there was a rush for the dinghies and escape, but the
crowded boats capsized in the heavy seas, horrible disasters
showing those still on the beach that safety could be won only
by fighting. So there was a courageous rally. The wild seas
prevented Haakon, who was aboard, from landing proper reinforcements, but nevertheless a few brave warriors from the ships
succeeded in joining their comrades ashore and the end of this
remarkable skirmish was that the Norsemen, thus heartened,
advanced against the Scots and drove them from the field.
This done, the gallant remnant of Haakon's land-force rowed
out in small boats to their ships and safety. The Scottish army
withdrew and next day Haakon was able to bury his dead at
the old kirk of Largs ; on the following day he was joined by
the fleet under Magnus, and after burning the ships run aground
at Largs, the whole flotilla weighed anchor and returned to
Lamlash on Arran.

   There he received an invitation from the Irish Ostmen to
winter in Ireland at their expense, they still hoping for his help
against the English ; but his Norwegians had now been many
months from home, and though Haakon himself was eager for
the Irish adventure he complied, after some debate, with the
wishes of his people and announced the forthcoming break-up
of the great armada. Accordingly the island-princes returned
DEATH OF to their domains, and Haakon, now grand overlord
HAAKON   of all the Isles (for the Scots had in no wise crushed
IN THE   this flotilla that had come to establish the Norse
ORKNEYS   suzerainty), even conferred Bute and Arran, dearly
prized of the Scottish king, upon chieftains who had served
him. Then with the Norwegians he returned to Orkney where
he purposed to winter with twenty of his ships ; but shortly

after his arrival there a sickness seized him, and on the 15th of November this great and distinguished monarch died.

With the passing of Haakon the political domination of Norway over western Scotland was at an end. For Magnus, his youthful heir, had neither the inclination nor the power to enforce upon Scandinavia the colonial policy of his grandfather. And Alexander knew that at last his opportunity had come, so speedily collecting his armies and a fleet he prepared to attack the Isle of Man; there was no hope now of succour from outside for the little island thus threatened by a Scottish force of overwhelming strength, so that King Magnus of the Isles had no other choice than to sue for peace. He was compelled to surrender all the islands over which he ruled, except Man itself; and this he held henceforth only as vassal of the king of Scotland whom he undertook to supply with ten ships of war as often as they should be required of him. But this considerable triumph did not satisfy Alexander; in the same year MAN AND THE WEST-ERN ISLES CEDED TO SCOTLAND 1266 he forced all the western islands one by one to submit to him (though he could not capture nor crush King Dugald), and finally he re-established Scottish supremacy over the unhappy people of Caithness. In Norway it was soon realized that the easiest way of ridding the state of the embarrassment of colonies that could no longer be defended and were fast slipping from her hold was to sell them, so it came about that in July of 1266 a treaty was made whereby Magnus ceded to Alexander his now worthless overlordship of the Isle of Man and all the Sudreys in return for a payment of 4,000 marks (to be delivered in four yearly instalments) and of 100 marks annually thereafter, a bargain that brought to an end a period of more than four hundred years of Norse dominion in western Scotland. Yet still, in the north, the Orkneys and Shetlands remained faithful to the Norwegian crown.

And long did they remain faithful to their Scandinavian overlord. For though Caithness, now Scottish territory, was sometimes ruled by the Orkney earl as vassal of the king of Scotland, yet over the islands themselves the Scottish monarch exercised no practical authority. The male line of Harald SCOTTISH EARLS OF ORKNEY Maddadhsson had ended with the death of his son Earl Jon in 1231, and the new earl, also governor of Caithness, was a Scot, son of the earl of Angus who had married, it may be, a daughter of Harald. This Angus dynasty was in turn succeeded by that of the Scottish Stratherne family, and late in the fourteenth century the earldom passed into the keeping of the St. Clairs. Of this family, William, invested in 1434 by King Eric of Pomerania, sovereign of the united kingdoms of Norway, Sweden, and Denmark, was the last ruler of Orkney under Scandinavian suzerainty.

But the severing of the bond was a money bargain of remote statesmen, an inconclusive and embarrassing diplomatic exchange that in no wise was prompted by, nor reflected, the personal inclinations of the almost Norse folk of the islands. For the Scots had defaulted over a period of many years in their payment of the annual dues for their holding of the Sudreys, and when King Christian I of the united kingdoms was angrily insisting upon payment, it seemed the best way out of a difficult THE MORT- position that the heir to the Scottish crown should GAGE OF wed the Danish king's daughter. But though first THE proposed in 1457, it was not until 1468 that the NORTHERN treaty was signed, and the prince, now James III, ISLES 1468 took Margaret of Denmark to wife, and by the terms of this treaty as pledge for a part of the bride's enormous dowry Christian handed over the Orkneys to Scotland. And then, as still he could not conveniently pay up the remainder of the dowry, he pledged the Shetlands too. So it came about that in 1472 the islands were formally annexed by the crown of Scotland, though the right to redeem them, whether fanciful or real, was jealously guarded by the Scandinavian throne, even until the seventeenth century.

It was by treaty, then, here as in the western islands, that the Norse overlordship was ended. But the politics and bargains of the mainland did little to alter the hearts of the islanders, their loyalties, their customs, or their speech. Norse in spirit they remained and little-loving of the Scots, even though Scottish clerics had done much to soften them in the fifteenth century, when the Norse tongue began to die out in Orkney. Indeed it was not until the days of James I of England and Scotland that these mettlesome and unruly folk of the Nordreys and of the Sudreys submitted finally to Scottish authority.

CHAPTER XI

WALES

O F the Celtic lands Wales, the modern Wales, that is, without Strathclyde Wales in North Britain or West Wales (Cornwall), suffered not the least from the marauding vikings of the ninth and tenth centuries ; for on their way to Ireland, whether Danes coming from the south or Norwegians from the north, Cambria lay open to their attack, and there can be little doubt that from Anglesey and from the monasteries and settlements of the north and south coasts the vikings took a full toll of life and plunder. Yet the records of the raids are scarce and there is no coherent history of viking Wales, the reason being that this is the Celtic country that most successfully withstood the attack of the Northmen in the early colonizing period, yielding less to them than did Scotland or Ireland, and showing to the invader a fiercer and a firmer front. Thus upon the first appearance of the vikings (they were Danes) in 795, when after ravages in England they came to Glamorganshire to lay that county waste with fire and sword, manfully rose the Cymry against them, routed them in battle, and, driving them back to the sea with heavy loss, saw them sail off to Ireland in search of an easier prey. And thereafter followed a period of peace, if the chronicles are to be trusted, until the '50s and '60s of the ninth century when Anglesey in the north and Gower in the south were attacked, though in Gower it is known that the Northmen, like the first viking invaders of South Wales, were repulsed.

That the foreigners made no permanent settlements of historical import in the south at this period when the Irish colonies were founded must be due to this resolute defence of the stalwart Cymry, and that they likewise failed to gain a lasting foothold in the north, so temptingly close to Ireland and to Man, may be RHODRI owing in no small degree to the energy and example MAWR AND of a gallant Welshman, Rhodri Mawr, prince of THE IRISH Gwynedd, who, succeeding to the throne in 844, reigned VIKINGS until 878 and died as lord of the whole of North Wales. His best-known exploit in the wars with the vikings was the slaying of Orm (who perhaps gave his name to the Ormes Heads at

Llandudno), the leader of a great Danish invasion from Ireland that had been directed against Anglesey and that in 855 was terrorizing the mainland of North Wales. Yet though Rhodri was strong enough to prevent viking colonization of a serious kind, he was not always successful in his struggle with the Northmen inasmuch as a later viking attack in 877 forced him to take temporary refuge in Ireland.

It was not only the Irish vikings who menaced Wales, for in 876 came Ubbe, son of Ragnar Lodbrok, from Northumbria with his Danes to Pembroke, this just before the attack on Devonshire, and there put many of the Christian population to death ; and Danes from England they were who in 894 plundered in North Wales (p. 244), and who in 896, upon the break-up of the force RAIDS that had wintered at Bridgenorth, broke into and laid FROM THE waste the south-eastern counties of the Principality. ENGLISH But more serious was an attack in 915 when a viking DANELAW host from Brittany, after sailing into the estuary of the Severn, landed on the south coast of Wales and penetrated far inland to the neighbourhood of Hereford, capturing in their progress the Bishop of Llandaff whom they took as prisoner to their ships, later to be ransomed by Edward the Elder for 40 pounds. Yet they met with defeat, these vikings, at the hands of the men of Hereford, Gloucester, and the border towns, so that they turned away to attack the Devonshire coast, and then, by way of Pembroke, went off to Ireland.

In North Wales too, now that Rhodri Mawr was gone, the vikings appeared again, and there these Gaill from Ireland thirsted for a conquest of the land rather than for mere plunder, such an intending colonist being Ingimund who in 902, after a victory of the Irish over the Dublin settlers, crossed to Anglesey and ANGLESEY there took land for himself and his followers. But in ATTACKED due course he was driven out of the island and next 902 is heard of attacking Æthelfleda's newly repaired fortress of Chester. Thereafter Anglesey was left in peace until 915 when the Dublin Gaill once more attacked the island.

Yet there was no serious attempt to hold Anglesey as a Norse colony and a long period of respite from the viking raids followed. For this was a time when another great prince, much honoured of posterity, was already advancing to a fame and dominion such as few of the early kings in Wales enjoyed and to an authority HOWELL that seems to have made his lands temporarily THE GOOD secure from foreign attack. Hywel dda (Howell the d. 950 Good) was originally a king in Cardigan, but by the annexation of Pembroke about 920 he had become lord of all south-west Wales and by 942 he had made himself master also of the north, overlord, indeed, of the whole Principality. Supreme over all Wales, founder of Welsh unity not less by his law-giving than by the strength of his arm, staunch friend of the English, Hywel made of Cambria a realm that only the rashest of adventurers dared attack, and so at this very period wherein vikings abroad were seeking land in which to settle rather than to plunder it could only have been by the peaceful admission of a few of them as well-disposed traders that the wandering Norsemen might hope for access into the stalwart kingdom of Wales.

But with Hywel's death in 950 his mighty kingdom collapsed, at once rent asunder by civil wars. And upon Wales thus weakened by internal strife the Gaill descended with a fury and persistence that makes the second half of the tenth century the period of the worst sufferings of the country at their hands. Four notable viking chiefs who plundered Wales in this half-century were Eric Bloodaxe, who twice raided Cambria, the great Orkney earl Turf-Einar, Olaf Tryggvason, future king of Norway, and Svein Forkbeard, the future conqueror of England, who after much victorious fighting in Wales was later captured and imprisoned by the Welsh. But most of the attacks came from the settlements near at hand in Ireland or in Man, and it was most of all upon Anglesey and Carnarvonshire in the north and upon Pembroke in the south that their onslaughts fell. Holyhead was plundered in 961, Towyn in Merioneth in 963, Penmon in Anglesey in 971 by Magnus Haraldsson of Man, and to Anglesey in 972 came Godfred Haraldsson (p. 310), his brother, who made himself master of the island. Not that he could have held it for long, for in 980 he returned, this time in league with a Welsh chieftain, to lay Mona waste anew and to march with fire and sword throughout the Lleyn peninsula of Carnarvon. In 982 this same prince of the Isles invaded Pembroke, and in 987 for the third time he turned against Anglesey, gaining a memorable victory over the Welsh in which he took two thousand prisoners. Next year his, or other, vikings despoiled five rich monasteries of the west and south coasts, and in 989 Maredudd ab Owain (986–999), King of Deheubarth and overlord of all Wales, paid to the foreigners a tribute of a penny per head to redeem the Welsh prisoners of the invaders. In 992, in the wars against the English, Maredudd bribed some of the Gaill into his own service, but here, as in Ireland, alliances of this kind were no guarantee of immunity from the attacks of other vikings. Thus on Ascension Day in 993 Anglesey was raided

VIKING ATTACKS RENEWED

once more, and in 999 most of the population of St. David's was either put to the sword or captured and its bishop murdered.

There cannot be much doubt that the period of the chief viking attack upon Wales, the half-century following the death of Hywel dda, must have witnessed something more than mere raid after raid, and it was at this time in all probability VIKING that many viking adventurers won some temporary SETTLE- that many viking adventurers won some temporary MENTS IN power and status in the land, especially along the coast WALES from Newport to Neath, in the Gower Peninsula and in Pembroke, where Scandinavian place-names are common.[1] Thus there is a King Sigferth, surely some Scandinavian Sigfrid, in Wales who with Welsh princes attested a charter of Eadred in 955, and it was not much later (960) that the Danish viking Palnatoki, on visiting Wales, found one Stefni, with a foster-son Björn and a daughter Alof, established there in possession of an estate of some size.[2] For in Ireland Celt and Northman were learning to live side by side in harmony, and it well may be that some Scandinavians, making their home in Wales, even in these days of frequent attack upon the Cymry, were allowed to settle down in unchallenged ownership of land, their presence perhaps attracting profitable visits to Welsh harbours of the trading-ships bound for Dublin and the Norse towns of Ireland.   Indeed it was perhaps the busy Norse and Danish trade in the Bristol Channel preceding, or resulting from, this Scandinavian settlement upon its north coast that led to the development of such sea-ports as Cardiff and Swansea into towns of no small significance in the commercial system of the British Isles.

The viking attacks upon Wales continued in the first half of the eleventh century, and especially in the '30s and '40s the Northmen of Ireland and the Scottish Isles were still an ever-present danger to the Principality. Yet gradually conditions changed, for in Ireland the Gaill were already long-established and universally recognized members of the state, so that when ALLIANCES Wales, later in the century, was in danger of English OF VIK- or Norman attack the Irish Gaill were as much the INGS AND allies of the Cymry as were the native Irishmen them-WELSH selves. Gruffydd ap Cynan, the king whose stormy and interrupted reign over Gwynedd lasted from 1075 to 1137,

[1] There is no satisfactory evidence of vikings earlier established in Wales. Hring and Adils, kings in Bretland and vassals of Æthelstan who fought against their overlord at Brunanburh in 937 (*Egils saga*, LI, 4), were probably Welsh princes. Hring has not been identified, but Adils must have been Idwal, king of Gwynedd.

[2] For an attempt to localize this in Pembroke, see *Saga-book of Viking Club*, III, 163.

was, in fact, brought up in the Scandinavian settlement at Dublin, and by the marriage of his father Cynan to the Dublin princess Ragnhild was great-grandson of Sigtryg of the Silken Beard, king of Dublin at the time of the Battle of Clontarf. Norsemen and Irishmen together fought for him at every one of his battles in Cambria, whether against Welsh usurper or Norman invader, and it was to the Irish Norse that he fled whenever, as often happened, he needed asylum or fresh recruits.

The Norse attacks, therefore, of this period, the second half of the century, were few in number and were made not so much by the Irish foreigners as by the turbulent vikings of the western isles. In the '70s, St. David's was pillaged twice, and Bangor once, by 'pagans' who came probably from the Nordreys or Sudreys, and, indeed, when in 1090 St. David's was sacked for a third time the chronicles expressly record that it was the doing of 'pagans of the Isles'. And so too from the north came the attack of King Magnus Barefoot of Norway in 1098 who in the course of an invasion of the western sea had reached Man and thence sailed south to Anglesey. He found the island to be in the hands of two Norman earls, Hugh of Chester and Hugh of Shrewsbury, and these he fought in the battle of 'Anglesey Sound' wherein Hugh of Shrewsbury fell and the Normans were put to flight. Thereat King Magnus made Anglesey his own, so says

KING
MAGNUS
BAREFOOT
IN ANGLE-
SEY 1098

his saga, as far south as ever the kings of Norway of old had owned it, but his overlordship was of negligible import, his fleet sailing away almost immediately and leaving the island to the struggles between the English and the Welsh. Yet it is said that Magnus came a second time to Anglesey during a later raid upon the west in order to obtain timber for the rebuilding of three fortresses in Man that he himself had previously demolished. But this, it seems, was the last of the visits of hostile viking fleets to Wales, except for such minor attacks as those of the Orkney Svein, and Holdbodi of the Isles in the twelfth century.

CHAPTER XII

THE FAROE ISLANDS

DICUIL, the Irish monk who lived in Francia and who wrote a treatise on geography in the year A.D. 825, is the first to tell of the Faroes, saying that they might be reached from North Britain if the wind were favourable after a voyage two days and two nights long. In these islands, said he, Irish hermits had been wont to dwell for a space of about a hundred years, but at the time when he wrote he supposed that men lived no longer there since Norse robbers had made it impossible for the hermits to stay. Only the sheep, he thought, and the countless sea-birds now inhabited this remote archipelago.

So there were Irishmen in the Faroes as early as about A.D. 700,[1] and it was just about a century later that the visits of the vikings drove them forth, these newcomers doubtless giving the archipelago its present name of *Faereyjar*, Norse words meaning Sheep Islands. But the first Scandinavian colonist of whom there is record was Grim Kamban and it was not until Harald Fairhair's days, towards the end of the ninth century, that he GRIM KAMBAN came. In his lifetime he was a renowned person, and after his death the other settlers in the islands are said actually to have worshipped him, believing that his spirit could bring them good seasons ; they were impressed, perhaps, by his Christian lore, apart from his natural wisdom and authority, for because his second name (Camman) is Irish it is probable enough that he was a baptized viking who had been directed to the Faroes from Ireland. Yet there must have been others of the early colonists who had learnt something of Christianity from Ireland or Britain, even though the majority may have been heathen who had migrated direct from Norway.

The wealthiest and noblest family of the Faroe Islands were the Gateskeggs (Gatebeards) who dwelt at Gata on Austrey ;

---

[1] There is no *papa* element (see p. 339) surviving in Faroes place-names, but it may be that the first element of Baglahólm off Sudrey is derived from the Irish *bachall*, crozier. The name Dimon, *two mountain*, is believed to be of Celtic origin, but this does not necessarily date back to the pre-Norse period.

they had the blood of Aud the Deepminded in their veins, for this
remarkable woman, widow of a Norse king of Dublin,

THE GATE-
SKEGGS
coming to the Faroes on her way to Iceland, gave her
granddaughter in marriage to one of the settlers, and
it was of this union that the Gateskeggs were sprung. But of the

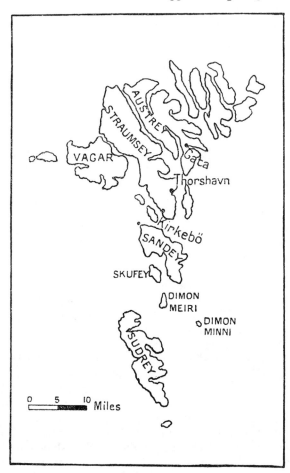

FIG. 35.—The Faroe Islands

history of the settlement period nothing is known and it is said
simply that men went to live in the Faroes in order to escape from
the oppression of Harald Fairhair in Norway, a statement that
is probably only half the truth as the fuller history of the first
colonization of Iceland, set forth in the next chapter, may be

deemed to show.   In the Faroes the story of the tenth century is
likewise a blank, though it is at least certain that on each of
the principal islands there dwelt by this time a chieftain with his
family and servants and that this community of scattered families
was so far developed as a corporate society as to possess a central
thing-place, doubtless with a temple too, for the general assembly
of the islanders.   This *thing* was at Thorshavn where is now the
capital town of the Faroes.

Whether Harald Fairhair was acknowledged as overlord of
this Norse colony of the Faroes history does not record, but it
seems that at a very early date the Norwegian royalties owned
these islands and possessed here a far greater authority than
they ever had in Iceland.   For in King Harald Greycloak's time
(*c.* A.D. 965) a chieftain called Hafgrim, who dwelt in Sudrey,
ruled over one half of the islands as a vassal of the king, while
the other half was held by two brothers, Breste and Beine, of the
Gateskegg family, as vassals of Jarl Haakon Sigurdsson of
Lade, the redoubtable rival of the king.

The great saga of the Faroe Islands, the story that is preserved
in chopped and separated pieces in the Flatey Book, is concerned
with this Breste's son and another member of the same family,
Thrond, the younger son of Thorbjorn Gateskegg who was
himself the son of Aud the Deepminded's granddaughter.   Thrond
had come into possession of the homestead at Gata
and after travelling in Norway and Denmark had
returned to the Faroes with great riches ; he was a tall
red-headed man with freckles and a beard, a gloomy
and grim-looking person of whom the island folk were much
afraid.   When Hafgrim quarrelled with Breste and Beine,
Thrond, although these two were his cousins, took Hafgrim's side
and together they made a cowardly attack with three boatloads of armed men upon the brothers whom they caught alone
with their two young sons sheep-tending on uninhabited Dimon
minni.   Breste and Beine were killed, but the two boys were
spared and Thrond took them back to Gata with him, but in the
same summer he had them sent out of the islands to Norway.
As Hafgrim had fallen in the fight on Dimon minni and the
Gateskegg brothers were dead, both of the two halves of the
colony had lost their rulers, so Thrond very easily became lord
of all the Faroes ; nevertheless, when he had established his
leadership throughout the islands, he granted to Össur Hafgrims-
son, whom he had fostered, the right to his father's possessions.

In Norway the two boys, Sigmund Brestesson and Thore
Beinesson, came at length to the court of Jarl Haakon who now

SAGA OF
SIGMUND
AND
THROND

held the reins of power, Harald Greycloak having been slain. They were well received and in the course of time, as young men in their twenties, they went back to the Faroes with two ships and an armed following given to them by Haakon. Sigmund attacked Össur in his fortified homestead on Dimon meiri and killed him, and then, accompanied by Thore, he met Thrond at Thorshavn and forced him to submit their quarrel to Haakon's arbitration. The result was that the crafty old Thrond, who had to protest his willingness to secure peace, was heavily fined and given to understand that Sigmund and the great jarl were now lords of the Faroes in his stead. Nevertheless he was allowed to retain his own estate at Gata as long as he obeyed the terms of Haakon's settlement.

But all this was only prelude to the great drama that was to be played in the Faroes at the time of the introduction of Christianity ; for it was Sigmund who was evangelist to the islands while suspicious and resentful old Thrond stood forth at the head of the conservative and heathen party to withstand the coming of the new faith and the everlasting meddling by Norway in the affairs of the islanders.

It was in A.D. 987, after Olaf Tryggvason had been king of Norway for two years, that that urgent and tremendous missionary sent suddenly for Sigmund Brestesson and promised him SIGMUND the royal favour if he would be baptized. Sigmund IS BAP- dutifully went to court and, like most of Olaf's visitors, TIZED agreed that a religion good enough for so mighty a monarch must be good enough for himself ; so he became a Christian and the king thereupon renewed his title to the lordship of all the Faroes.

But Sigmund was also asked to undertake the conversion of his fellow-islanders and to this request he agreed only with considerable reluctance, as did also Leif Ericsson three years later when Olaf bade him convert the Greenlanders, for the task of persuading these conservative Norsemen abroad to abandon their old faith was THROND one such as might daunt even a trained and enthusiastic AS LEADER missionary ; yet Olaf paid no heed to his protests and OF THE excuses, but sent him off with priests in his company HEATHEN to do the best he could for the Christian cause. So PARTY Sigmund, on his return, summoned the chieftains of the Faroes to a *thing* and asked them to accept Christianity, but he found at once that popular opinion, headed by Thrond, was unmistakably against him, and so angry was the temper of the meeting that Sigmund only escaped with his life by swearing that he would never again ask the Faroe folk to become Christian,

He took this defeat at the *thing* very much to heart, but he dared not abide by his oath nor abandon his mission, and as he now realized that a general appeal was not only useless but dangerous he determined upon a more practical plan of piecemeal conversion. This he put into operation in the following spring and began his campaign with a surprise attack upon Gata where he took Thrond prisoner. Sigmund had the man at his mercy and forced him to be baptized ; then he took this unwilling convert with him and made a tour of all the Faroes, seeing to it that one by one the terrified colonists accepted Christianity.

King Olaf fell at Svold in the year A.D. 1000 and the two jarls, Eric and Svein, sons of Jarl Haakon of Lade, who then became the rulers of Norway, likewise extended their favour to Sigmund, the lord of the Faroes. And Sigmund, in his turn, built a church close to his homestead on Skufey and made sure that at least the members of his own household were good Christians. But the other colonists, though nominally converted, lived much as they would and were most of them still heathen at heart ; Thrond, especially, hated the faith he had been forced so shamefully to accept and plotted to have his revenge.

The first move was an attack by Thrond and eleven followers upon Sigmund and his cousin Thore and a third man called Einar when they were alone upon Dimon minni, the scene of the tragic death of Breste and Beine. But Sigmund and his companions outwitted their assailants and, making off with Thrond's boat as well as their own, left them marooned upon the island so that they had to light a beacon before they were rescued. Thrond made another attack the same summer and caught Sigmund in a boat with the same two companions ; but once again Sigmund triumphed by the exercise of his cunning and his great strength, for he succeeded in capsizing Thrond's boat. Some of the crew were drowned, and Thrond and the others who were saved so marvelled at their luck in escaping Sigmund's sword, for he would not slay them helpless in the water, that they felt fortune was upon their side and were encouraged to make yet a third attempt against the Christian chief.

Therefore, in the autumn of this year, A.D. 1002, Thrond gathered together sixty men and landed one night after dark with this force upon Sigmund's island of Skufey. He took the homestead completely by surprise and set upon it with fire and weapons ; those within, Sigmund and Thore with Sigmund's wife and the whole household, defended themselves boldly and there was hard fighting for a while. Then Sigmund's wife called out, ' How long are

THROND
ATTACKS
SIGMUND
ON SKUFEY

you going on fighting with headless men, Thrond ? ', and Thrond knew from this that Sigmund must have escaped. He ran round the houses whistling after them and then he came to the mouth of an earth-house a little way off the homestead. There he stopped and began feeling the ground, the while raising his hand and sniffing it. At last he cried, ' Three men have gone this way and they are Sigmund, Thore, and Einar ! ', and he continued snuffling around as though he were a dog tracking them ; then, bidding no one follow him, he made his way to a point near the cliff-edge where the ground was broken by a sudden and steep drop [1] and he realized that the fugitives must be lurking at its foot. He summoned his men and called out, ' Now is the time to show yourself, Sigmund, if you have a brave heart and would be thought as bold as men have long believed you to be ! '. The answer to this taunt was that a man suddenly appeared among them, although it was quite dark, and struck down one of Thrond's men, after which he was as suddenly lost again in the night ; whereupon Thrond and his men stumbled down the slope in pursuit. By this time Sigmund and his companions had taken refuge upon a rock that jutted out over the sea, but soon they heard the voices of their pursuers close upon them ; then Thore said, ' Let us stand at bay here '. Sigmund, however, had lost his sword in the fight when he had appeared among Thrond's company, so he could battle no longer. ' Let us jump from the rock and swim ', he cried, and thereupon he and his two companions leapt down into the sea. Thrond heard the splashes and shouted directions to his men who hurried down through the darkness to the beach and tried to follow, some on the shore and some in a boat ; but it was too late and they found nothing.

Sigmund and his friends swam on in the dark. They may have intended to make Dimon, but as they were swept by the current in the direction of Sudrey it was for this island that they made, the distance being some six or seven miles. About half-way across Einar gave up, saying ' We must part here ' ; but Sigmund said that should never be and bade Einar hold on to him ; so they swam on for a while until Thore said, ' Sigmund, how long are you going to carry a corpse on your back ? ' And Sigmund realized that the devoted Einar was dead, so he loosed him into the water. They swam on until only a quarter of the crossing remained and then Thore said, ' All our lives we have been together, cousin, and great has been the love between us ; but now our

ESCAPE BY
SWIMMING
AND
DEATH OF
SIGMUND

---

[1] A rift crossing the island, says the saga ; but actually there is no cleft of this kind on Skufey near ' Sigmund's Leap '.

life together is over, for I can go no further. But you, dear Sigmund, look to yourself and take no heed of me.' Sigmund answered, ' We will never part thus, Thore ', so he put his cousin's arm around his shoulder and struggled forward. At last he reached Sudrey ; but by this time he was so completely exhausted that he was washed ashore in a helpless condition and Thore slipped from his grasp and was drowned. Sigmund lay on a heap of sea-weed and was there till the morning when he was discovered by the sons of a man called Thorgrim who lived at a neighbouring farmstead and was a tenant of Thrond's. These folk, although he told them who he was, murdered him for the gold ring and sodden clothes that he wore, and when Thore's body was cast ashore, they buried these two cousins side by side in a bank close to the sea. Some years later Thrond found out the true story of their death, for it was long supposed that Sigmund had been drowned at sea ; he had the cruel murderers hanged and the bodies of the two cousins taken up and laid to their final rest upon Skufey near to the church that Sigmund had built. And there on Skufey can be seen to-day a stone that marks the grave of Sigmund Brestesson, the ever-beloved hero of the Faroe Islands.

The immediate sequel to Sigmund's death was that Thrond once more became lord of the Faroes, though he shared his power with Leif Össursson, his foster-son and the grandson of that Hafgrim who had once owned a half of the islands. These two did not share Sigmund's loyalty to the Christian rulers of Norway and for many years the islands were a self-ruled and largely heathen colony. But after the accession of King Olaf the Saint in 1015 the small royalist and Christian party in the Faroes began to have friends at court, and in 1024 many of the Faroe chieftains journeyed to Norway to swear allegiance to Olaf and to promise him the tax that was his due as their overlord. But old Thrond held aloof and did all that he could to interrupt the collection of the necessary money from the islanders, and though Olaf threatened and sent messengers to take by force the sum owing to him, Thrond held out against the king and the islands paid nothing into the royal exchequer.

TEMPORARY TRIUMPH OF THROND AND THE HEATHEN PARTY

Yet when Thrond died in the '30s, humbled by the women of Sigmund Brestesson's family and broken-hearted at the kidnapping from him of Sigmund's little grandson whom he had fostered and dearly loved, the conservative and anti-Christian party of which he had so long been the head could hold out no longer against the chieftains who knew the advantages of the royal

friendship. For Leif Össursson now ruled all the Faroes and he
CHRISTI- acknowledged the overlordship of King Magnus Olafs-
ANITY son the Good (1035–1047), journeying to Norway that
AT LAST he might pay allegiance to him in person. Neverthe-
ACCEPTED less, the complete triumph of Christianity was long
delayed and although a bishopric was established in the islands
in 1105, with the episcopal seat at Kirkebö, there were many
quarrels between the bishops and their stubborn flock, the most
unfortunate of the island-prelates being Erlend (1268–1308) who
was starved to death in his own unfinished cathedral, a ruin that
is still to be seen.

Once only in this later time do the Faroes win more than a
passing notice from the historians of Norway and that is in connexion with the parentage of the great King Sverre (1177–1202).
For though this monarch boasted himself the illegitimate son of
KING King Sigurd Mouth (d. 1155), his mother, a Norwegian
SVERRE lady of good birth, was wed to a Faroese comb-maker
AND THE called Unas, and the future king, her eldest son, was
FAROES given the humble Faroese name of Sverre. And whether
or no he was of Faroese birth, the youth spent much of his time
in the islands, for his uncle, Roe, was bishop of the Faroes from
1162 onwards, and with Roe at Kirkebö Sverre was trained for the
priesthood, not returning to Norway until 1174.

The rest of the story of the Faroes there is no need to recount,
for the Norse stock has been little altered by the changing political
and economic conditions of the centuries. Yet at the time of the
union of the Scandinavian powers at the end of the fourteenth
century the Faroes, like Iceland, passed under the control of the
Danish sovereigns, and under the rule of the king of Denmark
they still remain.

CHAPTER XIII

ICELAND

TRADITION tells that it was Gardar Svavarsson, a Swede with estates in Denmark, who, first of the vikings, discovered and explored Iceland, having been driven there by wind and storm after a voyage to the Hebrides. But it was not much later that the Norwegian Naddod, sailing with his company to the Faroe, was also storm-driven upon Iceland ; he gave the country the name of Snowland, and when at last he was safely back in Norway he had much to say in praise of it. Then followed the voyage of the viking Floki Vilgerdsson who sailed by way of Scotland to Iceland ; unlike Naddod, he did not speak very highly of the new country on his return, because his few cattle had all died for want of fodder during the winter and he had had several other unpleasant experiences in the course of a lengthy sojourn there. It was Floki who gave this country the name it still bears.

Nevertheless the Norsemen were not long in peopling the far-off island that Naddod had found so agreeable ; for it must have been shortly after the middle of the ninth century that these voyages of discovery took place and it was as early as the year A.D. 874 [1] that the first of the Norwegian colonists in Iceland came as emigrants to their new home. These were Ingolf Arnarson and Leif Hrodmarsson.

The story goes that Ingolf and Leif, who were foster-brothers and cousins, after a viking voyage in the company of three young nobles, the sons of Jarl Atli of Gaular, quarrelled with them and killed two of them in battle. As a result of this the law demanded the confiscation of Leif's goods (for he was the cause of the quarrel) and the two foster-brothers soon found THE FIRST that life in Norway was henceforth going to be a NORSE miserable business for them, so they decided upon SETTLERS emigration and as a first step they sailed off to the 874 new country of which there was so much talk with the intention of seeing for themselves what Iceland was really like.

[1] Ari's *Libellus Islandorum* antedates the first settlement by four years. And see note as to possibility of still earlier settlements in Iceland and Greenland, p. 362.

336

They passed a winter there and returned to Norway fully satisfied that they could live in this land ; so Leif went off to Ireland
on a viking raid in order to recuperate his fortunes and Ingolf
sold his possessions in Norway. When Leif came back rich
with Irish plunder and having ten Irish slaves in his following,
the foster-brothers could afford to fit out two ships, and taking
with them their wives, a selected band of both freemen and
thralls, some cattle, and all their worldly goods, they set sail
for their new home. On reaching Iceland the ships parted
company ; Ingolf made a temporary settlement at Ingolfshöfdi

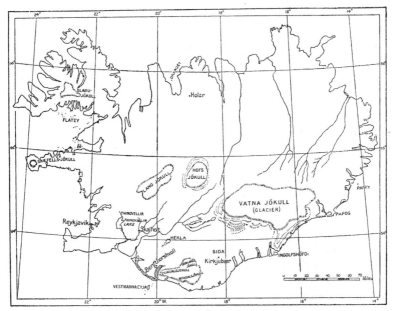

FIG. 36.—Iceland

on the south coast at the foot of the great Vatna glacier, while
Leif went much further to the west along this same stretch of
coast before he found a suitable place to live ; but at last he
made his choice and built two large houses on the selected site.

Before his departure from Norway Ingolf had duly sacrificed
to the gods, and upon sighting Iceland, determined that the
gods should direct him to his home, he had cast the pillars of
his high-seat, whereon their sacred figures were carved, into
the sea, vowing that wheresoever they came to shore there would
he take up his abode. But Leif, perhaps because he had learnt
something of Christianity in Ireland, would not sacrifice before

he sailed to the new country, nor, when he came there, would he allow the pillars with their heathen carvings to decide for him where he should live.   And miserable, therefore, was his fate, for in the spring after his arrival he and his companions were treacherously murdered by the Irish slaves in their party who subsequently fled to some neighbouring islands with the Norse women and what possessions they could lay hands upon. Some of Ingolf's men, during their search along the coast for the missing pillars, came upon Leif and his men lying dead, and Ingolf, who was brought to the scene of the tragedy, after moralizing upon the horrible fate of those who would not sacrifice to the gods, buried his unfortunate countrymen and took their ship ; then he went in search of the slaves and put them to death.   The islands where he found them are the beautiful and steep-cliffed Vestmannaeyjar, and they are so called because the Celtic slaves were known as *Vestmenn*, men from the West.

Ingolf took into his care the women who had been carried off and spent the winter at Leif's settlement.   In the following year he sailed westwards along the coast and in the spring of

INGOLF   875 his pillars were found far away in Faxafjord on
ARNARSON the south-west coast.   And here this pious heathen
AT REY- made his permanent dwelling, calling the place,
KJAVIK   because of the steamy hot-springs there, Reykjavik
875   (smoky creek).   So came the first colonist to that
lovely bay where on a low and grassy isthmus now stands the capital of Iceland.

Iceland, when Ingolf Arnarson arrived in the van of the Norse colonists, was not entirely uninhabited, for there were a few Irishmen living there, chiefly in the south-east of the country,

IRISH   hermits whom the vikings called *papar*, that is priests,
HERMITS because of the white gowns that they wore.   This
THE FIRST was the Thule of the Irish monk Dicuil who, in A.D.
INHABI- 825, recorded that some thirty years before he wrote
TANTS OF a number of Irish clerics had spent a summer there.
ICELAND
Celtic anchorites, too, said Dicuil, had lived in the Faroe Islands for a hundred years past, and he tells how one of these had made the voyage thither in a two-oared boat, taking only two summer days and a night for the journey.

Perhaps it was the Norse raids upon the religious houses of Ireland that had driven these pious men from Erin, sending them first to the Scottish islands, where also came the vikings, and then north to the Faroes, where for a while they found peace, and then north again to Iceland.   But whatever impelled them to go thus far abroad, and withholding nothing of the respect properly due to the Norse as navigators of unknown seas, there surely can have been few more remarkable voyages in the whole history of European seamanship than these amazing journeys of the Irish anchorites who, in frail little boats and with the aid of no stalwart warrior crew, sought these far-away empty lands of the north, there in loneliness and quiet to worship Almighty God.

But the advent of the vikings even to their Thule drove them forth again. They would not live among the heathen, says Ari the Learned (not telling whether these heathen would allow their further sojourn), and soon sailed away, leaving behind them (such is his charitable expression) Irish books, bells, and croziers that proved the country of their origin. There is also mention of the *papar* in the Icelandic *Landnámabók*, where, besides recording [1] how these books and other relics were found in Papey and Papýli,[2] it is told how the *papar* had dwelt at a certain homestead known as Kirkjubaer in Sida in the south of the country ; no heathen man thereafter could live upon this hallowed place and it was not inhabited again until the coming of the Christian viking Ketil Fíflski from the Hebrides. Subsequently, when all Iceland was Christian, it became the site of a nunnery.

The *landnáma* period of Icelandic history, the time of the settlement, the *taking up of the land*, by the early colonists, occupies a space of some sixty years following upon the coming LANDNÁMA of Ingolf Arnarson. And nowhere else in the world PERIOD is there so complete a record of the first peopling of 870–930 a country in ancient times, for the tale of it is fully told in the *Landnámabók*, set down in writing in the thirteenth century, wherein are preserved the names of some 400 of the original chieftain-settlers, together with those of over 2,500 other inhabitants. At the close of the *landnáma* time, that is about A.D. 930, there must have been, on the showing of the book and the sagas of early Iceland, a population in the new colony of not less than 20,000 souls, perhaps even half as many again.

[1] But in one MS. only.

[2] This name is *papa-býli*, priest's dwelling, but the place itself has not been identified ; the island of Papey is on the east coast and there are said to be ruins of Irish religious cells upon it. The element *papa* (the same word as the Greek παππάς, Latin *papa*, the O. Slav. ПОПЪ, and our *pope*) is to be found in other Icelandic place-names such as Papos, Papafjord, and Papavik; it also occurs in the Orkneys and Shetlands, e.g. Papa Stour, Papilwater, etc.

It is little likely that colonization on such a scale, so eager a rush to take land in the recently discovered island, could be due solely to the emigration of the truculent and exasperated chiefs who hated the harsh rule of Harald Fairhair. CAUSES OF THE EMI-GRATION TO ICE-LAND Yet this the Icelandic historian, Snorri Sturlason, alleges to have been the chief cause of the flocking of the Norwegian folk to Iceland, saying that after the battle in Hafrsfjord Harald laid all Norway under him and that those who would not submit to him fled to the Faroes and to Iceland and to the Scottish Isles, or to the remote and sparsely populated districts of their own country. Certainly some of the early settlers, in rebellion against Harald, chose a voluntary exile in Iceland rather than remain in a Norway no longer safe for them. Ketil Haeng was one ; he migrated in the *landnáma* time with his wife and son because he was guilty of the murder of friends of King Harald ; Kveldulf and his son Skalla-Grim were likewise at feud with the king ; Thorolf Örnolfsson, Geirmund Heljarskinn, and many another of the Icelandic colonists had also incurred his displeasure ; moreover, Harald's violent attack upon the vikings of the Scottish islands undoubtedly drove forth many of these already exiled folk to seek a new home in the great island of the north. But all this, much though it impressed Snorri, is not to say that Harald's conquest of western Norway and his expedition to the islands of the west were more than contributory causes of the great outpouring of the Norwegians into Iceland.[1] Ingimund the Old, another early colonist, had fought at Hafrsfjord on the king's side, and yet another, Hrollaug, son of Harald's good friend, Ragnvald Möre-jarl, made his home in Iceland at the suggestion of the king himself. So that not mere hostility to Harald, but some greater impulse was the cause of this notable emigration of the vikings. This was, in its practical expression for the Norse emigrants to Iceland, the wellnigh irresistible appeal of large estates, easily to be taken and free from all complications and restrictions of inherited tenures, in a land where each man was as good as his neighbour and none was lord ; but in its larger setting the peopling of Iceland must be nothing

[1] This subject has been debated again recently ; for a summary of the arguments, see Johan Schreiner (who believes that Harald's harsh rule *was* the cause of the emigration), *Historisk Tidsskrift*, XXVIII (1928), p. 190. Note that Professors Finnur Jónsson and Halvdan Koht take the opposite view, and that if Hafrsfjord can be post-dated to the '90s, as Professor Koht believes, it is clear that the emigration to Iceland must have begun nearly twenty years before the decisive battle that brought all Norway under his strong arm.

but a single aspect of that unrest, that longing for a freedom and a wealth greater than their own poor countries could offer, that for a hundred years past had sent the men of the north exploring and plundering west-over-sea and east-over-sea, had fired them to the winning of lands abroad in the hostile kingdoms of the Celt and the Englishman and the Frank and in the country of the Slavs, and had made their name to be feared on every coast in Christendom.

Familiar to the readers of the sagas are many of the names of the first Icelandic settlers. There was Skalla-Grim whose son, the great poet Egil, is hero of one of the best-known Icelandic tales ; there was the family of old Ketil Flatneb (p. 304), the governor of the Hebrides, including Aud the Deepminded, his daughter, who was the widow of King Olaf of Dublin and subsequently the founder of a noble Icelandic family. There was Thorolf Mostrarskegg (Mostr-beard), the devout servant of Thor, exiled by Harald because he had harboured Ketil's son Björn the Easterner. There was Önund Tree-foot (p. 305), who had lost a leg at Hafrsfjord, from whom is descended Grettir Asmundarson, hero of the finest saga of them all. Also there was the widow Asgerd, who with her children and her brother took land in Iceland and whose son, Thorgeir, was the father of wise old Njal of Bergthorshvoll, the noble and tragic Burnt Njal of the famous saga. And many others there were whose names and deeds are told in the naive and enchanting literature of Iceland.

What Harald thought of the new-born colony where so many of his enemies now dwelt in security history does not reveal. He deplored, beyond a doubt, the loss to his own kingdom of so many members of the aristocracy with their retinues, and he attempted to stop the wholesale emigration to Iceland that was draining Norway ; but his decree of prohibition was soon altered into a demand for a tax from all who journeyed thither. He must have believed himself, whether formally acknowledged or not, the legitimate overlord of Iceland, and once he sent Uni, son of Gardar, the discoverer of the country, to bring the island under the king's direct authority, promising him a jarldom if he succeeded. But the Icelanders boycotted Uni and he accomplished nothing. On another occasion Harald made a show of his supposed power over the colony, for upon hearing the complaints of later emigrants that the original settlers had taken to themselves too large a share of the land, he decreed that no one should possess more land in Iceland than he and his ship's crew could circumambulate in a day. Whether he was obeyed, or by what means he intended to enforce this ruling, are alike unknown, and it may be that this order was but a gesture on his part to secure the adherence of at least the later emigrants inasmuch as the king must have known that he had not many loyal subjects among the early settlers. But what mattered most of all to Harald was that during the *landnáma* period the Icelanders were much too busily employed in developing their new land, and much too far off, to return, as did the Scottish vikings, to harry their mother-country ; therefore Norway and Iceland lived at peace, Harald recognizing the hopelessness of controlling, or interfering more than occasionally with, the government of this remote and contented island.

But it was not long before the Icelanders found that the business of the government of their own country was no easy task. The island is large, the little settlements were scattered far apart, and communication between them was slow ; moreover, the folk of these settlements were not inclined to submit to any authority other than that of their local chieftain, for these landholders were most of them of equal rank and none might consider himself by virtue of birth or station as entitled to a supreme power.

Yet for the purposes of a rough-and-ready local administration of justice, these colonists had quickly formed themselves into *godords*, confederacies of neighbouring estates loosely knit together under the leadership of the foremost resident,
GODI AND GODORDS a chieftain who had assumed the office of *godi*, that is priest of the temple. By common consent this godi was first among the landowners around, though his powers were ill-defined and his official dignity but small ; nevertheless he conducted the ceremonies at the temple and this, since in most instances it was he who had built the temple and who maintained it, meant that his priestly office was but the sign of his wealth and importance. So he also presided over the thing, or folk-moot, of the district and appointed the judges who were to try the cases brought before it.

The problem, then, was to unite these godords by some lasting and respectable political bond, since the chaos resulting from the independence of such small communities was soon distressing the land. For although there were localized attempts to set up hundred-things as a court of appeal for the members of a group of godords, there was no uniform action on these lines, and so long as a common code of law was wanting disputes between members of different godords meant a quarrel that usually ended in war. Men might desert from one godord to another and those sufficiently powerful might fearlessly make their own strong arm the law, so that in the bitter feuds that followed such flouting of authority the arbitration of a merely local thing counted for nothing. But more serious still, matters concerning the public welfare of the whole colony had to be neglected since there was no popular assembly of the island where they could be debated.

To the more public-spirited and thoughtful of the godar it was soon plain that if there was to be order and justice at all only a national assembly could ensure a reasonable measure of respect for the simple laws and ordinances that were sufficient to secure this end. And among these godar was one Ulfljot, originally from Hordaland in Norway, to whom, more than to any other, is due the foundation of that celebrated FOUNDA- parliament, a thousand years old in 1930, that is TION known as the Althing. For upon his suggestion, and OF THE with the approval of his fellows, he journeyed back ALTHING to Norway there most diligently to study the constitutions and legal codes of the different assemblies of his mother-country ; three years he devoted to this task, most of all in the Gula-thing (p. 104), and this done, he returned to Iceland, prepared to frame a code of laws and, more important, having formulated the principles of a constitution for the future republic. This, in its simplest outline, involved the convocation of a national assembly, the Althing, to meet annually for two weeks in the summer and to be attended by all the godar and freeholders, though its powers were to be exercised by an inner body, the *lögrétta*, or legislative council, formed of forty-eight godar, representing the four Quarters of the island, and ninety-six others. This was to be possessed of complete power within its own sphere and was to act without the general sanction of the whole assembly ; but as head of this and director of procedure Ulfljot recommended the election of a *lögsögumaðr*, or lawspeaker, who was to preside over the *lögrétta*, proclaim the new laws from the *lögberg*, the law-mount, and whose duty it also should be to recite to the people the whole of the law in the course of three years.

While Ulfljot was in Norway his foster-brother Grim Geitskor was commissioned to explore the whole island in order to discover a suitable meeting-place for an assembly of the kind that was contemplated ; the Icelanders were asked to pay him a penny per man for undertaking this task, but Grim would not take this money for himself and preferred that the sum collected should be given to the temple that was later to be built upon

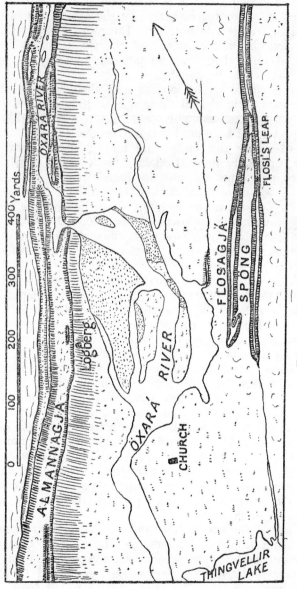

Fig. 37.—Plan of Thingvellir

the chosen place of assembly. And well, indeed, did he perform his search, for the site he chose at last, some 30 miles to the east of Reykjavik, takes high rank among the noblest pilgrimage-places of the world ; *Thingvellir*, Plain of the Thing, THING-VELLIR is a five-mile-long level greenness that is ribboned by the white waters of the many-channelled Öxará and seamed suddenly by the grey lava-ridge, the Spöng, where through steep-sided ravines the narrow rivers pass on their journey to the huge Thingvalla lake. Here, on the western boundary of the plain, rises a dark and frowning wall of rock, 100 feet in height, that overhangs a long and deep rift, the *Almannagjá*, Cleft of all Men, and from the 50-foot high eastern cliff of this an abrupt grassy slope descends to the plain, a slope that was to be the meeting-place of the Althing. At its top was *lögberg*, or law-mount, and arrayed at its foot the *lögrétta* was to sit in debate, while in the *Almannagjá*, on the plain below, and on the eastern lava-ridge in the plain, there was room for the booths of the thingmen, their families and attendants, room for the contests and races of the multitude, and room for all the excitements and activities of a thronged and lively national fête.[1]

Such, then, was the theatre chosen, a fair plain with the boundary of towering cliffs, and there in A.D. 930 for the first time met the Althing, the grand assize of Iceland. And there the Althing continued to meet year after year almost without interruption until 1798.

The initial success of the newly constituted gathering, however, depended not so much upon its effectiveness as an instrument of government as upon its social usefulness. It became, in fact, a joyous and eagerly awaited assembly of the whole nation, for, there being as yet no town life, no capital of the THE AL-THING AT WORK country, this annual union of legislators, judges, and litigants, was attended by all classes of people, including merchants and marketers, athletes and entertainers, so that Thingvellir during the two summer weeks of the meeting became the temporary and crowded capital of Iceland.

[1] From the point of view of acoustics and comfort there is much to be said for Mr. Eggert Briem's notion that *lögberg* was a little to the west of the position as marked on the map (Fig. 37) and that the assembly sat not on the steep slope facing up-hill but in the Almannagjá itself. For an account of the topography of Thingvellir see Matthías Thórdarson, *Fornleifar á Thingvelli*, Reykjavik, 1922. As to the booths, it should be noted that most of the foundations now to be seen are those of eighteenth century structures ; but it is believed that the foundations known as Byrgi's Booth on Spöng and Snorri's booth near *lögberg* may date back to the saga-period.

But from the point of view of efficient government it was soon plain that the Althing, in spite of Ulfljot's excellent intentions, was not going to be all that men had hoped of it. And the cause of its failure in this respect was simply that the aristocratic oligarchy of the godar, functioning through this primitive parliament, was provided with no adequate executive power. However perfect was the machinery of debate, of the promulgation of laws, of trial and of the declaration of judgements, this was of little avail without a sufficient power to ensure its smooth working ; for the godar, though they might act in assembly as the state, had no armed force at their disposal, no police or government agents, to enforce the observance of the laws they made or to compel the performance of the sentences they passed. They trusted to the goodwill of the people, and though this was not always failing, there was in some respects little improvement upon the lawlessness of the old days when justice could be obtained only at a local court. Violent disputes, bloodshed even, took place before the judges of the Althing and its decrees could be, and often were, safely disregarded by any powerful chieftain who had armed followers at his call.

The difficult and peculiar conditions of social life in Iceland seem to have made it impossible to remedy this disastrous weakness in the government of the Free State and the various attempts that were made to strengthen the authority of the Althing were reforms of the judicial system, for it was this that was the chief source of the troubles that arose. Thus in 965 the four Quarters of the country were each represented by their own court at the Althing, and about 1004 there was added a fifth and supreme tribunal as an ultimate court of appeal. But the main mischief, the lack of executive power, was never remedied, and it was this in the end that caused the downfall of the commonwealth as an independent state.

The institution of the Althing in A.D. 930 is, as is natural, the principal event in early Icelandic history, but another notable landmark is the adoption by the Althing in the year A.D. 1000 of Christianity as the religion of the commonwealth. INTRODUC- There had, of course, been Christians of a kind among TION OF the first Norse settlers, such as Aud the Deepminded, CHRISTI- ANITY who had come to Iceland from the colonies in the Celtic lands, and Örlyg Hrappsson, brought up by Bishop Patrick of the Hebrides, who was given by this prelate when Örlyg went to Iceland timber, a bell, a gospel, and consecrated soil, in order that he might build a church there. But the tale goes that these few Christians wore their faith but lightly and

PLATE X

THE LÖGBERG, THINGVELLIR, ICELAND

VIEW FROM THE LÖGBERG OVER THINGVELLIR

that upon their death the paganism of their forefathers triumphed in their families, so that Landnámabók can record how for a period of about a hundred years the country was entirely heathen. Yet it may be that there was more Christianity in Iceland in these early days than Landnámabók will allow,[1] for certainly many Icelanders abroad, whether soldiers of fortune or traders, found it profitable to be baptized ; 'such were the brothers Egil and Thorolf Skallagrimsson who accepted Christianity in England, and Gisli Sursson and his two companions who became Christians at Viborg. Nor was missionary endeavour wholly lacking, for the Irish, whose holy *papar* had first found Iceland, did not forget the northern isle, and one Asolf Alskik, who was of mixed Norse and Irish descent, journeyed to Iceland with twelve Irish monks ; but he made no converts and died as a hermit, though later generations of Icelanders venerated him as a saint.

EARLY MISSION-ARIES: ASOLF ALSKIK

But another missionary was more successful, baptizing many folk and disturbing the trust of the islanders in their ancient gods. This was Thorvald Kodransson, Iceland-born but a great traveller, who returned in the year 981 to the land of his birth in the company of the Saxon bishop who had baptized him. There, because the bishop had no Norse, Thorvald himself preached the new faith, persuading many Icelanders to receive baptism. For four years these missionaries laboured, but in the end their good works proved to be their undoing, for so indifferent towards the old gods did some of their hearers become that they no longer paid the accustomed temple dues, and this earned for Thorvald and the bishop the uncompromising enmity of the older and more conservative of the godar and chief men. At last, in 984, when Thorvald dared to preach Christianity at the Althing, there was serious trouble, and the end of it all was that in 986 the missionaries found themselves compelled to leave Iceland. Thorvald himself set out upon his journeys again ; far and wide he travelled, and finally this first Icelandic evangelist died as a monk in Russia.

THORVALD KODRANS-SON

Ten years later came the next missionary to Iceland; but the bitterness of the chieftains against Christianity was not yet allayed, and though some of the folk had not forgotten Thorvald's teaching, the newcomer was received but coldly and his robust methods speedily made the faith he had come to spread more unpopular than before. His name was Stefni

[1] On this subject, see Dr. Jón Helgason, *Islands Kirke*, Copenhagen, 1925, p. 17 ff.

Thorgilsson and he was a great-great-grandson of Ketil Flatneb;
STEFNI   like Thorvald he was Iceland-born, but he had been
THORGILS- baptized in Denmark and now came as a missionary
SON   from the court of Olaf Tryggvason. At once he
began a crusade against heathendom in Iceland such as that
pugnacious proselyte, his royal master, would have lovingly
approved, for when he found that little heed was paid to his
preaching he employed rougher methods to overthrow paganism,
breaking the images of the gods and defacing and destroying
the temples. This was more than the Icelanders, even those
who might have listened sympathetically to the new doctrines,
could endure, and at the meeting of the Althing in the year
after Stefni's arrival a law was passed authorizing relatives of a
Christian to take legal action against the blasphemer of the
gods and thus rid their family of disgrace, a law sounding as
though it heralded the beginning of a fierce and organized state
resistance against the Christian faith, but in reality engineered
against Stefni who was at once summoned by four of his kin.
The result was that he was promptly outlawed and expelled.

But Olaf Tryggvason, already encouraged by the conversion
of a few Icelanders travelling in Norway, had by this time made
up his mind that, even though he had no temporal authority
over Iceland, he would at any rate ensure the spiritual salvation
of those scions of the Norwegian stock who dwelt there ; so,
when Stefni returned having accomplished nothing, the king
         forthwith sent Thangbrand to preach Christianity in
THANG-   the far-away island. This new missionary was a
BRAND   truculent German robber who had once been in high
favour with Olaf but was now in disgrace as a result of the frauds
and piracy he had committed after being installed as priest on
the island of Mostr in Norway ; yet, like Stefni, he was a fearless
and determined man such as the king loved and well suited for
the enterprise, Olaf believing that force rather than gentleness
was essential for the conversion of a reluctant and godless people.
As punishment for his offences, therefore, Thangbrand went to
Iceland.

At first he did badly, but he soon made an important convert, Sidu-Hall, the chieftain of Thvotta, by whom he was most
hospitably entertained, and after this he was successful in winning
over a number of influential men, including wise old Njal of
Bergthorshvoll, who had already foreseen the ultimate triumph
of Christianity, so that the new faith began steadily to gain
ground. But although Icelanders returning from Norway could
vouch for the advantages of adopting the royal and official

religion of the mother-country, there was still much of the old opposition to the Christian doctrines, and the violent and quarrelsome missionary was speedily involved in various unpleasant brawls that often ended in bloodshed. The result was that when the Althing assembled in 998, though the Christians in the state were by this time strong in numbers, Thangbrand was prosecuted by his enemies and only escaped with his life because Njal saved him from the relatives of the men he had slain. He remained in the country, nevertheless, for another year and then escaped to Norway in A.D. 999.

Olaf was seriously angry at the apparent failure of his second missionary and in his wrath he ordered some heathen Icelanders whose boats had lately arrived at Nidaros to be seized and put to death ; but it happened that at this time there were several other influential Icelanders, who were Christians, in Norway and these worthies prayed for the release of their countrymen, promising not only that these men should receive baptism but also that they themselves would see to it that Christianity was adopted as the official religion of their land. GIZUR So in the year A.D. 1000 two of them, Gizur the White AND and his son-in-law Hjalti Skeggjason, returned home HJALTI with the express intention of inviting the Althing SKEGGJA- to sanction a general change of faith. The meeting SON was about to assemble when they arrived and there was no time for diplomacy ; the heathens in the state threatened resistance and it seemed as though there would be an ugly conflict between the two parties ; but the Christians showed themselves plainly as ready to take up arms and at length it was agreed that a fair hearing should be given to the newly arrived spokesmen. On Sunday the 23rd of June a priest was allowed to celebrate mass and afterwards the Christians, with their clergy vested and with two crosses held aloft, moved in procession to *lögberg*, the law-mount, whence the sweet odour of their incense stole down upon the assembled folk of Iceland as Gizur and Hjalti began to explain their mission.

It was a strange thing that Hjalti, who had been sentenced to banishment at the Althing of the previous year, should have been heard unchallenged, and, in truth, it seems that the more AT THE thoughtful of the heathen godar were at last beginning ALTHING to realize the hopelessness of opposing the new religion. A.D. 1000 They knew that Christianity had already found favour in Norway, where it was now the state religion, and that the folk of the Celtic lands, and most of the Norsemen dwelling there, had long been Christian, while on the Continent Christianity, as they were aware, was the age-old and unchallenged faith of all men ; to remain heathen, therefore, was to run the risk of a spiritual isolation that could not fail to be attended by the most serious political and economic disadvantages. For behind the mission of Gizur and Hjalti there was unmistakably the sanction of Olaf Tryggvason's might, and this for a country so dependent as was Iceland upon the goodwill of Norwegian traders was formidable indeed. Moreover, apart from the danger of a boycott by merchants from the now Christian lands of Norway and Britain, it was no longer possible to ignore the disturbing fact that already the new faith was threatening to break asunder the government in Iceland, for already no less than nine of the godar had received baptism and were thereby disqualified from fulfilling their duties at the things and courts where heathen oaths and customs were the rule ; indeed, with the steady growth of the number of converts there had arisen a movement on the part of the Christians to set up a general thing of their own. No man doubted, then, the utmost gravity of the situation on this June Sunday in the year 1000, and there was good reason for the heathen party to grant to Olaf's two ambassadors, Icelanders like themselves, at least full freedom of speech.

In the fierce and anxious debate that followed Sidu-Hall, the Christian, and Thorgeir, a heathen godi, were the spokesmen of the rival parties ; but Thorgeir was one of those who realized the fundamental importance of safeguarding the constitution of Iceland from disruption by the establishment of an independent Christian thing, and all his counsel was directed to this end. His word it must have been that finally, on the 24th of June, persuaded the heathen folk that it was wisest to yield to Olaf's wishes at any rate in the letter, if not in the spirit, for the result of the long argument was an agreement that, though sounding as a noble triumph for Christianity, was in effect nothing but a compromise. The new faith was adopted as the official religion of Iceland, the heathens were one and all to be baptized, temples and images were to be destroyed, and open worship of the old gods was forbidden ; but it was clear enough that there was neither clergy nor state machinery to enforce these changes and no rule was made forbidding the heathen to worship in private according to their ancient faith, while the continuance in secret of certain heathen practices, such as the exposing of children and the eating of horse-flesh, were expressly sanctioned. In becoming a Christian state, then, Iceland had avoided the chaos that was threatened by the secession of the Christian party from the Althing and had cemented her friendship with the mother-country of Norway. But that she had instantly and at one stroke changed the hearts of all her children no man believed.

King Olaf Tryggvason died at the battle of Svold in this same year and the Icelanders were left alone with this artificial and imperfectly understood Christianity until such time as their continued heathen practices began to create scandal abroad.

FURTHER LEGIS- LATION AGAINST HEATHEN- DOM 1016 Then in 1016, the year that he came to the throne, King Olaf the Saint intervened, calling upon the law-speaker of the Althing to introduce legislation against the offending heathen customs, and when the necessary laws had been passed Saint Olaf was so pleased that he sent to Iceland timber for the building of a church upon Thingvellir and a bell for this church; also he sent an English priest, Bishop Bernard Vilradsson, to tend this neglected community.

The first bishop dwelt in Iceland for five years and was then succeeded by a Norwegian; the third bishop was an Englishman again, Rudolf, who, after nineteen years in Iceland, returned to EARLY BISHOPS England to become Abbot of Abingdon. But little is known of the work of these early prelates in the north and it is unlikely that they, foreigners labouring under most difficult conditions in a land where churches and priests were few, could do more than urge the formal observance of the Christian sacraments upon those pagans-at-heart who were now legally bound to live according to the Church's teaching. Only among the followings of a few of the chieftains with whom the bishops associated frequently did the new faith find its outward expression in a godly behaviour such as the continental Church would approve, and only there, if anywhere at all in Iceland, did the doctrines of Christianity comfort and enlighten the soul.

But ecclesiastical administration was made easier by the appointment in 1056 of Isleif, son of Gizur the White, as bishop, for a native had advantages in the matters of language and authority that were denied to the foreign prelates. Isleif had ISLEIF GIZURAR- SON been ordained in Germany and had then returned to Iceland where eventually he succeeded his father as godi of the little church of Skalholt; his learning and ability much impressed his countrymen and it was at their request that he went abroad to beg from the Emperor Henry III and from the Pope an appointment as bishop of Iceland. At Whitsuntide of 1056 he was consecrated to this office by Archbishop Adalbert of Bremen and in 1057 he went back to Iceland, there to take up his residence once more at Skalholt. One of his first cares was to establish a school for the training of clergy chosen from among the Icelanders, and by so doing he laid the foundations of a national church in Iceland.

He died in 1080, having been bishop for twenty-four years, and two years later he was succeeded by his son, Gizur, who is justly honoured as the greatest of the early churchmen of the island. In Gizur's day, for the first time, the Church in Iceland GIZUR was administered as a single disciplined body ; the ISLEIFS- chieftains who elected him were made to promise a SON full obedience to his ecclesiastical jurisdiction ; Skalholt was permanently endowed as a seat for himself and his successors ; a system of tithes was introduced, thus giving the Church a fixed revenue, and the better management of the great diocese was ensured by its division into two, Jon Ögmundsson, a pupil of his father's school, being installed as bishop of a new northern diocese of Holar. Gizur Isleifsson, therefore, is a noble figure in Icelandic history, one of those rare political princes of the Church whose temporal power was no less than their spiritual authority. There was peace in his time, a peace so secure that it was no longer necessary for men to walk armed, and Ari the Learned wrote of Gizur that he was more honoured by his countrymen than any other man known to have lived in Iceland.

When, amid the universal sorrow of his people, the great bishop was laid to rest in the year 1118 the Icelandic Church was already a stable body, and it needed only the passage of a special code of ecclesiastical laws by the Althing in 1125 to confirm the authority of this Church as a national institution. But that the development of the ecclesiastical machinery outraced the spiritual education of the Icelandic congregations is certain, and it is improbable that, even in Gizur's day, Christianity had laid anything but the lightest hold upon the hearts of the common folk. That this was still so must perhaps be explained as chiefly the fault of the priests, for these were men always much more occupied with secular affairs, their estate-management and their trading, than with the cure of souls, and though among them were numbered such dignified and responsible persons as Ari Thorgilsson the Learned (1067–1148) and Saemund Sigfusson the Wise (1056–1133), the brawls and violences of others are sufficient to show how poor a thing must have been the spiritual leadership of some of the clergy, even if they were, as occasionally happened, chieftains with considerable temporal power. The establishment of a national Icelandic Church, in a word, is an event of the early saga-history of the

country, but many centuries were yet to pass, all the courage,
patience, and example of the Catholic Church were required,
before the agnosticism and indifference of the Icelander was at
last changed into a real and lively Christian faith.

The two centuries following upon the creation of the Althing,
the first popularly known as the Saga Period and the second as
the Peace Period, together form the grandest and most famous
epoch in Icelandic history ; yet it was an epoch that
SAGA
PERIOD was prelude to one of rapid decline and ultimate
(930–1030) collapse. But the domestic politics of early Iceland,
AND PEACE whether they be of state or of Church, are the small
PERIOD concerns of a lonely and primitive community, and
though the failure of the Icelandic experiment in self-government
most deservedly possesses much interest for the student of
constitutional history, in this book, where all the viking world
is under survey, the further story of the remote colony must
be compressed into a few words.

But there remain two things still to be told of Iceland in the
famous days of the Saga and Peace Periods, the one a brief
mention of the activities of Icelanders abroad and the second a
reference to the literature that Iceland has given to the world.
On the first score it is sufficient to state simply that in spite
of the geographical remoteness of their country the Icelanders
never held themselves aloof from the world, for always the
spirit of adventure burned strong within them.   Greenland they
found and in Greenland some of their number established a
colony ; others of them made the long and perilous journey to
Wineland the Good, a lovely country in North America.   In
Norway Icelanders were ever to be found, for many of them
had kin, or owned estates, in this their mother-country, while
some, even, had been appointed officials of the royal court.
Travellers from Iceland journeyed all over the viking lands from
Scotland to Constantinople.   In Ireland and the Western Isles
were they known ; there were Icelanders taking part in the
battle of Clontarf ; with Cnut when he won England there were
Icelandic poets ; with Æthelstan at Brunanburh there were
Icelanders, Egil Skallagrimsson, his brother, and their company ;
there were Icelanders with Harald Hardradi in the Balkans
and in the Mediterranean ; there were Icelanders in the Varangian guard of the Greek emperor ; with King Sigurd on the
crusades there were Icelandic poets who made verses by the
waters of Jordan.

Yet however valorous and exciting were the adventures of
the Icelanders abroad, however interesting the domestic history

of the colony may be, that which is most wonderful in the story of early Iceland is assuredly the fact that from this lonely country a great literature was given to the world. For from Iceland comes the precious legacy of the sagas.

Not that the saga itself, a narrative in prose, was an Icelandic invention, for the telling of these tales was the common pastime of the unlettered world, German and Celtic, European and THE Asiatic ; but the Icelandic saga, by the time it was ICELANDIC set down in writing, was something more than a SAGAS familiar and often repeated tale such as the other German peoples told ; it was a narrative constructed according to a peculiar literary convention, a special treatment of which the Icelander alone had won the secret.

Perhaps the very remoteness of the island was the cause of this remarkable development in the art of saga-telling here in the distant north. For the chieftains, now isolated from their Norwegian kin, were interested not only in local affairs, but in their own aristocratic traditions, and, furthermore, they were avid for news from Norway and the Continent, so that the three needs of preserving genealogical data, of familiarizing themselves with life and politics abroad, and of maintaining a consistent record of past and present Icelandic history, could be best met by the single expedient of combining the necessary information into a saga that was to be learnt by heart and repeated down the ages. There was, therefore, a practical incentive for the composition of these sagas, one that was distinct from that other impelling motive, the wholesome and childish love of all the folk to be entertained by the telling of a tale.

Usually there was some notable central theme throughout the saga, such as the biographies of a family and their neighbours, but a long and rambling tale it was, burdened with tedious tables of descent, and elaborated with accounts of journeys abroad and every discursion and irrelevancy that could possibly be deemed of interest to the listeners. Clearly a story thus encumbered cannot be the highest form of prose narrative, yet this tiresome flavour of the journal or historical record is almost the only fault of the Icelandic saga, and it would be an injustice to a noble literature not to say at once and without hesitation that the typical saga is nevertheless a composition in narrative style that for simplicity and beauty, for honesty, for humour and sympathy, has seldom been surpassed. All the drama, be it comedy or tragedy, in the lives of the central characters is mirrored with a faithfulness and an understanding that both amazes and enthralls, and with a tenderness and a directness

that has won for these simple northern folk the no uncertain
honour of immortality. For Njal, Egil, Grettir, Gisli, and the
rest, will live so long as men love a fine story bravely told.

The popularity of saga-telling at the things and festivals
and during the long winter evenings in the home, and the high
esteem in which a clever narrator was held, are sufficient to
explain the rapid growth of these Icelandic oral records into a
very large collection of stories that formed the material of which
the written sagas are composed. For the sagas in their present
form are hardly likely to have been copied exactly from the
traditional oral version ; instead they bear in most instances the
stamp of the author's art, being a carefully edited collation of
the current stories. This, at any rate, is how the early histories
such as Ari the Learned's *Íslendingabók*, written in the beginning
of the twelfth century, must have been composed, and it was
certainly the method of the more pretentious written sagas of
the thirteenth century like those of Njal and Egil, only a very
few historical stories such as Hrafnkel's seeming to be free of
the author's manipulation and representing the oral tradition
in a narrative that is little changed. For this reason the crucial
question as to how much of the sagas in their present form can
be accepted as exact history is one that only rarely can be
answered with any confidence and that demands for the answer-
ing a most delicate and critical judgement. Certainly it is not
hard to find instances of what must be deliberate fiction or of
the insertion of obviously supernatural occurrences in many of
the stories, while in others the inaccuracies of certain facts can
be plainly proved, and from this it follows that no saga can be
accepted at its face value as an entirely truthful tale. Some—
Grettir's saga is an example—cannot at the best be ranked in
this respect as better than a tale that is based on history, and
in these stories realism and wealth of detail must be credited to
literary skill rather than to the long memory of tradition. Yet,
on the whole, it may be asserted with some confidence that
Scandinavian and Icelandic studies are more likely to suffer
from an over-hasty denial of saga-evidence than by too great
a trust in its historical value.

But here it is as literature that the saga is above all to be
commended, and under this heading those that most deserve
the attention of the reader are the tales of the Icelanders themselves, such as that of the Laxdale Men or of the Ere Dwellers,
or that of Egil Skallagrimsson, or that (perhaps best of all) of
Njal, or (another masterpiece) that of the morose and sarcastic
giant Grettir whose death as a hunted and pitiful outlaw on

Drangey is related with a stark and savage simplicity that has made of this awful climax one of the most remarkable and moving examples of the saga-teller's art. Such sagas as these do not, of course, represent the whole scope of early Icelandic literature ; for there are the great histories, such as the noble *Heimskringla* of Snorri Sturlason, and there are besides many duller works, of both local and foreign interest, and also tales of the heroic age, to say nothing of certain late fictitious compositions or of mere translations of continental mediaeval romances and legends. But it is in the tales of the Icelanders, fortunately a large and lovely series, that the art of the native story-teller is seen at its best ; for here, in describing his own folk, the narrator's uncanny gift of effortless yet vivid presentation of character brings an added life and zest to the story he has to tell. It may be true that for the most part these sagas of Iceland are made up of the grim stuff of tragedy, but wit and humour are in no wise lacking, and of the whole great body of these tales, all of them written down in unadorned and simple prose, it may be truly said that their naive Icelandic authors have made a rich and memorable contribution to the literature of Europe.[1]

The dismal affairs of Iceland in the years following the Peace Period, the brave days of Bishop Gizur, need only short mention here. It has already been said that the Althing lacked executive power and that it depended for its successful functioning upon the goodwill and loyalty of the chieftains whose united godords formed the state ; it follows then that the warring of these chieftains, or the too great power of any one of them, would quickly put an end to the authority of the courts, and it was, indeed, the quarrels between the godar and the contempt of the DECLINE   victors for constitutional government that brought OF THE   the existence of the Free State to an end.   The period FREE   of the decline begins shortly after the death of Bishop STATE   Gizur (1118), for then it was that these quarrels first became serious, and though perhaps in the beginning they did not seem likely to shake the foundations of Icelandic society, yet they rapidly assumed the alarming characteristics not merely of family feud but of civil strife. Especially in the first half of the thirteenth century was Iceland torn by civil war, for this was the time when the Sturlungs, the kin of the great chieftain

[1] When I wrote this chapter I included some short extracts from English translations of the sagas, but I have since omitted them as the inexperienced reader anxious for a first taste of saga literature can now turn to an excellent little book that has recently been published ; this is *The Northern Saga*, by E. E. Kellett (London, 1929).

and historian Snorri Sturlason, had grasped so large a power and so dominated Icelandic affairs that the period and its horrible wars are named after them. The long struggle between Snorri and his brother Sighvat and Sturla Sighvatsson, with its many battles, ended, after a temporary triumph that left Sturla supreme in Iceland, in the defeat and death of Sighvat and Sturla at the battle of Örlygsstadir in the year A.D. 1235 where an army of 1,680 men had collected to overthrow these ambitious and dangerous chiefs. Whereupon Snorri, who had previously fled to Norway, returned to Iceland; but now another chieftain, Gizur Thorvaldsson, was his rival for the supremacy among the godar, and by the hands of this man's assassins Snorri was slain in 1241. *Sturlungasaga*, the story of these factions and conspiracies, is a tale of Iceland torn by the struggles of lawless chiefs, of a chaos and an anarchy far worse than the conditions at the end of the *landnáma* Period before the setting up of a central government.

Under such conditions there was only one remedy and that was to place this unhappy country under the protection of the Norwegian crown. For many years the kings of Norway had sought to lay Iceland under their dominion, knowing that the Free State was in origin but a colony of their own countrymen. Harald Fairhair had sent Uni Gardarsson to establish his authority; Olaf Tryggvason in his brusque missionary zeal had treated the Icelanders exactly as his own subjects; King Olaf the Saint, after making a treaty in 1022 with the Icelandic leaders whereby Norwegians and Icelanders were given full rights of citizenship in each other's countries, two years later definitely invited the Althing to recognize him as the overlord and ruler of Iceland. But the Free State had maintained its independence, and for another hundred years and more the interference of the Norwegian king was resisted; yet at the end of this period the passing of the Icelandic Church under the jurisdiction of the Archbishop of Nidaros brought the ultimate union with Norway perceptibly nearer, while the chaotic condition of domestic affairs in the early thirteenth century made the guidance of a strong royal hand more and more welcome to the Icelanders. Nevertheless many of them, even in their most desperate straits, were reluctant to surrender their independence, and King Haakon Haakonsson (1217–1263), great monarch though he was, had long to occupy himself in negotiations and intrigue before the king's party in Iceland was of one purpose and large enough to force an issue at the Althing. Perhaps the deciding factor was the arrogance of Gizur Thorvaldsson, Snorri's slayer, who

THE STUR-
LUNGS

had been made a jarl by Haakon and official representative of the king, for so greedy was this chief of power that he turned against his master, plotting to make himself supreme ; but the Icelanders knew him for their own equal and among themselves decided that they would prefer to give allegiance to Haakon rather than to an upstart from their ranks. To the Althing came Gizur with an army of 1,440 men, intending to stake all upon the people's love of independence, but it was only to find that the popular temper had changed. At least, men said, Haakon could offer that which no Icelander, however powerful, could bestow, namely law and security and trade-privileges ; so Gizur, accepting the now general desire for union with Norway, suddenly changed his plans and himself initiated the proposal that Haakon should be their king.

THE FIRST FREE STATE COMES TO AN END

Thus it came about that in the year 1262 Haakon and the Icelanders made a bond. For their part the Icelanders pledged themselves to grant to the king of Norway ' lands, thanes, and taxes in perpetuity ' and to respect the authority of the king's jarl, or governor. On the king's part it was stipulated that he should allow the colonists to obey their own laws, that he should repeal the tax upon persons leaving Norway for Iceland and send at least six ships to the colony during each of the following summers, that he should accord special privileges to Icelanders when in their mother-country, that he should respect their claims, if any, as heirs to property in Norway, and, finally, that he should maintain peace for them in Iceland. Only the thingmen of southern and northern Iceland were present when this momentous decision was made, but by 1264 the whole of the country had offered submission to Norway on these terms and had acknowledged the king's sovereignty.

SUBMIS- SION TO NORWAY

This union of Iceland and Norway, though later history suggests that it may have been an imprudent step, was rendered almost inevitable by local conditions and did certainly bring about some temporary amelioration in domestic affairs, for the power of the overbearing Icelandic chieftain Gizur was restricted and an earnest endeavour was made by Haakon to establish order in the land ; but Haakon himself died in the Orkneys in 1263 and it was his son, King Magnus Lagaböter (1263–1280), who initiated the greatest changes. For ignoring the stipulation of the Icelanders that they should retain their own legal code, in 1271 this great jurist submitted for the acceptance of the Althing a code drawn up by himself,

NEW LEGAL CODES

and ten years later, because this hastily constructed statute-book was far from perfect and obviously had been adopted in Iceland with considerable reluctance, he supplanted it by another, the *Jónsbók*, which was brought to Iceland in 1280. This was accepted by the Althing in 1281 and is a stern and noble document that not only threatened crime with punishments of salutary severity but also most profoundly affected the constitution of Iceland, for it broke the power of the godar and placed the business of government largely in the hands of state officials appointed by the king. The whole character of the Althing as a grand national assembly was thereby altered, and instead of a large and rowdy confabulation of the godar and their followers, henceforth a small body met under the guidance of the royal representatives to discharge the various legislative and judicial duties. And at last the government was provided with proper executive powers, for now the king lent the force of his own royal sanction to the laws that were propounded, and with the disappearance of the old office of law-speaker the monarch was left as the sole constitutional source both of law and of justice.

Yet the union brought Iceland no lasting prosperity. For the power of Norway herself was already on the wane and inevitably the colony suffered in the slow eclipse of her mother-country. The Norwegian government, as the years passed, became greedy and ineffective, the Norwegian Church more selfish and tyrannical, and, worst of all, shipping and merchant-enterprise rapidly declined so that the imports into Iceland were totally insufficient for the needs of the colonists. Once more the old violence of the jealous chiefs flamed forth and where there had been peace and order now there were brawls and bloodshed that the functionaries of the king dared neither interrupt nor punish. Then, to add to the distress of the unhappy colony, a series of horrible disasters, devastating volcano-eruptions, calamitous earthquakes, and deadly plagues took each a heavy toll of life.

ICELAND IN DECLINE AND MISFORTUNE

But worse was to come, for the union of the Scandinavian crowns in 1397 left the enfeebled state of Norway in the hands of distant kings of Danish or German family who had little interest in Icelandic affairs and neglected the colony except as a source of revenue ; the result was that in this unhappy fifteenth century taxes were increased, trade with Iceland was further restricted by the royal monopoly, and gradually intercourse with Norway grew less and less frequent. Only the vigorous revival of trade with Britain, England especially, saved Iceland from economic ruin, and even this was hindered by the jealous

Scandinavian government and was the source of constant friction between the loyalist Icelanders and the Englishmen.

Here then the history of this viking colony, a gloomy tale until the brighter days of the nineteenth century, must stop, and it remains to note only a few landmarks such as the transference of Iceland to the Danish crown in 1814 as a result of the Treaty of Kiel, when the King of Denmark ceded Norway to Sweden but himself retained the colonial possessions of the ancient Norwegian kingdom. Another notable event was that the Althing, whose legislative power was now gone, met for the last time upon Thingvellir in 1798 and was abolished by the Danish government in 1800 ; but this ancient assembly, henceforth to meet in Reykjavik, was re-established as a parliament in 1843. Iceland received a new constitution upon the occasion of the millenary of its first colonization in 1874, and in 1918 the country became a free and sovereign state in union with the Danish realm and owing allegiance to the king of Iceland and Denmark.

CHAPTER XIV

GREENLAND

A GREAT adventurer was Eric the Red. With his father, because they were implicated in a murder-suit, he had left his home in the Jaeder in Norway and fared to Iceland where he had settled and married ; but here too ill-luck had attended him, and in 981 or 982 a stormy and quarrelsome sojourn ended in his being outlawed. Accordingly Eric prepared his ship for departure, telling his friends that it was his purpose to seek for the land that one Gunnbjörn had sighted nearly a century ago when he had been driven far west past Iceland.

DISCOV-
ERY BY
GUNN-
BJÖRN
AND FIRST
EXPLORA-
TION BY
ERIC THE
RED

This country, of which there was still talk, was Greenland, and thither Eric turned his prow when he put out to sea, intending to prove or disprove the tale of Gunnbjörn's accidental discovery. The voyage was successful ; he soon sighted the ice-bound eastern coast of Greenland, sailed south, rounded Cape Farewell, and following the ice to the north-west eventually found an opening through the floes and put in to land at a point on the west coast probably about the latitude of Cape Desolation ; thence he explored many of the fjords in the search for a habitable district and spent his first winter at Ericsey which lies opposite the entrance to Ericsfjord not far from the modern Julianehaab. In the summer he explored large tracts of the western coast, giving names to many places that he visited, and the second winter he spent at Ericsholm near Cape Desolation ; the next summer he explored northwards as far as the modern Unatok. Then he returned to Ericsey and penetrated inland up to the head of Ericsfjord, and the third winter he abode once more at Ericsey. The following summer he returned to Iceland.

There he was soon involved again in the quarrels that had led to his being outlawed, and though he eventually patched up a peace with his principal enemy, he left Iceland the summer after his return with the express purpose of founding a colony in the new country west-over-sea, this being called by him Greenland for the reason that a good name might attract other

361

settlers to join him. And, indeed, so favourable were his accounts

ERIC
ESTAB-
LISHES
A COLONY
c. 985

of the place that in the summer twenty-five ships bearing emigrants and their wives left Iceland for Greenland, though it is told that only fourteen of these reached their destination. Not all of these joined Eric at his 'eastern settlement' near Julianehaab,

for some went further on to establish a 'western settlement'

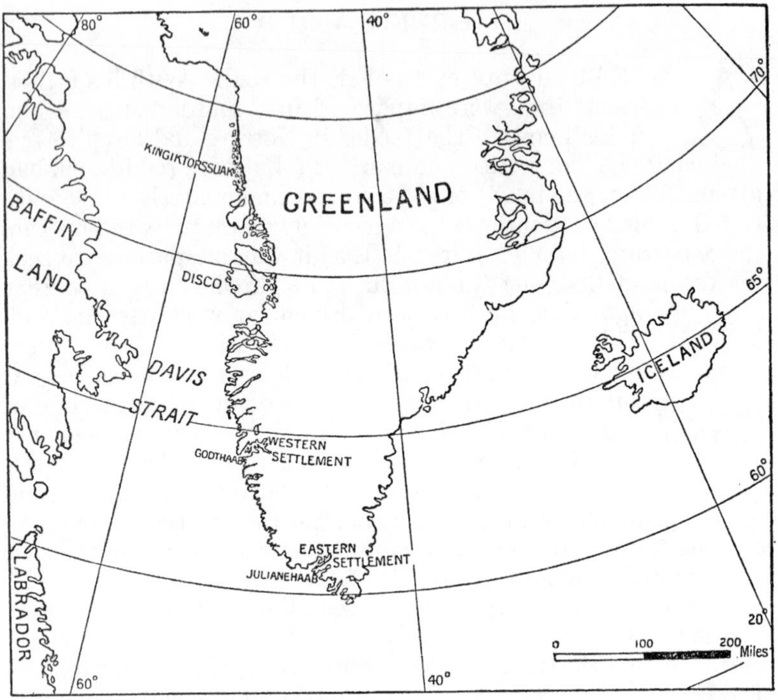

FIG. 38.—The Greenland Settlements

around the modern Godthaab. And thus, in 985 or 986, was Greenland first colonized.[1] They were all heathens, save for a

[1] Note that W. M. Peitz, *Untersuchungen zu Urkundenfälschungen des Mittelalters, I, Die Hamburger Fälschungen,* Freiburg, 1919, p. 93 ff., has sought to prove that Greenland, and Iceland too, had been discovered and explored at least as early as 832, for both countries are named as being under the ecclesiastical jurisdiction of the archbishop of Hamburg in papal letters of 832 and 834. Though Peitz's contention has received some support, the fact remains that the letters in question are inadmissible as evidence, since it is common ground that they have been doctored, if not deliberately falsified. Yet Peitz has much ingenious argument to bring forward in their favour.

single Christian from the Hebrides, these first colonists, and Red
Eric was accepted as their chief.

The two settlements lay to the west of Cape Farewell for
the reason that the east coast of Greenland is ice-locked for the
greater part of the year and was consequently uninhabitable ;
but even on the west and south-west coast, where the pack-ice thins
out so that ships can make land, the great ice-cap that lies upon
the country leaves only a narrow strip of bleak and mountainous
sea-board, on an average some fifty miles in width, to sustain
human life. This western littoral, however, is broken by fjords into
a maze of necks and islands, and on the lower margins of these
fjords, and at their heads, there is grass in plenty, so that cattle
can be fed, and a scrub of small birch-trees and willows.   In such
districts lived the early colonists, depending for their livelihood
on the breeding of their scraggy cattle, eking out their larders
with the salmon of the rivers and the fish of the fjords and sea,
and hunting, too, the reindeer, hares, and foxes of the mountains.
They were able to extract iron from the local ore and, if there
was fuel enough to keep the furnaces going, could make for themselves such simple articles as knives, hooks, and nails ; but corn
they had none, though in later days attempts were made to
induce a little barley to grow ; wood was precious and scarce ;
soapstone had to suffice for the making of their pots and pans.
Yet they were not without valuables, skins of seal and bear,
walrus-tusks, and the like, to offer to the few trading-ships that
came their way, and so, for two centuries or more, the little
colony of thrifty and simple souls managed to hold their own on
this remote and horrid shore.

The eastern settlement, extending along the coast from Cape
Farewell to Arsuk, was the larger and the more important of the
two Norse establishments ; in the heyday of the Greenland
EASTERN   vikings it boasted nearly two hundred homesteads, and,
SETTLE-   because these were far scattered and travel between
MENT   them took long, by the fourteenth century there were
a dozen churches and two monastic foundations.   Here, in the
old days, dwelt the founder of the colony, Eric the Red, at
Brattahlid (now Kagssiarsuk) in Ericsfjord (now Tanugdliarfik),
and here, on the low isthmus separating Ericsfjord and Einarsfjord
(now Igalikofjord), was Gardar, the place of the meeting of the
Althing, the grand assize of Greenland, and, some time after
Christianity was introduced, the site of the cathedral and the
bishop's seat.

The western settlement lay about 170 miles to the north of
Arsuk and was made up of some ninety homesteads and four

churches, so that in all, even in the period of her utmost prosperity, the Norse population of Greenland could not have num-
WESTERN   bered much more than two or three thousand souls.
SETTLE-   Much further to the north, around Disko Island, were
MENT   the cabins of the summer hunting and fishing grounds,
the headquarters of some of the colonists during the short season
they spent in hunting seals, whales, and walrus, in preparing
' seal-tar ' (congealed blubber), and in collecting driftwood.   And
right up the coast, perhaps far into Baffin Bay, these Greenland
farmers explored ; thus, on the island of Kingiktorsuak in latitude
72° 55′ there was found in 1824 a tiny stone, only 4 inches in
length, bearing a Runic inscription that recorded how, on a certain
day probably in the fourteenth century, Erling Sighvatsson and
Bjarni Thordarson and Eindridi Jonsson built cairns there.

The introduction of Christianity among the Greenland vikings
in the year A.D. 1000 was the work of Leif, son of Eric the Red.
For in 999 he went on an expedition to Norway and there joined
INTRODUC- the court of that great proselytizing king, Olaf Trygg-
TION OF   vason, where he was, of course, speedily converted to
CHRISTI-   the new faith.   When, in the following year, he proposed
ANITY   to return to Greenland, he was invited by the king to
preach Christianity to the people of this far-off colony, and this,
though not without some misgivings, Leif said he would do ; so
he was given a priest to take with him.   Soon after his arrival in
Greenland he set about his task and it was not long before his
mother, Thjodhild, consented to be baptized ; she had a church
built in the neighbourhood of their Brattahlid homestead, but
old Red Eric himself was stubborn and preferred that his wife
should live away from him rather than that he should betray
the gods beloved of his fathers.   Nevertheless Leif and the
priest sent by King Olaf made many converts.

No doubt here, as in Iceland, Christianity soon received the
formal sanction of the Althing as the official religion of the republic, for by the middle of the eleventh century the colony, together
with Scandinavia and Iceland, was recognized as a part of the
great archbishopric of Bremen, and as early as the time of Archbishop Adalbert (1043–1073) came messengers from Greenland
to the prelate at Bremen begging him to send them clergy.   In
1103 the Greenland Church was transferred to the ecclesiastical
province of Lund, but in the '20s of the twelfth century the pious
and neglected colonists, dismayed at the lack of priests in their
remote country, subscribed together for the endowment of a
bishop's see and obtained the permission of the Norwegian
king that Greenland should have its own resident prelate.   In

PLATE XI

IKIGAIT (HERJOLFSNESS), GREENLAND
SHOWING RUINS OF NORSE CHURCH

IGALIKO (GARDAR), EINARSFJORD, GREENLAND
SITE OF CATHEDRAL AND BISHOP'S HOUSE

the saga of Eric the Red it is related that the custom in Greenland was to bury men on the farms where they died, in unconsecrated ground, and to set a stake rising up from the corpse's breast ; then, later on, when the priest came, the stake would be drawn up and holy water poured down the cavity and a funeral service sung over them. Sometimes this happened a very long time after the burial of the body. In 1124 the Norwegian Arnald was FIRST consecrated to the new see by the archbishop of Lund BISHOP and in 1126, after two years of travel and delay, the OF GREEN- first bishop of Greenland landed in his far-off diocese. LAND He dwelt at Gardar and there was built the cathedral, a little cruciform church between 70 and 80 feet in length, that was dedicated to St. Nicholas. Arnald proved himself to be an able and influential man ; indeed, when he departed from his diocese in 1150 he had created for his successors in the see an authority that established the bishop of Greenland henceforth as the chief personage in the colony, its temporal, and not merely its spiritual head. Ten years after his leaving the already close bond between Greenland and Norway was strengthened by the transference from the ecclesiastical jurisdiction of Lund to that of the archbishop of Nidaros.

It was just over a hundred years later, in 1261, that the free state of Greenland, after more than 250 years existence as an independent republic, became a crown colony of Norway. This was an inevitable sequel to the now almost complete economic dependence of Greenland upon Norway, and the promise of the payment of taxes to the Norwegian king was little more than a desperate measure to secure by purchase that frequent coming and going between Europe and Greenland necessary for the supply to this distant land of such vital commodities as corn and timber. But it was a political move with disastrous and disappointing results, for shortly afterwards there came about a decline in Norse trading-enterprise, largely the result of the rapidly increasing power of the Hanseatic League, and the isolation of Greenland was now made more terrible inasmuch as the Scandinavian kings, jealous of their rights, forbade private commerce with the Greenlanders. Only the royal *knerrir* (merchant-ships), sailing from Bergen, were allowed to trade with the colony, and in the THE fifteenth century, upon the further decline of Norway COLONY as a sea-power, even this kingly monopoly was ABAN- neglected and rare indeed became the visit of a *knörr*. DONED TO At last, forgotten of the civilized world, these poor ITS FATE dwellers in the distant north knew themselves faced with ruin and extinction ; then slowly and inexorably this worst tragedy of all viking history played itself out ; alone and unwatched of men, without hope of help, the Greenland vikings died.

The last record of a foreign vessel having reached Greenland, an Icelandic boat driven out of her course by storm, and the last recorded sailing of a *knörr* from Bergen, date from the first decade of the fifteenth century, but before this date shadows of the doom impending had darkened over the far-off colony. In 1345 the Greenlanders, because of their extreme poverty, were excused by the pope the payment of a tithe, and ten years later it was reported to the king of Norway that some of the colonists were forsaking Christianity and Christian behaviour for the faith and habits of the Eskimo ; so a *knörr* was hastily equipped and sent off to them, the first for nine years. From 1349 to 1368 there was no resident bishop of Greenland, and in 1377 died Alf, the last prelate who lived in the country. In 1492 a papal letter of Alexander VI declared that the inhabitants of Greenland lived on dried fish and milk, that there was no knowledge of a ship having visited them during the previous eighty years, and that most of them had abandoned their Christian faith, having nothing else to remind them thereof save an altar-cloth (*corporale*) which was exhibited once a year and whereon the body of Christ had been consecrated at the last mass said in the country a hundred years ago.[1]

But though the history of the decline of the colony is incomplete, and the story of its final extinction lost, yet the archaeologist has something to tell about the life of these poor colonists in the fourteenth and fifteenth centuries, this thanks to those EXCAVA- pathetic and wonderful discoveries that fill several TIONS AT wall-cases of the National Museum at Copenhagen, HERJOLFS- the result of the extraordinary excavations of Dr. NESS AND GARDAR Poul Nörlund of this museum at Herjolfsness in 1921 and at Gardar in 1926.[2] The first site was the cemetery of Herjolfsness (now Nassarmiut) near Fredericksdal, and here, indeed, though poverty and sickness were fast undermining the little settlement,

---

[1] J. C. Heywood, *Documenta selecta e tabulario secreto vaticano, etc.* Rome, 1893, No. 10, p. 12 ; trans. in F. Nansen, *Northern Mists*, II, p. 121.

[2] *Meddelelser om Grønland*, LXVII (1924) and LXXVI (1929) : in English. For a summary of the Gardar excavations see *Geografisk Tidskrift*, XXXI (1928), p. 46. At Gardar the ruins of the little cathedral and bishop's dwelling have been investigated, and the tomb of Bishop Jon Smyrill (d. 1209) found, this containing besides the skeleton the episcopal ring and a fine English-looking crozier-head of walrus ivory.

HOOD FOUND AT HERJOLFSNESS, GREENLAND
(FOURTEENTH CENTURY)

DRESSES (WOMAN'S *LEFT* AND MAN'S *RIGHT*) FOUND AT HERJOLFSNESS,
GREENLAND
(FOURTEENTH CENTURY)

the unhappy remnant of the people was still faithful and devout Christians. In the hundred odd graves that were explored it was found that the burial-customs of the Church were most scrupulously observed, and no less than fifty-eight of the bodies had wooden crosses laid upon their breasts, most of them ornamental and carefully made, some even bearing inscriptions in runes. ' God the Almighty guard Gudleif well ' ran the prayer of one, and ' Thorleif made this cross in praise and worship of God the Almighty ' said another.

The dead were laid to rest, some in wooden coffins and the remainder directly in the earth, shrouded in the miserable clothes, often threadbare and patched, that they had worn in life. These garments (Pl. XII) were woven of sheep's wool, and, for both men and women, were long skirted gowns with full sleeves, following the European fashions of a somewhat earlier date ; the common head-dress was a hood and cape combined, having a tail at the back, but there were five capes of simpler cut, and one of conical shape that cannot have been in vogue in Greenland long before the end of the fifteenth century. The skeletons of twenty-five individuals survived for examination, and it was found that the folk represented were of short stature (5 foot was tall for a man, while all the women were under 4 foot 9 inches) and of feeble build. Only five seem to have been of ordinary health, and of the twenty folk over eighteen years of age a half had died before their thirtieth year. Plainly did these miserable bones of a dying race betray the hard life and chronic under-nourishment that had ruined the sturdy physique of the old Norse settlers.

And at this time the end was near, for already nearly all intercourse with Europe had ceased. But there remains one tragic picture of the passing of these lonely colonists. About the year 1550 an Icelander, aboard a German merchant-ship, was blown far out of his course and found himself off the coast of Greenland. The ship put into a fjord where there were many islands, some inhabited by Eskimos, and these natives the European crew dared not approach. But they landed on a seemingly uninhabited island upon which were some ruins, boat-houses and walls such as were familiar objects in Iceland. And there they found a man lying dead. He wore a well-made hood and clothing of coarse woollen material and sealskin ; by his side lay an iron knife, almost worn away by long use and much resharpening. Who he was they knew not, but this stiffened and lonely corpse must have been the last Norseman of the old colony who was seen by Europeans, and there he lay, dead and unburied, by his deserted dwelling with the wasted knife at his side, a pitiful emblem of the civilization to which he belonged, the civilization that had forgotten and deserted him.[1]

There were, however, two contributory causes, in addition to European neglect, that had made life for the Norse in Greenland too hard to be endured. One was a gradual and serious DETERI- deterioration of the climate during the centuries follow-ORATION ing the original settlement, and the other, itself a con-OF THE sequence of the now increasing cold, was the southward CLIMATE AND movement of the Eskimo. When the Norsemen first SOUTH- came to Greenland they found the ruined dwelling-WARD MOVEMENT places and stone implements of the Skraelings, as they OF THE called these nomad native folk, but discovered that the ESKIMO Eskimo themselves were then living far away to the north. But by the thirteenth century the southward movement had begun and finally, about 1325, the western settlement was abandoned by the white men. In 1355 it was told in Norway that many of the Greenland Norse had become tainted with Eskimo heathendom ; but there was, nevertheless, a continued hostility between the two races, and another attack by the Skraelings took place in 1379, this time upon the eastern settlement, where a large number of the white men were killed.

What finally happened is unknown. The Eskimos never seem to have been a naturally quarrelsome folk and there was perhaps some ordinary and peaceful intercourse with the Skraelings, enough at any rate to lend some probability to the belief of Dr. Nansen that the Norse, finding themselves deprived of the comforts of their own civilization, were compelled by the hard necessity of imitating the Eskimo manner of life to abandon what had survived of their own faith and customs, this ending at last in the complete absorption of the remaining white men by the far more numerous Eskimos. Yet the excavations at Herjolfsness revealed nothing that pointed to an intermingling of the two races, and it seems more likely that the children of the vikings died surrounded by natives who regarded unmoved and without sympathy the sufferings of the enfeebled and starving folk who clung so desperately to this inhospitable country where now only the hardy Skraelings dared hope to live.

And so it was almost as an unknown country that Greenland was rediscovered in 1576 by Martin Frobisher. He landed on

[1] This story, which is admittedly of dubious historical value, is taken from an account written in 1625 by Björn Jónsson, a noted Icelandic author, wherein it is related how this adventure befell ' within living memory ' another Icelander named Jón Greenlander (*Grönlands historiske mindesmaerker*, III, 1845).

the west-coast in 1578, and finding that the Eskimos had a few
REDIS- pieces of iron, some spearheads of this metal, a bronze
COVERY button or two, and knew gold when they saw it, he
OF GREEN- concluded that they must have had intercourse at
LAND BY some time with Europeans. But of these he knew
FRO- and heard nothing. Yet the memory of the Norse
BISHER
settlers had not wholly passed away, for in 1721 the Norwegian
missionary Hans Egede landed in Greenland to discover, if he
could, their fate and to preach to them the Christianity that Leif
Ericsson had first taught in the country over seven hundred years
before. But Hans Egede found only the Skraelings in the land
where once his countrymen had lived.

CHAPTER XV

AMERICA

THERE is no chapter in the history of the Norsemen abroad that is finer reading than the tale of those brave and simple seamen who discovered America. For they were only poor Greenlanders and Icelanders, these first white men in the New World, not commanding for their explorations a well-equipped and magnificent fleet from Norway, but embarking upon their audacious enterprise, a most fearless navigation of unknown seas, if not in a single ship, at most only in tiny companies of two or three vessels.

Their names are Bjarni Herjolfsson of Iceland, who in the hazard of the winds and storm found America when he sought Greenland ; Leif Ericsson of Greenland who discovered ' Wineland the Good ', the fair and pleasant country of Maryland and Virginia ; Thorvald Ericsson, his brother, who was killed out in Wineland by the Indians ; and Thorfinn Karlsefni, an Icelandic merchant who spent three years in America and whose son, Snorri, was born there.

But before the narratives of these brave voyages are repeated, it is necessary to say something about the historical worth of the passages in the sagas that record them. At the outset one may with a full confidence dismiss any uncertainty as to whether the Norsemen really did discover America, for this few have dared to doubt. And in that matter there is an early testimony that is independent of the sagas since the pious geographer, Adam of Bremen, declared, less than half a century after the voyage of Karlsefni, that he had been told by Svein Estridsson, king of Denmark, of the existence in the Atlantic of an ' island ', discovered by many, and called Wineland because grapes were found growing there. Moreover, he had heard that there was also self-sown corn abounding, and this report he knew depended not on mythical tales but on trustworthy information from the Danes.

Nevertheless it is the wild vine and the self-sown corn of Wineland that laid the saga-tales of the voyages under the suspicion of containing much legendary matter, and on this score

Dr. Fridtjof Nansen has been their harshest critic. For though
he did not deny the Norse discovery of America, yet this most
WINELAND distinguished scholar claimed that the rich and pleasant
THE GOOD Wineland is a country that existed only in Norse
AND THE imagination, a fictitious paradise that was the result
ISLANDS
OF THE of too much hearing of the *Isles of the Blest*, the lovely
BLEST archipelago in western Ocean that in ancient days
Horace and Plutarch, and, in the seventh century, Isidore His-
palensis, praised. And certainly it is true that the unusual name
Vinland hit góða, though in fact only very rarely used, may be
some muddled Norse equivalent of the classical *Insulae Fortunatae*
where, in cornfield and vineyard, the wheat and the grapes
ripened under the hot sun.

It is, of course, an injustice to the learned and closely-reasoned
dissertation wherein Dr. Nansen expounds his views [1] to sum
up his charge against the historicity of the Wineland-sagas in a
sentence, yet it chances that there is little need to debate the
matter at great length inasmuch as the case against the Norse
tales has been tried and, in the opinion of most students of the
subject, a verdict won for their sincerity as travel-records. But
if the reader would himself be judge, let him, after Dr. Nansen
has been heard, turn to Mr. G. M. Gathorne-Hardy's *Norse
Discoverers of America* [2] and there read the admirable and convincing defence that most manfully opposes, point by point, the
contentions of Dr. Nansen.

It is not, of course, wholly unknown to saga-literature, even
though the tales are normally couched in the most simple and
direct of all narrative styles, that legendary matter should be
introduced. But in this special instance it does seem unlikely
that make-believe voyages of the kind posited by Dr. Nansen
could have been paraded before the attentive and critical ears
of the listeners as historical fact ; for cogent arguments to support
a declaration of faith in the Wineland stories are not wanting,
since it is assured that although their writing down is of comparatively late date (thirteenth and fourteenth centuries),[3] yet the
Icelanders of a much earlier time must have been familiar with
them. It has been said that the self-sown corn and the grapes
of Wineland were known to Adam of Bremen by about 1070,
and so too in Iceland when, about 1130, Ari the Learned, the first
of the great Icelandic historians, wrote his *Íslendingabók,* he was
aware that his countrymen would understand a casual allusion

[1] *In Northern Mists,* London, 1911, I, p. 312 ff. (esp. p. 345 ff.) ;
II, p. 1 ff.
[2] Oxford, 1921, p. 147 ff.   [3] See note 3, p. 373.

to Wineland ;[1] for he says of Greenland that the first Norse settlers found there ruins of houses and the stone implements of a people such as inhabited Wineland. He knew, then, and most Icelanders knew, the stories of the voyages, and that he could only know a reasonably accurate and strictly historical version of them is nearly certain since Ari was the grandson of Karlsefni's cousin and he wrote his book to interest, among others, the grand-son of that Snorri, Karlsefni's son, who was born in America. It is difficult to imagine any accretion of classical and Celtic legend around the narratives of the voyages up to the time of Ari's death in 1148, and as only just over sixty years later there is a written saga-reference to Leif Ericsson's adventure in Wineland, there must have been a continued oral repetition of the narrative until the time of its first setting down in writing. Thus in the thirteenth century, when the archetype of the saga of Leif's father, Eric the Red, was committed to manuscript, it is improbable that it would depart in any noteworthy degree from the versions of the tales known to Ari, tales that may even have been related in his hearing by members of Karlsefni's expedition.

THE HIS-
TORICITY
OF THE
WINELAND
STORIES

Not, of course, that anything approaching a sustained and detailed accuracy can be claimed for the written tales after this long interval and this passing from mouth to mouth. Indeed, some of the stories are twice-told in manuscript, appearing in sources that are independent of one another, and they are found, when compared, to present all those puzzles and discrepancies that are to be expected of distinct versions of ancient and often repeated travellers' yarns. Yet these contradictions must be held to give the collection of stories a most satisfactory stamp of honesty, for nowhere do they show suspicious signs of the too facile agreement that might easily betoken a common legendary basis. It is, in fact, not the skeleton of the narratives that convinces the reader of their underlying truth ; rather is it an occasional detail, abbreviated, perhaps, and out of place, that, standing forth suddenly as a sentence of the real story that in ancient days the returned sailor himself had told, prove the intended veracity of the whole account.

Leaving generalities aside, then, the content of the Wineland sagas is in itself sufficient to demonstrate that they are based not upon legend but upon fact. Thus in one story a scrap of information concerning solar movement as observed in Wineland establishes the certainty that the observers had travelled as far south as Maryland. And beyond a doubt there are wild vines in these

[1] Wineland is also casually mentioned in *Landnámabók*.

southern latitudes, so that a genial country of the grape was assuredly known to the Norse of Greenland and Iceland. This much granted, it is perverse to scorn those other details in the narratives that may reasonably be held to apply to this land and the voyage thither ; for the references to the Indians, the descriptions of the coast and climate of North America, the remarkable reference in the sagas to the formidable Indian ballista,[1] and the mention of the self-sown corn that was likewise noted by later European explorers,[2] these are in themselves almost convincing enough to win for the Wineland sagas a full value as the secondhand history of real expeditions to the New World.

The chief problem, then, is to decide not whether the substance of the Wineland tales is true, but what parts of them are to be selected for the narrative that follows, and this is a matter that has to be decided summarily, for the long and intricate essays in textual criticism that the debate involves cannot be analysed here. The choice lies between what is known as the *Hauk's Book* version and that contained in the *Flatey Book*,[3] and the reader will find their respective merits discussed in Mr. Gathorne-Hardy's work and he will learn that Mr. Hardy is prepared to defend the superiority of the *Flatey Book* throughout. This version, then, for it has the added attraction of being fuller and more picturesque, is adopted as the principal source of the Wineland voyages now to be set forth ; but it is only just to the memory of a very distinguished scholar and a profound student of saga-literature, Professor Gustav Storm, to observe that he saw reason to criticize severely the *Flatey Book* narratives,[4] rejecting, for example, the whole story of Bjarni Herjolfsson, who, according to the source preferred here, was the first Norseman to reach America. It will be important, therefore, to indicate in the following pages the divergences between the *Flatey Book*

---

[1] See p. 384.

[2] There is, however, some difficulty about this self-sown corn. See Gathorne-Hardy, *op. cit.*, p. 159 ff.

[3] The sources for the detailed accounts of the Norse voyages to America belong to two traditions, the one (A) contained in two MSS., namely *Hauk's Book* (early fourteenth century) and Arne Magnusson 557 (fifteenth century), both being derived in all probability from a thirteenth-century archetype ; the second (B) is contained in the *Flatey Book*, which was not compiled until the end of the fourteenth century. A is therefore the older source and in some respects it certainly does give an impression of greater trustworthiness ; yet, contrary to expectations, the independent and later *Flatey Book* version reads as circumstantial and explicit fragments of history that compel the prior attention of the student.

[4] *Studier over Vinlandsreiserne*, Aarb., 1887.

FIG. 39.—North-east America

account and those of the rival version,[1] but having thus cautioned the reader, with Bjarni the tale shall begin.

This, then, is the story. The discovery of America was a chance result of the peopling of Greenland in 986 and the hero of the first voyage was Bjarni, the son of one of Red Eric's colonists called Herjolf. When his father emigrated to Greenland, Bjarni was away with his trading-ship in Norway and it was a sad blow to him when he returned to Iceland to find his parents gone, for it was his wont to pass every winter with them ; so he refused to unload his cargo and decided instead to follow them to Greenland. This was a perilous enterprise, for Bjarni knew little or nothing of the course to be followed except that somewhere in the west he would discover his people in a country of mountains and large glaciers, and very soon, thanks to northerly gales and fogs, he found himself lost in unknown seas. For many days his ship was driven by the winds or drifted aimlessly in fog, and when at last the sun appeared so that Bjarni could take his bearings a day's sail in the direction in which he had headed on leaving Iceland brought him in sight of land. But it was not Greenland, thought Bjarni, on sailing close in, because it was wooded and had low hills ; and, indeed, he was right, for it was America that he had found, the currents and the winds having swept him past the Newfoundland Banks and Nova Scotia to the neighbourhood of the Cape Cod peninsula between Boston and New York. He must have known that he was now too far south, so he sailed for two days to the north-east and this brought him to land again, a flat wooded country that was probably the south of Nova Scotia ; the crew wanted to land, saying that they were short of wood and water, but Bjarni refused to stay in spite of their grumbles and, realizing that once again he had failed to find Greenland, continued on his course for three more days before a south-westerly breeze until a third land, Newfoundland, was sighted. This certainly was mountainous, and there was ice about,[2] but Bjarni would not put in to shore, for the country

BJARNI HERJOLFS-SON DISCOVERS AMERICA

---

[1] The major discrepancies between the two authorities are these : (1) A knows nothing of Bjarni's voyage, which is recorded only in B (*Flatey Book*). (2) Leif's voyage is represented as the accidental result of a storm in A and as a deliberately undertaken exploration in B. (3) Thorvald Ericsson's independent voyage to extend the discoveries of his brother Leif is not mentioned in A, where it is merely said that Thorvald died a quite incredible death during the later voyage of Karlsefni. (4) B alone gives the story of Freydis's second voyage to America.

[2] The word *jökul* ordinarily means *glacier*, but Mr. Gathorne-Hardy has rightly observed (*op. cit.*, p. 249) that this need not necessarily rule

seemed to him to be good for nothing, and when, by sailing on, he discovered that it was an island, he headed for the open sea, bearing north. There was a strong following wind and in four days' time he sighted land again. Of all the countries he had seen it was most like the Greenland Bjarni was expecting to find and when at length he landed he realized that it was indeed his goal, for he had made the coast close to the eastern settlement where Herjolf lived, and that same night, so the story runs, Bjarni, the discoverer of America, was once more reunited with his father.

The second Norse voyage to America (1002–3), some fifteen or sixteen years later, was made by Leif, son of Eric the Red, the Leif who first brought Christianity to Greenland. All accounts save one assert that during his return from Norway in the summer of the year A.D. 1000 as the bearer of Olaf Tryggvason's mission
LEIF   to his fellow-colonists he was driven out of his course
ERICSSON'S and carried by winds and currents to the shores of
VOYAGE   the New World ; yet the *Flatey Book* version of the
1002–3   discovery of America tells the story differently, saying
that after Leif's return to Greenland direct from Norway he found that men were now talking much about Bjarni's discoveries and eventually determined to become explorer himself ; so he bought Bjarni's boat, engaged a crew of thirty-five men, and set out to find these new lands of which the Herjolfsness folk talked so much.

He came first to a barren and ice-capped country that he called Helluland (land of flat stone) and this, presumably, was the eastern coast of Labrador. Then he sailed off to a second land that was low-lying and wooded with a gentle slope to the sea and wide stretches of sand, a description that applies well enough to the south-western end of Nova Scotia in the neighbourhood of Cape Sable. This Leif named Markland (land of woods). Then two days' sail before a north-east wind brought the ship to a pleasant country where Leif made a camp and passed the winter. There was no want of salmon in the river and lake near which they built their booths, the pasturage was excellent, and there was no frost in winter-time ; the men explored a little bit

out Newfoundland, where there are no glaciers, as Bjarni's third land, since the term might refer simply to *icebergs*. Professor Hovgaard, on the other hand, makes Newfoundland Bjarni's first land and the third Resolution Island off Baffin Land ; on this view *jökul* can certainly be read as glacier, but there still remain serious objections to the itinerary proposed by Hovgaard (*Voyages of the Norsemen to America*, New York, 1915, p. 245).

of the country in the immediate neighbourhood of the camp, and
DISCOVERY one evening a German sailor of the party, native of a
OF WINE- wine country, discovered wild grapes growing, so Leif
LAND named this most agreeable territory Wineland. In the
spring, with a cargo of liquor [1] and wood, he returned to Greenland and there abode for the rest of his days, wealthy and much
honoured.

The discovery of the wild grapes establishes the position of
Wineland as somewhere at any rate south of Passamaquoddy
Bay in latitude 45°, the northern limit of the vine in America.
But the approximate locality of Leif's camp can be determined
with much greater precision by means of the once obscure statement in the *Flatey Book* that on the shortest day the sun, as
observed from the camp, had ' eykt ' place and ' dagmála ' place.
To Mr. M. Mjelde belongs the honour of having satisfactorily
solved the riddle of this sentence, for he has shown [2] that the
positions at which Leif observed the sun rise and set in Wineland
on the shortest day of a year about A.D. 1000 were the points on
the horizon 60° east and 60° west of south, and on this basis it
can be calculated that the most northerly point at which Leif
could make his observation was somewhere about latitude 37° N.
This places Leif's camp in Virginia or Maryland on the shores of
Chesapeake Bay.

According to the *Flatey Book*, the third Norse voyage to
America (1004–7) came about in this wise. There was much talk
in Greenland about Leif's expedition after he had returned, and
his brother, Thorvald, said that he was of the opinion that the
exploration of the new country had been confined to too small
an area. So Leif gave Thorvald his ship and a crew of thirty was
THOR- chosen, including, no doubt, several of the men who
VALD'S had been on the previous voyages. With the aid of
VOYAGE these experienced sailors Thorvald managed to reach
AND
DEATH IN Leif's camp in Wineland without much difficulty and
AMERICA, there, like Leif before him, he passed the winter. But
1004–7 in the spring Thorvald began preparations for a summer
exploration of the country to the west ; the party made their way
along a wooded coast where there were many islands, but they
found no sign of human beings although on one island there was
a deserted hut or wigwam. Thorvald therefore returned to
Leif's camp in the autumn and in the next summer explored to
the east, arriving at length in a very beautiful bay where he told
his men he would dearly like to make his home. But there

---

[1] In the saga *grapes*.
[2] *Saga-Book of the Viking Society*, X, pt. I (1919–24), p. 57.

were Indians living here and the Norsemen, having come upon nine of them hiding under three canoes,[1] killed eight of them, one alone escaping. That same night they were attacked by large numbers of the natives; Thorvald and his men defended themselves behind the shield-wall of their boat, and after a little while

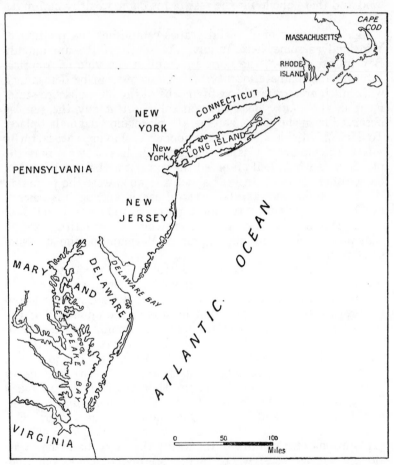

FIG. 40.—Wineland the Good

the Indians, having spent their spears and arrows, withdrew. Then Thorvald asked his men if any of them were wounded and

[1] Made of skin according to the saga, but probably of birch-bark, for the writer was no doubt confusing the Indians with the Eskimos since both peoples are referred to by the same name (*Skraelings*).

they answered that they were all safe and sound. ' I have got a wound under the arm ', said he ; ' an arrow passed between the gunwale and the shield and struck me. It is here and it will be my death. Now my advice to you is that you make ready to depart as soon as you can, but first you must carry me to that headland where I wanted so much to make my home, for it seems that it was the truth I spoke when I said that I should stay there awhile. Bury me there with a cross at my head and at my feet, and let the place be called Crossness hereafter '. So Thorvald died and was buried in America ; his crew cut a harvest of grapes in the autumn and in the next spring returned to Greenland where they had much news to tell Leif.

Thorvald's company arrived back with the news of their leader's death in the spring of A.D. 1007 and Thorstein, his brother, the third of the sons of Eric the Red to set out on the voyage to America, declared that he would go to Wineland to bring home the body of his brother. So he and his wife took the same ship and put to sea with a crew of twenty-five carefully chosen men ; but they were driven out of their course and soon lost their bearings. They sailed the open sea for many weeks with no idea of their whereabouts but by the beginning of winter they found themselves once again off Greenland and landed in Lysufjord in the western settlement.[1]

THOR-STEIN'S UNSUCCESS-FUL VOY-AGE 1007

The Wineland voyage most famous of all is that of Thorfinn Karlsefni, a wealthy Icelandic merchant and a sailor of considerable reputation. One summer (about A.D. 1020 [2]) he fitted out his ship for a trading expedition to Greenland and, in company

---

[1] In describing Thorvald's voyage and that of Thorstein I have followed the *Flatey Book*, not without some misgivings. I can commend the ingenious view of Professor William Hovgaard (*Voyages of the Norsemen to America*, New York, 1915, p. 101) who ignores Thorvald entirely and describes the events in this manner. After Leif's return from Wineland there was much talk of further exploration in the new country and Thorstein prepared to make a voyage of discovery, even persuading old Eric to join the expedition. He fitted out the ship of one Thorbjorn, lately arrived from Iceland, and set sail, but leaving Eric behind at the last moment because of an accident that happened to him on the way to the ship. Thorstein was at sea all the summer, was driven completely out of his course, sighted Iceland, and saw birds from Ireland ; finally the boat returned to Ericsfjord at the beginning of winter. Thorstein then married Gudrid, the daughter of Thorbjorn the Icelander, and went to live at Lysufjord in the western settlement where Thorstein died of sickness.

[2] The dating of this voyage is largely a matter of conjecture and some authorities place it as early as 1107–11. But see Gathorne Hardy, *op. cit.*, p. 137 ; the late dating used here was first proposed by Vigfusson.

with another Icelandic boat, he arrived in Ericsfjord where Eric the Red received him with great hospitality and invited the crews of both boats to spend the winter at Brattahlid, his home.   This offer the Icelanders accepted and they had a very merry

KARLS-
EFNI'S
VOYAGE
c. 1020–1024 time with Eric ; they lent their host malt and meal and corn for a grand Christmas feast which is said to have been one of the most magnificent ever given in this poor country, and they passed many long evenings in playing draughts and telling stories ; meanwhile Karlsefni courted and married Gudrid, Thorstein's widow and the daughter of Thorbjorn. The conversation had, of course, often been concerned with the adventures of the members of Eric's family in Wineland and the upshot was that Karlsefni and his companion Snorri resolved to go to look for this country, for by all accounts it seemed a profitable place to visit.   The other Icelandic boat, commanded by Bjarni Grimolfsson and Thorhall Gamlason, was also fitted out to take part in the expedition, and there was a third boat that joined the enterprise.   This was commanded by Thorvard, a Greenlander who had married a most remarkable woman of the name of Freydis, an illegitimate daughter of Red Eric ; Freydis accompanied her husband, and with them went a surly old Greenlander known as Thorhall the Hunter.   By this time Bjarni Herjulfsson's old boat, that had already made three Wineland voyages, was no longer seaworthy, so Thorvard obtained the ship of Gudrid's father, Thorbjorn, who had settled in Greenland not very long before this time.   In all the little fleet of three ships had a total strength of 160 men, and besides this there were women on board, including Gudrid, Karlsefni's wife.

The three boats first made their way up the coast of Greenland to the western settlement, perhaps deliberately to escape the strong current that had swept Thorstein out of his course when, on leaving Ericsfjord, he had headed straight for America.[1] Then they sailed south across Davis Strait and made the coast of Labrador ; there they landed and found the country strewn with immense boulders and the home of arctic foxes, so they concluded that it was Leif's Helluland.   Thereupon they sailed off in a south-easterly direction until, after passing through the Strait of Belle Isle, they found themselves off a wooded land that they assumed to be Markland ; then they came to Cape Whittle, and at this or some other promontory near by they landed and found

[1] On the other hand, it may have been necessary this year to go first along the Greenland coast in order to penetrate the ice.   Or the journey to the western settlements may have been undertaken in order to transact some business of Gudrid's, for she had property there.

the keel of a ship stranded on the shore so that they called the place Keelness. Afterwards they sailed along the desolate sands of the south coast of Labrador, and these they called Wonderstrands because the sail past them took so long a time. At length they realized that they were going too far to the west and, turning south across the Gulf of St. Lawrence, perhaps west of Anticosti Island, they came to the east coast of the great bay-indented Gaspé peninsula ; then the beautiful Chaleur Bay opened before them and as it was now late summer there, in Straumfjord, as they called it, they prepared to stay.

STRAUM-
FJORD

At first it proved to be a very agreeable place. There was grass in plenty for the cattle they had brought from Greenland and the members of the expedition passed some happy weeks in exploring this beautiful country at their leisure. But the winter, when it came, brought disillusionment, for it was very severe ; the water froze, the fishing and hunting failed, and because they had done nothing to provide against this misfortune it was not long before food grew scarce.

They tried to live on an island in the mouth of Straumfjord, for it was the home of enormous numbers of sea-birds and they hoped that there might be some fishing there and that they might pick up some sort of jetsam that would help to keep them alive. But though their cattle throve when taken across to the island, they themselves were as badly off as before and soon they found themselves faced with starvation. They called upon God to send them food ; but their prayers were not answered as speedily as the impatient and desperate men desired.

So one day a member of their company disappeared. This was Thorhall the Hunter, an ill-tempered lout who had been in the service of Eric the Red, and when after three whole days of searching for him he was at length found, he was discovered on a crag lying in a rigor with staring eyes and open mouth and dilated nostrils, though sometimes he relaxed in order to writhe and pinch himself, muttering a recitation as he turned and twisted. It took some time to bring him to his senses and when at last they were able to ask him why he had come there, he replied shortly that it was no business of theirs. So they took him home and left this surly creature to his own devices. But shortly afterwards a whale was stranded in the shoal waters and though it was of a species that none of them recognized they cut it up and the cooks boiled it. Now the finding of the beast was just what Thorhall expected. ' Is not the Red-Beard (Thor) of more use than your Christ ? ' he asked, and then he shouted, ' This is my reward for my chanting and spells, since Thor has seldom failed me '. Some of the eaters were ill already, but when they heard this they one and all refused to have anything more to do with the whale-flesh and immediately cast it away from them over the cliffs, committing themselves, as they did so, to the keeping of Almighty God.

Soon after this the weather improved and the ice melted ; they were able to row out to sea and henceforth there was no lack of provisions ; by the time spring came fish, game, and eggs, were once more plentiful. But they could not afford to stay on here for they had not yet found Wineland, so there was a consultation as to how their voyage was to be continued. Thorhall, thoroughly disgruntled and objectionable, pointed out that so far he had not tasted a drop of the wine he had been promised, that he had had a very uncomfortable time with little to eat and nothing but hard work to do, and that he did not intend accompanying Karlsefni if he chose to proceed in what he himself considered to be quite the wrong direction for Wineland ; so while Karlsefni coasted southwards with two ships, Thorhall with nine malcontents renounced the quest of the grapes, taking the third ship first to explore the country to the west and then to set off northwards to Wonderstrands and Keelness on their way back to Greenland.

Karlsefni and his people left Straumfjord and followed the coast first to the south, after which they rounded Cape Breton and made their way south-west along Nova Scotia ; at last they came to a river-mouth, probably the estuary of the Hudson (if it was not further south in Leif's Wineland), that they called HOP *Hóp*,[1] a name meaning *inlet* or *creek*. Here on the low ground was wild wheat and on the hills were vines ; the streams were full of fish, and by digging pits at high-water mark

[1] The Hudson mouth is the Hop of Mr. Gathorne Hardy. Professor Hovgaard, who does not believe that Karlsefni ever got to Wineland at all, makes Straumfjord Sandwich Bay on the east coast of Labrador, and Hop White Bay in Newfoundland. Professor Steensby puts Straumfjord and Hop in the St. Lawrence estuary ; Mr. W. H. Babcock (*Smithsonian Misc. Coll.* 59, 1913, No. 19, pp. 124, 139) places Straumfjord in Passamaquoddy Bay and Hop in Mount Hope Bay. Gustav Storm placed both Straumfjord and Hop on the south-east coast of Nova Scotia. And this illustrates the almost hopeless difficulty of describing these voyages in a coherent story that does not at some point run counter to the narratives in the sagas. I cannot defend the identifications I have chosen here, but I have picked out what seem to me to be the best guesses, and I earnestly commend to the student a very excellent little paper by Professor Halldór Hermannsson (*Geographical Review*, New York,

in the estuary they were able to catch fine halibut when the tide ebbed ; there was game of every variety and good pasture for their remaining cattle. So they built themselves houses and settled down to enjoy themselves.

After they had been a fortnight at Hop nine canoes loaded with Indians appeared ; the natives were swinging their rattle-sticks [1] sunwise, that is from east to west, and Karlsefni and THE INDIANS Snorri interpreted this as a sign of peace so they displayed a white shield in answer. The Indians proved to be friendly, but they were very timid and soon took themselves off ; the Norse described them as swarthy men, ugly to look at and with unkempt hair, large eyes, and broad cheeks. Nothing more was heard of them during the winter.

At Hop, unlike Straumfjord, the weather remained mild and there was no snow ; so the tiny settlement prospered, the men busy chiefly with the cutting of timber for transport to the northern colonies. At the beginning of spring the Indians returned, this time in large numbers, and began to trade with the Norsemen, bartering their furs for red cloth and for milk ; they wanted also to buy swords and spears, but Karlsefni wisely forbade his men to part with their weapons. For a good skin the natives got a span of the cloth, which they then tied round their heads ; when the cloth got scarce the Norsemen began to cut it into smaller and smaller pieces until at last the fragments measured

January, 1927, p. 107) who begins his study by the novel and ingenious method of plotting Leif's course *back* to Greenland. To Professor Hermannsson is due the identification that I have adopted here of Straumfjord as Chaleur Bay. The trouble, of course, is that the sources are in no sense sailing directions ; they are narratives, as muddled and misleading as any other stories set down in writing some two or three hundred years after they were first told, and the plain truth is that the identification of the viking settlements in America will only be conclusively settled, if ever, by the actual discovery of the Norse booths. Unfortunately, the search for Scandinavian remains in the New World has so far yielded no results in spite of various extravagant claims. The old stone mill at Newport, Rhode Island, thought to date from the time of the Norsemen, proves to have been built in the seventeenth century, the alleged runes on the Dighton Rock and the Yarmouth Stone are certainly not Norse, the Kensington runic inscription in Minnesota is a forgery, and there is no hope for the painted boulder at Spokane, Washington. Excavation has failed to show that certain ruins on the Charles River at Cambridge, Massachusetts, are Norse, as was at one time believed, and other ruins and graves on the east coast of Labrador near Nain and Amitok Island, also thought to be of Norse origin, are now known to be the work of other peoples.

[1] The word *trjóna* is usually translated pole or stave, but I adopt here Mr. Gathorne Hardy's suggestion (*op. cit.*, p. 182).

not more than a finger's breadth.   Yet the Indians gave as much, or even more, for these little scraps.

The trading, however, was interrupted by two most unfortunate incidents : one the frightening of the natives by Karlsefni's bull and the other the murder of one of the Indians by a Norseman whose weapons he had tried to steal.   The result was that the THE FIGHT Indians departed in an obviously angry mood, so WITH THE Karlsefni saw nothing for it but to erect a strong INDIANS pallisade around the settlement and make ready for its defence.   At the end of three weeks came the expected attack. The Indians were in even greater numbers, and this time they were shouting and waving their rattles not sunwise but widdershins.   Karlsefni saw that this meant war and so he raised a red shield as a sign that he also was ready to fight, and there followed a battle.   The savages had a very peculiar engine of war, a variety of ballista that was worked by several men,[1] and this so terrified the Norsemen that they fled.   But they were rallied by the woman Freydis and in the end they beat off the Indians, killing four of them and losing only two of their own number.

After this it was plain that however attractive the land might be Karlsefni and his people would live henceforth in constant danger of attack by the Indians.   So the Norsemen packed up and sailed off to Straumfjord, and here, now that they were well stocked with provisions, they passed their third winter ; but it was not a happy one as there were quarrels of a serious nature over the women.   Karlsefni himself took one ship and went off to look for Thorhall the Hunter, sailing, it seems, westwards up the St. Lawrence estuary.[2]   But Thorhall, who had left the expedition two years previously with the intention of exploring to the west, that is up the St. Lawrence, had changed his mind and had tried to return to Greenland ; on his way back he had met with misfortune as storms had driven him far out of his course and he is said to have landed eventually in Ireland where

[1] The Norsemen described this as a large ball, resembling a sheep's paunch and dark-coloured, which was slung from a pole and made a horrible noise when it descended.   Modern Indians use no such weapon, but Algonquin tradition has preserved the memory of a formidable ballista which was made of a boulder sewn up tight in a skin and slung at the end of a long rod, H. R. Schoolcraft, *Indian Tribes of the United States*, I (1851), p. 85.

[2] Karlsefni is said to have sailed northward to Keelness and then westwards, having land on his port side.   This probably means that he sailed across the Gulf of St. Lawrence and then back again in a westerly direction to the Gaspé peninsula and thence westward along the south bank of the St. Lawrence.

he was taken prisoner and killed. Karlsefni, therefore, saw
nothing of his former companion ; so he returned to
RETURN
OF KARL-
SEFNI Straumfjord and then with the second boat began his
return journey to Greenland. For this boat of Bjarni
Grimolfsson the homeward trip was disastrous, for
he was storm-driven far out into the western Atlantic where his
ship foundered and only a half of the crew escaped with their lives.
But Karlsefni came safely to Greenland and there spent the
winter (1023–4) with old Eric the Red.

The story of the next voyage to Wineland is less the narrative
of a journey than the tale of an evil woman and her doings ;
for though America was indeed the stage whereon her worst
villainy was played, yet of the travelling thither and the discoveries or fortunes of the voyage there is nothing told.

Perhaps it is largely for this reason that the historicity of this
last adventure in Wineland has been challenged, and it is certainly
true that the story is related by the *Flatey Book* alone. There
may be some reasonable misgivings, furthermore, over the circumstance that the cruel woman who dominates the almost
unbelievable drama now to be unfolded herself accompanied
Karlsefni. For it is Freydis, the wild and valorous daughter of
Eric, who inspired and directed this next enterprise, and as she
has already been heard of as rallying Karlsefni's Norsemen when
the Indians pressed them it is easy to suspect that the new tale
of her adventures in America may likewise be an episode happening
during Karlsefni's voyage, perhaps on the return journey when
the leader himself was away searching for Thorhall.

This, however, is the *Flatey Book* tale. After Karlsefni's
return to Greenland, Freydis, who seemingly could make her rich
and stupid husband do whatever she wanted, determined to go
VOYAGE OF
FREYDIS back to Wineland, and she persuaded two brothers,
Helgi and Finnbogi, Icelanders lately arrived in Greenland, to accompany her with their ship, this on the
condition that she and they should share the profits of the expedition. It was agreed that the brothers should take thirty men of
fighting age, besides women, and Freydis thirty also in her own
ship ; but Freydis began her cheating by smuggling five extra
men on board.

The two boats sailed for Leif's camp and the brothers, arriving
first, took up their belongings to the booths where they imagined
the crews of both ships would make their home. But Freydis,
when she came, had them turned out. ' Leif lent the houses to
me and not to you ', said she. ' We are certainly no match for
you in wickedness ', replied Helgi, and he and his brother carried

away their goods and built a camp for themselves some distance away. By the time winter came the arrogance of Freydis had made friendly relations between herself and the brothers impossible and soon the quarrel of the leaders spread into an open hostility between the two settlements. This was exactly what Freydis desired to happen, and now it was that this woman did her foulest deed ; she had long coveted, it seems, the brothers' ship, for it was a bigger and better boat then her own, and early one morning she went over quite alone to their house and bargained for it. Evidently she was refused, as she had every reason to expect she would be, and she returned to her husband, Thorvard, and roused him to tell him that the brothers had so abused and ill-treated her that the insult could only be wiped out with blood. The miserable Thorvard was at length goaded into action and, summoning his men, he let Freydis lead them off to attack the camp of the brothers. They took the place by surprise and having captured every single man, including the wretched brothers, they led them out and killed them one by one. But the five women of the camp remained, and though they had been witnesses of the atrocity, yet no one of Thorvard's men could bring himself to slay them. And then it was that Freydis stood forth. ' Give me an axe ', she cried, and when they put one in her hand she went up to the five women and killed them every one.

Freydis said to her men, ' If we have the luck to get back to Greenland I shall certainly contrive the death of anyone who speaks of this event. We shall say that the crew of the other ship stayed behind here when we came away '. But when, after fitting out and loading the brothers' ship, they sailed back in the spring to Ericsfjord the story of this utterly abominable massacre leaked out. Yet Leif could not bring himself to punish his sister as she deserved, though from that time onwards she and her husband were everywhere regarded with loathing.

She was not the last of the Greenlanders, this remarkable Freydis, to sail for the New World. It is related that in 1121, just about a hundred years later, Eric Gnupsson, said to have been Bishop of Greenland, went in search of Wineland, maybe to preach the gospel to the Indians or Eskimos of America ; but he never returned and there was nothing heard of his fate. Probably Markland was visited more than once during the period of the decline of the colony in order that wood might be obtained and there is, indeed, record of a voyage thither in the fourteenth century, for in the year 1347 it was reported that there arrived in Iceland a little Greenland ship with a crew of seventeen or

eighteen men that had been to Markland and subsequently driven
out of her course on the return journey. So it must be counted
to the credit of the sickly colony of the thirteenth and fourteenth
centuries that the Greenlanders still dared to make the perilous
crossing to the great continent their ancestors had found. But
that they made their way far enough south to visit Wineland
no man knows.[1]

[1] It is sometimes said that Harald Hardradi journeyed to Wineland
during his celebrated voyage to investigate the breadth of the northern
ocean (Adam of Bremen, IV, 38), but actually there is no reason for supposing that he reached America. Nor is the Honen rune-stone in Ringerike
of any historic importance even though an uncertain reading seems to
record an expedition to Wineland by explorers who lost themselves
among the ice of uninhabited countries. Nor, moreover, can anything
be made of a projected expedition to discover the ' New Land ' found in
the northern seas by Icelandic explorers about 1290. On this, and Harald's
voyage, see F. Nansen, *In Northern Mists*.

SELECT BIBLIOGRAPHIES

(For a more complete guide to the literature concerning the history of the vikings, both modern works and sources, see *Cambridge Mediaeval History*, III, p. 618 ; various other useful bibliographies that should be consulted are indicated in the following short list of well-known books and articles.)

GENERAL

R. NORDENSTRENG : Vikingafärderna. 2nd. ed., Stockholm, 1926.
ALLEN MAWER : The Vikings. Cambridge, 1913.
—— The Vikings. Cambridge Mediaeval History, III, 1922, Ch. XIII, p. 309.
HALFDAN KOHT : The Scandinavian Kingdoms until the end of the thirteenth century. Cambridge Mediaeval History, VI, 1929, Ch. XI, p. 362.
AXEL OLRIK : De nordiska folken under vikingatiden och den äldsta medeltiden. Stockholm, 1926 (Swedish trans. by H. Ellekilde in Världskulturen, III, 1907).
K. T. STRASSER : Wikinger und Normannen. Hamburg, 1928. See Bibliography, p. 207.
M. W. WILLIAMS : Social Scandinavia in the Viking Age. New York, 1920. See Bibliography, pp. 431–44.

DENMARK

ERIK ARUP : Danmarks Historie. I, Copenhagen, 1925.
J. C. H. R. STEENSTRUP : Danmarks Riges Historie. I, Copenhagen, 1904.
VILH. GRØNBECH : Nordiske Myter og Sagn. Copenhagen, 1927. See p. 172 ff.
L. WEIBULL : Kritiska undersökningar i Nordens historia omkring år 1000. Lund, 1911.
OTTO SCHEEL AND PETER PAULSEN : Schleswig-Haithabu. Kiel, 1930 (note especially important Bibliography, p. 149).
L. JACOBSEN : Svenskevaeldets Fald. Copenhagen, 1929.

NORWAY

A. BUGGE AND OTHERS : Norges Historie. I and II, Oslo, 1912–16.
KNUT GJERSET : History of the Norwegian People. 2 vols. in one, New York, 1927.
JOHAN SCHREINER : Saga og Oldfunn. Oslo, 1927 (in Vid.-Akad. Skrifter II, Hist.-Filos. Klasse, I).
—— Olav den hellige og Norges Samling. Oslo, 1929.
HALFDAN KOHT : Innhogg og utsyn i norsk historie. Oslo, 1921.

SWEDEN

H. Schück and others : Svenska Folkets Historia. I, Lund, 1914.
Carl Hallendorf and A. Schück : History of Sweden. London, 1929.
Birger Nerman : Det svenska rikets uppkomst. Stockholm, 1925.
A. Schück : Det svenska stadsväsendets uppkomst och äldsta utveckling. Stockholm, 1926 (full Bibliography p. ix ff.).

EAST BALTIC, RUSSIA, BYZANTIUM, AND THE EAST

Birger Nerman : Die Verbindungen zwischen Skandinavien und das Ostbaltikum in der jüngeren Eisenzeit. Stockholm, 1929 (K. Ant. Akad. Handl. 40 : 1).
T. J. Arne : La Suède et l'Orient. Uppsala, 1914 (Arch. d'études orientales, vol. 8).
—— Det stora Svitjod. Stockholm, 1917.
C. Kadleč : The Empire and its northern neighbours. Cambridge Mediaeval History, IV, 1923, Ch. VII, pp. 200–210 ; note especially Bibliography, pp. 819–821.
V. Thomsen : The Relations between Ancient Russia and Scandinavia. Oxford, 1877.
A. A. Vasiliev : La Russie primitive et Byzance (in L'Art byzantin chez les Slaves, Ie rec. Uspenskij, I, pp. 8–19). Paris, 1930.
V. O. Kluchevsky : History of Russia. I, London, 1911.
B. Pares : A History of Russia. London, 1926.
M. Hruchevsky : Geschichte des ukrainischen Volkes. I, Leipzig, 1906.
—— Geschichte der Ukraine. I, Lemberg, 1916. French summary, Paris, 1920.
L. Niederle : Manuel de l'Antiquité slave. I, Paris, 1923. See p. 198 ff.
V. G. Vasilievsky : Trydy (Works). I, St. Petersburg, 1908. For Varangians in Constantinople see p. 177 ff.
B. Dorn : Caspia. St. Petersburg, 1875. In Mem. Acad. imp. des Sciences, 7 S., XXIII, 1877.

WESTERN EMPIRE AND SPAIN

J. C. H. R. Steenstrup : Normannerne. Copenhagen, 1876–82. I, Chs. 7, 8 ; II, Chs. 6–11.
C. F. Keary : The Vikings in Western Christendom. London, 1891.
Walther Vogel : Die Normannen und das Fränkische Reich bis zur Gründung der Normandie (799–911). Heidelberg, 1906.
Jan de Vries : De Wikingen in de lage landen bij de Zee. Haarlem, 1923.
R. Poupardin : Cambridge Mediaeval History, III, 1922, Chs. I–III passim.
L. Halphen : ibidem, Ch. IV passim.
E. Wadstein : Norden och Västeuropa i gammal tid. Stockholm, 1925.
J. H. Holwerda : Dorestad en onze vroegste middeleeuwen. Leiden, 1929.
P. C. J. A. Boeles : Friesland tot de elfde eeuw. Hague, 1927. See p. 220 ff.
Jón Stefánsson : Vikings in Spain. In Saga-book of the Viking Club, VI, 1908–9, p. 31.

ENGLAND

C. F. KEARY : op. cit., s.v. Western Empire.
W. J. CORBETT : Cambridge Mediaeval History, III, 1922, Chs. XIV and
   XV *passim*. Note also Bibliographies p. 625 ff.
T. HODGKIN : Political History of England. I (to 1066), London, 1920.
C. OMAN : England before the Norman Conquest. 7th. ed. London, 1929.
W. G. COLLINGWOOD : Scandinavian Britain. London, 1908.
J. C. H. R. STEENSTRUP : Normannerne Copenhagen, 1876–82. II, Chs.
   2–4 ; III, Chs. 3, 7, 9–12.
F. M. STENTON : The Danes in England (Raleigh Lecture, British Academy,
   1927 : Proc. Vol. XIII).

IRELAND

A. WALSH : Scandinavian Relations with Ireland during the Viking Period.
   Dublin, 1922. Note Bibliography, p. 77.
ALICE STOPFORD GREEN : History of the Irish State to 1014. London,
   1925.
EOIN MACNEILL : Phases of Irish History. Dublin, 1920 (especially Ch.
   IX).
ELEANOR HULL : The Gael and the Gall. In Saga-book of Viking Club,
   V, 1906–7, p. 362.
E. CURTIS : History of Mediaeval Ireland. London, 1923.
J. H. TODD : War of the Gaedhil with the Gaill. Rolls Series : London,
   1867. See especially Introduction and Appendices.
L. J. VOGT : Dublin som Norsk By. Oslo, 1896.
C. HALIDAY : The Scandinavian Kingdom of Dublin. Dublin, 1884.

SCOTLAND AND MAN

A. O. ANDERSON : Early Sources of Scottish History. Edinburgh, 1922.
   Vol. I.
R. L. BREMNER : The Norsemen in Alban. Glasgow, 1923.
G. HENDERSON : The Norse Influence on Celtic Scotland. Glasgow, 1910.
A. W. BRØGGER : Ancient Emigrants. A History of the Norse Settlements
   in Scotland. Oxford, 1929.
W. G. COLLINGWOOD : Norse Influence in Dumfriesshire and Galloway. In
   Trans. Dumfries and Galloway Nat. Hist. and Ant. Soc. 3 S. VII,
   1921, p. 97.
D. W. HUNTER MARSHALL : The Sudreys in Early Viking Times. Glasgow,
   1929. Bibliography, p. 46.
JAMES GRAY : Sutherland and Caithness in Saga-time. Edinburgh, 1922.
   Bibliography, pp. ix–xii.
A. W. JOHNSTON : Orkney and Shetland Folk 880–1350. In Saga-book
   of the Viking Society, IX, 1914–18, p. 372.
SYMINGTON GRIEVE : The Book of Colonsay and Oronsay. Edinburgh,
   1923. Especially Vol. II, pp. 1–128.
A. W. MOORE : History of the Isle of Man. London, 1900.

WALES

J. E. LLOYD : A History of Wales. London, 1911. Especially Vol. I, Ch. IX, p. 320 ff.
D. R. PATERSON : Early Cardiff. Exeter, 1926.
—— The Pre-Norman Settlement of Glamorgan. In Archaeologia Cambrensis, 1922, p. 37. Cf. The Scandinavian Settlement of Cardiff, ibidem, 1921, p. 53, and a study of the Scandinavian placenames of Glamorgan, ibidem, 1920, p. 31.

FAROE ISLANDS

F. YORK POWELL : The Tale of Thrond of Gate (Faereyinga Saga). London, 1896. See especially Introduction.
A. BUGGE : Norges Historie. Oslo, 1910. Vol. I, Pt. 2, p. 151 ff., p. 265 ff., p. 370 ff.

ICELAND

KNUT GJERSET : History of Iceland. London, 1924.
D. BRUUN : Fortidsminder og nutidshjem paa Island. Copenhagen, 1928.
VALTÝR GUDMUNDSSON : Island i Fristatstiden. Copenhagen, 1924.
ARI THORGILSSON : The Book of the Icelanders (Íslendingabók) : Islandica, Vol. XX. Ithaca, N.Y., 1930, ed. Halldór Hermannsson.

GREENLAND

F. JÓNSSON, D. BRUUN, AND P. NØRLUND : Greenland (ed. M. Vahl). II, Copenhagen and London, 1928, p. 331 ff. See especially Bibliography, p. 361.
TH. N. KRABBE : Greenland : its nature, inhabitants, and history. London, 1930. English trans. ; also in Danish, Copenhagen, 1930.
FRIDTJOF NANSEN : In Northern Mists. 2 vols. London, 1911.
P. NØRLUND : Meddelelser om Grønland, LXVII, 1924, p. 1 (for Herjolfsness) ; ibidem, LXXVI, 1929, p. 1 (for Gardar).
IVAR BARDSSON : Det gamle Grønlands Beskrivelse (ed. F. Jónsson). Copenhagen, 1930. See particularly the detailed maps of the Norse settlements.

AMERICA

W. HOVGAARD : The Voyages of the Norsemen to America. New York, 1915 (American-Scandinavian Foundation : Scandinavian Monographs I). See Bibliography, p. 279.
G. M. GATHORNE-HARDY : The Norse Discoverers of America. Oxford, 1921. Bibliography, p. 299.
FRIDTJOF NANSEN : In Northern Mists. London, 1911.
H. HERMANNSSON : The Wineland Voyages. Geographical Review, New York, 1927, p. 107.
J. FISCHER : Catholic Encylopedia. I, 1907. S.v. America, Pre-Columban Discovery of.

INDEX OF AUTHORS

GENERAL INDEX

A CATALOG OF SELECTED
DOVER BOOKS
IN ALL FIELDS OF INTEREST

A CATALOG OF SELECTED DOVER
BOOKS IN ALL FIELDS OF INTEREST

CONCERNING THE SPIRITUAL IN ART, Wassily Kandinsky. Pioneering work by father of abstract art. Thoughts on color theory, nature of art. Analysis of earlier masters. 12 illustrations. 80pp. of text. 5⅜ x 8½.   0-486-23411-8

CELTIC ART: The Methods of Construction, George Bain. Simple geometric techniques for making Celtic interlacements, spirals, Kells-type initials, animals, humans, etc. Over 500 illustrations. 160pp. 9 x 12. (Available in U.S. only.)   0-486-22923-8

AN ATLAS OF ANATOMY FOR ARTISTS, Fritz Schider. Most thorough reference work on art anatomy in the world. Hundreds of illustrations, including selections from works by Vesalius, Leonardo, Goya, Ingres, Michelangelo, others. 593 illustrations. 192pp. 7⅛ x 10¼.   0-486-20241-0

CELTIC HAND STROKE-BY-STROKE (Irish Half-Uncial from "The Book of Kells"): An Arthur Baker Calligraphy Manual, Arthur Baker. Complete guide to creating each letter of the alphabet in distinctive Celtic manner. Covers hand position, strokes, pens, inks, paper, more. Illustrated. 48pp. 8¼ x 11.   0-486-24336-2

EASY ORIGAMI, John Montroll. Charming collection of 32 projects (hat, cup, pelican, piano, swan, many more) specially designed for the novice origami hobbyist. Clearly illustrated easy-to-follow instructions insure that even beginning papercrafters will achieve successful results. 48pp. 8¼ x 11.   0-486-27298-2

BLOOMINGDALE'S ILLUSTRATED 1886 CATALOG: Fashions, Dry Goods and Housewares, Bloomingdale Brothers. Famed merchants' extremely rare catalog depicting about 1,700 products: clothing, housewares, firearms, dry goods, jewelry, more. Invaluable for dating, identifying vintage items. Also, copyright-free graphics for artists, designers. Co-published with Henry Ford Museum & Greenfield Village. 160pp. 8¼ x 11.   0-486-25780-0

THE ART OF WORLDLY WISDOM, Baltasar Gracian. "Think with the few and speak with the many," "Friends are a second existence," and "Be able to forget" are among this 1637 volume's 300 pithy maxims. A perfect source of mental and spiritual refreshment, it can be opened at random and appreciated either in brief or at length. 128pp. 5⅜ x 8½.   0-486-44034-6

JOHNSON'S DICTIONARY: A Modern Selection, Samuel Johnson (E. L. McAdam and George Milne, eds.). This modern version reduces the original 1755 edition's 2,300 pages of definitions and literary examples to a more manageable length, retaining the verbal pleasure and historical curiosity of the original. 480pp. 5⁵⁄₁₆ x 8¼.   0-486-44089-3

ADVENTURES OF HUCKLEBERRY FINN, Mark Twain, Illustrated by E. W. Kemble. A work of eternal richness and complexity, a source of ongoing critical debate, and a literary landmark, Twain's 1885 masterpiece about a barefoot boy's journey of self-discovery has enthralled readers around the world. This handsome clothbound reproduction of the first edition features all 174 of the original black-and-white illustrations. 368pp. 5⅜ x 8½.   0-486-44322-1

STICKLEY CRAFTSMAN FURNITURE CATALOGS, Gustav Stickley and L. & J. G. Stickley. Beautiful, functional furniture in two authentic catalogs from 1910. 594 illustrations, including 277 photos, show settles, rockers, armchairs, reclining chairs, bookcases, desks, tables. 183pp. 6½ x 9¼. 0-486-23838-5

AMERICAN LOCOMOTIVES IN HISTORIC PHOTOGRAPHS: 1858 to 1949, Ron Ziel (ed.). A rare collection of 126 meticulously detailed official photographs, called "builder portraits," of American locomotives that majestically chronicle the rise of steam locomotive power in America. Introduction. Detailed captions. xi+ 129pp. 9 x 12. 0-486-27393-8

AMERICA'S LIGHTHOUSES: An Illustrated History, Francis Ross Holland, Jr. Delightfully written, profusely illustrated fact-filled survey of over 200 American light-houses since 1716. History, anecdotes, technological advances, more. 240pp. 8 x 10¾. 0-486-25576-X

TOWARDS A NEW ARCHITECTURE, Le Corbusier. Pioneering manifesto by founder of "International School." Technical and aesthetic theories, views of industry, economics, relation of form to function, "mass-production split" and much more. Profusely illustrated. 320pp. 6⅛ x 9¼. (Available in U.S. only.) 0-486-25023-7

HOW THE OTHER HALF LIVES, Jacob Riis. Famous journalistic record, exposing poverty and degradation of New York slums around 1900, by major social reformer. 100 striking and influential photographs. 233pp. 10 x 7⅞. 0-486-22012-5

FRUIT KEY AND TWIG KEY TO TREES AND SHRUBS, William M. Harlow. One of the handiest and most widely used identification aids. Fruit key covers 120 deciduous and evergreen species; twig key 160 deciduous species. Easily used. Over 300 photographs. 126pp. 5⅜ x 8½. 0-486-20511-8

COMMON BIRD SONGS, Dr. Donald J. Borror. Songs of 60 most common U.S. birds: robins, sparrows, cardinals, bluejays, finches, more—arranged in order of increasing complexity. Up to 9 variations of songs of each species.
Cassette and manual 0-486-99911-4

ORCHIDS AS HOUSE PLANTS, Rebecca Tyson Northen. Grow cattleyas and many other kinds of orchids–in a window, in a case, or under artificial light. 63 illustrations. 148pp. 5⅜ x 8½. 0-486-23261-1

MONSTER MAZES, Dave Phillips. Masterful mazes at four levels of difficulty. Avoid deadly perils and evil creatures to find magical treasures. Solutions for all 32 exciting illustrated puzzles. 48pp. 8¼ x 11. 0-486-26005-4

MOZART'S DON GIOVANNI (DOVER OPERA LIBRETTO SERIES), Wolfgang Amadeus Mozart. Introduced and translated by Ellen H. Bleiler. Standard Italian libretto, with complete English translation. Convenient and thoroughly portable–an ideal companion for reading along with a recording or the performance itself. Introduction. List of characters. Plot summary. 121pp. 5¼ x 8½. 0-486-24944-1

FRANK LLOYD WRIGHT'S DANA HOUSE, Donald Hoffmann. Pictorial essay of residential masterpiece with over 160 interior and exterior photos, plans, elevations, sketches and studies. 128pp. 9¼ x 10¾. 0-486-29120-0

THE CLARINET AND CLARINET PLAYING, David Pino. Lively, comprehensive work features suggestions about technique, musicianship, and musical interpretation, as well as guidelines for teaching, making your own reeds, and preparing for public performance. Includes an intriguing look at clarinet history. "A godsend," *The Clarinet,* Journal of the International Clarinet Society. Appendixes. 7 illus. 320pp. 5⅜ x 8½. 0-486-40270-3

HOLLYWOOD GLAMOR PORTRAITS, John Kobal (ed.). 145 photos from 1926-49. Harlow, Gable, Bogart, Bacall; 94 stars in all. Full background on photographers, technical aspects. 160pp. 8⅜ x 11¼. 0-486-23352-9

THE RAVEN AND OTHER FAVORITE POEMS, Edgar Allan Poe. Over 40 of the author's most memorable poems: "The Bells," "Ulalume," "Israfel," "To Helen," "The Conqueror Worm," "Eldorado," "Annabel Lee," many more. Alphabetic lists of titles and first lines. 64pp. 5$\frac{3}{16}$ x 8¼. 0-486-26685-0

PERSONAL MEMOIRS OF U. S. GRANT, Ulysses Simpson Grant. Intelligent, deeply moving firsthand account of Civil War campaigns, considered by many the finest military memoirs ever written. Includes letters, historic photographs, maps and more. 528pp. 6⅛ x 9¼. 0-486-28587-1

ANCIENT EGYPTIAN MATERIALS AND INDUSTRIES, A. Lucas and J. Harris. Fascinating, comprehensive, thoroughly documented text describes this ancient civilization's vast resources and the processes that incorporated them in daily life, including the use of animal products, building materials, cosmetics, perfumes and incense, fibers, glazed ware, glass and its manufacture, materials used in the mummification process, and much more. 544pp. 6⅛ x 9¼. (Available in U.S. only.) 0-486-40446-3

RUSSIAN STORIES/RUSSKIE RASSKAZY: A Dual-Language Book, edited by Gleb Struve. Twelve tales by such masters as Chekhov, Tolstoy, Dostoevsky, Pushkin, others. Excellent word-for-word English translations on facing pages, plus teaching and study aids, Russian/English vocabulary, biographical/critical introductions, more. 416pp. 5⅜ x 8½. 0-486-26244-8

PHILADELPHIA THEN AND NOW: 60 Sites Photographed in the Past and Present, Kenneth Finkel and Susan Oyama. Rare photographs of City Hall, Logan Square, Independence Hall, Betsy Ross House, other landmarks juxtaposed with contemporary views. Captures changing face of historic city. Introduction. Captions. 128pp. 8¼ x 11. 0-486-25790-8

NORTH AMERICAN INDIAN LIFE: Customs and Traditions of 23 Tribes, Elsie Clews Parsons (ed.). 27 fictionalized essays by noted anthropologists examine religion, customs, government, additional facets of life among the Winnebago, Crow, Zuni, Eskimo, other tribes. 480pp. 6⅛ x 9¼. 0-486-27377-6

TECHNICAL MANUAL AND DICTIONARY OF CLASSICAL BALLET, Gail Grant. Defines, explains, comments on steps, movements, poses and concepts. 15-page pictorial section. Basic book for student, viewer. 127pp. 5⅜ x 8½. 0-486-21843-0

THE MALE AND FEMALE FIGURE IN MOTION: 60 Classic Photographic Sequences, Eadweard Muybridge. 60 true-action photographs of men and women walking, running, climbing, bending, turning, etc., reproduced from rare 19th-century masterpiece. vi + 121pp. 9 x 12. 0-486-24745-7

ANIMALS: 1,419 Copyright-Free Illustrations of Mammals, Birds, Fish, Insects, etc., Jim Harter (ed.). Clear wood engravings present, in extremely lifelike poses, over 1,000 species of animals. One of the most extensive pictorial sourcebooks of its kind. Captions. Index. 284pp. 9 x 12. 0-486-23766-4

1001 QUESTIONS ANSWERED ABOUT THE SEASHORE, N. J. Berrill and Jacquelyn Berrill. Queries answered about dolphins, sea snails, sponges, starfish, fishes, shore birds, many others. Covers appearance, breeding, growth, feeding, much more. 305pp. 5¼ x 8¼. 0-486-23366-9

ATTRACTING BIRDS TO YOUR YARD, William J. Weber. Easy-to-follow guide offers advice on how to attract the greatest diversity of birds: birdhouses, feeders, water and waterers, much more. 96pp. 5³⁄₁₆ x 8¼. 0-486-28927-3

MEDICINAL AND OTHER USES OF NORTH AMERICAN PLANTS: A Historical Survey with Special Reference to the Eastern Indian Tribes, Charlotte Erichsen-Brown. Chronological historical citations document 500 years of usage of plants, trees, shrubs native to eastern Canada, northeastern U.S. Also complete identifying information. 343 illustrations. 544pp. 6½ x 9¼. 0-486-25951-X

STORYBOOK MAZES, Dave Phillips. 23 stories and mazes on two-page spreads: Wizard of Oz, Treasure Island, Robin Hood, etc. Solutions. 64pp. 8¼ x 11. 0-486-23628-5

AMERICAN NEGRO SONGS: 230 Folk Songs and Spirituals, Religious and Secular, John W. Work. This authoritative study traces the African influences of songs sung and played by black Americans at work, in church, and as entertainment. The author discusses the lyric significance of such songs as "Swing Low, Sweet Chariot," "John Henry," and others and offers the words and music for 230 songs. Bibliography. Index of Song Titles. 272pp. 6½ x 9¼. 0-486-40271-1

MOVIE-STAR PORTRAITS OF THE FORTIES, John Kobal (ed.). 163 glamor, studio photos of 106 stars of the 1940s: Rita Hayworth, Ava Gardner, Marlon Brando, Clark Gable, many more. 176pp. 8⅜ x 11¼. 0-486-23546-7

YEKL and THE IMPORTED BRIDEGROOM AND OTHER STORIES OF YIDDISH NEW YORK, Abraham Cahan. Film Hester Street based on *Yekl* (1896). Novel, other stories among first about Jewish immigrants on N.Y.'s East Side. 240pp. 5⅜ x 8½. 0-486-22427-9

SELECTED POEMS, Walt Whitman. Generous sampling from *Leaves of Grass.* Twenty-four poems include "I Hear America Singing," "Song of the Open Road," "I Sing the Body Electric," "When Lilacs Last in the Dooryard Bloom'd," "O Captain! My Captain!"—all reprinted from an authoritative edition. Lists of titles and first lines. 128pp. 5³⁄₁₆ x 8¼. 0-486-26878-0

SONGS OF EXPERIENCE: Facsimile Reproduction with 26 Plates in Full Color, William Blake. 26 full-color plates from a rare 1826 edition. Includes "The Tyger," "London," "Holy Thursday," and other poems. Printed text of poems. 48pp. 5¼ x 7. 0-486-24636-1

THE BEST TALES OF HOFFMANN, E. T. A. Hoffmann. 10 of Hoffmann's most important stories: "Nutcracker and the King of Mice," "The Golden Flowerpot," etc. 458pp. 5⅜ x 8½. 0-486-21793-0

THE BOOK OF TEA, Kakuzo Okakura. Minor classic of the Orient: entertaining, charming explanation, interpretation of traditional Japanese culture in terms of tea ceremony. 94pp. 5⅜ x 8½. 0-486-20070-1

FRENCH STORIES/CONTES FRANÇAIS: A Dual-Language Book, Wallace Fowlie. Ten stories by French masters, Voltaire to Camus: "Micromegas" by Voltaire; "The Atheist's Mass" by Balzac; "Minuet" by de Maupassant; "The Guest" by Camus, six more. Excellent English translations on facing pages. Also French-English vocabulary list, exercises, more. 352pp. 5⅜ x 8½. 0-486-26443-2

CHICAGO AT THE TURN OF THE CENTURY IN PHOTOGRAPHS: 122 Historic Views from the Collections of the Chicago Historical Society, Larry A. Viskochil. Rare large-format prints offer detailed views of City Hall, State Street, the Loop, Hull House, Union Station, many other landmarks, circa 1904-1913. Introduction. Captions. Maps. 144pp. 9⅜ x 12¼. 0-486-24656-6

OLD BROOKLYN IN EARLY PHOTOGRAPHS, 1865-1929, William Lee Younger. Luna Park, Gravesend race track, construction of Grand Army Plaza, moving of Hotel Brighton, etc. 157 previously unpublished photographs. 165pp. 8⅞ x 11¾. 0-486-23587-4

THE MYTHS OF THE NORTH AMERICAN INDIANS, Lewis Spence. Rich anthology of the myths and legends of the Algonquins, Iroquois, Pawnees and Sioux, prefaced by an extensive historical and ethnological commentary. 36 illustrations. 480pp. 5⅜ x 8½. 0-486-25967-6

AN ENCYCLOPEDIA OF BATTLES: Accounts of Over 1,560 Battles from 1479 B.C. to the Present, David Eggenberger. Essential details of every major battle in recorded history from the first battle of Megiddo in 1479 B.C. to Grenada in 1984. List of Battle Maps. New Appendix covering the years 1967-1984. Index. 99 illustrations. 544pp. 6½ x 9¼. 0-486-24913-1

SAILING ALONE AROUND THE WORLD, Captain Joshua Slocum. First man to sail around the world, alone, in small boat. One of great feats of seamanship told in delightful manner. 67 illustrations. 294pp. 5⅜ x 8½. 0-486-20326-3

ANARCHISM AND OTHER ESSAYS, Emma Goldman. Powerful, penetrating, prophetic essays on direct action, role of minorities, prison reform, puritan hypocrisy, violence, etc. 271pp. 5⅜ x 8½. 0-486-22484-8

MYTHS OF THE HINDUS AND BUDDHISTS, Ananda K. Coomaraswamy and Sister Nivedita. Great stories of the epics; deeds of Krishna, Shiva, taken from puranas, Vedas, folk tales; etc. 32 illustrations. 400pp. 5⅜ x 8½. 0-486-21759-0

MY BONDAGE AND MY FREEDOM, Frederick Douglass. Born a slave, Douglass became outspoken force in antislavery movement. The best of Douglass' autobiographies. Graphic description of slave life. 464pp. 5⅜ x 8½. 0-486-22457-0

FOLLOWING THE EQUATOR: A Journey Around the World, Mark Twain. Fascinating humorous account of 1897 voyage to Hawaii, Australia, India, New Zealand, etc. Ironic, bemused reports on peoples, customs, climate, flora and fauna, politics, much more. 197 illustrations. 720pp. 5⅜ x 8½. 0-486-26113-1

THE PEOPLE CALLED SHAKERS, Edward D. Andrews. Definitive study of Shakers: origins, beliefs, practices, dances, social organization, furniture and crafts, etc. 33 illustrations. 351pp. 5⅜ x 8½. 0-486-21081-2

THE MYTHS OF GREECE AND ROME, H. A. Guerber. A classic of mythology, generously illustrated, long prized for its simple, graphic, accurate retelling of the principal myths of Greece and Rome, and for its commentary on their origins and significance. With 64 illustrations by Michelangelo, Raphael, Titian, Rubens, Canova, Bernini and others. 480pp. 5⅜ x 8½. 0-486-27584-1

PSYCHOLOGY OF MUSIC, Carl E. Seashore. Classic work discusses music as a medium from psychological viewpoint. Clear treatment of physical acoustics, auditory apparatus, sound perception, development of musical skills, nature of musical feeling, host of other topics. 88 figures. 408pp. 5⅜ x 8½. 0-486-21851-1

LIFE IN ANCIENT EGYPT, Adolf Erman. Fullest, most thorough, detailed older account with much not in more recent books, domestic life, religion, magic, medicine, commerce, much more. Many illustrations reproduce tomb paintings, carvings, hieroglyphs, etc. 597pp. 5⅜ x 8½. 0-486-22632-8

SUNDIALS, Their Theory and Construction, Albert Waugh. Far and away the best, most thorough coverage of ideas, mathematics concerned, types, construction, adjusting anywhere. Simple, nontechnical treatment allows even children to build several of these dials. Over 100 illustrations. 230pp. 5⅜ x 8½. 0-486-22947-5

THEORETICAL HYDRODYNAMICS, L. M. Milne-Thomson. Classic exposition of the mathematical theory of fluid motion, applicable to both hydrodynamics and aerodynamics. Over 600 exercises. 768pp. 6⅛ x 9¼. 0-486-68970-0

OLD-TIME VIGNETTES IN FULL COLOR, Carol Belanger Grafton (ed.). Over 390 charming, often sentimental illustrations, selected from archives of Victorian graphics–pretty women posing, children playing, food, flowers, kittens and puppies, smiling cherubs, birds and butterflies, much more. All copyright-free. 48pp. 9¼ x 12¼. 0-486-27269-9

PERSPECTIVE FOR ARTISTS, Rex Vicat Cole. Depth, perspective of sky and sea, shadows, much more, not usually covered. 391 diagrams, 81 reproductions of drawings and paintings. 279pp. 5⅜ x 8½. 0-486-22487-2

DRAWING THE LIVING FIGURE, Joseph Sheppard. Innovative approach to artistic anatomy focuses on specifics of surface anatomy, rather than muscles and bones. Over 170 drawings of live models in front, back and side views, and in widely varying poses. Accompanying diagrams. 177 illustrations. Introduction. Index. 144pp. 8⅜ x11¼. 0-486-26723-7

GOTHIC AND OLD ENGLISH ALPHABETS: 100 Complete Fonts, Dan X. Solo. Add power, elegance to posters, signs, other graphics with 100 stunning copyright-free alphabets: Blackstone, Dolbey, Germania, 97 more–including many lower-case, numerals, punctuation marks. 104pp. 8⅛ x 11. 0-486-24695-7

THE BOOK OF WOOD CARVING, Charles Marshall Sayers. Finest book for beginners discusses fundamentals and offers 34 designs. "Absolutely first rate . . . well thought out and well executed."–E. J. Tangerman. 118pp. 7¾ x 10⅝. 0-486-23654-4

ILLUSTRATED CATALOG OF CIVIL WAR MILITARY GOODS: Union Army Weapons, Insignia, Uniform Accessories, and Other Equipment, Schuyler, Hartley, and Graham. Rare, profusely illustrated 1846 catalog includes Union Army uniform and dress regulations, arms and ammunition, coats, insignia, flags, swords, rifles, etc. 226 illustrations. 160pp. 9 x 12. 0-486-24939-5

WOMEN'S FASHIONS OF THE EARLY 1900s: An Unabridged Republication of "New York Fashions, 1909," National Cloak & Suit Co. Rare catalog of mail-order fashions documents women's and children's clothing styles shortly after the turn of the century. Captions offer full descriptions, prices. Invaluable resource for fashion, costume historians. Approximately 725 illustrations. 128pp. 8⅜ x 11¼. 0-486-27276-1

HOW TO DO BEADWORK, Mary White. Fundamental book on craft from simple projects to five-bead chains and woven works. 106 illustrations. 142pp. 5⅜ x 8. 0-486-20697-1

THE 1912 AND 1915 GUSTAV STICKLEY FURNITURE CATALOGS, Gustav Stickley. With over 200 detailed illustrations and descriptions, these two catalogs are essential reading and reference materials and identification guides for Stickley furniture. Captions cite materials, dimensions and prices. 112pp. 6½ x 9¼. 0-486-26676-1

EARLY AMERICAN LOCOMOTIVES, John H. White, Jr. Finest locomotive engravings from early 19th century: historical (1804–74), main-line (after 1870), special, foreign, etc. 147 plates. 142pp. 11⅜ x 8¼. 0-486-22772-3

LITTLE BOOK OF EARLY AMERICAN CRAFTS AND TRADES, Peter Stockham (ed.). 1807 children's book explains crafts and trades: baker, hatter, cooper, potter, and many others. 23 copperplate illustrations. 140pp. 4⅝ x 6. 0-486-23336-7

VICTORIAN FASHIONS AND COSTUMES FROM HARPER'S BAZAR, 1867–1898, Stella Blum (ed.). Day costumes, evening wear, sports clothes, shoes, hats, other accessories in over 1,000 detailed engravings. 320pp. 9⅜ x 12¼. 0-486-22990-4

THE LONG ISLAND RAIL ROAD IN EARLY PHOTOGRAPHS, Ron Ziel. Over 220 rare photos, informative text document origin (1844) and development of rail service on Long Island. Vintage views of early trains, locomotives, stations, passengers, crews, much more. Captions. 8⅞ x 11¾. 0-486-26301-0

VOYAGE OF THE LIBERDADE, Joshua Slocum. Great 19th-century mariner's thrilling, first-hand account of the wreck of his ship off South America, the 35-foot boat he built from the wreckage, and its remarkable voyage home. 128pp. 5⅜ x 8½. 0-486-40022-0

TEN BOOKS ON ARCHITECTURE, Vitruvius. The most important book ever written on architecture. Early Roman aesthetics, technology, classical orders, site selection, all other aspects. Morgan translation. 331pp. 5⅜ x 8½. 0-486-20645-9

THE HUMAN FIGURE IN MOTION, Eadweard Muybridge. More than 4,500 stopped-action photos, in action series, showing undraped men, women, children jumping, lying down, throwing, sitting, wrestling, carrying, etc. 390pp. 7⅞ x 10⅝. 0-486-20204-6 Clothbd.

TREES OF THE EASTERN AND CENTRAL UNITED STATES AND CANADA, William M. Harlow. Best one-volume guide to 140 trees. Full descriptions, woodlore, range, etc. Over 600 illustrations. Handy size. 288pp. 4½ x 6⅜. 0-486-20395-6

GROWING AND USING HERBS AND SPICES, Milo Miloradovich. Versatile handbook provides all the information needed for cultivation and use of all the herbs and spices available in North America. 4 illustrations. Index. Glossary. 236pp. 5⅜ x 8½. 0-486-25058-X

BIG BOOK OF MAZES AND LABYRINTHS, Walter Shepherd. 50 mazes and labyrinths in all–classical, solid, ripple, and more–in one great volume. Perfect inexpensive puzzler for clever youngsters. Full solutions. 112pp. 8⅛ x 11. 0-486-22951-3

PIANO TUNING, J. Cree Fischer. Clearest, best book for beginner, amateur. Simple repairs, raising dropped notes, tuning by easy method of flattened fifths. No previous skills needed. 4 illustrations. 201pp. 5⅜ x 8½. 0-486-23267-0

HINTS TO SINGERS, Lillian Nordica. Selecting the right teacher, developing confidence, overcoming stage fright, and many other important skills receive thoughtful discussion in this indispensible guide, written by a world-famous diva of four decades' experience. 96pp. 5⅜ x 8½. 0-486-40094-8

THE COMPLETE NONSENSE OF EDWARD LEAR, Edward Lear. All nonsense limericks, zany alphabets, Owl and Pussycat, songs, nonsense botany, etc., illustrated by Lear. Total of 320pp. 5⅜ x 8½. (Available in U.S. only.) 0-486-20167-8

VICTORIAN PARLOUR POETRY: An Annotated Anthology, Michael R. Turner. 117 gems by Longfellow, Tennyson, Browning, many lesser-known poets. "The Village Blacksmith," "Curfew Must Not Ring Tonight," "Only a Baby Small," dozens more, often difficult to find elsewhere. Index of poets, titles, first lines. xxiii + 325pp. 5⅜ x 8¼. 0-486-27044-0

DUBLINERS, James Joyce. Fifteen stories offer vivid, tightly focused observations of the lives of Dublin's poorer classes. At least one, "The Dead," is considered a masterpiece. Reprinted complete and unabridged from standard edition. 160pp. 5³⁄₁₆ x 8¼. 0-486-26870-5

GREAT WEIRD TALES: 14 Stories by Lovecraft, Blackwood, Machen and Others, S. T. Joshi (ed.). 14 spellbinding tales, including "The Sin Eater," by Fiona McLeod, "The Eye Above the Mantel," by Frank Belknap Long, as well as renowned works by R. H. Barlow, Lord Dunsany, Arthur Machen, W. C. Morrow and eight other masters of the genre. 256pp. 5⅜ x 8½. (Available in U.S. only.) 0-486-40436-6

THE BOOK OF THE SACRED MAGIC OF ABRAMELIN THE MAGE, translated by S. MacGregor Mathers. Medieval manuscript of ceremonial magic. Basic document in Aleister Crowley, Golden Dawn groups. 268pp. 5⅜ x 8½. 0-486-23211-5

THE BATTLES THAT CHANGED HISTORY, Fletcher Pratt. Eminent historian profiles 16 crucial conflicts, ancient to modern, that changed the course of civilization. 352pp. 5⅜ x 8½. 0-486-41129-X

NEW RUSSIAN-ENGLISH AND ENGLISH-RUSSIAN DICTIONARY, M. A. O'Brien. This is a remarkably handy Russian dictionary, containing a surprising amount of information, including over 70,000 entries. 366pp. 4½ x 6⅛. 0-486-20208-9

NEW YORK IN THE FORTIES, Andreas Feininger. 162 brilliant photographs by the well-known photographer, formerly with *Life* magazine. Commuters, shoppers, Times Square at night, much else from city at its peak. Captions by John von Hartz. 181pp. 9¼ x 10¾. 0-486-23585-8

INDIAN SIGN LANGUAGE, William Tomkins. Over 525 signs developed by Sioux and other tribes. Written instructions and diagrams. Also 290 pictographs. 111pp. 6⅛ x 9¼. 0-486-22029-X

ANATOMY: A Complete Guide for Artists, Joseph Sheppard. A master of figure drawing shows artists how to render human anatomy convincingly. Over 460 illustrations. 224pp. 8⅜ x 11¼. 0-486-27279-6

MEDIEVAL CALLIGRAPHY: Its History and Technique, Marc Drogin. Spirited history, comprehensive instruction manual covers 13 styles (ca. 4th century through 15th). Excellent photographs; directions for duplicating medieval techniques with modern tools. 224pp. 8⅜ x 11¼. 0-486-26142-5

DRIED FLOWERS: How to Prepare Them, Sarah Whitlock and Martha Rankin. Complete instructions on how to use silica gel, meal and borax, perlite aggregate, sand and borax, glycerine and water to create attractive permanent flower arrangements. 12 illustrations. 32pp. 5⅜ x 8½. 0-486-21802-3

EASY-TO-MAKE BIRD FEEDERS FOR WOODWORKERS, Scott D. Campbell. Detailed, simple-to-use guide for designing, constructing, caring for and using feeders. Text, illustrations for 12 classic and contemporary designs. 96pp. 5⅜ x 8½. 0-486-25847-5

THE COMPLETE BOOK OF BIRDHOUSE CONSTRUCTION FOR WOODWORKERS, Scott D. Campbell. Detailed instructions, illustrations, tables. Also data on bird habitat and instinct patterns. Bibliography. 3 tables. 63 illustrations in 15 figures. 48pp. 5¼ x 8½. 0-486-24407-5

SCOTTISH WONDER TALES FROM MYTH AND LEGEND, Donald A. Mackenzie. 16 lively tales tell of giants rumbling down mountainsides, of a magic wand that turns stone pillars into warriors, of gods and goddesses, evil hags, powerful forces and more. 240pp. 5⅜ x 8½. 0-486-29677-6

THE HISTORY OF UNDERCLOTHES, C. Willett Cunnington and Phyllis Cunnington. Fascinating, well-documented survey covering six centuries of English undergarments, enhanced with over 100 illustrations: 12th-century laced-up bodice, footed long drawers (1795), 19th-century bustles, 19th-century corsets for men, Victorian "bust improvers," much more. 272pp. 5⅜ x 8½. 0-486-27124-2

ARTS AND CRAFTS FURNITURE: The Complete Brooks Catalog of 1912, Brooks Manufacturing Co. Photos and detailed descriptions of more than 150 now very collectible furniture designs from the Arts and Crafts movement depict davenports, settees, buffets, desks, tables, chairs, bedsteads, dressers and more, all built of solid, quarter-sawed oak. Invaluable for students and enthusiasts of antiques, Americana and the decorative arts. 80pp. 6½ x 9¼. 0-486-27471-3

WILBUR AND ORVILLE: A Biography of the Wright Brothers, Fred Howard. Definitive, crisply written study tells the full story of the brothers' lives and work. A vividly written biography, unparalleled in scope and color, that also captures the spirit of an extraordinary era. 560pp. 6⅛ x 9¼. 0-486-40297-5

THE ARTS OF THE SAILOR: Knotting, Splicing and Ropework, Hervey Garrett Smith. Indispensable shipboard reference covers tools, basic knots and useful hitches; handsewing and canvas work, more. Over 100 illustrations. Delightful reading for sea lovers. 256pp. 5⅜ x 8½. 0-486-26440-8

FRANK LLOYD WRIGHT'S FALLINGWATER: The House and Its History, Second, Revised Edition, Donald Hoffmann. A total revision—both in text and illustrations—of the standard document on Fallingwater, the boldest, most personal architectural statement of Wright's mature years, updated with valuable new material from the recently opened Frank Lloyd Wright Archives. "Fascinating"–*The New York Times*. 116 illustrations. 128pp. 9¼ x 10¾. 0-486-27430-6

PHOTOGRAPHIC SKETCHBOOK OF THE CIVIL WAR, Alexander Gardner. 100 photos taken on field during the Civil War. Famous shots of Manassas Harper's Ferry, Lincoln, Richmond, slave pens, etc. 244pp. 10⅝ x 8¼. 0-486-22731-6

FIVE ACRES AND INDEPENDENCE, Maurice G. Kains. Great back-to-the-land classic explains basics of self-sufficient farming. The one book to get. 95 illustrations. 397pp. 5⅜ x 8½. 0-486-20974-1

CATALOG OF DOVER BOOKS

A MODERN HERBAL, Margaret Grieve. Much the fullest, most exact, most useful compilation of herbal material. Gigantic alphabetical encyclopedia, from aconite to zedoary, gives botanical information, medical properties, folklore, economic uses, much else. Indispensable to serious reader. 161 illustrations. 888pp. 6½ x 9¼. 2-vol. set. (Available in U.S. only.)   Vol. I: 0-486-22798-7   Vol. II: 0-486-22799-5

HIDDEN TREASURE MAZE BOOK, Dave Phillips. Solve 34 challenging mazes accompanied by heroic tales of adventure. Evil dragons, people-eating plants, blood-thirsty giants, many more dangerous adversaries lurk at every twist and turn. 34 mazes, stories, solutions. 48pp. 8¼ x 11.   0-486-24566-7

LETTERS OF W. A. MOZART, Wolfgang A. Mozart. Remarkable letters show bawdy wit, humor, imagination, musical insights, contemporary musical world; includes some letters from Leopold Mozart. 276pp. 5⅜ x 8½.   0-486-22859-2

BASIC PRINCIPLES OF CLASSICAL BALLET, Agrippina Vaganova. Great Russian theoretician, teacher explains methods for teaching classical ballet. 118 illustrations. 175pp. 5⅜ x 8½.   0-486-22036-2

THE JUMPING FROG, Mark Twain. Revenge edition. The original story of The Celebrated Jumping Frog of Calaveras County, a hapless French translation, and Twain's hilarious "retranslation" from the French. 12 illustrations. 66pp. 5⅜ x 8½.   0-486-22686-7

BEST REMEMBERED POEMS, Martin Gardner (ed.). The 126 poems in this superb collection of 19th- and 20th-century British and American verse range from Shelley's "To a Skylark" to the impassioned "Renascence" of Edna St. Vincent Millay and to Edward Lear's whimsical "The Owl and the Pussycat." 224pp. 5⅜ x 8½.   0-486-27165-X

COMPLETE SONNETS, William Shakespeare. Over 150 exquisite poems deal with love, friendship, the tyranny of time, beauty's evanescence, death and other themes in language of remarkable power, precision and beauty. Glossary of archaic terms. 80pp. 5³⁄₁₆ x 8¼.   0-486-26686-9

HISTORIC HOMES OF THE AMERICAN PRESIDENTS, Second, Revised Edition, Irvin Haas. A traveler's guide to American Presidential homes, most open to the public, depicting and describing homes occupied by every American President from George Washington to George Bush. With visiting hours, admission charges, travel routes. 175 photographs. Index. 160pp. 8¼ x 11.   0-486-26751-2

THE WIT AND HUMOR OF OSCAR WILDE, Alvin Redman (ed.). More than 1,000 ripostes, paradoxes, wisecracks: Work is the curse of the drinking classes; I can resist everything except temptation; etc. 258pp. 5⅜ x 8½.   0-486-20602-5

SHAKESPEARE LEXICON AND QUOTATION DICTIONARY, Alexander Schmidt. Full definitions, locations, shades of meaning in every word in plays and poems. More than 50,000 exact quotations. 1,485pp. 6½ x 9¼. 2-vol. set.
Vol. 1: 0-486-22726-X   Vol. 2: 0-486-22727-8

SELECTED POEMS, Emily Dickinson. Over 100 best-known, best-loved poems by one of America's foremost poets, reprinted from authoritative early editions. No comparable edition at this price. Index of first lines. 64pp. 5³⁄₁₆ x 8¼. 0-486-26466-1

THE INSIDIOUS DR. FU-MANCHU, Sax Rohmer. The first of the popular mystery series introduces a pair of English detectives to their archnemesis, the diabolical Dr. Fu-Manchu. Flavorful atmosphere, fast-paced action, and colorful characters enliven this classic of the genre. 208pp. 5³⁄₁₆ x 8¼.   0-486-29898-1

THE MALLEUS MALEFICARUM OF KRAMER AND SPRENGER, translated by Montague Summers. Full text of most important witchhunter's "bible," used by both Catholics and Protestants. 278pp. 6⅝ x 10. 0-486-22802-9

SPANISH STORIES/CUENTOS ESPAÑOLES: A Dual-Language Book, Angel Flores (ed.). Unique format offers 13 great stories in Spanish by Cervantes, Borges, others. Faithful English translations on facing pages. 352pp. 5⅜ x 8½. 0-486-25399-6

GARDEN CITY, LONG ISLAND, IN EARLY PHOTOGRAPHS, 1869–1919, Mildred H. Smith. Handsome treasury of 118 vintage pictures, accompanied by carefully researched captions, document the Garden City Hotel fire (1899), the Vanderbilt Cup Race (1908), the first airmail flight departing from the Nassau Boulevard Aerodrome (1911), and much more. 96pp. 8⅞ x 11¾. 0-486-40669-5

OLD QUEENS, N.Y., IN EARLY PHOTOGRAPHS, Vincent F. Seyfried and William Asadorian. Over 160 rare photographs of Maspeth, Jamaica, Jackson Heights, and other areas. Vintage views of DeWitt Clinton mansion, 1939 World's Fair and more. Captions. 192pp. 8⅞ x 11. 0-486-26358-4

CAPTURED BY THE INDIANS: 15 Firsthand Accounts, 1750-1870, Frederick Drimmer. Astounding true historical accounts of grisly torture, bloody conflicts, relentless pursuits, miraculous escapes and more, by people who lived to tell the tale. 384pp. 5⅜ x 8½. 0-486-24901-8

THE WORLD'S GREAT SPEECHES (Fourth Enlarged Edition), Lewis Copeland, Lawrence W. Lamm, and Stephen J. McKenna. Nearly 300 speeches provide public speakers with a wealth of updated quotes and inspiration–from Pericles' funeral oration and William Jennings Bryan's "Cross of Gold Speech" to Malcolm X's powerful words on the Black Revolution and Earl of Spenser's tribute to his sister, Diana, Princess of Wales. 944pp. 5⅜ x 8⅜. 0-486-40903-1

THE BOOK OF THE SWORD, Sir Richard F. Burton. Great Victorian scholar/adventurer's eloquent, erudite history of the "queen of weapons"–from prehistory to early Roman Empire. Evolution and development of early swords, variations (sabre, broadsword, cutlass, scimitar, etc.), much more. 336pp. 6⅛ x 9¼. 0-486-25434-8

AUTOBIOGRAPHY: The Story of My Experiments with Truth, Mohandas K. Gandhi. Boyhood, legal studies, purification, the growth of the Satyagraha (nonviolent protest) movement. Critical, inspiring work of the man responsible for the freedom of India. 480pp. 5⅜ x 8½. (Available in U.S. only.) 0-486-24593-4

CELTIC MYTHS AND LEGENDS, T. W. Rolleston. Masterful retelling of Irish and Welsh stories and tales. Cuchulain, King Arthur, Deirdre, the Grail, many more. First paperback edition. 58 full-page illustrations. 512pp. 5⅜ x 8½. 0-486-26507-2

THE PRINCIPLES OF PSYCHOLOGY, William James. Famous long course complete, unabridged. Stream of thought, time perception, memory, experimental methods; great work decades ahead of its time. 94 figures. 1,391pp. 5⅜ x 8½. 2-vol. set.
Vol. I: 0-486-20381-6 Vol. II: 0-486-20382-4

THE WORLD AS WILL AND REPRESENTATION, Arthur Schopenhauer. Definitive English translation of Schopenhauer's life work, correcting more than 1,000 errors, omissions in earlier translations. Translated by E. F. J. Payne. Total of 1,269pp. 5⅜ x 8½. 2-vol. set. Vol. 1: 0-486-21761-2 Vol. 2: 0-486-21762-0

MAGIC AND MYSTERY IN TIBET, Madame Alexandra David-Neel. Experiences among lamas, magicians, sages, sorcerers, Bonpa wizards. A true psychic discovery. 32 illustrations. 321pp. 5⅜ x 8½. (Available in U.S. only.) 0-486-22682-4

THE EGYPTIAN BOOK OF THE DEAD, E. A. Wallis Budge. Complete reproduction of Ani's papyrus, finest ever found. Full hieroglyphic text, interlinear transliteration, word-for-word translation, smooth translation. 533pp. 6½ x 9¼.
0-486-21866-X

HISTORIC COSTUME IN PICTURES, Braun & Schneider. Over 1,450 costumed figures in clearly detailed engravings–from dawn of civilization to end of 19th century. Captions. Many folk costumes. 256pp. 8⅜ x 11¾. 0-486-23150-X

MATHEMATICS FOR THE NONMATHEMATICIAN, Morris Kline. Detailed, college-level treatment of mathematics in cultural and historical context, with numerous exercises. Recommended Reading Lists. Tables. Numerous figures. 641pp. 5⅜ x 8½.
0-486-24823-2

PROBABILISTIC METHODS IN THE THEORY OF STRUCTURES, Isaac Elishakoff. Well-written introduction covers the elements of the theory of probability from two or more random variables, the reliability of such multivariable structures, the theory of random function, Monte Carlo methods of treating problems incapable of exact solution, and more. Examples. 502pp. 5⅜ x 8½. 0-486-40691-1

THE RIME OF THE ANCIENT MARINER, Gustave Doré, S. T. Coleridge. Doré's finest work; 34 plates capture moods, subtleties of poem. Flawless full-size reproductions printed on facing pages with authoritative text of poem. "Beautiful. Simply beautiful."–*Publisher's Weekly.* 77pp. 9¼ x 12. 0-486-22305-1

SCULPTURE: Principles and Practice, Louis Slobodkin. Step-by-step approach to clay, plaster, metals, stone; classical and modern. 253 drawings, photos. 255pp. 8⅜ x 11.
0-486-22960-2

THE INFLUENCE OF SEA POWER UPON HISTORY, 1660–1783, A. T. Mahan. Influential classic of naval history and tactics still used as text in war colleges. First paperback edition. 4 maps. 24 battle plans. 640pp. 5⅜ x 8½. 0-486-25509-3

THE STORY OF THE TITANIC AS TOLD BY ITS SURVIVORS, Jack Winocour (ed.). What it was really like. Panic, despair, shocking inefficiency, and a little heroism. More thrilling than any fictional account. 26 illustrations. 320pp. 5⅜ x 8½.
0-486-20610-6

ONE TWO THREE . . . INFINITY: Facts and Speculations of Science, George Gamow. Great physicist's fascinating, readable overview of contemporary science: number theory, relativity, fourth dimension, entropy, genes, atomic structure, much more. 128 illustrations. Index. 352pp. 5⅜ x 8½. 0-486-25664-2

DALÍ ON MODERN ART: The Cuckolds of Antiquated Modern Art, Salvador Dalí. Influential painter skewers modern art and its practitioners. Outrageous evaluations of Picasso, Cézanne, Turner, more. 15 renderings of paintings discussed. 44 calligraphic decorations by Dalí. 96pp. 5⅜ x 8½. (Available in U.S. only.) 0-486-29220-7

ANTIQUE PLAYING CARDS: A Pictorial History, Henry René D'Allemagne. Over 900 elaborate, decorative images from rare playing cards (14th–20th centuries): Bacchus, death, dancing dogs, hunting scenes, royal coats of arms, players cheating, much more. 96pp. 9¼ x 12¼. 0-486-29265-7

MAKING FURNITURE MASTERPIECES: 30 Projects with Measured Drawings, Franklin H. Gottshall. Step-by-step instructions, illustrations for constructing handsome, useful pieces, among them a Sheraton desk, Chippendale chair, Spanish desk, Queen Anne table and a William and Mary dressing mirror. 224pp. 8⅛ x 11¼.
0-486-29338-6

NORTH AMERICAN INDIAN DESIGNS FOR ARTISTS AND CRAFTSPEOPLE, Eva Wilson. Over 360 authentic copyright-free designs adapted from Navajo blankets, Hopi pottery, Sioux buffalo hides, more. Geometrics, symbolic figures, plant and animal motifs, etc. 128pp. 8⅜ x 11. (Not for sale in the United Kingdom.)   0-486-25341-4

THE FOSSIL BOOK: A Record of Prehistoric Life, Patricia V. Rich et al. Profusely illustrated definitive guide covers everything from single-celled organisms and dinosaurs to birds and mammals and the interplay between climate and man. Over 1,500 illustrations. 760pp. 7½ x 10⅛.   0-486-29371-8

VICTORIAN ARCHITECTURAL DETAILS: Designs for Over 700 Stairs, Mantels, Doors, Windows, Cornices, Porches, and Other Decorative Elements, A. J. Bicknell & Company. Everything from dormer windows and piazzas to balconies and gable ornaments. Also includes elevations and floor plans for handsome, private residences and commercial structures. 80pp. 9⅜ x 12¼.   0-486-44015-X

WESTERN ISLAMIC ARCHITECTURE: A Concise Introduction, John D. Hoag. Profusely illustrated critical appraisal compares and contrasts Islamic mosques and palaces—from Spain and Egypt to other areas in the Middle East. 139 illustrations. 128pp. 6 x 9.   0-486-43760-4

CHINESE ARCHITECTURE: A Pictorial History, Liang Ssu-ch'eng. More than 240 rare photographs and drawings depict temples, pagodas, tombs, bridges, and imperial palaces comprising much of China's architectural heritage. 152 halftones, 94 diagrams. 232pp. 10¾ x 9⅞.   0-486-43999-2

THE RENAISSANCE: Studies in Art and Poetry, Walter Pater. One of the most talked-about books of the 19th century, *The Renaissance* combines scholarship and philosophy in an innovative work of cultural criticism that examines the achievements of Botticelli, Leonardo, Michelangelo, and other artists. "The holy writ of beauty."–Oscar Wilde. 160pp. 5⅜ x 8½.   0-486-44025-7

A TREATISE ON PAINTING, Leonardo da Vinci. The great Renaissance artist's practical advice on drawing and painting techniques covers anatomy, perspective, composition, light and shadow, and color. A classic of art instruction, it features 48 drawings by Nicholas Poussin and Leon Battista Alberti. 192pp. 5⅜ x 8½.
0-486-44155-5

THE MIND OF LEONARDO DA VINCI, Edward McCurdy. More than just a biography, this classic study by a distinguished historian draws upon Leonardo's extensive writings to offer numerous demonstrations of the Renaissance master's achievements, not only in sculpture and painting, but also in music, engineering, and even experimental aviation. 384pp. 5⅜ x 8½.   0-486-44142-3

WASHINGTON IRVING'S RIP VAN WINKLE, Illustrated by Arthur Rackham. Lovely prints that established artist as a leading illustrator of the time and forever etched into the popular imagination a classic of Catskill lore. 51 full-color plates. 80pp. 8⅜ x 11.   0-486-44242-X

HENSCHE ON PAINTING, John W. Robichaux. Basic painting philosophy and methodology of a great teacher, as expounded in his famous classes and workshops on Cape Cod. 7 illustrations in color on covers. 80pp. 5⅜ x 8½.   0-486-43728-0

CATALOG OF DOVER BOOKS

LIGHT AND SHADE: A Classic Approach to Three-Dimensional Drawing, Mrs. Mary P. Merrifield. Handy reference clearly demonstrates principles of light and shade by revealing effects of common daylight, sunshine, and candle or artificial light on geometrical solids. 13 plates. 64pp. 5⅜ x 8½. 0-486-44143-1

ASTROLOGY AND ASTRONOMY: A Pictorial Archive of Signs and Symbols, Ernst and Johanna Lehner. Treasure trove of stories, lore, and myth, accompanied by more than 300 rare illustrations of planets, the Milky Way, signs of the zodiac, comets, meteors, and other astronomical phenomena. 192pp. 8⅜ x 11. 0-486-43981-X

JEWELRY MAKING: Techniques for Metal, Tim McCreight. Easy-to-follow instructions and carefully executed illustrations describe tools and techniques, use of gems and enamels, wire inlay, casting, and other topics. 72 line illustrations and diagrams. 176pp. 8¼ x 10⅞. 0-486-44043-5

MAKING BIRDHOUSES: Easy and Advanced Projects, Gladstone Califf. Easy-to-follow instructions include diagrams for everything from a one-room house for bluebirds to a forty-two-room structure for purple martins. 56 plates; 4 figures. 80pp. 8¾ x 6⅜. 0-486-44183-0

LITTLE BOOK OF LOG CABINS: How to Build and Furnish Them, William S. Wicks. Handy how-to manual, with instructions and illustrations for building cabins in the Adirondack style, fireplaces, stairways, furniture, beamed ceilings, and more. 102 line drawings. 96pp. 8¾ x 6⅜. 0-486-44259-4

THE SEASONS OF AMERICA PAST, Eric Sloane. From "sugaring time" and strawberry picking to Indian summer and fall harvest, a whole year's activities described in charming prose and enhanced with 79 of the author's own illustrations. 160pp. 8¼ x 11. 0-486-44220-9

THE METROPOLIS OF TOMORROW, Hugh Ferriss. Generous, prophetic vision of the metropolis of the future, as perceived in 1929. Powerful illustrations of towering structures, wide avenues, and rooftop parks–all features in many of today's modern cities. 59 illustrations. 144pp. 8¼ x 11. 0-486-43727-2

THE PATH TO ROME, Hilaire Belloc. This 1902 memoir abounds in lively vignettes from a vanished time, recounting a pilgrimage on foot across the Alps and Apennines in order to "see all Europe which the Christian Faith has saved." 77 of the author's original line drawings complement his sparkling prose. 272pp. 5⅜ x 8½. 0-486-44001-X

THE HISTORY OF RASSELAS: Prince of Abissinia, Samuel Johnson. Distinguished English writer attacks eighteenth-century optimism and man's unrealistic estimates of what life has to offer. 112pp. 5⅜ x 8½. 0-486-44094-X

A VOYAGE TO ARCTURUS, David Lindsay. A brilliant flight of pure fancy, where wild creatures crowd the fantastic landscape and demented torturers dominate victims with their bizarre mental powers. 272pp. 5⅜ x 8½. 0-486-44198-9

Paperbound unless otherwise indicated. Available at your book dealer, online at **www.doverpublications.com**, or by writing to Dept. GI, Dover Publications, Inc., 31 East 2nd Street, Mineola, NY 11501. For current price information or for free catalogs (please indicate field of interest), write to Dover Publications or log on to **www.doverpublications.com** and see every Dover book in print. Dover publishes more than 500 books each year on science, elementary and advanced mathematics, biology, music, art, literary history, social sciences, and other areas.